Beginning at April 17, 1915, and ending at July 21, 1915, Volume 33 brings together for the first time all the significant documents relating to the conclusion of the Far Eastern crisis of 1915; the crisis set off by the torpedoing of *Lusitania* on May 7; Wilson's, Bryan's, and Lansing's collaboration in the writing of the first and second *Lusitania* notes; Bryan's resignation; the writing of the third *Lusitania* note; and Wilson's secret direct negotiations with the German government during this crisis. Mexico continues to be torn by civil war, and the President's efforts to avoid intervention and prevent counterrevolutions are well documented, as is the conclusion of Colonel House's peace mission.

This volume marks the beginning of Wilson's courtship of Edith Bolling Galt, and their letters to each other are printed for the first time. Among the most important letters in presidential literature, Wilson's letters to Mrs. Galt reveal not only his love for her but also his innermost thoughts about war and peace, individuals, and domestic affairs. He describes events day by day: cabinet meetings, confidential conferences, and his most secret plans for policies concerning the European belligerents.

Arthur S. Link is George Henry Davis '86 Professor of American History at Princeton University.

THE PAPERS OF

WOODROW WILSON

VOLUME 33
APRIL 17–JULY 21, 1915

SPONSORED BY THE WOODROW WILSON
FOUNDATION
AND PRINCETON UNIVERSITY

THE PAPERS OF

WOODROW
WILSON

ARTHUR S. LINK, *EDITOR*

DAVID W. HIRST, *SENIOR ASSOCIATE EDITOR*

JOHN E. LITTLE, *ASSOCIATE EDITOR*

ANN DEXTER GORDON, *ASSISTANT EDITOR*

PHYLLIS MARCHAND AND MARGARET D. LINK,
EDITORIAL ASSISTANTS

Volume 33
April 17–July 21, 1915

PRINCETON, NEW JERSEY
PRINCETON UNIVERSITY PRESS
1980

Note to scholars: Princeton University Press
subscribes to the Resolution on Permissions of
the Association of American University Presses,
defining what we regard as "fair use" of copyrighted works. This Resolution, intended to encourage scholarly use of university press publications and to avoid unnecessary applications
for permission, is obtainable from the Press or
from the A.A.U.P. central office. Note, however,
that the scholarly apparatus, transcripts of
shorthand, and the texts of Wilson documents
as they appear in this volume are copyrighted,
and the usual rules about the use of copyrighted materials apply.

    Publication of this book has been aided by a
grant from the National Historical Publications
and Records Commission.

Printed in the United States of America
by Princeton University Press
Princeton, New Jersey

INTRODUCTION

THIS volume opens during a period of unusual quietude in Washington. There is hope for peace in Mexico because Venustiano Carranza's best general, Álvaro Obregón, has just smashed Pancho Villa's Division of the North in several battles at Celaya. Congress is in adjournment after a memorable session. Colonel House is in London and helps to improve already good relations with the British government. Even German-American relations are calm. Wilson politely answers Bernstorff's protest against the sale of war materials by American firms to the Allies; more important, Wilson decides not to make a formal protest in the *Falaba* case. Negotiations for a Pan-American Pact, to unite the United States and Latin America in a treaty of nonaggression, seem to be getting off to a good start. The one dark cloud is on the far eastern horizon: Japan seems still determined to impose demands upon China that will make her virtually a protectorate of Japan. However, Wilson's and Bryan's forceful protests soon cause the Tokyo government to withdraw the demands that threaten Chinese sovereignty most portentously.

It is the proverbial calm before the storm. At one o'clock (Greenwich time) in the afternoon of May 7, 1915, just off the Irish coast, Commander Walter Schwieger, *U-20*, without warning, sends a torpedo into the starboard side of *Lusitania*, pride of the Cunard Line. The front part of the ship explodes; she sinks in eighteen minutes; and nearly 1,200 persons, including 124 American citizens, are killed or drown.

Unbelief and anger sweep over the American people; Wilson is momentarily in a state of shock. But he quickly recovers his poise and sets to work with Bryan and Lansing to find a diplomatic solution. Bryan, as ever, wants a peaceful settlement; Lansing urges Wilson to send a stern demand. Wilson, responding more to Bryan than to Lansing, sends a note to Berlin on May 13 that appeals to the German government to abandon the submarine campaign on the high ground of humanity and asserts the right of Americans to travel on *unarmed* merchantmen. At the same time, Wilson, at Bryan's urging, attempts, unsuccessfully, to negotiate an agreement between the British and German governments by which the latter would abandon its submarine campaign and the former would permit the Central Powers to import food freely.

The German Foreign Office answers Wilson's first *Lusitania* note on May 28. The German note expresses regret for the loss of American lives but is otherwise captious and argumentative. So

Wilson, Bryan, and Lansing set to work on a second note. At the same time, Wilson opens secret negotiations with the German Ambassador, Count von Bernstorff, looking toward a definitive settlement. In effect, Wilson offers the Germans his right hand of fellowship and cooperation in an effort to establish and enforce international law at sea, provided the Germans will abandon ruthless undersea warfare. Wilson's second note, sent to Berlin on June 9, reiterates his appeal for abandonment of the submarine campaign. Bryan, who fears that reiteration of the appeal carries the risk of war, resigns and is replaced by Lansing.

The Germans reply on July 8. They promise protection for American ships but refuse to disavow Commander Schwieger. Wilson now brings the correspondence to a temporary close in a third note to Berlin on July 21. He rejects the earlier German notes as unsatisfactory. However, he concedes that the submarine is a legitimate weapon of war and says that recent events have demonstrated that submarine warfare can be conducted with due regard for human life. Moreover, he eloquently appeals to the German authorities to join him in a campaign to re-establish the freedom of the seas. Finally, he warns that a repetition of the *Lusitania* sinking will cause a break in German-American relations.

Meanwhile, Wilson presses his courtship of Mrs. Galt in increasingly passionate letters. He professes his love for her on May 4. She replies that she is "dead to love" on account of an unhappy first marriage. Wilson kindles in her the capacity for love and convinces her that she is fully capable of being First Lady and absolutely indispensable to him as a lover and counselor. Mrs. Galt pledges her troth to Wilson at Harlakenden, the presidential summer home, on June 29: "I promise with all my heart absolutely to trust and accept my Lord, and unite my life with his without doubts or misgiving."

"VERBATIM ET LITERATIM"

In earlier volumes of this series we have said something like the following: "All documents are reproduced *verbatim et literatim*, with typographical and spelling errors corrected in square brackets only when necessary for clarity and ease of reading." The following essay explains our textual methods and review procedures.

We have never and do not intend to print critical, or corrected, versions of documents. We print them exactly as they are, with a few exceptions which we always note. We never use the word *sic* except to denote the repetition of words in a document; in fact, we think that a succession of *sics* simply defaces a page.

We usually repair words in square brackets when letters are missing. As we have said, we also repair words in square brackets for clarity and ease of reading. Our general rule is to do this when we ourselves cannot read the word without stopping to determine its meaning. Jumbled words and names misspelled beyond recognition of course have to be repaired. We are usually able to correct the misspelling of a name in the footnote identifying the person. Moreover, all misspelled names, place names, names of ships, etc., are corrected in the Indexes.

However, when an old man writes to Wilson saying that he is glad to hear that Wilson is "comming" to Newark, or a semiliterate farmer from Texas writes phonetically, we see no reason to correct spellings in square brackets when the words are perfectly understandable. We do not correct Wilson's misspellings unless they are unreadable, except to supply in square brackets letters missing in words. For example, for some reason he insisted upon spelling "belligerent" as "belligerant." Nothing would be gained by correcting "belligerant" in square brackets.

We think that it is very important for several reasons to follow the rule of *verbatim et literatim*. Most important, a document has its own integrity and power, particularly when it is not written in perfect literary form. There is something very moving in seeing a Texas dirt farmer struggling to express his feelings in words, or a semiliterate former slave doing the same thing. Second, in Wilson's case it is crucially important to reproduce his errors in letters that he typed himself, since he always typed badly when he was in an agitated state. Third, since style is the essence of the person, we would never correct grammar or make tenses consistent, as one correspondent has urged us to do. Fourth, we think that it is obligatory to print typed documents *verbatim et literatim*. For example, we think that it is very important that we print exact transcripts of Charles L. Swem's copies of Wilson's letters. Swem made many mistakes (we correct them in footnotes from a reading of his shorthand books), and Wilson let them pass. We thus have to assume that Wilson did not read his letters before signing them, and this, we think, is a significant fact. Finally, printing letters and typed documents *verbatim et literatim* tells us a great deal about the educational level of the stenographical profession in the United States during Wilson's time.

We think that our series would be worthless if we produced

unreliable texts, and we go to considerable effort to make certain that the texts are authentic.

Our typists are highly skilled and proofread their transcripts carefully as soon as they have been typed. The Editor sight proofreads documents once he has assembled a volume and is setting the annotation. The editors who write the notes read through documents several times and are careful to check any anomalies. Then, once the manuscript volume has been completed and all notes checked, the Editor and Senior Associate Editor orally proofread the documents against the copy. They read every comma, dash, and character. They note every absence of punctuation. They study every nearly illegible word in written documents.

Once this process of "establishing the text" is completed, the manuscript volume goes to our editor at Princeton University Press, who checks the volume carefully and sends it to the printing plant. The volume is set by linotype by two typographers who have been working on the Wilson volumes for years. The galley proofs go to the proof room, where they are read orally against copy. And we must say that the proofreaders at the Press are extraordinarily skilled. Some years ago, before we found a way to ease their burden, they used to query every misspelled word, absence of punctuation, or other such anomalies. Now we write "O.K." above such words or spaces on the copy.

We read the galley proofs three times. Our copyeditor gives them a sight reading against copy to look for remaining typographical errors and to make sure that no line has been dropped. The Editor and the Senior Associate Editor sight read them against documents and copy. We then get the page proofs, which have been corrected at the Press. We check all the changes twice. In addition, we get *revised* pages and check them twice.

This is not the end. Our indexer of course reads the pages word by word. Before we return the pages to the Press, she comes in with a list of queries, all of which are answered by reference to the documents.

Our rule in the Wilson Papers is that our tolerance of error is zero. No system and no person can be perfect. We are sure that there are errors in our volumes. However, we believe that we have done everything humanly possible to avoid error; the chance is remote that what looks at first glance like a typographical error is indeed an error.

We are greatly indebted to Professors John Milton Cooper, Jr., William H. Harbaugh, and Richard W. Leopold and to Katharine E. Brand for reading the manuscript of this volume and making helpful suggestions. And we continue to benefit from the careful work of Judith May, our editor at Princeton University Press.

THE EDITORS

Princeton, New Jersey
October 4, 1979

CONTENTS

Collateral Materials

ILLUSTRATIONS

Following page 298

Wilson's shorthand draft of the second *Lusitania* note
Library of Congress

William Jennings Bryan
Library of Congress

Photographic Portrait of Edith Bolling Galt by Arnold Genthe
Princeton University Library

ABBREVIATIONS

AL	autograph letter
ALI	autograph letter initialed
ALS	autograph letter signed
CC	carbon copy
CCL	carbon copy of letter
CCLS	carbon copy of letter signed
CLS	Charles Lee Swem
CLSsh	Charles Lee Swem shorthand
CLST	Charles Lee Swem typed
EAW	Ellen Axson Wilson
EBG	Edith Bolling Galt
EBW	Edith Bolling Wilson
EMH	Edward Mandell House
FR	*Papers Relating to the Foreign Relations of the United States*
FR-LP	*Papers Relating to the Foreign Relations of the United States, The Lansing Papers*
FR-WWS 1915	*Papers Relating to the Foreign Relations of the United States, 1915, Supplement, The World War*
Hw	handwriting, handwritten
HwC	handwritten copy
HwLS	handwritten letter signed
JPT	Joseph Patrick Tumulty
JRT	Jack Romagna typed
MS	manuscript
RG	record group
RL	Robert Lansing
T	typed
T MS	typed manuscript
TC	typed copy
TCL	typed copy of letter
TL	typed letter
TLI	typed letter initialed
TLS	typed letter signed
TS	typed signed
WHP	Walter Hines Page
WJB	William Jennings Bryan
WW	Woodrow Wilson
WWhw	Woodrow Wilson handwriting, handwritten
WWsh	Woodrow Wilson shorthand
WWT	Woodrow Wilson typed
WWTL	Woodrow Wilson typed letter
WWTLI	Woodrow Wilson typed letter initialed
WWTLS	Woodrow Wilson typed letter signed

ABBREVIATIONS FOR COLLECTIONS AND REPOSITORIES

Following the National Union Catalog of the Library of Congress

CLO	Occidental College
CtY	Yale University

DLC	Library of Congress
DNA	National Archives
EBR	Executive Branch Records
FO	British Foreign Office
GFO-Ar	German Foreign Office Archives
MH	Harvard University
MH-Ar	Harvard University Archives
MHi	Massachusetts Historical Society
MdHi	Maryland Historical Society
NHpR	Franklin D. Roosevelt Library
NjHi	New Jersey Historical Society
NjP	Princeton University
NNC	Columbia University
PRO	Public Record Office
PSC-P	Swarthmore College Peace Collection
RSB Coll., DLC	Ray Stannard Baker Collection of Wilsoniana, Library of Congress
SDR	State Department Records
WC, NjP	Woodrow Wilson Collection, Princeton University
WP, DLC	Woodrow Wilson Papers, Library of Congress

SYMBOLS

[April 22, 1915]	publication date of a published writing; also date of document when date is not part of text
[*May 3, 1915*]	composition date when publication date differs
[[May 26, 1915]]	delivery date of speech if publication date differs
* * *	text deleted by author of document

THE PAPERS OF
WOODROW WILSON
VOLUME 33
APRIL 17–JULY 21, 1915

From William Jennings Bryan, with Enclosure

My dear Mr. President: Washington April 17th, 1915.

I am sending you a memorandum left with me by Governor Lind, after a conversation with Arredondo.[1] The book to which Mr. Lind refers is rather an interesting one. Its preface as quoted in Mr. Lind's memorandum calls attention to the fact that histories of Mexico have exalted the military chieftians. This book contains biographical sketches of ten men who have achieved prominence in civil life; rather a good indication I think.

I am also sending you a letter which Mr. Lansing has received from Portland, Oregon.[2] I thought it might rest your mind for a moment to see how one man—I do not know whether he is an American citizen or not—looks upon the course which we are pursuing.

With assurances of high respect, I am, my dear Mr. President,
Very sincerely yours,   W. J. Bryan

TLS (W. J. Bryan Papers, DNA).
[1] Eliseo Arredondo, Carranza's diplomatic agent in Washington.
[2] It is missing.

E N C L O S U R E

John Lind to William Jennings Bryan

My dear Mr. Secretary: Washington, D. C., April 16, 1915.

Pursuant to the arrangement which I mentioned to you Wednesday afternoon, I met Mr. Arredondo last night at Mr. Douglas' house and had a most interesting talk with him, in fact, I deemed it of sufficient importance to take full notes, and to make this memorandum of the points discussed and the views he expressed.

First of all, I sought to take a mental measurement of Mr. Arredondo as I talked with him. I saw him last February, but only for a short time. He then used the English language very indifferently. Now he understands readily. I plied him with questions for hours. He responded with remarkable clearness and to the point and he has one quality which even Mexicans of extensive culture seem to lack, and that is to look facts squarely in the face and to reason accordingly. Instead of so doing, they seem anxious to satisfy their hopes by glossing over the inevitable. I was the more interested in Arredondo when I learned that he is a near relative of Carranza—that the two men have grown up together in the same environment, under the same influences, and that they have, to a large extent, read the same books and held the same political views. Mr. Douglas had previously expressed to me the conviction that Arredondo had the confidence and the intimacy of Carranza in a greater degree probably than any other man in Mexico.

After my questions directed to the measurement of the man, for I had begun to feel that I was virtually talking with Carranza himself, I said: "Mr. Arredondo, why were you sent here in place of Zubaran—he was a good man?"

He answered in substance—yes, Zubaran is a good man, the special work he did I can do no better, perhaps not so well, but Mr. Carranza believed that I might be able, knowing him as I do, to refute the calumnies that had become current in the United States as to his character and views, and especially in respect of his attitude toward the American people and the American government. Carranza's last words and his only instructions to me, as I recall, were "If possible, make the American people and government know me as I am, my views, my aims for my country, and the esteem I have for the American people, their government and their President. You know me as well as I know myself."

"Well," I said "do you think there is any general misunderstanding of Carranza in the United States?" He answered with warmth—"Of course there is everywhere, in the press, among the people, and I fear in the Department. It is very unfortunate but it was almost inevitable that this should be so. Carranza has been at the head of the Constitutionalist government from the beginning,—all the lies, all the denunciations of the Cientifico element and of the Concessionaires, whose privileges were threatened, have been levelled against him. He was the arch-fiend, he was the rebel, he was the author of all the disturbances. If Madero had lived he would have rebelled against him, it is said,—the people under him are poor, deluded, ignorant wretches, whose lives he was willing to sacrifice for the gratification of his own ambition, and that no obligations of law or of humanity or of religion, appealed to his gross and selfish nature. This is the way he has been characterized by the Huertistas, and by the selfish interests in charge of the Villa publicity campaign. They have even gone so far as to represent him as a senile old egoist who is despised by the best men of the Constitutionalist movement."

"Well," I remarked, "what about his age? Is he as old as his whiskers look?"

"He is fifty-five years old—physically he is as well and as fit as any man in Mexico. He is a man of splendid attainments and culture. He is well informed as a lawyer though he has not practiced the profession. He is a practical farmer and was prosperous, though not wealthy, when he entered public life. He has been a student all his life and has always interested himself in social and educational work and progress. He has been a close student of affairs in the United States and has spent a portion of many years as a student and observer in this country. He has educated his family here. He is a very quiet man, almost taciturn —his going and coming has never been heralded in the press. He was a loyal friend and supporter of Madero. He foresaw the treason of the Cientifico element before many others did. He remembered the Maxmillian episode. He cautioned Madero. As governor of Coahuila, he was prepared for eventualities and that very preparedness on his part has been used against him as the basis of a charge that he was planning to rebel against Madero —a most infamous falsehood."

"What about the charge that he is against the Catholic Church" I said.

It is false in every particular. Our whole family are Catholics. Carranze was married in Church—his children were baptized and we are all members of the Church, but we are as determined as was Juarez, that Church and State must be and remain separated. We have no quarrel with the Church but our laws and the Constitution forbid monasteries, convents, nunneries and religious orders in Mexico, and the law must be observed. You Americans can hardly appreciate our feelings on this point. You have had no Maxmillian, and I say to you, and I challenge contradiction, that during this whole disturbed period there has been no single instance where a priest or a member of a religious order has suffered loss of life or punishment, though their political offenses have in many instances been aggravated. You may recall that when General Obregon, as a measure of military safety in Mexico City, as he viewed it, caused the arrest and temporary confinement of a large number of priests in Mexico City, Mr. Carranza, on learning the facts, promptly modified the order and liberated the priests.

Mr. Carranza is a mild and sympathetic man. He has not, during this whole disturbed period, ordered or suffered the taking of a single life for a political crime. I repeat this statement with emphasis. It is the fact. Nothing would cause him greater pleasure than a situation which would justify general amnesty for all political offenses. I do not mean to say that unfortunate incidents have not occurred at the hands of some of his subordinates—how could anything else be expected. When Carranza had to assume the responsibility of civil or military administration, in localities hundreds and thousands of miles distant, he could not personally supervise. He had to do the work with the material available. In many instances he was compelled by the force of circumstances, to leave important work to men without skill, without training, and without discipline. What could be expected in such emergencies in a country where the masses of the people had been kept in ignorance and degradation.

No one realizes this more keenly than Mr. Carranza, for this reason his solicitude for popular education. We have some good schools in the cities but no facilities for popular education in the rural communities. "Next to peace" said Carranza to me "we need teachers." One of his first acts of civil activity was to send a large number of promising young Mexicans to an American normal school in Massachusetts. They are there now, and it is our hope that they will return with the return of peace, and that they will come equipped with the spirit of peace and of progress.

The first general publication by the Carranza government was a school reader. It contains the biography of ten great Mexican civilians—men of the type of your Franklin, your Horace Mann. I will send you a copy of this book tomorrow. More books of the same character and others suited to the needs of our people, young and old, will follow as rapidly as our means and organization permit.

This morning Mr. Arredondo sent me the little volume, and I turn it over to you herewith. It is not a very attractive specimen of Mexican typographic art, but turning to the introduction my eye fell on the very first paragraph which I underscore. It reads:

"The instruction in National History in the past has had the ill and grave defects of universally exalting men of arms, the deeds of war and military actions. We have peopled the pages of our text books with heroes, pretended or real, but have diverted the youthful mind from the fecundity of labor in the shop and on the farm."

When I read this sentiment, which I render in English as well as I can, I could not help reflect that possibly the stress and the suffering of the last two years may not have been wholly in vain.

But to resume the report of my conversation.

I said to Mr. Arredondo, I wish you would tell me frankly not only your hopes but your basis in fact for your many hopeful expressions that peace is not far distant. He said I hope that peace may come before it can be compelled by military operations. I have advices that are full of promise. We all trust that this hope may be realized. No one is more anxious than Mr. Carranza. He will yield at any point and make any concession that will not jeopardize the reforms for which the Constitutionalists have fought and suffered. He bears none of those in opposition any personal ill will. Even in the case of Villa he feels that if he had been left to himself, if he had not been misguided by selfish men and influenced by selfish interests, who cared nothing for the welfare of the people of Mexico, he would not have been in arms against his unfortunate brethern. But if these interests cannot be detached, he feels confident, nevertheless, of final success, though peace through military means will necessarily be delayed longer.

Carranza has over one hundred thousand men under arms, but of course they are not all available for the field. Many are in garrisons from Guatamala to the border on the North. Obregon and Gonzales have efficient arms in the field, much superior to Villa's, both in numbers and in supplies.

In the battles that took place last week the Carranza troops were victorious in every instance and the victories were decisive.[1] If military operations must be continued there may occur temporary set-backs, but they will be trifling, and I venture to predict that Mr. Carranza will have complete military control of the whole country within ninety days.

I then asked him about the land question—whether there had been any change in the Constitutionalist's program in that regard. He replied that there had not. That, on the contrary, its importance was appreciated more than ever, but it had become evident to Mr. Carranza with fuller study and investigation, that the execution of their plans for land reform would not be as difficult as it appeared at first. In the localities where the ques-

[1] Arredondo was correct. In two battles at Celaya between Obregón and Villa on April 6-7 and April 13-15, Obregón virtually decimated Villa's forces when the latter threw his men against entrenched machine guns and artillery. The second battle resulted in Villa's rout and withdrawal northward. Thereafter he was no longer a major military and political factor in Mexico. See Arthur S. Link, *Wilson: The Struggle for Neutrality, 1914-1915* (Princeton, N.J., 1960), pp. 465-66, and Charles C. Cumberland, *Mexican Revolution: The Constitutionalist Years* (Austin, Tex., 1972), pp. 200-202.

tion is most acute, it grew out of the illegal resurveys by which communities and individuals were deprived of their holdings. In those instances where the lands have not passed into the hands of innocent foreign ownership, the lands can be easily and promptly restored to their true owners. The remaining public lands will also be equitably distributed, and wherever additional lands are required they will be obtained by expropriation and compensation or purchase, as the case may be. There will be no confiscation. Mr. Carranza and his advisers are all agreed that the land problem generally can best be solved by the introduction and efficient administration of an adequate system of taxation of unoccupied lands which have hitherto escaped taxation.

In regard to their plans for inaugurating permanent civil government in Mexico, it still seems necessary that most of the important and far-reaching reforms, such as the land question, education and others, be put in operation by military decrees during a period of military administration, and this wholly for political and practical reasons. Parliamentary debates and delays might defeat or seriously hinder their speedy establishment. But with those questions settled, it is Carranza's firm determination and also the view of his advisers that the operation of the Constitution shall be restored at once and civil administration entered upon. To that end free and fair elections will be held under and in accordance with the Constitution at the earliest practicable moment.

At this point Mr. Arredondo added with emphasis, I wish to repeat also what Mr. Carranza has frequently told me and his intimates—that he never has sought and never will seek any position except the position of leading this movement to success. He feels that a change of leadership at this time might be disastrous to the reforms in view as well as to an early peace in Mexico. As to who is likely to be selected for the presidency, it is impossible to predict at this time. Circumstances and the future must control that selection. The only statement that he can make on that question is the assurance that one candid man makes to his fellows, and it is this "that he does not seek nor does he wish the presidency of Mexico, nor will he suffer himself to be led into any position or attitude that will hamper the peace or welfare of Mexico."

Concerning the future relations between the two countries, Mr. Arredondo said that Carranza and his personal and political friends were not only sanguine but that they are confident of the most cordial and confidential relations with the United States in the future. The troubles of the last two years, as he pointed out, in this regard, as in many other respects, had been a period of mutual education. American observers must concede that in the circumstances of the generally unsettled conditions the lives and rights of Americans have, on the whole, been protected as well as could be hoped for. These facts give the lie to the wicked charge that Carranza and his followers are hostile to the United States. On the other hand, the occupation of Veracruz and its prompt and generous surrender to Mexican authority has also forever allayed any lingering suspicion in the hearts of the Mexican people that the United States wanted Mexican territory or political control. You who have never lived neighbor to a rich and powerful nation cannot appreciate the value of this object lesson to our people.

In addition to this, your President has put our present and future relations on a basis that appeals strongly to the sentimental side of our people. He has put those relations on the basis of neighborhood. To this every Mexican says "amen," and is determined to do his share to make it a relation of good, loyal and confidential neighborhood.

But now, said Mr. Arredondo, I want to speak about another matter, a delicate one, which lies wholly in the hands of your government, but it is so vital to us that I cannot refrain from bringing it up. You know and Mr. Carranza and all of us appreciate that at all times Mexico needs the goodwill and friendly cooperation of the United States, but at this moment we need more than we can express in words also the neighborly sympathy and confidence of your government. With that aid peace and orderly government are in sight in Mexico. Without it, we see protracted bloodshed and menace. We have no fears of Villa, and we do not fear any mili[t]ary operations that Huerta can inaugurate but we fear that Huerta will involve other factors in the situation that will make our work more difficult and that will inevitably tend to render more difficult the good understanding between the citizenship of the two people. I wish you could make it clear to your government how vitally we need your official support in the present crisis. We do not assume to suggest what form it should take but it is essential that Carranza's government should be recognized as the temporary organ of the Mexican people. By his military control such recognition seems fully justified.

Carranza at this moment controls fully nine-tenths of the settled portion of Mexico, as you will see by the marking of the map which I will send you in the morning.

Mr. Carranza personally, and all his co-laborers are fully determined to observe and discharge all international obligations to the fullest extent, but he is in no position to demonstrate his purposes in this regard so long as he is not recognized as representing the Mexican nation. He cannot take up negotiations for any purpose looking to that end in an orderly way. The just claims of foreigners for losses suffered cannot be adjusted. No commissioners can be appointed to take or perpetuate the evidence with regard to these claims or to pass upon their genuineness, so long as his government is not recognized as such.

I just wish to add one more vital fact which should appeal to the American people more strongly than any mere words that I can utter,—it is this,—Carranza himself and every man connected with him in any important function of government, has either been educated in the United States or has spent considerable time in the country. Each one of these men has learned to look upon the institutions and the ideals of your people as his pattern to strive for. Mr. Carranza and all of his associates realize the assistance that the goodwill of your government has been to the cause of freedom and the progress in Mexico, and we hope and beg that the full fruition of that good will and assistance will not be deferred at this vital moment in the history of our nation.

I deemed the foregoing statement so clear and comprehensive that I concluded to not submit it to you until Mr. Arredondo had read and verified his views as rendered by me. To that end I submitted this manuscript to him this morning. He made no changes, no corrections and only added, "Do you think, Mr. Lind, that it is possible for me to disabuse the American mind of the falsehoods that have been circulated about Carranza?" I said to him "Mr. Arredondo, I hope so, but the greatest and best refutation of all calumnies, is to prove their falsity by action."

John Lind

TLS (W. J. Bryan Papers, DNA).

From Edward Mandell House

Dear Governor: Paris, France. April 17th, 1915.

I have just cabled you of my interview with Poincare.[1] I had been told that he was austere in his manner and I was quite unprepared for the warmth with which he welcomed me.

He seemed to understand my relation to you and he expressed his appreciation of your having sent me to France.

When I wrote the cable to you on Thursday I made a request

that you send some message that could be repeated to him and to Delcasse. I afterwards struck this out for fear lest it might give you too much trouble. When I received your cablegram yesterday sending messages to them both, it seemed almost like a case of telepathy.

Poincare was visibly pleased. I have not seen Delcasse since, but will do so in a day or two in order to discuss with him the second convention. There is nothing you could do that would promote better feeling than to occasionally send some word that I may repeat to those in authority in the country in which I happen to be. We are all susceptible to these little attentions.

I find your purposes badly misunderstood in France. They believe the American public largely sympathetic to the Allies, but there is a feeling, which I am sorry to say is almost universal throughout France, that you, personally, are inclined to be pro-German. It is the most illogical conclusion that one could imagine and I can scarcely keep within the bounds of politeness when I discuss it.

I have just had lunch with one of the most influential men here, and he was surprised when I gave him the real facts. They also believe that it is your purpose to attempt to intervene in order to save Germany. It is discouraging to find such ignorance among intelligent people, but God being willing, we will straighten them out before we are through. That is why I am lingering in Paris.

It is harder to change a set opinion here than it is in England where our language is the same.

There is a feeling in Europe that there will be more or less a cleavage among the nations after this war is over, and that those, be they neutral or otherwise, that are not in sympathy with one or the other of the belligerents now, will be, as it were, beyond the pale afterwards.

After I get through with England I have it in mind, with your sanction, to go to Holland, Denmark, Sweden and Russia to pursue the work there.

Affectionately yours,   E. M. House

There is an extraordinary confidence in France that the Allies will win. It is thought by many that the war will last through another year. No prediction is safe until we see what happens during the next few months.

TLS (WP, DLC).
1 EMH to WW, April 17, 1915, T transcripts of WWsh decode (WC, NjP; WP, DLC) of T telegram (WP, DLC).

To William Jennings Bryan

My dear Mr. Secretary,   The White House. 18 April, 1915.

I have read this with the deepest interest, and lay it down with a ray of hope penetrating the darkness. If it should prove to be true that the Carranza forces have defeated Villa, there is much to meditate upon in the closing plea.

Faithfully Yours,   W.W.

WWTLI (W. J. Bryan Papers, DNA).

From Edward Mandell House, with Enclosure

Dear Governor: Paris, France. April 18th, 1915.

I am enclosing you a copy of a letter which has just come to me from Sir Edward Grey[1] and which is in answer to the one, a part of which I sent you.

You will notice how dispassionately and fairly he discusses the question. The better I know him the more the hope grows that you and he together may have the dominant voice in peace measures.

Unless all signs fail, Germany cannot win in this contest. Page writes me from Rome that Italy will soon go in. Then will come Greece and Roumania, and Austria and Turkey will be put out of the running. It must then be patent to the Germans that there can be but one conclusion. The sad part of the situation is that the German authorities already recognize the straits they are in, but they do not dare give the people any insight into the true state of affairs.

If Germany continues to resist, with all the force that the Allies can bring, I do not believe they can decisively defeat her within a year, unless she has internal troubles. If the German people would change their military autocracy into something akin to a democracy, England and France I believe would be glad to make terms with her, for there is no feeling against the people themselves.

Franklin Bouillon, the brilliant socialist leader, with whom I lunched yesterday told me one reason why France was not prepared for this war was that the military authorities concluded that an army in excess of two million was not practicable. That more than that could not be properly fed or manoeuvred. They learned their mistake almost immediately.

He also said that the reason Russia did not have her troops closer to the German Frontier, was because she did not have sufficient transportation facilities to feed and maintain them.

The French during the past few years have been insistent that Russia keep a larger force near the Eastern Frontier, and there was some feeling between the French and Russian Military Authorities upon this point. The war has proven that Russia was right, and that if her army had not fallen back beyond the Vistula Germany would have had a decisive victory at the very beginning.

Bouillon said that France's misinformation concerning England was as dense as it was concerning you and America, that the general belief here was that England was not doing her part. He went to England two weeks ago in order to report what was actually being done, and since his return he has been telling the French people that England is doing so much more than France that he almost felt like apologizing.

He said that the French before the war had calculated that 13,500 shells a day was the maximum that could be used. They find now that 150,000 can be used and, it is said, that the English at Neuve Chappelle fired 200,000 shells a day.

By shelling the trenches is the only possible way that a position can be taken, and that is how the Allies expect to win.

I have a feeling that Germany's resentment towards America for supplying munitions of war may be an indication that she is suffering a shortage.

Your affectionate,   E. M. House

TLS (WP, DLC).
    [1] House summarized Grey's letter in EMH to WW, April 18, 1915, T transcript of WWsh decode (WC, NjP) of T telegram (WP, DLC).

E N C L O S U R E

Sir Edward Grey to Edward Mandell House

Private.

Dear Colonel House: London [c. April 15, 1915]

Thank you very much for your letter of the 12th.

I shall be delighted to see you and to discuss the situation in the light of what you say, whenever you come to London.

At present it seems that the German people will not contemplate terms of peace except on the assumption that they are both the aggrieved and the victorious party.

We on the other hand feel deeply that moral wrong has been done *by* Germany and not *to* Germany; we believe that the longer this war continues the more will the prospect of German success fade till even to German eyes it disappears, and that the [longer the] war continues the greater will be the financial crash in Germany after the war and the worse it will be for her, though everybody will suffer.

As long as there is this great divergence between the German estimate of the situation and that of the Allies, terms of peace acceptable to one party will not be so to the other.

As to security for the future to be obtained by something bigger than the actual terms of peace between belligerents, what I desire to see is some security against aggressive war being made again.

The three wars made by Prussia were admittedly deliberate. Bismarck said in later days that he made them. I am sure this war was planned and intended in Germany and we cannot have war made in this way again. But anything that secures us against aggressive war would give Germany the same security against war being made upon her.

If such security can be found by agreement between leading nations of the world in a form that we can trust, many things about reduction of expenditure on armaments and "freedom of the sea" would in my opinion become possible.

I note what you say about meeting the American position concerning blockade. We recognize the friendly and courteous tone of the Note from Washington about our Order in Council, and are considering a reply to it in the same spirit. When German submarines are sinking merchant ships and drowning noncombatants crews and passengers off our coasts, public opinion is naturally indignant at the idea of goods to and from Germany whether through neutral ports or not passing our doors openly and unhindered.

But we are trying to avoid interference with bona fide neutral commerce and in the case of some German goods such as dyestuffs are making exceptions for particular cargoes.

Yours very sincerely,   E. Grey.

TCL (WP, DLC).

A Welcome to the Daughters of the American Revolution[1]

April 19, 1915

Madam President, ladies and gentlemen: You need not be welcomed to Washington by me, because you have a permanent home here and I have not. You have your own house, and I am your guest; and I am exceedingly glad once more to be your guest and to express my very great interest in this notable association. In these times, when unusual things are happening and there are many queries as to the future, I suppose that those associations whose business it is to commemorate the past must be asking themselves what part they have in the future. Our business, of course, is not merely one of recollection, not merely the business of remembering and reverencing the traditions of the country that we love. There is no dignity in a tradition which has lost its practical energy, and our interest in traditions is that they should bear fruitage in the present and a still richer fruitage in the future.

Your society is particularly intended to commemorate the circumstances of the birth of this nation, but I take it for granted that it is not your thought to create an exclusive company of those whose recollections by heredity run back to that great day,[2] but that your thought is also of the constant rebirth of the nation. In a peculiar degree, the United States seems to be reborn from generation to generation, because renewed out of all the sources of human energy in the world. There is here a great melting pot in which we must compound a precious metal. That metal is the metal of nationality, and if you will not think I am merely playing upon words, I would like to spell the word "metal" in two ways, for it is just the *mettle* of this nation that we are now most interested in. There are many tests by which a nation makes proof of its greatness, but it seems to me the supreme test is self-possession, the power to resist excitement, to think calmly, to think in moments of difficulty as clearly as it would think in moments of ease—to be absolutely master of itself and of its fortunes.

Therefore, it seems to me that the object of traditions such as this society cherishes and means to assist in perpetuating is to show us the bases of principle upon which we shall keep our poise. We are interested, in the United States, politically speaking, in nothing but human liberty. We are not interested in polities or governments for their own sake. I venture to say that, if there should ever be discovered a better form of government than the democratic, we should wish to adopt it because it was better, for our object is not to stick in the bark, our object is not merely to preserve forms, but to preserve a precious essence —and that is the essence of equal opportunity and essential human rights. Such ideals cannot be maintained with steadiness of view amidst contest and excitement, and what I am constantly hoping is that every great influence, such as you ladies exercise, for example, will be exercised to produce the sober second thought upon every critical matter that arises. The first thought is apt to proceed from impulse, is apt to proceed from prejudice, from predilection, from some transient sympathy, but we cannot afford to sympathize with anybody or anything except the passing generation of human beings. America forgets what she was born for when she does exactly the way every other nation does—when she loses her recollection of her main object, as sometimes nations do and sometimes, perhaps, she herself has done, in pursuing some immediate and transitory object.

I cannot speak, ladies, as you know, in more than general terms. Indeed, it is indiscreet for me to speak at all. But I can ask you to rally to the cause which is dearer in my estimation than any other cause, and that is the cause of righteousness as ministered to by those who hold their minds quiet and judge according to principle. We must preserve the judicial temperament, not because we would sit in judgment upon others, but because we would ultimately wish to sit in judgment upon ourselves, because we should ultimately wish to be justified by our own consciences and by the standards of our own national life. Do you wonder that, hoping for such things and expecting such things from bodies of people like this, I should be glad to come and greet you, that I should esteem it an honor to say that I hope I shall have some part in the great things that you are trying to do and to create in the field of the national spirit?

T MS (WP, DLC).
1 Wilson addressed the opening session of the twenty-fourth Continental Congress of the D.A.R. in their Memorial Continental Hall in Washington. Jean Jules Jusserand also spoke. Daisy Allen (Mrs. William Cumming) Story, president-general of the organization, presided. There is a WWsh outline of these remarks, dated April 19, 1915, in WP, DLC.
2 In his shorthand outline, Wilson wrote: "I take it for granted they do not wish to set up an aristocracy or an exclusive caste."

To Edward Mandell House, with Enclosure

Dear Friend,   The White House. 19 April, 1915.

Here is a letter which I wanted you to see as soon as possible, so I hurry it off. I will not try to write a letter until I receive the one from you which you hoped w'd reach me on the twenty-fourth.

Your letters, added to your cables, make me independent of rumours and irresponsible informants in general, and constantly serve to steady my thinking and clarify it, too. The[y] are an incalculable help, even though the situation alters as they cross the ocean.

I am well. I think constantly of you with gratitude and deep affection.   Affectionately Yours,   Woodrow Wilson

WWTLS (E. M. House Papers, CtY).

E N C L O S U R E

From Hugo Münsterberg

Cambridge, Massachusetts,
Dear Mr. President: April 13, 1915.

Once more I write to you in a strictly confidential way, and I say at once what you would take for granted anyhow, but which it is my duty to emphasize in this case, that I am speaking as an individual in no way authorized by any government or governmental agents. Let me start with the following facts which have been kept secret and which I should not divulge to anyone but to the President. I do venture to unveil these hidden facts to you, because I am convinced that they can lead to an action which might bring unlimited good to the world.

About six weeks ago President Eliot, whose fanatical utterances on the war I have sharply criticized in my writings, sent to me a lawyer with a written introduction. The lawyer came to hear from me what the probable stand of Germany would be in case that President Eliot organized a committee of truly leading non-political men who would propose to the belligerent nations a programme on which they could agree before they enter into peace negotiations. The idea was that as soon as all nations have agreed on the programme as a whole they could at once enter on a truce and negotiate the details. The second part of this mission was to find out what in my opinion the German stand would be with regard to certain detailed questions like the permanent opening of the Dardanelles, and so on. As the list for the committee contained names like Andrew D. White, Cardinal Gibbons, Charlemagne Tower, David J. Hill, J. J. Hill,[1] Joseph Choate, Justice White and others, I saw that this would be a group of men whose right to speak as unofficial representatives of the American people could hardly be denied. I therefore entered into a certain co-operation with the lawyer, who in the meantime had three further conversations of several hours with

[1] Those not previously identified in this series are Charlemagne Tower, a wealthy Philadelphian, who served successively as Minister to Austria-Hungary and Ambassador to Russia and to Germany between 1897 and 1908, and James Jerome Hill, the railroad executive and financier.

me in my house. President Eliot, whose first programme was preposterous and without the slightest chance of success, yielded more and more to sane arguments. For a while he was checked by Choate, who wanted no peace to be discussed until Germany is utterly crushed. But finally Eliot seems to have decided to go on. The platform which Eliot is now ready to offer expresses that minimum which possibly might be gained from all nations and which involves, of course, concessions on all sides. I have formulated the points with that lawyer as follows. First: No territorial changes in Europe. Second: Belgium to receive indemnity. Third: The open sea to be neutral. Eliot's pet addition that no nation is to claim world dominance is, of course, nothing but an empty phrase.

As to point one, Eliot wanted only an agreement on Germany's withdrawing from Belgium, but that would leave open questions like Alsace-Lorraine or Galicia, and no peace is at present possible if these questions are not ruled out. Therefore if Germany is to give up Belgium, it must be made sure beforehand that no other territorial change will be demanded. Second, Eliot's first proposal was that Belgium be indemnified by Germany. That is again out of the question. Germany would not think of such an arrangement, the more as fantastic figures would be demanded. Belgium sacrificed itself for France and England. A fair solution would thus be that Germany, France and England pay equal indemnity. I formulated it therefore in the simplest terms, leaving every detail to the further discussion after making truce. As to the third point, the open sea would be, of course, a concession of England, but it is the one demand on which Germany and America have always agreed and it would be England's concession in exchange for Germany's not holding Antwerp. It would not involve the opening of the Dardanelles, and of course still less Eliot's idea of internationalizing the Kiel Canal. In this form the proposal for an agreement would have a certain chance.

Yet probably weeks would pass before Eliot would succeed in bringing his selfappointed committee to complete agreement, the more as I insisted from the start that some German sympathizers like Lehman or Nagel or Burgess,[2] etc., would have to join the committee, if it is not to awake suspicion in Central

2 "Lehman" was perhaps Frederick William Lehmann, prominent German-born lawyer of St. Louis, although there is no evidence that he was a German sympathizer, and it is unlikely that Münsterberg would have misspelled his name. The leading members of the prominent Lehman family of New York were outspoken in their condemnation of German militarism. The others were Charles Nagel, lawyer of St. Louis and Secretary of Commerce and Labor in the Taft administration, and John William Burgess, former professor and Dean of the Graduate Faculties at Columbia University.

Europe of being an anti-German war manoeuvre. Moreover, while the personnel of such a committee would impress the European nations as authoritative, it is not improbable that the governments would refuse to react on it and would simply suggest that committees of representative men from the midst of the nations give an answer. It is evident that such an answer would not mean more than a private opinion and the real policies of the nations would not be furthered by such unofficial responses at all. If the events are really to be brought to a great turn, America must speak through the President. I may add that just Eliot's personality is the last which would awake confidence in continental Europe. In this matter his expectations go far beyond the compass of his actual influence. Friends have tempted him by the suggestion that he is called to write a Declaration of International Dependence which is to bring peace to Europe and is to figure in American history with the Declaration of Independence and with Lincoln's Emancipation Proclamation. If in this great historic hour a new declaration of human freedom has to be written, all Europe would hope to have it signed by your name and not by Eliots.

I have not the slightest right and not the slightest intention to give advice to the President of the United States. I think that I have the right to give you notice of these intentions of private men who want to reach for a goal which would appear to the world as naturally yours. Moreover, most intimately familiar with the actual situation in Europe on both sides—the Englishman who has written the sharpest book against Germany this winter is the husband of my niece[3]—and viewing the peoples from my standpoint as professional psychologist, I may be permitted to add that this is the true psychological moment for the proposition of an armistice to negotiate peace on the basis of those three points which I formulated above. A few weeks hence that chance will probably have slipped away. It is quite probable that the next few weeks will bring great decisions, but nobody is able to foresee for which side. If they brought victory to the allies, they would no longer listen to terms which were not humiliating to Germany; and if Germany were victorious, the German nation would insist on humbling England. At such a stage any interference from without might be hopeless, but at this moment both are aware of the tremendous task and a proposition for peace which does not humiliate anyone and which in-

[3] William Harbutt Dawson, author of numerous books on German life and institutions. His latest work was *What is Wrong with Germany?* (London and New York, 1915). His wife was Else Münsterberg Dawson.

volves certain concessions from everyone would have the prospect of moral and political success. By the very fact that the solution offered by those three points would include at the same time a tremendous gain for the United States and would reduce the dangers of the future to a minimum, I feel still more convinced that this great opportunity ought to be made use of by the authorized leader of the nation before a group of selfappointed dilettantes tampers with the greatest task of the century.

Very respectfully yours,   Hugo Münsterberg.

TLS (E. M. House Papers, CtY).

To William Jennings Bryan, with Enclosure

My dear Mr. Secretary,   The White House. 19 April, 1915.

Here is my try at a note in reply to Bernstorff. Please let me know what you and Lansing think of it. I shall be at my desk again on Wednesday and we might finish this at that time.

I enclose the other, earlier, papers in the case.

Faithfully Yours,   W.W.

WWTLI (W. J. Bryan Papers, DLC).

ENCLOSURE

DRAFT of a reply to the note of the German Ambassador of the fourth of April, 1915.

I have given thoughtful consideration to Your Excellency's note of the fourth of April, 1915, enclosing a memorandum of the same date, in which Your Excellency discusses the action of this Government with regard to trade between the United States and Germany, and the attitude of this Government with regard to the exportation of arms from the United States to the nations now at war with Germany.

I must admit myself somewhat at a loss how to interpret Your Excellency's treatment of these matters. There are many circumstances connected with these important subjects to which I would have expected Your Excellency to advert but of which you make no mention, and there are other circumstances to which you do refer which I would have supposed to be hardly appropriate for discussion between the Government of Germany and the Government of the United States. But I believe that I am safe in assuming that what you desire to call forth is a frank statement of the position of this Government in regard to its obligations as a neutral power. I had hoped that that position had been made abundantly clear, but I am, of course, perfectly willing to state it again.

I shall take the liberty of regarding Your Excellency's references to the course pursued by the Government of the United States with regard to such interferences with trade from this country as the Government of Great Britain has attempted as intended merely to illustrate more fully the situation to which you desire to call our attention, and not as an invitation to discuss that course. Your Excellency's long experience in international affairs will have suggested to you that the relations of two great governments with one another cannot wisely be made a subject of discussion with a third government, which cannot be fully informed as to the facts and which cannot be fully cognizant of the reasons for the course pursued.

But the general attitude and course of policy of this Government in the maintenance of its neutrality I am particularly anxious that Your Excellency should see in their true light. This seems to me the more necessary and desirable because, I regret to say, the language which Your Excellency employs in your memorandum is susceptible of being construed as impugning the good faith of the United States in the performance of its duties as a neutral. I take it for granted that no such implication was intended, but it is so evident that Your Excellency is laboring under certain false impressions that I cannot be too explicit in setting forth the facts as they are, when fully reviewed and comprehended.

In the first place, this Government has at no time and in no manner yielded any one of its rights as a neutral to any one of the present belligerents. It has acknowledged, of course, the right of visit and search and the right, within certain well defined limits, to declare certain goods contraband of war. It has, indeed, insisted upon the use of visit and search as an absolutely necessary safeguard against mistaking neutral vessels for vessels owned by an enemy and legal cargoes for illegal. It has admitted the right of blockade if actually exercised and effectively maintained. These are merely the well known limitations which war places upon commerce on the high seas. But nothing beyond these has she conceded. I call Your Excellency's attention to this notwithstanding it is already known to all the world as a consequence of the publication of our correspondence in regard to these matters with several of the belligerent nations because I cannot assume that you have official cognizance of it.

In the second place, this Government attempted to secure from the German and British Governments mutual concessions with regard to the measures those Governments had respectively adopted for the interruption of trade on the high seas. This it did, not of right, for it had no right in the matter, but merely as exercising the privileges of a sincere friend of both parties and as indicating its impartial good will. The attempt was unsuccessful; but I regret that Your Excellency did not deem it worthy of mention in modification of the impressions you expressed. We had hoped that this act on our part had shown our spirit in these times of distressing war as our diplomatic correspondence had shown our steadfast refusal to acknowledge the right of any belligerent to alter the accepted rules of war at sea.

In the third place, I am sincerely sorry to note that, in discussing the sale and exportation of arms by citizens of the United States to the enemies of Germany, Your Excellency seems to be under the impression that it was within the choice of the Government of the United States, notwithstanding its professed neutrality and its diligent efforts to maintain it in other particulars, to inhibit this trade, and that its failure to do so manifested an unfair attitude towards Germany. This Government holds, as I believe Your Excellency is aware, and as it is constrained to hold in view of the present indisputable doctrines of accepted international law, that any change in its own laws of neutrality during the progress of a war which would affect unequally the relations of the United States with the nations at war would be an unjustifiable departure from the principle of strict neutrality by which it has consistently sought to direct its actions. And I respectfully submit that none of the circumstances urged in Your Excellency's memorandum alters the principle involved. The placing of an embargo on the trade in arms at the present time would constitute such a change and be a direct violation of the neutrality of the United States. It will, I feel sure, be clear to Your Excellency that, holding this view and considering itself in honor bound by it, it is out of the question for this Government to consider such a course.

I hope that Your Excellency will realize the spirit in which I am writing. The friendship between the people of Germany and the people of the United States is so warm and of such long standing, the ties which bind them to one another in amity are so many and so strong, that this Government feels under a special compulsion to speak with perfect frankness when any occasion arises which seems likely to create any misunderstanding, however slight or temporary, between those who represent

thc Governments of the two countries. I shall be very glad if I
have removed from Your Excellency's mind any misapprehension
you may have been under regarding either the policy or the
spirit and purposes of the Government of the United States. Its
neutrality is founded upon the firm basis of conscience and good
will.

Accept, Exccllency, the renewed assurances of my highest consideration.

T MS (SDR, RG 59, 763.72111/1930, DNA).

To William Jennings Bryan, with Enclosure

Personal and Confidcntial.

My dear Mr. Secretary: [The White House] April 19, 1915

For fear you have not had a similar letter to this from Bishop
Bashford, I am taking the liberty of sending you the enclosed for
your perusal and comment. I must say I am at a loss just how
to answer friends like this without going into a long and full and
perhaps not very wise exposition of just how the thing stands as
a matter of international politics.

          Always   Faithfully yours,   Woodrow Wilson

TLS (Letterpress Books, WP, DLC).

                    E N C L O S U R E

From James Whitford Bashford

Dear Mr. Wilson,   Peking, China. March 12, 1915.

You were kind enough to ask me in 1911 to write you about
Chinese matters of interest to the United States. I am sending
by accompanying mail a letter to Secretary Bryan which I hope
you may read.[1] I add this word about missions because you and
Mr. Bryan appreciate mission work.

The Japanese demands upon China specify that in the interior
of China the Japanese shall have the right to ownership of land
for the building of Japanese hospitals, churches, and schools.
Another article specifies that Japanese subjects shall have the
right to propagate Buddhism in China. Inasmuch as all religious
organizations—Buddhists from India, Parsees from India or
Persia, and Christians from America, have the right to hold prop-

[1] It is printed as an Enclosure with WJB to WW, April 19, 1915 (fifth letter
of that date).

erty for religious purposes and to propagate their faiths in China, it is difficult to interpret the meaning of these two articles unless they indicate a purpose upon the part of the Japanese Government to advance the interests of Buddhism in China at the expense of other faiths. It is unfair to announce publicly that the Japanese Government has such a purpose, and it would be unfair to suggest it had not the Japanese Government clearly revealed its purpose in Korea. In the official volumne entitled Results of Three Years Administration of Chosen Since Annexation, published by the Governor-General of Korea in January 1914 he announces the government policy ultimately to close all mission schools in Korea. On page 60 he uses the following language: "If the separation of education and religion be enforced all at once those mission schools will be obliged to close their doors, and there being a dearth in the government and public schools able to take their place, their closure will leave a great gap in the educational work in Chosen. For this reason, for the time being the authorities concerned pay attention only to the prevention of evil that may occur on account of the presence of these schools, intending later to enforce the principle of education standing aloof from religion." Here is an official announcement by the Japanese Governor-General of Korea that later the Japanese Government is to close all mission schools in that land. When the government will have the courage to put this program into effect we do not know. But the announcement shows the attitude of the Japanese Government toward mission work in Korea. Upon the contrary, the government attitude toward Buddhism in Korea is shown by a sentence found on page 61, viz. "Provisions were also included in the ordinance for reviving Buddhism and its propagation. Thanks to this ordinance, more than 20,000 priests and nuns living in about 1,400 temples and monasteries were enabled to engage in their work." It is at least natural, therefore, that Christian missionaries in China should feel anxiety as to the significance of these demands which relate to Buddhism.

In the very nature of the case, every American missionary, Catholic and Protestant, sympathizes with the Chinese Republic in its desire to preserve its independence and integrity. Indeed, while our missionaries are not preaching politics, our usefulness with the Chinese would be immediately at an end if they felt that we were out of sympathy with their aspirations to preserve their national freedom and independence. The Japanese Government understands that all missionaries, and especially Americans whether they express it or not feel in their hearts hostility to any effort on their part to secure the control of China by threats of force. Christianity inspires individuals to be loyal to God rather than to men, and to contend for freedom to worship Him according to the dictates of their consciences. Such convictions necessarily are in conflict with any attempt at military dictation to a nation by an alien government and race. The Japanese Government as instinctively feels the antagonism of Christianity to her program in Korea and in China as the Roman Government felt the antagonism of early Christianity to her imperial despotism. Hence, Japan's attempt through threats of force and through her efforts to impose secrecy upon China to secure the control of this nation in the very nature of the case will lead her also to hinder, cripple and if possible destroy the work of Christian missionaries in China.

All we beg you to do is to notify the Japanese Government of your anxiety over her negotiations with China, of your expectation that she will not press by threats of force conditions upon China compromising her dignity as a nation or in any degree infringing upon her sovereignty, and assuring Japan in the most friendly spirit but with absolute frankness that any conditions extorted from China now in regard to exclusive control by Japan of all new railways, mines, and internal improvements in China and also demanding freedom of residence in parts of China without the surrender of extra-territoriality by the Japanese, and the joint control by Japan and China of the Chinese police in important places, must seriously affect the trade and political relations of other nations with China, and in the very nature of the case must therefore come up for revision at the close of the present European war. In view of the fact that Japan and the United States are 5,000 miles apart, and especially of Japan's heavy national debt, we do not believe that such a firm but friendly note can possibly involve war between the two nations. Besides, no man sees more clearly than do you that it is safer for nations as well as for individuals in the face of any possible dangers to do their duty rather than to shirk. And no President ever has shown more courage than yourself in acting upon this conviction.

In case our appeal to you fails, which seems incredible, it can fail only through your conviction that our people are unwilling to see you put forth any effort to guard American interests and the interests of humanity in the Far East. In that case, greatly as we dread appearing in print upon any subject which may appear controversial, we are willing to assist in all possible ways in letting the American people know of the events which are transpiring in the Far East. Our people have a right to this knowledge and we shall be unwilling longer to stand idly by and see consummated plans which will bring to naught that for which we have given our lives and that which we count dearer than life itself. Nor can we remain dumb oracles and witness this national outrage of Japan upon China. An influential body of China's missionaries are willing to state the facts thus clearing our consciences before God and man, and to leave the consequences with Him who controls the destinies of men and of nations. We feel sure that you sympathize with us, that you share our conviction that the Christian religion has a great mission among the millions of China, and that you will do your utmost to prevent at once an outrage upon China and the bringing to naught of mission work in this land.

Cordially Yours,   J. W. Bashford

TLS (WP, DLC).

To Seth Low

My dear Mr. Low: The White House April 19, 1915

I thank you sincerely for your interesting letter of April sixteenth with regard to the situation in Colorado and am gratified by what it contains.

Do I understand that the bill to create an industrial commission and the bill for workmen's compensation have passed and become law in the state? If so, the outlook is indeed much more encouraging.

Cordially and sincerely yours,   Woodrow Wilson

TLS (S. Low Papers, NNC).

From William Jennings Bryan, with Enclosures

My dear Mr. President: Washington April 19, 1915.

I enclose flimsy of a telegram from Santo Domingo, with draft of a reply, for your consideration.

With assurances of high respect I am, my dear Mr. President,
Yours very sincerely,   W. J. Bryan

TLS (W. J. Bryan Papers, DNA).

E N C L O S U R E   I

[Santo Domingo] April 18, 11 P.M.

Dominican Government advises that the Horatian party is secretly preparing to start a revolution immediately. The pretext will be a failure of Dominican Government to keep its pledges to hold a constitutional convention for reforms. Dominican Government requests immediate advance thirty thousand dollars for preparations. Dominican Government anxious to suppress expected revolution themselves without calling for open assistance of the United States until assistance is absolutely necessary. Munitions of war should be purchased and money expended under observation of the United States. I believe the Department should take positive action at the outset of any actual outbreak to convince revolutionists American Government will itself suppress revolts. Opposition do not believe American Government will interfere notwithstanding all assertions by us. This crisis has solidified Dominican Cabinet for the present.   Sullivan

T telegram (SDR, RG 59, 839.00/1687, DNA).

E N C L O S U R E   I I

Washington, April 19, 1915 2 p.m.
Answering your April Eighteenth, eleven p.m.
It is not wise to authorize the expenditure of additional money for military purposes. Unless this Government assists the Jiminez Government the insurrection would be likely to spread, reviving the old conditions of lawlessness. As our Government must furnish assistance it would be better to do so at once and thus save the Jiminez Government needless expense. You will therefore advise President Jiminez to demand the resignation of Arias and any other members of the Cabinet who are conspiring with the insurrectionists. Also advise him to arrest these conspirators at once if they attempt to interfere with the orderly administration of his Government. You will see these revolution leaders also and notify them that this Government will hold them personally responsible for any attempt which they make to interfere with the Government whether that attempt is made by them directly or through their supporters. This Government meant what it said when it declared that it would tolerate no more insurrections in Santo Domingo and it will furnish whatever force may be necessary to put down insurrections and to punish those guilty of exciting or supporting insurrections.   Bryan

T telegram (SDR, RG 59, 839.00/1687, DNA).

To William Jennings Bryan

My dear Mr. Secretary,   The White House. 19 April, 1915.

I return this at once, thinking that time is probably of the essence.

This is the best way. There is no use postponing the test. It had better be made at once.   Faithfully Yours,   W.W.

WWTLI (W. J. Bryan Papers, DNA).

Three Letters from William Jennings Bryan

My Dear Mr President   [Washington] April 19th 1915

As a matter of preca[u]tion I return these letters & answer your note concerning them with my pen. The one sent by O Laughlin[1] is frank and bears evidence of correctly stating the situation. There is no doubt as to the sentiment in Germany and the view they take is a natural one. 1st They have warned Americans not to travel on British ships—why do Americans take the risk? Not an unreasonable question. 2nd If we allow the use of our flag how can we complain if, in the confusion, one of our boats is sunk by mistake? 3d Why be shocked at the drowning of a few people, if there is no objection to starving a nation? Of course, Germany insists that by careful use she will have enough food, but if Great B can not succeed in starving the non-combattants, why does she excite retaliation by threatening to do so? If we are to prove our neutrality—and unless we do we are likely to be drawn into the conflict by the growing feeling in Germany— it seems to me we must prevent the misuse of our flag and warn Americans not to use British vessels in the war zone unless we can bring pressure on Gt B to withdraw threat about making bread or food contraband. Our identical note was well intended & Germany indicated a willingness to negotiate—would it not be wise to make another effort to pursuade Gt B. to join in some agreement which will, by permitting food to go into Germany, do away with the torpedoing of merchant vessels? Otherwise the continued export of arms is likely to get us into trouble. So much for the O Laughlin letter.

The Munsterberg letter[2] indicates that Germany is ready for peace. I doubt if the terms he proposes are possible, and I doubt if it wise to propose terms but I feel & have felt for some time, that we should urge the allies to consent to a conference at which terms shall be discussed. It is impossible for either side to annihilate the other and a continuation of the struggle not only adds to the horrors but endangers neutrals who have already suffered greatly. I doubt if secret proposals will suffice—a *public* appeal strongly worded might have effect, and would it not be justified considering the nature of the contest and our relation to the nations at war? All the neutral nations I am sure would at once endorse it and it might end the war—I do not see that it could do harm.

I agree with Munsterberg that *you* are the one to act—no self-appointed committee could or should take the lead. "Who knoweth whether thou art come to the kingdom for such a time as this?" With assurances etc

I am my dear Mr President   Yours truly   W. J. Bryan

ALS (WP, DLC).
    1 A TCL dated March 25, 1915 (WP, DLC), from an unnamed aide of Prince von Bülow in Rome to John Callan O'Laughlin, Washington correspondent of the *Chicago Herald*, enclosed in J. C. O'Laughlin to JPT, April 16, 1915, TLS (WP, DLC). Bryan lists some of its main points below. In addition, the writer stressed the growing hostility in Germany toward the United States and outright contempt for the Wilson administration on account of its allegedly unneutral policies and failure to do anything about preparations for war. He warned of massive uprisings of German and Irish Americans in case of war with Germany. Finally, he threatened that a German submarine would sink *Lusitania*, with considerable loss of American lives.
    2 Printed as an Enclosure with WW to EMH, April 19, 1915.

My dear Mr. President.   Washington April 19, 1915.

I enclose two flimsies—the one from Aguascalientes[1] indicates a severe defeat for Villa. The Carranza people claim that it was a disastrous defeat. You will notice that Schmutz says that Villa himself arrived in Aguascalientes and "says that he will reorganize here." He also states that the railroad track was destroyed behind him, which indicates that he is afraid of being pursued.

I understand (confidentially) that Carranza is preparing to issue a statement giving assurances along the line of your telegram to Him which, by the way, his representative says he is sure Carranza himself never saw. Now might be an opportune time for Carranza to make a statement promising amnesty, religious freedom, etc.

The flimsey from Carrothers[2] saying he will reach El Paso Monday night would also indicate that he has a defeat to report.

With assurances of high respect I am, my dear Mr. President,
                    Yours very sincerely,   W. J. Bryan

P.S. I enclose two other telegrams—one from Brownsville[3] and a second one from Schmutz.[4]

TLS (WP, DLC).
    1 G. Schmutz to WJB, April 18, 1915, T telegram (WP, DLC).

² Z. L. Cobb to WJB, April 19, 1915, telegram (WP, DLC), repeating a message from Carothers dated Torreón, July 18, 1915.
³ J. H. Johnson to WJB, April 19, 1915, T telegram (WP, DLC).
⁴ This second telegram from Schmutz is missing.

My dear Mr. President: Washington April 19th, 1915.

I am sending you a letter which I have just received from Father Kelley.¹ He has already authorized the release of our letter and in his letter (bottom of page 2) he refers to that passage in the communication to Carranza and Villa saying that this Government "was friendly to the Constitutionalists." It is too late therefore to leave out the sentence and since they do not take advantage of that sentence to criticize it, it will, I think, do no harm. I was afraid they were going to withhold publication of the letter because that statement appeared in it. Father Kelley's letter is on the whole quite moderate I think, but there is one proposition in it which would seem to be untenable, namely, that the revolutionists should be asked *to repeal the laws which they have there on the separation of the church and state.* I do not see how we could insist upon a change in their laws on that subject, as a condition precedent to recognition. Those laws have been enforced since the time of Juarez, and I do not believe that it would be possible to secure their repeal even if it were proper for us to attempt to change their laws other than by advice. I have suggested to those speaking for the Mexicans that no objection should be raised to private schools; that is, while they have public schools there should be no prohibition of private schools, if the church there desire to establish private schools as in this country.

I do not know that any extended answer is necessary to Father Kelley's letter but I would like to have your views before making reply.

With assurances of high respect, I am, my dear Mr. President,
                          Very sincerely yours,   W. J. Bryan

TLS (W. J. Bryan Papers, DNA).
¹ F. C. Kelley to WJB, April 17, 1915, TCL (WP, DLC), saying that the administration's efforts to protect clergymen, members of religious orders, etc., in Mexico had been admirable but usually futile; that the land question could be easily solved without confiscations; that the anti-religious laws had been largely responsible for the Mexican failure in education; and concluding:
"It is reassuring to note your promise, that the principles [principles] which have governed the political life of the American people will 'govern the Administration in handling every question that affects its relations with Mexico, including the final question of the recognition of any government that may issue out of the present revolution and give promise of stability and justice.' For those who represent religion there has hitherto been no justice; and stability can scarcely be expected while follow-countrymen are busy cutting each other's throats. But your declaration of policy may, and I hope will, force upon Revolu-

tionary leaders in Mexico a knowledge of the fact that there can be neither stability nor justice in any country where there are basic injustices in its laws; where men and women are persecuted and where individual liberty is trampled upon. Our own republic could not exist as a democracy under such laws, how then could we expect that any other democracy can exist with them?

"Permit me, then, in thanking you for your assurances, to express the hope that Mexican leaders will yet come to see that no democracy can exist which, to satisfy the tyrannical prejudices of two percent of its population, tramples on the dearest rights of ninety-eight percent, as is being done in Mexico now. We all look forward with hope to the day when those who aspire to lead a government for Mexico, shall realize that their country can count on American recognition and American sympathy, only when their actions conform to the principles of justice and morality."

From William Jennings Bryan, with Enclosure

Dear Mr. President: Washington April 19, 1915.

In accordance with the request of Bishop Bashford I am sending for your perusal a letter just received from him relating to the demands which Japan has made upon China.

                    Very truly yours,   W. J. Bryan

TLS (WP, DLC).

E N C L O S U R E

James Whitford Bashford to William Jennings Bryan

Dear Mr. Bryan,   Peking, China. March 12, 1915.

I have in hand a copy of the twenty one demands made on January 18, 1915, by the Japanese Minister to China upon Yuan Shi-kai. . . .[1]

I am sure that you will agree with me that while in form these demands maintain the independence and integrity of China, in substance they transfer the sovereignty of the nation to Japan.

Some Americans may say that the United States deeply regrets the overthrow of Chinese nationality by a rival government, but that the United States is not concerned save as a friendly neighbor in the maintenance of Chinese sovereignty. But you can easily point out the error of this conclusion. So long as the integrity of China and the Open Door are maintained, then whether China charges 5% upon imports as at present, or whether the tariff rises to ten times that amount, it applies equally to the imports of all foreign nations and leaves the United States upon an equality with every other nation in winning her fair share of the foreign trade of China. But if Japan, who herself is a manu-

[1] He here summarized the demands.

facturing rival of the United States, secures control of China, she inevitably secures for her subjects the advantages over outside competitors, and we shall thus lose our fair share of the foreign trade of China.

Commercially, the United States is no longer independent of the rest of the world. Our foreign trade in 1913 amounted to $4,538,000,000, of which $2,615,000,000 consisted of exports. If this two and a half billion dollars were taken annually from the products of the American people, many of our industries would be paralyzed and many of our workmen out of employment. The maintenance of our foreign trade is essential to our prosperity and the growth of our foreign trade is essential to the growth of the United States.

The possibilities of our Pacific trade are shown in the fact that twenty five years ago Japan's foreign trade amounted to one dollar per inhabitant; whereas now it amounts to ten dollars per inhabitant; and it probably will increase to three or four times that amount, inasmuch as the foreign trade of the United States now amounts to over forty dollars per inhabitant. Considering the high industrial and commercial capabilities of the Chinese, the fertility of the soil of China and the wealth of her coal and iron resources, China ought to have as great an increase in the growth of her foreign commerce as Japan has enjoyed during the last twenty five years, and as Japan is likely to gain during the next twenty five years. An increase of ten fold in China's foreign commerce during the next twenty five years would lift it to six billion dollars by 1940, a little over half of which would consist of imports. T. H. Whitehead's Expansion of Trade in China[2] fully confirms this estimate. Von Schierbrand, in his volume entitled America, Asia and the Pacific, published in 1904,[3] estimates that the exports of the United States to China will increase six fold each twenty years for probably a century to come. Taking our present exports to China, direct and indirect, and using Von Schierbrand's estimates, our exports to China would reach $1,229,000,000 by 1955, and $7,374,000,000 by 1975. Sir Thomas Jackson, Manager-in-Chief of the Hongkong and Shanghai Banking Corporation, said recently, "China is at the beginning of a commercial development which in its magnitude cannot be estimated."

An additional factor must be borne in mind. In 1913 China took less than eight and a half percent of her imports direct from

2 Thomas Henderson Whitehead, The Expansion of Trade in China (London, 1901).
3 Wolf von Schierbrand, America, Asia and the Pacific, With Special Reference to the Russo-Japanese War and its Results (New York, 1904).

the United States, though she took some more indirectly through raw material shipped to Europe, manufactured and shipped to China. The completion of the Panama Canal puts the whole eastern coast of the United States 3,000 miles nearer China than the western coast of Europe. No geographical cause will ever destroy this advantage in distance between us and the Far East, because the building of another canal will only open a second gateway which, so far from destroying, will simply enlarge the advantages of the United States. If, therefore, we adopt a shipping and commercial policy, putting American vessels in some measure upon a par with the shipping of other countries, it is possible for us not simply to hold the eight and a half percent of China's increasing trade during the next quarter of a century, but to win two or three times this proportion of China's foreign trade. Mr. John Barrett in 1904 summed up the possibilities of Far Eastern trade in the following sentences: "The foreign trade of the coast line in the Far East from Vladivostock to Singapore is now one billion dollars and it is only in its infancy. The foreign trade of Australia and Oceanica reaches another billion dollars per year, and of the Dutch East Indies a quarter of a billion more." Hence, Mr. Barrett maintained that with the immense increase of foreign commerce through the industrial development of China and Malaysia, through the advantages of the Panama Canal and through our wealth, our inventions and our industries, our opportunities for expansion in the twentieth century may approach the opportunities enjoyed by us in the nineteenth century through the development of our internal resources.

I realize that all of these statements in regard to the future commerce of China are in the very nature of the case only estimates. But no man with any vision can fail to see: first, the growing importance to the United States of her foreign trade; and second, the immense importance of our foreign trade with China which has either the largest or the second largest coal and iron resources of any nation on earth, with three or four hundred million of the most industrious and economic people on earth, in a different stage of civilization from ourselves, and with a semitropical climate the products of which will always differ from our own. All arguments to the effect that this foreign trade with China will be greater under Japanese control concedes our first contention of Japan's purpose to control China; and rests upon the further assumption that there is no commercial advantage accruing to a nation from its control of another nation—an assumption which neither the United States nor any other government ever has conceded. Any Administration which fails to face the conditions now confronting us on the Pacific and fails to preserve the opportunities for the commerce of the United States with China will be condemned to shame and contempt by the future historians of the United States.

Moreover, we have an historic policy in regard to the Pacific Basin. Anson Burlingame in 1868 made the treaty between the United States and China which admitted China into the family of nations. It was the influence of this treaty and the determination of Great Britain to stand with the United States upon it which led Sir Michael Hicks-Beach[4] to write January 17, 1898: "The Government of Great Britain is absolutely determined at whatever cost, even if necessary at the cost of war, that the door of China shall not be shut." It was the adherence of western nations to this principle which led Secretary Hay to secure in 1900 a treaty signed by every leading nation in the world pledging them all to respect the integrity of the Chinese Empire and to maintain the Open Door. It is not to be wondered at, therefore, that in March 1901 when Russia was concluding a bargain with China for the occupation of Manchuria, Secretary Hay protested against the conclusion of any agreement between any foreign nation and China which in any way affected unfavorably either of these principles. Again, Secretary Root, November 30, 1908, secured a firm agreement between the United States and Japan to preserve the integrity of China and the Open Door, and a further pledge that in case any complication arose in China neither Japan nor the United States would take any step without frank and full discussion with the other. We are not advocating the grasping of any privileges or opportunities by the United States in China which are not equally open to the other nations. But the maintenance of our historic policy in favor of the integrity of China and of the Open Door is an absolutely essential condition for equal opportunity for our commerce in the Pacific Basin.

Again, the Alaska Purchase gave us a line of islands with open ports free from ice during the winter, and of sufficient size to accomodate the largest navies of the world, all the way across the northern border of the Pacific from the United States to within 750 miles of Asia. Moreover, the distance from San Francisco to Tokyo is 243 miles shorter by this route along the Aleutian Islands than by what appears upon the map to be a straight line between these two cities. Harold Bolce[5] says of Dutch Harbor,

---

[4] Sir Michael Edward Hicks Beach, who became Viscount St. Aldwyn in 1906. He was Chancellor of the Exchequer in 1898.

[5] Harold Bolce, a free-lance journalist of New York. Bashford probably referred to Bolce's *The New Internationalism* (New York, 1907).

Waterfalls, Constantine Bay, Lost Harbor, Baldwin Bay, and Glory of Russia, that these splendid harbors—of inestimable value for trade upon the Pacific—may prove in the twentieth century the greatest geographical discovery of the nineteenth century. The acquisition of Hawaii, the key to the Pacific, was another step taken toward the maintenance by the United States of a strategic position in the Pacific Basin. Once more, the Philippine Islands fell into our lap in 1898 without any planning upon our part and when we little dreamed of their value for strategic purposes upon the Pacific. If we grant the Filipinos independence as soon as they are prepared for it as we expect to do, nevertheless our historic connection with them and the service we are rendering them, and our probable future relations with them, especially if we keep a single port among them, must in the end contribute to our commercial and political influence in the Pacific Basin. Finally, the completion of the Panama Canal gives even the eastern coast of the United States a geographical position 3,000 miles nearer Japan and China than the seaports along the western coasts of Europe; and just as trade between the western world and Asia made Venice, made Spain, and has contributed to the greatness of Britain, so trade in the Pacific Basin will make the great nations of the twentieth century and after.

Rising to higher moral considerations, surely the United States is acting in the best interests of China in quietly but firmly protesting against her absorbtion by Japan; and China though weak today will be an exceedingly powerful factor before the century is half through. Hence, Chinese friendship will add immensely to the moral, financial and political influence of the United States during the twentieth century. Gratitude exists among nations as well as among individuals; and the gratitude of this truly great people numbering more than a fifth of the human race may become a priceless asset to us in the centuries to come.

Moreover, the United States is acting quite as truly in the best interests of Japan as of China. It is simply impossible for Japan long to dominate by military force a population seven or eight times as numerous as her own and, man for man, quite as strong as her own people. I made a trip of between three and four thousand miles in China at the outbreak of the revolution in 1911 and also at the outbreak of the second revolution or rebellion in 1913. On the first trip, out of perhaps a thousand judgements expressed by Chinese I found only one person favoring the Manchus. On the second trip, out of almost a similar number of judgements expressed by Chinese I found only one favoring the second uprising of Hwang Hsing and Sun Yat Sen. Subsequent events amply confirmed the judgement formed by these two trips. I have just completed another four months trip of China. The Chinese are eagerly discussing the situation with Japan, and on this trip not a single person favored Japanese control. Upon the contrary, every Chinese expressing an opinion was willing to fight for China's integrity and independence. History confirms this conviction of the impossibility of Japan placating the Chinese. Formosa, occupied by Japan in 1895, is not yet pacified. The Chinese started over fifty rebellions for the overthrow of the Manchus, one of them, the Taiping Rebellion, costing over twenty million lives, and all of them costing probably the lives of over a hundred million persons. Two thousand years of Chinese history show a war upon the average every fifteen years, and the Chinese will not surrender their independence to Japan without many, many, many uprisings and revolutions. Thus the universal sentiment of China today and the history of China lead to the strong conviction that Japan can never succeed in pacifying China by force.

The indebtedness of Japan in proportion to her wealth is sixteen fold heavier than the indebtedness of the United States. It was the pressure of this indebtedness and the danger of revolution, unrecognized by the world but very real, which led to Count Okuma's recall to office after eighteen years of retirement. It is simply impossible for Japan to exploit China without a large increase of her army, involving an increase of this indebtedness. Even should the present Administration out of false sentimentality instead of real friendship for Japan fail to warn her of the seriousness of her proposed demands upon China, future Administrations of the United States and the other governments of the world at the close of the present struggle as well as constant uprisings in China will make impossible Japan's permanent maintenance of the authority she is now trying to seize in China through secrecy and threats of force. Moreover, Japan's true policy in the Far East is to strive to gain the commercial and industrial leadership in the Pacific Basin in the twentieth century as Great Britain gained the commercial and industrial leadership in the Atlantic Basin in the nineteenth century. Japan should also aim at intellectual leadership in the Pacific Basin similar to that which Greece secured in the Mediterranean, only she ought to aim at such leadership through the arts and applied sciences rather than through philosophy. We believe that the Japanese are capable of philanthropic leadership in the Pacific Basin, Leadership in the three directions of commerce, of intellect, and of philanthropy will make Japan one of the greatest nations upon earth. But leadership in any one of these directions is clearly impossible through any attempted military control of the Chinese nation. We believe also that the Japanese leaders and the Japanese people are essentially a reasonable people, and that they are capable of a scientific estimate of their possibilities and limitations. A firm policy at the present time will conserve interests of priceless value to humanity and will win lasting renown and the just gratitude of posterity for the statesmen who maintain it.

Cordially Yours,   J. W. Bashford

TLS (WP, DLC).

Remarks to the Associated Press in New York[1]

April 20, 1915

Mr. President,[2] gentlemen of the Associated Press, ladies and gentlemen: I am deeply gratified by the generous reception you have accorded me. It makes me look back with a touch of regret to former occasions when I have stood in this place and enjoyed a greater liberty than is granted me today. There have been times when I stood in this spot and said what I really thought, and I cannot help hoping that those days of indulgence may be accorded me again. I have come here today, of course, somewhat restrained by a sense of responsibility which I cannot escape. For I take the Associated Press very seriously. I know the enormous part that you play in the affairs, not only of this country, but of the world. You deal in the raw material of opinion and, if my convictions have any validity, opinion ultimately governs the world.

It is, therefore, of very serious things that I think as I face this body of men. I do not think of you, however, as members of the Associated Press. I do not think of you as men of different parties, or of different racial derivations, or of different religious denominations. I want to talk to you as to my fellow citizens of the United States, for there are serious things which, as fellow citizens, we ought to consider. The times behind us, gentlemen, have been difficult enough; the times before us are likely to be more difficult still, because, whatever may be said about the present condition of the world's affairs, it is clear that they are drawing rapidly to a climax, and at the climax the test will come,

1 In the Waldorf-Astoria Hotel.
2 Frank Brett Noyes, publisher of the Washington *Evening Star* and president of the Associated Press.

not only for the nations engaged in the present colossal struggle—
it will come to them, of course—but the test will come for us
particularly.

Do you realize that, roughly speaking, we are the only great
nation at present disengaged. I am not speaking, of course, with
disparagement of the greatness of those nations in Europe which
are not parties to the present war, but I am thinking of their
close neighborhood to it. I am thinking how their lives, much
more than ours, touch the very heart and stuff of the business,
whereas, we have rolling between us and those bitter days across
the water three thousand miles of cool and silent ocean. Our
atmosphere is not yet charged with those disturbing elements
which must permeate every nation of Europe. Therefore, is it
not likely that the nations of the world will some day turn to us
for the cooler assessment of the elements engaged? I am not now
thinking so preposterous a thought as that we should sit in judgment upon them—no nation is fit to sit in judgment upon any
other nation—but that we shall some day have to assist in recon-
structing the processes of peace. Our resources are untouched; we
are more and more becoming, by the force of circumstances, the
mediating nation of the world in respect to its finance. We must
make up our minds what are the best things to do and what are
the best ways to do them. We must put our money, our energy,
our enthusiasm, our sympathy into these things, and we must
have our judgments prepared and our spirits chastened against
the coming of that day.

So that I am not speaking in a selfish spirit when I say that
our whole duty, for the present, at any rate, is summed up in this
motto: "America first." Let us think of America before we think
of Europe, in order that America may be fit to be Europe's friend
when the day of tested friendship comes. The test of friendship
is not now sympathy with the one side or the other, but getting
ready to help both sides when the struggle is over. The basis of
neutrality, gentlemen, is not indifference; it is not self-interest.
The basis of neutrality is sympathy for mankind. It is fairness,
it is good will at bottom. It is impartiality of spirit and of judgment. I wish that all of our fellow citizens could realize that.
There *is* in some quarters a disposition to create distempers in
this body politic. Men are even uttering slanders against the
United States as if to excite her. Men are saying that if we should
go to war upon either side, there would be a divided America—an
abominable libel of ignorance! America is not all of it vocal just
now. It is vocal in spots, but I, for one, have a complete and
abiding faith in that great silent body of Americans who are not

standing up and shouting and expressing their opinions just now, but are waiting to find out and support the duty of America. I am just as sure of their solidity and of their loyalty and of their unanimity, if we act justly, as I am that the history of this country has at every crisis and turning point illustrated this great lesson.

We are the mediating nation of the world. I do not mean that we undertake not to mind our own business and to mediate where other people are quarreling. I mean the word in a broader sense. We are compounded of the nations of the world. We mediate their blood, we mediate their traditions, we mediate their sentiments, their tastes, their passions; we are ourselves compounded of those things. We are, therefore, able to understand all nations; we are able to understand them in the compound, not separately as partisans, but unitedly, as knowing and comprehending and embodying them all. It is in that sense that I mean that America is a mediating nation. The opinion of America, the action of America, is ready to turn, and free to turn, in any direction. Did you ever reflect upon how almost every other nation has through long centuries been headed in one direction? That is not true of the United States. The United States has no national momentum. It has no history back of it which makes it run all its energies and all its ambitions in one particular direction. And America is particularly free in this—that she has no hampering ambitions as a world power. We do not want a foot of anybody's territory. If we have been obliged by circumstances, or have considered ourselves to be obliged by circumstances, in the past, to take territory which we otherwise would not have thought of taking, I believe I am right in saying that we have considered it our duty to administer that territory, not for ourselves, but for the people living in it, and to put this burden upon our consciences —not to think that this thing is ours for our use, but to regard ourselves as trustees of the great business for those to whom it does really belong, trustees ready to hand it over to the *cestui que trust* at any time, when the business seems to make that possible and feasible. That is what I mean by saying we have no hampering ambitions. We do not want anything that does not belong to us. Isn't a nation in that position free to serve other nations, and isn't a nation like that ready to form some part of the assessing opinion of the world?

My interest in the neutrality of the United States is not the petty desire to keep out of trouble. To judge by my experience, I have never been able to keep out of trouble. I have never looked for it, but I have always found it. I do not want to walk around trouble. If any man wants a scrap that is an interesting scrap and worthwhile, I am his man. I warn him that he is not going to draw me into the scrap for his advertisement, but if he is looking for trouble that is the trouble of men in general, and I can help a little, why then, I am in for it. But I am interested in neutrality because there is something so much greater to do than fight: there is a distinction waiting for this nation that no nation has ever yet got. That is the distinction of absolute self-control and self-mastery. Whom do you admire most among your friends? The irritable man? The man out of whom you can get a "rise" without trying? The man who will fight at the drop of the hat, whether he knows what the hat is dropped for or not? Don't you admire and don't you fear, if you have to contest with him, the self-mastered man who watches you with calm eye and comes in only when you have carried the thing so far that you must be disposed of? That is the man you respect. That is the man who, you know, has at bottom a much more fundamental and terrible courage than the irritable, fighting man. Now, I covet for America this splendid courage of reserve moral force, and I wanted to point out to you gentlemen simply this:

There is news and news. There is what is called news from Turtle Bay, that turns out to be falsehood, at any rate in what it is said to signify, but which, if you could get the nation to believe it true, might disturb our equilibrium and our self-possession. We ought not to deal in stuff of that kind. We ought not to permit that sort of thing to use up the electrical energy of the wires, because its energy is malign, its energy is not of the truth, its energy is of mischief. It is possible to sift truth. I have known some things to go out on the wires as true when there was only one man or one group of men who could have told the originators of that report whether it was true or not, and they were not asked whether it was true or not for fear it might not be true. That sort of report ought not to go out over the wires. There is generally, if not always, somebody who knows whether the thing is so or not, and in these days, above all other days, we ought to take particular pains to resort to the one small group of men, or to the one man, if there be but one, who knows whether those things are true or not. The world ought to know the truth; the world ought not at this period of unstable equilibrium to be disturbed by rumor, ought not to be disturbed by imaginative combinations of circumstances, or, rather, by circumstances stated in combination which do not belong in combination. You gentlemen, and gentlemen engaged like you, are holding the balances in your hand. This unstable equilibrium rests upon scales that are in your hands. For the food of opinion, as I began by saying, is the news of the day. I have known many a man to go off at a tangent on information that was not reliable. Indeed, that describes the majority of men. The world is held stable by the man who waits for the next day to find out whether the report was true or not.

We cannot afford, therefore, to let the rumors of irrresponsible persons and origins get into the atmosphere of the United States. We are trustees for what I venture to say is the greatest heritage that any nation ever had—the love of justice and righteousness and human liberty. For, fundamentally, those are the things to which America is dedicated and to which she is devoted. There are groups of selfish men in the United States, there are coteries, where sinister things are purposed, but the great heart of the American people is just as sound and true as it ever was. And it is a single heart; it is the heart of America. It is not a heart made up of sections selected out of other countries.

What I try to remind myself of every day, when I am almost overcome by perplexities, what I try to remember, is what the people at home are thinking about. I try to put myself in the place of the man who does not know all the things that I know and ask myself what he would like the policy of this country to be. Not the talkative man, not the partisan man, not the man that remembers first that he is a Republican or a Democrat, or that his parents were German or English, but the man who remembers first that the whole destiny of modern affairs centers largely upon his being an American first of all. If I permitted myself to be a partisan in this present struggle, I would be unworthy to represent you. If I permitted myself to forget the people who are not partisans, I would be unworthy to be your spokesman. I am not sure that I am worthy to represent you, but I do claim this degree of worthiness, that before everything else I love America.

T MS (C. L. Swem Coll., NjP), with WWhw emendations and editorial corrections.

From William Jennings Bryan, with Enclosure

My dear Mr. President: Washington April 20, 1915.

I am enclosing a note from Mr. Lansing explaining the changes which he suggests. They refer to the form of expression rather than to the merits of the proposition, and I am inclined to agree with him except in one particular.

On page 8 he suggests the substitution of *"conscious right"* for *"conscience."*[1] I prefer your phraseology for I think the word "conscience" harmonizes with the good will which follows it better than the phrase "conscious right."

The only change which I have to suggest is in regard to the right of American citizens to export arms. You will remember that Bernstorff, in his note, bases his whole argument in favor of an embargo on the ground that a nation should not increase its plants for the manufacture of arms, etc. Of course this position is entirely unsound but as we reiterate our position would it not be well to conclude the statement of our position with a statement something like this—*"We can find no justification in international law for the restrictions upon the export of arms which your Excellency suggests."*? And the answer would be still further strengthened by adding—*"and even if the position taken by your Excellency were tenable, it would only relate to the amount of arms and ammunition which it would be proper for belligerents to purchase in a neutral country, and would involve the apportionment of such purchases among belligerents, a thing which would seem to be impossible."*[2]

Mr. Lansing does not think it necessary to make any answer to the Ambassador's argument on this subject, but it seems to me that in restating our position we cannot well ignore the argument upon which he bases his criticism of our position.

With assurances of high respect I am, my dear Mr. President,
Yours very sincerely,   W. J. Bryan

TLS (SDR, RG 59, 763.72111/1930, DNA).
[1] "Conscience" was retained in the final draft.
[2] Bryan's suggested additions were not incorporated in the final draft.

E N C L O S U R E

Robert Lansing to William Jennings Bryan

Dear Mr. Secretary: [Washington] April 20, 1915.

I enclose herewith a copy of the draft reply[1] to the note of the German Ambassador of April 4, 1915, prepared by the President.

The principal change is in the re-arrangement of the sentences in the second, third and fourth paragraphs of the draft. None of them has been omitted, but it seemed to me that the harmony of ideas would be more complete by a change of order, such as suggested. The revised draft of the paragraphs is appended to the reply and is marked X in blue pencil.

On page 4 I wish to call your attention to the change made in regard to the acknowledged rights of belligerents referred to.

We have thus far carefully avoided any discussion of the articles included in the lists of contraband, and therefore it would not seem advisable to me for us to say "within well defined limits." In place of that portion of the sentence, I have inserted my idea as to what should be said.

On pages 4 and 5, it seemed to me well to limit our consideration of belligerent action to neutral rights and interests. Also on page 5, I suggest the omission of the words "for it had no right in the matter," because I am not sure we did not have a right, since it affected our trade. It is possible that the inclusion of the phrase might open the Government to a further charge of weakness in failure to insist on its just rights.

On page 8, I offer the suggestion that the word "conscience" be changed to "conscious right." It seems to me that we should convey the idea of righteousness, including in the thought justice.

A minor correction which I have made is to give precedence to the United States over Germany when the two are connected by a conjunction. This is according to the practice of the Department, and is customary with other governments, who give precedence to their own countries.

You will perceive that I have been very free in my suggestions, as I assume that is your wish and also the President's.

Faithfully yours,   Robert Lansing.

TLS (SDR, RG 59, 763.72111/1930, DNA).
¹ Lansing's emended draft bears the same file number as this letter.

From William Jennings Bryan, with Enclosures

My dear Mr. President: Washington April 20th, 1915.

I am enclosing a copy of a statement which I am told the Constitutionalists are considering with a view to having it issued by Carranza. It strikes me as a very well written document, and will, I think, put the Carranza Government in a very good light. You will notice that private schools are to be allowed and freedom of worship protected.

With assurances of high respect, I am, my dear Mr. President,

Very sincerely yours,   W. J. Bryan

I also enclose a statement prepared by Lind

TLS (SDR, RG 59, 812.00/17536, DNA).

E N C L O S U R E   I[1]

It is deemed proper for the Constitutionalist government, for the guidance of our own citizens, as well as for the assurance of the foreigners among us, and for the information of the Nations with whom the Mexican State has treaty and commercial relations to make public declaration, by this proclamation, of the attitude and policy of the provisional (military) government of Mexico with respect to the following matters:

1st. *This government will accord all foreigners in Mexico every guaranty to which they are entitled by treaty, and full protection of life, liberty and in the enjoyment of their lawful property rights.*

All legitimate financial obligations, as well as the claims of foreigners and nationals growing out of the disturbed conditions of Mexico, since the assumption of power by Huerta, will be assumed to the extent that they shall be found just and fair by a method to be hereafter agreed upon.

2nd. The first solicitude of the government is to restore peace and a reign of law and order; to that end it asks cooperation of the people of Mexico, foreigners, as well as citizens. The Commission of common crimes will not go unpunished but a most generous amnesty will be extended to all political opponents of the present government who will accept the same in a spirit of patriotic desire to further the peace and progress of Mexico.

3rd. *The Constitution and Laws of Mexico demand the separation of Church and State and guarantee to the individual the untrammeled right to worship according to the dictates of his own conscience. In so far as these rights have been interrupted or denied, they shall be restored and no individual shall be made to suffer in property, in life or in liberty on account of his religious views.*

4th. In the adjustment of the agrarian problem no confiscations will be resorted to. Land for the homeless will be obtained, by the reclamation of such tracts as have been illegally taken from individuals and communities in the past, when such lands are not now in the hands of innocent holders; by the equitable distribution of the remaining government lands; by the purchase or expropriation of larger tracts, if necessary. The Constitution of Mexico forbids privilege. The lands of all owners, whether occupied or not, must hereafter, be taxed and this in itself, the government is convinced, will be the essential reform.

5th. Property legitimately acquired, whether from individuals

---

[1] Italicization in the following document by Wilson or Bryan.

or from the government, will be protected. The government will, however, unrelentingly assail those privileges which tend to produce unmerited wealth on the one hand and undeserved poverty on the other.

6th. The peace and safety of a republic depends on the intelligence of its citizenship. In order to insure that intelligence the opportunity for education at public expense must be extended to all sections of the land. The first duty of the government is to afford instruction to the masses and to aid in this work the cooperation of all private schools under law is earnestly invoked.

7th. While it is not possible to fix a date at this time for the inauguration of the permanent civil government under the constitution, it is the fixed determination of this government to proceed with the rehabilitation of the country along the lines indicated with the greatest expedition that the delicacy of the work permits. So soon as conditions warrant (and before the end of the current presidential term) an election will be called and held under the constitution, and the laws in that behalf, for the election of a president and other elective federal officials and the government guarantees that the election will be fair and free and so conducted and supervised that every qualified elector shall be protected in his right to express his choice as a freeman.

E N C L O S U R E I I

MEMORANDUM SUBMITTED BY JOHN LIND

My judgment is that no action taken by our Government at this junction would be so conducive to peace and order in Mexico as the speedy recognition of the Carranza Government as the legitimate provisional government of Mexico—and this for the following reasons:

1. Villa's complete military defeat will not only remove him as a factor in the military situation but it will tend to insure the return of the Constitutional elements who have sympathized with him to the Carranza fold, especially if the latter's government has the open approval of the United States.

2. General Angeles, if he feels that he can look for sympathy from the United States, will attempt to consolidate the remnants of the Huerta army to continue the opposition against the Carranza government—recognition of the latter government by the United States will cause him to hesitate before starting warfare on his own account, and will probably result

in his retirement, especially if the embargo along the border is reimposed.

3. The recognition of the provisional government would at once command the respect and cooperation of the foreign representatives and the foreigners in Mexico. They would cease their unreasonable harping, bow to the inevitable, and become factors for peace and order instead of being the most disturbing element in the Mexican situation as they are now. The salutary influence of the "divinity that hedges about Kings" cannot be overestimated in the practical administration of government.

4. The justification for the recognition of Carranza's provisional government is well-founded in precedent.

The numerous business interests and relations between the Mexican State and our own government are suffering inestimable injury because of the absence of regular channels and orderly methods for the transaction of international affairs. Considerations of this character prompted our government to recognize the Rivas-Walker government of Nicaragua under circumstances infinitely less persuasive than here presented.[1]

Moore's Digest, Vol. 1, p. 142 & 3. It is hardly necessary to refer to our action in connection with the Papal States[2] or the recognition of the Republic of Panama for like reasons.[3]

5. Under circumstances not unlike the present Mr. McLane recognized the Government of Benito Juarez when the latter had little more than a foothold at Vera Cruz.[4] McLane was instructed that it was not necessary that the government should be in possession of the capital but that it was enough if it was "obeyed over a large majority of the country, and the people, and is likely to continue."

Moore's Digest 1-147.

Surely the general situation and the circumstances are more promising for the Carranza government at this time than were the prospects for that of Benita-Juarez at the time he was recognized.

6. To my mind the most persuasive argument in favor of prompt action at this time is the fact that at this moment

[1] About this matter, see William O. Scroggs, *Filibusters and Financiers: The Story of William Walker and His Associates* (New York, 1916), pp. 196-217.

[2] For the diplomatic relations between the United States and the Papal States, see Leo Francis Stock, *United States Ministers to the Papal States: Instructions and Despatches, 1848-1868* (Washington, 1933), pp. xxi-xxxix.

[3] See Dwight Carroll Miner, *The Fight for the Panama Route: The Story of the Spooner Act and the Hay-Herrán Treaty* (New York, 1940), pp. 335-91.

[4] See J. Fred Rippy, *The United States and Mexico* (New York, 1926), pp. 212-29.

there is no competitor of the Carranza government worthy of international consideration. His government can now be recognized without subjecting the administration to the charge of partiality or unneutral conduct. If the Angeles and the Huertas are encouraged by our non-action, a condition of affairs may again arise where our government will be called upon to express a choice of preference.

T MSS (SDR, RG 59, 812.00/17536, DNA).

From Edward Mandell House

Dear Governor: Paris, France. April 20th, 1915.

At dinner last night among others I met the Infanta Eulalia[1] and the Spanish Ambassador.[2]

I found the Infanta a warm admirer of the Kaiser. She has a liking for France, but an antagonism for England. I also found that she and the King of Spain are not on good terms. I suggested that she come to the peace congress wherever it might meet and form something of a salon. The idea met with her warm approval and, while we agreed that it should be between us and the angels, I have no doubt but she will be found there. She is a very intelligent woman, and very progressive in her ideas and I can see where she could be useful.

The Spanish Ambassador told me that the King of Spain wished him to meet me and ask me to come to Madrid. He confirmed what Willard had said, and that is the King would like to take some part in peace negociations and that he was willing to follow your lead.

I told the Ambassador that you did not desire me, at the moment, to visit the neutral countries and that I was confining myself to the belligerents, and that you were not making any peace overtures but were simply studying conditions.

I told him, however, that after visiting Russia, I might go to San Sabastian and meet the King. This makes it indefinite and many things may happen to prevent my going.

I am getting enough information here concerning the Pope and Alfonso to justify my remaining for awhile. It is my purpose to use this data in a way to eliminate them from consideration if possible.

Evidence still comes to me each day of the misunderstanding which the French people at large have of our position. They are very much afraid that peace will be made over night, and that the Germans will not receive the punishment for their misdeeds which they feel they so richly deserve.

In the course of the next two or three months the conviction will break in upon them that the wonderful things they expect the army to do, have not happened and they will then become more reasonable in their attitude.

I notice that Dernberg has taken the cue from Berlin and is saying that Belgium must be retained unless the "freedom of the seas" is established. Yesterday I noticed that a prominent Hamburger said the same thing and it looks as if the German Government had accepted the suggestion that this was the best way to save their faces before the people.

I took lunch today with Joseph Reinach. He is a German-French Jew whose people have lived in France some sixty years He is said to be thoroughly patriotic and is a man of influence.

He writes for the Figaro and I outlined some things I thought it would be well for him to incorporate in his next article. I drew his attention to the fact that it was more to France's interest to have the United States come in at the final settlement and exercise its moral influence than it was for us.[3]

I also made him the same talk I have made to others concerning you and your purposes.

He said that Clemenceau[4] was largely responsible for the anti-Administration articles that had appeared in France,[5] that he was an impossible person to handle, and that he got his views from his wife who had much of the prejudice of her American connections.[6]

Reinach gets German papers from friends in Switzerland and he said he saw a great change within the last two weeks in their attitude towards England. I am wondering whether what I said to them in Berlin has begun to bear fruit, and they see the wisdom of modifying their hate campaign in that direction.

Your affectionate,   E. M. House

TLS (WP, DLC).

[1] Sister of the late King Alfonso XII of Spain, the Infanta, who lived in Paris, had published two books espousing democracy, her own brand of socialism, and woman's independence. An intimate at all the courts of Europe, she remained neutral throughout the war.

[2] Carlos Espinosa de los Monteros, Marqués de Valtierra.

[3] Reinach did not write an article incorporating House's suggestions.

[4] Georges Eugène Benjamin Clemenceau, at this time publisher of *L'Homme Enchaîné*, formerly *L'Homme Libre*.

[5] See, for example, Clemenceau's editorial in *L'Homme Enchaîné*, May 15, 1915.

[6] In June 1869, at the conclusion of a four-year sojourn in the United States, Clemenceau married nineteen-year-old Mary A. Plummer. Little is known about her except that she was born in Springfield, Mass., was residing in New York

at the time of her marriage, and had been a student of Clemenceau's at a girls' school in Stamford, Conn., where he taught French to supplement his income as a journalist. They immediately sailed for France. Clemenceau's biographers differ greatly on the course of the marriage, but it is clear that it was not a success, despite the birth of three children, and that husband and wife saw little of each other after the early 1870s and separated permanently either in the late 1870s or the 1880s. Clemenceau never remarried.

From Seth Low

Dear Mr. President: New York, April 20th, 1915.

In reply to your question, I am happy to be able to say that both of the bills to which I referred in my letter of April 16th have been passed, and are now laws of the State of Colorado.
                   Sincerely yours,   Seth Low, Chairman.

TLS (WP, DLC).

Remarks to Potomac Presbytery[1]

April 21, 1915.

Mr. Moderator, my friends: I have not come here tonight to make an address, for I feel that an address by me would merely be an interruption to the business of the presbytery, which is very much more important, I can say with sincere conviction, than anything I might be able to say to the presbytery. Moreover, I have not come here as representing the office which I now occupy, because just so soon as Doctor Taylor asked me if I could meet with the presbytery, my thought went back to a time long before I had any thought of occupying public office, when throughout a very happy boyhood I was associated with one of the most inspiring fathers that ever a lad was blessed with, who during practically the whole of my youth was the Stated Clerk of the southern General Assembly and who, therefore, among other things, edited the minutes of the Assembly. I did a lot of the hard work, let me say, of editing those minutes, and I still retain in the back of my head certain grudges against some moderators of some presbyteries. I do not remember whether the moderator of Potomac Presbytery was among them or not; certainly not the present one.

I remember that the clerks of those presbyteries gave me a great deal of trouble. Some of them, particularly of the country presbyteries, did not consult the almanac. They would say that the presbytery would convene on the second Monday after full moon, at early candlelight. My father exacted of me that I should find which Monday that was and calculate the probable hour of early candlelight. It was before the days when I had studied the mathematical aspects of astronomy, and I was not perfectly familiar with the hours which the sun kept. It was, therefore, necessary for me constantly to resort to very puzzling almanacs and to make calculations the correctness of which I was by no means certain.

Then, these same clerks gave me a great deal of practice in addition. I had to add up the columns of their reports to see whether they had added them correctly or not. I have sometimes suspected that I may have substituted errors other than their own. But, at any rate, I remember the many hours of somewhat tedious labor which I devoted to the matters of the southern Presbyterian Church—to the statistical and not to the more entertaining parts—because at that time I had not the imagination to give significance to large bodies of statistics.

All of this, however, is merely a playful allusion to what was a very delightful experience with me. My father, because of his office, had an extraordinarily wide acquaintance with the active membership of the southern Presbyterian Church, its ministers and elders, of course, in particular. Their names were familiar in our household; and anecdotes about them made their personality very real to us; the visits of a great many of them gladdened us from time to time. My father was a very lively companion and seemed to provoke and draw out liveliness in other people. He had the very risky habit of always saying exactly what he thought, a habit which I in part inherited, and of which I have had diligently to cure myself. But he was the best instructor, the most inspiring companion, I venture to say, that a youngster ever had, and, in facing a southern presbytery, I cannot think of myself as the President of the United States; I can only think of myself as the son of Joseph R. Wilson. And I only wish that I could claim some of the vital connection with the church which he could claim, because those of us who stand outside the active ministrations of the church, so to say, get an illegitimate usury from it. We do not seem to add a great deal to its capital, but we do live on its investments; we do live on its great investments of spirit and of the kind of energy which keeps the world alive, which makes us different from the beasts of the field.

When I think of the great bodies of opinion which sustain the affairs of the world, it seems to me that the heart and nucleus of them is the principle of Christianity and that, therefore, the conservation of that great fountain of all that is just and righteous is one of the most important things conceivable, infinitely more important than the things which those of us do who attempt to take some part in administering the external affairs of the world. And when I hear men like Mr. Stuart² pleading for the means to introduce this great influence into a part of the world now for the first time feeling its connection with the rest of mankind, now first wakening to the possibilities of the power that lies latent in it, I wonder if it is possible that the imaginations of Christian people will fail to take fire. Why, this is the most amazing and inspiring vision that can be offered you, this vision of that great sleeping nation suddenly cried awake by the voice of Christ. Could there be anything more tremendous than that? And could there be any greater contribution to the future momentum of the moral forces of the world than could be made by quickening this force which is being set afoot in China? China is at present inchoate; as a nation it is congeries of parts in each of which there is energy, but which are unbound in any essential and active unit, and just as soon as its unity comes, its power will come in the world. Should we not see that the parts are fructified by the teachings of Christ?

But that is quite apart from what I had come to say. I had not come to speak on foreign missions. I am not competent to speak on foreign missions. I am merely competent to utter my deep allegiance to the things which are represented by bodies of people like this and to express my thanks to God that as a youth and as a man I have been permitted to have some part in them.

T MS (WP, DLC).
  ¹ Which met in Central Presbyterian Church in Washington. The moderator was the Rev. Dr. Robert F. Fleming, pastor of Dickey Memorial Presbyterian Church of Baltimore.
  ² The Rev. Warren Horton Stuart, Presbyterian missionary to China, at this time Professor of Religion at Hangchow College.

Three Letters to William Jennings Bryan

My dear Mr. Secretary,   The White House. 21 April, 1915.

I agree with you in thinking this an excellent document calculated to make a very good impression indeed.

Gov. Lind's argument is very persuasive, but the right moment is not here yet. Many things may happen in the next few days, and I am anxious to get *West's* first hand impressions before we act.   Faithfully Yours,   W.W.

WWTLI (SDR, RG 59, 812.00/17536, DNA).

My dear Mr. Secretary,   The White House. 21 April, 1915.

I agree with you entirely. No other position is possible for us, and I think the whole country will agree with us, and not with Father Kelley.   Faithfully Yours,   W.W.

My dear Mr. Secretary,   The White House. 21 April, 1915.

I am glad to accept the emendations suggested (except where I have run my pencil through them) and also the rearrangement of paragraphs, and hasten to return the note to be copied and delivered.

I took advantage of your suggestion to add the words (p. 6) "and I respectfully submit that none of the circumstances urged in Your Excellency's memorandum alters the principle involved."[1]

In haste,   Faithfully Yours,   W.W.

[1] The letter was sent to Bernstorff on April 21 and published in the American press on April 22. It is printed in *FR-WWS 1915*, pp. 160-162.

From William Jennings Bryan, with Enclosure

My dear Mr. President: Washington April 21, 1915.

I am sending you copy of the communication which we have received from the Chilean Ambassador; and I will call your attention to it proposition by proposition.

In the *first* place—you will notice that in the paragraph marked "1" he does not expect the matter to be proposed to the other governments unless it is approved by the three to whom it was first submitted—Brazil, Argentina and Chile.

I think it would be well for us to correct this impression and say to him that while we feel that it was wise to submit it to the three larger countries before submitting it to the others, we would not feel justified in refusing to enter into an agreement with such nations as would desire to become parties to such an agreement, merely because one or more of the nations did not see fit to join, and that we feel sure that no nation which for any reason feels that it cannot come in would desire to deny to the other nations such benefits as might result from the negotiation of such a treaty.

Second: You will notice that he objects—(and his Government supports his objection)—to a guarantee of a republican form of government.

There is force in the objection which he makes—namely, that the form of Government is a matter for the people of the country and not a matter in which outside countries should interfere. At the same time, as all these governments are republican in form and as none of them have any intention of returning to any other form I do not believe that the objection which he makes would be entertained by other countries and it would be a great advantage to have this endorsement given to the republican idea of government; and, moreover, we might have difficulty in securing the ratification of a treaty which pledged us to assist in maintaining the independence of a monarchy.

We might meet his objection, it occurs to me, by saying that the treaty will doubtless provide for its denunciation by any of the contracting parties upon notice—which is generally one year —so that any country desiring to change its form of government can give notice of its desire and withdraw, and when released from the treaty can then make such change in its form of government as it desires.

Third: The question which he raises about the guarantee of territorial integrity is more difficult to deal with, and yet I think it is even more important than the guarantee of a republican form of government.

The purpose of the treaty is to insure peace in the western hemisphere and nothing will go further in this direction than a guarantee of territorial integrity. While we are confident as to our own intentions, it will be a very acceptable thing to Latin-America to have us agree that we will respect the territorial integrity of all the other nations, and it will be a great protection to the little countries to have their territorial integrity guaranteed.

The thing that troubles Chile, of course, is the controversy between Chile and Peru and I suggest that we might meet this proposition as follows:

Let those nations sign which will agree to sign and let the guarantee cover all questions that may arise *after* the settlement of existing disputes or disagreements, each nation to set forth specifically the excepted dispute.

This will enable Chile to sign and in doing so make an exception of the dispute with Peru. Peru may or may not desire to make an exception of the dispute with Chile. If we make a guarantee covering all future disputes I do not think it will be necessary to go further than have the nations agree to use their best endeavors to reach a settlement of any disputes which may exist, without fixing a time limit on those disputes.

If Peru is guaranteed against any further invasion of its territory I believe it will be possible for the Peruvian government to accept the settlement offered by Chile, which is that the control of the disputed territory be submitted to an election within a year, no one being permitted to vote who is not a resident at the time the agreement is made; the nation securing the disputed territory to pay a fixed sum to the nation losing. The sum of ten millions is proposed, but Chile has indicated a willingness to go beyond that. If Peru can be assured of territorial integrity after the settlement of this dispute it is more than likely that a settlement can be soon effected.

While it would be desirable to have a time limit fixed for the settlement of existing disputes that is not so essential as the agreement that when the disputes are settled there shall be no more forcible taking of territory.

I believe that nearly all the countries would enter into such a treaty and it should be left open for others to sign afterwards.

You will notice that the Chilean Ambassador makes a distinction between original boundaries and disputes of territory arising from other sources. I see no insuperable objection to that distinction, but believe it would be better to let it rest with an agreement on the part of the nations to try and adjust their disputes. Possibly we might make the provision for arbitration as to original boundaries, and then add the promise as to other boundary disputes.

Fourth: You will notice that the objection he makes in regard to the provision of monopoly of arms. I do not think his objection is sound but as the purpose of this paragraph is to prevent the shipping of arms from one American country into another it might be sufficient if the agreement provided for legislation which would enable each country to so control the export of arms as not to permit export of arms to be used by one of the contracting parties as against another. The Chilean Ambassador is afraid that we might have difficulty in securing the ratification of the treaty if it provided for a radical change in this respect, and he does not want to have the treaty fail on account of a provision which would incite opposition.

I might add, in closing, that the Argentine Ambassador is in favor of the draft of the treaty just as it was presented by you and the Brazilian is desirous of that form, with the exception of the question of arbitration of differences, and upon this they have not yet given their final answer.

With assurances of high respect I am, my dear Mr. President,
Yours very sincerely,   W. J. Bryan

TLS (SDR, RG 59, 710.11/200½a, DNA).

E N C L O S U R E

MEMORANDUM

Confidential.

The Government of Chile was informed on time of the plan confidentially and privately suggested by Colonel E. M. House, on behalf of the White House, before the Governments of Chile, Argentina and Brasil, through their Ambassadors in Washington. The Government of Chile replied that the idea of a continental accord was considered by them worth[y] of the warmest applause, generous and advantageous to the panamerican solidarity; and, that, consequently, they were perfectly willing to accept in principle, though reserving the privilege of carefully revising the plan at the time when a final form would be given to it. (This was so verbally stated by the Ambassador of Chile to the Secretary of State in interview of January 19th).

To precisely appreciate the reply of the Government of Chile, it is convenient to know the terms in which the suggestion initiated through Mr House was transmitted to Santiago by the Chilean Ambassador in Washington. In his cablegram of December 21st, after informing of the explanations given by Mr House on the text of the two original propositions, the Ambassador of Chile said to his Government:

"My visitor (Col. House) insisted that this initiative ought to be considered as strictly confidential and private until it should deserve approval by the Governments, and that, if objected, it should be considered as *"non avenue,"* as it was only a personal advance of the President, as shown by the fact that no official intervention yet had been taken by the Department of State.

"He also added that the President had desired to previously consult this matter with the Representatives in Washington of Chile, Argentina and Brasil and, through them, with the Governments themselves; and that, once accepted by these Governments, there would remain for the three of them to seek the accord of the other Governments of America, as an action by the United States to that end might be wrongfully construed.

"After carefully reading the Memorandum, I expressed to the presidential emissary that neither I nor my Government could fail to recognize the great significance of the initiative and the high spirit of american solidarity that inspired it; that it meant to eliminate from the very begining the troublesome factor of the Monroe Doctrine in the form and reach that its application is contemplated by many people in this country; that it set the lines of a sort of political federation which would certainly result in bringing forth a greater approachment and commercial activity in the Continent. But, that the terms of the first proposition, particularly in its final sentence, suggested [to] me "prima facie" a serious objection originated by the special position of Chile and the problems it has yet pending in the Continent. I intimated that possibly the proposition could be conceived in a sense to generalize the Monroe Doctrine, making of all other american countries solidary supporters of its true spirit. Col. House expressed the certainty that it would not be difficult to avoid the objection I referred to when the final terms would be discussed. Regarding the Monroe Doctrine,—he said,—in fact it is now a panamerican doctrine and this plan would really only come to protocolize that fact. He requested and I offered to wire to my Government, as the desire of the President is to officialize this suggestion as soon as possible, if consistent."

The Government of Chile, therefore, had to consider the initiative of the White House on [in] the light of the informations transmitted by their own Representative in Washington, and consequently, understood that their acceptance in principle would allow them to utter afterwards any remark the plan could be motive of, in their judgment, and that until no final agreement would be reached about the terms of said plan, it should be looked upon merely as a tentative suggestion.

The 1st of February, the Ambassadors of Chile, Argentina and Brasil received from the Secretary of State, for their confidential examination, a draft of Convention, that, in four articles, gave form to the ideas contained in the original proposition and to some new ones.

At the same time the Secretary of State requested the Ambassadors to meet in his residence in order to go over the text of the plan before this was submitted to the Governments.

In that meeting the Ambassador of Chile stated:

1st. That the two ideas contained in the first article were of nature to give rise to some remarks, as far as Chile is concerned. These remarks were of a doctrinary character in that they regard the mutual guarantee of political independence *under a republican form of government*, and pertained to the opportunity of the proposition in that they refer to the mutual guarantee of territorial integrity. Concerning the former, is to say, the guarantee of political independence under a republican form of government, he signified that the establishment of a form of government did not seem to be an adequate matter for international treaties. Whichsoever may be the belief about the advantages of the republican form of government to insure the welfare of nations,—the Ambassador said,—there can be no doubt that the institution of a form of government is of the essence of popular sovereignty and to make this question a matter of an international treaty, whichever terms may be employed, it will ever purport an alienation of sovereignty. And, as the republican form of government in America does not seem to be jeopardized, probably there is no need to relate to this matter, likely to arouse protests, being preferable to circumscribe only to the guarantee of political independence. Regarding the guarantee of territorial integrity, the Ambassador of Chile signified that the original proposition was considered by him as merely involving an extension or generalization of the Monroe Doctrine as to be converted into a continental doctrine; but, if it was to be understood as a guarantee of the american countries, ones against the others, such a proposition, as far as Chile is concerned and by obvious reasons, would seem improper on its terms and unacceptable on its ground while Chile may not have definitively settled the territorial problem it has now pending in the Pacific; and that even after that problem would be adjusted, it would involve yet the danger,— unless length of time did elapse,—to awake retrospective resentments and feelings unpleasant to Chile.

As a matter of illustration, he referred to the present situation between the United States and Columbia, intimating that under the circumstances being the United States surely would not feel in a position to advance to Colombia a similar proposition.

2nd. That the settlement of all questions of boundaries now pending among american countries would meet with the full assent of the Chilean Government. Only it would be necessary to clearly define that it applies to the questions derived from the original frontiers, as there exist other territorial controversies that are not precise boundary questions and for whose solutions it has been provided with special means.

3rd. That the monopoly of arms and ammunitions of war could interfere with constitutional provisions in some countries, so far as it would restrict the freedom of commerce. Furthermore, outside of the United States, there is practically no manufacture of arms and ammunitions of war in America by industrial or commercial concerns,—the present manufacturing belonging exclusively to the Governments, and being intended for the supply of their military forces. Regarding the control of *interned* arms and ammunitions, it is at the hand of every Government through the Custom Houses, that permit to regulate the importation as it is deemed suitable. Yet the proposition would have the danger to arouse great resistance in the Congress of the United States, where the vast interests invested in this line of industry in this country would very likely move its influence; and such resistance against this proposition or its failure to be passed by Congress would affect the prestige of the treaty and would divide, instead of uniting, the public sentiment of the countries of the Continent.

4th. That the system of investigation for the settlement of future difficulties among american countries,—which is the extension of the peace plan suggested to the world by the United States and carried into effect until now only in bilateral treaties with this country, deserved the warmest approval of Chile.

The Secretary of State was pleased to consider these remarks, (some of which were sustained by other of the Ambassadors there present) and after some exchange of ideas, he decided to refer them to the President.

Some days after the Secretary of State requested the three Ambassadors to transmit to their Governments the text of the draft of Convention in the terms it was presented to them on February 1st, and adding on their part those suggestions that each one might deem proper. Thus, it was thought, this Government would be in a better position to consider the changes that may be recommended.

The project of Convention having been transmitted to the Government of Chile, they have expressed to the Ambassador their entire approval to the manner in which he has viewed the several ideas therein contained; and, consequently, have directed the Ambassador to suggest those changes that, in their judgment, would be necessary to carry through, without any sacrifice of interests or doctrines, the great and beneficial initiative of the President of the United States to unite the American countries in a continental accord that will mutually guarantee the maintenance of their sovereignty, efficaciously contribute to a reciprocal and friendly understanding, and thus aggregate greater efficiency to its international action and a proper and more representative character to the Continent.

Within these lines, the Ambassador of Chile believes that the proposed Convention presented by the Secretary of State on February 1st ultimo, could be modified in the following manner:

I

That the contracting parties to this covenant and agreement hereby join in a common and mutual guarantee to one another on complete political independence; and, as a consequence of this agreement and recognizing the greatly favorable influence for the development and welfare of american countries of the declaration that, known as the Monroe Doctrine, condemns any occupation, colonization or intervention by other Continent's nations in America, give to said declaration their solemn acceptance and solidary support.

II

That to the end of securing the most perfect understanding among the american nations for the sustenance of the guarantee and declarations referred to in article I, as well as to the most effective promotion of the interests of peace and civilization among them, it is covenanted and agreed that all disputes now pending between any two or more of the contracting parties regarding the demarcation of its original boundaries, shall be brought to a final settlement within one year, in the manner prescribed by treaties or conventions presently in force, or, on its defect, by those methods agreed upon within three months after the ratification of this Convention by the parties interested in each case.

If at the expiration of the three months' term no agreement had been adopted, the following method will be put into operation:

Each of the parties to the dispute shall select two arbiters and those thus selected shall select by vote, or in case of a tie, by drawing lots, an additional arbiter or umpire; to the tribunal thus constituted the question or questions at issue shall be submitted and the decisions and findings of this tribunal shall be final and conclusive as between the parties to the dispute. The findings of such tribunal or tribunals shall be arrived at and officially announced and accepted within not more than one year after the formal constitution of the tribunal and the tribunal shall be constituted no more than three months after the ratification of this Convention.

III

That the contracting parties further agree: First, that all questions of whatever character, arising between any two or more of them which cannot be settled by the ordinary means of diplomatic correspondence shall, before any declaration of war or beginning of hostilities, be first submitted to a permanent international commission for investigation, one year being allowed for such investigation; and, second, that, if the dispute is not settled by investigation, to submit the same to arbitration, provided the question in dispute does not affect the honour, independence or vital interests of the nations concerned or the interests of third parties; and the contracting parties hereby agree, where this has not already been done, to enter into a treaty, each with all of the others severally, to carry out the provisions of this article.

IV

Finally, that the contracting parties agree that in case of any question arising from a claim by a foreign power against an american nation, the latter shall be entitled to lay the matter for its consideration before the Governing Board of the Pan American Union, to the sole effect that this Body may pronou[n]ce itself, if so it is deemed advisable, as to the equity of the claim.

It seems that in these suggestions there is platform large enough as to a first step in the continental accord.

After the full settlement of all boundary questions and other pending territorial disputes, the condition of the national sentiment in those countries before engaged into controversies shall show eventually the propitious moment to sign such conventions on which it would not seem adequate to insist at present.

T MS (SDR, RG 59, 710.11/200½a, DNA).

To Mary Allen Hulbert

Dearest Friend,   [The White House] 21 April, 1915.

I of course had not the least idea you were in New York yesterday (perhaps you had already gone to Trenton), but I was there for so short a time,—only three hours,—that I do not know how I could have managed to look you up. How can I *ever* look *anybody* up without carrying the whole world along with me to see them in any case? But I am none the less deeply disappointed that I could not get a little glimpse of you. And now you are in Trenton, helping your friend, as usual!

This is just a line to say that for two weeks I have been trying to get time, and strength, to sit down and write you a real letter, and that every hour of my time, every bit of my strength has been used, and more than exhausted, by our friends, the people of the United States.

I keep well, keep going, and, I think, with undiminished force, but it is costing all the while, I imagine, just a little more than I have without drawing on reserves.

Has the Nantucket house been rented? Please keep me posted about everything in which I can help or sympathize even, and believe that this little note carries all the friendship of a long letter.   Your devoted friend,   Woodrow Wilson

WWTLS (WP, DLC).

From Sylvester Woodbridge Beach

Dear Wilson: Princeton, N. J. April 21, 1915.

I am writing this line to thank you most heartily for the words you spoke yesterday in New York to the Associated Press. No one could use the English language with more strength and grace or to nobler purpose than you do in that address. More than ever do I realize how greatly favored is our beloved country that none other than Woodrow Wilson has "come to the kingdom for such a time as this." Yours is the firm and steady hand so necessary if the elements in the present critical situation are to be held in solution until the exact moment shall arrive to act. The silent, thoughtful masses of the American people trust you, and are therefore confident and unafraid.

Please do not stop to acknowledge this note, which is a way of saying once more, God bless Woodrow Wilson.

As ever, faithfully yours,   Sylvester W. Beach

TLS (WP, DLC).

Two Letters to William Jennings Bryan

My dear Mr. Secretary,   The White House.   22 April, 1915.

Although I have been silent for a long time about the case, I have had it much in my mind, as I have no doubt you have, to work out some practicable course of action with regard to the death of Thrasher; and I have the following to suggest as the outline of a note to the German Government:

(1) State the circumstances, as we have officially received them.

(2) We take it for granted that Germany has had no idea of changing the rules (or, rather, the essential principles) of international law with regard to the safety of non-combatants and of the citizens of neutral countries at sea, however radical the present change in practical conditions of warfare; and that she will, in accordance with her usual frankness in such matters, acknowledge her responsibility in the present instance.

(3) Raise in a very earnest, though of course entirely friendly,

way the whole question of the use of submarines against merchant vessels, calling attention circumstantially to the impossibility of observing the safeguards and precautions so long and so clearly recognized as imperative in such matters: the duty of visit and search; the duty, if the vessel proves to belong to an enemy and cannot be put in charge of a prize crew, to secure the safety of the lives of those on board; etc.

(4) On these grounds enter a very moderately worded but none the less solemn and emphatic protest against the whole thing, as contrary to laws based, not on mere interest or convenience, but on humanity, fair play, and a necessary respect for the rights of neutrals.[1]

My idea, as you will see, is to put the whole note on very high grounds,—not on the loss of this single man's life, but on the interests of mankind which are involved and which Germany has always stood for; on the manifest impropriety of a single nation's essaying to alter the understandings of nations; and as all arising out of her mistake in employing an instrument against her enemy's commerce which it is impossible to employ in that use in accordance with any rules that the world is likely to be willing to accept.   Faithfully Yours,   Woodrow Wilson

WWTLS (SDR, RG 59, 462.11 T 41/21½, DNA).
   [1] There is a WWsh draft of this letter to this point in WP, DLC.

My dear Mr. Secretary,   The White House. 22 April, 1915.
   Just a preliminary word about the Chilean memorandum.
   I shall cable to House to-day to ask whether he intended to convey the impression the Chilean Ambassador received.
   My present judgment is, that it is best to draft something to which Argentina and Brazil will warmly subscribe and then go ahead with that, leaving Chile free to decide whether she will come in or not, either now or at some future time. I do not think that it would be wise to trim and dilute it to suit her special and singular case.   Faithfully Yours,   W.W.

WWTLI (SDR, RG 59, 710.11/202½, DNA).

To Edward Mandell House

[The White House, April 22, 1915]
   Chilean Ambassador claims that you left the impression upon him that at your conference with the three ambassadors concerning the American agreement that it was not to be proposed to the

other American governments unless first assented to by all of
the three first consulted. Argentine and Brazil are willing to enter
the agreement in substantially the terms proposed; Chile wishes
serious modifications because of her present relations with Peru.

Did you intend to give the implied assurance he understood
you to give?

T transcript of WWsh (WC, NjP).

From Edward Mandell House

Dear Governor: Paris, France. April 22nd, 1915.

I received the following code message from Gerard yesterday.
"Had a talk with von Jagow. He thinks peace could be made if
Germany could keep from Belgium to include Namur, Liege and
the Valley of the Meuse. Indemnity from France and a part of
Congo."

While, of course, I knew such terms were absolutely impossible
from the Allies viewpoint, I arranged for an interview with
Delcasse.

He smiled when he read the message and said that von Jagow
was joking and that tomorrow he would perhaps deny having
made such a statement. I tried to make him understand that
while the terms were impossible it was an indication that they
were beginning to think of peace.

In regard to the indemnity which von Jagow suggested that
France pay, Delcasse told me to tell him to come and get it. Of
course I shall not send any such message, but I shall indicate to
them that there is no use proposing such terms. They do not understand France's attitude at all and I have never been able to
make them see it. They think she is in much the same position as
the Allies think of Austria and they believe that she is eager for
almost any sort of peace.

I read Delcasse your message and he expressed his appreciation very warmly. He said again and again that France was well
satisfied with your attitude and that he reciprocated your good
wishes and hopes that the friendship existing between the two
nations would continue uninterrupted. He took occasion to thank
you for sending me over, just as Poincare had done, and and
[sic] said he appreciated it and understood your high and unself-
ish purposes.

I spoke of the second convention and told him what great
good could come out of it by France and the United States work-

ing hand in hand. He said he understood this perfectly and he was in cordial sympathy with the idea.[1]

I told him Sir Edward Grey had also expressed his approval and he replied: ["]that goes without saying."

It is my purpose to return to England next week and begin to formulate some of the things that we will want to propose at the second convention.

Lord Loreburn is one of the foremost Admiralty lawyers and it is my intention to go over that side of it with him. If we can get a conplete program ready and digested before the convention meets it should not be difficult to put it into execution. These things are so often left for the last moment and are not given sufficient consideration.

Lord Murray of Elibank has at last run me to cover. He is as you know Lord Cowdrey's right hand man. I managed to avoid them both last year, but they are so close to the present Liberal Government that I do not think it wise to offend them.

Your affectionate,   E. M. House

TLS (WP, DLC).
  [1] House summarized the contents of his letter to this point in EMH to WW, April 22, 1915, T transcripts of WWsh decode (WP, DLC; WC, NjP) of T telegram (WP, DLC).

From James Ford Rhodes

My dear Mr. President   Boston April 22 1915

Admiration of the thoroughly patriotic and American tone of your Tuesday speech leads me to an expression of approval of the neutral position you have taken in this terrible European War. I am trying to consider your speech and course from a historical point of view and I have not found it difficult as, making just now a fresh study of Lincoln, I am asking what he would do and say in a similar case.

I believe that posterity will heartily approve your Tuesday speech and your foreign policy. Fortunately you have not that long to wait for appreciation as, unless I am greatly mistaken, you have the country at your back in your sane and dignified attitude.

An unvarying supporter of your foreign policy, I have had occasion to commend it in my letters to Sir George O. Trevelyan[1] and, from an intimation made to me last week by his son,[2] I feel sure that my most significant letter found its way to Trevelyan's warm friend, Sir Edward Grey.

I have just read the Secretary of State's reply to Count von

Bernstorff. Its friendly tone, decisive character and gentle sarcasm could not be improved.

With the expression of my high respect I am

Very truly yours   James F. Rhodes

ALS (WP, DLC).
1 Sir George Otto Trevelyan, historian, former M.P. and cabinet member, now in retirement.
2 George Macaulay Trevelyan, then visiting the United States.

From Edward Mandell House

Paris, 23 April [1915]

I did not intend to give the assurance indicated. His misunderstanding probably arose from my suggestion that if Brazil, Argentine, and Chile consented they might prefer to approach the smaller republics themselves rather than have you do so direct. I am glad you are pushing that matter to a conclusion, for it may have a decided influence for good on the situation here.

I will leave for London April 28th.   Edward House.

T transcript of WWsh decode (WC, NjP) of T telegram (WP, DLC).

Two Letters from William Jennings Bryan

My dear Mr. President: Washington April 23d, 1915.

I am sending you a report just received from Mr. West after a visit at Vera Cruz. I think you will find his views of the men and the situation interesting.[1]

With assurances of high rexpect I am, my dear Mr. President,

Yours very sincerely,   W. J. Bryan

TLS (W. J. Bryan Papers, DNA).
1 Duval West to WJB, April 5, 1915, TLS (SDR, RG 59, 812.00/20721, DNA). West first reported about a cordial meeting with Carranza in Veracruz on March 29 and commented in a highly complimentary way upon the manner in which the First Chief and his aides were setting about to establish orderly government. He was high in his praise of Luis Cabrera and of Carranza's patriotism. He added, however, that there was much disorder in the areas controlled by the *Carrancistas* and that it was reported that commanders often disregarded Carranza's orders. He concluded as follows:
"*CONCLUSIONS.* The conclusions stated, being based upon a partial consideration and investigation of the country, must be taken as tentative and as in comparison only with the investigations made and the conclusions reached after an inspection of the Northern country.
"The Constitutionalist Government, under its present leaders, cannot establish peace in Mexico, because of the failure of its military leaders to obey the orders and decrees of the First Chief. Law and order must be first physically established by the exercise of force. General Carranza, personally, has not the qualifications for military leadership and, even if the movement were successful, the military leaders themselves would, undoubtedly, set General Carranza aside and bring about further differences.

"The great majority of leaders *believe* they are actuated by patriotic motives, but actually they are not wholly so, and the main factor in the revolutionary game is purely selfish. The common people are bearing the burden; they are paying the price and their interests *are not* being advanced by the revolution. The leaders thus far met are not capable of bringing about the reforms indicated in the Plan of Guadalupe, even if they were actuated by patriotic motives.

"There is evident everywhere a strong dislike especially to Spaniards and next to Americans, largely fostered by I.W.W. agitators and irresponsible newspapers. The outlook for any good results to Mexico under this revolutionary movement is most discouraging."

My Dear Mr President,   [Washington] April 23 1915

In a note to you this afternoon I stated that Mr Lansing would take your instructions[1] to Old Point Comfort and prepare a tentative draft of note in the Thrasher case during his stay there. As I have not been able to reach the conclusion to which you have arrived in this case I feel it my duty to set forth the situation as I see it.

The note which you propose will, I fear, very much inflame the already hostile feeling against us in Germany, not entirely because of our protest against Germany's action in this case but in part because of its contrast with our attitude toward the allies. If we oppose the use of the submarine against merchantmen we will lay down a law for ourselves as well as for Germany. If we admit the right of the submarine to attack merchantmen but condem this particular act or class of acts upon the ground that the action is inhuman we will be embarrassed by the fact that we have not protested against Great Britains defense of the right to prevent food reaching non-combatant enemies. We suggested the admission of food and the abandonment of torpedo attacks upon merchant vessels; Germany seemed willing to negotiate but Great Britain refused to consider the proposition. I fear that denunciation of one and silence as to the other will be construed by some as partiality. You do not make allowance for the fact that we were notified of the intended use of the submarine, or for the fact that Thrasher knowingly took the risk of travelling on an enemy ship. I can not see that he is differently situated from those who, by remaining in a belligerent country, assume risk of injury. Our people will, I believe, be slow to admit the right of a citizen to involve his country in war when by ordinary care he could have avoided danger.

The fact that we have not contested Great Britain's assertion of the right to use our flag has still further aggravated Germany and we cannot overlook the fact that the sale of arms and amunition, while it could not be forbidden under neutrality, has worked so entirely for the benefit of one side as to give Germany—not justification but an excuse—for charging that we are favoring the allies. I have mentioned these things to show the atmosphere through which the Thrasher note will be viewed by Germany.

Believing that such a note as you propose is, under the conditions that now exist, likely to bring on a crisis, I venture to suggest an alternative, namely, an appeal to the nations at war to consider terms of peace. We can not justify waiting until both sides, or even one side, ask for mediation, and as a neutral we can not have in mind the wishes of one side more than the wishes of the other side. The neutral nations have both rights and duties, and we are the neutral nation looked to to give expression to these.

Nearly nine months have passed since the war began and after the expenditure of over ten billion dollars and the sacrifice of several millions of the flower of Europe the war is a draw. Surely the most sanguinary ought to be satisfied with the slaughter.

I submit that it is this nation's right and duty to make, not a secret, but an open appeal for the acceptance of mediation. All the neutral nations would support the appeal—several have suggested it. Our own interests justify it—we may be drawn into the conflict if it continues. Our obligation to the neutral nations demands it. Our friendship for the nations at war requires it. They can not reason calmly and neither side is in a position to ask for mediation. As the well-wisher of all we should act; as the leader of the peace propaganda we should act; as the greatest Christian nation we should act—we can not avoid the responsibility. The loss of one American, who might have avoided death, is as nothing compared with the tens of thousands who are dying daily in this "causeless war"   Is it not better to try to bring peace for the benefit of the whole world than to risk the provoking of war on account of one man?

We can not foresee the result of such an appeal as you can make, but if it is *right* there ought not to be lacking the faith to try. You have such an opportunity as has not come to any man before. I most earnestly urge you to make the appeal.

With assurances of high esteem I am, my dear Mr President,
Very truly yours   W. J. Bryan

ALS (WP, DLC).
¹ That is, WW to WJB, April 22, 1915.

From Joseph Patrick Tumulty

[The White House] April 24th [1915].
The Secretary thinks the President should write some sort of a letter showing that he did not approve the "Birth of a Nation."
WFJ.[1]

TL (WP, DLC).
[1] Warren F. Johnson, Tumulty's secretary.

To Joseph Patrick Tumulty

Dear Tumulty: [The White House, April 24, 1915]
I would like to do this if there were some way in which I could do it without seeming to be trying to meet the agitation which in the case referred to in this clipping was stirred up by that unspeakable fellow Tucker.[1]   The President.

TL (WP, DLC).
[1] The unidentified newspaper clipping contained a report of a hearing before Mayor James Michael Curley on April 7 to determine whether "The Birth of a Nation" should be shown in Boston. William Monroe Trotter was among those testifying against the film. The Mayor decided that it could be shown, provided that a few scenes were cut. The film began its run on April 10. There was a near riot at the Tremont Theatre a week later, resulting in the arrest of Trotter and ten other protesters. Two days later, April 19, Trotter and others sought the assistance of Governor David I. Walsh and secured his promise to prosecute the manager of the theater under a censorship law of 1910 and, if that proved ineffective, to seek a stronger censorship law. All of these events were well publicized. See Stephen R. Fox, *The Guardian of Boston: William Monroe Trotter* (New York, 1971), pp. 191-94, and Thomas Cripps, *Slow Fade to Black: The Negro in American Film, 1900-1942* (New York, 1977), pp. 58-60.
Swem consistently wrote "Trotter" in shorthand as "Tucker." Wilson undoubtedly said "Trotter."

Two Letters to William Jennings Bryan

My dear Mr. Secretary,   The White House. 26 April, 1915.
I cabled House to ask whether he had intended to convey to the Chilean Ambassador the impression that we would not act in our American plan unless we had the assent of all three of the A.B.C., and their assent to the same terms, and this is his reply:
"I did not intend to give the assurance indicated. His misunderstanding probably arose from my suggestion that if Brazil, Argentine, and Chile consented they might prefer to approach the smaller republics themselves rather than have you do so direct. I am glad you are pushing that matter to a conclusion for it may have a decided influence for good on the situation here."
This misunderstanding removed, we can go forward without regard to what Chile proposes, though earnestly desirous that she should come in.   Faithfully Yours,   W.W.

My dear Mr. Secretary,   The White House. 26 April, 1915.

I think we sent the right man. This report carries conviction. It is disappointing, of course, but what we wanted was the truth. I hope that West is to be here soon.

Faithfully Yours,   W.W.

WWTLI (W. J. Bryan Papers, DNA).

To James Ford Rhodes

My dear Mr. Rhodes: The White House April 26, 1915

Your letter of April twenty-second gratifies me very deeply and I want to thank you for it most warmly. It heartens me not a little to be thus supported by those who have really given serious study to the history and interests of our country. I have to thank you, therefore, for a piece of deep encouragement.

Cordially and sincerely yours,   Woodrow Wilson

TLS (J. F. Rhodes Papers, MHi).

From William Jennings Bryan

My dear Mr. President: Washington April 26th, 1915.

I am sending you a copy of a message which has just been brought to the Department.[1] You will notice the language in Sections 3 and 6 regarding the church. I heard today that the movement which I reported to you a few weeks ago has not made much progress since they found they could secure no assurances from the government.

With assurances of high respect, I am, my dear Mr. President,

Very sincerely yours,   W. J. Bryan

TLS (W. J. Bryan Papers, DNA).
[1] V. Carranza to E. Arredondo, April 23, 1915, T translation of telegram (W. J. Bryan Papers, DNA), repeating in slightly different language the seven points in the Enclosure printed with WJB to WW, April 20, 1915. Carranza's telegram ended with a new paragraph: "The above articles are a part of the program of the Revolution and constitute a pledge to the country, which the Constitutionalist Government will not fail to observe."

From Edward William Bok

My dear Mr. President: Philadelphia April 26, 1915

I have a ten year old boy—Cary, by name—who is essentially a "Wilson boy"! That is, he has fastened his interest on you, and follows everything you do with the keenest joy. His older brother

is a Roosevelt boy so that between them there is no danger of my
suffering from any monotony in the way of home discussion of at
least two public men. This younger boy is very keen to see his
divinity in the flesh, and as there are one or two little matters—
non-political, believe me—I would like to talk to you about, I wondered if you could give me fifteen minutes on some day of *next
week* when I could see you on the little matters in my mind and
bring the little chap and his mother with me? Would this be at
all possible? I know you are not making any engagements and if
you can't do it, please have no hesitation in saying so, and I will
understand. Or perhaps you would prefer me to board your train
at Baltimore or Wilmington when you come to Philadelphia on
the 10th of May as I understand is your plan?

Will you please say, frankly, which, or No to both suggestions
as you feel?

With every personal regard, believe me,

Very cordially yours   Edward Bok

ALS (WP, DLC).

Remarks at a Press Conference

April 27, 1915

Mr. President, is it true that you have endorsed the plan looking
to a gathering in the United States of the representatives of the
neutral governments for the purpose of inaugurating a peace
propaganda?

No, sir. That's the first I have heard of it. That is Cain compounded. It hasn't been brought to my attention at all.

Has any reply been made to the cablegram, to the mystery that
the United States demand the right to participate in the Japanese-
Chinese situation?

No. I understood that the Secretary of State did—has intended, for our information, in calling for their reply, but of
course—

Mr. President, would you care to say anything about the Chinese-
Japanese negotiations?

No, sir, there is nothing new in that aspect of it.

This morning's dispatches seem to indicate that Japan is pressing
very hard.

Yes. But that has been indicated again and again. I don't
know what that may turn out to signify. . . .

Mr. President, there is a good deal of speculation as to what you
are doing in seclusion at the White House these days. Can you
give us any light?

Well, there's no secrecy about it that I know of, or mystery. I am doing what I was not permitted to do when Congress was in session. I am really reading all the dispatches. I am keeping in touch with everything that is going on and expressing an opinion when I am obliged to, and keeping silent when I am not obliged to.

One of the problems of the District of Columbia is the Recorder of Deeds.

I wish, Price,[1] I could help you out on that.

JRT transcript (WC, NjP) of CLSsh (C. L. Swem Coll., NjP).
[1] William W. Price, White House correspondent of the Washington *Evening Star*. His comment was a reference to the controversial issue of whether or not another Negro should be appointed Recorder of the Deeds of the District of Columbia, as had been the tradition for many years.

To William Jennings Bryan

My dear Mr. Secretary,   The White House. 27 April, 1915.

This is a very sensible document and I hope is sincerely meant, though West's report, which you sent me the other day, does not seem to afford much prospect of real control by Carranza.

The position taken about the Church seems to me entirely justified in view of the history of that matter in Mexico.

Do you hear anything about Huerta's movements and plans which seems like business? Is he acting with Church people in this country, do you think?

I understand he expects to visit Washington, but *not* to see us!

Faithfully Yours,   W.W.

WWTLI (W. J. Bryan Papers, DNA).

From William Jennings Bryan, with Enclosures

My dear Mr. President: Washington April 27, 1915.

I am enclosing the tentative draft of a note in the Thrasher case, together with a letter from Mr. Lansing. Mr. Lansing has followed the instructions contained in your note and I do not see that it is susceptible of material improvement if the line indicated is to be followed.

You will notice that on pp 9 and 10 he takes the position that the submarine cannot be used against merchant vessels because, like the torpedo boat, it is not capable of furnishing means of escape to passengers on board the ill-fated vessel.

I am not sure that this reasoning is conclusive. If a submarine is employed near enough to land to permit of a reasonable hope of escape in the ship's boats it might be a sufficient compliance with the laws of humanity to give those on the vessel sufficient time to leave the vessel and embark in smaller boats. In this particular case the time given was *not* sufficient and, as stated, there is no evidence that the shortness of time was necessitated by the presence or proximity of other vessels.

Unless you think it necessary to oppose the use of the submarine entirely for attacking merchantmen I think it is worth while to consider whether the use might not be allowable if the time is sufficient in a particular case to give the passengers a chance to escape by *any* means—not necessarily by the use of the attacking vessel.

As stated in my letter to you I think the alternative which I suggested is, for the reasons stated, better than the sending of any note on this subject, although if a note such as is proposed in the Thrasher case were sent at the same time that the proposition I suggest, the Thrasher case would be lost sight of in the discussion of the larger proposition. Each day new dangers arise and we know not how soon some catastrophe, like the sinking of an American ship by mistake, may so arouse our people as to make it difficult to apply diplomatic remedies. The course which I submitted for your consideration is, of course extraordinary, but the situation is extraordinary—nothing like it has ever occurred before and, therefore, it is permissible to venture away from the beaten track.

With assurances of high respect I am, my dear Mr. President,
Yours very sincerely,   W. J. Bryan

TLS (WP, DLC).

ENCLOSURE   I

Robert Lansing to William Jennings Bryan

Dear Mr. Secretary: [Washington] April 27, 1915.

I hand you herewith a draft instruction to Ambassador Gerard on the Thrasher case, which I prepared while at Old Point Comfort. I have tried to follow as closely as possible the President's memorandum of the 22nd instant.

In the preparation of this instruction it has been my endeavor to soften the language as far as consistent with a plain and emphatic statement of disapproval of the use of submarines against merchant ships. However gently our views are expressed I am convinced that the German Government and press will inter-

pret our communication as unfriendly, and as further evidence
of our partiality for the Allies.

Of course this result cannot be avoided if we say anything at
all; but it is certainly the Government's duty to make representations to the German Government as to the death of Thrasher.
Silence in this case would, I think, be severely condemned by the
American people.

As I have said before, the Thrasher case is the most disturbing, in my opinion, of any with which the Department has had
to deal. It can not be ignored, and yet any possible action is bound
to increase the hostile feeling of Germany for this country. Every
day the German press is becoming more and more bellicose in
commenting on the neutral conduct of the United States. Even
the considerate and temperate reply to the German Ambassador's
memorandum of April 4th has been received with general condemnation and sarcastic remarks by the German press.

The tension in our relations with Germany is becoming
greater; the situation more and more difficult; almost anything
we say or do will be distorted into unfriendliness. For that reason
I can but be apprehensive of sending an instruction like the one
enclosed, and yet it seems impossible to avoid doing so in the
circumstances. Altogether the case is one to cause grave anxiety.

Faithfully yours,   Robert Lansing.

TLS (WP, DLC).

E N C L O S U R E   I I[1]

MEMORANDUM April 24, 1915.
DRAFT INSTRUCTION TO THE AMERICAN AMBASSADOR AT BERLIN

You are instructed to convey textually the following to the
Minister of Foreign Affairs.

The Government of the United States has now received re
ports from London, and the official statement given to the United
States naval attache at Berlin, relative to the sinking by a German submarine of the British passenger steamship FALABA on
March 28, 1915. It does not appear where the attack on the vessel took place except that it was upon the high seas. Though the
reports and statement differ in details they agree substantially as
to the following facts:

1. The submarine appeared in the wake of the FALABA, out-

---

1 Words in the following document in angle brackets deleted by Wilson; words
in italics added by him. Words in square brackets deleted by Bryan; words in
double square brackets added by him.

ward bound from a British port, and signalled her to stop immediately.

2. The FALABA did not obey the signal but attempted to escape by flight, being pursued by the submarine.

3. Fifteen minutes after the signal was given a second signal directed the FALABA to stop immediately or the submarine would fire, and the commander of the submarine by megaphone ordered the vessel to be abandoned within ten minutes.

4. On receipt of the second signal the engines of the FALABA were stopped, and the crew at once began to lower her boats.

5. Within ten minutes, according to testimony of witnesses at the inquest, or twenty-three minutes according to the ⟨German⟩ statement *from Berlin*, after the second signal was given, and while some of the FALABA's boats hung at their davits, and many persons were on the vessel's deck, a torpedo was discharged from the submarine, which was lying a short distance off the FALABA's quarter. The torpedo struck the vessel, causing her to sink almost immediately.

6. By [[the]] torpedoing [[of]] the FALABA before the crew and passengers had time to take to the boats and leave the vessel over one hundred persons were drowned.

7. Among the passengers drowned was Louis C. Thrasher, a citizen of the United States.

In addition to the foregoing facts it is reported that the FALABA was unarmed and made no attempt at resistance, but hastened to lower her boats on receipt of the second signal from the submarine.

The fact that the commander of the submarine allowed several minutes for the persons on the FALABA to escape shows [conclusively] that he was not apprehensive of an attack from the vessel and that such apprehension was not the cause of torpedoing it without further delay.

Furthermore it does not appear from the evidence at hand that the action of the submarine in discharging the torpedo before the FALABA was abandoned was induced by any imminent danger of attack by other British vessels or through fear that the FALABA would be rescued by such vessels, since none capable of attacking the submarine is shown to have been in the vicinity or approaching.

The facts and circumstances of the sinking of the FALABA, by which Thrasher and other non-combatants were drowned, are of such an unusual nature, and are so contrary to the generally accepted rules of naval warfare, that this Government, inspired by a sincere desire to remove all causes of possible difference

between it and the Imperial German Government, would be wanting in its duty as a friend if it refrained from earnestly impressing upon the Imperial Government the grave international complications which [can hardly be avoided] [[may arise]], if the[ir
present] policy of sinking unarmed merchant vessels on the high
seas is continued [[adopted]], without safeguarding the lives of
inoffensive non-combatants on such vessels.

The Government of the United States is unwilling to believe
that the German Imperial Government, whose past has been
distinguished by strict observance of their legal obligations, intend to cease to conform to those essential principles of international law, the application of which insure safety to citizens of
neutral countries and other non-combatants when on the high
seas.

Whatever change in the general conduct of naval warfare has
resulted from the introduction of new methods of offense and
defence, this Government takes it for granted that the Imperial
Government will not intentionally deviate from the rules of war
founded on these principles, but will confine their operations to
acts which are not opposed to the practice of nations and the
dictates of humanity.

The Government of the United States, relying upon the Imperial German Government's respect for international law and
their usual frankness in dealing with questions of legality, confidently expects that Government to acknowledge their responsibility in the case of the FALABA and to make full and just
restitution for the death of Leon C. Thrasher caused by their
naval authorities in the manner above stated.

This Government, in submitting to the Imperial Government
this case, in which a citizen of the United States lost his life by a
seemingly indefensible act of the German naval authorities,
believes it to be in the interest of the mutual regard and friendship, which it hopes will continue to characterize the intercourse
between the two governments, to state plainly and without
reservation its views as to the use of undersea craft in intercept-
ing and destroying commercial vessels bound for or departing
from the ports of an enemy.

The citizen or subject of a neutral state, whether he embarks
on a merchant vessel of neutral or belligerent nationality, is,
when on the high seas, entitled to the protection furnished by
the exercise of the right of visit and search in the event that the
vessel is stopped by the naval authorities of a belligerent; and, in
case the vessel, on which he has embarked, is subject to capture
on account of its nationality, destination or cargo, the neutral

as well as other non-combatants on the vessel are entitled to be placed in safety, whatever disposition may be made of the vessel and its cargo.

These rules governing the conduct of a belligerent in its treatment of an alien merchant ship and the persons on board of it, have been so long and clearly recognized by civilized nations that they are imperative. They cannot be ignored or violated without inviting universal condemnation and imposing full liability for their breach upon the Government which permits it.

The high seas are the property of all mankind. Neutrals as well as belligerents are entitled to their common use in time of war under those restrictions, and only those restrictions, which have been sanctioned by the universal consent of nations. If a belligerent power has acquired a means of destroying vessels engaged in peaceful commerce, but is unable, if it employs such means, to observe the precautions which international law imposes as safeguards to neutral rights and to the lives of non-combatants on the high seas, those means can not be legally employed, and ought not to be employed, however expedient they may appear to the belligerent possessing them.

For the past forty years the maritime powers have used torpedo-boats in prosecuting a naval war, but they have never, so far as this Government is advised, employed them to destroy merchant vessels on the high seas. Unfitted as torpedo-boats are to exercise the belligerent right of visit and search, and to safeguard the lives of the crews and passengers of merchant vessels, their offensive operations have been confined to attacks upon the warships of the enemy.

To the same class of warcraft, in the opinion of this Government, belong submarines, whose chief weapon of offense is the torpedo. Like the torpedo-boat the submarine evidently lacks the necessary size and equipment to exercise the right of visit and search and to protect non-combatants. Its use, therefore, should be subject to the same limitations as those which are applied to the use of the torpedo-boat.

Since it is the general opinion, in which it is understood the Imperial Government concurs, that it is impossible to utilize submarines to interrupt effectively commerce on the high seas without a breach of the principles of international law, to which Germany and all other civilized nations have given an unqualified assent, the Government of the United States relying upon the justness of those principles which are founded not alone on material interests, but on humanity, fairness, and the common rights of mankind, appeals solemnly and earnestly to the German Imperial Government to refrain from a practice which law and morality alike condemn, or to modify that practice so that it will not be adverse to those accepted principles of international right, which Germany has steadfastly advocated and respected, and which are essential to the perpetuation of international order and amicable relations between belligerent and neutral powers.

Robert Lansing.

TS MS (WP, DLC).

From William Jennings Bryan, with Enclosure

My dear Mr. President: Washington April 27, 1915.

I am enclosing for your consideration draft of a letter to the Chilean Ambassador. His answer covered so much that I thought it best to put our reply in writing so that there will be less likelihood of his misunderstanding your views.

If you will return it with such changes as you think should be made, I will have the corrected copy put into the form of a letter and sent to him.

With assurances of high respect I am, my dear Mr. President,
Yours very sincerely, W. J. Bryan

TLS (SDR, RG 59, 710.11/2021½A, DNA).

E N C L O S U R E

William Jennings Bryan to Eduardo Suárez-Mujica

My dear Mr. Ambassador: [Washington, April 27, 1915]

I have laid before the President your counter-proposition and at his request present the situation as he views it.

First: He has communicated with Mr. House and finds that Mr. House did not intend to convey the impression that the presentation of this plan to the republics of Latin-America would depend upon its acceptance by any one or more countries. The misunderstanding on this subject probably arose from the suggestion made by him to the effect that if approved by the three countries to which he presented it these countries might assist in presenting it to the other countries.

The President would not feel justified in making the negotiation of a treaty so important to all the countries dependent upon the action of any one country—an action that might be dependent entirely upon circumstances which, while justifying the refusal of one country to enter into the agreement, might not affect other countries. And besides, it would be unfair to any country to assume that it would be willing to stand in the way of the negotiation of such a treaty merely because it, for any reason, was not able to join in the convention.

Second: The President feels that the agreement would be greatly strengthened by the guarantee of a republican form of government and he doubts whether it would be possible to secure the ratification of the treaty by the Senate if this guarantee were omitted.

While it is true, as you suggest, that the form of government is, in the first instance, a matter to be decided by the people of the country still, in view of the fact that all of these countries have adopted the republican form of government, and in view of the further fact that the trend of the world is toward the idea of popular government, it would seem that the right of return to monarchy is one that need not be considered. It is not likely that officials of any government would be willing to create uneasiness in the minds of the people of that country by any action which would even suggest the possibility of an abandonment of the government's representative character.

Third: The President feels that the guaranty of territorial integrity is an essential part of the plan and that it would be unwise to eliminate it.

History has shown that nearly all wars have resulted in changing the territorial boundaries of the nations engaged—in fact, many wars have had such changes as their object. Nothing would go further to insure peace among the nations of the western hemisphere than an understanding that force would not be recognized as a legitimate means of acquiring territory.

The United States is not only willing to give assurances of its purpose in this respect, but is willing, if desired, to join with the Latin-American republics in giving specific and definite assurances that it will not be forced to part with any of its territory.

Fourth: It is necessary, of course, to recognize the fact that there are existing disputes in regard to territory, and boundaries which have to be taken into consideration and the plan you propose of distinguishing between original boundaries and territorial boundaries arising from other sources may point to a solution. The guaranty of territorial integrity might read something like this:

> "*One*: All territorial boundaries now agreed upon shall remain unchanged, and their establishment shall be a guaranty by the contracting parties.

"*Two*: All disputes as to original boundaries shall be determined in accordance with the plan set forth in the proposition submitted by the President, such exceptions to be set forth specifically by the nations concerned.

"*Three*: Territorial disputes which have arisen from any other cause than disputes over original boundaries shall be specifically stated by the parties interested, and shall be adjusted as soon as circumstances will permit; the parties to the dispute pledging themselves to do everything to promote an early adjustment of these disputes, all boundaries, when finally determined, to be accepted in like manner as those already established, and to be for the future guaranteed."

You will notice that the plan above outlined guarantees the permanence of the boundaries now agreed upon, provides for an early settlement of disputes over original boundaries and relieves those nations from embarrassment over territorial disputes that arise from other causes.

As to the matter of arms we do not anticipate any difficulty of securing the ratification of a treaty pledging the contracting governments to an endeavor to secure legislation which will enable each government to prevent the export of arms intended for use by one of the contracting parties against another of the contracting parties. The provision above referred to, guaranteeing territorial integrity and national independence would, of course, be a protection to the contracting parties against foreign powers, as well as against each other.

While the United States has, for a century, borne alone the responsibility for preventing aggression from countries in the eastern hemisphere, and while the purpose of the proposed treaty is not to secure relief from these responsibilities, it will be gratifying to this country to have the republics of Latin-America join in the upholding of what is known as the Monroe Doctrine, because such a recognition of the doctrine by them would prevent for the future any misunderstanding of its purpose and underestimating of its value.

I have not mentioned the provision for the embodying in the proposed treaty of the principles of the treaties already negotiated, providing for investigation of all disputes. This we regard as of great value. The three countries so far interviewed agree to this and we have no doubt that all the rest will accept it.

The President hopes that your Government, upon full consideration of the subject, will find it possible to join in this treaty at this time. If, however, existing conditions are such as to prevent your Government, or any other Latin-American government, from signing now, provision will be made in the treaty for the subsequent signing by such governments as may find it advisable to delay becoming parties to the convention.

Assurances, etc.   [W. J. Bryan]

CCL (SDR, RG 59, 710.11/203½A, DNA).

To William Jennings Bryan

My dear Mr. Secretary,   The White House. 27 April, 1915.

This seems to me excellent. I agree with you that it is wise to be explicit and that it is well to put these views in writing, as you have done.

I think it would be wise, however, to state that the provisions as to territory as you restate them in this letter are not definitively proposed (for we have not yet shown them to Argentine and Brazil, upon whose cooperation we are depending) but are formulated by way of suggestion of what we would be quite willing to discuss, if in that form they commended themselves to the Chilean government.[1]   Faithfully Yours,   W.W.

WWTLI (SDR, RG 59, 710.11/203½, DNA).
    [1] In the letter sent (WJB to E. Suárez-Mujica, April 29, 1915, CCL [SDR, RG 59, 710.11/203½A, DNA]), Bryan added the following paragraph:
    "The provisions relating to existing disputes have not been submitted to Brazil or Argentina but are suggested to you tentatively by way of indicating what we would be quite willing to discuss if, in that form, they commend themselves to your Government."

From William Jennings Bryan

My dear Mr. President: Washington April 27, 1915.

I had a talk with Bishop Bashford today and he is very deeply concerned about the situation in China. I told him, confidentially, what we had done and he felt very much relieved, but he feels that the increase in the troops sent to China is having a very bad effect and he is afraid that it may result in a conflict there which he thinks would be very disastrous.

I am sending you for your consideration and amendment a communication[1] along the lines that we have talked. I am not entirely satisfied with it but it sets forth the things which we have discussed.

With assurances of high respect I am, my dear Mr. President,
                Yours very sincerely,   W. J. Bryan
    Mr Lansing, being away, has not seen this.

TLS (W. J. Bryan Papers, DNA).
    [1] It is printed in expanded form as an Enclosure with WJB to WW, April 28, 1915.

Two Letters to William Jennings Bryan

My dear Mr. Secretary,   The White House. 27 April, 1915.

I think this excellent, and I think all that you have said ought to be said. It certainly can give no offense as you have put it, and may do good.

But I was thinking yesterday in Cabinet, as Lane was presenting his views, that the real weakness of our influence in this matter lay in the *privacy* of our representations to Japan with regard to it. I think, therefore, that it would be wise to say to the Japanese Ambassador that our position with regard to these important matters, of which treaties with China as well as our general interest in the position China is to take in the economic development of her resources give us a right to speak, has been so generally misunderstood and so misleadingly speculated about that we feel that it may become immediately necessary to make our views public, *perhaps* in conjunction with other nations whose interests and sympathies are equally involved; and that we are on that account the more anxious to have a perfectly clear and cordial relationship of mutual understanding between ourselves and Japan, so that it may be evident from the first that no friction from this source is involved so far as our two governments are concerned.

This, I am convinced, is the only means we have of reassuring China, our own people, and other governments at present less free than we to protest.

I think, too, that we ought to instruct Reinsch to assure the Chinese government that it has our sympathy in resisting any demands which too seriously impinge upon its sovereignty, its administrative independence, or its territorial integrity.

Faithfully Yours,   W.W.

My dear Mr. Secretary,   The White House. 27 April, 1915.

This is significant news.[1]

I am, as you know, keeping in as close touch as possible with what the men in authority at Berlin, Paris, and London have in mind, and I am sorry to say that there is only one thing we can truthfully say to the Japanese Ambassador in reply to his inquiry,—and perhaps it will be useful to say it,—namely, that there are no terms of peace spoken of (at any rate in Germany) which are not so selfish and impossible that the other side are ready to resist them to their last man and dollar. Reasonableness has not yet been burned into them, and what they are thinking of is, not the peace and prosperity of Europe, but their own aggrandizement, an impossible modern basis (it might be well for Japan to reflect) for peace.

Faithfully Yours,   W.W.

WWTLI (W. J. Bryan Papers, DNA).
1 WJB to WW, April 26, 1915, FR-LP, I, 12-13, saying that he had received a very confidential communication from the Japanese Ambassador to the effect that the Japanese Minister in Stockholm had been approached by the Austrian envoy on the subject of Japan concluding a treaty of peace with Germany, and that the Japanese Minister had replied that his government would do nothing independently of its allies. "He wanted to know," Bryan added, "whether we had seen any indications of a desire on the part of either side for a cessation of hostilities and I told him that while we had heard rumors we were unable to find any authority for such rumors and that so far as we knew no indication of a desire for peace had been given by either side."

From William Jennings Bryan, with Enclosure

My dear Mr. President: Washington April 28th, 1915.

I enclose a draft of Section 4 in compliance with the suggestion which you make. I have not inserted the phrase, "perhaps in conjunction with other nations whose interests and sympathies are equally involved," but can add it if, after you hear my reason for omitting it, your judgment is in favor of including it in the statement. None of the Allies are in position to join us in anything that we say or do and of course we could not invite Germany to join us in view of the relations existing between Japan and Germany. That being the case, I am inclined to think that any suggestion of union with them would divert attention from the course which we desire them to consider, the only course open to us, namely, action taken by ourselves alone but action which we feel sure the Allies would favor if they were free to express themselves. I await your opinion before adding the enclosed to the letter.

With assurances of high respect, I am, my dear Mr. President,

Very sincerely yours,   W. J. Bryan

TLS (W. J. Bryan Papers, DNA).

E N C L O S U R E

William Jennings Bryan to Viscount Sutemi Chinda

My dear Mr. Ambassador: Washington April 27, 1915.

This Government entertains for both Japan and China a feeling of such sincere friendship and is so deeply interested in their prosperity and progress, that it feels that it is its duty to present the situation to you as it sees it, with the earnest hope that it may contribute to that amity and good will which must exist between Japan and China if the legitimate aspirations of the people of the two countries are to be realized.

It will, with equal pleasure, discuss with China any matters which stand in the way of understanding.

First: It is feared that the increase in the number of soldiers stationed in China has been misunderstood and caused an irritation, unintended by Japan and embarrassing to China. There is every reason why the relations between Japan and China should be of the most friendly and neighborly character, and this is hardly possible if China feels that the presence of additional troops at this time evidences an intention upon the part of Japan to resort to force to secure such an agreement as it may regard as desirable.

This Government feels sure that Japan has no such intention and that in taking this action she was not fully informed as to the apprehension felt in China.

Second: This Government is led to believe that the distinction which Japan has made to the United States, Great Britain, France and Russia, between the "demands" and the "requests," has not been made sufficiently clear to the Chinese Government and is of opinion that much of the irritation caused in China is due to the fact that the Chinese Government has misunderstood the real purpose and intention of Japan. The propositions submitted by Japan, having been published as *demands*, and no distinction having been made between the two classes of propositions, a great deal of discussion has been indulged in as to the possible conflict between certain propositions and treaty stipulations entered into by China with the other Powers.

Third: There is one demand, namely the one affecting the mines at Hanyehping, which might be construed to interfere with both the sovereignty of China and the equal rights of other countries. The mines referred to are owned by a Chinese company which has borrowed a large amount of money from certain Japanese capitalists. The obligation thus created is merely a pecuniary one and would be fully satisfied by a payment of the money borrowed. The loaning of this money would hardly seem to justify a demand for joint ownership of the mining property.

When it is remembered that iron ore is the basis of one of the great industries, and when it is remembered further that the mines are located in the very heart of the Chinese Empire, a *demand* for alien ownership may seem inconsistent with that sovereignty and independence which China can rightfully claim, and which Japan has repeatedly recognized. As joint ownership would vest in the Japanese Government, or in its nationals, a power to control an industry essential to the prosperity of China, a demand for such control cannot fail to alarm the people of China, especially if that demand is accompanied by the presence of an increased military force. And since the demand includes a control over all mines in the neighborhood there would seem to be an interferance with the equal rights of other countries having dealings with China.

We are informed that the Japanese Government has a contract running for some years, and covering a considerable amount of ore, indicating the Government's pecuniary interest in the working of these mines. The interest of Japan would seem to be protected by the terms of the contract and insofar as the contract fails to meet the requirements of Japan, either as to quantity or time, the rights of Japan are protected by treaty the same as the rights of other countries.

Fourth: The embarrassment caused to both our Government and yours by the privacy of our representations to Japan and by the fact that we have not felt free to confer with China regarding matters covered by treaty between the United States and China raises the question whether it might not be better for all parties for us to make our views public. Your Government has felt it necessary to give out statements from time to time and our silence has invited speculation and misrepresentation. Since we may find it necessary to make some announcement we are the more anxious to have a perfectly clear and cordial relationship of mutual understanding between ourselves and Japan, so that it may be evident from the first that no friction from this source is involved so far as our two governments are concerned.

In presenting these suggestions I beg to repeat that this Government is actuated by a cordial desire to see these two great empires in the Orient achieve the high destiny which lies before them—a destiny which requires for its complete realization the fullest cooperation between the two countries upon a basis of confidence and good will.

Accept, Excellency, the renewed assurances of my highest consideration.   W. J. Bryan

TLS (W. J. Bryan Papers, DNA).

Two Letters to William Jennings Bryan

My dear Mr. Secretary, The White House. 28 April, 1915.

I dare say you are quite right.

Perhaps what I had in mind might be better accomplished by your handing this communication to the Ambassador in person and taking occasion to say to him, that, inasmuch as the subject matter of the relations of China to the rest of the world had more than once been the subject of correspondence between the United States and the chief European powers, it might become our duty to make our position clear (and invite comment) by means of a circular note. I mean, just to intimate this to him as something we had in mind as possible.

Faithfully Yours, W.W.

WWTLI (W. J. Bryan Papers, DNA).

My dear Mr. Secretary, The White House. 28 April, 1915.

I have thought a great deal about the contents of the letter you wrote me (the letter written in your own hand) about the Thrasher case. It of course made a deep impression on me.

As I told you yesterday at Cabinet, I am not at all confident that we are on the right track in considering such a note as I outlined for Mr. Lansing to work on. I am not sure that my outline really expressed what I would myself say in the note, for, after all, the character of a note is chiefly in the way the thing is said and the points developed. Perhaps it is not necessary to make formal representations in the matter at all.

What I have been thinking about most is your alternative proposition, that we publicly call upon the belligerants to end the war.

I wish I could see it as you do. But in view of what House writes me I cannot. It is known to every government concerned that we believe the war should be ended and that we speak for all neutral nations in that wish. It is known to them that we are seeking to help and that anything they want to say to one another which they are too proud or too prudent to say directly and officially they can say privately through us. They are at present most appreciative and cordial,—ready to accept help when they think they can accept it. We know their minds and we know their difficulties. They are dependent upon their own public opinion (even Germany) and we know what that opinion is. To insist now would be futile and would probably be offensive. We would lose such influence as we have for peace.

I am afraid, Mr. Secretary, that there is much in this that will seem to you disputable; but I can only state my conviction in the matter, and God knows I have searched my mind and conscience both to get the best, the nearest approach to wisdom, there is in them.

With warmest regard and appreciation,

                    Faithfully Yours,   Woodrow Wilson

WWTLS (CLO).

To Joseph Patrick Tumulty

Dear Tumulty: [The White House, April 28, 1915]

I would suggest as an answer to this letter[1] the following:

"It is true that 'The Birth of a Nation' was produced before the President and his family at the White House, but the President was entirely unaware of the character of the play before it was presented and has at no time expressed his approbation of it. Its exhibition at the White House was a courtesy extended to an old acquaintance."[2]   The President.

TL (WP, DLC).
    [1] T. C. Thacher to JPT, April 17, 1915, TLS (WP, DLC), enclosing F. T. Hammond and J. M. Hollowell to Annie Fisher, April 15, 1915, TCL; Anna P. Williams To Whom It May Concern, April 14, 1915, TCL; and a typed extract of a hearing before James M. Curley, April 7, 1915, all in WP, DLC. All of the enclosures stated that, at the hearing before Mayor Curley, the counsel for the promoters of "The Birth of a Nation" had said that the President and members of the cabinet had viewed the film at the White House and had either expressed their approval of the production or, at least, had voiced no objection to it. Thomas Chandler Thacher, a former Democratic congressman from Massachusetts, reiterated this statement in his covering letter and asked Tumulty to let him know whether or not it was true.
    [2] JPT to T. C. Thacher, April 28, 1915, TCL (WP, DLC), repeated Wilson's words.

To Edward William Bok

My dear Mr. Bok: [The White House] April 28, 1915

Thank you for your interesting note of April twenty-sixth. Please present my warmest compliments to Cary and tell him how proud I am to have such a partisan. I shall hope some day to placate his older brother.

I shall be very happy indeed to see Mrs. Bok and you and the youngster next week. I suggest that, if convenient, you come on Monday, the third of May, and come direct to the house at 12:30.

        Cordially and sincerely yours,   Woodrow Wilson

TLS (Letterpress Books, WP, DLC).

To Edith Bolling Galt

My dear Mrs. Galt,   The White House 28 April, 1915

I have ordered a copy of Hamerton's "Round My House"[1] through the bookseller, but while we are waiting for it I take the liberty of sending you a copy from the Congressional Library. I hope it will give you a little pleasure. I covet nothing more than to give you pleasure,—you have given me so much!

If it rains this evening, would it be any fun for you to come around a[nd] have a little reading,—and, if it does *not* rain, are you game for another ride? If you are not in when this gets to you, perhaps you will be gracious enough to telephone Margaret.

Your sincere and grateful friend,   Woodrow Wilson

ALS (WP, DLC).
[1] Philip Gilbert Hamerton, *Round My House: Notes of Rural Life in France in Peace and War* (London, 1876).

From Edith Bolling Galt

My dear Mr. President: [Washington] April 28th, 1915.

How very good of you to remember my desire to read "Round My House," and take the trouble to send to the Congressional Library to gratify me.

Your wish to give me pleasure has been so abundantly fulfilled already, that for you to take time to send a personal note is only generous good measure with which you fill my goblet of happiness. Thank you.

I am very tired tonight, and can think of nothing more restful than to come and have you read to us, or—in case it clears,—blow away the cobwebs in another way, by another life-giving ride. *But*—(that word that so often destroys my pleasure) I have promised my dear mother to spend this evening with her, so must not yield to the impulse to come.

Just a word more to tell you how deeply I value the assurance with which you end your note. Such a pledge of friendship blots out the shadows that have chased me today, and makes April twenty eighth a red letter day on my calendar.

Faithfully and proudly your friend   Edith Bolling Galt.

ALS (WP, DLC).

From William Jennings Bryan

My dear Mr. President: Washington April 30, 1915.

His Excellency the Ambassador of Austria-Hungary has asked me to convey to you an expression of his respectful gratitude for complying with the wish of his Government in appealing personally to the Czar of Russia on behalf of the Austro-Hungarian prisoners of war in Russia and especially in Siberia.

I remain, my dear Mr. President,
Very sincerely yours,   W. J. Bryan

TLS (WP, DLC).

From Edward Mandell House[1]

Dear Governor: [London] April 30th, 1915.

I arrived here Wednesday night. I have already had two conferences with Sir Edward Grey and I am to have the first formal one with him by appointment through Page this afternoon at five o'clock.

Of course no one is to know but you of the other two conferences.

I have outlined to him the full plan of the freedom of the seas and how best it can be brought to Berlin's attention and what concessions they must give in return. I shall not let them know how receptive he is to the idea, but shall try to impress upon them how hard we are working to accomplish the desired end, and give them little dribblets of hope from time to time. The thing thus is held within our hands.

Sir Edward tells me that public opinion here will have to be educated in this direction, particularly the conservatives, and I shall endeavor to do this.

I also outlined to him the plan, about which I wrote you, of formulating ideas and reducing them in some concrete way so as to have them ready for the peace convention.

I have told him of the idea of consolidating the two conventions. He approves of all this and has suggested the proper people for me to see in order to work out these different problems. As I get them started I shall transmit them to you.

The first one I shall take up will be the rules regarding the freedom of the seas. Sir Edward agreed that my suggestion regarding Lord Loreburn was good as far as one person, but he thought he had too broad a view to make it entirely feasible to have him alone. He suggested my discussing this feature with

Lord Mersey,[2] and also with Balfour, and later perhaps with Bonar Law and Austen Chamberlain.[3] The last two have narrow views, but must be reckoned with.

We will have to keep this program absolutely confidential between yourself, Sir Edward and myself, and even the men I shall discuss these things with will not know the full purposes.

I wish I had a first class American mind who knew Admiralty Law to confer with. Do you know of anyone? Charles Burlingham of New York is the only one, for the moment, I can think of. However, this is something that is not pressing and we have ample time.

I told Sir Edward I felt sure that the Berlin Government wanted peace and that they were deterred mainly by German public opinion which will have to be educated to the making of concessions.

I am in a great rush to get this to you by the St Louis so I cannot go into further details.

Your affectionate,   E. M. House

TLS (WP, DLC).
  [1] House conveyed the gist of the following letter in EMH to WW, April 30, 1915, T transcript of WWsh decode (WP, DLC; WC, NjP) of T telegram (WP, DLC).
  [2] John Charles Bigham, 1st Baron (later Viscount) Mersey, former judge of the King's Bench Division of the High Court of Justice, at this time serving as head of the judicial committee which heard appeals from the prize court.
  [3] M.P. and former cabinet member, soon to become Secretary of State for India in the coalition cabinet.

From Oscar Solomon Straus

Dear Mr. President   New York City. April 30/1915.

This evening General Huerta called upon me with his interpreter. I was glad to have the opportunity of meeting him and "sizing him up." I wish briefly to convey to you the substance of his talk and the impression he made. He is 58 years of age medium stature, very dark bronze complexion denoting considerable Indian blood, with great vitality and apparently a man of nervous force vigor and decision. He gave me a a [sic] sketch of his life. At 17 he went to the Military School and graduated after 4 years as a military and topographical engineer, after that passing up through various grades until he became general under Diaz and afterwards President of Mexico.

He is living here at the Ansonia Hotel awaiting his family which is expected shortly from Europe. He informed me he is devoting much of his time in studying English and apparently making progress.

He described to me the conditions in Mexico, saying there is neither government nor security there only rival bandits. He says Mexico needs a strong government under a firm hand determined to do justice, and that the right man will be supported by public opinion. He is very modest and reserved in manner but rather oratorical & emphatic in speech.

I asked him if he intended while here to visit Washington, he said no, as his going there would doubtless be misinterpreted by the press. Yet if he knew that the President would receive him, nothing would give him more pleasure.

My own opinion is, and his interpreter intimated as much that in a few weeks he will go to Mexico leaving his family here.

He said a strong man can bring peace out of chaos and I am quite sure, without his having said so, he regards himself *as that man*.

I asked what in his opinion the United States could do, if anything, in bringing about peace, he replied—absolute neutrality, keep hands off. I asked him whether to pacify Mexico would necessitate the spilling of much blood? He said no, and indicating by his fingers, only the hanging of not more than ten men at most, and Mexico will have peace.

I would not be surprised, if after all he should prove to be "the man of the hour" Mexico needs, for the lack of a better.

If I can be of any service, command me, should you desire me to speak further with him

Very truly yours   Oscar S. Straus

ALS (WP, DLC).

To Edith Bolling Galt

Dear Friend,   The White House 30 April, 1915

I am sorry I could not find a fresh copy of this book, but this copy is in fairly good condition. I hope it will give you some of the same pleasure it gave me years ago when I first read it.

It is a great privilege to be permitted to share any part of your thought and confidence. It puts me in spirits again and makes me feel as if my *private* life had been recreated. But, better than that, it makes me hope that I may be of some use to you, to lighten the days with wholehearted sympathy and complete understanding. That will be a happiness indeed.

Your sincere and grateful friend,   Woodrow Wilson

Don't trouble to acknowledge this.

ALS (WP, DLC).

From William Jennings Bryan, with Enclosure

My dear Mr. President: Washington May 1, 1915.

I am enclosing a memorandum from Mr. Lansing in regard to the attack upon the CUSHING,[1] and the publication which appeared in this morning's papers.

The dropping of the bomb on the CUSHING is, I think, a matter which should be at once called to the attention of the German Government and I am cabling Van-Dyke's telegram to Berlin[2] and asking for a report on it.

As to the second[3]—I do not take the same views of it as Mr. Lansing does. I do not see that it is a matter of offense, in fact, I think it is a fortunate thing to have it published, and the publication is evidence of a friendly desire to evade anything that might raise a question between Germany and the United States. I see no more reason why an American citizen should take the risk involved in going in one of these vessels than there is for taking the risks that are involved in going near the fighting on land.

I am sending this, however, for your consideration.

With assurances of high respect I am, my dear Mr. President,
                    Yours very sincerely,   W. J. Bryan

TLS (WP, DLC).
    [1] A German airplane bombed an American merchant ship, *Cushing*, in the North Sea on April 29. Only one bomb struck the vessel; it caused some damage but no loss of life.
    [2] H. van Dyke to WJB, April 30, 1915, *FR-WWS 1915*, p. 378.
    [3] The German Embassy had just published a warning in the American press stating that vessels flying the flag of Great Britain or her allies were liable to destruction in the zone of war surrounding the British Isles, and that travelers sailing in the war zone on such ships did so at their own risk. See, for example, the *New York Times*, May 1, 1915.

E N C L O S U R E

Robert Lansing to William Jennings Bryan

Confidential.

Dear Mr. Secretary: [Washington] May 1, 1915.

Two events have occurred which bear upon the Thrasher case and which should be called particularly to the attention of yourself and the President in connection with that case and the policy which should be adopted.

The first of these is the attack April 29th by a German aeroplane on the American s.s. CUSHING, which is reported by Dr.

Van Dyke in a telegram dated April 30th, a copy of which is enclosed.

The second is the publication this morning in some fifty newspapers of a notice to American citizens not to take passage on British vessels which will traverse the German "war zone." The notice, a copy of which is enclosed, is signed by the Imperial German Embassy, and, as I am informed was a paid advertisement prepared about a week ago by that Embassy.

While no lives were lost by the attack on the CUSHING, one bomb is reported to have struck the vessel and caused considerable damage. It is, therefore, not so serious in one sense as the attack on the FALABA which caused the death of Thrasher. On the other hand, it is a more flagrant violation of neutral rights on the high seas, and indicates that the German naval policy is one of wanton and indiscriminate destruction of vessels regardless of nationality. The fortunate outcome of this attack in no way removes the grave possibilities which may result from future attacks of the same character.

The question arises, therefore, what course should be pursued by this Government. Should we make representations in this case *before* we do in the *Thrasher* case? And, if we do, will it not appear that we care less for an American life than we do an American ship? I fear that this course would arouse a great deal of criticism, and might be interpreted as an admission that an American citizen had no right to take passage on a British vessel. Such an admission would appear to me to be a serious mistake. An American citizen legally has such a right and in my opinion the Government ought to uphold it.

The published notice of the German Embassy has an even more direct bearing on the Thrasher case. It is a formal threat that American citizens, exercising their just rights on the high seas will not be protected from the intended attack on all British ships without visiting them or giving the persons on board ample opportunity to escape.

If we do not take up the Thrasher case, in what position are we placed in the event other American passengers lose their lives? Will not the answer be that we acquiesced by our silence in the propriety of the sinking of the FALABA, and that Americans were publicly warned of the danger, and that, therefore, Germany is not to be blamed?

Another thing, the using of the American press to warn Americans not to exercise their legal rights, for a violation of which this Government has said that it would hold Germany to "a strict accountability" seems to me to be highly improper. It is an even more insolent proceeding than the making public of diplomatic correspondence. Communications of this sort should be sent to the Department, which can make the contents public if it pleases, but not to address the Department at all is an impertinent act, which would warrant summary action if it was expedient.

In this case, however, it would seem to me unwise to act, as I believe that would be playing into Count von Bernstorff's hands. I cannot but feel that these two events are in line with Germany's attitude toward the United States, to which I directed attention in my memorandum of February 15th.[1] Everything seems to point to a determined effort to affront this Government and force it to an open rupture of diplomatic relations. I hope that I am wrong, but I have that feeling.

For the present, however, the question is how do these events affect the Thrasher case. Do they compel action, or is it wise to continue silent?

Faithfully yours,   Robert Lansing.

TLS (WP, DLC).
[1] See WW to WJB, April 5, 1915 (first letter of that date), n. 1, Vol. 32.

To Edward Mandell House

[The White House, May 3, 1915]

Referring to your letter of 12th April from Paris, I think the suggestion you make for starting correspondence between the belligerents excellent. I shall be glad to play any part circumstances suggest or permit.

Your cable of May 1st[1] gives me some hope that the first of your alternative suggestions may be about to work. I would welcome any advice you may have to give as to the best way to handle the matter of the sinking of American oil boat in view of all you have learned.   Wilson.

T transcript of WWsh telegram (WC, NjP).
[1] That is, the cable of April 30, which arrived on May 1. See EMH to WW, April 30, 1915, n. 1.

From William Jennings Bryan, with Enclosure

My dear Mr. President: Washington May 3, 1915.

I am enclosing a confidential suggestion from Mr. Lansing in regard to the Thrasher, CUSHING and GULFLIGHT[1] cases.

We have made inquiry in regard to the CUSHING and today will make inquiry in regard to the GULFLIGHT. I think it better

to wait till we have information in regard to the CUSHING and
GULFLIGHT before deciding on the action to be taken.

    With assurances of high respect I am, my dear Mr. President,
                    Yours very sincerely,   W. J. Bryan

TLS (WP, DLC).
    ¹ A German submarine torpedoed the American tanker *Gulflight* without
warning in the Irish Sea on May 1. Although the vessel remained afloat, the
captain died of heart failure, and two sailors were drowned when they jumped
into the ocean.

                    E N C L O S U R E

Confidential.

Dear Mr. Secretary: [Washington] May 3, 1915.

    In view of the aerial attack on the American s.s. CUSHING and
of the reported torpedoing of the s.s. GULFLIGHT, of which no
official confirmation has yet been received, I think it should be
considered whether the draft instruction to Ambassador Gerard
regarding the death of Leon C. Thrasher through the sinking of
the British s.s. FALABA should be sent.

    The death of Thrasher loses much of its importance in com-
parison with these two attacks on American vessels if it is true
that three of the crew of the GULFLIGHT lost their lives by reason
of the vessel's being torpedoed.

    If these attacks are confirmed officially, I can not see how this
Government can avoid making a vigorous protest; a mere appeal or a deferential complaint will, in my opinion, neither satisfy
the American people nor be in accord with the duty of the Government or with the rights of the United States.

    The course pursued by the Germans seems to be based on a
policy intended to provoke radical action by this Government,
which will result in the severance of diplomatic relations. I may
be wrong and I most sincerely hope so, but recent events appear
to tend strongly in support of that view.

    It may be deemed advisable to proceed with the Thrasher case
separately. If so, the instruction should be sent without delay,
provided it is sent at all, so that it could go out before official
reports are received on the facts of the other two cases.

    Another course would be to treat all three cases in one in-
struction. While the draft instruction in the Thrasher case might
be taken as a basis for a new instruction covering the three cases,
it would require very considerable amendment, and would have
to be put in stronger and less conciliatory language.

    I need not say to you, Mr. Secretary, that I believe the situa-

tion is critical and one to cause the gravest anxiety. We are being
forced near to the breaking point in our relations with Germany;
and I am thoroughly convinced that it is being done wilfully
through a misconception of the result here in the United States.

Faithfully yours,   Robert Lansing.

TLS (WP, DLC).

Two Letters from William Jennings Bryan

My dear Mr. President: Washington May 3, 1915.

Referring to the confidential memorandum left by the Japanese Ambassador on the morning of April 30th,[1] a copy of which
I gave you at the Cabinet meeting, I beg to call your attention
to the changes which have been made and to submit comments
thereon.

I do not see that we have any substantial reason for objecting
to the claim which Japan makes, that Japanese subjects should
be permitted to buy land in South Manchuria; and the same as
to paragraph "b" in regard to travel, residence, and the carrying
on of business there.

Paragraph "c" raises two questions: You will notice that the
Japanese are to produce passports to the Chinese local authorities, and to observe China's police laws—"or regulations approved
by the Japanese consuls" and they are to pay to Chinese authorities "taxes approved by the Japanese consuls."

I called the Ambassador's attention to the fact that the two
clauses which I have placed in quotation marks are susceptible
of abuse. To say that the Japanese shall not obey police laws
unless those laws are approved by Japanese consuls is to take
away from China the right to make laws controlling Japanese
residents, and to say that Japanese need not pay taxes *except
as approved by the Japanese consuls* is to say that in the sovereign
matter of taxation the Japanese shall be subject to Japanese
orders. If the Japanese desire to protect themselves against unfair legislation they might ask that Chinese police laws *be not
more severe against Japanese than against Chinese*; or that the
Chinese police *laws shall not be more severe than the police laws
enacted by the Japanese for the control of foreigners residing
in Japan.* Japan has a right to object to discrimination as between
Chinese and Japanese, and in view of the unusual punishment

---

[1] T MS (SDR, RG 59, 793.94/551, DNA), printed in FR 1915, pp. 128-30,
reporting on the progress of the Sino-Japanese negotiations to date. Bryan summarizes the memorandum very well.

that may be employed in China, she might even justify a demand that her citizens be not subject to more severe laws than those prescribed by Japan herself under the same circumstances; but to say that the regulations must be approved by the Japanese consuls transfers the right of making laws to Japan, acting through her consuls, and may result in serious discriminations in favor of Japanese, which could not fail to create trouble in China.

In regard to taxation, it seems to me it would be sufficient to provide that Japanese should not be *subject to greater taxation than Chinese*. I suggested this to Chinda and he expressed a fear that China might institute special taxes, applicable only to the business in which Japanese are engaged; but this might be prevented by a provision that the taxes levied on industries in which Japanese are engaged should not be greater than taxes levied upon the same industries elsewhere.

In other words—what Japan has a right to ask is that there shall be no discrimination against Japanese, but not that exceptional rules shall be made in favor of her people as compared with the rules governing Chinese.

The long paragraph following gives, as I understand it, the rule in such cases, and the final clause of the paragraph indicates an intention to leave Japanese to the Chinese courts as soon as the Chinese judicial reforms are brought about.

I do not see that we need to refer to Section 3, in regard to Eastern Inner Mongolia.

Section 4 relates to the Hanyehpin'g Company. I think it might be well to express gratification that that demand has been so modified as not to include an option on, or refusal of, mines in the "neighborhood." They drop that out of consideration of our suggestion. The demand as it now stands is very much softened. Paragraph "a" stipulates that China shall approve an agreement that *may* be concluded in the future between the Company and the Japanese capitalists. This leaves the matter to the Company and the capitalists. China can avoid the joint undertaking if the Chinese stockholders in the Company fail to conclude an agreement with the capitalists of Japan for the joint holding of the mines.

The provision "b," not to confiscate, is, in my opinion, unobjectionable, but to insist that (c) China shall not nationalize the mines—"without the consent of the interested Japanese capitalists"—is to deny to China the right of eminent domain, which is essential to sovereignty. Every nation, every state and every municipality ought to have the right of eminent domain, and so far as I know, they have that right conditioned, of course, upon the payment of damages—no property being taken for public use without just compensation. I do not think that China ought to surrender the right to appropriate any property or industry within her domain upon the payment of just compensation to the owners.

Paragraph "d" is unnecessary. If this Company is a joint organization nothing can be done without the consent of both the Chinese and Japanese stockholders, and, therefore, it is unnecessary to say that no loan shall be permitted from any other than Japanese. If China permits the organization of the Company she ought not to prohibit the Company from borrowing from other than Japanese because that would permit the Japanese creditors to close out the Chinese holders at any time.

Section 6 deals with the provisions of former Article V, which covered the "requests." It seems to me that the language of these new requests which are to be "kept on record" is unfortunate. Take "a," for instance: It reads—"That the Chinese Government will, in case of necessity in the future, employ Japanese advisors." This might be construed to mean that China engages not to employ any advisors in the future except Japanese advisors, in case advisors are necessary. The Ambassador says that this was not the intention, but in view of the feeling over there it is not well to have any ambiguous language employed.

Our suggestion on that point is the only fair basis, it seems to me, namely: that China will not discriminate against Japan in the matter of advisors.

I do not see any objection to paragraph "b," provided it is understood that the land leased or purchased for school buildings and hospitals shall not be used for any other purpose—that is, that they shall not be used for commercial or military purposes.

Paragraph "c" is very ambiguous and is quite sure to result in further irritation. Our suggestion here, too, seems to be the only rational basis of agreement—namely, that China shall not discriminate against Japan in the matter of purchase of arms.

The request for the establishment of an arsenal in China under Japanese and Chinese management is naturally offensive to China, and if she agreed to send military officers to Japan for that purpose, it would be difficult for the military officers to refuse to make the arrangement when they reached Japan.

The request for railways in south China, contained in paragraph "d," relates to lines about which Great Britain has been consulting, and Japan asks that she be granted these if no objection is made by other powers—evidently relying upon her ability to secure the consent of Great Britain.

In view of the fact that all railroad lines at once demand a sphere of influence, and in view of the danger that these spheres of influence will, if continued to be granted, ultimately deprive China of her own country, I am inclined to think we ought to advise China to build her own railroads with money borrowed by general loans and *not by the mortgage of particular property*. I think our capitalists will loan on China's general credit and if our capitalists will loan on this security other capitalists will be compelled to loan on the same terms. This will make China's loans national, like the loans of other governments, and relieve her of the danger which follows in the wake of these concessions.

Paragraph "e," in regard to the freedom of preaching, is left for future discussions—that would seem to be the most easily granted of all the requests.

You will notice that the original proposal for joint administration of police is withdrawn, but I can understand why the Chinese would object more to the privilege which Japan asks for her subjects in Manchuria and Mongolia than she did to the demand for joint police supervision.

The provision as to Fukien is in line with our suggestion if the word "other" is left out, so that China will not grant the right to build shipyard, coaling or other naval or military establishment on the coast of Fukien to *any* Government. The last part of that clause, however, would seem to bind the Chinese Government not to allow any such establishment to be build with any foreign capital. It seems to me that it would be sufficient to provide that China should not give *any agreement or pledge upon any harbor, coaling station, or naval base to any other foreign government*.

You will notice that Japan makes no reference to the development of the interior of Fukien. This is in line with our suggestions.

The return of Kiaochou to China is, I think, a valuable concession and I do not see that there is any objection to the conditions—first, as to the opening of Tsingtao as a commercial port; and second, to the establishment of a Japanese concession—(that is a place for Japanese settlement)—in the locality to be designated by Japan. I suggested to the Ambassador that this, of course, did not mean that Japan would select the fort, and he said, of course not. If the space selected is not too large and is intended for commercial use and residence, like the foreign settlement at Shanghai and the foreign settlement contemplated in these last proposals, I do not see any objection.

Taking the document as a whole, and considering the concessions which Japan has made, I think we are justified in believing that she will modify such of the demands as are still unreasonable, and that we ought to so change the letter that we wrote as to call attention to these points.

The Ambassador was very earnest in his expressions of fear that our reference to the use of the soldiers would be embarrassing, because his Government could not, at this time, withdraw the soldiers lest it might seem an act of weakness, and he evidently did not like to have us make a request which they would have to refuse. I believe that this new statement gives us ground enough for a strong letter and it would seem desirable to make it as soon as possible.

I would like your opinion on the points to which I have called attention, and the impressions which you have received from reading this latest statement from the Japanese.

With assurances of high respect I am, my dear Mr. President,
Yours very sincerely,   W. J. Bryan

Mr Lansing & Mr Lockhart[2] of the Far East approve of these suggestions   W.J.B.

TLS (W. J. Bryan Papers, DNA).
2 Frank Pruit Lockhart, Assistant Chief of the Division of Far Eastern Affairs.

My dear Mr. President: Washington May 3, 1915.

I send you a letter which Mr. B. Howell Griswold, Junior, of Baltimore, Maryland, desires.[1] It is in connection with the loan about which he and Doctor Goodenow spoke with you.

I have suggested that the first paragraph be so changed as not to make reference to the six-Power group. As they desire all the banking aid they can get I thought it might not be advisable to bring up the other case as it is no longer a matter under consideration.

I have also stated to them that you might not care to go into detail to the extent that they have in in [sic] this letter but I see no objection to the general line of the letter. What they especially desire to have brought out is that you recommend the opening up of the loan to such a number of bankers as possible, in order that it may be more in the nature of a popular loan.

In talking with them you suggested that it might be well to let knowledge of this proposed loan get to the public in order to test out the Japanese attitude on it. They ask that the time and place of such announcement be left to them. They are afraid we may not be able to judge the effect of such an announcement or the opportunities of making it. They would rather leave it to the judgment of the man who is acting for them in China. I presume there would be no objection to this.

With assurances of high respect I am, my dear Mr. President,
                    Yours very sincerely,   W. J. Bryan

TLS (WP, DLC).
    ¹ For the letter and its ultimate fate, see WW to WJB, June 7, 1915 (third letter of that date).

From Edward Mandell House

Dear Governor: London, May 3rd, 1915.

Thank you for sending me the Munsterburg letter. I do not think it indicates anything except that he wishes to prejudice you against Eliot.

Eliot and his commission cannot do anything—no one would listen to them. They would not be in good favor in Germany and we have the situation here so well in hand that no one in Governmental circles would talk to them seriously.

Sir Edward tells me that Straus is again talking to Bernstorff and trying to inject himself into the situation.

I saw Lord Loreburn this morning. He is not only a man that can be thoroughly trusted, but I believe he is my friend. He told me that he thought if we could bring about the freedom of the seas it would be the greatest act of statesmanship that had been accomplished in centuries. He thought it would be "of 100% value to other nations and 120% to England," though we would have great difficulty in getting the English mind to see this.

He spoke of Balfour as having great ability, but thought his mind was too feminine to grasp the significance of such a measure. He advised, just as Sir Edward did, that I see Bonar Law, whom he said had an inferior mind, but who was practical and could probably be convinced sooner on that account.

He said if we could incorporate this idea into the peace convention, it would not only be a great act of statesmanship, but "it would be perhaps the greatest jest that was ever perpetrated upon an unsuspecting nation"; having, of course, Germany in mind.

I told him I shivered in Berlin when I proposed it to the Chancellor and the Foreign Office for fear they would see that it was more to England's advantage than their own, and would therefore not be willing to make any concessions because of it.

Loreburn told me in the deepest confidence that England would not be averse to letting Germany have a strip in Africa running across the Continent from sea to sea. He cautioned me not to mention this to anyone, because it seems to be one of the

Governmental secrets which he did not feel that he should tell, but which he felt justified in telling me because of the advantage it would give us in dealing with Germany.

I cannot quite fathom the significance of this unless it be that England is afraid of France in Africa, and may wish to use Germany as a buffer between North and South Africa. Germany could get this through the purchase of the Belgian and Portuguese possessions, which she is willing to pay for and which it seems England might be willing to agree to.

Lord Loreburn is one of the warmest admirers you have in Great Britain, which is naturally a great bond of sympathy between us. Your affectionate, E. M. House

TLS (WP, DLC).

From William Jennings Bryan, with Enclosure

My desr [dear] Mr President: Washington May 4, 1915.

I enclose you draft of the letter to Chinda. I have had to frame it in the midst of interruptions and would take more time on it but for the desire you expressed that it reach you tonight.

I also enclose for your criticism a statement to be given to the press after I have shown it to the Ambassador.¹ In speaking to him I think it would be well to say that we cannot believe that the newspapers correctly report the situation in China when they say that Japan is contemplating an ultimatum and that there is every reason why the doctrine that "Nothing is final between friends" should ne [be] applied to this situation.

With assurances of high respect I am, my dear Mr President,
Yours very sincerely, W. J. Bryan

TLS (W. J. Bryan Papers, DNA).
¹ It was a statement issued to the press on May 6. It said that the Japanese government had confidentially informed the State Department about its negotiations with China at their outset and had given assurances that it had no intentions of interfering with the political independence or territorial integrity of China or with the "open door" policy. The statement then defined American policy in the present situation as follows:
"This Government has not only had no thought of surrendering any of its treaty rights with China, but it has never been asked by either Japan or China to make any surrender of these rights. There is no abatement of its interest in the welfare and progress of China and its sole interest in the present negotiations is that they may be concluded in a manner satisfactory to both nations, and that the terms of the agreement will not only contribute to the prosperity of both of these great Oriental empires but maintain that cordial relationship so essential to the future of both, and to the peace of [the] world." *FR 1915*, p. 143.

E N C L O S U R E

William Jennings Bryan to Viscount Sutemi Chinda

My dear Mr. Ambassador: May 5th, 1915.

The confidential memorandum left by you on April 30th has been carefully examined, and, by direction of the President, I beg to submit the following comment upon the same:

This Government entertains for both Japan and China a feeling of such sincere friendship and is so deeply interested in their prosperity and progress, that it feels it is its duty to present the situation to you as it sees it, with the earnest hope that it may contribute to that amity and good will which must exist between Japan and China if the legitimate aspirations of the people of the two countries are to be realized.

It will, with equal pleasure, discuss with China any matters which stand in the way of an understanding.

First: The provision that the police laws or regulations, applying to Japanese subjects in South Manchuria, and also the taxes, shall be approved by Japanese Consuls, would seem to interfere with the sovereignty of China, whereas, we take it for granted, Japan only desires to protect from discrimination such of her subjects as choose to reside in China.

The desired end could be reached by an agreement that police rules and regulations applicable to Japanese should not be more severe than those obeyed by Chinese, or more harsh than those which Japan applies to foreign residents under similar circumstances; and, in like manner, protection from unjust taxation might be secured by an agreement that the rate of taxation imposed upon Japanese subjects should not be greater than the tax imposed upon citizens of China; or to meet the fear which Your Excellency expressed, should not be different from, or greater than, taxes levied on like industries in other parts of China.

Second: It is gratifying to note that one of the provisions of the former demand, in regard to the Hanyehpi'ng mines, has been withdrawn, namely: that the Hanyehpi'ng Company should have an option upon, or the refusal of, other mines in the neighborhood. It would seem to us clear, however, that one of the demands, namely: "c" is inconsistent with the political independence of China; and that another, namely: "d" is a discrimination against the nationals of other countries. The right of eminent domain is essential to sovereignty, every nation and every political unit having the right to take private property for public purposes upon the payment of just compensation. No nation would willingly surrender this right and no nation should be asked to do so. To invest any group of foreigners with the right to refuse to surrender for public use any property desired by the Government is to create within the country a power superior to the Government.

Paragraph "d" not only asks China to discriminate against the nationals of other countries, in favor of the nationals of Japan, but makes the value of the property of Chinese stockholders of the Company dependent upon the willingness of Japanese creditors to make or renew loans.

Third: This Government understands from previous memorandums, and interviews relating thereto, that the items enumerated in Section 6, and described as "points to be kept on record" are presented as *requests* and are not to be urged if objected to by China.

This Government has already expressed itself in regard to the employment of Japanese advisors and also as to the purchase of arms. It understands that Japan's only purpose is to protect herself against discrimination and that she has no desire to secure the employment of Japanese advisors out of proportion to those selected from other treaty powers.

Likewise, in the matter of arms, we understand that Japan's only purpose is to protect herself from discrimination in the purchase of arms, not to secure for her Government or manufacturers a disproportionate share of the arms purchased, as compared with purchases from other treaty powers.

Fourth: This Government understands that the request for railway concessions in southern China is not presented as a demand upon the Chinese Government, but is merely an expression of a wish that these concessions be granted, if agreeable to China, and not inconsistent with her obligations to other countries.

Fifth: As to Fukien. We take it that the word "other" is a mistake in translation, it not being the desire of Japan to reserve for herself that which is denied to other powers. What is intended, as we understand it, is that the Chinese Government will undertake not to grant to *any* power the right to build shipyards, coaling or naval station, or any other military base, on or along the coast of Fukien.

The second provision, that the Chinese Government will not allow any such establishment to be built with foreign capital may not, as Your Excellency suggested, be a correct translation. We presume that it is intended by this only to preclude the mortgaging or pledging of any property on the coast in return for foreign capital borrowed; or is it the desire of Japan to secure a promise that China shall use for such coast development only money raised by taxation and not the proceeds of any foreign loan?

Sixth: This Government feels sure that the announcement of Japan's intention to return Kaiochow to China will be accepted as an evidence of Japan's regard for China's welfare, as well as for the protection of her territorial integrity.

While paragraph two of the provision relating to Kaiochow provides for the establishment of a Japanese concession, or settlement, to be designated by Japan, such concession, we of course presume, would not be unreasonable in amount and would not include the fortified portion.

We cannot but feel that the effort, well intended of course, to conduct the negotiations in secret, has been unfortunate in that the press has felt licensed to speculate as to the communications that have passed back and forth between the Governments of Japan and China. This tendency on the part of sensational newspapers, however reprehensible, is a matter that must be taken into account. In this respect this Government has suffered along with the Governments of Japan and China for, not having taken the public into our confidence, our silence has been misinterpreted and our position misunderstood. The papers, according as it suited their purpose, have represented us as agreeing to proposals submitted, or as objecting to demands made. We are convinced that a frank statement of this Nation's position will contribute to a solution of the problems involved, and that the time has come when we must make such a statement.

In presenting these suggestions I beg to repeat that this Government is actuated by a cordial desire to see these two great empires in the Orient achieve the high destiny which lies before them—a destiny which requires for its complete realization the fullest cooperation between the two countries upon a basis of confidence and good will.

Accept, Excellency, the renewed assurances of my highest consideration.   [W. J. Bryan]

CCL (W. J. Bryan Papers, DNA).

Paul Samuel Reinsch to William Jennings Bryan

Peking. May 4, 1915. Recd 4:32 p.m.
STRICTLY CONFIDENTIAL.

The Chinese Government has been advised that tonight or tomorrow it will receive from Japan an ultimatum requiring absolute compliance with the revised demands as reported in my telegram of April 27, 8 p.m.[1]

It has also learned that the Japanese reservists in Mukden have been ordered to their stations and others instructed to leave Chinese territory and gather in the railway zone and that Japanese residents in Peking have been told to hold themselves in readiness for similar orders.

It is not yet possible to foresee whether the Chinese Government will comply with the ultimatum.   Reinsch

T telegram (W. J. Bryan Papers, DLC).
    [1] P. S. Reinsch to WJB, April 27, 1915, printed in FR 1915, p. 127.

To William Jennings Bryan

My dear Mr. Secretary,   The White House. 5 May, 1915.

Thank you for your prompt compliance with my desire to see this letter sent to the Japanese Ambassador.

I am returning it and the announcement for the press with my entire approval.

I also think it very important that you should say to the Ambassador what you suggest about the alleged ultimatum, and ask him to repeat it to his Government.

Faithfully Yours,   W.W.

I suppose the letter will be sent and the interview sought today.

WWTLI (W. J. Bryan Papers, DNA).

To Edward Mandell House

[The White House, May 5, 1915]

There is something I think ought to be said to Sir Edward Grey of which I wish you would speak to Page, but which I cannot convey through him but must convey through you because I wish it to be absolutely unofficial and spoken merely in personal friendship. A very serious change is coming over the public sentiment in this country because of England's delays and many wilful interferences in dealing with our neutral cargoes. The country is listening with more and more acquiescence, just because of this unnecessary irritation, to the suggestion that an embargo be placed upon the shipment of arms and war supplies, and if this grows much more before Congress assembles it may be very difficult if not impossible for me to prevent action to that end,

Please present to Sir Edward Grey very earnestly the wisdom and necessity of giving utmost freedom to our commerce in neutral goods to neutral ports, and the permanent settlement of all questions concerning cargoes seized or detained. More detaining will probably bankrupt many in the South.   Wilson

T transcript of WWsh telegram (WC, NjP).

To Joseph Patrick Tumulty

My dear Tumulty: [The White House] May 5, 1915

I cannot let your birthday go by without sending you a message of deep affection. I need not tell you what daily comfort and support it gives me to have you at hand, so thoughtful of every interest of the administration and of the country, and so constantly alert to keep me in touch with the things that I ought to know and ought to do. My warm affection goes out to you, my dear friend. May you have many, many happy returns of the day!
                Faithfully yours,   Woodrow Wilson

TLS (Letterpress Books, WP, DLC).

To Oscar Solomon Straus

Personal.

My dear Mr. Straus: The White House May 5, 1915

I thank you sincerely for your interesting account of your interview with General Huerta. I read it all with the greatest interest, but the concluding portion with a great deal of concern. It disturbs me to think that it is possible that you should deem this man, after the record he has already made in Mexico, to be the man to bring ordered peace and justice to that country. This seems to me inconceivable and impossible and I can at present imagine no circumstances which would make it possible for this administration to recognize him. I should deem it a great danger to the peace of both countries if he should return to Mexico.
                Sincerely yours,   Woodrow Wilson

TLS (O. S. Strauss Papers, DLC).

From William Jennings Bryan, with Enclosure

My Dear Mr President,   Washington May 5 [1915]

I am sending you a memorandum from Mr Lansing. Since hearing your statement at Cabinet meeting indicating an intention to postpone final settlements until after the war, in case present efforts fail, I am not so much afraid of representations—it is the *possibility* of *war* from which I shrink & I think we have a good excuse for asking that the disputes be settled when reason reigns. It occurs to me that the effect might be softened on both if we make a protest against the holding up of our trade with neutrals at the same time we protest against the submarines. I gave the letter to Chinda this afternoon. He found no fault with the proposed press notice but asked that we wait long enough to get the dispatch to Japan so that they can issue a statement also. He asked two days[.] I gave him *one* & told him we [will] decide tomorrow about second day. With assurances etc I am my dear Mr President   Yours truly   W. J. Bryan

ALS (WP, DLC).

E N C L O S U R E

Robert Lansing to William Jennings Bryan

CONFIDENTIAL.

Dear Mr. Secretary: [Washington] May 5, 1915.

I have been reading over the annexed instruction to Ambassador Gerard of February 10th[1] to determine how far a course of action was declared by that document in case of submarine attack.

The important statements are contained in the three paragraphs at the top of page 2 which I have underscored in red ink and the key words I have made "black-faced." They are "indefensible violation," "strict accountability" and "steps * * * necessary * * * to safeguard."

The term *"indefensible violation"* eliminates in my opinion any argument as to the justification of the German naval or aerial authorities for their action in attacking American vessels without warning. It leaves no room for debate, but is an assertion that the act constitutes an international crime.

"Strict accountability" can only mean that the German Government must make full reparation for the act of their naval force and must also repudiate the act, apologize for it and give ample assurance that it will not be repeated.

*"Steps * * * necessary * * * to safeguard"* can have no other meaning than to protect American lives and property by force unless the German Government guarantee that American lives and property will not be molested on the high seas.

In view of these declarations, which are substantially unqualified, a representation covering the attacks on the CUSHING and the GULFLIGHT would leave little opportunity to discuss the subject of submarine or aeroplane activities in the "war zone." Those cases would seem to require brief and positive protests and demands based on the declarations of February 10th.

In the *Thrasher* case the circumstances are different. There is room for argument and a discussion of the use of submarines would be appropriate since it is open to question whether the declarations apply to that particular case.

I suggest, therefore, the advisability of acting in the Thrasher case before the full reports are received in the other cases, so that a more moderate and less rigid representation may be made before action is taken in the other cases, which, if the reported facts are confirmed, leaves little opportunity for a conciliatory note, unless we recede from our former statements, a course which I assume will not be done.

Faithfully yours,   Robert Lansing.

TLS (SDR, RG 59, 763.72/1434, DNA).
1 WW to J. W. Gerard, Feb. 10, 1915, Vol. 32.

To William Jennings Bryan

My dear Mr. Secretary,   The White House. 5 May, 1915.
Thank you sincerely for letting me see this.

Faithfully Yours,   W.W.

WWTLI (W. J. Bryan Papers, DNA).

From Edward Mandell House

[London, May 5, 1915]

I believe that a sharp note indicating your determination to demand full reparation would be sufficient in this instance. I am afraid a more serious breach may at any time occur, for they seem to have no regard for consequences.

Edward House

T transcript of WWsh decode (WC, NjP) of T telegram (WP, DLC).

From Edith Bolling Galt

[Washington] May the Fourth [fifth], 1915.
"Your dear love fills me with a bliss untold,
Perfect, divine.

I did not know the human heart could hold
    Such joy as mine.
But it does more for me, it makes
    the whole world new
Dreams and desires within my Soul
    it wakes more high and true
Than aught I have ever known.
For I do see, with sad surprise,
    how far I am beneath your thought of me
For, lover-wise, you've crowned me queen
    of grace and truth and light
All pure and good.
In utter faith have set me on the
    height of womanhood
Since you exalt me thus, I must
    not prove your wisdom vain.
Unto these mighty heights, oh help me
    wondrous love I must attain!
Since love invests me with such royal dower
The marvel sweet, shall in my
    own life, by the same power
Be made—complete!"[1]

This little poem I learned years ago, little thinking how perfectly it would express what is in my heart tonight. It is long past midnight. I have been sitting in the big chair by the window, looking out into the night. Ever since you went away my whole being is awake and vibrant!

I wish you were here so I could talk to you, for then I know you would understand, and a written word is so cold, so capable of conveying more or less than we can express in speech. But I will try to tell you. How I want to help! What an unspeakable pleasure and privilege I deem it to be *allowed* to share these tense, terrible days of responsibility, how I thrill to my very finger tips when I remember the tremendous thing you said to me tonight,[2] and how pitifully poor I am, to have nothing to offer you in return. Nothing—I mean—in proportion to your own great gift!

I am a woman—and the thought that you have *need* of me—is sweet!

But, dear kindred spirit, can you not trust me and let me lead you from the thought that you have forfeited anything by your fearless honesty to the conviction that, with such frankness between us, there is nothing to fear—we *will help* and hearten each other. There will be no subterfuge

You have been honest with me, and, perhaps, I was too frank

with you, but if so—forgive me! and know that here on this white page I pledge you all that is best in me—to help, to sustain, to comfort—and that into the space that seperates us I send my spirit to seek yours.

Make it a welcome guest?   E.B.G.

ALI (WP, DLC).
¹ The Editors have been unable to identify the author of this poem.
² Wilson had professed his love for Mrs. Galt.

Two Letters to Edith Bolling Galt

[The White House, May 4-5, 1915]

"When to the Sessions of sweet silent thought
I summon up remembrance of things past,
I sigh the lack of many a thing I sought,
And with old woes new wail my dear time's waste:
Then can I drown an eye, unused to flow,
For precious friends hid in death's dateless night;
And weep afresh love's long-since-cancell'd woe,
And moan th' expense of many a vanish'd sight:
Then can I grieve at grievances forgone,
And heavily from woe to woe tell o'er
The sad account of fore-bemoaned moan,
Which I new pay as if not paid before.
But if the while I think on thee, dear friend
All losses are restored and sorrows end."¹

W.W.

"I lay awake and listened, ere the light
Began to whiten at the window pane.
The world was all asleep: earth was a fane
Emptied of worshipers; its dome of night,
Its silent aisles, were awful in their gloom.
Suddenly from the tower the bell struck four,
Solemn and slow, how slow and solemn! o'er
Those death-like slumberers, each within his room.
The last reverberation pulsed so long
It seemed no tone of earthly mould at all.
But the bell woke a thrush; and with a call
He roused his mate, then poured a tide of song;
'Morning is coming, fresh, and clear, and blue,'
Said that bright song; and then I thought of you."²

I did my best to do your bidding, for [it] is in pleasing you; but grief and dismay are terrible companions in the still night, with hope lying dead and I could not endure them beyond the dawn. I will do better. They shall not conquer me. I shall get used to them, as I have to so many others like them, and be by degrees stronger than they are,—with God's help, and yours! I wonder what God means to do with me, having cast me off?

Please promise *not* to go to the Orient! Don't put *every* burden on me!

Your devoted friend, and your *dependent* friend,
                                                                W.W.

ALI (WP, DLC).
¹ Shakespeare, Sonnet XXX.
² Wilson evidently composed this sonnet; the Editors have been unable to find it in any collections.

Dear, dear Friend,   [The White House] 5 May, 1915.

I am infinitely tired to-night,—brain and body and spirit,—for it is still, for me, practically the same day on which I put my happiness to the test,—and I do not know that I can say anything as I would say it; but there are some things I must *try* to say before the still watches come again in which the things unsaid hurt so and cry out in the heart to be uttered. It was this morning —while I lay awake thinking of you in all your wonderful loveliness and of my pitiful inability to satisfy and win you, to show you the true heart of my need, and of my nature,—that you wrote that wonderful note Helen brought me to-day, with its fresh revelation of your wonderful gifts of heart and mind,—the most moving and altogether beautiful note I ever read, whose possession makes me rich; and I must thank you for that before I try to sleep,—thank you from the bottom of a heart that your words touch as if they knew every key of it. I am proud beyond words that you should have thought of me in such terms and put the thoughts into such exquisite, comprehending words. God has indeed been good to me to bring such a creature as you into my life. Every glimpse I am permitted to get of the sweet depths of you I find them deeper and purer and more beautiful than I knew or had dreamed of. If you cannot give me *all* that I want—what my heart finds it hard now to breathe without—it is because I am not worthy. I know instinctively you *could* give it if I were—and if you understood,—understood the boy's heart that is in me and the simplicity of my need, which you could fill so that all my days would be radiant. Browning speaks somewhere of a man having two sides, one that he turns to the world, another that he shows a woman when he loves her. I think you have not opened your eyes to see that other side yet, though I laid it bare to you without reserve and I must have a chance to show it to you. These are the supreme years of my life. Minutes count with me now more than days will some time,—and my *need* is supreme. I know that you can fill it because you do fill it every moment I am with you. Every power in me is happily free when you are by, with the light in your eyes I love so. You have not stopped thinking of me as the public man! You have not yet looked with full comprehension on your friend and lover, Woodrow Wilson, whose heart must be satisfied if his life is to tell for all it might tell for and who would want you—oh with *such* a longing—whether he had ever been heard of or not. What you have given me is inestimable, precious to me beyond all words, beautiful and a very fountain of happiness. Perhaps the rest will come when you see how simple, how natural, how inevitable an addition it is—always provided you think me worthy of love and of all a woman can give. You will not *forbid* the thought to come, will you? Here stands your friend, a longing man, in the midst of a world's affairs—a world that knows nothing of the heart he has shown you and which would as lief break it as not, but which he cannot face with his full strength or with the full zest of keen endeavor unless you come into this heart and take possession, not because he is exposed but because, simply and only because, you love him. *Can* you love him? You have given him all but that —in what wonderful measure, with what exquisite insight—and he has all but the utmost of what he needs (this precious note and the sweet words you spoke, the sweet touch of your hand last night prove that). Will you come to him some time, without reserve and make his strength complete?

Forgive all errors in what I have said,—read it with your heart, as I know you can, and will, and know that, whatever happens, you will have the companionship, the gratitude, the loyalty and the devoted, romantic love of

Your devoted friend   Woodrow Wilson

What would I not give for words that would really make you see and feel what is in my heart! You *could* not shrink!

W.W.

How much of my life has gone into this note you will never know unless, some day—

Do not misunderstand. What I have now at your generous hands is infinitely precious to me. It would kill me to part with it,—I could not and I hope you could not. And I will be patient, patient without end, to see what, if anything, the future may have to store for me.

ALS (WP, DLC).

From William Jennings Bryan, with Enclosures

My dear Mr. President: Washington May 6th, 1915.

I enclose the proposed message to Count Okuma, also draft of a telegram to Great Britain, France and Russia. If you will return them with your corrections I will send them as soon as I have called Ambassador Chinda to the State Department and communicated their contents to him. I know he shares our desire to avoid war and he may be able to assist.

I suppose I ought to send Reinsch at Peking for his information both the telegram to Okuma and the telegram to the other powers. Don't you think it might be well for me to send a telegram to the Chinese Government also, somewhat along the line of my telegram to Count Okuma, leaving out the personal part and saying that it is done by your direction?

With assurances of high respect I am, my dear Mr. President,
            Yours very sincerely,   W. J. Bryan

TLS (W. J. Bryan Papers, DNA).

E N C L O S U R E   I

Amembassy Tokio.   Washington, May 6th, 1915. 6 pm

Please deliver the following message to His Excellency, Count Okuma, as a personal and unofficial communication from me: Quote. Relying upon the personal acquaintance with you, so pleasantly formed when I was in Japan, and the friendship for and confidence in you which have been built upon that acquaintance, I take the liberty of appealing to you personally and unofficially to use your great influence with your Government to have it deal with China in the spirit of patience. It would be most distressing if China and Japan who, because of their geographical position, must remain neighbors, and because of their mutual interests must be friends, should be brought into armed conflict, especially at this time when so large a portion of the world is at war. Fully sharing your well known attachment to the cause of international peace I most respectfully and most earnestly urge you to counsel a continuation of negotiations until some amicable solution of existing disputes is found. I am sure that such a course will, in the end, prove best for both China and Japan and for the world as well.

With assurances of high esteem I am,
            Very sincerely yours,   W. J. Bryan. Unquote.

T telegram (SDR, RG 59, 793.94/405a, DNA).

ENCLOSURE I I

Amembassy Tokio   Washington, May 6, 1915. 7 pm

I am sending you a personal telegram to be delivered to Count Okuma, and for your information am repeating to you a telegram which we are sending to Great Britain, France and Russia. You will be governed by the purpose expressed in the telegram to Count Okuma and insofar as opportunity offers will urge patience and a continuance of the negotiations. It is of the highest importance that the friendly relations existing between Japan and China should not be interrupted. (Quote Okuma telegram and telegram to London Paris and Petrograd, of May 6, 7 pm)

Bryan

T telegram (SDR, RG 59, 793.94/402a, DNA).

ENCLOSURE I I I

Amlegation Pekin.   Washington, May 6, 1915. 6 pm

The President desires that you call upon the Foreign Office and urge that the negotiations between China and Japan shall be conducted in a spirit of patience and friendliness, and be continued until an amicable solution of the existing disputes is found. China and Japan, because of their geographical position must remain neighbors and because of their mutual interests must be friends. It would be most unfortunate if they should be brought into armed conflict, especially at this time when so large a portion of the world is at war. Peaceful means are urged in the conviction that they will, in the end, prove best for both China and Japan and for the rest of the world as well.   Bryan

T telegram (SDR, RG 59, 793.94/400a, DNA).

ENCLOSURE I V

Amembassy—London 1519
    "   —Paris 790
    "   —Petrograd. 315

Washington, May 6th, 1915. 7 pm

Please call at the Foreign Office and inform the Government that we are both alarmed and distressed at the news from Japan and China. Ask whether the (*) Government will join us in a friendly but earnest appeal to Japan and China to continue their negotiations in the spirit of patience and friendship until a satisfactory conclusion is reached, representing that it would be unfortunate beyond expression if these nations should be drawn into armed conflict; and that as a friend of both nations we feel it our duty to ask the cooperation of other friendly nations in an effort to prevent such a calamity. A similar message is being sent to (**).   Bryan

(*) Government to which telegram is sent.
(**) Other two Governments to which telegram is sent.

T telegram (SDR, RG 59, 793.94/393a, DNA).

To William Jennings Bryan

My dear Mr. Secretary,   The White House. 6 May, 1915.

I fully approve these telegrams and have made only a very slight verbal alteration in each.[1]

I think it wise, and indeed, necessary that Reinsch should know exactly what we are doing, for the information of the Chinese government, and no doubt it would be well for him to convey a message of friendly advice there as Wheeler[2] is to do in Japan.   Faithfully Yours,   W.W.

WWTLI (W. J. Bryan Papers, DNA).
[1] They were slight indeed.
[2] Post Wheeler, Secretary of the American embassy in Tokyo.

From William Jennings Bryan, with Enclosure

My dear Mr. President: [Washington] May 6th, 1915.

I am enclosing you a draft of a letter to Mr. Fuller[1] drawn according to the line of our conversation with him. Will you please return it to me with your corrections. I had hoped to get it to you last night but it was crowded out by some other matters.

I shall either enclose herewith, or send you separately, the letter for which Mr. Fuller asked authorizing him to formally recognize the government of the present president[2] by the delivery of the necessary letters when a satisfactory agreement is reached. I feel very much concerned that we shall get matters in Haiti upon a proper basis and Fuller impresses me as a good man to do the work.

With assurances of high respect, I am, my dear Mr. President,
                    Very sincerely yours,   [W. J. Bryan]

CCL (W. J. Bryan Papers, DLC).
[1] Paul Fuller, Jr., a lawyer with the firm of Coudert Brothers in New York. Bryan had requested him in late April to go to Haiti as a special representative of the President.
[2] Vilbrun Guillaume Sam.

William Jennings Bryan to Paul Fuller, Jr.

Dear Mr. Fuller: [Washington] May 6th, 1915.

By direction of the President I submit the following for your guidance on your visit to Haiti as Special Representative of the President:

You will please state to the President of Haiti that you have come in the spirit of friendship and good will to arrange with him for a basis of action which will have these ends in view:

First: You will make clear to the President that Haiti, being a part of the western hemisphere and included in the protection offered by the Monroe Doctrine, this Government not only can but will do what no other European Government is in position to do—namely: protect the independence of Haiti from outside attack, and aid the Government of Haiti to suppress insurrection from within, so long as the government is worthy of confidence and support.

Second: You will assure him of the disinterestedness of our efforts, as indicated by the fact that we ask no special favors for Americans, but, on the contrary, insist upon the equal treatment of all foreigners, to the end that the people of Haiti may have the benefit of competition between the nationals of all countries, and that good-will which is possible only when there is such equal treatment.

Third: The honest and efficient administration of a government in Haiti, according to the Constitution and the laws of that Republic—a government which will give expression to the will of the people of Haiti, protect their rights and interests, and respect international obligations.

Fourth: This government will give effective support to such a government in Haiti by the employment of such force as may be necessary to prevent insurrection and insure stability.

The third condition is necessary to the fourth, because only an honest and efficient government deserves support. The Government of the United States could not justify the expenditure of money or the sacrifice of American lives in support of any other kind of government.

As a guarantee that an honest and efficient government will be administered by the present President and his associates, it is necessary that there shall exist between the American Legation in Haiti and the President of Haiti such an intimate and confidential relationship as will enable the American Legation to advise as to such matters as affect the honest and efficient administration of the government—the President of Haiti agreeing that he will follow the advice so given to the extent of requiring honesty and efficiency in officials and of removing those found to be dishonest and inefficient.

Fifth: We take it for granted that the President of Haiti will continue the understanding which this Government has had with preceding Presidents—namely: That no rights of any kind concerning the use of Mole St. Nicholas will be granted to any other foreign government, or to the nationals of any other foreign government.

While this Government would be willing to lease directly, or through a Haitien Company in which the United States would be a controlling stockholder, the right to use Mole St. Nicholas, it will not insist upon such lease if objectionable to Haiti, but it can not consent to the lease or use of such harbor by any third power, or by the nationals of a third power.

Sixth: It is also taken for granted that the President of Haiti will arrange for the settlement or arbitration of such claims as American citizens or other foreigners may have against the Government of Haiti.

This letter is accompanied by a document signed by the President of the United States which authorizes you to give formal recognition to the President of Haiti upon the conclusion of satisfactory arrangements with him for the carrying out of the purposes hereinbefore set forth.[1]

With assurances of respect, I am,

Yours very truly,   W J Bryan.

CCL (SDR, RG 59, 838.00/1393a, DNA).
[1] WW to V. G. Sam, May 6, 1915, HwLS (SDR, RG 59, 838.001 G94/1, DNA).

To Edith Bolling Galt

[The White House] 6 May, '15

Oh, dear kindred spirit, my sweet incomparable friend, what would I not give this morning for just one clasp of your hand, just one little greeting exchanged face to face, one word with the sound of your voice in it! But I have slept a little now and can speak more clearly than I did last night, when my need, my fathomless need, was crying out in me. I was thinking of myself then, now I can think of you (and, ah, how sweet it is to think of you!). That note you wrote me yesterday before the dawn ("before the dawn"!) lies before me, my little charter of liberty!

and I realize that I have not answered it—except in my heart. I can hardly see to write for the tears as I lift my eyes from it,—the tears of joy and sweet yearning. *Yes*, dear loving friend, "we *will* help and hearten each other." My heart sends you back your words—oh, with what gladness and pride,—"I pledge you all that is best in me—to help, to sustain, to comfort." "Into the space that separates us I send my spirit to seek yours. Make it a welcome guest!" How welcome a guest your spirit is, my dear, I hope God will give me the grace to show you—without selfishness of any sort. And how proud I am to be its host—and its haven of welcome—how proud and how happy! For there never was a more beautiful spirit, a spirit more altogether lovely. I will be its knight, —serve it, not myself, and feel myself grow a better, purer man in the service!

"I claimed and claim thee; ready now to pay
  The perfect love that leaves no self to slay!"[1]
Yesterday, in my deep need and longing, I let myself think of my own life and the work I need the full, unbounded equipment to do that I can have only when my heart is satisfied; but now what I hope is my real and finer self is awake in response to your sweet pledge. It goes out to meet you, with outstretched hands. I love *you*, not myself. I shall live to help *you*—"to help, to sustain, to comfort," to gladden, not burden or distress,—to help you, if I can, to realize the lovely things that are in you and you have not seen yourself. It grieves me that you should ever have been unhappy, that clouds should ever have shadowed you who are by nature and every sweet gift so radiant and full of the perfect light that shines in the heart of a completely gifted woman. If I can never have the privilege of shielding you from all the world, I can at least shield you from anything that is selfish in me and let no shadow darken your thoughts that may gather in my sky. It will be my study and my joy to make you *glad* that you met me. My love shall never stand in your way. You have had too little joy in your life; I shall try to add to its stock, not take away from it! The wonderful woman I recognized and loved, and sought selfishly to claim, I shall seek to enrich, not impoverish. Nothing that she demands of me, though it were utter sacrifice, will seem hard to give if she desires or needs it or will be made happier by it. I would rather see light—the light of joy and complete happiness—in those eyes than have anything I can think of for myself.

I seem to have been put into the world to serve, not to take, and serve I will to the utmost, and demand nothing in return.

It is so a man may show himself worthy, perhaps, to call himself
Your devoted friend,   Woodrow Wilson

"Being thy slave, what should I do but tend
Upon the hours and times of your desire?
I have no precious time at all to spend,
Nor services to do, till you require.
Nor dare I chide the world-without-end hour
Whilst I, my sovereign, watch the clock for you,
Nor think the bitterness of absence sour
When you have bid your servant once adieu;
Nor dare I question with my jealous thought
Where you may be, or your affairs suppose,
But, like a sad slave, stay and think of nought
Save, where you are how happy you make those!
So true a fool is love, that in your Will,
Though you do any thing, he thinks no ill."[2]

W.W.

ALS (WP, DLC).
[1] The Editors have been unable to identify the author of these lines.
[2] Shakespeare, Sonnet LVII.

From Edith Bolling Galt

[Washington] May 6th, 1915

I have just read and read again your triumphant note of the
early morning—so full of tenderness, of yearning, of the "hunger
and thirst of the heart"—and yet vibrant with *strength* and the
blessed surety that you have *found yourself*!

This is what makes me so proud of you, and so sure that all's
right with the world! You could not *be* yourself and not feel as
you do today. It is so worthy of you to forget your own hurt in
helping me, and my heart is singing with the wonder of your
revelation of yourself.

Forgive a pencil[.] I am in my car waiting for Mother so ink
is impossible.

On my heart rests a golden rose, and in my heart is a treasure
of purer gold. May I never tarnish this pure trust, but guard it
with my life, and leave the rest to God.   E.B.G.

ALI (WP, DLC).

To Mary Allen Hulbert

My dear Mrs. Hulbert,   [The White House] 6 May, 1915.

I am immensely interested to hear about the cook book. I hope that when you consult a publisher about it you will tell them that in my opinion they will miss a mighty good thing if they do not take it.

I can guarantee it without seeing it; for I have tested your knowledge of such things when I had the privilege of being your guest, and of having my palate appealed to and satisfied in more ways than I supposed possible or within the law of mere cooking.

Please, if you will, use this letter as a letter of introduction, not only as an accomplished house-keeper, but as my friend.

Cordially and sincerely Yours   Woodrow Wilson

WWTLS (WP, DLC).

To Hugh Lenox Scott

My dear General Scott: The White House May 7, 1915

Let me say again how sincere my pleasure has been in being instrumental in conferring upon you honors which I felt have been all too long delayed in view of the character and length of your distinguished service.[1]

With warmest regard,

.   Cordially and sincerely yours,   Woodrow Wilson

TLS (Hugh L. Scott Papers, DLC).
[1] Wilson had promoted Scott to the rank of major general on April 30, 1915.

From William Jennings Bryan

My dear Mr. President: [Washington] May 7th, 1915.

I am sending you a suggestion which Mr. Lansing makes in regard to the Eastern situation.[1] I hope that an agreement is going to be reached and that it will not be necessary for us to send it. It is only prepared as a matter of precaution.

With assurances of high respect, I am, my dear Mr. President,

Very sincerely yours,   [W. J. Bryan]

CCL (W. J. Bryan Papers, DLC).
[1] See WW to WJB, May 10, 1915 (third letter of that date) enclosing RL to WJB, May 7, 1915.

From Edward Mandell House, with Enclosure

Dear Governor: No. 2 [London] May 7th, 1915.

Your cablegram concerning the delaying of cargoes came to me yesterday. I already had an engagement with Sir Edward Grey for this morning so I did not make an earlier appointment.

I read him your message and told him that in my opinion the situation was critical and that it would not do to temporize with the matter; that the Germans were doing everything possible to embarrass you and to force you to place an embargo upon arms.

He said he understood the situation perfectly. He took a memorandum which he read to me afterwards and which was to be sent to each Member of the Cabinet in the form of a communication. He put it strongly and urgently and he told me he would do all that was possible.

He said he had to contend with public sentiment here that demanded a complete blockade of Germany. I think, too, he has opposition in the Cabinet with Kitchener and Winston Churchill.

I am showing the cablegram to Page so that he may also press the matter with Grey. I shall tell Page, however, that I have already spoken to Sir Edward so our record may be kept clean.

Sir Edward wants to do everything that is possible, but he desired me to let you know that he had great difficulties here to contend with.

I had an interesting talk with him about Japan and China. He tells me that Japan did not let him know concerning their negociations with China, and that they were inclined to keep their plans to themselves. He finally sent for the Japanese Ambassador[1] and had a frank talk with him concerning Japan's intentions and of England's interest in the situation. The Ambassador then told him pretty much what was going on, and gave him a clear idea of the difficulties they were having with China.

He said after getting at the bottom of the matter, China seemed to be acting in a very stupid and foolish way diplomatically. That she said, at one time, she was willing to accept the terms which Japan had offered with the exception of Clause 5, which Sir Edward thought was really the only thing she could reasonably object to. After Japan agreed to eliminate Clau[s]e 5, then China raised a lot of minor and trivial objections.

Sir Edward told the Ambassador that England was very desirous that good relations between China and Japan should be maintained, and that she would view with concern any rupture between them, and that she was willing to do all that was possible to better relations.[2]

The feeling here is that Japan is taking advantage of the war to further her own ends. She sees clearly that Europe is in no position to object, and that we are not much better off.

Sir Edward said he felt there was some excuse for Japan wanting an outlet in Manchuria for the reason that North and South America, Africa and the British Colonies were closed against her citizens.[3]

I have seen a great many people since I last wrote you, among them the Russian Ambassador.[4] I found him a very able man, but as ignorant of your purposes as the people of France. He seemed delighted when I told him that you were not seeking to aid Germany by insisting upon an early peace, and that you were not influenced in your actions in the slightest by the so called German sentiment in America.

When I came over here it was practically the universal opinion in France and England, and I find now in Russia also, that you were inclined to be pro-German, even though the American people as a whole, were otherwise. I have a feeling that Sir Cecil has fostered this sentiment, because what I have heard here sounds very much like what he said to me on several occasions. He told Norman Hapgood that the Administration was pro-German and he has told others the same thing.

I took occasion to tell Sir Edward that Sir Cecil was very nervous and was constantly seeing spooks, and that he had told me that we would all be pro-German before the end of the war. I did this because I was sure he had written the same thing to Sir Edward.

I saw Balfour last night and had some talk with him. I am to take lunch with him next Thursday and will try to show him that it would not be to England's disadvantage to grant the freedom of the seas. If I can get him right on this question it will go a long way towards bringing the Conservatives into line. I think Sir Edward is now well convinced, and that we may count upon his influence.

There are some things I have learned that may interest you, which were told me in deepest confidence.

England now has a total of 2,300,000 men, outside of the National Reserve (which is composed of men beyond regular army age) for home defense, and enlistment is going on at the rate of 30,000 a week. They expect tp [to] get through the Dardanelles within a month.

Russia is very deficient in munitions of war. The opening of the Dardanelles will be of great advantage to her in this regard. England is manufacturing enormous amounts of war materials so as to help Russia out whenever they can reach her. For instance, she has 4,000,000 million [*sic*] pairs of boots on hand, and 39,000,000 yards of khaki.

The feeling between Russia and France is not too cordial. Joffre insisted upon the Grand Duke[5] changing his whole plan of campaign, which was to throw up strong entrenchments along the German front and to go after Austria actively. Joffree demanded that they strike at Prussia in order to relieve the French situation.

The Grand Duke thought this a mistake, and he considers the losses the Russians have had and the lack of success they have made in the Carpathians has been due largely to this policy.

Both the French and British are confident that they can turn the tide soon against Germany despite their immediate reverses.

I give you the above not as gossip, but as first hand information which may be relied upon, therefore please do not let it go beyond yourself.

I had a note yesterday from Lord Stamforham, the King's Private Secretary, saying the King would be glad to see me at the Palace this morning. I had nearly an hour's conversation with him. He was exceedingly cordial and communicative, but the conference was not important. I do not know why he asked me to call for there was nothing that was said that would indicate any important purpose.

I am sending you a copy of a letter from Sir Edward Grey which I received just as I left Paris. Also a copy of a letter from Willard which I have just gotten.[6] You will see from Willard's that Germany is trying to induce Spain to side against the Allies. I am also keeping in close touch with the Italian situation.

As I told you once before, I am greatly impressed by the lack of coordination between the Allies. They do not seem to altogether know each others plans, sentiments or purposes. This lack of coordination leads me to believe that under favorable circumstances you will be able to largely dominate the peace convention.   Your affectionate,   E. M. House

This letter is *No* 2, since May first. I shall number them hereafter so that you may know if any are missing.

TLS (WP, DLC).

1 Katsunosuke Inouye.

2 Grey conveyed this advice in E. Grey to C. Greene, April 29, 1915, printed telegram (FO 371/2323, No. 52466, PRO).

3 House summarized this letter to this point very briefly in EMH to WW, May 7, 1915, T transcripts of WWsh decode (WP, DLC; WC, NjP) of T telegram (WP, DLC).

⁴ Alexander Constantovich, Count Benckendorff.
⁵ Grand Duke Nicholas Nicholaevich, commander in chief of the Russian armies.
⁶ J. E. Willard to EMH, May 2, 1915, TCL (WP, DLC), reporting on an audience with King Alfonso XIII of Spain. He noted that the King generally agreed with House's peace plans, so long as they did not interfere with Spain's own political ambitions, which had recently become generally aroused by German propaganda regarding Tangier and Gibraltar. The King had also expressed his desire that House come to Spain.

E N C L O S U R E

Sir Edward Grey to Edward Mandell House

Private.

Dear Colonel House,   London, April 24th, 1915.

I sent you a letter by Sir F. Bertie as you desired a week ago. I have now received yours of the 21st. I shall be very glad to see you again.

Your news from Berlin is not encouraging: it reduces Bernstorff's peace talk at Washington to "Fudge." What you heard from Berlin and found there is confirmed to me from another source neutral but not American.

As to "Freedom of the Seas," if Germany means that her commerce is to go free upon the sea in time of war, while she remains free to make war upon other nations at will, it is not a fair proposition.

If on the other hand Germany would enter after this war some league of nations where she would give and accept the same security that other nations gave and accepted against war breaking out between them, then expenditure on armaments might be reduced and new rules to secure "freedom of the sea" made. The sea is free in times of peace anyhow.

Yours sincerely,   E. Grey.

TCL (WP, DLC).

Two Letters to Edith Bolling Galt

[The White House] 7 May, 1915

Ah, my precious friend and comrade, what happiness it was to be with you last night! While your hand rested in mine I felt as if I could stand up and shout for the strength and joy that was in me. When I told you in halting words (for words come hard from the deepest places in a man) the ideals of public duty I hold myself to and saw the answering light in your eyes (thank God for the lamps on that road!) I knew where I could get the solace that would ease the strain and felt fit for any adventure of the spirit. God comes to a man, I think, through the trust and love of a sweet, pure woman. Certainly God seems very near when I am with you. I have tried to put selfishness away, sweet lady—even at the moments of greatest yearning, when it seemed intolerable to let go your hand and walk alone—but surely the desire to be complete and free is not selfish. The selfishness would come in seeking to be or do *any*thing at another's cost. I cannot be complete until I have what I lack, or free until I am strong with a supporting happiness: but I can master my fate and be captain of my own soul without these. Such strength is not beautiful, is not filled and informed by the real sources of life; it is hard and grim, without grace and zest and inspiration; but it is at least self-conquest; but the glory of it does not satisfy. It is fortitude, but it is not happiness!

   "When Nature sinks, as oft she may,
Through long-lived pressure of obscure distress,
Still to be strenuous for the bright reward,
And in the soul admit of no decay,
Brook no continuance of weak-mindedness—
Great is the glory, for the strife is hard!"[1]

But a man cannot *live* on glory and strength: they may even kill him with their sheer strain and stress!

In this clear morning air the world seems less in the way, seems less to stand between us. It seems as if my voice could carry to you and no one hear but your own heart,—that sweet understanding heart which I *know* to be the mate to mine, but which I would not take by force but only by its own wish and recognition of the wonderful love God has given us. I *cannot* be mistaken! God *has* given it to us. Why, otherwise, should that exquisite scribbled note my sweet lady sent me yesterday seem to me to be my own heart speaking—only its tones more perfectly tender and delicate than my masculine thought could have uttered? It shot back every bolt and seemed to make me complete and free, as I have prayed to be. For I *have* prayed, dear, that God would give me this, my heart's desire. If you come to me, I shall know that it is he who is leading us, and that he is willing that I should give all that is best in me to make you happy!

What a dull pen this is! It cannot speak to you in the tones that ring in my heart as I write. I must *speak* the deepest things of all to you. And you will let me—if only for my heart's ease and for the joy and pride it gives me to reveal to you the depth and pure enduring passion of my love for you. You are beyond measure generous, as you are beyond measure lovely!

Your devoted—Woodrow Wilson

ALS (WP, DLC).
¹ William Wordsworth, "To B. R. Haydon."

Beloved Friend,   [The White House] 7 May, 1915

There is something I must say to you before I go to bed. It is the cruel compulsion of circumstances that I must write it instead of speaking it in your sweet presence and with the interpretation it might receive from the tones of the voice. I have felt, rather than known, the movement of your thought during the last few days and know that it involves so many possibilities of infinite loss and mistake that that [sic] I dare not delay or fail to say what is in my heart with perfect candor. I must do everything I *can* for your happiness and mine

To begin with, make your mind perfectly at ease about one thing: I cannot take back what I have given, but you can command the *form* of my allegiance. If—not now, but when you know me better, and see more clearly than you do now what all this means—you decide that all that you *can* give is a deep and tender friendship, I pledge myself to accept that decision and live up to it with utter loyalty and devotion to what *you* want, forgetting myself in my allegiance to you. The one thing I *cannot* do is to give you up altogether and turn away from a spirit of which I know myself to be part—but, come what may, we shall at least have a wonderful friendship till death parts us. That is fixed and manifest fate, no matter what compulsion you put upon yourself.

But, my dear, dear friend, that must not be all, great and wonderful as it would be. You gave me that much with such poignant sweetness, grace, and frankness, so spontaneously, with such an instant glow of recognition and welcome, that I *know* you can give me more, if you will but think only of your own heart and me, *and shut the circumstances of the world out*. You owe it to me, to both of us, to the very conscience of the heart I already know so well, to to [sic] shut the circumstances out in that great decision. It would be cruel, it would be wrong, to make it, and mar our lives, upon any ground of *expediency*; do you not see that it would? Especially since the expediency of the whole situation can be taken care of anyway. My happiness absolutely depends upon your giving me your entire love; but the moment I know I have it—the moment, even, I know I may hope for it—my happiness has come already, and we have a precious secret we can keep in any way we please and as long as we please, pledged and secure, without disquiet of mind or heart, together or separated, till we choose to let the world know. And what sweet fun it would be—to be absolutely secure in each other's love and yet keep the cynical world at arm's length, to know nothing of our sacred troth and understanding! All that you have to determine, all that you have a right to decide, if you are going to be fair to me is, *can you love me for my own sake and do you want me for your life's joy?* All the rest it will be easy to take care of.

What I am afraid you are doing is using your splendid strength and conscience to determine *what is best for me*—when the only thing that is best for me is your love—and what you should *do*— what our actions and outward relations to one another should be is quite another matter.

I am pleading for my life, dear friend. I am strong enough to endure unhappiness—and not cry out, but (I say it with infinite tenderness) you have no right to make me endure it, *if*, forgetting everything else, *you think you can love me*—and set me free!

Please think of *me* and not of the circumstances. We can take care of them, if we have one another for motive!   W.W.

Do not *answer* this argument till we can *talk*, and *please hold it in your inmost heart.*

ALI (WP, DLC).

From Edith Bolling Galt

Friday night [May 7, 1915] 8:15

I did not mean to write to you tonight, but something whispers you will understand, and know that it is because of—many things

First that you *will* me to do it. I feel it, and love to obey.

Second that, in the awful possibilities the extra papers hint at,[1] I know you need all the help and tender comprehension I can give.

And oh! do you know what a flood of happiness sweeps over me when you say I am really a help, a haven to you and sanctuary for your tired spirit?

This seems so marvelous a blessing to me you will not think me blasphemous when I say the wonder of it is as gracious as the shining presence of the Angel when he came in gleaming whiteness to the Virgin.

Why should I be chosen among all women to help you in your masterful strength to serve—and serve so worthily, so unselfishly a great nation. The thought makes me tremble and grow afraid, and I long to come and have you answer my question.

What worlds are crowded into one little week of time. Last Friday you were our host at dinner, gracious, courteously interested.

You were the *President*, which high office set you apart, and to whom I paid my obedient homage. Tonight, you are—YOU[.] And I come to you as trustingly, as restfully as the tiny child you told me of, who wanted the warm human touch of a loved hand to bring assurance of safety in a vast crowd.

I trust you absolutely, and am so infinitely proud of you and the splendor of your purpose.

I have by me your morning messenger. Should I try to answer it my note would be too long, but I want you to know that every word of it is dear to me and brings you to me in the strangest, but happiest reality. You seem here—in this room—and I stretch out my hand to welcome you, and behold, instead of your strong clasp, my fingers close on a golden-hearted rose whose exquisite fragrance takes me, on a breath of purfume, back to *our* loved Southland, and I close my eyes to dream and fear to open them lest you go away and leave me.

Thank you for the dear flowers. They make an empty house vocal with their message.

Goodnight. I am still thrilled by the beauty of our ride last night, and the peace of the forest and the strength of the pines beneath the stars has remained with me.

I hope it brought you all this and more.

Always,   E.B.G.

ALI (WP, DLC).
¹ That is, the possibility of war between the United States and Germany. The German submarine *U*20, Walter Schwieger, commander, torpedoed the Cunard Line steamship *Lusitania*, 30,396 tons, in the Irish Sea without warning near Old Head of Kinsale on May 7. The ship sank in only eighteen minutes. The dead numbered 785 passengers and 413 members of the crew, a total of 1,198, including 270 women, 94 children, and 124 American citizens. The survivors included 472 passengers and 289 members of the crew, 761 in all. See Link, *Struggle for Neutrality*, pp. 369-72. The most exhaustive and scholarly study of all aspects of the sinking of *Lusitania* is Thomas A. Bailey and Paul B. Ryan, *The Lusitania Disaster: An Episode in Modern Warfare and Diplomacy* (New York and London, 1975).

To Edith Bolling Galt

P.S.   [The White House] Saturday, [May 8, 1915] 7 A.M.

After I had written what goes before your longed-for note, written last evening, came, to bless me and make me calm and happy. What depths of poetry and tenderness and comprehending sympathy there are in you, my adorable friend,—what limitless store of everything I need! And how sure what you write, in the quiet of your own room and heart, makes me of what *I* tried to say last night. What you have to determine is not whether you can make me happy (that is my part, and about that there is no conjecture) but whether I can make you happy. How proud, how complete, how re-inforced in everything that fits a man for achievement and the exercise of serene strength I shall be if I can! I know that you will put doubt away and come to me if I can give you happiness, and I know that to give you happiness will crown my life and quicken and enhance every force in me. Every glimpse I get of your wonderful heart makes me lonelier without you. You dare not refuse me entrance if you *want* me in! You stretched out your hand to me last night, this sweet note lying before me says, (while I was pacing the streets to get my mind and purpose in hand):[1] will you not stretch out your arms and let me come, at such sweet time as we shall have a right to be with one another always?

Prudence is an impertinent intruder *this week*, and Wisdom intolerable! We can open the door wide to them when we are sure, and can make the welcome genuine, not grudging—even yield them serene obedience *then*!   W.W.

Why is it I always see what I write you through a veil of sweet tears?

ALI (WP, DLC).
    1 "The news was almost more than Wilson could bear. Before the Secret Service men knew what he was doing, he walked quietly out the main door of the White House. Crossing Pennsylvania Avenue, he started northward up Sixteenth Street. Thoughts must have whirled in confusion in his mind, pictures of horror that he could not suppress. He seemed oblivious to the light rain that was falling and to the voices of newsboys in the streets. From Sixteenth Street the President turned into Corcoran Street and then into Fifteenth and back to the White House and his study. At ten o'clock a fresh bulletin came saying that probably 1,000 souls had perished on the ship." Link, *Struggle for Neutrality*, p. 379.

From Walter Hines Page

London May 8, 1915.

Following is in Secretary's private code:

2068. CONFIDENTIAL in the extreme. For the President and the Secretary only.

As nearly as I can interpret public opinion here as affected by the sinking of the LUSITANIA, it is as follows, which I transmit for your information: A profound effect has been produced on English opinion in general regarding both the surprising efficiency of the German submarine work and the extreme recklessness of the Germans. The sinking of the LUSITANIA, following the use of poisonous gas and the poisoning of wells and the torpedoing of the GULFLIGHT and other plainly marked neutral ships the English regard as the complete abandonment of war regulations and of humanity in its conduct as well as of any consideration for neutrals. Sir Edward Grey said to me last night "They are running amuck." It is war under the black flag. Indignation in the aggregate reached a new pitch.

Official comment is of course reticent. The freely expressed unofficial feeling is that the United States must declare war or forfeit European respect. So far as I know this opinion is universal. If the United States come in, the moral and physical effect will be to bring peace quickly and to give the United States a great influence in ending the war and in so reorganizing the world as to prevent its recurrence. If the United States submits to German disregard of her citizens' lives and of her property and of her neutral rights on the sea, the United States will have no voice or influence in settling the war nor in what follows for a long time to come. This, so far as I can ascertain, is the practically unanimous opinion here. The Americans in London are outspoken to the same effect.

Much the profoundest depression is felt today that has been felt since the war begun and British opinion is stirred to its depths.

The foreign editor of the TIMES,[1] a usually well-informed and trustworthy man, who knows all the principal European statesmen, is just returned from a week in France. He tells me in strictest confidence that England, France and Russia made a bargain with Italy on April thirtieth, agreeing to cede to Italy very large parts of Austrian territory, some of which has a Slavic population, if Italy comes into the war within a month. This was done without consulting Servia and against her wishes. Italy will soon come in if she keeps her agreement, to be followed by Roumania. I have heard unofficial confirmation of this agreement here.

The same editor informs me that General Joffre told him that he is confident that he would break through the German lines within a month.

I have heard the opinion expressed today in several well-informed but unofficial quarters that warlike action by the United States would be a signal for other neutral nations whose rights Germany has disregarded especially the Scandinavian countries and possibly Holland. For the correctness of this view I cannot vouch but I know it is widely entertained.

American Ambassador London.

T telegram (SDR, RG 59, 763.72/2541, DNA).
[1] Henry Wickham Steed.

From William Jennings Bryan, with Enclosure

My dear Mr. President:　　　　　　　　Washington May 8, 1915.

I am enclosing a communication from Ambassador Page (London) sent in the confidential cipher. I have no doubt that the despatch had its influence in Japan in helping to reduce the severity of the demands. Our despatches from there indicate that the matter is now all settled, which is a great relief at such a time as this.

With assurances of high respect I am, my dear Mr. President,
Yours very sincerely,　 W. J. Bryan

I also enclose despatch from Tokio.[1] Chinda called with a note similar to Okuma's reply.[2] I told him we were not contemplating sending any *advise* to China & that our information was to the effect that terms would be accepted by China. I expressed gratification that group five had been withdrawn.

TLS (SDR, RG 59, 793.94/392½, DNA).
　[1] P. Wheeler to WJB, May 8, 1915, T telegram (SDR, RG 59, 793.94/3721½, DNA), reporting on Count Okuma's favorable reception of Bryan's personal message to him (printed as an Enclosure with WJB to WW, May 6, 1915). Okuma said that Japan had presented its ultimatum to China only after having exhausted "all methods of diplomacy" and in the conviction that China was negotiating "in a spirit of insincerity." However, since Japan was now offering new concessions, Okuma hoped for a "peaceful outcome." Wheeler also reported that the British Ambassador in Tokyo had informed him of Sir Edward Grey's actions discussed in the enclosure printed below.
　[2] S. Chinda to WJB, May 9, 1915, TLS (W. J. Bryan Papers, DNA), enclosing "Cable Message from Count Okuma, dated Tokio, May 8, 1915," T MS (W. J. Bryan Papers, DNA).

ENCLOSURE

London, May 7, 1915.
2062. The following is in the Secretary's private code.

Your telegram No. 1519, May 6th. Sir Edward Gray informs me that he gave the following memorandum to the Japanese Ambassador here yesterday. He asks that it be made known only to you and the President in the strictest confidence.

"His Majesty's Government are very much concerned at the prospect of a war between China and Japan. They feel this may imperil the independence and integrity of China which is one of the main objects of the Anglo-Japanese Alliance. In view of Article One of the Alliance, we trust that the Japanese Government will not finally shut the door upon the possibility of agreements with China without consulting with us and giving us an opportunity of promoting a friendly settlement."[1]

Sir Edward Gray further informs me that the Japanese Government have withdrawn the demands classified under Group Five and left them for subsequent discussion and settlement, thus leaving a way open for the Chinese acceptance of the demands as they now stand.

Sir Edward Gray expressed the hope today to the Chinese Minister[2] that his Government would find itself able to accept them.　　　　　　　American Ambassador, London.

T telegram (SDR, RG 59, 793.94/392½, DNA).
   [1] Grey also added in the telegram actually sent: "I added that war between Japan and China must be very serious for China, and might mean the break up of China. I did not know what China's last reply to Japan had been, but I assumed China had not refused everything, and if we could know what points were left in dispute something might be done to secure agreement. Sir J. Jordan [British Minister in Peking] had already given most conciliatory advice when sounded by the Chinese at Peking in general terms." E. Grey to C. Greene, May 6, 1915, printed telegram (FO 371/2324, No. 56360, PRO).
   [2] Sao-ke Alfred Sze.

To Edith Bolling Galt

[The White House] 8 May, '15

There is a question in your note of last evening which my heart bids me answer at once, if only for its own joy in the answer. "Why," you ask, in your sweet modesty, "should I be chosen to help you? * * * the thought makes me tremble and grow afraid, and I long to come and have you answer the question." How delightful it is to have the privilege of answering it and showing you my heart! There is nothing to make you tremble or grow afraid. It is all very simple and very beautiful. I have seen you, I have known you to be of my essential kith and kind (though much finer—the *woman* of all that is in me), and I have loved you beyond all power to doubt or hold back, oh, with such an instant intuition, such an irresistible power of comprehending love, and I know that no one can help me as you can. I know that you may be my haven and the sanctuary in which my heart may realize all the purest passions that are in it, just as one knows (*how* does he know, do you think?) moving music when he hears it, or the voice of true prayer, or the tones of sympathy and affection,— just as he would know that he had reached *home* the moment the door opened and he stepped within the sacred and yet familiar and beloved place where his spirit had been bred. You are my haven because I love you. Please accept that great fact in all its simplicity. The passion and the longing of my heart are yours. You understand and I feel *at home*. That is why there is no reason to tremble or to be afraid. You long to come and have me answer the question? Then come! With what joy I shall answer it

and how *I* shall tremble with the great hope that when you come
you will stay and be the guest of my heart forever!¹

AL (WP, DLC).
¹ There is a WWsh draft of this letter in WP, DLC.

From Edith Bolling Galt

[Washington] Saturday May 8, 1915 11:30 P.M

When all the world is quiet and I am alone, face to face with
my thoughts, I love to read over again your messenger of the
day and to drink deep of its tenderness.

This has been such a wonderful day and I have been so happy.

You asked me not to answer your questions in the note you
wrote last night. I have read it over and over, and am glad you
do not want a written answer—glad, because I want to drift—to
feel myself as free as a child not yet fit to decide its own future,
but resting secure in the heaven-given sense of protecting love.

If this is unworthy of me forgive it?

Sunday morning

I hope you are as refreshed as this early day, and that the
cares and responsibilities that bulk so large unceasingly will lie
dormant this *rest* day and you will be at peace. I see in the papers
that you are to go to Philadelphia tomorrow. If I do not see you to
tell you let this little note whisper that my thoughts go with you
and hover close until I know you are safe home again.

I did not half thank you Thursday night for trusting me
enough to talk to me of the perplexities these awful conditions
put upon you. It is so stimulating to talk to you, always, and
these questions are so tremendous that I was as eager as a thirst-
ing man for water, but feared to express my fierce interest lest
I seem impertinent and overreaching, but I loved your telling me.

The little note you gave me in the car last night is infinitely
precious to me but it will take me still a long time to accept what
you say—"is such a simple fact"—that is that you, Woodrow Wilson, love *me*! I hardly dare write the words they seem so impossible, and yet (I would not be fair if I did not add) so wonderful!

Let me have time to accept this fact, to hold it close in very
tender hands, and to try to warm and ease the great heart that
puts into my keeping such a dower of gold.

Always,   E.B.G.

ALI (WP, DLC).

To Thomas William Hardwick

[The White House] May 9, 1915.
Strictly confidential. The situation not yet fully developed but need not if wisely handled involve a crisis.[1]

Woodrow Wilson.

T telegram (Letterpress Books, WP, DLC).
[1] The telegram to which this is a reply is missing. Hardwick was in Hawaii.

From Edward Mandell House

[London, May 9, 1915]
It is now certain that a large number of American lives were lost when *Lusitania* was sunk. An immediate demand should be made upon Germany for assurance that this shall not occur again. If she fails to give such assurances, I should inform her that our government expected to take whatever measures were necessary to insure the safety of American citizens. If war follows, it will not be a new war but an endeavor to end more speedily an old one. Our intervention will save rather than increase the loss of life. America has come to the parting of the ways, when she must determine whether she stands for civilized or uncivilized warfare. Think we can no longer remain neutral spectators. Our action in this crisis will determine the part we will play when peace is made, and how far we may influence the settlement for the lasting good of humanity. We are being weighed in the balance, and our position amongst the nations is being assessed by mankind.   Edward House

T transcript of WWsh decode (WC, NjP) of T telegram (WP, DLC).

From William Jennings Bryan

My Dear Mr President   Washington May 9th 1915
As you do not read the Post I am taking the liberty of enclosing an editorial that appeared in it this morning.[1] You will notice that it calls attention to Germany's action in endorsing the requirement of notice to passengers. But my special reason for calling your attention to this editorial is that it makes a suggestion for which I ask your consideration, namely, that ships carrying *contraband* should not be permitted to carry passengers. The idea occurred to me last night (it was not, of course communicated to the Post) that some such rule should be adopted. Germany has a right to prevent contraband going to the allies

and a ship carrying contraband should not rely upon passengers to protect her from attack—it would be like putting women and children in front of an army.

You will notice from another clipping[2] that the manifest showed 4200 cases of cartridges & ammunition valued at $152,-400. I learned from Mr Lansing last night that the Lusitania carried ammunition,[3] and this information suggested to me the rule which seems to have suggested itself to the editor of the Post also. You will notice that Germany refers to this war material in the Lusitania cargo.

One result will be to make the world realize more fully the horrors of war and pray more earnestly for peace. Ridders comments which I enclose are suggestive.[4] Our people will, I think, be the more thankful that a believer in peace is in the White House at this time.

With assurances of esteem I am my dear Mr President

Yours truly   W. J. Bryan

ALS (WP, DLC).

[1] This clipping from the *Washington Post* is missing. Bryan summarizes two of its more distinctive suggestions below. In general, while stressing that not all the facts were yet known, the editorial strongly condemned the sinking of *Lusitania*. It also expressed faith in "the courage, patience and wisdom of President Wilson," asserting that, while he was not one to act hastily or without knowledge of the facts, he would in due time "uphold the honor and interests of the United States."

[2] This enclosure, also from the *Washington Post*, May 9, 1915, is missing.

[3] In addition to the 4,200 cases of rifle cartridges, *Lusitania* carried 1,250 cases of shrapnel, 18 cases of fuses, 3 cases of shell castings, and one package of empty high explosive shells. Neither the shrapnel nor the fuses contained explosives. There were no explosives or explosive ammunition on the vessel. See D. F. Malone to W. G. McAdoo, June 4, 1915, *FR-LP*, I, 428-36, and Bailey and Ryan, *The Lusitania Disaster*, pp. 96-113. Bailey and Ryan point out that repeated tests and practical experience, both before and since the sinking of *Lusitania*, have shown that rifle cartridges packed in cases cannot explode in the mass even when subjected to great heat and cannot be detonated by jarring. *Ibid.*, pp. 101-102.

[4] This enclosure is missing. Herman Ridder, editor of the *New Yorker Staats-Zeitung*, published a signed article, "Vale Lusitania," in his newspaper on May 8. It was printed in English translation in the *New York Times* and summarized in the *Washington Post* on the same date. Ridder regretted the loss of American lives; however, he pointed out that the American passengers on the ship had ignored two clear warnings from the German Government: the declaration of the German Admiralty of February 4, 1915, making the waters around Great Britain and Ireland a war zone, and the notice which the German Embassy in Washington had widely published on May 1. The sinking of *Lusitania*, Ridder continued, would at least have the salutary effect of forcing both Great Britain and the United States to take seriously the German submarine campaign. The lesson of the tragedy for American policy makers was, at least to Ridder, clear:

"Whoever sails the seas in these war times, taking passage under the British flag, assumes the risk attaching thereto. There can be no responsibility of the Government of the United States to protect British shipping in British waters. There is one way to safeguard American life, and that is by staying at home."

Two Letters to Edith Bolling Galt

[The White House]

My sweet, sweet friend,   Sunday morning. 9 May [1915].

Not write any more notes? How the thought dismays me! How am I to know what you are thinking? So long as we are in this prison of circumstances, how else are we to show our inmost hearts to one another? I *cannot* give up your notes, if you want to write them! They are wonderful in their revelation of your sweetness and of all the lovely thoughts and emotions that speak so eloquently of what you are. Every line in them makes me love you more deeply and admire you more ardently and delightedly. I almost laughed aloud yesterday when you said you could not write what was in your thought. If that is true, some special inspiration has created the notes you have written to me. They are a perfect delight to me! They bring you into my very presence in all your radiant loveliness, and thrill me with the happiness of being with you. And, oh, what a happiness that is! Did you not see and feel yesterday how happy I was because you were close to me and I could look into your eyes and feel the touch of your hand,—how I let myself *go* in the full freedom of a delightful gayety? It seems as if I could talk to you as I can talk to no one else and as if a light played through all my thought while you listen. And your thought comes out to meet mine so gayly, so happily, so naturally, so like a mate to its own self! And, with this instant and joyous and irresistible joining of spirits, you ask why *you* have been chosen to help me! Ah, dear love, there *is* a mystery about it, of course (there is a sweet mystery about all love!) but there is no mistake and there is no doubt!

At any rate, for myself, I cannot help being altogether

Your lover,   W.W.

No more notes? Impossible!

"When, in disgrace with Fortune and men's eyes,
I all alone beweep my outcast state,
And trouble deaf heaven with my bootless cries,
And look upon myself, and curse my fate,
Wishing me like to one more rich in hope,
Featured like him, like him with friends possesst,
Desiring this man's art and that man's scope,
With what I most enjoy contented least;
Yet in these thoughts myself despising—
Haply I think on thee: and then my state,
Like to the lark at break of day arising
From sullen earth, sings hymns at Heaven's gate;

For thy sweet love remember'd such wealth brings
That then I scorn to change my state with Kings."[1]

W.W.

Please don't refuse to come to lunch to-morrow. I *must* have a *little* talk with you. Helen and I will be alone here for the day. W.W.

ALI (WP, DLC).
[1] Shakespeare, Sonnet XXIX.

[The White House] Sunday [May 9, 1915] P.M.

Your note written last night and this morning seems, dear friend, to have a little tremor in it, as if I had frightened you, and fills me with the impulse to go to you and reassure you with all the inexpressible tenderness that wells up in me whenever I think of you (and when do I *not* think of you?). *Please* have no fear of any kind in your thought of me. You may take as long a time as you need to accept in your heart the fact of my love, 'holding it in tender hands,' as you so sweetly phrase it, but you must accept it *as a fact*. The only question is, may I have your love in return, to treasure and live upon? Why should the fact of my deep love for you be even for a moment strange or incredible to you? You are altogether lovely. You are such a woman as any man would bless God to have known and been allowed to love who had any touch of the same nobility in him. You 'warm' my heart, whether you will or not; but you cannot 'ease' it until some day you come to me with faith and utter acceptance in your eyes.

And why should you thank me for speaking to you the other day of the great problems I am facing these terrible days (when I can think of nothing bright but you)? If I could but have you at my side to pour my thoughts out to about them, I would thank God and take courage, and bless you that you cared and comprehended and gave me leave to make you my confidante! Everything about you is a blessing and a help to me and seems to deliver me from all weakness and discouragement,—from worry and even from thought of fatigue. Ah, how shall I ever open my heart to you in *words*! I can do it only in life and act! My love for you passes present expression. I *need* you. I need you as a boy needs his sweetheart and a strong man his help-mate and heart's comrade. Do not *doubt* the blessed fact! And when you have accepted that, God grant you may see your way to my side. I am not seeking to hurry you, my precious friend, or to take you by storm or to put any, even the least, pressure on you,

—but only to make you understand to the utmost. For I *love* you, with a love as pure as it is irresistible, which exists for your sake. I love *you*, not myself! You *must* be conscious that your mind and spirit are the perfect mates of mine, that our thoughts and instincts and affections fit one another, suit and complete one another, as the light and the flame. Do you think it an accident that we found one another at this time of my special need and that it meant nothing that we recognized one another so immediately and so joyously? And think what the last year has been for me, its days counting for more than weeks of an ordinary life (even an ordinary life here in this great office), and its months as if they were years—and I struggling through dark ways alone—*no* one understanding altogether, with the heart as well as with the mind. Do not these extraordinary circumstances alone and of themselves explain a great many things for you which you did not understand at first?

I hope that you will think of me to-night. I shall be working on my speech for to-morrow evening and on our note to Germany. Every sentence of both would be freighted with greater force and meaning if I could feel that your mind and heart were keeping me company!   W.W.[1]

ALI (WP, DLC).
 [1] There is a WWsh draft of this letter in WP, DLC.

From the Shorthand Diary of Charles Lee Swem[1]

May 10 [1915]

The President read the telegrams pressing on him the suggestion that we should go to war with Germany. He declared that some men are carried off their feet. Reading a telegram which bet that Americans would not be stampeded, he mused, "You may bet your head that this American nation won't be stampeded."

One telegram read: "In the name of God and humanity, declare war on Germany," to which the President said, "War isn't declared in the name of God; it is a human affair entirely."

I called his attention to the expression in a telegram which read, "Worst outrage in history. Redskins were gentlemen." He shook his head and said it was a terrible thing.

Before dictating, he stopped to read a funny story about an Irishman who was threatened by Bridget with being turned into a rat for getting drunk and coming home drunk. He asked Bridget, if she loved him, "To keep an iron on the kettle." He laughed heartily at the story.

Upon coming to the study to have my letters signed, I found him busily engaged in composing a note about the *Lusitania*.

Transcript (WC, NjP) of CLSsh in bound desk diary (C. L. Swem Coll., NjP).
¹ Swem made only three entries in this diary. The other two shed no light on Wilson.

To Herbert Bruce Brougham

Personal.

My dear Mr. Brougham: [The White House] May 10, 1915

I do not feel that I have any right to say whether I would approve of your writing on a particular subject or not and I hope that you will feel perfectly free to do anything that your judgment dictates.¹ My only thought is that this time of deep irritation is hardly a time when suggestions will be of any real service, no matter how wise they are. The air may clear enough for your article by the time it is ready to appear, but at present men are not listening to reason.

Cordially and sincerely yours,   Woodrow Wilson

TLS (Letterpress Books, WP, DLC).
¹ Brougham's letter to Wilson is missing.

To William Jennings Bryan

My dear Mr. Secretary,   The White House. 10 May, 1915.

After all, this* does not express Page's own opinion, but what he takes to be public opinion at the moment in Great Britain.

It is a very serious thing to have such things thought, because everything that affects the opinion of the world regarding us affects our influence for good.   Faithfully Yours,   W.W.

* Page's despatch about the Lusitania, which I find I have burned.

WWTLI (SDR, RG 59, 763.72/2541, DNA).

To William Jennings Bryan

My dear Mr. Secretary,   The White House. 10 May, 1915.

This¹ needs no comment now, since the whole suspicious business has lost for the time being its critical character.

I think Sir Edward Grey acted very well and very wisely in the matter, and I believe that your personal message to Count Okuma will have more than a temporary effect on his mind.

Faithfully Yours,   W.W.

WWTLI (SDR, RG 59, 793.94/392½, DNA).
¹ P. Wheeler to WJB, May 8, 1915, about which see WJB to WW, May 8, 1915 (first letter of that date), n. 1.

To William Jennings Bryan, with Enclosures

My dear Mr. Secretary,   [The White House] 10 May, 1915.

In view of the situation as a whole (I mean the situation of the world, politically) I think that it would be wise to file such a caveat as Mr. Lansing suggests. It will not do to leave any of our rights indefinite or to seem to acquiesce in any part of the Japanese plan which violates the solemn understandings of the nations with regard to China.

It may favourably affect the Japanese official mind with regard to the wisdom of postponing the discussion of Group V for a very long time indeed.   Faithfully Yours,   W.W.

TCL (SDR, RG 59, 793.94/343½, DNA).

E   N   C   L   O   S   U   R   E   I

Robert Lansing to William Jennings Bryan

CONFIDENTIAL.   [Washington] May 7, 1915.

Dear Mr. Secretary:

In the event that the Allied Powers refuse to unite in a joint representation to Japan, which I am afraid will be their reply, I think that we should be prepared to act immediately.

I suggest, therefore, that a notice in the sense of the one annexed be sent to Tokio and also to Peking. While it might not prevent Japan from carrying out her purpose of coercing China to submit to her demands, it would constitute a complete reservation of all possible rights affecting American interests and Chinese interests as well, so that any agreement forced upon China at the present time could properly become the subject of discussion in the future when the conditions are more propitious.   Faithfully yours,   Robert Lansing.

TLS (SDR, RG 59, 793.94/339½, DNA).

ENCLOSURE II

Draft of notice to be sent to the Governments of Japan and China in case the Allied Powers fail to unite in a joint representation.

In view of the circumstances of the pending negotiations between Japan and China, the Government of the United States has the honor to notify the Imperial Japanese Government that it cannot recognize any agreement or undertaking entered into between Japan and China which impairs the treaty rights of the United States and its citizens in China, the political or territorial integrity of the Republic of China, or the international policy relative to China commonly known as "the open door policy." An identical notice has been sent to the Chinese Government.[1]

T MS (SDR, RG 59, 793.94/339½, DNA).
[1] This note, with several minor revisions, was sent to Japan and China on May 11, 1915, and is printed in *FR 1915*, p. 146.

From William Jennings Bryan

My dear Mr. President: Washington May 10, 1915.

I am sending you a memorandum by Mr. Lansing in regard to the question of "Warning."[1] As you and I have gone over this matter together I need not re-state my views.

Mr. Villard, of the New York Evening Post, called this morning. I do not know what value you attach to his opinions but he presented the idea of calling a conference of neutral nations to discuss the interferance with trade, of which both sides have been guilty.

I explained to him that the difficulty about calling a neutral conference was that any position taken by such a conference during the war would be considered, not upon its merits, but as it affected one side or the other. He thought that both sides had done enough so that complaint could be made against the action of both sides.

With assurances of high respect I am, my dear Mr. President,
                    Yours very sincerely,   W. J. Bryan

TLS (SDR, RG 59, 763.72111/2236½, DNA).
[1] RL to WJB, May 9, 1915, TLS (SDR, RG 59, 763.72111/2236½, DNA), printed in *FR-LP*, I, 387-88. Lansing was responding to a suggestion from Bryan that Americans taking passage on a British vessel bound for a British port and passing through the war zone might be considered to have done so at their own peril and therefore were not entitled to the "full protection" of the United States Government. Lansing argued that, since the American government had made no distinction between belligerent and neutral vessels in its "strict accountability" note to Germany of February 10 and had at no time since that date given any warning to American citizens against traveling on British or other belligerent vessels, adopting such a position now would lead to much public criticism.

From William Jennings Bryan, with Enclosures

My dear Mr. President: Washington May 10th, 1915.

I am sending you a memorandum prepared by Mr. Lansing, together with a letter to me, suggesting courses to be pursued. While I presume you have already prepared an outline of the note, these may be suggestive.

With assurances of high respect, I am, my dear Mr. President,
            Very sincerely yours,   W. J. Bryan

P.S. I am enclosing also an editorial from the Springfield Republican which probably has more weight than any other paper of the same circulation in the country.[1]

TLS (SDR, RG 59, 763.72/1771½, DNA).

[1] It is missing; however, Bryan referred to the editorial, "Banish Thoughts of War," in the *Springfield*, Mass., *Republican*, May 9, 1915. While wholeheartedly condemning the "murderous atrocity" of sinking *Lusitania* without warning, the editorial denied that this act would necessarily lead to war between Germany and the United States. The precise issue between the two nations was not that a British liner had been sunk, but that the American citizens who lost their lives thereon "did not receive the advantage they were entitled to under the law of nations in being warned and given the opportunity to escape from the doomed ship before she was struck." The newspaper warning published by the German Embassy did not meet this requirement. However, it was true that the German government had had no desire to cause the death of these Americans. "There was no deliberate attack, therefore, on the honor of the United States in the primary sense of the words. Our government will necessarily demand suitable redress from the German government because of the American lives lost, but a war for redress or reprisal would not be within the bounds of reason."

E N C L O S U R E   I

Memorandum on sinking of the S.S. LUSITANIA. May 10, 1915.
POSSIBLE GERMAN DEFENSES.

First. The Lusitania carried in its cargo a large quantity of munitions of war for Great Britain and was, therefore, properly destroyed.

This fact, in order to be effective in defense, must be shown to have been communicated to the German naval force making the attack on the vessel.

If so communicated the information came from the representatives of Germany in this country showing the ability to communicate with Berlin.

The presence of munitions of war in the cargo does not in itself relieve the German naval authorities from stopping the vessel and permitting those on board to take to the boats before the torpedo was launched.

The necessity for attack without warning and without delay must rest upon some other defense, which is stated to be—

Second. The Lusitania naturally carried guns to resist attack by German war craft.

This defense must be based on actual knowledge or justifiable suspicion.

The fact is that the *Lusitania* had no guns mounted or unmounted and so was entirely unarmed (Collector Malone's statement).[1]

As the German representatives in this country had means of communicating the fact of the presence of munitions of war on board to their Government they had equal facilities to notify them that the vessel was unarmed. They cannot avoid responsibility by claiming that they suspected the vessel was armed, when they had the means of obtaining actual knowledge showing that the suspicion was unwarranted.

The first defense must rest on *knowledge*; the second defense on *ignorance*. If the German Government had knowledge in one case, they are chargeable with knowledge in the second case.

Third. The German Embassy gave public warning through the press to American citizens not to travel through the "war zone" on British vessels.

The German Government cannot relieve themselves of responsibility for doing an illegal and inhuman act by announcing that they intend to violate the principles of law and humanity.

The communication was not addressed to the Government of the United States. The German Embassy went over the head of the Administration and addressed the American people. Such procedure was an act of insolence similar to the giving of publicity to his memorandum by the German Ambassador.[2] Advantage was taken of the American doctrine of the right of freedom of the press to ignore the Government and to address the people directly. A foreign diplomatic representative is accredited to the Government of the United States, not to the People of the United States. An Ambassador's means of communication is through the Department of State. The conduct of the German Ambassador in this case is an indefensible breach of propriety, an insult to this Government.

If the warning had been delivered to this Government, it would have been compelled to decide whether it should be made public. It had no opportunity to do this. It did, however, have opportunity to advise the American people to heed the warning. This it did not do. It ignored the warning, and by remaining silent gave the impression that the warning might be ignored.

Robert Lansing.

TS memorandum (SDR, RG 59, 763.72/1770½, DNA).

¹ This statement by Dudley F. Malone is embodied in A. J. Peters to RL, May 8, 1915, printed in *FR-LP*, I, 385-86. The relevant passage reads as follows: "3. Whether the vessel had any guns mounted on board. Neutrality men were on board every day. No guns at any time found mounted, nor, so far as they knew, on board."

² That is, Bernstorff's protest against American export of munitions to the Allies.

E N C L O S U R E   I I

Robert Lansing to William Jennings Bryan

CONFIDENTIAL.

Dear Mr. Secretary: [Washington] May 10, 1915.

I offer the following course of procedure in the LUSITANIA case as a basis of discussion:

An earnest protest against the torpedoing of an unarmed passenger steamship on the high seas without giving warning of attack or placing non-combatants in a place of safety.

A declaration that the act violated the established rules of international law and the principles of humanity.

A reaffirmation of the assertion made in the note of February 10th that the German Government would be held to a strict accountability for loss of American lives and property.

A demand (1) that the German Government disavow the act and apologize for it; (2) that the officers guilty of the offense be punished; (3) that the German Government acknowledge liability and promise to pay a just indemnity; and (4) that the German Government will guarantee that in the future ample measures will be taken to insure the safety of the lives of American citizens on the high seas unless they are traveling on a vessel of belligerent nationality, which is armed or being conveyed by belligerent war craft.

In case the German Government refuse to comply with these demands, diplomatic relations could be severed.

The severance of diplomatic relations does not necessarily mean war. It may mean that a government is unwilling to continue intercourse with another government, which has grievously offended against law and right and which refuses to rectify the offense by making proper amends. It is an evidence of extreme displeasure but is not a hostile act.

In presenting the foregoing outline of action for consideration I do not express any opinion.

There is another course of action, which I think worthy of consideration.

The neutral powers, Netherlands, Denmark, Sweden, Norway,

Italy and the United States, might jointly agree to send identic notes to Germany and also to Great Britain protesting vigorously against the violations of international law with which each is charged. The protest to Germany would have to cover breaches of inhumanity as well as of international law. The protest to Great Britain would cover illegal interruption of trade between neutrals.

If such a course is wise, the present would seem to be an opportune time. I do not think, however, that this would relieve the Government of a separate protest to Germany on the LUSI-TANIA case, but it might give a chance to make it more moderate in tone.   Faithfully yours,   Robert Lansing.

TLS (SDR, RG 59, 763.72/1771½, DNA).

From Edith Bolling Galt, with Enclosure

[Washington] Monday morning [May 10, 1915]

I wrote this card last night and this morning. It seems so perfectly inadequate to what I felt in my heart, that I am showing how truly humble I am by sending it to you as an evidence of my statement that I *cannot* write.

You will never contradict me again when I make this assertion, but I throw myself on your mercy and trust you to find the "crock of gold" that is hidden some where in the roots of these halting sentences

I am coming to lunch and we can then talk instead of trusting to my untrained pen.   E.

ENCLOSURE

From Edith Bolling Galt

[Washington] Sunday midnight [May 9-10, 1915]

I *was* with you tonight; in thoughts, in mind, in spirit, yearning to help you, close to your chair, where, when you lifted your tired eyes, I could hold them with my own, and rest them by the very force of my longing to be of service.

I know what you have written Germany will go ringing down the ages, and making your name greater as time goes on. Would it not thrill even those in high places to feel that, even remotely, they had shared that message to the waiting world—how much more then it means to me. It is so exciting, so virile that I cannot sleep. So I have come to talk to you instead.

You know, in our service[1] there is a special prayer for the President of the United States, and this morning when I knelt and heard these words, "Most heartily we beseech thee with thy favour to behold and *bless* thy servant The President of the United States," I forgot your office and thought only of yourself. The very special blessing I held in my heart was your ultimate happiness. And then such a wave of shame came over me, that I dared think of you there, save as the choice of a great people who had put in your keeping the destinies of millions, and that you, in your loneliness had offered me those same strong hands to put my own in, and told me I, in my weakness, could give them strength. I hated myself, and came home humbled.

E.B.G.

ALI (WP, DLC).
[1] She was an Episcopalian.

From Edith Bolling Galt

[Washington] May 10, 1915. 12:15

In just ten minutes I am leaving the house to come and have a minute alone with you, and I am going to try so hard to make you understand and not be disheartened or hurt. You will try to understand, dear kindred Spirit, won't you? and know that I would not add one feather weight to the burden you are carrying. Still I must tell you the truth. And together we will trust the future.

We both deserve the right to try, and if you, with your wonderful love can quicken that which has laid dead so long within me, I promise not to shut it out of my heart, but to bid it welcome, and come to you with the joy of it in my eyes.

On the other hand, if I am dead (as I believe) you will not blame me for seeking to live, even if it means pain in your own tender heart when my pulses refuse to beat in unison with yours. Goodby, and know that you carry away with you all that brings me happiness.   Edith

ALS (WP, DLC).

To Edith Bolling Galt

Adorable Lady,   [The White House] 10 May, 1915

When I know that I am going to see you and am all aquiver with the thought, how can I use this stupid *pen* to tell you that

I love you? That is all there has been in any of my notes. Each one has simply striven to make you realize what is to me the greatest and the most delightful thing in the world—that I am permitted to *love you*.   W.W.

ALI (WP, DLC).

An Address in Philadelphia
to Newly Naturalized Citizens[1]

[May 10, 1915]

Mr. Mayor,[2] fellow citizens: It warms my heart that you should give me such a reception; but it is not of myself that I wish to think tonight, but of those who have just become citizens of the United States.

This is the only country in the world which experiences this constant and repeated rebirth. Other countries depend upon the multiplication of their own native people. This country is constantly drawing strength out of new sources by the voluntary association with it of great bodies of strong men and forward-looking women out of other lands. And so, by the gift of the free will of independent people, it is being constantly renewed from generation to generation by the same process by which it was originally created. It is as if humanity had determined to see to it that this great nation, founded for the benefit of humanity, should not lack for the allegiance of the people of the world.

You have just taken an oath of allegiance to the United States. Of allegiance to whom? Of allegiance to no one, unless it be God—certainly not of allegiance to those who temporarily represent this great government. You have taken an oath of allegiance to a great ideal, to a great body of principles, to a great hope of the human race. You have said, "We are going to America, not only to earn a living, not only to seek the things which it was more difficult to obtain where we were born, but to help forward the great enterprises of the human spirit—to let men know that everywhere in the world there are men who will cross strange oceans and go where a speech is spoken which is alien to them, if they can but satisfy their quest for what their spirits crave; knowing that, whatever the speech, there is but one longing and

Printed in *Address of the President . . . at Convention Hall, Philadelphia, Pa. . . .* (Washington, 1915), with corrections and additions from the CLSsh notes (C. L. Swem Coll., NjP).
    [1] Wilson spoke in the evening before a crowd of some 15,000 persons, including 4,000 newly naturalized citizens, in Convention Hall, Philadelphia. Secretary of Labor William B. Wilson also spoke.
    [2] Rudolph Blankenburg.

utterance of the human heart, and that is for liberty and justice."
And, while you bring all countries with you, you come with a
purpose of leaving all other countries behind you—bringing what
is best of their spirit, but not looking over your shoulders and
seeking to perpetuate what you intended to leave behind in them.
I certainly would not be one even to suggest that a man cease
to love the home of his birth and the nation of his origin—these
things are very sacred and ought not to be put out of our hearts.
But it is one thing to love the place where you were born, and it
is another thing to dedicate yourself to the place to which you
go. You cannot dedicate yourself to America unless you become
in every respect and with every purpose of your will thorough
Americans. You cannot become thorough Americans if you think
of yourselves in groups. America does not consist of groups. A
man who thinks of himself as belonging to a particular national
group in America has not yet become an American, and the man
who goes among you to trade upon your nationality is no worthy
son to live under the Stars and Stripes.

My urgent advice to you would be, not only always to think
first of America, but always, also, to think first of humanity. You
do not love humanity if you seek to divide humanity into jealous
camps. Humanity can be welded together only by love, by sympathy, by justice—not by jealousy and hatred. I am sorry for the
man who seeks to make personal capital out of the passions of
his fellow men. He has lost the touch and ideal of America, for
America was created to unite mankind by those passions which
lift, and not by the passions which separate and debase. We came
to America, either ourselves or in the persons of our ancestors, to
better the ideals of men, to make them see finer things than they
had seen before, to get rid of the things that divide, and to make
sure of the things that unite. It was but an historical accident,
no doubt, that this great country was called the "United States";
and yet I am very thankful that it has that word "united" in its
title, and the man who seeks to divide man from man, group
from group, interest from interest in the United States is striking
at its very heart.

It is a very interesting circumstance to me, in thinking of
those of you who have just sworn allegiance to this great government, that you were drawn across the ocean by some beckoning
finger of hope, by some belief, by some vision of a new kind
of justice, by some expectation of a better kind of life. No doubt
you have been disappointed in some of us. Some of us are very
disappointing. No doubt you have found that justice in the United
States goes only with a pure heart and a right purpose, as it does

everywhere else in the world. No doubt what you have found here did not seem touched for you, after all, with the complete beauty of the ideal which you had conceived beforehand. But remember this: If we had grown at all poor in the ideal, you brought some of it with you. A man does not go out to seek the thing that is not in him. A man does not hope for the thing that he does not believe in. And if some of us have forgotten what America believed in, you, at any rate, imported in your own hearts a renewal of the belief. That is the reason that I, for one, make you welcome. If I have in any degree forgotten what America was intended for, I will thank God if you will remind me. I was born in America. You dreamed dreams of what America was to be, and I hope you brought the dreams with you. No man that does not see visions will ever realize any high hope or undertake any high enterprise. Just because you brought dreams with you, America is more likely to realize dreams such as you brought. You are enriching us if you came expecting us to be better than we are.

See, my friends, what that means. It means that Americans must have a consciousness different from the consciousness of every other nation in the world. I am not saying this with even the slightest thought of criticism of other nations. You know how it is with a family. A family gets centered on itself if it is not careful and is less interested in the neighbors than it is in its own members. So a nation that is not constantly renewed out of new sources is apt to have the narrowness and prejudice of a family, whereas America must have this consciousness— that on all sides it touches elbows and touches hearts with all the nations of mankind. The example of America must be a special example. The example of America must be the example, not merely of peace because it will not fight, but of peace because peace is the healing and elevating influence of the world, and strife is not. There is such a thing as a man being too proud to fight.[3] There is such a thing as a nation being so right that it does not need to convince others by force that it is right.

So, if you come into this great nation, as you have come, voluntarily seeking something that we have to give, all that we have to give is this: We cannot exempt you from work. No man is

[3] Frederick A. Duneka of Harper & Brothers later proposed publishing a small book, *The Man with a Country: Ideals of American Citizenship, Three Addresses by President Woodrow Wilson*. The addresses were Wilson's speeches at Congress Hall, Oct. 25, 1913; at Convention Hall, May 10, 1915; and to the D.A.R. in Washington, Oct. 10, 1915. Duneka sent Wilson newspaper texts of the speeches. Wilson edited them slightly and deleted this sentence entirely. F. A. Duneka to WW, Oct. 29, 1915, TLS (WP, DLC), with enclosures. The little volume was never published.

exempt from work anywhere in the world. I sometimes think he is fortunate if he has to work only with his hands and not with his head. It is very easy to do what other people give you to do, but it is very difficult to give other people things to do. We cannot exempt you from work; we cannot exempt you from the strife and the heartbreaking burden of the struggle of the day—that is common to mankind everywhere. We cannot exempt you from the loads that you must carry. We can only make them light by the spirit in which they are carried, because that is the spirit of hope, it is the spirit of liberty, it is the spirit of justice.

When I was asked, therefore, by the Mayor and the committee that accompanied him to come up from Washington to meet this great company of newly admitted citizens, I could not decline the invitation. I ought not to be away from Washington, and yet I feel that it has renewed my spirit as an American. In Washington, men tell you so many things every day that are not so, and I like to come and stand in the presence of a great body of my fellow citizens, whether they have been my fellow citizens a long time or a short time, and drink, as it were, out of the common fountains with them and go back feeling what you have so generously given me—the sense of your support and of the living vitality in your hearts of the great ideals which have made America the hope of the world.[4]

4 There is a WWsh outline of this address, dated May 10, 1915, in WP, DLC.

From William Howard Taft

PERSONAL.

My dear Mr. President: New Haven, Conn May 10, 1915.

The heavy weight of responsibility that has fallen on you, in view of the Lusitania disaster, leads me to write to you to express, in a deeply sympathetic way, my appreciation of the difficult situation which you face. It seems to me that it is the duty of every thoughtful, patriotic citizen to avoid embarrassing you in your judgment and not to yield to the impulse of deep indignation which the circumstances naturally arouse, and demand at once a resort to extreme measures which mean war. It may be that the attitude of Germany will ultimately require us, in the defense of our honor and our legitimate interests, to join the Allies and punish the ruthless spirit in her conduct of war which breaks every accepted law of war and every principle of international justice to neutrals. But have we reached that point yet? War is a dreadful thing. It would involve such enormous cost of life

and treasure for us that if it can now be avoided, in a manner
consistent with the dignity and honor of our country, we should
make every effort to this end. Is there no alternative between
a mere protest and the presentation of a claim on the one hand,
and the summoning of Congress to consider the question of our
entering the world conflict, with all that that involves, on the
other? In view of Germany's bold assertion of the—up to this time
—unheard of rights of a belligerent in the use of mines, torpedoes
and submarines, and her justification of attacks upon defence-
less people, a mere protest may seem to be hardly less than an
acquiescence. If you concur in this view and believe that something must be done, could it not be done in this way? Your demand for explanation, reparation and disavowal will doubtless
meet with a refusal. Could you not then, on the ground that you
wish to sever diplomatic relations with a power conducting war
in a manner so utterly inhumane, withdraw our Ambassador
from Berlin and give to the German Ambassador in Washington
his passports? That would certainly give force to your protest.
But it would not necessarily involve us in war. Such a severing
of relations has precedents in which war did not result. Germany
in her madness might insist on making this a *casus belli*. I doubt
if she would. Of course if she did, war could not be avoided. Our
other Ambassadors who have undertaken to represent German
interests in belligerent countries could decline further responsibility in that regard. You might then await the meeting of Congress in December and submit the situation to it for its action.
The country meantime would have a chance to recover its calm
and consider the *pros* and *cons* before Congress meets. Of course
I am not in a position to measure the disadvantage we would
sustain by this cutting off diplomatic relations. But I can not
think it would be very burdensome for us.

I presume if you were to call Congress together now, it would
be difficult to avoid a war; but if you take such a step as I suggest, it might save the necessity for an immediate call. Time is
a great solvent of many of these troubles.

The practical result of our going to war would not be great.
Germany is so cooped up that our Navy could do little to make
the navies of the Allies more effective, and it would certainly
take us six months or a year to prepare an army which could be
of any assistance to the Allies. Such a severing of relations might
have as much moral effect as a declaration.

I met Governor Simeon E. Baldwin on the street to-day, and he
suggested that you might invite a submission of the question of
the violation of international law involved in the sinking of the

Lusitania to a tribunal of arbitration, under the rules of the first Hague Conference, and that upon failure of Germany to accept such a suggestion, you might take the course which I have outlined above. I am doubtful whether with war flagrant, with no possibility of securing an impartial tribunal, such a suggestion would be thought to be in good faith or would satisfy public opinion, though it would be most gratifying to have our nation take the position in favor of a peaceful mode of settling difficulties in the midst of war.

You have able Counsellors about you, and these suggestions of mine of course are made without the study which they have been able to give. Perhaps reasons will occur to you for rejecting at once what I have suggested, but, even so, I am glad to have the opportunity of expressing to you my confidence that you will take the wise and patriotic course and that you will avoid war, if it is possible. If you see no other course open than now to summon Congress and declare war, of course the whole people will be with you without regard to party.

With earnest prayer that you may good deliverance make, believe me, my dear Mr. President,

Sincerely yours,   Wm H Taft

TLS (WP, DLC).

From Paul Fuller

My dear Mr President: New York 10 May 1915

I have been with you in spirit since the hour when the sinking of the Lusitania put its appalling burden upon you.

I have no stronger wish that [than] to be of help to you if in any way I could. Thank Heaven that in despite of the little cavillings that are unavoidable, the country has learned to trust to you in a real crisis, for even unfair critics know that you have but a single purpose: to labor for the country's good and to uphold its honor & its usefulness, and all know that you are not to be swerved by clamor nor swayed by political ambition

I will not trouble you with counsel or opinion, but simply say that if I can in any way serve you, I am at your call. With great regard & greater sympathy

Cordially Yours   Paul Fuller

ALS (WP, DLC).

Remarks at a Press Conference

May 11, 1915

We all have the same thing in mind this morning, Mr. President.
 Yes, sir, I dare say we have, all of us, but I have nothing
 yet to add to what was said on Saturday.[1]
As far as that goes, it may be regarded as a declaration of our
policy, may it not—as far as you went yesterday?
 I didn't mean yesterday; I was not thinking of our policy in
 any particular matter yesterday. I was thinking wholly of
 the people I was addressing, and of the Cain some people
 have been trying to raise. I did not mean that as a declara-
 tion of policy of any sort.
Mr. President, has anything been done yet in the way of com-
municating with the German government with regard to recent
events?
 I have nothing more to say about that until I speak finally.
One of the morning papers has what purports to be a report of
Duval West with reference to Mexico.
 That must be a fake. None has been received, so far as I
 know. Is it in the form of an interview?
It isn't clear—yes, I think it is, although he isn't quoted.
 I sincerely doubt its authenticity.
It claims to present his ideas and conclusions, Mr. President.
 That is pretty certainly not so. He is not the sort of man who
 would do that.
Have you seen him?
 No, he was to arrive on Sunday, I think. Probably he is in
 town, but I haven't seen him.
He would see you first, naturally?
 I shouldn't think he would tell anybody else what he thought
 before he told me.
Mr. President, now that the Japanese-Chinese situation has ad-
justed itself, can you say anything about our part in it?
 No, I think not. Better let it alone as it stands for the present.
Mr. President, does the Japanese-Chinese situation guarantee our
commercial rights as they have existed under the Open Door
policy?
 Well, I can't answer that in the way I would like to be prepared to answer it, because I haven't yet studied the effects
 of what China has granted. I haven't been properly advised
 as to how far-reaching it would be. Of course, we shall expect that nothing will interfere with our treaty rights, either
 with China or with Japan.

If it is proper to ask, have you been informed by both governments as to what those demands are?

Yes, sir.

And they agree now, do they?

Yes, sir, they agree now.

Mr. President, going back to the first subject of conversation, I would like to know whether we may expect soon a decision as to our policy.

Just as soon as it is possible to be sure I have all the elements in mind.

Then, Mr. President, your statement in Philadelphia about a man sometimes being too proud to fight had no reference to the policy we might adopt?

I was expressing a personal attitude, that was all. I did not really have in mind any specific thing. I did not regard that as a proper occasion to give any intimation of policy on any special matter.

Mr. President, do you expect to see the German Ambassador?

No, sir, I have no appointment to see him.

T MS (C. L. Swem Coll., NjP).

¹ Wilson's first public response to the *Lusitania* disaster was a brief message to the American people released by Tumulty on the evening of May 8:

"Of course the President feels the distress and the gravity of the situation to the utmost, and is considering very earnestly, but very calmly, the right course of action to pursue. He knows that the people of the country wish and expect him to act with deliberation as well as with firmness." *New York Times*, May 9, 1915.

To William Jennings Bryan

My dear Mr. Secretary,   The White House. 11 May, 1915.

Mr. Lansing's argument seems to me unanswerable. Even if it were just to take the position that a warning that an unlawful and outrageous thing would be done might operate as an exemption from responsibility on the part of those who issued it, so far as our citizens were concerned, it is now too late to take it. We defined our position at the outset and cannot alter it,—at any rate so far as it affects the past.   Faithfully Yours,   W.W.

Mr. Villard's suggestion interests me very much; but the objections you make are certainly very vital ones. We can turn the matter over in our minds.

WWTLI (SDR, RG 59, 763.72111/2237½, DNA).

To William Jennings Bryan, with Enclosure

My dear Mr. Secretary,   The White House. 11 May, 1915.

Both in mind and heart I was deeply moved by what you said in Cabinet this morning.[1] I have gone over it again and again in my thoughts since we separated; and it is with no sort of confidence that I am right, but, on the contrary with unaffected misgivings that I may be wrong, that I send you the enclosed[2] with the request that you and Mr. Lansing will be generous enough to go over it and put it into shap[e] for transmission to the German government, making such suggestions of improvement as occur to you. But I am following my best judgment in the light of the situation as I see it now.

Time seems to me of the essence just now because cimmitments of opinion are taking place upon every apprearance of the newspapers and I would be very much obliged if this note might be made ready to be sent at the earliest possible hour.

I was deeply grateful for the generous things you said this morning.   Faithfully Yours   W.W.

WWTLI (CLO).
[1] For a summary of what is known about this cabinet meeting, see Link, *Struggle for Neutrality*, pp. 383-84.
[2] There is also a WWT outline of this draft in WP, DLC and a WWsh draft, dated May 11, 1915, in *ibid.*

E N C L O S U R E

A Draft of the First *Lusitania* Note

In re Lusitania.

(RECITAL of the facts of the death of Thrasher, the attacks on the Cushing and Gulflight, and the loss of American lives by the sinking of the Lusitania.)

The Government of the United States has observed this series of events with growing concern, distress and amazement. Recalling, as it did, the humane and enlightened action of the Imperial German Government hitherto in all matters of international right and particularly with regard to the freedom of the seas; having learned to recognize the German views and the German influence in the field of international obligation as always engaged upon the side of justice and humanity; and having understood the instructions of the Imperial German Government to its naval commanders to be upon the same plane of humane action prescribed by the naval codes of other nations, it was loath to believe, it cannot now bring itself to believe, that these acts, so absolutely contrary to the rules, the practices, and the spirit of modern warfare, could have the countenance or sanction of that great Government. It feels it to be its duty, therefore, to address the Imperial German Government concerning them with the utmost frankness and in the earnest hope that it is not mistaken in expecting action on the part of the Imperial German Government which will correct the unfortunate impressions which have been created and vindicate once more the position of that Government with regard to the sacred freedom of the seas.

The Government of the United States has been apprised of the feeling of the Imperial German Government that it has been obliged by the extraordinary circumstances of the present war and the drastic measures of its adversaries in seeking to cut its coasts off from all commerce to adopt methods of retaliation which go much beyond the ordinary methods of warfare at sea, in the proclamation of a war zone from which it has warned neutral ships to keep away. But the waters of that zone touch the coasts of many neutral nations, and this Government has already had the honour of informing the Imperial German Government that it cannot admit the adoption of such measures or such a warning of danger to operate as in any degree an abreviation of the rights of American ship masters or of American citizens bound on lawful errands as passengers on merchant ships of belligerant ownership; and that it must hold the Imperial German Government to a strict accountability for any infringement of those rights, direct or incidental. It does not understand the Imperial German Government to question those rights. It is confident, on the contrary, that the Imperial German Government accepts, as of course, the rule that the lives of non-combatants, whether they be of neutral citizenship or citizens of one of the nations at war, cannot lawfully or rightfully be put in jeopardy by the capture or destruction of an unarmed merchantman, and recognizes as all other nations do the obligation to take the usual precaution of visit and search to ascertain whether a suspected merchantman is in fact of belligerant ownership or is in fact carrying contraband of war under a neutral flag.

The Government of the United States, therefore, takes the liberty of calling the attention of the Imperial German Government with the utmost earnestness to the fact that the danger of its present method of attack against the trade of its enemies lies in the practical impossibility of employing submarines in the destruction of commerce in conformity with what all modern opinion regards as the imperative rules of fairness, reason, justice, and humanity. It is practically impossible for the officers of a submarine to visit a merchantman at sea and examine her papers and cargo. It is practically impossible for them to make a prize of her; and, if they cannot put a prize crew on board of her, they cannot sink her without leaving her crew and all on board of her to the mercy of the sea in her small boats. In the instances of which we have spoken time enough for even that poor measure of safety was not given, and in at least two of the cases cited not so much as a warning was received. Submarines, we respectfully submit, cannot be used against merchantmen without an inevitable violation of many sacred principles of justice and humanity.

There was recently published in the newspapers of the United States, we regret to inform the Imperial German Government, a formal warning, purporting to come from the Imperial German Embassy at Washington, addressed to the people of the United States, and stating, in effect, that any citizen of the United States who exercised his right of free travel upon the seas would do so at his peril if his journey should take him within the zone of waters within which the Imperial German navy was using submarines against the commerce of Great Britain and France, notwithstanding the respectful but very earnest protest of his government, the Government if [of] the United States. We do not speak of this for the purpose of calling the attention of the Imperial German Government at this time to the surprising irregularity of a communication from the Imperial German Embassy at Washington addressed to the people of the United States through the newspapers, but only for the purpose of pointing out that no warning that an unlawful and inhumane act will be committed can possibly be accepted as an excuse or paliation for that act or as an abatement of the responsibility for its commission.

Long acquainted as this Government has been with the character of the Imperial German Government and with the high principles of equity with which it has been actuated and guided, the Government of the United States cannot believe that the commanders of the vessels which committed these acts of lawlessness did so under orders from the Imperial German naval authorities or with their approval. It takes it for granted that, at least within the practical possibilities of every such case, the commanders even of submarines were expected to do nothing that would involve the lives of non-combatants or the safety of neutral ships, even at the cost of failing of their object of capture or destruction. It confidently expects, therefore, that the Imperial

German Government will disavow the acts to which the Government of the United States takes the liberty of calling its attention, that it will make reparation so far as reparation is possible for injuries which are without measure, and that it will take immediate steps to prevent the recurrence of anything so obviously subversive of the principles of warfare for which the Imperial German Government has always itself so wisely and so firmly contended.

American citizens act within their indisputable rights in taking their ships and in travelling wherever their legitimate business calls them upon the high seas, and exercise those rights in what should be the well justified confidence that their lives will not be endangered by acts done in clear violation of universally acknowledged international obligations, certainly in the confidence that their own Government will sustain them in their exercise. The Government of the United States looks to the Imperial German Government for just, prompt, and enlightened action in this vital matter with the greater confidence because Germany and the United States are bound together by special ties of friendship not only but also by special stipulations of explicit treaty. (Here cite treaty with Prussia so far as pertinent). The Imperial German Government will not expect the Government of the United States to omit any necessary representation or any necessary act in sustaining the rights of its citizens or in safeguarding the sacred duties of international obligation.

WWT MS (WP, DLC).

From Edward Mandell House

Dear Governor: No. 3. [London] May 11th, 1915.

I cabled you on Sunday for the reason that I felt you would like to know what I thought was best in the situation that confronts you.

I cannot see any way out unless Germany promises to cease her policy of making war upon non-combatants. If you do not call her to account over the loss of American lives caused by the sinking of the Lusitania, her next act will probably be the sinking of an American liner, giving as an excuse that she carried munitions of war and that we had been warned not to send ships into the danger zone.

The question must be determined either now or later and it seems to me that you would lost [lose] prestige by deferring it.

Germany has either one or two things in mind. She may believe that we will not go to war under any provocation or will be impotent if we do, or she desires us to enter. The first is more understandable than the second, although she probably thinks if we became involved we would stop the shipment of munitions in order to equip ourselves.

She may also think that in the peace conference we would be likely to use our influence to settle upon broader and easier terms for Germany.

Or she may think that by being able to torpedoe our ships it would contribute to the isolation of England.

If, unhappily, it is necessary to go to war I hope you will give the world an exhibition of American efficiency that will be a lesson for a century or more. It is generally believed throughout Europe that we are so unprepared and that it would take so long to put our resources into motion, that our entering would make but little difference.

In the event of war we should accelerate the manufacture of munitions to such an extent that we could supply not only ourselves, but the Allies, and so quickly that the world would be astounded.

You can never know how deeply I regret the turn affairs have taken, but it may be for the ultimate good. My heart goes out to you at this time as never before, and I think of you every hour of the day and wish that I was by your side. My only consolation is that I may be of greater service here.

Your affectionate,   E. M. House

TLS (WP, DLC).

From William Henry Cardinal O'Connell[1]

Dear President,   Boston May 11, 1915

I have just finished reading your wonderful words to the men of Philadelphia—words so sublime that I am still trembling from their echo in my heart.

The spirit of Christ breathes in those lofty yet stately simple sentiments, and all America every human being must feel reminded of a great duty—a duty clear enough yet so easily clouded by self-interest.

Again you have lifted up the soul of the whole nation, and I beg God to bless you.

Your humble servant   W. Card. O'Connell

ALS (WP, DLC).
1 Archbishop of Boston.

From Henry Albert Stimson[1]

My dear Mr. President   New York City May 11/15

There is not a Sunday morning service in our church in which we do not pray for you by name. We can rejoice that the answer to our prayer is in the noble address you gave in Philadelphia yesterday, no less than the way in which you have been kept from mistake and manifestly guided by God through the critical hours of the past Autumn and Winter. The heart of the nation is certainly beating in you. Your address, so strong in its grasp of the situation, and so nobly Christian in the best sense, will be a power for righteousness & peace in the chancelleries of the nations and an uplift to people of good will everywhere

With gratitude to God & to you I am

Very respectfully yours   Henry A. Stimson

ALS (WP, DLC).
  [1] Pastor of the Manhattan Congregational Church.

From Samuel Allen Harlow

My dear Tommy: Grafton Mass., May 11th, 1915.

I absolutely *must* sit down and express to you my profound and sincere admiration of your noble address yesterday in Philadelphia. Nothing finer, more elevated in spirit, more beautiful in thought and sentiment, more inherently American and patriotic in essence, more happy in expression, has been delivered in this nation for years. One's heart can not help but respond to such splendid and statesmanlike utterance as this:

"America was created to unite mankind by the passions that lift and unite, and not by the passions that separate and debase mankind."

It is all, my dear Tommy, full of the spirit, the poetry, the elevation, which remind one of Gettysburg and Lincoln's undying words.

May God give you great wisdom and strength in these days.

I am, Very sincerely yours,   Samuel Allen Harlow.

ALS (WP, DLC).

To Edith Bolling Galt

The White House 11 May [1915], Tuesday, 7 A.M.

I do not know just what I said at Philadelphia (as I rode along the street in the dusk I found myself a little confused as to

whether I was in Philadelphia or New York!) because my heart
was in such a whirl from that wonderful interview of yesterday
and the poignant appeal and sweetness of the little note you
left with me; but many other things have grown clear in my
mind. You have seen me from the top of your tower, on one of
your visits to the sweet air and the life about you, where men and
women are free, and you have stretched out your hands to me
and called to me to rescue you—*and I will*; unless there is some
secret passage in which you will hide yourself in sudden panic
when I have made my way into the tower. Even that I am sure
I could find! I might be better equipped for the fight—I would to
God I were! It may be that, if the knight were younger and had
a beauty of person that matched his love and his courage, you
would save him the agony of the siege and come out with shining eyes to deliver him the keys with your own hands. And yet
the very fact that he looks grey and grim and yet has the indomitable spirit of the knight in him and loves without limit
and without thought of being said nay may stand him in sufficient stead. Nay it must. He has been permitted a sacred enterprise: there is a heart to be rescued from itself—a heart that
never made complete surrender and is wounded by the cage
it has made for itself,—which has never known that final divine
act of self-surrender which is a woman's way to love and happiness. If she cannot be taken—taken away from herself—by
siege, she must be taken by storm—and she shall be!

Please read Arnold's "The Buried Life," dear, that I read to you
once, and let the meaning of it grow very clear to you.

Was it not interesting that the very day I spoke of it—and
before I had actually spoken of it—you changed your signature,
first to 'E' and then to 'Edith'? Is it not thrillingly interesting to
see how our hearts draw together whenever you come to the top
of your tower! I dream that some day you will take down the
rusty keys and come out to me, as sweetly and naturally as a
child, with utter faith in your shining eyes and no quiver of
doubt or dismay—coming of course, because I am waiting and
am already your own   W.W.

ALI (WP, DLC).

From Edith Bolling Galt

[Washington] May 11, 1915

Welcome home! How I wish I could really come and put both
hands in yours and tell you how proud, how infinitely proud I am

of you. Your message to the people last night is all I knew it would be.

I will keep the little sheet of characters you gave me,[1] and always love the day they went out to the world. Perhaps it may mean another awakening!

I am *so so* glad you are back   Last night Helen took me for a ride in the park. It was a subtle thing to do, for I missed you so I could hardly talk. And you must have felt my need of you.

                                                        Edith

ALS (WP, DLC).
[1] The WWsh outline of his address in Philadelphia on May 10. It is in the EBW Papers, DLC.

To Edith Bolling Galt

                                        The White House
                        Tuesday evening, 9 p.m. 11 May [1915]

The words of that e[x]quisite note you sent me by Helen to-day sing in my heart as I write to-night, dearest one. They say that you were lonely without me, that you are happy because I am back, that you would love to come and put your hands in mine and speak the pride in *me* (bless you!) that is in your sweet heart, that you had need of me and were sad because I was away, and, above all, that yesterday may have meant for you another awakening! Of course it did: and it meant as much for me as for you, my wonderful, true, fearless sweetheart! You thought sleep was death, because there was no hope in the dreams! It has been a week of self-revelation for both of us, since I poured my love out to you in the half light there where we sat in the still evening, and I found the sweet lady I spoke to a prisoner in her own thoughts; and now you are awake and free! The little god is blind himself, but he has made us see. And, oh, how happy he has made me! My heart echoes every syllable of what you have written and knows what was unspoken. I felt that I was at home again this morning because I was where you were. If I said what was worth saying to that great audience last night it must have been because love had complete possession of me. I did not know before I got up very clearly what I was going to say, nor remember what I had said when I sat down; but I knew that I had left the speech in your hands and that you needed me as I needed you. And, ah, I have needed you to-night, my sweet Edith! What the touch of your hand and a look into your eyes would have meant to me of strength and steadfast-ness as I made the final decision as to what I should say to

Germany! You must have felt it. You must have heard the cry of
my heart to you and known in every fibre of you that I needed
you. And I know that you would have come if you could and
would have given me the full solace of all that is in your woman's heart, and I have been happy in spite of my loneliness,—
you *have* helped me. I did not need to be told of your love, my
heart only ached because I could not feel your touch and see
you. I have looked into your eyes, dear, while the veil was over
them, until I was fairly faint with thirst. The veil is not over them
now, for you are awake and I love you beyond measure! God
bless you! We shall help each other henceforth whether we can
touch hands or not.   W.W.[1]

ALI (WP, DLC).
   [1] There is a WWsh draft of this letter in WP, DLC.

From Edith Bolling Galt

[Washington] May 11, 1915 midnight
   I cannot go to sleep until I tell you how completely you have
been with me all day and what fun it has been to hear everyone talking of you.
   It began by 8 oclock this morning when I went to market
and heard this greeting from my butcher.
   "Well! Mrs. Galt have you read the President's speech made
in Philadelphia? He is the greatest man this country has ever
produced and he is going to stay right where he is another
four years"
   Then, groups of people standing near me, all discussing your
speech, and all filled with admiration.
   Then I came home and Helen brought me something which
made this thing I call a heart, for lack of a better word, beat to
words that thrill and burn—and when I read that you did "*not
know just what I said in Philadelphia*, because my heart was
in such a whirl from that wonderful interview of yesterday"—
well, I didn't *want* to be a worm, I *was* a worm with no head to
lift from the dust at your feet.
   You—to be in a whirl—from an interview with me! The very
thought is presumption.
   But, I must go on with my story. At noon I had an appointment with my lawyer,[1] whose opinion I value as much as anyone
I know, and he could talk to me of nothing but you, and what
you had said. Lifting the paper from my desk where, I had been
reading, he held it in his hand and said: "This is the finest ut

terance I have ever read. The English is so clear, so simple, and yet so magnificent in its principles, in the man's conviction to do right at any personal cost and in his profound comprehension of the greatest burden that has ever come to any President, that it seems inspired."

He waited a long minute, and then he turned and took my hand and said, "Child, I don't know why, but I feel that you are destined to hold in this woman's hand a great power—perhaps the weal or woe of a country. You can be an inspiration and a force if you do not willfully shut your eyes to opportunity. In order to fit yourself for this thing that I feel will come to you, you must work—*read, study, think*! Don't shut yourself up in this house alone, because you are afraid to go into the larger life, for fear of failure."

Doesn't this seem almost uncanny? And I tried so hard to keep the pride out of my eyes and voice when he praised you, and yet he seemed to be looking through and through me.

Don't think from this that he can imagine the wonderful thing you have given into my keeping. I know he could not do that, but it is a possibility of the future to his mind because he knows and trusts me. It would not be fair not to tell you that he has said very much the same thing to me for four or five years, and it is only because of what was singing in my heart that it is freighted with such meaning.

I cannot read "The Buried Life" tonight. I want only to be alive, to feel the thrill of extacy that must come to one who has been in darkness, and suddenly—even in the far distance—sees the gleaming of a light.   Edith.

ALS (WP, DLC).
  1 Nathaniel Wilson, a prominent attorney of Washington and a close friend and adviser of Mrs. Galt.

To William Jennings Bryan

My dear Mr. Secretary,   The White House. 12 May, 1915.

I am sincerely obliged to you for these papers,[1] and would appreciate it if you would ask Mr. Lansing to let me have a copy of these suggestions as to alternative courses of action.
                              Faithfully Yours,   W.W.

WWTLI (SDR, RG 59, 763.72/1772½, DNA).
  1 The enclosures in WJB to WW, May 10, 1915 (second letter of that date).

From William Jennings Bryan

My Dear Mr President   [Washington] May 12 1915.

Your more than generous note received with draft of protest to Germany.

I have gone over it very carefully and will give it to Mr Lansing at once, for I agree with you that it is well to act without delay in order to give direction to public opinion. I do not see that you could have stated your position more clearly or more forcibly. In one sentence I suggest addition of words "as the last few weeks have shown," so that it will read: "Submarines, we respectfully submit, can not be used against merchantmen, as the last few weeks have shown, without an inevitable violation of many sacred principles of justice and humanity." The only other amendment that occurs to me relates to the Cushing and Gulflight. Would it not be wise to make some reference to the rules sent us yesterday and the offer to apologize and make reparation in case a neutral ship is sunk by mistake?[1] I suggest some thing like this: "Apology and reparation for destruction of neutral ships, sunk by mistake, while they may satisfy international obligations, if no loss of life results, can not justify or excuse a practice, the natural and almost necessary effect of which is to subject neutral nations to new and immeasurable risks, for it must be remembered that peace, not war, is the normal state, and that nations that resort to war to settle disputes are not at liberty to subordinate the rights of neutrals to the supposed, or even actual, needs of belligerents." I am in doubt about the propriety of referring to the note published by Bernsdorf.

But, my dear Mr President, I join in this document with a heavy heart. I am as sure of your patriotic purpose as I am of my own, but after long consideration, both careful and prayerful, I can not bring myself to the belief that it is wise to relinquish the hope of playing the part of a friend to both sides in the role of peace maker, and I fear this note will result in such a relinquishment—for the hope requires for its realization the retaining of the confidence of both sides. The protest will be popular in this country, for a time at least and possibly permanently, because public sentiment, already favorable to the allies, has been perceptibly increased by the Lusitania trajedy, but there is peril in this very fact. Your position, being the position of the government, will be approved—the approval varying in emphasis in proportion to the feeling against Germany. There being no intimation that the final accounting will be postponed until the war is over, the jingo element will not only predict, but demand, war—see enclosed editorial from Washington Post of this morning[2]—and the line will be more distinctly drawn between those who sympathize with Germany and the rest of the people. Outside of the country the document will be applauded by the allies, and the more they applaud the more Germany will be embittered, because we unsparingly denounce the retaliatory methods employed by her without condemning the announced purpose of the allies to starve the non-combattants of Germany and without complaining of the conduct of Great Britain in relying on passengers, including men, women and children of the United States, to give immunity to vessels carrying munitions of war—without even suggesting that she should convoy passenger ships as carefully as she does ships carrying horses and gasoline. This enumeration does not include a reference to Great Britain's indifference to the increased dangers thrown upon us by the misuse of our flag or to her unwarrented interference with our trade with neutral nations. Germany can not but construe the strong statement of the case against her, coupled with silence as to the unjustifiable action of the allies, as partiality toward the latter—an impression which will be deepened in proportion to the loudness of the praise which the allies bestow upon this government's statement of its position. The only way, as I see it, to prevent irreparable injury being done by the statement is to issue simultaneously a protest against the objectionable conduct of the allies which will keep them from rejoicing and show Germany that we are defending our rights from aggression from both sides. I am only giving you, my dear Mr President, the situation as it appears to me—and am praying all the while, that I may be wholly mistaken and that your judgment may be vindicated by events. With assurances of respect I am my dear Mr President,   Very truly yours   W. J. Bryan

ALS (WP, DLC).

[1] J. W. Gerard to WJB, May 9, 1915, printed in *FR-WWS 1915*, pp. 387-88, stating that specific instructions had repeatedly been issued to German war vessels to avoid attacks on neutral ships in the war zone which had "been guilty of no hostile act." However, if a neutral ship should come to harm by mistake through the action of German submarines or aircraft, the German government would "unreservedly recognize its responsibility therefor," express its regrets, and pay damages without the usual prize court action. The note also outlined briefly the procedure for establishing responsibility in such cases.

[2] "If War Should Come," *Washington Post*, May 12, 1915. "The plain truth is," the editorial declared, "that the United States is in no condition to declare war upon Germany. It could not make its demands effective by force of arms, because it has no navy and no army capable of waging war on the scale that would be required." President Wilson was right in his strong desire to maintain peace. But the nation was in no position to "command peace." In its present state, it could have only "a peace of weakness, preserved at the expense of national humiliation, purchsed by the surrender of national rights." America was becoming involved in the war in spite of itself, and Americans would have to decide whether they wished a peace of weakness or a peace of strength.

Protests against violations of American rights were meaningless unless backed up by military power. The editorial concluded with a plea for the creation of an adequate army and navy and called for a special session of Congress to begin the task at once.

From William Jennings Bryan, with Enclosures

My dear Mr. President: Washington May 12, 1915.

I am enclosing copy of the draft of the note made according to your instructions. In most of the cases it is simply a choice of words and usually the words used by Mr. Lansing are a little harsher than words used by you, and I incline to the milder statement where it is clear and certain.

In one case, on page 5, I very much prefer your word to his, namely, the use of the word "unarmed" instead of the word "unresisting"—(line 3, page 5). The difference is quite an important one. If the vessel is armed that, as I understand it, establishes her character and it is not necessary to wait to see whether she will resist. It is presumed that an armed vessel will resist—that is what the arms are for.

At the bottom of page 5 he has substituted—"the civilized world" for "modern opinion." I like your phrase—"modern opinion" better. In his phrase—the word "civilized" would be more offensive because it will virtually charge Germany with being uncivilized. There is no use calling names—there is sufficient force in the plain statement.

About the middle of page 6 the phrase which he leaves out strengthens the statement. It might be qualified a little by adding after "was" and before "not giving," the phrase—"according to our information."

You will notice that he has inserted on page 6—fifth line from the bottom—the suggestion which I made to you in my letter of this morning—namely: "as the last few weeks have shown." This, of course, is put in subject to your approval.

He has also indicated a place at the beginning of page 11 for the insertion of "A" which I suggested in my letter this morning, only, he leaves out the phrase "sunk by mistake" which broadens the phrase—an improvement.

He also suggests the ommission of the last sentence but I am inclined to think that it is worth while to set it forth as a principle. It will be difficult for her to reply that she is "at liberty to subordinate the rights of neutrals to the supposed or even actual needs of the belligerents," and, if she does not deny it, it may be of value to have it taken as admitted.

On page 11 you will notice that he uses the words—"must

realize that" instead of "will not expect, etc." I like your phrase better; it is more polite to say that the German Government *will not expect* us to surrender our rights, rather than to say that the German Government *"must* realize" that we will not.

Mr. Lansing prefers to leave in the reference to von Bernstorff about the propriety of which there is, as I wrote you this morning, a question in my mind.

A question arises as to making the matter public. I think it advisable to have the statement issued as soon as possible— do you think it would be improper to give it out here as soon as it is cabled to Berlin? I presume there is no use of putting it in cipher if we give it out here when it is sent. I am inclined to think that, desirable as it would be to give it out at once, it might be better to put it in cipher and send it by cable and then give it out when it has had time to reach Berlin. It occurs to me it would be a little better to have them in possession of it when it was given out here, rather than have them receive the information by news before it reaches them officially. They gave their last statement to us to the Press there when it was filed for transmission, at least it reached the newspapers here in the evening before it reached the Ambassador, and we read it in the newspapers before it was delivered, but the Ambassador explained that he brought it as soon as he could.

With assurances of high respect I am, my dear Mr. President,
Yours very sincerely,   W. J. Bryan

TLS (W. J. Bryan Papers, DNA).

E N C L O S U R E   I

Robert Lansing to William Jennings Bryan

Dear Mr. Secretary: [Washington] May 12, 1915.

I enclose herewith the draft prepared by the President in re LUSITANIA.

The method which I have adopted in making suggestions is to put in brackets the portions of the President's draft which I would omit, and underscoring the words which I would add.

I feel that the communication loses some of its strength by being too long, but I have not been very successful in the short time I have had to consider it in reducing the length.

You spoke to me about omitting any reference to the public warning given by the German Embassy here. My own view is that it would be a mistake to do so, as at once the German Gov-

ernment would employ that as an argument. It might as well
be met to begin with as later.

Faithfully yours,   Robert Lansing.

TLS (SDR, RG 59, 763.72/1774½, DNA).

E N C L O S U R E   I I

American Ambassador, Berlin.

Please call on the Imperial German Foreign Minister and after
reading to him this communication leave with him a copy if
he so desires.

In view of the recent acts of the German authorities viola-
tive of American rights on the high seas which culminated in the
torpedoing and sinking of the British steamship LUSITANIA on
May 7, 1915, by which over one hundred American citizens lost
their lives, the Government of the United States and the Imperial
German Government must come to a clear and full understanding as to the grave situation which has resulted.

The sinking of the British passenger steamer FALABA by a
German submarine on March 28th, through which Leon C.
Thrasher, an American citizen was drowned; the attack on April
28th on the American vessel CUSHING, by a German aeroplane;
the torpedoing on May 1st of the American vessel GULFLIGHT
by a German submarine, by which two or more American citizens
met their death; and, finally, the torpedoing and sinking of the
LUSITANIA, constitute a series of events, which the Government of the United States has observed with growing concern,
distress and amazement.

[The Government of the United States has observed this series
of events with growing concern, distress and amazement.] Recalling [, as it did,] the humane and enlightened *attitude assumed
hitherto by* [action of] the Imperial German Government *in*
[hitherto in all] matters of international right and particularly
with regard to the freedom of the seas; having learned to
recognize the German views and the German influence in the
field of international obligation as always engaged upon the side
of justice and humanity; and having understood the instructions
of the Imperial German Government to its naval commanders
to be upon the same plane of humane action prescribed by the
naval codes of other nations, *the Government of the United
States* [it] was loath to believe, it cannot now bring itself to
believe, that these acts, so absolutely contrary to the rules, the
practices, and the spirit of modern warfare, could have the

countenance or sanction of that great Government. [It feels it to be its duty, therefore, to address the Imperial German Government concerning them with the utmost frankness and in the earnest hope that it is not mistaken in expecting action on the part of the Imperial German Government which will correct the unfortunate impressions which have been created and vindicate once more the position of that Government with regard to the sacred freedom of the seas.]

The Government of the United States has been apprised *that* [of the feeling of] the Imperial German Government *considered themselves to be* [that it has been] obliged by the extraordinary circumstances of the present war and the [drastic] measures *adopted by their* [of its] adversaries in seeking to cut [its coasts] off *Germany* from all commerce, to adopt methods of retaliation which go much beyond the ordinary methods of warfare at sea, in the proclamation of a war zone [from] which it has warned neutral ships to *avoid*. [keep away. But the waters of that zone touch the coasts of many neutral nations, and] This Government has already *informed* [had the honor of informing] the Imperial German Government that it cannot admit the adoption of such measures or such a warning of danger to operate as in any degree an abbreviation of the rights of American ship masters or of American citizens bound on lawful errands as passengers on merchant ships of belligerent *nationality* [ownership]; and that it must hold the Imperial German Government to a strict accountability for any infringement of those rights. [, direct or incidental. It does not understand the Imperial German Government to question those rights.] It *assumes* [is confident, on the contrary,] that the Imperial German Government accept[s, as of course,] the rule that the lives of non-combatants, whether they be of neutral citizenship or citizens of one of the nations at war, cannot lawfully or rightfully be put in jeopardy by the capture or destruction of an *unresisting* [unarmed] merchantman, and recognize[s] *also*, as all other nations do, the obligation to take the usual precaution of visit and search to ascertain whether a suspected merchantman is in fact of belligerent *nationality* [ownership] or is in fact carrying contraband of war under a neutral flag.

The Government of the United States, therefore, *calls* [takes the liberty of calling] the attention of the Imperial German Government with the utmost earnestness to the fact that the *objection to their* [danger of its] present method of attack against the trade of *their* [its] enemies lies in the practical impossibility of employing submarines in the destruction of commerce *without disregarding those* [in conformity with what all modern opinion regards as the imperative] rules of fairness, reason, justice, and humanity, *which the civilized world regards as imperative.* It is practically impossible for the officers of a submarine to visit a merchantman at sea and examine her papers and cargo. It is practically impossible for them to make a prize of her; [and, if they cannot put a prize crew on board of her,] They cannot sink her without leaving her crew and all on board of her to the mercy of the sea in her small boats. *These facts it is understood the Imperial German Government frankly admit.* [In the instances of which we have spoken time enough for even that poor measure of safety was not given, and in at least two of the cases cited not so much as a warning was received.] *Manifestly* submarines [, we respectfully submit,] cannot be used against merchantmen, as the last few weeks have shown, without an inevitable violation of many sacred principles of justice and humanity.

American citizens act within their indisputable rights in taking their ships and in traveling wherever their legitimate business calls them upon the high seas, and exercise those rights in what should be the well justified confidence that their lives will not be endangered by acts done in clear violation of universally acknowledged international obligations *and* [−] certainly in the confidence that their own Government will sustain them in *the* [their] exercise[.] *of their rights.*

There was recently published in the newspapers of the United States, *I* [we] regret to inform the Imperial German Government, a formal warning, purporting to come from the Imperial German Embassy at Washington, addressed to the people of the United States, and stating, in effect, that any citizen of the United States who exercised his right of free travel upon the seas would do so at his peril if his journey should take him within the zone of waters within which the Imperial German Navy was using submarines against the commerce of Great Britain and France, notwithstanding the respectful but very earnest protest of his government, the Government of the United States. *I* [We] do not *refer to* [speak of] this for the purpose of calling the attention of the Imperial German Government at this time to the surprising irregularity of a communication from the Imperial German Embassy at Washington addressed to the people of the United States through the newspapers, but only for the purpose of pointing out that no warning that an unlawful and inhumane act will be committed can possibly be accepted as an excuse or palliation for that act or as an abatement of the responsibility for the commission.

Long acquainted as this Government has been with the character of the Imperial German Government and with the high principles of equity [with] by which [it has] they have in the past been actuated and guided, the Government of the United States cannot believe that the commanders of the vessels which committed these acts of lawlessness did so *except under a misapprehension of the orders issued by* [under orders from] the Imperial German naval authorities [or with their approval. It takes it for granted that, at least within the practical possibilities of every such case, the commanders even of submarines were expected to do nothing that would involve the lives of non-combatants or the safety of neutral ships, even at the cost of failing of their object of capture or destruction.] It confidently expects, therefore, that the Imperial German Government will disavow the acts *of* [to] which the Government of the United States *complains* [takes the liberty of calling its attention]; that *they* [it] will make reparation so far as reparation is possible for injuries which are without measure, and that *they* [it] will take immediate steps to prevent the recurrence of anything so obviously subversive of the principles of warfare for which the Imperial German Government *have in the past* [has always itself so wisely and] so firmly contended.

[American citizens act within their indisputable rights in taking their ships and in traveling wherever their legitimate business calls them upon the high seas, and exercise those rights in what should be the well justified confidence that their lives will not be endangered by acts done in clear violation of universally acknowledged international obligations *and* [–] certainly in the confidence that their own Government will sustain them in *the* [their] exercise. *of their rights*].

The Government of the United States looks to the Imperial German Government for just, prompt, and enlightened action in this vital matter with the greater confidence because the United States and Germany are bound together *not only* by special ties of friendship [not only] but also by *the* [special] stipulations of *the Treaty of 1828 between the United States and the Kingdom* of Prussia. [explicit treaty]

A

Insert A

[An] Expressions of regret and [an act] offers of reparation in case of the destruction of neutral ships [, sunk by mistake,] while they may satisfy international obligations, if no loss of life results, can not justify or excuse a practice, the natural and necessary effect of which is to subject neutral nations *and neutral persons* to new and immeasurable risks; [for it must be remembered that peace, not war, is the normal state, and that nations that resort to war to settle disputes are not at liberty to subordinate the rights of neutrals to the supposed or even actual needs of belligerents.]

The Imperial German Government *must realize that* [will not expect] *this* [the] Government *will not* [of the United States to] omit any *word* [necessary representation] or any [necessary] act *necessary to the performance of its sacred duty of maintaining* [in sustaining] the rights of *the United States and* its citizens *and of safeguarding their free exercise and enjoyment.* [or in safeguarding the sacred duties of international obligation.]

T MS (SDR, RG 59, 763.72/1774½a, DNA).

From William Jennings Bryan

My Dear Mr President,   Washington May 12 1915

I am so fearful of the embarassment which the jingoes will cause by *assuming* that your note means war– an interpretation which might affect the *tone* of Germany's reply, as well as make it more difficult to postpone final settlement—that I venture to suggest the propriety of meeting the issue *now* by a statement given out at the time the statement is published or before. To explain what I mean I give the following—*not* as a draft of such notice or interview but as an illustration: "The words 'strict accountability' having been construed by some of the newspapers to mean an *immediate* settlement of the matter I deem it fitting to say that that construction is not a necessary one. In individual matters friends sometimes find it wise to postpone the settlement of disputes until such differences can be considered calmly and on their merits. So it may be with nations. The United States and Germany, between whom there exists a long standing friendship, may find it advisable to postpone until peace is restored any disputes that do not yield to diplomatic treatment. Germany has endorsed the principle of investigation embodied in the thirty treaties signed with as many nations. These treaties give a years time for investigation and apply to *all* disputes of every character.["]

From this nations stand point there is no reason why this policy should not control as between the United States and Germany.

I believe such a statement would do great good. With assurances etc I am my dear Mr President

Yours truly   W. J. Bryan

The Allies having signed such treaties could not object to applying their principle to Germany

ALS (WP, DLC).

To William Jennings Bryan, with Enclosure

My dear Mr. Secretary,   The White House. 12 May, 1915.

I am sending you herewith the final form of the note to Germany.

I want to express my deep appreciation of the work you and Mr. Lansing have done on it and the splendid spirit in which you have acquiesced in my decision in this grave matter, which gives me as deep concern as it does you.

I am thinking over the suggestion of your manuscript letter very deeply. If the statement is made, I think it should accompany the publication of the note Friday morning, so I will take the day to revolve the matter a little further in my mind.

Faithfully Yours,   W.W.

WWTLI (SDR, RG 59, 763.72/1775½, DNA).

E N C L O S U R E[1]

American Ambassador, Berlin.

Please call on the Imperial German Foreign Minister and after reading to him this communication leave with him a copy ⟨if he so desires⟩.

In view of ⟨the⟩ recent acts of the German authorities ⟨violative⟩ *in violation* of American rights on the high seas which culminated in the torpedoing and sinking of the British steamship LUSITANIA on May 7, 1915, by which over one hundred American citizens lost their lives, *it is clearly wise and desirable that* the Government of the United States and the Imperial German Goverment ⟨must⟩ *should* come to a clear and full understanding as to the grave situation which has resulted.

The sinking of the British passenger steamer FALABA by a German submarine on March 28th, through which Leon C.

[1] In the following document, Wilson edited Lansing's edited version of Wilson's first draft. Words in angle brackets were deleted by Wilson; words in italics were added or restored by him.

Thrasher, an American citizen was drowned; the attack on April 28th on the American vessel CUSHING, by a German aeroplane; the torpedoing on May 1st of the American vessel GULFLIGHT by a German submarine, ⟨by⟩ *as a result of* which two or more American citizens met their death; and, finally, the torpedoing and sinking of the *steamship* LUSITANIA, constitute a series of events, which the Government of the United States has observed with growing concern, distress and amazement.

Recalling the humane and enlightened attitude *hitherto* assumed ⟨hitherto⟩ by the Imperial German Government in matters of international right and particularly with regard to the freedom of the seas; having learned to recognize the German views and the German influence in the field of international obligation as always engaged upon the side of justice and humanity; and having understood the instructions of the Imperial German Government to its naval commanders to be upon the same plane of humane action prescribed by the naval codes of other nations, the Government of the United States was loath to believe, it cannot now bring itself to believe, that these acts, so absolutely contrary to the rules, the practices, and the spirit of modern warfare, could have the countenance or sanction of that great Government. *It feels it to be its duty, therefore, to address the Imperial German Government concerning them with the utmost frankness and in the earnest hope that it is not mistaken in expecting action on the part of the Imperial German Government which will correct the unfortunate impressions which have been created and vindicate once more the position of that Government with regard to the sacred freedom of the seas.*

The Government of the United States has been apprised that the Imperial German Government considered themselves to be obliged by the extraordinary circumstances of the present war and the measures adopted by their adversaries in seeking to cut Germany *off* from all commerce, to adopt methods of retaliation which go much beyond the ordinary methods of warfare at sea, in the proclamation of a war zone *from* which they have warned neutral ships to ⟨avoid⟩ *keep away.* But the waters of that zone touch the coasts of many neutral nations, and this Government has already ⟨informed⟩ *taken occasion to inform* the Imperial German Government that it cannot admit the adoption of such measures or such a warning of danger to operate as in any degree an abbreviation of the rights of American ship masters or of American citizens bound on lawful errands as passengers on merchant ships of belligerent nationality; and that it must hold the Imperial German Government to a strict accountability for any infringement of those rights, ⟨direct⟩ *intentional or incidental. It does not understand the Imperial German Government to question those rights.* It assumes, on the contrary, that the Imperial Government accept, *as of course*, the rule that the lives of noncombatants, whether they be of neutral citizenship or citizens of one of the nations at war, cannot lawfully or rightfully be put in jeopardy by the capture or destruction of an ⟨unresisting⟩ *unarmed* merchantman, and recognize also, as all other nations do, the obligation to take the usual precaution of visit and search to ascertain whether a suspected merchantman is in fact of belligerent nationality or is in fact carrying contraband of war under a neutral flag.

The Government of the United States, therefore, ⟨calls⟩ *desires to call* the attention of the Imperial German Government with the utmost earnestness to the fact that the objection to their present method of attack against the trade of their enemies lies in the practical impossibility of employing submarines in the destruction of commerce without disregarding those rules of fairness, reason, justice, and humanity, which ⟨the civilized world⟩ *all modern opinion* regards as imperative. It is practically impossible for the officers of a submarine to visit a merchantman at sea and examine her papers and cargo. It is practically impossible for them to make a prize of her; *and, if they cannot put a prize crew on board of her*, they cannot sink her without leaving her crew and all on board of her to the mercy of the sea in her small boats. These facts it is understood the Imperial German Government frankly admit. ⟨In⟩ *We are informed that in the instances of which we have spoken time enough for even that poor measure of safety was not given, and in at least two of the cases cited not so much as a warning was received.* Manifestly submarines cannot be used against merchantmen, as the last few weeks have shown, without an inevitable violation of many sacred principles of justice and humanity.

American citizens act within their indisputable rights in taking their ships and in traveling wherever their legitimate business calls them upon the high seas, and exercise those rights in what should be the well justified confidence that their lives will not be endangered by acts done in clear violation of universally acknowledged international obligations, and certainly in the confidence that their own Government will sustain them in the exercise of their rights.

There was recently published in the newspapers of the United States, I regret to inform the Imperial German Government, a formal warning, purporting to come from the Imperial German

Embassy at Washington, addressed to the people of the United States, and stating, in effect, that any citizen of the United States who exercised his right of free travel upon the seas would do so at his peril if his journey should take him within the zone of waters within which the Imperial German Navy was using submarines against the commerce of Great Britain and France, notwithstanding the respectful but very earnest protest of his government, the Government of the United States. I do not refer to this for the purpose of calling the attention of the Imperial German Government at this time to the surprising irregularity of a communication from the Imperial German Embassy at Washington addressed to the people of the United States through the newspapers, but only for the purpose of pointing out that no warning that an unlawful and inhumane act will be committed can possibly be accepted as an excuse or palliation for that act or as an abatement of the responsibility for ⟨the⟩ *its* commission.

Long acquainted as this Government has been with the character of the Imperial German Government and with the high principles of equity by which they have in the past been actuated and guided, the Government of the United States cannot believe that the commanders of the vessels which committed these acts of lawlessness did so except under a misapprehension of the orders issued by the Imperial German naval authorities. *It takes it for granted that, at least within the practical possibilities of every such case, the commanders even of submarines were expected to do nothing that would involve the lives of non-combatants or the safety of neutral ships, even at the cost of failing of their object of capture or destruction.* It confidently expects, therefore, that the Imperial German Government will disavow the acts of which the Government of the United States complains, that they will make reparation so far as reparation is possible for injuries which are without measure, and that they will take immediate steps to prevent the recurrence of anything so obviously subversive of the principles of warfare for which the Imperial German Government have in the past *so wisely and* so firmly contended.

The Government of the United States looks to the Imperial German Government for just, prompt, and enlightened action in this vital matter with the greater confidence because the United States and Germany are bound together not only by special ties of friendship but also by the ⟨special⟩ *explicit* stipulations of the Treaty of 1828 between the United States and the Kingdom of Prussia.

Expressions of regret and offers of reparation in case of the destruction of neutral ships, *sunk by mistake*, while they may satisfy international obligations, if no loss of life results, can not justify or excuse a practice, the natural and necessary effect of which is to subject neutral nations and neutral persons to new and immeasurable risks.

The Imperial German Government ⟨must realize that⟩ *will not expect* ⟨this⟩ *the* Government ⟨will not⟩ *of the United States to* omit any word or any act necessary to the performance of its sacred duty of maintaining the rights of the United States and its citizens and of safeguarding their free exercise and enjoyment.

T MS (SDR, RG 59, 763.72/1764a, DNA).

From Edith Bolling Galt

[Washington] May 12, 1915 7 30 P.M.

"I could not love thee dear so much

Loved I not honor more."

This must be my excuse for the shock and disappointment I gave you this afternoon. I wonder now how I had the courage to tare down my own image, that you had made in your thoughts of me, and shatter it in the dust at your feet but it is done, and I feel like poor Humpty Dumpty. "All the King's horses and all the king's men, can never put *me* together again![")

The only real harm though is for you, and the shock of re-adjusting your thoughts

Tell me frankly if you would rather I did not go on the trip.[1] Whatever is best for you will be my happiness, and I will always trust and understand you. Don't say I am morbid, and love darkness better than light.

Now I want to ask you a real favor in fact two favors. The first one is do'nt ask anybody how I know this, and say nothing about its coming from me until I can tell you more about it when I see you; and do'nt think for a minute that our loyal little Helen told me, for she *did not*, and I only learned it by the mearest accident yesterday. It is this that Helen wants very much to ask two or three people[2] aboard in New York for the Review,[2] and will not ask you to let her for fear you would rather not have them, and would do it just because you wanted to please her.

If you don't *really* mind, will you tell her tonight she can ask them? I know you will, and it makes me so happy to have *you* make *her* happy.

Trust me in this, and don't let her know I asked. I will tell you the whole story when we are together again. Oh! it has been such a tense but such a perfect afternoon. Your note this morning[3] would dispel any shadow, and I have read it until I know every word in my heart, and know that I l– y–!   Edith

ALS (WP, DLC).
  [1] Wilson was going to New York aboard *Mayflower* on May 14 for a luncheon on May 17 and a review of the Atlantic Fleet on May 18.
  [2] The party aboard *Mayflower* included Wilson, Miss Bones, Mrs. Galt, Mrs. Howe, Mrs. Cothran, Josephine Cothran, and Alice Gertrude Gordon, an intimate friend of both Miss Bones and Mrs. Galt. Dr. Grayson was courting Miss Gordon very warmly at this time.
  [3] That is, WW to EBG, May 11, 1915, 9 P.M.

To Edith Bolling Galt

The White House, Wed. evening, 12 May [1915].

I have just put the final touches on our note to Germany, and now turn—with what joy!—to talk to you. I am sure you have been by my side all evening, for a strange sense of peace and love has been on me as I worked—maybe brought by that note you wrote last night (you are a bad girl to sit up so late!) with its story of the day!

I cannot put into words the happiness with which that dear note filled me! To have brought you out of darkness into the light, my sweetheart, seems to me the crowning privilege of my life; and to have your day filled with me,—how that makes my heart sing and all work grow easy! And your lawyer—hurrah for him! I am glad a man of such insights and sound sense and vision should bear the name of Wilson. That was truly one of the most interesting and thrilling incidents I ever heard of. How true every word he said,—how full of wisdom and of comprehending affection for you,—except the advice "Work—read, study, think!" Heaven forbid you should *prepare* for me as for a business! You think I do not know you; but you know that *he* does and that he conceived the sweet thing possible that has happened "because he knows and trusts you." I must tell him some day of my admiration and gratitude. And, my lovely sweetheart, the light is *not* "in the far distance": you are already standing in it! I have seen it shine in your radiant face, shine all about you, when you moved out of the shadow; and, God helping me, it shall shine about you always henceforth,—and my burdens will be made light by standing in it with you.

You are so funny, as well as so delightful! I could laugh out loud as I read these passages in your happy note (it *is* a happy note—it is that that makes my heart sing as I read it) in which you express your amazement (you blind dear!) that my heart should be preoccupied with you. Do you really know so little about me? Are you really so unconscious of your supremacy over my heart? Well, it may be just as well that you should *not* know your power, and the things that your eyes and your speech and every gesture and attitude of your sweet person can do to me!

"The things you call your heart"! Edith, my sweetheart, *do* not say such things: make it impossible to say them by not *thinking* them. They hurt me. They are morbid. You have tried to crush your heart, you have left it without air to breathe, but it has broken from you and triumphed in spite of you. You must acknowledge the victory. Neither your happiness nor mine will be full until you do. I ask Helen every day how you look (alas! that I should have to *ask* instead of going to see for myself) and she says now that you *look* happy. How glad, how proud, how deeply thankful that makes me! I would give my life to make you happy. I want you to be as happy as you are adorable,—and I know that the happier you are the more adorable you will become!   W.W (read here only the name Woodrow)[1]

ALI (WP, DLC).
[1] There is a WWsh draft of this letter in WP, DLC.

From William Jennings Bryan

My dear Mr. President: Washington May 13, 1915.

In going over the draft of the note which you sent over this morning Mr. Lansing discovered that you had left in the sentence saying that this German war zone touched the coasts of many neutral countries. He calls attention to the fact that the war zone does not touch the coast of any neutral nation. The Netherlands is the only neutral nation affected and thirty miles is left along the coast.

We take it for granted that you would desire to have that sentence left out, but I bring it to your attention so that it can be inserted if you think it best.

In talking over the phone with Mr. Tumulty I said I was very much pleased with the statement you are going to have made—meaning the newspaper statement which you have prepared—and I found that he did not know about it. I told him he would find it out from you and did not attempt to give him the contents of it. I was sorry afterwards that I had said anything about it. While I presume he would not mention the matter you might, if you think it necessary, caution him.

With assurances of high respect I am, my dear Mr. President,
Yours very sincerely,   W. J. Bryan

TLS (W. J. Bryan Papers, DNA).

To William Jennings Bryan

My dear Mr. Secretary,   The White House. 13 May, 1915.
Of course whatever is not a fact must be left out. It was my mistake.
In haste,   Faithfully Yours,   W.W.

WWTLI (W. J. Bryan Papers, DNA).

To William Jennings Bryan, with Enclosure

My dear Mr. Secretary,   The White House. 13 May, 1915.
After sleeping over your suggestion, I have this to propose:
It would not be wise, I think, to give out a direct statement; but I think the same purpose would be served by such a "tip" as the enclosed, accompanying the publication of the note. And it would be best that this tip should be given out from the Executive Office, while the note was given out by the Department of State. What do you think?
If you will return the paper in the course of the morning, I will make the necessary arrangements.
Faithfully Yours,   W.W.

WWTLI (CLO).

ENCLOSURE

There is a good deal of confidence in Administration circles that Germany will respond to this note in a spirit of accommodation. It is pointed out that, while Germany is not one of the many nations which have recently signed treaties of deliberatiion and inquiry with the United States upon all points of serious difficulty, as a means of supplementing ordinary diplomatic methods and preventing, so far as feasible, the possibility of conflict, she has assented to the principle of such a treaty; and it is believed that she will act in this instance in the spirit of that assent. A frank issue is now made, and it is expected that it will be met in good temper and with a desire to reach an agreement, despite the passions of the hour,—passions in which the United

States does not share,—or else submit the whole matter to such processes of discussion as will result in a permanent settlement.[1]

WWT MS (WP, DLC).
[1] There is a WWsh draft of this statement in WP, DLC.

From William Jennings Bryan, with Enclosure

My dear Mr. President: Washington May 13, 1915.

Enclosed you will find a copy of the telegram which I have prepared in accordance with your instructions. I will call you over the phone when you have had time to read this and see if there are any changes which you would suggest in the introductory words, explaining the telegrams.

I find it will only take two or three hours to put the note to Germany in cipher. That will enable us to send it by one or two o'clock, and if you give it to the papers for release tomorrow morning Germany ought to have ample time to receive it before it reaches her through the press or reaches any of the other countries.

With assurances of high respect I am, my dear Mr. President,
Yours very sincerely,   W. J. Bryan

Mr Lansing approves of the statement which the newspapers are to use.

TLS (W. J. Bryan Papers, DNA).

E N C L O S U R E

Amembassy Rome   May 13, 1915.

(Forward Berlin)

I am sending you a statement which will be issued from the White House at the time the note to Germany is made public, which will probably be in time for tomorrow (Friday) morning papers. This will not be published as a statement given out by the President, but will appear as a newspaper report describing the situation. It is sent to you in advance so that you can deliver it at the time you deliver the note, which will be sent you as soon as it can be transmitted. Quote There is a good deal of confidence in Administration circles that Germany will respond to this note in a spirit of accomodation. It is pointed out that, while Germany is not one of the many nations which have recently signed treaties of deliberation and inquiry with the United States upon all points of serious difficulty, as a means of supplementing ordinary diplomatic methods and preventing, so far as feasible, the possibility of conflict, she has assented to the principle of such a treaty; and it is believed that she will act in this instance in the spirit of that assent. A frank issue is now made, and it is expected that it will be met in good temper and with a desire to reach an agreement, despite the passions of the hour,—passions in which the United States does not share,—or else submit the whole matter to such processes of discussions as will result in a permanent settlement. unquote.

T MS (W. J. Bryan Papers, DNA).

To William Jennings Bryan

My dear Mr. Secretary,   The White House. 13 May, 1915.
     Thank you. This is altogether right.
                         Faithfully Yours,   W.W.

     May I have back the original of the statement?

WWTLI (W. J. Bryan Papers, DNA).

From William Jennings Bryan

My dear Mr. President: Washington May 13, 1915.
     I beg pardon for not sending the original of the notice which is being copied to Berlin. I enclose it herewith.
     With assurances of high respect I am, my dear Mr. President,
                    Yours very sincerely,   W. J. Bryan

P.S. Do you think it worth while to repeat this telegram to Page at London and Sharp at Paris so that it can be published there at the same time the note is published.

TLS (WP, DLC).

To William Jennings Bryan

My dear Mr. Secretary,   The White House. 13 May, 1915.
     Since I expressed my approval of the statement you suggested for the press I have heard something, indirectly, from the German Embassy which convinces me that we would lose all chance of bringing Germany to reason if we in any way or degree indicated to them, or to our own public, that this note was merely

the first word in a prolonged debate. I will tell you what I have in mind when I do not have to write it.

In the meantime, I beg that you will pardon me for changing my mind thus. I am sure that it is the safer course, the one more likely to produce the results we are all praying for. Please withdraw the message (the supplementary statement) altogether. If we say anything of the kind it must be a little later, after the note has had its first effect.[1]   Faithfully Yours,   W.W.

WWTLI (CLO).
[1] About this episode of the so-called *Lusitania* postscript and Wilson's reasons for canceling it, see Link, *Struggle for Neutrality*, pp. 385-89. For Wilson's substitute, see WW to WJB, May 14, 1915, n. 1.

To William Howard Taft

My dear Mr. Taft: [The White House] May 13, 1915

I have read your letter of May tenth with the deepest appreciation. I think the whole country admires, as I do, the generous spirit in which you have sunk all considerations of party and have come to my support at this critical juncture in our history.[1]

You may be sure that the suggestions you make have great weight with me and that they will constitute part of my most serious thought in this time of perplexity. All the light I can get is welcome, as I am sure it would be to you in similar circumstances, and I am hoping and praying that we may work out a successful solution.

Cordially and sincerely yours,   Woodrow Wilson

TLS (Letterpress Books, WP, DLC).
[1] Taft had made a brief statement to the press in Milwaukee on May 8 regarding the *Lusitania* crisis. The event was "most distressing" and created a diplomatic situation "of the most difficult character." "I do not wish," he concluded, "to embarrass the President or the Administration by a discussion of the subject at this stage of the information, except to express confidence that the President will follow a wise and patriotic course." *New York Times*, May 9, 1915.
  In a speech to the Union League of Philadelphia on May 11, Taft urged the American people not to be hurried into the sacrifices of war until it was clear that they wished it and knew what they were doing when they wished it. He closed with an expression of faith in President Wilson:
  "He will not surrender our country's rights. . . . The national honor and interests may ultimately demand it [war], but time for serious thought and clearly weighing the consequences will not prejudice the justice of our cause or the opportunity to vindicate it, and this the President may be counted on to secure. . . . It is the people's cause, not his alone, and he does well, when quick action is of no critical importance, to allay excitement, and to await the regular and studied action of the people's representatives.
  "Let us stand by him in this juncture. Our honor is safe with him." W. H. Taft, "Address before the Union League of Philadelphia," May 11, 1915, T MS (W. H. Taft Papers, DLC).

From William Jennings Bryan

My dear Mr. President: Washington May 13, 1915.

I have received from the White House, without comment, the following telegram:

"Chicago, Ills. May 11, 1915. THE PRESIDENT: Our citizens are aboard the British Steamship Transylvania. Our Government gave the ship clearance from our waters. It is claimed that the vessel carries war munitions and that the captain has said he will ram any undersea boat thereby threatening the German craft and preventing any notice being given to the vessel. We would suggest that our Government at once call upon the British Ambassador to cable by wireless to the Transylvania and request that our citizens be disembarked at the Portugese Azo[r]es. (Signed) James T. Clark, President, United Irish Societies; Patrick H. O'Donnell, President, Irish Fellowship Club; Horace L. Brand, Chairman, German-Irish Central Legislative Committee; Ferdinand Walter, President, German-American National Alliance; (Chicago Branch); G. F. Hummel, Member of German-American National Alliance."

Do you think it would be wise to take any action pending the negotiations with Germany? It will probably be some days before an answer is received to the note which we are sending today. Do you think it would be advisable to give out a statement saying that while these negotiations are in progress American citizens are advised not to take passage upon belligerent ships entering the danger zone?

This ship, as I remember it, sailed the day after the Lusitania disaster but before it was known that any passengers were lost. It would very much increase the tension if another disaster occurred before we reached an understanding with Germany.

With assurances of high respect I am, my dear Mr. President,
                    Yours very sincerely,   W. J. Bryan

TLS (W. J. Bryan Papers, DLC).

To William Jennings Bryan

My dear Mr. Secretary,   The White House. 13 May, 1915.

My own judgment is that it would be very unwise to act upon the suggestion of this message (which I had not seen). It would create the impression that we expected further trouble. With things standing at such an uncertain balance it seems to me that nothing at all should be done that throws a doubt upon our perfect self-possession. And, besides, I do not believe that it is feasible for the British Ambassador to do anything of the kind.

Faithfully Yours,   W.W.

WWTLI (W. J. Bryan Papers, DLC).

Two Letters from William Jennings Bryan

My dear Mr. President: Washington May 13, 1915.

I have received from the White House another telegram[1] which you may not have read. I presume your action in regard to the message from Chicago would indicate a negative action on this also, but I venture to lay it before you. As my own views have been made known on former occasion it is not necessary to repeat them.

With assurances of high respect I am, my dear Mr. President,
Yours very sincerely,   W. J. Bryan

I am very sorry that your judgment is against using the statement you prepared this morning. I fear the use the jingo element will make of the German note

TLS (W. J. Bryan Papers, DNA).
[1] R. P. Hobson to WW, May 13, 1915, T telegram (W. J. Bryan Papers, DNA), urging that the United States Government immediately request the British government to instruct the captain of the British steamship *Transylvania*, as well as those of all other British ships carrying American passengers, not to resist if challenged by enemy submarines. If the British government refused, then it should be requested to halt all vessels with American passengers beyond the war zone until these passengers could be removed. Also, notice should be given to American citizens to avoid traveling on British vessels in the future so long as their commanders were under instructions to ram enemy submarines.

My dear Mr. President: Washington May 13, 1915.

When I looked at the last sentence of the note to Germany I was struck with the fact that there is no concluding reiteration of our friendship as in the other messages that we have sent. I called Mr. Lansing's attention to it and he said he did not think there ought to be, but as it will probably be an hour yet before it is all in type   I venture to ask you whether, on reflection, you think it would be wise to conclude the statement with any formal expression referring to friendly relations. If so, will you please send over what you desire added?

With assurances of high respect I am, my dear Mr. President,
Yours very sincerely,   W. J. Bryan

TLS (W. J. Bryan Papers, DNA).

To William Jennings Bryan

My dear Mr. Secretary,   The White House. 13 May, 1915.

I am sorry to say that in this matter my judgment is with Mr. Lansing. I think the body of the note contains a sufficient tone of sincere friendliness.

In haste,   Faithfully Yours,   W.W.

WWTLI (W. J. Bryan Papers, DNA).

From William Jennings Bryan

My dear Mr. President: Washington May 13, 1915.

I am sending you copy of the final report of Mr. West.[1] You have seen the partial report which he sent from Aguascalientes[2] and from Vera Cruz.[3] He is here and asks whether you wish to see him. I have told him you were very busy just now but thought you would like to see him within a few days. Can you fix a time when you can give him an hour?

I have not kept a copy of the report which I am sending you but if you will return it when you are through I will keep it with the others.

With assurances of high respect I am, my dear Mr. President,
                    Yours very truly,   W. J. Bryan

TLS (SDR, RG 59, 812.00/19181, DNA).
    [1] Duval West, "Report to the President. . . . ," May 11, 1915, TS MS (SDR, RG 59, 812.00/19181, DNA). This document briefly described the Conventionist government of Roque González Garza, characterized Emiliano Zapata, and described in some detail the shortages of food in and the general devastation of Mexico. His conclusions were as follows:
                    "REMEDIES.
    "It is more important to remedy the conditions than to fix the responsibility for them. The people do not wish that character of intervention that will involve a physical invasion of their country, nor that character of intervention which will affect their future national integrity. They are confidently relying upon the help and aid of the United States to bring about a condition of peace and order, so expressed by all classes. The military leaders want the help to take the form of a recognition of this, that, or the other party. Property owners desire it to take any form that will permit the continuance of business occupations without undue taxation or interference. The peon class want to be permitted to have regular employment, and the right to own and cultivate a little land so that they may feed their families and provide their simple necessaries.
    "The remedies most frequently suggested by Mexicans are:
    "1 That the United States should lend its moral and financial support to some of the existing parties in the field.
    "2 To select its own person, party, or faction as being best representative of the desires of the Mexican people.
    "3 A third suggestion, coming from jurists, statesmen and conservatives, all Mexican citizens, is that the Constitution provides who shall succeed to the presidency in the event of vacancy; that the assassination of President Madero and Vice President Pino Suarez, occasioned such vacancy and since the Huerta Government had no legal existence, the Constitution should be

looked to to see what officer of the government still survives upon whom the succession of President has legally fallen. Assuming that this interpretation is correct, the position seems to be based upon sound reason and is worthy of consideration. It is in line with the policy of our Government in asserting that the action of Huerta in obtaining control of the government was usurpation and without validity. If the United States will lend its aid to the individual who is entitled to the presidency, by virtue of the letter of the Constitution, its position would be logical and ultimately receive the support of the great body of the Mexican people.

"From a knowledge of Mexican character, acquired through an experience of forty years, and after a study of the conditions in Mexico upon the ground and from reliable information received during the last few years, it is my conviction that a condition of permanent peace and order and the establishment of a stable government, administering justice upon recognized civilized lines cannot be brought about by any of the contending parties in Mexico without the aid or assistance of the United States.

"The great mass of our people and the great mass of the Mexican people do not desire physical intervention, and while it may be true that the difficulties in aiding one or another of the existing parties, or in selecting some new party or individual will be great and may perhaps fall in the end, yet in deference to the wishes of those most interested, it would seem the right and just thing to make an attempt to bring about the desired condition conforming to the suggestions mentioned."

2 See the enclosures printed with WW to WJB, March 16, 1915 (first letter of that date), Vol. 32.

3 See WJB to WW, April 23, 1915, n. 1.

From Robert Latham Owen

My dear Mr. President: Muskogee, Oklahoma, May 13, 1915.

I believe it my duty to say to you that I profoundly believe that the United States can be of much greater service to humanity by keeping at peace than by taking preliminary steps which may lead inevitably to war, and therefore I wish to endorse your attitude as explained in the public press.

Everybody agrees to the enormity of the Lusitania incident but every one may not see the extremity of the military necessity with which the German government is confronted, and while the military necessity does not excuse the conduct in destroying this vessel without notice and the neutrals on board, we should seek in every way possible to get satisfaction without going to the extremity of war or to the steps which must eventuate in war.

The entire country will look to you with confidence to solve this extremely difficult problem, and we believe that you will receive Divine guidance in its wise solution.

Yours faithfully,   Robt. L. Owen

TLS (WP, DLC).

A Letter and a Telegram from Edward Mandell House

Dear Governor: No. 4. London, May 13th, 1915.

I had a talk with Kitchener yesterday. There has been much speculation here as to whether it would be best for the United States to enter the war, or to remain a sympathetic neutral and Kitchener fell to talking of this phase of the situation.

He said, "God forbid that anyone should want America to come in, but if she does come in I cannot see how anybody but a fool could think that it would not be of benefit to the Allies."

He paid a high tribute to American valor and resourcefulness, and went so far as to say that together with the English, the western line could be held without a single French soldier. He thought it would shorten the war enormously, and thereby save an infinite number of lives on both sides. He asked me to tell you this as being his opinion, but he wanted it particularly understood that he expressed no desire for us to enter, for that was something that we must determine for ourselves, and even if he could influence our action he would not do so.

He could not understand what the Germans were thinking of by pushing us so far in the direction of war, and he could not believe that they desired to have us against them.

He gave me the number of men under arms, which coincided with the information I gave you the other day, and which was gotten from one of the Chiefs of Staff. He told me, however, of the distribution of his forces which no one here knows and which will interest you.

There are about 550,000 men now in France and about 650,-000 that are soon to go over. There are 120,000 in the Dardanelles. He said that the recruiting was entirely satisfactory and he was getting as many men as he needed.

He still thinks the war may be a long one. His original estimate was three years. Nearly one year has already gone by. He said if America should go in, that he would issue a statement, and stake his military reputation upon it, cutting down his original estimate to a large extent.

He spoke with much bitterness concerning the German mode of warfare, and said no one could have made him believe in advance that they would have struck below the belt in the way in which they have. He thought it was imperative that the Allies should use asphyxiating gases in order to hold their own. Shells of this description, I take it, are being manufactured in both France and England. The prevailing wind in France is from the west which will give the Allies the advantage in the use of these shells.

I have talked to a good many people since I last wrote concerning "the freedom of the seas" and it surprised me to find how easily they are convinced that it would not be a bad thing for England. I tried it out yesterday on two of Kitcheners Aides, where I thought I would certainly get negative results, but was surprised and gratified that they could see the force of my argument.

I had a conference with Balfour today and outlined it to him. He was noncommittal, but not antagonistic. If we can put this achievement to your credit, it will perhaps be the most far-reaching result of the peace conference.

Your affectionate,   E. M. House

TLS (WP, DLC).

[London, May 13, 1915]

The forecast of your note to Berlin seems to me in every way admirable. It should lessen the chances of war unless Germany is bent upon it. Yesterday I had a long conference with the Minister of War. He expressed no opinion as to whether we had reason to come in but he wished me to say [to you]¹ that if we did decide to do so that in his opinion it would cause the war to end much sooner and would thereby save countless lives. I hope Germany may give the United States necessary assurances so that some way out may yet be found.   Edward House

T transcript of WWsh decode (WP, DLC).
    ¹ Text in brackets in the telegrams between Wilson and House supplied from copies in the E. M. House Papers, Cty.

From Jessie Woodrow Wilson Sayre

Williamstown Massachusetts

Dearest, dearest Father,   [c. May 13, 1915]

How much I love you and how constantly I think of you these days! The feeling everywhere in this community is one of such quiet confidence in you and in God whom they know is with you. It seems to me this same feeling prevails everywhere. Some of the things the old people say are so beautiful and touching, and even the trades people, the old farmer who brings the butter & eggs, for instance, say such naive and quaint things all showing how earnestly and eagerly they are back of you. Dear, dear, father!

You will get this on the blessed fifteenth[1] and I hope you will think of us way off here whose little home owes so much of its potentialities for happiness to her and to her spirit abiding with us and to the knowledge of your love and thought of us. Oh how I long to be with you all, sometimes, precious Father. Such a little glimpse of you—and yet more than I deserve when the country and the world need you so![2]

Frank sends his dearest love to you and to all,

Your adoring and devoted daughter   Jessie.

ALS (WC, NjP).
[1] Ellen Axson Wilson's birthday.
[2] Wilson had spent the weekend of May 1-2 with the Sayres in Williamstown.

To William Jennings Bryan

My dear Mr. Secretary,   The White House. 14 May, 1915.

I was as sorry as you can have been to withdraw the "statement" which we had intended for the press. It cost me a struggle to do so. But the intimation was plain from the German Embassy (and I cannot doubt the source of my information) that we were not in earnest, would speak only in a Pickwickian sense if we seemed to speak with firmness, and I did not dare lend colour to that impression. You will notice that hope of a pacific settlement was expressed. That, in the circumstances, was as far as I dared to go.[1]   Faithfully Yours,   W.W.

TCL (SDR, RG 59, 763.72/1758¾, DNA).
[1] "You will notice that hope of a pacific settlement was expressed" has traditionally been interpreted as referring to the portion of the *Lusitania* note expressing Wilson's hope for a peaceful settlement. However, it seems highly probable that, in view of the context of the exchange between Wilson and Bryan about the so-called *Lusitania* postscript and other evidence, Wilson was, in fact, referring to an action that he had just taken, and that he was referring to this action when he wrote, "That, in the circumstances, was as far as I dared to go."

David Lawrence, Washington correspondent for the New York *Evening Post*, had, as his letter printed below reveals, an hour's talk with Bernstorff, undoubtedly during the morning of May 14. He probably took his letter to Wilson by hand. Wilson undoubtedly read it at once and then called Lawrence back to the White House. The fact that there was no reply to this letter lends credence to this supposition.

Lawrence immediately sent a special dispatch to the New York *Evening Post*, a reading of which makes it clear that what he said could only have come from Wilson himself. The report said there was a "hopeful tone in Washington to-day" as to Germany's attitude in replying to the *Lusitania* note. "At any rate," the report went on, "there is in official circles a determination to await the reply from Berlin calmly and coolly and to give time for legitimate delay and consideration. There is not going to be any blustering or moving about of the fleet or any other military measures during the interval, but there is no intention, on the other hand, on the part of the Administration, to tolerate an unreasonable delay, or an answer short of a reasonable compliance with all demands." This story appeared of course on the front page of the *Evening Post*, May 14, under the headline: "Hopeful Tone in Washington Regarding Berlin Government's Reply to Wilson's Note."

Another special dispatch appeared on the front page of the *New York Times* on May 15 under the dateline "Washington, May 14." It, too, undoubtedly was written by Lawrence (he described Wilson as "tired and showed it") and was an even fuller account of so-called official opinion in Washington. The most significant portions of this report follow:

"It was apparent throughout official circles today that a feeling of hopefulness prevailed, and this feeling pervaded the regular meeting of the Cabinet, which was devoted, in part, to a discussion of the critical situation that had been reached in the relations of the nation with Germany. While there are some officials who are pessimistic, it is not going beyond the fact to say that generally the idea that the differences with Germany will be adjusted without war is in the ascendant.

"While officials are extremely anxious to ascertain the German view of the note as soon as possible, they are inclined to the opinion that the longer the German Government delays its response, although it is hoped that due regard will be paid to the President's request for prompt action, the better will be the prospect that Germany's decision will be for peace. The American note was filed for cabling to Berlin as quickly as it could be in the circumstances, the desire being to have it reach the German Government as expeditiously as was feasible, so that it might serve to warn the German naval authorities of the manner in which this Government regarded submarine warfare and possibly have the effect of causing a suspension, at least, of the submarine attacks on merchant vessels."

One of the headlines of this report read: "Feeling in Washington Is Strongly Hopeful of Peace."

It is significant that these reports appeared only in the New York *Evening Post* and the *New York Times*. It is also suggestive to read these reports alongside the proposed statement.

If our above reconstruction of these events of May 14 is correct, then Wilson was obviously sending a signal to Berlin, as he had originally intended to do through the so-called postscript. This, then, is probably what he meant when he said that he had gone as far as he dared to go in the circumstances.

No telegrams from Bernstorff to the German Foreign Office concerning these news reports are extant. However, such a fact is of little significance. Bernstorff's communications with Berlin were at this time extremely difficult. Moreover, he well knew that German correspondents in New York would send summaries of the stories by wireless to their newspapers in Germany. After Wilson broke diplomatic relations with Germany in 1917, Bernstorff used one reporter to send diplomatic messages as news stories to his newspaper. Perhaps he did the same thing on May 14 and 15, 1915.

From William Jennings Bryan, with Enclosure

My dear Mr. President: [Washington] May 14, 1915.

I am sending you a letter from Mr. Lansing. You will notice that he cannot possibly prepare the note before Monday. At my request he prepared a notice such as we discussed, warning passengers against taking these ships pending negotiations. He is doubtful about the wisdom of issuing the notice, fearing that it may raise the question as to why we did not issue an earlier notice. While this question may be asked, I think it is better for us to have the question asked and answered, rather than run the risk of any more attacks. I believe that the issuance of such a notice would not only be likely to protect the lives of some Americans and thus lessen the chances of another calamity, but would have its effect upon the tone of the German reply and might point the way to an understanding. At least it would probably prevent anything like a summary dismissal of our protest. I beg to submit the idea for your consideration and the tentative notice for your criticism in case the idea commends itself to you.

With assurances of high respect I am, my dear Mr. President,
                    Yours very sincerely,   [W. J. Bryan]

CCL (W. J. Bryan Papers, DNA).

E N C L O S U R E

Robert Lansing to William Jennings Bryan

Dear Mr. Secretary: [Washington] May 14, 1915.

The memorandum of vessels detained in British ports prepared by Mr. Johnson, which you handed to me this afternoon, covers only "*cotton* ships." There are a number of other vessels detained which carry different cargoes.

I do not think that it would do to confine a representation to Great Britain to vessels only laden with cotton. It would cause undoubtedly much criticism from owners of other vessels and cargoes. The data is being collected as rapidly as possible, but I do not see how a representation could be prepared before Monday, which would be at all complete.

In regard to your suggestion that the President give public notice advising, asking or directing Americans not to take passage on belligerent steamships while the controversy as to submarine warfare is pending, that could of course be prepared at once.

In compliance with your request that I draft a notice such as is suggested I submit the following:

"The President in view of the present diplomatic situation requests that American citizens, intending to proceed abroad and to traverse waters adjacent to the coasts of Great Britain and France, will refrain from taking passage on vessels of belligerent nationality pending the exchange of views between this Government and the Government of Germany regarding the use of submarines in interrupting vessels of commerce in those waters."

I think that this is the sort of notice, which you had in mind. I doubt if more than a request could be made, as I believe there is no law, by which Americans could be restrained from going on belligerent vessels if they saw fit or by which such vessels could be prevented from receiving American passengers. Furthermore a request like this would be, in my opinion, almost, if not quite, as effective as an order, and presents no legal difficulties.

Do you not think that, if this notice is given, it will be said "Why did the Government not give this notice before? Why did it wait after the sinking of the FALABA, CUSHING and GULFLIGHT until a hundred Americans lost their lives on the LUSITANIA?["] Even admitting that the effect on the German Government might be beneficial in influencing their reply, I think that the criticism in this country must be considered. It is a matter of policy which must be viewed from every standpoint.

Faithfully yours,   Robert Lansing

TLS (SDR, RG 59, 341.1153/11, DNA).

Four Letters to William Jennings Bryan

My dear Mr. Secretary,   The White House. 14 May, 1915.

It is hard to turn away from any suggestion that might seem to promise saftety for our travellers, but what is suggested seems to me both weak and futile. To show this sort of weak yielding to threat and danger would only make matters worse.

Faithfully Yours,   W.W.

WWTLI (W. J. Bryan Papers, DNA).

My dear Mr. Secretary,   The White House. 14 May, 1915.

I return this report from Mr. West because I think it ought to be in the files at your hand.

I have read it with close attention. It contains nothing new, but it contains the old things in authoritative form, and I am very glad indeed to have seen it.

I gather that Mr. West on the whole favours the third of the remedies he suggests. Has your own thought taken shap[e] about it at all?   Faithfully Yours,   W.W.

WWTLI (SDR, RG 59, 812.00/19181, DNA).

My dear Mr. Secretary,   The White House. 14 May, 1915.

Here is some extremely interesting matter from our Ambassador at Rome.[1]

The part which will especially arrest your attention, I dare say, as it did mine, is the information given by the representative of the Morgans as to the plans (not to say designs) of the French bankers. And if these plans were indeed entertained and given countenance by the French Government, I think Mr. Page is right in forecasting that France will be more troublesome after the war (provided, of course, the Allies are in any measure victorious) than she could have been before.

Faithfully Yours,   W.W.

Will you not be kind enough to have these papers returned to me.

WWTLI (WP, DLC).
  1 T. N. Page to WW, April 19, 1915, TLS (WP, DLC), enclosing TS minutes of a conversation between Page and Francisco León de la Barra on Mexican affairs. The significant portion of the letter dealt with an interview between Page and James Edward Dunning, the European representative of the National City Bank of New York. Dunning stated that he had been told by a French banker in June 1914 that the French government, at the instigation of a group of French banks with heavy investments in Mexico, had approached the British, Spanish, and German foreign offices about a plan to send a joint fleet to Mexico to intervene and re-organize the Mexican government, regardless of American wishes in the matter. The British Foreign Office refused to participate, Dunning said, and the outbreak of the European war had put an end to the plan for the time being. However, Dunning warned, the French banking interests had not altered their view of the Mexican situation and proposed to have this or some similar scheme carried out following the conclusion of the European conflict. Page added to this report the suggestion that large military forces would then be available to carry out such a plan.

My dear Mr. Secretary,   The White House. 14 May, 1915.

I quite understand why a note about the detained ships cannot be made ready before the beginning of next week.

As to the request to Americans not to take passage on belligerent ships (for I agree with Mr. Lansing that it could be nothing more than a request), my feeling is this: the request is unnecessary, if the object is to save lives, because the danger is already fully known and those who do not refrain because of the danger will not, in all probability, refrain because we request them to do so; and this is not the time to make it, not only for the reason Mr. Lansing suggests, but also because, as I urged this morning, it weakens the effect of our saying to Germany that we mean to support our citizens in the exercise of their right to travel both on our ships and on belligerent. If I thought the notice necessary, or effective, to save lives, the second objection might be waived, but since I do not, I think the second objection ought to prevail.   Faithfully Yours,   W.W.

TCL (SDR, RG 59, 763.72/1758½, DNA).

To William Birch Haldeman[1]

My dear Mr. Haldeman: [The White House] May 14, 1915

I have your letter of May fifth[2] and must apologize for not having replied to it sooner. I am sure that you will understand the pressure of circumstances I have been under.

The reply to your letter is very simple. My so-called Shannon[3] letter precisely defines my position with regard to the liquor issue, not only as it was when I wrote the letter, but as it is now, and the letter to Mr. Grogan[4] is, or was, at any rate, intended to be entirely consistent with it. What I intended to say to Mr. Grogan and think that I said with sufficient clearness was that, while the position I had taken in the Shannon letter expressed my fixed conviction in the matter, I was not self-confident or self-opinionated enough to say what the proper course of action was either in Texas or in any other state where I was not personally in touch with the conditions obtaining. I felt that it would be arrogant on my part to state that there were in my opinion no circumstances which justified an agitation for state-wide prohibition.

I am sure that you yourself felt that there was no inconsistency between the two letters and I am sincerely obliged to you for having afforded me the opportunity to make this very explicit.[5]

Cordially and sincerely yours,   Woodrow Wilson

TLS (Letterpress Books, WP, DLC).
 [1] Editor of the *Louisville Times*.
 [2] W. B. Haldeman to WW, May 5, 1915, TLS (WP, DLC).
 [3] WW to T. B. Shannon, May 1, 1911, Vol. 22.
 [4] WW to E. W. Grogan, July 6, 1911, Vol. 23.
 [5] For an amusing account of the background of this letter, which was published, see Arthur S. Link, *Wilson: The New Freedom* (Princeton, N. J., 1956), pp. 259-60.

To William Henry Cardinal O'Connell

                                        [The White House]
My dear Cardinal O'Connell: May 14, 1915

I read your letter of May eleventh about my speech in Philadelphia with a very full and thankful heart. It was very gracious of you to write me as you did and I can assure you that it has done not a little to strengthen and hearten me in these troublous days.

Cordially and sincerely yours,   Woodrow Wilson

TLS (Letterpress Books, WP, DLC).

To Henry Albert Stimson

My dear Doctor Stimson: [The White House] May 14, 1915

It was very generous of you to write me your letter of May eleventh and I thank you for it most sincerely. I know of no element of strength that serves me better than the support of good and thoughtful men.

        Cordially and sincerely yours,   Woodrow Wilson

TLS (Letterpress Books, WP, DLC).

To Samuel Allen Harlow

My dear Harlow: [The White House] May 14, 1915

That was a very generous note of yours of May eleventh and I thank you for it most warmly. It is very sweet to be praised in these days of deep difficulty.

        Cordially and sincerely yours,   Woodrow Wilson

TLS (Letterpress Books, WP, DLC).

Two Letters From Edward Mandell House

Dear Governor: *No 4—continued*   London, May 14th, 1915.

I took lunch with Sir Edward Grey today. The principal topic of our conversation was the Lusitania disaster and the action you might take in the premises.

Grey told me he did not see how you could do differently from what you had done, and he intimated that if we had done less we would have placed ourselves in much the same position which England would have been placed if she had not defended Belgian neutrality. In other words, that we would have been totally without friends or influence in the concert of nations, either now or hereafter. I am sure that this is true.

If we had failed to take action in a determined way it would have meant that we would have lost the friendship of the Allies on the one hand, and would not have mitigated any of the hate which Germany feels for us. Sooner or later we would have had to reckon with Germany unless she is completely crushed, and we would not have had a sympathetic friend among the great nations.

Grey asked me what I thought Germany's reply would be. I told him that if I were writing Germany's reply I would say that if England would lift the embargo on foodstuffs, Germany would

consent to discontinue her submarine policy of sinking merchantmen. Grey replied that if Germany would consent not only
to discontinue that mode of warfare, but would also agree to discontinue the use of asphyxiating gases and the ruthless killing
of non-combatants, England he thought would be willing to lift
the embargo on foodstuffs.

I am rushing a cablegram to you outlining this.[1] It distresses
me that I cannot have you, Grey and Berlin within talking distance. If that could happen so much could be accomplished that
is impossible under present conditions.

I am writing this hastily in order to catch tonight's mail. It
may interest you to know that Italy has signed an agreement with
the Allies to come into the war before the 26th. This agreement
will be carried out unless the Italian Parliament refuses to sanction it. I have had this information for ten days or more, but have
not written it because there seemed so many slips between the
agreement and its completion.

The King told me the other day that he wanted to send you a
message of sympathy over the loss of American lives on the Lusitania. I cautioned him not to do it unless you were given the privilege of keeping it private. He referred the matter to Sir Edward
Grey and he advised him not to do so for fear that you might
misunderstand his good intentions, particularly in view of the
critical decision which you had to make. I told Grey that I would
write you and explain the circumstances, and that I knew you
would appreciate it just as much as if the message had been sent.

Grey has given me one of his books for you, which I shall either
send or deliver in person.

Your affectionate,   E. M. House

[1] EMH to WW, May 14, 1915, T trancript of WWsh decode (WP, DLC) of T
telegram (WP, DLC).

Continuation of No. 4.
Dear Governor: London, May 14th, 1915.

I forgot to say that the Secretary at the Embassy who has
charge of the embargo on our shipping, tells me that since your
cablegram a marked change for the better has come about and
that we now have no cause for complaint.

Grey told me that he was doing all that he could, and I am
sure he is. He said, curiously enough, that during one period
fourteen *neutral* boats were attacked by submarines and twelve
of them were sunk, and during the same time only 5 British ships

were sunk, and yet the British tonnage of the world totals twenty-
one million tons as against sixteen million tons of the neutrals.

Your affectionate,   E. M. House

TLS (WP, DLC).

From David Lawrence

Dear Mr. President: [Washington] Friday May 14, 1915
I have just had an hour's talk with the German Ambassador
and am writing here my recollection of what was said while it is
fresh in my mind. It was, of course, not for publication and confidential in every sense. I asked him what he thought of the note.
"Honestly," he said, "I went to dinner last night with a sigh of
relief. I had been afraid from the newspaper stories that there
would be an ultimatum or that the tone of the note would be such
that it would offend the Government and the people of Germany.
It was very friendly—in fact, much friendlier than the other note
(the "strict accountability) and gives room for 'a clear understanding' and discussion."
"Of course," I said, "you realize the temper and feeling of the
people is such that a disputatious answer would probably stir
up more feeling, especially if the idea was merely to make the
usual prolonged diplomatic discussion of it."
He said he did and he believed the answer would be prompt.
"It's hard for me to know just what will be done" he said, "even
though I may have messages every day as to their feeling but I
have the conviction that my government will seize the opportunity afforded by your note with respect to the 'freedom of the
seas' and say "That's just what we are fighting for. If England
abandons her starvation policy, we will abandon our submarine
warfare because if we can get food—if this is to be a long war—
we can't be beaten."
"Well," I said, "you realize, of course, that Germany said the
same thing once before and a mere restatement of her position
wouldn't sit well with the American people especially if Germany
stipulated a condition for most folks believe and, I think, the
Government, too, has made it plain that our quarrel with Germany is one thing and our quarrel with England is another. I
don't think the people of this country will be satisfied unless they
get one thing—an abandonment of submarine warfare on merchant ships."
"But" he said, "the Lusitania legally is a doubtful case. We

would be willing to arbitrate the question of a neutral's right on board a belligerent ship."

"Assuming," I said, "that it is a doubtful case legally—it isnt a bit doubtful from the point of view of humanity and that's America's whole argument."

"I don't think" he said, "the American people would go to war for Great Britain and her ships."

"It isn't that," I said, "it is the *principle* involved—the principle of humanity. We went to war with Spain for that and we probably would go to war with anybody else for the same thing."

"But," he said, "the President doesn't want war."

"I know that," I said, "but that wouldn't prevent him from approving of it whether he *wanted* it or not if there was a repetition of the Lusitania disaster especially with an American ship."

"I have no doubt of that—but it all depends on whether the people of the United States want war. The war if it comes will be of their making."

"That's exactly," I said, "what everybody says about Germany. If there's to be war, it will be of Germany's making in refusing to accept the point of view of the United States in this matter. Some people have felt for a long time that the series of incidents have been a part of a plan to draw the United States into war because it would reduce the ammunition supply to the Allies."

"Well," he said, "I am thoroughly convinced that there is no such idea but I know my Government and the people of Germany feel that they haven't been getting a square deal here."

"We have been powerless," I said, "to do anything with England on the foodstuffs question without going to war about it and when the question of property is involved, there isn't the same haste as there is when lives are in danger."

"But England says they are doing this thing merely as a reprisal. If we gave up submarine warfare, they ought to give up the other."

I suggested that this might eventually be the way things would work out especially if this government, assisted by a big public opinion all over the world, were compelled by virtue of a German acceptance to take up the subject with Great Britain, although I expressed my own opinion that the United States might do this of its own initiative if Germany accepted our demands and wouldn't do so if it was an expressed condition. The safety of human lives, I said, must first be assured.

"Oh," he said, "of course we wouldn't use our submarines in that way while the diplomatic discussion was going on."

"An assurance like that," I said, "might make it possible for the United States to do something for if your answer was a guarantee of that kind, it would afford an opportunity for a resolution of the case quietly and with deliberation."

He said he was keeping his government informed by wireless of what was going on and that the wireless was working very well. I thought from his conversation that he realized clearly the deep feeling of the people and the fact that they would 'omit no word or act' to have their way in this thing.

"It would be a terrible tragedy," I told him, "if war with Germany resulted. The unhappiest of all would be thousands of innocent German-Americans. If they fight, they cannot entirely remove their personal feeling. If they don't fight, their countrymen will call them cowards. Their allegiance will be always doubted."

"I know that," he said—"and so does my government. But let me repeat—if there is to be war, it will be of your making, and not Germany's."

"Then there'll probably be no war," I said, and the interview ended.   Sincerely yours,   David Lawrence

P.S.—I spoke as I did because of the hope that he might be influenced to understand the situation clearly and not be confused by any previous events. I thought, too, that if he is making reports to his government daily, he might be an important factor in influencing its decision.

TLS (WP, DLC).

From Oswald Garrison Villard

My dear Mr. President,   [Washington] Friday, May 14, 1915

I tried to express to you the other morning[1] my deep sense of obligation for the uplifting character and the nobility of spirit of your Philadelphia address and now I find myself again thrilled by your note to Germany. In felicity of utterance, in charity of statement, as well as for its style, it must ever be a landmark in our foreign relations, and stand out above all else among our documents of State. If he who conquers his spirit is greater than he who taketh a city your achiev[e]ment of self-restraint in this message must surely put you far ahead of any of the generals of our history. But the force and power of the note gain all the more by this suppression of the emotions and the generosity of it all.

You are truly doing a service not merely to America but to all the world by setting such standards and uplifting us all with you.

That success may attend your efforts to show to all the nations that great wrongs may be redressed without the barbarism of human slaughter is the most heartfelt wish of

Yours sincerely,   Oswald Garrison Villard.

ALS (WP, DLC).
¹ Villard was present at the press conference on May 11. See "War Not Contemplated in President's Policy," a "Special Dispatch" datelined Washington, May 11, and signed "O.G.V.," in the New York *Evening Post*, May 11, 1915.

From John Pierpont Morgan, Jr.

My dear Mr. President: New York. May 14, 1915.

I am well aware that you are receiving far more letters and telegrams than you can read, but I cannot refrain from adding my word to the many in the expression of my intense satisfaction of both the substance and the manner of the note to the German Government, published this morning. I want also to assure you of my profound sympathy with you personally in the difficulty of the great questions which you have before you, and of my sincere hope that the German Government may be enabled by the clear statements in your note to perceive the position in which such acts as you have condemned place it, and may be inclined by the perfect courtesy of your communication to come to a wise decision in its answer.

I am, my dear Mr. President,

Yours very sincerely,   J. P. Morgan.

TLS (WP, DLC).

From Charles William Eliot

Dear Mr. President: Cambridge, Mass. 14 May, 1915

Your message to Germany is adequate and altogether admirable. Come peace, come war, you will have the American people at your back.

Sincerely yours,   Charles W. Eliot

TLS (WP, DLC).

From Joseph Rucker Lamar

Dear Mr. President   Washington, D. C. May 14 [1915]

I can recall no instance in our history presenting so many elements of difficulty as that with which you have had to deal in connection with the recent acts of Germany on the high seas. But your message to the Imperial German Government has given perfect expression to the deep feeling of the American people.

In dignity and firmness, in letter and spirit it reaches the height of this great occasion.

Sincerely yours   J. R. Lamar

ALS (WP, DLC).

To Edith Bolling Galt

[The White House]
6.30 A.M. Friday 14 May [1915].

Of course I want you to go on the trip. There is nothing I want more than to give you pleasure and happiness,—*lead* you to it, if I may,—lest in your blindness you miss it, and all the true meaning of life as well.

You love me (your own dear lips have said it,) and if that is true everything else is possible,—indeed it is impossible that you should *not* come to see and desire what all the truest, sweetest women in the world have seen and desired. On days like yesterday, when you see *every*thing wrong, your light is indeed a long way off, but there *are* times (particularly when you are alone) when it is nearer. I pray God you may day by day move towards it, with however faltering steps, and at last save yourself and me!

Woodrow

ALS (WP, DLC).

From Edith Bolling Galt

[Washington] May 14, 1915

Your note tells me so much, and yet so little!

I felt when I saw you in the Park I must come and nestle in your dear arms and cry out all the pain that is in my heart. I know it was wrong to let Helen follow you, but she suggested it, and I was so weak with longing for you that I could not say no.

I loved your going on in spite of us, and knowing your strength was greater than my own.

Please forgive my asking you things that were plainly not for me to interfere with.

Your silence is a rebuke and, I feel a just one.

Try to trust me.

The golden bud is a perfect flower this morning, and, last

night, when I could not sleep, I watched it unfold, while I read over again every line you have ever written to me, beginning with the little note about the book, and ending with the finest a man has to offer a woman. God bless and keep you—Edith

ALS (WP, DLC).

To Edith Bolling Galt

[The White House]
Friday, 6.30 P.M. [May 14, 1915]

Oh, my darling, my darling, thank you from the bottom of my heart for your little note! How the sweet, sweet woman comes out in you upon the slightest test! And I had already granted and acted on your request—so much as a matter of course that I *forgot* to speak of it this morning—thinking only of you and your deep, deep need. Helen's friends are going to join us. And some day, when God is good to us you will cry out or *laugh* out close in my arms everything that is in that wonderful inscrutable heart of yours. God grant it may be soon! Meantime, I love you, I love you, I love you! Smuggle me a line saying you love *me*.
Woodrow

ALS (WP, DLC).

From Edith Bolling Galt

[*U.S.S. Mayflower*] May 14 [15], 1915

It is now after midnight and I hope you are already asleep, for you looked so weary.

But you asked me to write, and your note made me so happy that I am just sending you my warmest thanks for granting my first request, and a tender good night   Edith
Oh! I almost forgot what I was to smuggle you a note for—
Of course I do!!
It is such fun to know we will be together in the morning.

ALS (WP, DLC).

To Edith Bolling Galt

[*U.S.S. Mayflower*] Sat. 6.40 [May 15, 1915]

Dearest, what a delight, what a solace, what a tonic to everything that is best and a source of happiness in me, it has been

to be near you all day! It has made me feel that the boat was
home and full of the sweet influences that *guide* a man and make
him sure of his anchorage and of the meaning of life for him.
And the more I see of you, the more the feeling grows, the feeling
of identification, and of being somehow made complete by your
presence! Has it been fun for you, too, dear? Do you feel that
I am your natural comrade and understand at every turn, catch
your thought by a mere exchange of glances, and respond without word or hint to what is in your heart? And do I succeed in
conveying to you what is between the lines in *my* remarks? But
I know that I do: I see the instant answering flash. And the more
I see of you the more I wonder. You have a vivid personality, carry
an atmosphere of your own as perceptibly as any person I ever
knew—so that your individuality can be felt as one is aware of
a sweet pervasive perfume—and yet, with all the suggestion that
naturally goes with such subtle, intangible things there is no intimation of your perplexity

AL (WP, DLC).

To Edward Mandell House

[The White House, May 16, 1915]
Deeply interested in your intimation that Sir Edward Grey
would be favorable to a raising of the embargo on foodstuffs to
Germany because that may afford a solution of a situation as
trying and difficult for England as it is for us.
Almost the same thing would be accomplished by action on
the part of the British government which would assure our practically unmolested access to neutral ports with noncontraband
cargoes, food being regarded as noncontraband.
It would be well to ascertain so soon as possible how far Sir
Edward Grey would be supported by his colleagues in the suggested action, for things are likely to move rapidly now.
                                                        Wilson.

T transcript of WWsh telegram (WC, NjP).

From William Jennings Bryan, with Enclosures

My Dear Mr President,   [Washington] May 16 1915
As my son-in-law[1] is coming to N. Y. I am sending a note
drafted by Mr Lansing along the line suggested by you. Aside
from its being deserved I think it will serve as a counter irritant.

Personally I would rather deal with the matter of carr[y]ing passengers on belligerent ships but knowing your views on that I turn to this as the only immediate remedy. You may be interested in a memorandum prepared by Mr Johnson[2] (I had not consulted with him on the subject) on the carrying of passengers and contraband together.

Bishop Cranston has issued to the Methodist churches the enclosed appeal[3]–I am sure you will have all the churches behind you in the effort to prevent war.

With assurances of respect I am my dear Mr President

Very truly yours   W. J. Bryan

ALS (WP, DLC).

[1] Richard Lewis Hargreaves, husband of Bryan's younger daughter, Grace Dexter Bryan Hargreaves.

[2] Cone Johnson, "A Suggestion," TS memorandum, May 15, 1915 (R. Lansing Papers, DLC), recommending that ships sailing from American ports with passengers aboard be prohibited from carrying munitions. Johnson further suggested that the President could establish such a policy himself by causing clearance to be refused to such ships. In addition, Johnson went on, the President might follow this with a vigorous note to Great Britain, warning her that the American government intended to pursue such a course and would take whatever action might be necessary and appropriate for the protection of American commerce on the high seas.

[3] E. Cranston, "An Urgent Call to Earnest Prayer. To the Ministers and People of the Methodist Episcopal Church," printed proclamation (WP, DLC) dated May 12, 1915, urging constant prayer for peace. Bryan had marked a passage in which Cranston said that America, as a haven of peace in a war-torn world, had a special obligation to beseech God for peace. Such prayers would also serve to restrain "the latent spirit of war" among Americans themselves.

E N C L O S U R E   I

Robert Lansing to William Jennings Bryan

Dear Mr. Secretary: [Washington] May 15, 1915.

I thought over our conversation of yesterday in regard to a note of complaint to Great Britain for violation of American rights on the high seas, and I came to the conclusion that the subject might be treated in a general rather than a specific way, which would avoid the necessity of waiting for complete data.

In accordance with that conclusion I have drafted an instruction to Ambassador Page, which is enclosed. It is an uncompromising presentation and "shows its teeth." Probably you will think it too strong, or rather too strongly expressed. In view, however, of the note to Germany a note to Great Britain ought not to be in more friendly or conciliatory language, if it is to give an expression of impartiality to the German Government which will effect in any way their reply.

I am in favor of sending some note similar to the one enclosed as the British treatment of our vessels and cargoes to neutral countries is in flagrant violation of law and contrary to Sir Edward Grey's assurances.

The opportune time to send a communication of this sort seems to me to be the present, as it will evince our impartial purpose to protect American rights on the high seas, whoever is the aggressor. We have just complaints against both. We have already been too complacent with Great Britain in the enforcement of the Order in Council. For two months they have been violating the rights of neutrals.   Faithfully yours,   Robert Lansing.

TLS (WP, DLC).

ENCLOSURE II

Draft note to Great Britain regarding Order
in Council of March 11, 1915.

You are instructed to address a note to His Britannic Majesty's Principal Secretary of State for Foreign Affairs in the following sense:

The Government of the United States in its note relative to the British Order in Council of March 11, 1915, expressed the expectation that the orders issued to His Majesty's naval forces charged with the duty of enforcing the Order in Council would be of such a nature as not, quote, to impose restrictions upon neutral trade more burdensome than those which have been regarded as inevitable when the ports of a belligerent are actually blockaded by the ships of its enemy, unquote.

Relying upon this expectation, which was amply warranted by the assurances contained in Your Excellency's note of March 15th transmitting the Order in Council, the Government of the United States has observed with increasing surprise and disappointment the method of enforcement of the Order in Council by the British authorities. Realizing that the institution of a policy of commercial non-intercourse with an enemy presented difficulties of exceptional character in view of the conditions prevailing in the present war the Government of the United States patiently awaited the adaptation of the actual practice under the provisions of the Order in Council to the continued exercise of rights of commerce between neutral nations.

Two months have now elapsed since the British authorities entered upon the enforcement of the Order in Council. The time has been ample for the British Government to put into practice the considerate policy toward neutral trade, which was assured in Your Excellency's note. Yet, in spite of these assurances, neutral rights are disregarded and the long-sanctioned rules of international law governing the freedom of the seas to neutrals are repeatedly violated. There has been no apparent abatement of the rigorous methods adopted at the outset by the British naval authorities.

American and other neutral vessels plying between neutral ports and laden with cargoes destined to neutral consignees have been stopped on the high seas and taken into British ports. American vessels and cargoes have been held without the cause of detention being made known to the Government of the United States. In some instances the cargoes have been preempted and, though compensation has been promised, the owners have been brought to the verge of financial ruin through failure of the British Government to recompense them promptly for the goods thus preempted. Furthermore, no reparation has been offered for irregular or undue detentions of vessels and cargoes which were subsequently released.

The unprecedented procedure of arresting neutral vessels and neutral cargoes on the high seas, though in trade between neutral ports, of unduly detaining them in British ports without disclosing the *prima facie* cause, of refusing to permit them in many instances to proceed to their destination, and of practically requisitioning cargoes consigned to neutrals, has caused a situation, which the Government of the United States can no longer view with patience or in silence.

Not only is grievous wrong being done to the American citizens interested in the vessels and cargoes, which have been detained without authority of the law or the usage of nations, but the menace of the British practice is forcing American citizens to incur unknown hazards in the special privileges which they are entitled to enjoy, and is threatening to disorganize if not to destroy regular traffic between the United States and the neutral countries of Europe, to which they should have full liberty to resort in trade and navigation.

The Government of His Britannic Majesty should realize that the practices of the British naval authorities in their enforcement of the Order in Council of March 11th has destroyed the expectation and hope of the Government of the United States, which were based on the assurances of Your Excellency in the note of March 15th; that the conditions of trade between the United States and other neutral nations as a consequence of these practices have become intolerable and can no longer be endured with-

out complaint; and that a continuance of these practices so subversive of neutral rights and so destructive of their enjoyment will
invite measures by the Government of the United States, which
will restore to American citizens the freedom of the high seas and
protect them in the exercise of their just rights.

The Government of the United States sincerely hopes that His
Majesty's Government, realizing the gravity of the situation and
appreciating the duty which this Government owes to itself and
to its citizens, will so modify the present practices of its naval
authorities that it will not become necessary for the Government
of the United States to make further representations or to take
any step to protect American citizens in their commerce with
neutral nations.

The Government of the United States, while making this appeal to His Majesty's Government in all friendliness and with a
full appreciation of the apparent purposes of their policy, desires
it to be distinctly understood that the rights of American citizens
on the high seas must be respected and that this Government will
not fail to adopt measures necessary to insure that respect and
to prevent any impairment of those rights which have been universally recognized by the principles of international law and the
usages of maritime nations.   Robert Lansing.

TS MS (WP, DLC).

Remarks at a Luncheon in New York[1]

[May 17, 1915]

Mr. Mayor, Mr. Secretary, Admiral Fletcher, and gentlemen
of the fleet: This is not an occasion upon which, it seems to me,
it would be wise for me to make many remarks, but I would
deprive myself of a great gratification if I did not express my
pleasure in being here, my gratitude for the splendid reception
which has been accorded me as the representative of the nation,
and my profound interest in the navy of the United States. That
is an interest with which I was apparently born, for it began
when I was a youngster and has ripened with my knowledge of
the affairs and policies of the United States.

I think it is a natural, instinctive judgment of the people of the
United States that they express their power most appropriately in
an efficient navy, and their interest in their ships is partly, I believe, because that navy somehow is expected to express their
character, not within our own borders, where that character is
understood, but outside our borders, where it is hoped we may

occasionally touch others with some slight vision of what America stands for.

But before I speak of the navy of the United States, I want to take advantage of the first public opportunity I have had to speak of the Secretary of the Navy, to express my confidence and my admiration, and to say that he has my unqualified support. For I have counseled with him in intimate fashion; I know how sincerely he has it at heart that everything that the navy does and handles should be done and handled as the people of the United States wish it handled, because efficiency is something more than organization. Efficiency runs into every well-considered detail of personnel and method. Efficiency runs to the extent of lifting the ideals of a service above every personal interest. So that when I speak my support of the Secretary of the Navy, I am merely speaking my support of what I know every true lover of the navy to desire and to purpose; for the navy of the United States is, as I have said, a body specially entrusted with the ideals of America.

I like to image in my thought this ideal: These quiet ships lying in the river have no suggestion of bluster about them, no intimation of aggression. They are commanded by men thoughtful of the duty of citizens as well as the duty of officers, men acquainted with the traditions of the great service to which they belong, men who know by touch with the people of the United States what sort of purposes they ought to entertain, and what sort of discretion they ought to exercise in order to use those engines of force as engines to promote the interests of humanity.

The interesting and inspiring thing about America, gentlemen, is that she asks nothing for herself except what she has a right to ask for humanity itself. We want no nation's property. We wish to question no nation's honor. We wish to stand selfishly in the way of the development of no nation. We want nothing that we cannot get by our own legitimate enterprise and by the inspiration of our own example. And, standing for these things, it is not pretension on our part to say that we are privileged to stand for what every nation would wish to stand for, and speak for those things which all humanity must desire.

When I think of the flag that those ships carry, the only touch of color about them, the only thing that moves as if it had a subtle spirit in it in their solid structure, it seems to me that I see alternate stripes of parchment upon which are written the rights of liberty and justice, and stripes of blood spilt to vindicate those rights; and, then, in the corner a prediction of the blue serene into which every nation may swim which stands for these great things.

The mission of America is the only thing that a sailor or a soldier should think about. He has nothing to do with the formulation of her policy. He is to support her policy whatever it is; but he is to support her policy in the spirit of herself, and the strength of our polity is that we who, for the time being, administer the affairs of this nation do not originate her spirit. We attempt to embody it; we attempt to realize it in action; we are dominated by it; we do not dictate it.

And so with every man in arms who serves the nation—he stands and waits to do the thing which the nation desires. Those who represent America sometimes seem perhaps to forget her programs, but the people never forget them. It is as startling as it is touching to see how, whenever you touch a principle, you touch the hearts of the people of the United States. They listen to your debates of policy, they determine which party they will prefer to power, they choose and prefer as between men; but their real affection, their real force, their real irresistible momentum is for the ideas which men embody. I never go on the streets of a great city without feeling that somehow I do not confer, elsewhere than on the streets, with the great spirit of the people themselves—going about their business, attending to the things which immediately concern them, and yet carrying a treasure at their hearts all the while, ready to be stirred, not only as individuals, but as members of a great union of hearts that constitutes a patriotic people. And so this sight in the river touches me merely as a symbol of all this; and it quickens the pulse of every man who realizes these things to have anything to do with them. When a crisis occurs in this country, gentlemen, it is as if you put your hand on the pulse of a dynamo; it is as if the things that you were in connection with were spiritually bred, as if you had nothing to do with them except, if you listen truly, to speak the things that you hear.

These things now brood over the river; this spirit now moves with the men who represent the nation in the navy; these things will move upon the waters in the maneuvers—no threat lifted against any man, against any nation, against any interest, but just a great solemn evidence that the force of America is the force of moral principle, that there is nothing else that she loves, and that there is nothing else for which she will contend.[2]

Printed in *Address of the President . . . at the Luncheon Tendered to Him by the Mayor's Committee . . .* (Washington, 1918); with corrections and additions from the complete text in the *New York Times*, May 18, 1915.

1 At the Hotel Biltmore in New York. This was one of several events during
Wilson's visit to the city to review the Atlantic Fleet in New York harbor.
Wilson was introduced by Acting Mayor George McAneny. For reports on this
and other events of the day, see the *New York Times*, May 18, 1915.
2 There is a WWsh outline of these remarks, dated May 17, 1915, in WP, DLC.

From William Jennings Bryan, with Enclosure

My dear Mr. President: Washington May 17, 1915.

As you will not return until Wednesday morning I think I
ought to let you know at once of a conversation which I had this
morning with Ambassador Dumba, of Austria. I am therefore
sending this by special messenger.

The Ambassador first expressed appreciation of your letter
to the Czar[1] and then asked me to say to you that he would be
pleased to give you any assistance he could in the negotiations
with Germany. He said he knew that Germany had no desire for
war but, on the contrary, was anxious to maintain friendly
relations with the United States and asked whether if assurances
were given for the future it would not be possible to arbitrate the
question so far as past transactions are concerned. I told him
I would not feel authorized to discuss the subject without first
getting your views, but suggested that he might say to the German Government that he felt sure there was no desire for war
in this country and that we expected Germany to answer the
note in the same spirit of friendship that prompted ours. He
then suggested it might make it easier for Germany if she could,
in her reply, say that she expected us to insist in the same spirit
upon freedom of trade with the neutrals. I pointed out to him
that such an expression in the answer might embarrass us and
also make it more difficult to deal with the Allies along that Line—
and that I thought Germany ought to *assume* that we would
live up to the position taken in our answer to the Orders in Council. He asked whether we could give any confidential assurances
of that kind and I told him it ought not to be necessary and suggested to him that if Germany desired to justify, before her own
people, her acceptance of the doctrine set forth in our note she
could publish her views in a statement—not to us but to the German people, and say that she took it for granted that we would
maintain the position taken in that statement and would insist
upon our right to trade with neutrals. I told him if this statement was made to the German people instead of to us it would
not require any answer from us and would not embarrass us, but
if Germany's answer contained any expression of opinion as to
how we would deal with Great Britain it would seemingly link

the two cases together and put us in the attitude of acting at Germany's suggestion instead of acting upon our own initiative and for the protection of our own interests, and it might also be construed as a sort of trade, whereby we would settle an account with Germany by opening an account with the Allies.

He saw the force of the objection. I emphasized the two points —first that it was important that Germany should answer in the same spirit in which we had addressed her; and second, that there should be no attempted connection between our dealings with Germany and our dealings with Great Britain.[2]

He asked whether we could not refuse clearance to ships that carried explosives and ammunition. He said that in Germany passenger trains were not allowed to carry explosives and that the regulation was made for the protection of the lives of passengers; he suggested we might, on the same ground, refuse to allow shipowners to carry explosives on passenger boats. I told him that Germany was, of course, at liberty to make any suggestions that she thought proper in her reply, but that we could not consider these suggestions in advance.

I think the call of the Ambassador was rather significant especially as I learned from Villard that he had received some of the same suggestions from von Bernstorff. I believe it will have a splendid effect if our note to Great Britain can go at once. It will give Germany an excuse and I think she is looking for something that will serve as an excuse. There is much discussion of the idea suggested by Dumba—in fact mentioned in the first explanation received from Germany, namely—that passengers and ammunition should not travel together. I have no doubt Germany would be willing to so change the rule in regard to submarines as to exempt from danger all passenger ships that did not carry munitions of war.

I am also enclosing a statement from Page. The closing sentence is interesting. Am glad to note that it will not take a generation to regain the respect with the loss of which we were threatened.

With assurances of high respect I am, my dear Mr. President,
Yours very sincerely,   W. J. Bryan

P.S. The bearer of this letter—Mr. Edward Yardley—will bring it to the Mayflower tonight and await instructions from you. If you have any answer to send back tonight he will return on the twelve-thirty train—if not, he will return early tomorrow afternoon. If you do not send an answer tonight but desire to send one tomorrow you can instruct him whether he is to call at the Mayflower for it or whether you can send it to the Holland House, Fifth Avenue near 28th street where he will stop.   W.J.B.

TLS (W. J. Bryan Papers, DNA).
  1 WW to Nicholas II, March 18, 1915, Vol. 32.
  2 Dumba gave a rather different cast to Bryan's remarks to this point in his telegram to the Austrian Foreign Minister of the same date. For the relevant portions thereof, see Link, *Struggle for Neutrality*, pp. 400-401. For the interpretation which Arthur Zimmermann put upon Dumba's version of Bryan's comment, see EMH to WW, May 24, 1915.

E N C L O S U R E

London, May 16, 10 P.M.

2104. Commendation of the note to Germany and gratification are universally expressed privately and in the press. The Times says: "It is a note that both in substance and expression recalls the best traditions of American diplomacy. The stand taken by President Wilson is something more than a declaration of national policy. Nothing less than the conscience of humanity makes itself audible in his measured and incisive sentences." The Times editorial ends in these words: "The moral interests of the United States and the allies are henceforward indissolubly linked." The Westminster Gazette says: "We count this note as from all human and moral points of view the greatest event of this war."

The following is in the Secretary's private code and confidential to the President and the Secretary:

Among the men whose private expressions of praise have come to me are most members of the government as well as Lan[s]-downe,[1] Balfour and Bonarlaw, of the opposition.

I think the practically unanimous expectation here is that the German government will give an evasive answer and decline to abbreviate the use of submarines against merchant ships.

The representatives of other neutral governments here privately express pleasure and gratitude. The Americans in London about whose impatience I telegraphed feel ashamed of their hasty fears.

May I be allowed to express my personal congratulations on the note?   American Ambassador, London.

CC T telegram (W. J. Bryan Papers, DNA).
  1 Henry Charles Keith Petty Fitzmaurice, 5th Marquess of Landowne, Foreign Secretary, 1900-1905.

From Robert Lansing

Dear Mr. President: Washington May 17, 1915.

In compliance with the request contained in your note of the

12th instant to the Secretary of State asking for copies of the suggestions as to alternative courses of action made in my letter to the Secretary on the 10th, it seemed to me better to repeat them in a more detailed form.

The suggestions apply to possible action in the event Germany refuses to comply with the demands made upon her.

First. Diplomatic relations could be severed by the withdrawal of our Ambassador. The natural course would be for the German Government to recall Count Bernstorff or at least to direct him to leave Washington and cease to communicate with this Government.

This action would not necessarily mean war. It might mean that this Government is unwilling to continue intercourse with the German Government because it has grievously offended against the principles of international law and humanity affecting American citizens and has refused to rectify the offense by making proper amends and giving proper assurances. It is an evidence of extreme displeasure but is not in itself a hostile act.

For this method of emphasizing a protest or demand there are several precedents, one of the most recent being the withdrawal of Baron Fava because of the failure of our Government to take steps to punish those persons guilty of lynching Italians at New Orleans and to pay a satisfactory indemnity.[1]

The severance of diplomatic relations may, however, be interpreted as an evidence of hostile purpose. As the interpretation of the course of action in this case would lie largely with Germany, it is necessary in taking this step to consider the present temper of the German Government. My own belief is that it would be viewed by them as unfriendly, if not hostile, and that they might consider it to be a practical declaration of war.

Second. The alternative course of action would be to approach the other neutral powers particularly affected by the submarine war, namely, Netherlands, Denmark, Sweden and Norway, as to the sending of identic notes to both Germany and Great Britain protesting vigorously against the disregard shown of neutral rights on the high seas and asserting that, unless ample assurances were given that these rights would be respected, the neutral nations would consider what joint action they should take to protect their citizens on the high seas in the enjoyment of their rights.

If this course of action should be decided upon, I think that as a preliminary step an immediate representation should be made to Great Britain pointing out the failure of the British Government to act in accord with Sir Edward Grey's assurances of consideration for neutral rights given in his note of March

15th. By doing this the disregard of Germany for law and humanity and of Great Britain for law would form substantial grounds for joint protest and, if necessary, for joint action. It would furthermore indicate entire impartiality toward the belligerents and show that the neutrals sought to secure the freedom of the seas for their people, whichever belligerent invaded their rights.

A copy of this letter has been given to the Secretary of State.

I am, Sir, with deep respect,

Sincerely yours,   Robert Lansing.

TLS (WP, DLC).
[1] Baron Saverio Fava, Italian Minister to the United States, 1881-91. See n. 6 to remarks at a press conference, printed at April 11, 1913, Vol. 27.

From Edith Bolling Galt

My dearest One: [U.S.S. *Mayflower*] May 17, 1915   2:10

I just must send you a real message that is too tender to trust to wireless transmission.

I have missed you every moment, but I think the proudest minute of my life was when you turned your wonderful eyes to *me* —in the midst of all the people and their praise of you.

I stood and watched you as you went away in the automobile, and I think even *you* would have been satisfied with my *heart* it was so warm, so bursting with emotion.

The others are coming.   Edith

ALS (WP, DLC).

A Statement on the Condition of the Atlantic Fleet

[May 18, 1915]

I was greatly struck by the appearance of the fleet and the quiet efficiency shown by the officers and men, as I am sure everyone must have been who had the pleasure of seeing it assembled at New York. There could have been no more interesting verification of Admiral Dewey's statement[1] that the navy was never in a better or more efficient condition and that the country has every reason to be proud of it, not only, but every reason to wish to go forward in its policy of steadily adding to its strength and equipment.

T MS (WP, DLC).
[1] At a dinner at the Waldorf-Astoria Hotel on May 15 honoring the officers of the visiting Atlantic Fleet, Secretary Daniels, in the course of a speech entitled "The Preparedness of the Navy," read aloud a letter from Admiral George Dewey. "The people of New York," Dewey had written, "have just cause to be proud in the fleet now assembled in their harbor. Not only is it

composed of the finest and most efficient warships we have ever had, but it is not excelled, except in size, by the fleet of any nation in the world; our officers are as good as any, and our enlisted men are superior in training, education, physical endurance, and devotion to duty to those of any other navy.

"As President of the General Board for fifteen years, I can say with absolute confidence that the efficiency of the fleet has steadily progressed and has never been so high as it is today. However we need more ships, more officers and men, and should continue the wise policy of increasing the size of our navy, which must ever remain our first and best line of defense. This defense, unless adequate, is impotent, and adequacy is not reached until the navy is strong enough to meet on equal terms the navy of the strongest possible adversary." *New York Times,* May 16, 1915.

To Edward Mandell House

[The White House, May 18, 1915]

It becomes more and more evident that it will presently become necessary for the sake of diplomatic consistency and to satisfy our public to address a note to Great Britain about the unnecessary and unwarranted interruption of our legitimate trade with neutral ports. It would be a great stroke on England's part if she would of her own accord relieve this situation and so put Germany alone in the wrong and leave her without any excuse that the opinion of the world could accept. It would be a small price to pay for the cessation of submarine outrages.

Wilson

T transcript of WWsh telegram (WP, DLC).

From Edward Mandell House

[London, May 18, 1915]

I am afraid we cannot bring about any immediate change in policy of this government in regard to foodstuffs. The feeling is running too high. They have no grounds for the government to take such action even if they desired to do so. No matter what Germany's answer to your note may be, the entire world will uphold you in the firm and just attitude you have taken and which I hope you will in no way recede from. Sir Edward Grey's eyes have given out, and he is leaving in a few days to be gone a month. This is unfortunate.   Edward House.

T transcript of WWsh decode (WC, NjP) of T telegram (WP, DLC).

Two Letters from William Jennings Bryan

My dear Mr. President: Washington May 18, 1915.

I enclose Mr. West's report of his visit to Zapata.[1] I sent you his conclusions the other day but I thought you might be interested in reading this account when you have a moment's spare time. I have asked Mr. West to remain until your return from New York, thinking that you might like to talk with him before he returns to Texas. After you have questioned him I shall be pleased to go over the situation with you.

I confess I have not been able to reach a conclusion very satisfactory to myself, although I find my mind inclined to a course of action which I shall be pleased to suggest to you whenever you have leisure for a conference on the subject. I think, however, you would better see Mr. West first because you may be able to draw from him by questions information in addition to that which he included in his reports and conclusions.

With assurances of high respect I am, my dear Mr. President,
Yours very sincerely,   W. J. Bryan

TLS (SDR, RG 59, 812.00/24272a, DNA).
[1] D. West, "Mexico City to Tlaltizapan," April 16, 1915, T MS (SDR, RG 59, 812.00/24272a, DNA), describing in detail both Zapata and his surroundings as well as the conversation between them. West remarked that he was "agreeably disappointed in Zapata." Zapata, West wrote, was deeply sincere in his desire to improve the lot of the peon class in his native Morelos; however, his limitations of education and outlook would prevent his being a large factor in Mexican politics, other than as the representative of the people of his own region.

My dear Mr. President: Washington May 19, 1915.

I am sending you Senator Phelan's report.[1] It seems to me that he has given undue weight to the testimony of some of the men who appeared against Mr. Sullivan. Some of them like Mr. Vick and Mr. Vance[2] were personally hostile to Sullivan, and others like Michelain,[3] Edwards[4] Mann[5] and Russell[6] are hostile to the State Department. There is in my judgment, however, enough testimony which is undisputed to justify the resignation of Mr. Sullivan. There is one thing alone—and upon which I have already consulted you—which would make his continuance in office inadvisable; namely, the letter to Gray in which Sullivan used disparaging language against the whole people, including their leaders, cannot but make him a *persona non grata*.[7] The fact that the letter was private and not intended for the public does not relieve the situation. When a man expresses himself in writing he puts his opinion out of his own hands and must take the chance of it becoming public property.

Nearly all of Senator Phelan's conclusions are based upon evidence that was brought out at the trial and are, therefore, no reflection upon the Department. One paragraph in his conclusions, however, does reflect upon the Department.

In stating the qualifications of a man for this particular place he expresses the opinion that Sullivan was not qualified—giving what he regards as lacking in Sullivan's qualifications for the position—one that of the twenty-seven foreign ministers and consuls in Santo Domingo Mr. Sullivan is the only one that cannot speak Spanish. While the speaking of Spanish would doubtless be an advantage I do not think it should be regarded as indispensable. We have not so regarded it in other appointments which we have made to ministerial positions. I do not think Page can speak Italian; Penfield German or Morganthau Turkish, and I am sure that very few of our ministers to South America can speak Spanish. I think we would have found no difficulty in finding a man for Santo Domingo who could speak Spanish, but it is not one of the most desirable of the legations—in fact we had few applications for the place. Sullivan impressed me as a man of rugged strength and honesty and I gave considerable weight to the fact that he is a Catholic, feeling that because of our intimate relationship with Santo Domingo it would be best to have someone religiously in sympathy with the people. I still feel that this factor ought not to be overlooked. It ought to be remembered, also, that Sullivan was endorsed by Governor Baldwin of Connecticut and by Henry Wade Rogers of the Law School. He was also endorsed by Senator O'Gorman, by Congressman Hamill, by Mr. Gray of Delaware whom I had known for eighteen years, and by Mr. Tumulty. I hardly feel, therefore, that the Department deserves the censure that is implied in that part of the report.

I am satisfied, from the testimony, that we were deceived as to the interests which supported Mr. Sullivan's candidacy. I was very anxious, as you will remember, that the person selected should not be biased toward either of the factions which he would have to meet there; and when something occurred which aroused a suspicion I made inquiry and was convinced by what I learned that there was no connection between Mr. Sullivan and the interests represented by Beer. I am now convinced by the testimony that there was a relationship which, had I known it, would have prevented my recommendation of him to you.

I presume that the report ought to be given to the public. The evidence was taken in public and of course the final action will be a matter of public noteriety, and I think Senator Phelan's findings might as well be given to the public. I am glad that we selected a Catholic to make the investigation for it relieves us of any possible charge that the finding was due to religious bias. I presume it would be better to ask for Mr. Sullivan's resignation before making the report public but await your instruction in the matter.

With assurances of high respect I am, my dear Mr. President,
Yours very sincerely, W. J. Bryan

TLS (WP, DLC).
¹ It must have been a manuscript copy of the report. A pencil notation on Bryan's letter indicates that it was sent to Robert Lansing on June 22, 1915. Phelan's report was summarized in the *New York Times*, the New York *World*, and other newspapers on July 27, 1915. It was later printed under the title *Santo Domingo Investigation. Copy of the Report, Findings and Opinion of James D. Phelan, Commissioner named by the Secretary of State, with the approval of the President, to investigate charges against the United States Minister to the Dominican Republic* (Washington, 1916). A copy of it is enclosed in J. D. Phelan to JPT, Feb. 18, 1916, TLS (WP, DLC).
Phelan concluded that James M. Sullivan was both corrupt and incompetent as a diplomat and recommended his immediate removal from his post. He also administered a severe rebuke to the State Department. For a summary of the charges against Sullivan, see Link, *The New Freedom*, pp. 108-110.
² John Thomas Vance, deputy Receiver General of Customs in the Dominican Republic.
³ Bryan undoubtedly referred to Santiago Michelena, a banker of Santo Domingo, who had acted as the representative of the National City Bank of New York in the Dominican capital.
⁴ J. H. Edwards, former deputy Receiver General of the Dominican Republic.
⁵ John L. Mann, former Director General of Public Works in the Dominican Republic.
⁶ William Worthington Russell, career diplomat, Minister to the Dominican Republic, July 1, 1911, to August 15, 1913, and from August 16, 1915, to 1925.
⁷ See WJB to WW, March 10, 1915 (first letter of that date), n. 1, Vol. 32.

From William Jennings Bryan, with Enclosure

My dear Mr. President: Washington May 19th, 1915.

I enclose you a copy of a memorandum which I have just received from the Brazilian Ambassador. You will notice that in the first paragraph reference is made to the guaranty of *national integrity* and the control of the manufacture and sale of arms. In the last paragraph reference is made to the Monroe Doctrine. The second paragraph, while not very clear, indicates that they do not think it wise to have a time set for the arbitration of existing disputes. In view of Chile's objection to this and Brazil's attitude on the subject, why would it not be well to modify the arbitration section to read something as follows:

"All boundaries now agreed upon are guaranteed for the future; all differences now existing as to boundaries will be specifically set forth in the treaty according to the views of the parties interested and the boundaries, when fixed, will be thereafter guaranteed. The parties will endeavor, according to their several interests, to reach an early settlement of existing disputes; all disputes arising in the future to be submitted to arbitration, provided those disputes do not affect the constitutions of the respective countries."

Do you think that some such wording would answer for the statement of the proposition? As this treaty is to be agreed to by the nations entering into it, it is entirely possible that in the exchange of views it may be necessary to accept some change in the wording.

This memorandum does not mention the guaranty of republican form of government. I have asked Ambassador da Gama to say to his Government that the guaranty of a republican form of government having been formerly endorsed by Brazil, and not being mentioned in this memorandum, we assume that the former endorsement still stands.

Now that we have Brazil's answer do you not think it would be wise to communicate this plan confidentially to the representatives of the other Latin-American countries so that they can be securing the opinions of their respective governments? The sooner we can get this before the public the better, for the influence it may have across the Atlantic. I am not sure but it might be well to give it to the public at the time we present it, as was done when we announced the peace plan which provides for investigation in all cases. I shall be pleased to have your instructions in this matter.

With assurances of high respect, I am, my dear Mr. President,
Very sincerely yours,   W. J. Bryan

TLS (SDR, RG 59, 710.11/204½, DNA).

ENCLOSURE

MEMORANDUM.   Washington, May 18th, 1915.

The Embassy of Brazil has received telegrams from Minister Lauro Müller, dated Buenos Aires, May 16th and 17th, confirming the previous acceptance of the proposal by the Government of the United States of America of a declaration of reciprocal guarantee of the integrity of national territories in America, and agreeing as well upon the control by their respective Governments of the manufacture and sale of arms and ammunitions of war in the contracting countries.

As for the decision of the territorial questions still pending between several American nations, the Minister thinks that it would not be possible to set a term for their solution, which largely depends upon the action of time, aided to some extent by the progress of Pan American sentiment and also by the action of the Governments, inasmuch as they do not interfere with the sovereignty of the interested countries. To allude to those difficulties or to seek a general solution for them might bring about criticisms, thus counteracting that same noble purpose of the Government of the United States, that well we understand.

The Minister's personal impression is that the joint action proposed by the President of the United States would be more solemn and greatly gain in moral strength if it were reduced to a declaration of solidarity in the defense of American national territories, thus transforming the Monroe Doctrine into what should be called the Wilson Doctrine. Nevertheless, the Minister will gladly consider a clause submitting to arbitration any disputes which may arise in future and do not affect the constitution of the respective countries.

T MS (SDR, RG 59, 710.11/204½, DNA).

From Edward Mandell House

[London, May 19, 1915]

After a conference with Sir Edward Grey this morning he agrees to use all his influence towards permitting staple foodstuffs to go to neutral ports without question providing Germany will cease submarine warfare on merchant vessels and discontinue the use of poisonous gas. I immediately cabled Gerard to get the German government to delay their answer to your note until the receipt of another cable, a copy of which I am sending for your information.[1] Germany must not know Sir Edward Grey is cognizant of this suggestion. The difficulty here is that the cabinet office is in solution and the proposal cannot be brought to the new ministry for several days. Sir Edward Grey seeks no advantage for England but is giving his personal support in order to conform to our wishes. Sir Edward Grey also says that the foodstuffs now detained would be brought before a prize court. Do you think it possible that payment for cotton cargoes now detained will be made as soon as shippers certify as to the real owners? I hope you approve my action. There was no time to confer.

T transcript of WWsh decode (WC, NjP) of T telegram (WP, DLC).
[1] "Have concluded to cable my suggestion rather than delay it by letter. Can you not induce the German Government to answer our note by proposing that if England will permit food stuffs in the future to go to neutral ports without question that Germany will discontinue her submarine warfare on merchant vessels and will also discontinue the use of poisonous gas. Such a proposal from Germany at this time will give her great advantage and in my opinion she will make a grave mistake if she does not seize it. Edward House" WHP to WJB, May 19, 1915, T telegram (WP, DLC), with the following introduction: "Rush for the President: Please transmit following to Berlin Embassy immediately."

To William Jennings Bryan

My dear Mr. Secretary,   The White House. 20 May, 1915.

I am glad to reply that I have no objection to these changes.

Faithfully Yours,   W.W.

WWTLI (W. J. Bryan Papers, DNA).

To Edward Mandell House

[The White House, May 20, 1915]

It seems to me very important indeed that we should not even seem to be setting off the one government against the other or trying by any means resembling a bargain to obtain from either of them a concession of our undoubted rights on the high seas. Each government should understand that the rights we claim from it have no connection which we can recognize with those we claim from the other, but that we must insist upon our rights from each without regard to what the other does or does not do. I should like to accomplish what you suggest in your message to Gerard, but that will have to be managed so as to be entirely free from the danger I have suggested. Can Gerard handle it in that way?   Wilson

T transcript of WWsh telegram (WC, NjP).

Three Letters to William Jennings Bryan

My dear Mr. Secretary,   The White House. 20 May, 1915.

As I intimated in the little scribbled note[1] I sent back by the special messenger whom you sent with this to New York, I think your position in the conversation with the Austrian Ambassador was admirable. We clearly cannot afford to consult with Germany as to our course toward Great Britain. The two must be kept carefully separate and distinct.

I am glad to be back and at my desk.

Faithfully Yours,   W.W.

[1] It is missing.

My dear Mr. Secretary,   The White House. 20 May, 1915.

The proposed note to Great Britain, drawn by Mr. Lansing, reached me in New York, and I shall at the earliest possible moment go over it and work it into what seems to me it[s] best expression.

But the more I think about this matter the clearer it becomes to me that we ought not to send this note, or any other on this subject, to Great Britain, until we have the reply of the Imperial German Government to our note to it, because we cannot afford even to seem to be trying to make it easier for Germany to accede to our demands by turning in similar fashion to England concerning matters which we have already told Germany are none of her business. It would be so evident a case of uneasiness and hedging that I think it would weaken our whole position fatally.

There is no reason to feel that our note to Germany is being looked upon by them as unfriendly; and it is right that we should oblige them to consider our rights upon the seas so far as they are concerned without regard to anything we mean to say or do in the case of England.

In every such decision I feel very keenly the force of your counter judgment and cannot claim that I feel cock sure of the rightness of my own conclusions; but I can only follow what grows more and more clear to me the more I think the matter out.   Faithfully Yours,   W.W.

My dear Mr. Secretary,   The White House. 20 May, 1915.

It is very interesting indeed that this course of action should have occurred to Mr. Johnson quite independently of any knowledge that it should have been in our minds as among the possibilities.

I think, however, as I did the other day, that this is at any rate not just the right moment to take such action, even if we have the legal right to take it.   Faithfully Yours,   W.W.

WWTLI (W. J. Bryan Papers, DNA).

To Robert Lansing

My dear Mr. Lansing: The White House May 20, 1915

May I not thank you very warmly for your kindness in sending me an amplified copy of your suggestions as to alternative courses of action should the Imperial German Government not respond as we hope it will to our note? I shall keep this by me.

Cordially and sincerely yours,   Woodrow Wilson

TLS (SDR, RG 59, 763.72/1777½, DNA).

To Robert Latham Owen

Personal and Confidential.

My dear Senator: [The White House] May 20, 1915

I thank you sincerely for your letter of May thirteenth. You may be sure that I share the sentiments which it expresses and that I shall school myself to such a course of action as will keep the country out of war if it is humanly possible to maintain our rights without it.

Cordially and sincerely yours,   Woodrow Wilson

TLS (Letterpress Books, WP, DLC).

To John Pierpont Morgan, Jr.

My dear Mr. Morgan: [The White House] May 20, 1915

It was certainly a most gracious act of thoughtful kindness on your part to write me your letter of May fourteenth, which I find on my desk upon my return from New York, and I thank you for it very warmly indeed.

Cordially and sincerely yours,   Woodrow Wilson

TLS (Letterpress Books, WP, DLC).

To Joseph Rucker Lamar

My dear Lamar: [The White House] May 20, 1915

Thank you with all my heart for your letter about the note. It warms me all through and strengthens me to get such expressions of approval and friendship from one whose judgment I value as I do yours. It was generous of you to think of writing.

Cordially and sincerely yours,   Woodrow Wilson

TLS (Letterpress Books, WP, DLC).

To Oswald Garrison Villard

My dear Mr. Villard: The White House May 20, 1915

Your letter of May fourteenth, which I find awaiting me on my return from the review in New York, seems to me singularly generous. I cannot thank you for it too warmly. I want you to know how sincerely I value your approval and when it comes with such warmth as it carries in this letter which I shall treasure, it contributes immensely to my strength and the steadiness of every process of my mind and heart.

Cordially and sincerely yours,   Woodrow Wilson

TLS (O. G. Villard Papers, MH).

To Charles William Eliot

My dear Doctor Eliot: The White House May 20, 1915

I want you to know how deeply gratified I was by your message of the fourteenth of May about our note to Germany. I am sure that you know how sincerely I value your approval.

Cordially and sincerely yours,   Woodrow Wilson

TLS (C. W. Eliot Papers, MH-Ar).

From Edward Mandell House

Dear Governor: No. 5. London, May 20th, 1915.

When your cable of the 17th[1] came I asked Page to make an engagement with Grey in order that we might protest against the holding up of cargoes and find definitely whether England would agree to lift the embargo on foodstuffs provided Germany would discontinue her submarine policy. Page promised to make the appointment. He did not do so and finally told me that he had concluded it was useless because, in his opinion, the British Government would not consider for a moment the proposal to lift the embargo.

It was then I sent you the discouraging cable.[2] However, when your second cable of Tuesday[3] came I went to see Sir Edward without further consultation with Page.

I found that Grey was even more receptive of the suggestion than when I saw him last and he promised to use all his influence in favor of such a proposal, provided one was made by Germany. He added, however, that the discontinuance of asphyxiating or poisonous gases must also be included in any agreement made.

He explained that the Cabinet was in solution and that he could only speak for himself and he did not want me to consider that he spoke for the Government. I expressed a willingness to accept his personal assurance in regard to his own endeavors with the understanding that it committed no one except himself [himself]. He said that in ordinary times if the Cabinet refused to acquiesce in his view, he would resign, but that he did not feel justified in doing this in time of war. I took occasion to express your high regard for him and to assure him that we would consider his resignation a calamity.

He dictated, while I wrote, the understanding between us which was literally this:

ıst. Permitting staple foodstuffs to go to neutral ports without question.

2md [2nd]. All foodstuffs now detained to be brought before the prize court as quickly as possible.

3rd. Claims for cotton cargoes now detained to be made as soon as shippers certify as to each cargo that they are the real owners to whom payment should be made.

Should England agree to the first proposition, Germany was to cease submarine warfare on merchant vessels and discontinue the use of asphyxiating or poisonous gases.

Proposition two and three are matters between this Government and ours and have no reference to Germany and will be carried out at once.

I told Grey that I would immediately cable Gerard asking Germany to withhold her answer to your Note until I could communicate with him further. I also told him I would suggest to the German authorities through Gerard that they answer the note by making the proposal in question.

I had no time to confer with you regarding it so I sent the messages to Gerard through you.

I assumed the entire responsibility so if things go wrong you and Sir Edward can disclaim any connection with it.

If Germany refuses to consider this proposal it will place you in the position of having done everything possible to avert war between the United States and Germany.

Sir Edward took a copy of the memorandum I made so that there might be no misunderstanding between us. Of course there would be none anyway for he remembers well what he says and never recedes from his word.

I dined with Lord Haldane last night and he said Grey had taken the matter up with him and that [if] he, Haldane, continued in the Cabinet we could count upon his support. I talked to Haldane about the freedom of the seas and he was sympathetic with that idea.

It is unfortunate that the Cabinet it [is] to be reformed for I am confident with the present members the plan would go through, provided Germany makes the proposal. The new element[4] to go in is less apt to favor the proposal than those already there.   Affectionately yours,   E. M. House

TLS (WP, DLC).
1 WW to EMH, May 16, 1915.
2 EMH to WW, May 18, 1915.
3 WW to EMH, May 18, 1915.
4 That is, Conservative members of the cabinet, notably Andrew Bonar Law, Arthur James Balfour, Edward Henry Carson, Austen Chamberlain, and George Nathaniel Curzon, Earl Curzon.

From Edith Bolling Galt

Washington, D. C. May 20th 1915

Oh! to be with you tonight my precious one—to put my arms 'round you and hold you close, and tell you how long the day has been without you.

I have been back in the prison. Instead of golden sunlight and silver waters there has been rain and wet streets. And my heart has been away—seeking you—and leaving me in a strange unfamiliar world, with nothing at 1308 20th Street[1] the same as when I left it a week ago.

You have been so vividly before me that I loose [lose] the sense of being alone, and find myself turning to welcome your coming if there is a noise or motion in the house.

Do you remember Wm. James Essay "On a Certain Blindness in Human beings"? I don't know what led me to read it again tonight, but, even with one eye still asleep, I found things in it that I never *really* read before—because I was *blind myself*. I mean the fable of the monk who heard the "bird in the woods break into song"—and then—"all that is not merely mechanical is spun out of two strands—*seeking* for that bird, and *hearing* him."

Dear Heart I have been seeking for so long for that bird. And now I am hearing him, clearer and sweeter is his call each day and if you will kiss the other eye into life, I believe I will see him, and

Tuesday [Friday] morning.

I did not mean to send you a penciled note today, but I was sick last night, and could not write any more. And now Helen is coming and I cannot let her go without a word. So forgive the medium and only know I have worked with you as you worked and felt you welcomed me.

I could not keep back the tears yesterday when my faithful servant brought me those dear flowers. There was no card, but I know *you* sent them to bring me a message you could not speak. They are so exquisite that the very possession of them would give me happiness but when I look into their hearts and find their message they seem warm, living things.　　　　　Edith

ALS (WP, DLC).
1 Her residence.

To Albert Bushnell Hart

My dear Professor Hart: [The White House] May 21, 1915

I thank you most warmly for your generous letter of May fifteenth. It has given me the deepest gratification.[1] It has certainly been splendid the way in which the country has stood back of the administration in this trying time, but it is only one more illustration of what the temper of America always is when challenged by a great situation.

I heartily agree with you that the talk about lack of loyalty on the part of American citizens of German blood and extraction has been a grand libel. I feel confident that we could completely count on them.

Cordially and sincerely yours,   Woodrow Wilson

TLS (Letterpress Books, WP, DLC).
[1] It is missing.

From Edward Mandell House

[London, May 21, 1915]

Your cable of yesterday is just received. I had lunch with Sir Edward Grey and he understands the point you make. I do not think it can be misunderstood in Germany. Sir Edward Grey has talked with the present cabinet ministers and with opposition members that are to come in, and he says in his opinion this government will now consider the suggestion you made to both England and Germany in your note of February 22, provided some additions be made to cover poisonous gas. There is no question as to bargaining, I think, as far as we are concerned. That is a matter between England and Germany, in which we are using our good offices. If successful it will close our contentions with both nations. It looks as if it might be successful if Germany consents to make the proposal. I would suggest it be now unofficially and confidentially taken up with Gerard from Washington. Gerard could then make it clear to the German government, as I have to the British government, that you in no way concede any of our rights in the premises.   Edward House.

T transcript of WWsh decode (WC, NjP) of T telegram (WP, DLC).

From Melancthon Williams Jacobus

My dear President Wilson: Hartford, Conn. May 21st, 1915

I have waited until your return to Washington and the flood of congratulations on your note to Germany had passed over your desk to add my word of praise for the statesmanship of that paper.

Of all that you have given to the world in these months since the war began, this is the greatest thing.

It is small wonder that you find behind you a calmly but proudly loyal people. The notes you may yet have to write before this matter is settled may bring us nearer to war, but they will not take us farther from you.

One thing has interested me in the talk of the people since the murderous attack upon the Lusitania's passengers: When your policy in the case of Mexico was disclosed the cry was raised, Why insist upon humanity in international relations! Now the same people are saying, How is humanity to be ignored in international relations!

To me it is a real satisfaction to see the idealism of your policy which was criticized then, commended now and I cannot but believe that your fellow countrymen are recognizing, in an unquestioned way, that your idea of what should constitute this Nation's relations with other Nations has been from the beginning as wise and noble as it has been consistent

May God give you heart and mind for whatever steps may yet have to be taken.

Yours devotedly   Melancthon W. Jacobus

ALS (WP, DLC).

From Thomas Nelson Page

Confidential

My dear Mr. President: Rome May 21, 1915

My telegrams will have given you all the important facts in skeleton; but I hope you will not mind my sending you such full letters.

Yesterday afternoon the Chamber of Deputies confided substantially plenary powers as to credits and everything else necessary to conduct the war, to the Ministry by a vote of 407 to 74. This about settles the matter, although the Senate has to vote on the proposition this afternoon, and although there is one chance, —how great I do not know,—that the Allies may ask so much of Italy in the way of sending troops to the Dardanelles or Egypt that matters may drag along until something occurs which may change the present status and open a way for new negotiations between Italy and Austria. In fact, although Italy has announced to Austria that she considers the Treaty with her at an end, the Treaty still holds undenounced between Italy and Germany. It hardly looks as though Austria or Germany would declare war on Italy. It seems evident that they will pursue a policy which will eventually lead to Italy being the first to make the breach.

A week or more ago it was intimated to us that Austria would, in the event of war with Italy, ask us to take charge of her interests. It was in fact longer ago than that. A week ago, however, I learned that Germany had requested Switzerland to look after her interests in the event of hostilities, and I have not believed since then that Austria would come to us.

This morning a Secretary of the latter Embassy came to see one of our secretaries whom he knows well and through whom the first intimation referred to came to me, and explained that owing to certain inconveniences which would result if the Austrian Embassy attached to the Vatican should confide its interests to Spain, while the Embassy attached to the Quirinal should confide their interests to us, they had decided to ask Spain to take over the latter's interests also.

He however confidentially admitted that another reason had arisen since the first conversation and that in fact it was the present relations between Germany and America which led them to fear some complication might arise should we have charge of their interests.

I have just had an interesting talk with a gentleman who has returned but now from Austria, where he was visiting an old friend of his, the editor of one of the Austrian papers. He is a lawyer of high standing in Chicago and a man of great intelligence, and I believe pretty clear-eyed. His name is Henry I. Furber, junior,[1] and he left Vienna only last Sunday.

He states that the Austrian people have been kept by the strict censorship completely in the dark as to the actual situation. He also understands that this is the case in Germany. He received a strong impression that they felt in Austria, and he understood it to be the same case in Germany, that if Italy should make war, Germany and Austria could not win, especially as it appears probable, that in this contingency Roumania and Greece also will enter the field.

He also has received this impression: That Germany considers that the United States would not be able,—even should a rupture occur between her and the United States, to do Germany any very great actual damage, at least, within the next six or eight months, and that she is quite ready to make a stand on the question of furnishing arms and munitions of war to Great Britain, believing that within the next six months or so, in which, as I say, she thinks America cannot injure her very much, she can do England & France more damage, through the cessation of the supplies of munitions of war from America, and will then have an opportunity to say to the German people that her plans failed because the whole world arrayed itself against her out of jealousy. Thus, she will be able to satisfy her people that her policy should have won and that she has really won the greatest glory, even though she was eventually forced to make peace.

This opinion is so much in accord with an opinion which I have myself formed from talking with others and from my reading that I am the more inclined to accept it as sound.

At least, I feel that Germany is so angry—on one side, and on the other feels so secure from immediate injury in the way of invasion that she will probably incline rather to increase her attitude of defiance than to consent to make reparation and cease from them.

Of one thing I am almost certain,—I try not to be too certain of anything,—that she has it in her mind to have a settlement with us in the future, and it may be in the not-distant future, and that this is an intention of much longer standing than the duration of this war, although she has inflamed her people against us since the war began by the argument of our furnishing war-materials to her enemies.

With regard to Roumania and Greece going in—to which I have alluded above, the present situation seems to rest on the point whether the Allies will, after the war, consent to such accession of territory on the part of those two countries as will satisfy them. Greece seems to have her heart set on the acquisition of certain territory, including Smyrna and its hinterland and Italy is said also to have aspirations in that direction,—at least, in the direction of the hinterland; while the division of Macedonia is a sort of apple of discord, and no one yet knows what the Allies will agree to with regard to its award.

I think it very likely, however, that all of these countries will go into the war if Italy goes in, and that Bulgaria will do so likewise if the Allies succeed in their enterprise along the Dardanelles.

I am, my dear Mr. President,

Always sincerely yours,   Thos. Nelson Page

TLS (WP, DLC).
1 Henry Jewett Furber, Jr.

From Frank Irving Cobb

Dear Mr. President: New York. May Twenty First [1915].

This information is submitted to you for whatever it may be worth.

Last night I dined with Captain [Franz] von Papen, the military attaché of the German Embassy, who is also a member of the German General Staff. He is a very intelligent and a very sane man.

His opinion of German diplomacy does not differ materially from our opinion. He has been much disturbed by the tense relations between the United States and Germany and is more than anxious that there shall be no break. He told me that he had been in direct communication with the German General Staff, making a personal appeal that the sentiment of the American people in this matter should not be misunderstood and that the Staff should use its influence with the Government. He told me further that he had reason to believe that the desire was increasing to conciliate the United States in the matter of submarine warfare. He added further that it was very possible that the German proposals would hold out an opportunity for the President of the United States again to offer his friendly offices in the way of mediation. I judged from what he said that they take the Italian situation with the utmost seriousness and believe that the beginning of the end has been reached. I am violating no confidence on his part in telling you this because he seemed to express a desire to have you know that a mediation proposal might be made and expressed his regret that the means of communication between the German Embassy and the United States Government were so unsatisfactory and inadequate from his point of view.   Sincerely yours,   Frank I. Cobb.

TLS (WP, DLC).

Two Letters to Edith Bolling Galt

[The White House] Friday morning,
My adorable sweetheart,   7.30   21 May [1915]

How hard, how *very* hard it has been to be separated from you and not to know what you were thinking about! I do not know when I have been so absolutely *tired out* as I was last night, but I went to bed at nine and have had nearly ten hours rest, so that I am renewed this morning. I hope you slept again as you did on the boat. The truth is that I have been under a terrible strain since a certain never-to-be-forgotten Tuesday night while a certain lady I deeply and tenderly love has been finding herself. She has not found herself yet and my heart still waits to live with a free breath until she comes to it with all her woman's heart in complete acceptance—as she will some day do if she is true to herself. But I am not impatient. I am willing to wait for a joy that will bring life more abundantly. For the joy of winning her complete love (in which there is no self to slay) will make every day of my life that follows full of a new power and zest and ease of action. For, oh, she is *so* sweet a spirit, so adorable a companion, so rewarding a comrade! The light that shines in her eyes—those deep, steady eyes that are always yielding something new out of their depths—is the light of everything I love and can draw strength and joy from. How I would love to draw inspiration from them to-day and kiss their lids for seal of my love!

Woodrow

[The White House]

My darling,   Friday afternoon 21 May [1915]

Was ever a lover blest with a sweeter love letter than this precious pencilled note dear Helen handed me this forenoon! Bless you for it! My heart aches to think that you were ill when you wrote it. Are you sure that you are all right now? How could I keep away from you if you were to fall ill and need me? *Please* keep well, as you value my peace of mind! Oh, my darling, my darling! You are in a lonely prison, but you are a prisoner no longer, and even with that one dear eye you let me kiss open you are seeing more than you ever saw before. How eager I am to kiss the other open! Those sweet eyes have sometimes seemed to me very tired, as if with their lonely vigil, their straining to see life through the murky darkness around them—and what a pure delight it has been to see the questioning go out of them and the light of love and discovery gleam in them, transforming your whole lovely face. May the loneliness of your little house (I will not call it your home) be now, for you, sweetheart, only a sweet peaceful silence in which to think and comprehend and make love sure of itself. You are right in thinking that I am there. Ah, if you only *could* touch me—if I only *could* take you in my arms and interpret by my kisses my love for you in all that I long to prove it to be!

My hand is tired from golf and will hardly guide the pen right, but I had to scribble these lines to keep from cracking my heart with the unspoken longing. I love you, I love you! I love you!!

Woodrow

How sweet of you to send a message of love, too, you adorable thing!

ALS (WP, DLC).

From Edward Parker Davis

My dear Woodrow,   [Philadelphia] May 22 1915

May I congratulate you on the birth of your granddaughter[1] and that she will bear Mrs. Wilson's name.

May she be like her, and so bring you joy.

Affectionately Yours   E P Davis.

ALS (WP, DLC).
[1] Ellen Wilson McAdoo, born at the McAdoo residence in Washington on May 21.

To Edith Bolling Galt

[The White House]

My darling,   Saturday morning, 22 May [1915]

What a *blissful* evening that was, and how deep the happiness of it sank into my heart,—a deeper, serener happiness than I have ever felt with you before, because I was aware of a new peace in *your* heart! Not once did a shadow of doubt or pain or misgiving pass over your face, but all through the evening it was either wonderful and radiant with love and content or else infinitely sweet with wistful longing,—and, oh, how glad I was, how proud, how full of every thought that gives a man life and the "joy of elevated thoughts." And how inexpressibly I loved and love you, —with what admiration, with what a sense of your ineffable sweetness and brightness! You seem to me a source of light and life. While I sit by you and feel the caress of your gentle touch there seems to go through me a glow and strength as of everything that is fine and inspiriting and charged with joy and reassurance. How shall I I [*sic*] ever be able to tell you what you are, what you have brought me, and how shall I ever be able to give you anything comparable in return! My darling, my darling!

Woodrow

ALS (WP, DLC).

From Edith Bolling Galt

[Washington]

Dearest One: Saturday midnight [May 22, 1915]

I have tried to go to sleep but can't until I have talked to you a little while. It seems horrid to send you another penciled note, but I am in bed and it is so hard to use ink. So please forgive it, one more time.

Your note of early this morning fulfilled its mission, if it was meant to bring me happiness, and I hope you did not miss my answer too much. It was just one of those days when my thoughts went too fast to admit of writing them. If we had been together I think I could have talked to you for hours but I simply *could* not write and I knew you would understand.

It seems so marvelously sweet that you knew early this morning, when you were writing, that I needed you today in tonic form. I needed to be loved, but in just the way you found—the way that made me feel you found in me what you need.

I told Helen this morning how incapable I am these past two weeks of doing anything, even the every day duties go unattended to. And therefore to have you say I reinforce you and give zest and inspiration to your work filled me with deep joy. Please, dearest heart, don't worry over my being sick. I do "value your peace of mind" entirely too much to do anything to disturb it, and I am sure I am going to be well.

I don't know why, but last night I could not concentrate when we were riding, and felt when I came home that you had been disappointed. There were so many things I wanted to ask you, but it seemed impossible to do more than just drink in the beauty of the night, feeling you were with me, and there was no need of speech. Did you see the wonderful sunset tonight? It was one of the most exquisite things I have ever seen. A perfect flood of gold breaking through black, angry clouds.

Then it changed, and a soft pink tone ran through the black, and suddenly the earth was transformed, for a radiant light like an Alpine glow spread over it, and the black clouds were gone, and seemed now only part of temples and spires of gold as they massed themselves in the glory of the light.

Goodnight, and God keep you.   Edith.

Sunday, May 23/1915

I have just waked and tried for a minute to readjust myself, for I was dreaming, and it was last Sunday, and I was asleep on the sofa and you were beside me in the big chair and just as

I wake[d] you were bending over me and I found your dear arm was my pillow, and you were saying, in that wonderful voice I love so, "Don't be frightened, I am here"

ALS (WP, DLC).

To William Jennings Bryan

My dear Mr. Secretary,   The White House. 23 May, 1915.

Here is at last a message from House (which I finished deciphering last last [sic] evening) which seems to afford a gleam of hope.

In compliance with its suggestion, I have prepared a despatch to Gerard. If you approve of it, I hope that you will have it sent at once to-day, since time would seem to be of the essence.

At the same time will you not take extraordinary precautions to keep all of this within the narrowest possible confidential circle and *prevent a leak at any cost*! I shall myself speak of it to absolutely nobody.

                              Faithfully Yours,   W.W.

From HOUSE, London May 21st.

"Sir Edward Grey has talked with the present cabinet ministers and with the opposition members that are to come in and he says in his opinion this government will now consider the suggestion you made to both Germany and England in your note of February twenty-second, provided some additions to cover poisonous gas. There is no question as to bargaining, I think, as far as we are concerned. That is a matter between England and Germany in which we are using our good offices. If successful it will close our contentions with both nations. It looks as if it might be successful if Germany consents to make the proposal. I would suggest it be now unofficially and confidentially taken up with Gerard from Washington. Gerard could then make it clear to the German government, as I have to the British Government, that you in no way concede any of our rights in the premises."

The above needs this explanation: House had intimated to me in an earlier despatch what he found Sir Edward Grey's views and disposition in this matter to be, and I had asked him to find out how far Sir Edward would be supported in those views. Then came his request that you send the message to Gerard about which you wrote me, asking for delay in the German reply to our recent note. I had heard from House to the same effect when I was in New York. I hastened to cable him that he must take pains to make it very clear indeed, not only in London but also in all that he said to Gerard, that we were proposing no bargaining, so far as our rights were concerned; that what England did to Germany or Germany to England did not release either of them from any part of their obligation to respect our rights.

This will make clear, I hope, the reference in the above.

W.W.

WWTLI (CLO).

To James Watson Gerard

The White House [May 23, 1915].

Despatches from House in London give us reason to hope that the new British ministry will be willing now to consider the proposals which we submitted to the governments of Germany and Great Britain in our identic note of February twenty-second last, if the German government will renew the proposals either through us or in any way it may prefer and will now include in its proposals a mutual agreement to discontinue the use of poisonous gases. Please take this up unofficially and very confidentially with the German foreign office but be careful at the same time to make it perfectly clear that while this action on the part of the German government if it lead to successful results would practically clear away the difficult questions now under discussion between ourselves and them we are conveying this information and making this suggestion only as the sincere common friend of Germany and England desirous of rendering any service to them and not as if we for a moment suggested a bargain or compromise with regard to our own rights upon the seas or were willing to make those rights contingent upon what England and Germany might agree upon. No matter what England does to Germany or Germany to England our rights are unaltered and we cannot abate them in the least. They cannot depend upon any circumstances of the war which do not by recognized international law constitute a necessary limitation. You will know how to make this clear at the same time that our services are most cordially offered and it is made evident that the adoption of this suggestion would furnish a happy way of clearing the field.[1]

WWT telegram (SDR, RG 59, 763.72/1500A, DNA).
[1] There is a WWsh draft of this telegram in WP, DLC.

To Edward Mandell House

[The White House, May 23, 1915]

Your cable of the 21st received. I have acted on your suggestion and have sent instructions to Gerard, though with some apprehension that it make the impression in Berlin of partial relaxation or unsteadiness in the firm tone of our recent note. In your conversation with Sir Edward Grey, please make it plain that it is not foodstuffs merely in which we are interested, but in all noncontraband shipments to neutral ports, and that the purchase of our cotton, illegally intercepted, does not help matters because it is the right and not the money we must insist upon. We feel that the blockade recently proclaimed has not been made in fact effective, and the impression prevails here that Sir Edward has not been able to fulfill assurances given us at the time of the Order in Council that the Order would not be carried out in such a way as to defeat our essential rights. There is accumulating public opinion here upon this matter which I think the ministers there should know, and the recent explanations do not touch the essentials or meet the opinion.   Wilson.

T transcript of WWsh telegram (WC, NjP).

To William Jennings Bryan

My dear Mr. Secretary,   The White House. 23 May, 1915.

As I said over the telephone, I think it would be unwise to give Garza too strong an impression of our personal approval.[1] I would suggest the following:

The statement made by General Garza is both important and significant. This Government welcomes every suggestion looking toward a unification of revolutionary factions and a union of patriotic men to put an end to bloodshed and anarchy, and hopes that you will in its name lend your encouragement to such views and purposes whenever you can do so with propriety.

I am very much disturbed about the condition of the people in Mexico City. I agree with you that it ought to be easy to obtain the most generous assistance from our people. Would it not be well for you to have a conference with Miss Boardman about it?
Faithfully Yours,   W.W.

WWTLI (W. J. Bryan Papers, DNA).
[1] J. M. Cardoso de Oliveira to WJB, May 21, 1915, FR 1915, pp. 690-691, which reported on Garza's speech to the Aguascalientes Convention on May 20. After

explaining the dire conditions in Mexico City and threatening to resign if his ministerial appointments were not confirmed by the Convention, Garza made "a warm appeal for the unification of all revolutionary parties including the Carrancistas to save the country and form a stable government saying that it was time for the army to give up fighting and go to work."

To Nancy Saunders Toy

My dear Friend,   The White House 23 May, 1915.

Helen has just given me your letter of the twentieth to her to read. How grateful we are for such letters, full of affection and of the things that we ought to know to keep us in heart, we shall never be able to tell you adequately. The only thing we have to quarrel with is that you should think for a moment that your letters give us anything but comfort and delight. And dear little Helen! If you could know how genuinely she admires you, how her face brightens when one of those letters comes, and how bitterly she chides herself because of her failure to answer them and the appearance of indifference that failure must wear, you would never doubt her! The plain fact is, that there are too many things for her to do in this complicated life of ours here to leave room for the things she *wants* to do. She foregoes all her private affairs and interests and desires to serve us all with unwearied love and loyalty. So you must understand, and be sure that she will write, and write with her heart in the writing, when she has a breathing time,—when, for example, she has acknowledged and replied to the messages now pouring in to Nell on the birth of her little daughter (for she has insisted on volunteering for that, among other things!). She sends her love, but does not know that I am sending her explanation.

Nell's baby is one of the most individual and engaging pieces of tiny humanity I ever saw, and I do not think that it is my partiality that dictates the verdict. She has touched and delighted me very deeply by naming it Ellen Wilson. And both mother and child are doing famously; have had no trouble at all from the first, which makes us additionally happy.

We are all well. That our domestic annals are quiet and happy is evidenced by the fact that there is nothing to chronicle about them. As for the public circumstances of the moment, I hardly know how to put my feelings into words. Of course it goes without saying that I am deeply touched and rewarded above my desert by the extraordinary and generous support the whole country has given me in this German matter; but you will understand when I say that the very completeness and generous fullness of the trust for the time reposed in me increases my sense of over-whelming responsibility,—and of a sort of inevitable loneliness; and that for a man like myself, who by no means implicitly trusts his own judgments, the burden of affairs is added to, not sub-tracted from, by such confidence. I know, moreover, that I may have to sacrifice it all any day, if my conscience leads one way and the popular verdict the other.

All join me in affectionate messages.

Your grateful friend,   Woodrow Wilson

WWTLS (WP, DLC).

To Lucy Marshall Smith

Dear Cousin Lucy,   The White House 23 May, 1915.

It was very, very sweet of you to write as you did,[1] and you do not know how much good it did me. We think and speak of you constantly, and know that you are thinking of us, but that does not make your messages of affection the less welcome and delightful, necessary to our content. For it is such understanding affection. It is the sort of affection that keeps the heart warm and creates a sense of companionship that makes hard days easier. I think I depend for strength amidst my tasks more on that sort of affection than on anything else in the world.

It is hard to think that we shall have to wait until September to see you: and who can tell whether I shall myself be able to be in Cornish in September or not? Who can predict anything, indeed, in this mad world? I feel that I dare not expect what a day will bring forth: for we are dealing with passion on the other side of the water, not with reason.

It is very delightful to me to hear praise of what I have done from those I love. I know that all the other praise is ephemeral: that it may turn into bitter censure to-morrow: that there is nothing to tie to or live on in popular approval: and I know that I must hold myself ready to do the right thing at the immediate sacrifice of it all, if the occasion should arise. And so you can imagine how I value the things I can count on through thick and thin.

We are all very happy over dear Nell's baby. She is really one of the most lovely and (already) charming little pieces of humanity I ever saw. Nell has named her Ellen Wilson, which has touched and delighted me very much. Everyt[h]ing is going perfectly with both mother and child, and has gone so from the first. Is it not fine? I know that Nell (and the baby) would send love if they knew I was writing, as do all of us, and a great deal of it.   Your devoted friend,   Woodrow Wilson

WWTLS (photostat in RSB Coll., DLC).
  1 Lucy M. Smith to WW [April 24, 1915], ALS (WP, DLC).

To Mary Allen Hulbert

Dearest Friend,   The White House 23 May, 1915.

I am startled to find on referring to your note that your address is to be Hot Springs only until to-day, the twenty-third. I had hoped that you would have a much longer rest there. Maybe they will keep you, in spite of yourself, and that this will be forwarded to you is my sincere hope. For what you need is the presence of friends to comfort and interest you, and rest, a great deal of healing rest. How I wish it were of any use to beg you to stop over here; but I know only too well what would happen, so far as I am selfishly concerned, and that is, that I would see you only at meals. For I am, during these distracted days, my own master only then,—if then. For we are dealing with passion on the other side of the water, not with reason. Nothing is calculable. One never knows what the next despatch will contain, or what a day or an hour will bring forth. And when anything does happen, it generally appears that it must be met at once, at the very hour one gets word of it. I ought at this moment to be at work on the answers to certain despatches which are only less clamorous for an answer than the most pressing, and I will probably have to pay for the indulgence of these few minutes of chat with you by sitting up till unseemly hours to do the postponed work.

The public news about us you of course know, and you probably know also our new happiness, in the birth of a little daughter to Nell day before yesterday. She has touched and delighted me very deeply by naming her Ellen Wilson; and the sweet little mite promises to be almost lovely enough to wear the name as it ought to be worn. I never before saw so minute a piece of humanity with so much individuality or so much charm. But I speak as a doting grandfather, and my testimony ought of course to be excluded. Both mother and daughter are doing as well as civilized mother and child ever can do; and that, too, makes us happy. Nell is so close to me, the tie between us so intimate and dear, that her baby must of course engage my special affection. It is deeply delightful to see her happiness. She is a wonderful young person, in my humble opinion.

I am the more sorry that you are leaving the Springs so soon because your note had in it that note of deep enjoyment of the country and of the freshness of Spring that I have learned to associate with your moments of refreshment and genuine recuperation, and I could wish that those moments might last a long, long time.

I must go to my tasks before it grows too late. All join me in affectionate messages. May the way clear before you, and before Allen, more and more. You deserve a time of real quiet and freedom from anxious care. You are so brave, so splendidly indomitable!

Your devoted friend,   Woodrow Wilson

WWTLS (WP, DLC).

To Edith Bolling Galt

[The White House]
Sunday afternoon 23 May [1915]

What is it, dear Heart? Is anything the matter? Do you *wish* to be left to silence and your own thoughts? I confess I feel embarrassed and fear to intrude. My heart is very lonely, but I loyally "wait upon the hour and time of your desire." I love you with a tenderness and devotion that are without limit. You need never fear what I am thinking   Woodrow.

ALS (WP, DLC).

From Edith Bolling Galt

[Washington]
Dearest Heart: Sunday, 6.45 [May 23, 1915]

There is nothing the matter, only I am missing you and cannot let you know if you don't feel and know it already.

I have just come in and found your note. Please don't be lonely, for I am always near.   Edith

ALS (WP, DLC).

From Edith Bolling Galt, with Enclosure

[Washington] Sunday night
Dearest,   8.45 May 23rd/1915

What do you suppose I have been doing since that minute, an hour and three quarters ago, when I saw you? (*How* I wanted to tell you to come and go 'round the Potomac Drive with me, and watch the sunset, and forget you had been lonely, forget everything Woodrow but the wonderful thing that we were together, and that I love you, and am prouder every day that you love me.)

That is an awfully long parenthesis isn't it? So, back to my first question.

Well, I have been *reading* about you, and this is the way the article ends.

"Mr Wilson is one of the most human and delightful of men, one in whom a fresh and sunny humor is of the essence of his nature, and *whose capacity for emotion is so great that it has to be vigi[l]antly suppressed.*"[1]

Do you know what it means to me to feel that such emotion has been caused by my humble and unworthy self as to make you "feel embarrassed and fear to intrude"

Bless your precious heart for the last lines—"I love you with a tenderness and devotion that are without limit. You need never fear what I am thinking."

It seems you are casting out all fear and I am living in a new world, which is bounded on the north, south, east and west by Woodrow Wilson! And the queerest part of the whole thing is that I like this new world, and feel *at home* in it.

And want neither to enlarge my borders nor annex any other country, content, where you are king!   Edith

P.S. The enclosed clipping from a letter I got yesterday from a good friend of mine, who is admirable in every way, save in being a Yankee and a Republican, pleased me, and I believe it will you. I *am so proud* of you!!

ALS (WP, DLC).

[1] Sydney Brooks, "President Wilson," London *Outlook*, XXXV (March 6, 1915), 298-99. For a summary of this article, see EMH to WW, March 5, 1915, n. 3, Vol. 32. Mrs. Galt was probably reading the reprint of the article in *The Living Age*, CCLXXXV (April 3, 1915), 56-58. She considerably condensed the sentence which she here quoted.

E N C L O S U R E

I say "*Mr* President" We did not consider him thus until he had managed the Lusitania scrape so splendidly. And then tho' we have taken the N. Y. Herald for years and years, we gave it up, after the first day they were so disloyal to him.

Hw MS (WP, DLC).

A Welcome to the Pan-American Financial Conference[1]

[May 24, 1915]

Mr. Chairman,[2] gentlemen of the American republics, ladies and gentlemen: The part that falls to me this morning is a very simple one, but a very delightful one. It is to bid you a very hearty welcome, indeed, to this conference. The welcome is the more hearty because we are convinced that a conference like this will result in the things that we most desire. I am sure that those who have this conference in charge have already made plain to you its purpose and its spirit. Its purpose is to draw the American republics together by bonds of common interest and of mutual understanding; and we comprehend, I hope, just what the meaning of that is. There can be no sort of union of interest if there is a purpose of exploitation by any one of the parties to a great conference of this sort. The basis of successful commercial intercourse is common interest, not selfish interest. It is an actual interchange of services and of values; it is based upon reciprocal relations and not selfish relations. It is based upon those things upon which all successful economic intercourse must be based, because selfishness breeds suspicion; suspicion, hostility; and hostility, failure. We are not, therefore, trying to make use of each other, but we are trying to be of use to one another.

It is very surprising to me, it is even a source of mortification, that a conference like this should have been so long delayed, that it should never have occurred before, that it should have required a crisis of the world to show the Americas how truly they were neighbors to one another. If there is any one happy circumstance, gentlemen, arising out of the present distressing condition of the world, it is that it has revealed us to one another: it has shown us what it means to be neighbors. And I cannot help harboring the hope, the very high hope, that, by this commerce of minds with one another, as well as commerce in goods, we may show the world in part the path to peace. It would be a very great thing if the Americas could add to the distinction, which they already wear, this of showing the way to peace, to permanent peace.

The way to peace for us, at any rate, is manifest. It is the kind of rivalry which does not involve aggression. It is the knowledge that men can be of the greatest service to one another, and nations of the greatest service to one another, when the jealousy between them is merely a jealousy of excellence, and when the basis of their intercourse is friendship. There is only one way in which we wish to take advantage of you, and that is by making better goods, by doing the things that we seek to do for each other better, if we can, than you do them, and so spurring you on, if we might, by so handsome a jealousy as that to excel us. I am so keenly aware that the basis of personal friendship is this competition in excellence that I am perfectly certain that this is the only basis for the friendship of nations—this handsome rivalry, this rivalry in which there is no dislike, this rivalry in which there is nothing but the hope of a common elevation in great enterprises which we can undertake in common.

There is one thing that stands in our way, among others—for you are more conversant with the circumstances than I am. The thing I have chiefly in mind is the physical lack of means of communication—the lack of vehicles, the lack of ships, the lack of established routes of trade, the lack of those things which are absolutely necessary if we are to have true commercial and intimate commercial relations with one another. And I am perfectly clear in my judgment that if private capital cannot soon enter upon the adventure of establishing these physical means of communication, the government must undertake to do so. We cannot indefinitely stand apart and need each other for the lack of what can easily be supplied, and, if one instrumentality cannot supply it, then another must be found which will supply it. We cannot know each other unless we see each other; we cannot deal with each other unless we communicate with each other. So soon as we communicate, and are upon a familiar footing of intercourse, we shall understand one another, and the bonds between the Americas will be such bonds that no influence that the world may produce in the future will ever break them.

If I am selfish for America, I at least hope that my selfishness is enlightened. The selfishness that hurts the other party is not enlightened selfishness. If I were acting upon a mere ground of selfishness, I would seek to benefit the other party and so tie him to myself; so that, even if you were to suspect me of selfishness, I hope you will also suspect me of intelligence and of knowing the only safe way for the establishment of the things which we covet, as well as the establishment of the things which we desire and which we would feel honored if we could earn and win.

I have said these things because they will perhaps enable you to understand how far from formal my welcome to this body is. It is a welcome from the heart; it is a welcome from the head; it is a welcome inspired by what I hope are the highest ambitions of those who live in these two great continents, who seek to

set an example to the world in freedom of institutions, freedom of trade, and intelligence of mutual service.[3]

Printed in *Address of the President* . . . *at the Pan American Financial Conference* . . . (Washington, 1916).
    [1] A conference of finance ministers and leading bankers of eighteen nations
of Latin America with officials of the Treasury Department, members of the
Federal Reserve Board and the Federal Trade Commission, other high officials
of the Wilson administration, and selected bankers and business leaders of
the United States, held at the Pan American Union in Washington, May 24-
29, 1915. The object of the conference, organized and presided over by Secretary McAdoo, was to discuss reciprocal trade relations. See *Proceedings of the
First Pan American Financial Conference. . . . Washington, May 24, to 29, 1915*
(Washington, 1915). McAdoo summarized the results of the conference in a
letter transmitting the proceedings to President Wilson, dated September 6,
1915, in *ibid.*, pp. 7-20.
    [2] McAdoo.
    [3] There is a WWsh outline of these remarks, with the composition date of
May 23, 1915, in WP, DLC.

To William Allen White

My dear Mr. White: The White House May 24, 1915

I cannot let your editorial headed "The President"[1] pass without expressing to you my very deep appreciation of its generous
attitude and assuring you that such things go a long way to keep
me in heart and steady my hand.
        Cordially and sincerely yours,   Woodrow Wilson

TLS (W. A. White Papers, DLC).
    [1] *Emporia*, Kansas, *Gazette*, May 13, 1915. This brief editorial urged that all
Americans support President Wilson in the *Lusitania* crisis. "As Americans," it
argued, "we must stand by our President. And so long as we must stand by
him in the end, why not back him up now, why not give him the strength of
our endorsement before he enters the final struggle as well as afterwards?" It
concluded with an eloquent tribute to Wilson:
    "A wise—an exceedingly wise—and brave man sits in the White House. The
greatest crisis that has visited this country since Lincoln's day confronts
President Wilson. A rash word would throw us into war, or force us to retire
from war in shame. We should be devoutly thankful that in this grave hour,
our President is of heroic size, of a great kind heart, and of a calm sagacity
that invites our trust and confidence."

From Edward Mandell House

[London, May 24, 1915]

Gerard cables me as follows: "Zimmermann told me yesterday that Dumba, Austrian Ambassador, had cabled him that
Bryan told him that America was not in earnest about Lusitania
matter."[1] Of course Mr. Bryan did not say that, but I think you
should know what Zimmermann told Gerard.

It is very difficult to communicate with Gerard from here,
and I have sent him nothing since first suggestion. Do you not

think it best for you to handle the matter direct so as to avoid complications? I will see Sir Edward Grey as soon as possible concerning holding up of cargoes, but I would suggest you cable Walter Page also in order to avoid transgressing upon his prerogatives. I think it unwise to show him your communications to me upon this subject.   Edward House.

T transcript of WWsh decode (WC, NjP) of T telegram (WP, DLC).
    1 See WJB to WW, May 17, 1915 and n. 1 thereto. Gerard also telegraphed Bryan about Zimmermann's interpretation of his remarks. Bryan then wrote to Dumba giving his recollection of the conversation and Dumba replied, giving another version of his controversial telegram to Vienna via Berlin. See J. W. Gerard to WJB, May 22, 1915, *FR-WWS 1915*, p. 407; WJB to C. Dumba, May 24, 1915, *FR-LP*, I, 413-14; C. Dumba to WJB, May 24, 1915, *ibid.*, pp. 415-16; WJB to WW, May 24, 1915, *FR-WWS 1915*, pp. 407-408; and WJB to J. W. Gerard, May 24, 1915, *ibid.*, p. 408.

To Edith Bolling Galt

[The White House] Monday morning,
Dear, dear Sweetheart,   7.15 24 May [1915]

Indeed I will pardon the pencil, as many times as you wish to use it. *Any* medium will content me that brings me the words of love my heart waits and longs for and my dear one knows how to utter so exquisitely! It is my longing that must excuse my dullness in not understanding (or, rather, in wondering about) your silence yesterday. You know you have sometimes, my darling, somewhat complicated states of mind, and not both of your eyes have yet been kissed awake! You have not yet completely surrendered to me as I have to you, but have let little queries have harbour in your heart. But letters like this unspeakably sweet one you brought last night reassure me, make me ashamed of my fears, and force me to comprehend.

Why *should* you have "concentrated" on that delightful ride the other night? I did not want you to concentrate: I wanted you to do exactly what you did, give yourself up to the delicious content which I felt was warming your heart as it warmed mine. You were wrong, you dear, in thinking that I was disappointed. Disappointed, indeed! I was happy and content to the core of my heart,—only full, also, of the pain that at last the inevitable moment must come and I must turn away from your lonely door and leave you, my precious one, there. There was no need of speech. Ah, darling, darling, how I wish it *were* again that dear Sunday on the boat and that your dream were true, and my arm actually your pillow while I watched over you!

Edith, my sweetheart, what we need is just to pour our hearts out to each other in these daily messages, without let or reserve. Do that, dearest,—do it always as you have done it in this wonderful letter before me—and my heart will never be sore or lonely, my work never hard, my thoughts never distraught, and the days full of strength and happiness, notwithstanding the infinite yearning for the time when you will be *all* mine, and actually and always by my side.

This note is only an echo of yours, dear; but that is what I want to do: I want to echo the sweet things in your own heart—that is what love is for. I am just begining to see the depths of that great heart and its infinite wealth of love. I do not *believe* that that wealth has any limits, now that it is unlocked and set free to be spent. Spend it without fear, dear One, and we shall both learn to be quiet and happy even while we wait for the sweet consummation of it all. Whenever you think of me cast all fear and questioning out. You are sure of the full love of my whole heart—and I am so proud and happy to give it to you.

Woodrow[1]

ALS (WP, DLC).
[1] There is a WWsh draft of this letter in WP, DLC.

From Edith Bolling Galt

Dearest One: [Washington] May 24, 1915 Monday night

Do you remember last Monday night? The exquisite happiness of finding you had come for us to the Dolphin—the absolute abstraction and forgetting there was *any*one else in the launch but *you*, and the beauty of the ships as we passed them all glorious with light. Oh! it all seems now to have been too ideal to have been real, and, but for the pain that followed, would still seem a dream, a castle in air.

But, with your dear love to comfort and protect me, the pain is growing less, and only the glory of this new happiness seems permanent and tangible.

This is not at all the way I meant to begin my talk with you tonight, my Lord. It was to 'specially tell you how wonderful these exquisite orchids are. I never before had an *entire box* of these lovely things, and I feel indeed like a princess, so rich am I in prodigal lovliness. I wish you could see my room as I write. You would forget it is a prison and mistake it for "my Lady's bower." Shall I tell you a little bit about it, since it can never be blessed with your dear presence?

Well, I have my piano up here, and that is open, with some tiny golden-hearted roses in a vase on the side. Then, there is a big square window with a broad window-seat and lots of cushions, and by this stands my "big chair," where I curl up to think. There is a table by this with a light and some books, and, tonight, there is a wonderful pale mauve orchid there looking like a spirit that had stayed its flight and paused there for a moment. Beyond this is a long couch—on which, I imagine you resting—while I am at my big-business-like looking desk opposite, where I have orchids either side of me to gladden my eyes when I have to turn away from you.

Besides these things the room is made livable by a wood fire, and more books, and a few household gods that I love.

It pleases me to feel you are here, and I find it hard to stay at my desk instead of coming over and kneeling beside you and whispering something you already know. I had to stop here and talk to a man who came to call, and it is now after 12, and I have just time to say goodnight and tell you how thrilled I was this morning when you came in to deliver your address of welcome.

Do you know I had never heard you, except in your first message to Congress, and I was so filled with pride that I had to hold on to myself not to stand right up and shout at the top of my voice—"Isn't he splendid, and don't everyone else seem commonplace compared to him, and *he loves me*, and I adore him." But I didn't, and contented myself by saying it inside, until I almost smothered.

It was splendid when all the audience responded so to you, and especially to watch their enthusiasm when you spoke of the lack of ships, of established routes of trade. No wonder you charm and fascinate me, when you never go astray or touch the wrong note even in a big audience where so many personalities are merged. Was I wrong—please be honest with me and say if I was—when I thought you were looking straight into my eyes, and saying this *one* thing to *me*—"We cannot know each other unless we see each other, we cannot deal with each other unless we communicate with each other: as soon as we do this we shall understand each other, and the bonds between the *Americas* will be such bonds that no influence the world may produce in the future will ever break them"

If I am right in thinking you meant this, partially to me, I salute you *America, the greatest America*, and take my humble place at your feet trusting that the warmth of the *South* will bring a glow to the *North* that will keep its great heart glowing and ex-

panding until the bond between us will be such a bond that
no influence in the future will ever break! Goodnight

Edith.

I hope you did not mind my coming to hear your speech. I
could not help it, and it was what I wanted it to be.   E.B.G.

ALS (WP, DLC).

Remarks at a Press Conference

May 25, 1915.

Mr. President, could you tell us anything about Mr. Duval West's
call on you last night?

> Yes, it was the first chance I had had to see him since he got
> back from Mexico. I had read his written reports, which
> had preceded him, but I just wanted to get some personal
> impressions which you can get only in a conversation. It was
> entirely for information.

Based upon the information received from Mr. West, have you
decided upon any change of policy?

> No.

Did Mr. West suggest the advisability of an embargo on arms and
ammunition?

> No, he did not.

Did he bring to you such reports as have shaken your confidence
in the conduct of the representatives of this government in
Mexico?

> Oh, no.

These questions, Mr. President, are all based on publications this
morning.

> Yes, I judged that they were.

Mr. President, can you give us any information in your own way
as to the relations with England or with the so-called blockade?

> No; that is what the physicians would call a chronic case.

I did not know but that you had some thought or suggestion that
you might care to volunteer.

> No, sir, nothing new.

Is there any information or intimation from Gerard as to when
the German note may be expected?

> No, none at all in this sense, that he has conjectured dif-
> ferent times, so that we are left to make our own conjec-
> tures.

The delay isn't disadvantageous?

> To whom?

I don't mean exactly that. I mean chances for an amicable settlement are increased with delay perhaps—a cooling off.

> I should think it was good to think about anything. But I
> don't know what the causes for the delay are. Of course, we
> can all conjecture—the new circumstances in the war, and
> so on.

Mr. President, Senator Lewis and Mr. Kitchin have suggested
the necessity of an extraordinary session of Congress to be called
in October. Do you share their opinion?

> Well, I hadn't brought my mind to that subject yet.

Mr. President, can you add to the statement of your address of
yesterday regarding the government undertaking lines of shipping communication?

> No; I said that merely to show my interest in a very practical
> aspect of the relations between the two continents.

Mr. President, if you will permit the question to be asked, can you
expect capital to go into foreign shipping with the navigation
laws unamended and the seamen's bill in force?

> I think I can—if they are up to snuff. We have the most dif-
> fident capital in the world.

Perhaps some of the $730,000,000 surplus lying in the banks
might be available for lines of communication?

> I don't know to whom that belongs. I met a banker the
> other day who had the view that deposits were liabilities, not
> assets. It is an old-fashioned view.

Mr. President, as to the development of the shipping situation,
do your ideas on the subject lead to the need of bringing the matter before Congress again at the next session?

> I had already stated what was all my thought at present. In
> answer to the question, I spoke of it yesterday to show that
> we comprehend one of the chief difficulties and know that
> it must be met, but it hadn't taken any new phase in my
> purpose at all.

Has your mind turned to any of the fiscal arrangements of the
United States, such, for instance, as the suggestion of Mr. Lewis,
the issue of $500,000,000 in bonds?

> No, sir, it has not.

Or the repeal of the free sugar provision?

> No, sir.

Mr. President, there has been some talk of reciprocity between
the United States and the South American countries. Have you
been giving that any consideration?

> Reciprocity in what matter?

Tariff, I think.

No, that hasn't assumed any concrete shape.

Does that idea appeal to you, Mr. President?

It hadn't entered my head before, sir. I have been very much absorbed, to tell the truth. I don't know all the things that are being talked about.

These matters with which you have been absorbed, would they be of interest to us?

Yes, sir, they would be if I could talk about them.

T MS (C. L. Swem Coll., NjP).

To Melancthon Williams Jacobus

My dear Friend: The White House May 25, 1915

Again I have to thank you for your generous thought of me and for sending me the kind of message which my heart needs. It was generous, not only, but full of the stuff that gives strength. I thank you with all my heart.

Cordially and faithfully yours,   Woodrow Wilson

TLS (RSB Coll., DLC).

A Telegram and a Letter from Edward Mandell House

[London, May 25, 1915]

I have the following cable from Gerard: "Gave your suggestion to von Jagow this morning. The proposition of permitting the passage of food [in return for] cessation of submarine methods already made and declined. If raw materials are added [matter] can perhaps be arranged. Germany in no need of food."

Of course the conditions they make are impossible. This takes away their contention that the starving of Germany justifies their submarine policy. I think this strengthens your already impregnable position.   Edward House.

T transcript of WWsh decode (WC, NjP) of T telegram (WP, DLC).

Dear Governor: No. 6. London, May 25th, 1915.

The reason I cabled you yesterday to also instruct Page concerning the delayed cargoes, was that he spoke to me concerning your message of some ten days ago in which you requested me to inform Sir Edward Grey unofficially of the situation in America, and also asked me to tell Page.

He showed some little feeling that the instructions were not given him direct. I replied that you wanted it done unofficially, and he said that nine tenths of the things he did were done unofficially.

I am very careful not to openly transgress upon any of his prerogatives, and Sir Edward understands this and aids me in every way possible.

There is nothing new to report here, and it looks as if things might be settling down for a long war. We shall probably be able to tell by the end of July whether it will last through another winter. If this seems apparent, unless you advise otherwise, I shall go home early in August. I want very much to see you and to go over the situation in person. There are so many things that cannot be written, and I think it would be well worth while for me to make the trip even if it is necessary to return within a short time.

There is no doubt that the position you have taken with both Germany and Great Britain is correct, but I feel that our position with the Allies is somewhat different, for we are bound up more or less in their success, and I do not think we should do anything that can possibly be avoided to alienate the good feeling that they now have for us. If we lost their good will we will not be able to figure at all in peace negociations, and we will be sacrificing too much in order to maintain all our commercial rights.

The situation, I know, is most trying and difficult and you have acted with extraordinary patience and good judgment.

Affectionately yours,   E. M. House

TLS (WP, DLC).

From Oswald Garrison Villard

Dear Mr. President: Washington, D.C., May 25, 1915.

I failed to lay stress today[1] upon what seems to me a very significant thing: The German Ambassador's constant saying that if the United States could induce both Great Britain and Germany to make concessions in their conduct of the sea war, an entering wedge would be driven for the beginning of mediation on the larger issues. Speaking today of the Italian plunge into the war he expressed the most earnest wish that somebody could be found now to offer mediation. Of course, he may not be in sufficiently close touch to Berlin to speak for the feeling there, but he has laid so much stress upon this possibility of our mediating *at the present time* that I deem it my duty to bring the matter to your attention for what it is worth.

Sincerely yours,   Oswald Garrison Villard.

TLS (WP, DLC).
   1 Villard had talked with Wilson after the press conference.

From Walter Hines Page

London, May 25, 5 P.M.

2175. Confidential to the Secretary and the President.

Following is in the Secretary's private code. I send the following for your information as an item in my report on broadcast opinions.

There is a feeling in official circles that some sinister influence is at work to cause misunderstandings at Washington of British feeling and action. The English were surprised at such a misunderstanding as occurred at Washington about the dealings of private American interests directly with the British Government about shipping. They had never considered our government a party to these dealings. There are plain intimations that the Chicago packers are, in British opinion, not playing a fair game but are "loading up" the British Government with products that are not marketable here, by taking advantage of the British willingness to buy cargoes rather than permit them to pass through neutral countries to Germany. The official feeling, as I gather it, is strong that German influence and special interests in the United States are pushing to bring about a public demand that a blow having been given to Germany a corresponding blow must now be given to England.

The Foreign Office has lately been more prompt and effective in giving answers to shipping questions than at any previous period in spite of the fundamental disturbance in the makeup of the cabinet and they show a keener appreciation of the need and justice of promptness. I remarked to Sir Edward Grey the other day that this was surely a good time to clean the slate and he almost effusively agreed with me.[1]

My feeling is that Balfour at the Admiralty will attain better for us than Churchill. He is more reasonable, less dictatorial and less vain. This is the most important change in the cabinet where it affects our dealings. I am doing everything possible to hurry action and with better results and better hope than I had awhile ago.   American Ambassador, London.

T telegram (WP, DLC).

¹ Page also wrote to Grey two days later: "I am sorry to be obliged to report to you that the public feeling in the United States about our shipping controversies does not subside. I take the liberty privately to express my opinion that as early an answer as possible to our Note about the Order in Council and the Blockade might have a good effect." WHP to E. Grey, May 27, 1915, TLS (E. Grey Papers, FO 800/85, p. 182, PRO).

To Edith Bolling Galt

[The White House]

My darling,   Tuesday morning, 7 25 May [1915].

You are an adorable lover! I knew you would be the minute you let go. If you were by while I read these dear notes of yours, or were ever to *say* such things to me, I would smother you with kisses for every sentence,—they make me so happy and reveal you as so altogether lovely!

And so you *were* at that meeting yesterday. The moment I entered the room I felt that you were there and my heart was all in a flutter, but I searched the audience in vain for your dear face after I got seated on the platform and could not find you, though I never lost the consciousness that you were there and searched again and again. Where were you sitting? I am sorry you heard so poor a speech—tame, without fire. Somehow I felt confused and could not get my forces mobilized. If I could have seen you it would have given me inspiration—if I could have thought at all of anything but *you*! Ah, Edith, my sweetheart, my darling, how you fill my life and brighten my thought all the day through —and all the night. I am conscious of you all the time, and now that you have given me your love with such largess, like a queen who knows *how* to spend and bless, that consciousness brings serenity and happiness,—longing, of course, oh, *what* longing, but, along with the longing, a confident hope that makes the longing sweet and a source almost of strength. Were ever two lovers disciplined as we are,—held apart not only by extraordinary circumstances but by thoughtful love itself—the love proved and tested by the self-restraint which is our chief pain and yet our chief proof that we are of the patriciate of love and love with a gallantry that is above self-indulgence! Oh, it is hard! I *need* you so. To be with you is the tonic of life and joy to me. But I *know* now that you love me and I keep myself in hand by thoughts of the knightly duty by which I seek to honour you as well as adore you. In all things, my darling, I am your lover,   Woodrow

ALS (WP, DLC).

To Edward Mandell House

[The White House, May 26, 1915]

The amazing misrepresentation about Bryan had already been corrected by cable to Gerard before your message of the 24th reached me.

Your suggestion that I cable Walter Page also instructions about the interferences of the British government with neutral trade is wise, but there are two serious difficulties. [First, I hoped] to influence the matter unofficially and avoid the strong note that must otherwise be sent, and, second, I am afraid of constant and hopeless leaks in the State Department.

Will you not explain this to Page and ask him for me whether he will not act also in presenting to Sir Edward Grey the many arguments for respecting our rights upon the seas and avoiding the perhaps serious friction between the two governments which it is becoming daily more and more evident cannot much longer be avoided if our access to neutral ports with neutral cargoes continues to be interfered with contrary to the assurances given us in Sir Edward Grey's note accompanying the Order in Council.   Wilson[1]

T transcript of WWsh telegram (WC, NjP).
[1] There is a WWT encode of this telegram in WP, DLC.

To Oswald Garrison Villard

Personal.

My dear Mr. Villard: The White House May 26, 1915

I thank you sincerely for your letter of yesterday.

My fear is, and the fear is based upon several experiences, that the German Ambassador is not in close enough touch with his government at home to be a safe guide as to their feeling or as to the possibilities of the situation. I am keeping in as close touch as possible with Berlin through other media and I can assure you am watching with eagerness for any chance for intervention of any kind which would bring about what we all so deeply and earnestly desire.

Cordially and sincerely yours,   Woodrow Wilson

TLS (O. G. Villard Papers, MH).

From William Jennings Bryan

My dear Mr. President: Washington May 26, 1915.

I have talked with Miss Boardman in regard to relief in Mexico. She says the Red Cross will be glad to take the matter up when assured that the contributions can reach the needy non-combatants. She suggests that the work would be very much aided by a public appeal from you and that the appeal should ask for contributions in foodstuffs as well as contributions in money. She says that many would give foodstuffs who would not give money and that when the matter is taken up for action the Red Cross will arrange in Galveston for a storehouse to which contributions can be shipped and will then take up with the War Department the matter of conveying the food by transport. It might be well to include this in the statement which you have in mind if you finally decide to make it. The information which we have from Mexico indicates that there is real distress in different parts of the country.

With assurances of high respect I am, my dear Mr. President,
Yours very sincerely,   W. J. Bryan

TLS (W. J. Bryan Papers, DNA).

From Franklin Knight Lane, with Enclosures

Dear Mr. President,   Washington [c. May 26, 1915]

Here is the result of two talks with Iturbide[1] & Snyman.[2] I believe absolutely in Iturbide's honesty, and his independence of Huerta & Co.

I have told them nothing of our concern nor even said that I would take the matter up with you.
Respectfully   Franklin K. Lane

ALS (WP, DLC).
[1] About Eduardo Iturbide, his counterrevolutionary plans, and the support that he enjoyed in high American and administration circles, see Link, *Struggle for Neutrality*, pp. 470-478.
[2] W. D. Snyman, former general in the Boer army, who fled to the United States and later to Mexico at the conclusion of the Boer War.

E N C L O S U R E   I

MEMORANDUM.   Washington May 26, 1915.

I have had a talk with General Snyman. He tells me that he has kept out of all intrigues in Mexico and has had nothing to do whatever with politics, nor contributed in any way to any fac-

tion. Things now, however, have come to a pass where he is willing to throw his lot with General Iturbide and try to restore order
in Mexico, but he will not do this under any other leader. He has
perfect and complete confidence in Iturbide's honesty and his
patriotism. He says that Iturbide is the one asset that Mexico
really has. He is the one man who stands out as a leader in whom
all have confidence, both for his courage and his patriotism. General Huerta has made several overtures to him. Iturbide has refused to see him or have anything whatever to do with his representatives. General Snyman says that he knows several of the
Federal Generals who have attempted on Huerta's behalf to
reach Iturbide, and Iturbide has said "I know those men to be
crooked, and I will not speak to them or have anything to do with
them." He says that Oscar Branniff,[1] who was a wealthy man, has
had nothing whatever to do with politics and holds no Mexican
concessions, and that he, General Snyman himself, induced
Branniff to join with Iturbide. Up to that time Branniff had no
notion whatever of going in to any movement on behalf of
Mexico.

I asked General Snyman what it was necessary to do to insure
Iturbide's success, and his reply was: "Nothing, excepting not to
interfere with him; let him raise his money and his men.
Iturbide's name has greater power among all classes in Mexico
than that of any other man, because all know him to be honest."

General Snyman says that nothing is needed to conquer
Mexico excepting money and food. All the men necessary can be
had and are all ready, but food must be brought in and should
be taken in under the protection of a force that will see it
distributed to the people themselves, or otherwise the armies of
Villa and Obregon would get it. General Snyman has no opinion
of Villa. He regards him as a murderous, thieving brigand. He
has much better opinion of Carranza, but he thinks that Carranza
has no strength and will not be able to stand up against Obregon
if Obregon should succeed, and he prophesies that they would
break. He is very emphatic upon the proposition that this Government need do nothing whatever; that the necessary money can
be raised. I said "Would it be enough if I said to you you won't be
interfered with?" and he said "Yes, that's all." General Iturbide,
he says, feels bound to make no move whatever toward the borrowing of money or anything else until he is satisfied that what
he may do will not be objectionable to this Government. Snyman
says that he has heard General Iturbide say this repeatedly to
those men with whom he has been in conference.

[1] He is identified in the next enclosure.

E N C L O S U R E   I I

MEMORANDUM.   Washington May 25, 1915.

I have had a talk with General Iturbide. He has no definite scheme of financing his enterprise, but thinks from talks that he has had with some bankers in New York that the money could be raised in two ways: first, by mortgaging his real estate and the real estate of those who are with him, which, he says, they are perfectly willing to do; second, by American bankers asking loans from those who are interested in Mexican property. I pointed out to him the danger in the second suggestion; that the oil interests, for instance, might be willing to put up money for an enterprise of this kind, but that this would bind him to a recognition of their claims, even though such claims were based upon alleged grants made by Huerta. His answer was that he would not accept any money from those who had Huerta claims but only from those who had genuine properties, such as mines, or mills, or lands, or stocks in Mexican railways. Nor would he consent to do more than pay a reasonable rate of interest, perhaps eight or nine percent, for the money. However, the whole scheme of financing has not been thought out, nor any effort made to raise money, because it was first regarded as necessary to learn whether such a scheme as proposed was practicable.

He would grant universal amnesty and call upon all, no matter of what faction, to join in the restoration of order. He says that the people no longer care for faction and have lost their enthusiasm even for such ideals as they have because of their terrible condition of hunger. Villa cannot hold his people because he has no money excepting his own personal fortune, which he thinks will not be spent to care for the people. Carranza, on the other hand, has money gained through the sale of sisal in Yucatan.

Bonilla[1] has not been seen. He is in Chihuahua and is ranked as a Villaista. Of course, Bonilla would have to be brought out of Chihuahua before the announcement was made that he would lead a movement for the restoration of the Madero regime. If Bonilla would not accept, General Iturbide thinks some of the other ministers would, but there are objections to some of the others. His theory is that the movement should proceed upon the assumption that Huerta never was legally the President, and that none of his acts should be recognized, but that order should be restored today upon the basis of the conditions that existed when Madero was killed.

[1] Manuel Bonilla, Minister of Communications and later of Agriculture in Madero's cabinet.

The men who are working on the committee with General Iturbide arc these:

Oscar Branniff, who lives in the City of Mexico and is a farmer and banker. His father was an American.

Manuel Calero, who was Minister of Justice and Foreign Affairs and Ambassador to the United States under Madero.

Flores Magon, who was Secretary of the Interior under Madero.

Calero and Magon are both lawyers in the City of Mexico. None of these three men have been identified either with Huerta, Carranza or Villa.

The forces which General Iturbide claims are already committed to his cause are scattered throughout the nation; 5,000 in Yucatan, 8,000 in Oaxaca, 5,000 in Mochoacan, and 10,000 in the border states of Nuevo Leon and Coahuila.

Argunedo,[2] who was formerly the Governor of Yucatan under Carranza, and now deposed by Carranza, has 10,000 arms interned in Yucatan. He is now in New York and has a ship at his disposal. He was ousted by Carranza, as he claims, so that Carranza could have a more pliable and more serviceable Governor. General Irtubide [Iturbide] says that there would be no lack of men if they could enter Mexico with food, and this is true as to officers as well as men, if they could be protected; that the word he gets from the followers of Villa is that they will desert.

The plan anticipates the restoration of the Government of Madero as far as is possible; that is to say, that the people who had property in Madero's time shall be regarded as still holding it, and the orders of confiscation & concessions made since shall be regarded as null. This is the meaning of the word "restitution." Subdivision of the lands is to be made by a system of taxation by which the unused lands will become the property of the Federal Government and given to the people. The people, however, need more than the land, and some method must be devised by which they can have implements and cattle with which to farm the lands, and these would have to be furnished at first by the Government. General Iturbide himself adopted this plan on his own irrigated lands ten years ago. He did not inherit these lands. He had when he left Mexico 22,000 acres of irrigated lands. These lands he had put under water himself, and they were the product of his own enterprise. He had no concession from the Government whatever. When he married his wife had $100,000. This he put into the purchase of lands, which he irrigated. These lands he sold, and with the profits bought more lands, until after

2 Abel Ortiz Argumedo.

twelve years he had made a small fortune, which consisted of several farms of irrigated lands, most of them free from mortgage. This idea of using the ignorant and poor native as a partner he thinks should be adopted by the Federal Government as the foundation of a new land scheme, under which the Mexican in the course of a few years would have a knowledge of how to work the lands, and would own the lands himself as well as the necessary implements.

General Iturbide says that he is known to the English Ambassador, the Spanish Ambassador, the Argentine Ambassador, the Brazilian Ambassador, and the Italian Ambassador. He is willing to agree in any way desired that he will not accept any office and that he will put himself at the service of anyone who might be named to restore order in Mexico. His first desire, he said, is to take in enough corn and wheat to put the people at work raising crops, for he says that temporary relief will not be sufficient to do any good. The famine will be as bad in the fall as it is now, because the people have not sown during the spring. He says that he will make no move whatever without feeling that he can have the moral support of the American Government. It was urged upon him some months ago that he should make an effort to gather the people around him and start a counter-revolution, but he refused to do this because he says it would be nonsense; that no man can succeed in Mexico in restoring order who does not have the support of this Government, and no man can maintain a Government in Mexico who does not have the support of this Government.

T memoranda (WP, DLC).

To Edith Bolling Galt

[The White House]
My adorable Sweetheart,   Wed. morning, 7. 26 May, '15

How empty this great house seems without you this morning, and how my heart turns back to that charming little house where I left you, standing lonely in the door-way, your lovely, lovely person clear and beautiful against the light,—left you with the thrill of your kiss on my lips,—left my heart with you and all the sweet hopes about you that now brighten the days before me. All night long, my darling, I was aglow with the sweet consciousness of you. It was a long time before sleep took full hold on me and in my half sleep I was aware of a deep, deep happiness and of a sort of transfiguration, as if I were filled with the love and beauty that last night filled those eyes, those wonderful eyes, I love so and made your face so radiant that I was fairly intoxicated with the beauty of it,—a spiritual beauty that seemed full of every fine and lovely thing that ever blessed a man's life. What memories were stored up then to feed my hungry heart with until I see you and hold you in my arms again; what minutes full of pure joy made the lovely evening holy and glorious! Ah, sweetheart, I do not know who wrote that article about me you were quoting the other day (I did not know that anyone outside the circle of those I love knew so much about me), but he was speaking nothing but the truth when he said that I have to keep vigilant watch on my emotions, but why should I keep watch on them where you are concerned? There is nothing to be afraid of in them: every one of them has made me a better man and put new light into my heart to guide it and purify it and prepare it for you. I had to hold myself tight while I was looking at those pictures. I was so carried away with delight that there *were* photographs from which your beautiful face could *speak* to me in all the long hours of our exile from one another that I could hardly refrain from taking you then and there in my arms (with that thoughtless shade up!) and expressing my emotion in the only way it could be adequately expressed! These are the best hours of the days when I do not see you, these quiet morning hours when I sit down in this great lonely study to pour out my heart to you, Edith,—and yet what a subtle disappointment they bring because I cannot find the words, there do not seem to *be* words, into which to put my thoughts of you,—the love that possesses my whole nature. I might as well try to define my life as to try to define my love. It is at once too complex and too simple. It seems like picking a flower to pieces to discover its perfume. It is the spirit of my life; and I can lay it at your feet, my darling, with pride and joy. I am altogether yours,   Woodrow

ALS (WP, DLC).

From Edith Bolling Galt, with Enclosure

[Washington]

Dear Heart: *Extra Editions* Wednesday A.M. [May 26, 1915]

I wrote you this stupid card last night when I hardly knew what I was saying (do you know why?) and so this morning I want to add another word. It is this—I love you.   Edith.

ENCLOSURE

[Washington] May 25th, 1915 midnight.

I am too happy tonight, dearest One, to write. Yes, absolutely *happy*, with the greatest content I have know[n] for years.

Your idea that I am more sure of myself away from you than when we are together may be right, but I am not a judge of that, for when I am with you I am so happy that I forget other things and just drink deep at the fountain of your love. You *are* right when you told me love would overcome fear. I feel now that with you by me, nothing can ever crush or really hurt me, for I have but to turn and find your dear eyes to have new strength and courage given me.

About the pictures my Lord, please tell me the numbers of the ones you like, and I will get them for you myself. I could not have it otherwise. All my love longs to go with this, and I am *so* happy that you have, at least, crossed my threshold. I wanted to bring you up here in my living room but knew it was best not.

Always Edith

ALS (WP, DLC).

To Edith Bolling Galt

Sweetheart,   The White House. [c. May 26, 1915]

The numbers of the pictures for which my heart waits are: $\frac{932}{2}, \frac{932}{3}, \frac{932}{5}$ but Genthe[1] charges such unconscionable prices for his pictures that it isn't *fair* to let you order all three for me. Please let us get two of them (Margaret can do it with perfect propriety) and get, yourself, for me the one you like best—please!

W.

ALI (WP, DLC).
[1] Arnold Genthe, the well-known photographer. See EAW to WW, Oct. 3, 1913, n. 2, Vol. 28.

To William Jennings Bryan, with Enclosure

My dear Mr. Secretary,   The White House. 27 May, 1915.

This is disappointing. House had cabled me a copy of what Gerard had sent him, and I was just about to send it to you.

I cannot help feeling that Gerard might have managed this better, so at least to give us a chance to act as intermediary in some way in an interchange between England and Germany that might have been the beginning of something.

The terms Zimmerman suggests are manifestly impossible of

acceptance by England so far as they concern things which, like copper, enter into the manufacture of munitions of war. It looks as if we were again in a blind alley.

What would you think of sending the following to Gerard:

> Please point out kindly and unofficially but very earnestly to the Foreign Office that the conditions now prevailing in the marine war zone are rapidly becoming intolerable to the whole world, that their rectification is in the interest of both parties to the present conflict, and that this Government, while it has nothing to propose as between the belligerants, but will confine itself to the protection of its own clear rights, will act with pleasure in conveying any proposals that either the one government or the other has to make for the correction of the present conditions fraught as they are with universal danger.[1]

We can do no more than this; we should, perhaps, do no less.

Gerard has got part of his instructions wrong. We did not say that the new Ministry in England would be willing. We said only that we had reason to hope that they would be. I suppose it would be well to make this clear to him, since he seems to need A B C.

Faithfully Yours,   W.W.

WWTLI (SDR, RG 59, 763.72/2478, DNA).
  [1] This was sent as WJB to J. W. Gerard, May 27, 1915, 3 P.M., T telegram (SDR, RG 59, 763.72/2478, DNA). There is a WWsh draft of this paragraph in WP, DLC.

E N C L O S U R E   I

Berlin via Copenhagen May 25, 1915.
Recd. May 26, 7.05 p.m.

2289   To be deciphered by the Secretary of State.
CONFIDENTIAL.

Referring to your 1723, May 23, 2 p.m., regret your telegram not quite clear because you say that House reports that new British Ministry now willing to consider the proposals which we made in our note received February 22nd last, and you then speak of getting the German Government to renew its proposals. The essential difference between the proposition made in our identic note and the German counter proposal is that we proposed that food stuff should be allowed to enter Germany and the German counter proposal demanded not only food stuff and forage but raw material also. Colonel House cabled me from London direct on May 18, the text of his telegram having been repeated in your 1622 to me. I immediately had interview with Von

Jagow and on May twenty-first cabled House as follows: "Gave your suggestion to Von Jagow this morning. This proposition of permitting passage food in return for cessation of submarine methods already made and declined. If raw material added matter can perhaps be arranged. Germany in no need of food. Ask Department to cable you my cable number 2305 of May 10, 5 p.m.["]

This disposes of the proposition if you mean that the British Government is willing to allow food stuffs but not raw material to enter Germany in return for cessation of torpedoing of merchant ships without notice by submarines. I had a talk to-day with Zimmerman, Von Jagow being out of town, and he reiterated what Von Jagow said but expressed himself as satisfied that an agreement might be reached on somewhat the following basis: Germany and England both agree not to use gases. Food, cotton, copper, rubber and such other raw material as does not directly enter into manufacture of munitions of war to be allowed to enter Germany. Germany to stop torpedoing of merchant vessels without notice but England to agree that merchant vessels shall not be armed and shall not attempt to ram submarines.

I think German answer to LUSITANIA note will be only in first place a statement of facts and we shall be asked if we agree that this statement correctly sets forth the facts.

Gerard, Berlin.

T telegram (SDR, RG 59, 763.72/2478, DNA).

To William Jennings Bryan

My dear Mr. Secretary,   The White House. 27 May, 1915.

I shall be very glad to issue such a public appeal as Miss Boardman refers to. I shall try to have one prepared.

I think we should press on with all possible means of relief. Are you hopeful that we can make arrangements that will really work for getting the relief we send safely through to Mexico City?

Faithfully Yours,   W.W.

WWTLI (W. J. Bryan Papers, DNA).

A Telegram and a Letter from Edward Mandell House

[London, May 27, 1915]

In re the shipping troubles, and in answer to your cable of 26th Walter Page says the British government is more prompt than

ever before and the Foreign Office is more effective in its desire
for great haste. The cabinet changes, he thinks, promise [much]
hope, and note now will retard rather than help matters. He
would like to know who is making complaint and about what
specific things. If the specific place where the shoe pinches is
indicated Walter Page believes the chances are he can fix it.

I understand that it is the principle to which you object as well
as the delay. I would suggest not sending another note until first
an answer is given to your note of some weeks ago for which Walter Page is now pressing and which will be forthcoming in a few
days; secondly, until Germany sends her answer to your note
concerning her submarine policy. While the two are separate, yet
they are in a way interrelated. I believe the new First Lord of the
Admiralty will be much more amenable to our contentions than
the one he supersedes.   Edward House

T transcript of WWsh decode (WC, NjP) of T telegram (WP, DLC).

Dear Governor: No. 7. London, May 27th, 1915.

I saw Sir Edward Grey yesterday and discussed the holding
up of cargoes.

As to cotton, he said this Government following precedent had
a right to make it contraband of war just as our Government did
during our Civil War. But out of consideration for our wishes
they had not done so and therefore he hoped we would be lenient.

He also said they were doing everything that was possible now
to avoid friction with us, and that orders had gone out to pass
upon all questions speedily so they could no longer be charged
with delay.

He told me some things of interest concerning the Balkan
States. One was that Rumania had agreed to come in, provided
the Allies would give her certain Hungarian territory. Sir Edward
refused to consider such terms for the reason that what she
wanted would be unfair to Serbia. His reply was that since Great
Britain went into this war to defend the rights of one small nation, it would not transgress upon the rights of another even
though great advantage to the Allied cause might accrue.

If it were not for Ferdinand Bulgaria would probably come in
with the Allies, and if she did, then Greece would also. They all
fear lest some one of the Balkan States will remain out and be in
a condition to take advantage of the exhaustion that may occur.

The other day Grey and I fell to talking of you. He expressed
the hope that you would come to England after you relinquished
your present office. He thought you would enjoy it here, and could
go about without any publicity whatsoever. He was interested

to hear me say that you and he would become friends at once and he feels this is true.

I am glad Balfour is in the new Cabinet. He is a man of the Grey type, and I feel sure there will be less trouble with the holding up of cargoes now than when the Admiralty was administered by Churchill.

Sir Edward leaves Monday to be gone a month, and Lord Crewe[1] will probably act for him during his absence. He is to arrange with Crew[e] for me to see him at any time I desire and at his home. He lives close by. I never go to the Foreign Office, or any of the other Government Offices, on account of the publicity. They all understand my reasons for this.

You will be pleased to know that the "Freedom of the Seas" grows apace, and I have but little doubt that when peace is concluded such a measure will be adopted. Grey speaks of it all the time and with growing fervor. His only reservation is that there shall be equal freedom of the land, which will doubtless also be brought about through the desire of all nations.

If we accomplish nothing else but this it will justify our being, for it will do more to lessen the chances of war than any one thing that seems possible.   Your affectionate,   E. M. House

Grey said he was glad we had made the suggestion to Germany regarding foodstuffs, and he was also glad that England had indicated her willingness to consent. He thought the proposal and rejection placed America and England in a better light and Germany in a worse. In presenting the matter to the Cabinet he said that England should do everything possible to avoid the appearance of trying to make trouble between America and Germany.

TLS (WP, DLC).
  [1] Robert Offley Ashburton Crewe-Milnes, Marquess of Crewe, long-time cabinet member and leader of the Liberal party in the House of Lords, at this time Lord President of the Council.

From David Lawrence

My dear Mr. President: Washington, D. C. May 27, 1915

I feel that it is my duty to write this memorandum to you of ideas that have suggested themselves to me as a result of my talks with men from the different factions in Mexico and others who are interested in the country. As you know, I have been studying the Mexican question for nearly five years, having had an opportunity to examine the situation when it first arose, at close range. Having an impartial point of view toward the Mexican problem, I have been able to keep my mind free from prejudices. In my observation recently I have come across such a state of affairs that, if you are not already aware of them, I think this memorandum may be of service to you.

First of all, let me describe present conditions as I understand them. The e[c]onomic situation in Mexico has been, as you know, going from bad to worse, and people who are in a position to know something of the crops and the resources of the country tell me that famine is a certain consequence of present conditions within another six months. The Mexican peso has depreciated in value, and not only has most of the gold been shipped out of the country, but all kinds of merchandise and produce, in order to gain revenues. Much of the cattle which would be used to till the land has been slaughtered, and a situation appears to be in prospect where a huge relief scheme costing many millions will become imperative.

As for the political situation, there are at least three separate and distinct intrigues going on now, apart from the two military movements in Mexico. These intrigues have more or less momentum. They are working at cross purposes. The curious part of it all is that they are gathering momentum on the pretension of having assurance of support from the United States Government. In one case, the facts of which I would prefer sometime to tell you in person, you, yourself, are being represented as supporting one particular faction, and the result is that false hopes are being raised and difficulties being accumulated for the future.

I have talked with some of the Mexicans in whom I have learned to have confidence—men who are not insensible to the fact that from the United States Government must come the real impetus which will make a settlement possible. I have had in mind a plan of a constructive character for the solution of the Mexican problem without the use of physical force, and have had occasion abstractly to sound out some of these men. I have found many who think the plan a feasible one—although, as I say, I have talked of it in such an abstract way as to leave no impression in the mind of anyone that it had any foundation except in a personal view. The success of the plan would, of course, depend upon exactly how it was executed and the selection of the psychological moment for its projection. Here are the essential features of it:

1. An investigation by the Department of Justice of all the financial or commercial interests in the United States which are in any way, remotely or otherwise, supporting any of the Mexican factions in Mexico or those which are in the United States conspiring to get a foothold. This should include, also, the

gathering of information concerning those American and other
interests in Mexico itself which are paying tribute to the Mexican
factions and, in a way, are assisting to support their military
movements. Much of this money, of course, is obtained by way
of taxation—and a good part of it illegally, and much of it would
not be paid, doubtless, if the foreign governments were in a position to insist upon only legal taxes.

2. The gathering of information as to the amount of war
munitions now in the possession of the Mexican forces and what
their prospects are for obtaining arms and ammunition from
American firms in view of the higher prices which European
countries are paying. All this information would give the American Government an idea of the sources of supply to the Mexican
factions, and influence and pressure could certainly be brought to
bear upon the interests in the United States to withdraw or, at
any rate, withhold support until other features of this plan are
worked out.

3. Separate and distinct negot[i]ation directly with representatives of the various elements in the Mexican situation—this to be
done in Washington and supplemented, perhaps, by our representatives in Mexico. It is well nigh impossible to bring representatives of the various factions together into any council or conference, because they are so diametrically opposed to one another
on the question of personalities. The most effective work can be
done by exerting pressure on separate elements. If the representatives now in Washington of these various elements are not
capable of speaking for the factions they represent, it might be
possible to have the leaders in Mexico indicate others who have
their confidence and would be the better able to speak for them.
The purpose of this negotiation would be to make clear to each
one of the elements concerned the necessity of establishing within the very near future a provisional government that could be
recognized and could hold an election in which all might participate. Knowing the American Government's sympathy for the
parties in Mexico which have proclaimed liberal principles of government in their platforms, those elements need have no fear
that any government which is brought into being through the
influence of the United States would be of a reactionary character. The chief value of the negotiation with the various elements
would be to impress upon them the fact that the United States
intends to press very earnestly for the establishment of a provisional government and that it must deal with those elements
which will deal with it. There are some leaders who will refuse to
come into such an arrangement, but they will not refuse long be-

cause as soon as they discover that the American Government
is in earnest and intends to use its influence to cut off all supplies,
financial and military, from the United States and intends to
throw all these factors into the scales in favor of those elements
which are *willing* to reach a compromise agreement, I feel sure
that the reluctant ones will come into the arrangement. One
of the difficulties of the situation has been that we have been
compelled to deal with leaders—Carranza and Villa and Zapata
as personalities—when below them are some respectable elements, military leaders and others, to whom a compromise plan
would not be unacceptable. We have, of course, no direct way of
reaching these elements. When I realize that the leaders of those
intrigues which are now going on are appealing to those very
military subordinates and are telling them that an amalgamation
of the liberal elements will be given the support of the United
States Government, it occurs to me that the most direct way
to accomplish results would be for the American Government to
undertake frankly to bring into harmony such elements as are
willing to harmonize. In the execution of this plan it would be
desirable after the conferences have begun in Washington with
the authorized spokesmen of the leaders to make known through
our consular representatives in several places in Mexico the
details of the plan with instructions to show it as a matter of information to the local authorities—this with the idea of informing these generals that the United States Government is earnestly
at work on a plan for the amalgamation of the different elements.
The allegiance of the subordinate generals to the larger chiefs in
Mexico is based on two things: first, the opportunity for personal advancement; and, second, the domination which a chief
might exercise over other powerful groups which could overcome
any defections in the ranks. It was proved, I think, after the
Aguascalientes convention that a majority of the military leaders
would support a plan for amalgamation but some of them believing Carranza had better means of support in the United States
feared to take the chance.

I am confident that as soon as it becomes generally known
that the United States Government intends to recognize soon an
amalgamation of the best elements in Mexico, there will be a
flocking of individual chiefs to the support of such a combination. I should expect Carranza to be stubbornly opposed to this
and with him the circle of politicians who have constantly
advised him against all manner of compromises. I have ever[y]
reason to believe, however, that General Obregon, who has lately
had personal differences with Carranza, would not stand by Car-

ranza. General Villa has shown himself amenable to compromises and one of his representatives here assured me recently that he would again be willing to fall in with any plan of amalgamation for the Constitutionalist cause. I do think in the working out of such a plan that some attention should be given to the thousands of Mexicans in the United States. Some of them, of course, are of the very undesirable *cientifico* class who would undermine any government newly-established along the lines of the original Constitutionalists, or liberals. There are others, however, whose connection with politics has been unimportant and who represent the intellectual and cultured side of Mexico. If, in the provisional government that is established, men are given Cabinet portfolios who would have the confidence of these thousands of cultured Mexicans in the United States, they would not distrust promises of amnesty, for, after all, the question of amnesty can never be settled by a mere proclamation. It must have behind it a man in whom foreign governments and the Mexicans themselves can have some confidence that they will be given justice. To put into operation a plan of this kind I think it is essential to select the proper moment. At present the military situation around Celaya is very uncertain. A victory by Carranza would not be decisive and would only complicate matters, as he has not, in my opinion, the personal capacity or elements strong enough to render any government stable even though he should temporarily obtain military control of the country. A victory by Villa would not injure, but would rather assist, a plan for an amalgamation. The one vital thing is to make clear to the Mexican factions that the American Government intends to *insist* on an early reestablishment of peace and *would use all the* influence at its disposal within the territory of the United States—such as the commercial and financial support—to bring about the desired result. As soon as the Government obtains some sort of control over these fundamental things, the factions in Mexico will feel the pinch immediately.

If affairs are permitted to continue as they are now, I think it will be difficult eventually to prevent physical intervention, because the economic situation will drive the people to excesses, and foreigners will not be safe. The various features of a plan of this sort would take several weeks to work out and as it developed, changes of process might be necessary.

I know that a great many ideas have been suggested to you in the Mexican situation and that it must be a very great source of worry to you. I sincerely hope that the ideas that I have outlined may be of value to you, or that they may suggest other ideas to you for a solution of this troublesome question. If I can be of any service further, please let me know, because there is a great deal of information I have gathered in my day-to-day talks which relates to other phases of this same problem. Being on the outside of the official circle looking in, I have noted some activities in Washington which are very discouraging and cannot but impair the influence of the American Government. Some day I should like to tell you of these things.

Very sincerely yours,   David Lawrence

TLS (WP, DLC).

To Edith Bolling Galt

[The White House]
Thursday morning, 7. 27 May [1915].

All the household is asleep, the study door is closed, and here I am alone with my darling, free to talk to her and think only of her, the tasks of the day unable yet to exercise their tyranny over me, and my heart full of what she said to me yesterday, that with me she was perfectly happy and that my prediction had come true, that love *had* cast out all fear—that, with me by her, nothing could ever crush or really hurt her, so that I can turn to her here in this quiet room as to my own sweet comrade and lover, no barrier any longer between us, my heart thrilling with pride and fairly melting with tenderness, dream that her dear, beautiful form is close beside me and that I have only to stretch out my arms to have her come to them for comfort and happiness and peace, my kisses on her lips and eyelids,—my *thought* of *her* and of all the incomparable wealth of beautiful things now released in her, to bless everyone with whom she comes in contact. I venture to say, my Lady, my Queen, that never in your life before have you looked so wonderfully beautiful as I have seen you look when the love tide was running in your heart without check, since you came to understand yourself and me. I have seen a transfiguration, and it has filled me with as much awe as ecstacy!

I can't think this morning,—I can only *feel*, only realize the exquisite thing that has happened to me, the beautiful love I have won, the ineffable charm of the sweet woman who has given it to me, the added value and joy that have come into life for me because of her, her spirit all about me, adding to the brightness and freshness and life-giving airs of the morning. Ever since I heard her voice and the little unconscious thrill in it last night

I have been as conscious of her as if her hand were in mine and she were signalling her love to me all the hours through, and I am happy, and proud, and strong because of her. Ah, I thank God for his unspeakable goodness! My darling, my darling! May he forever bless you and keep you! Your own Woodrow

ALS (WP, DLC).

From Edith Bolling Galt

[Washington] Thursday morning May 27, 1915

What a perfect model of discretion, my dearest One, you are becoming. And yet your guarded little talk over the phone was begun with *such* a superfluous statement, "Helen isn't here." Don't you think I could have guessed that, although the rest of the conversation was as though she were standing by with a club?

It was *so* nice to talk to you but you sounded weary and discouraged, and I knew this other old ship business was resting its great weight on you, so that I wanted to come and see if Love was stronger than any other thing—to put my arms about you, and whisper all the tenderness and sympathy that was in my heart. I do hope you went right to bed and to sleep some way. Somehow Dearest I must help when you need me, it breaks my heart not to. Just five minutes after I talked to you Dr. Grayson called me and said he had been riding with you, that he thought you were blue and awfully worried over the new situation, and that he wished you had Col. House or someone to talk things over with. That would be a relief and help. He, Dr. G., is certainly absolutely devoted to you and would give up anything to serve you. One thing he said pleased me, for it relieved a fear I had that he might know more than we believed. It was this—"Well, Mrs. Galt you seem to understand the President, and do him more good than anyone else. You don't *worry* him, and *I wish you would go* whenever they ask you, for he really needs all the diversion he can get" Bless your precious heart Your note yesterday was so exquisite, so perfect that I will not even *try* to answer.

The messenger has just come with your letter written at 7 this morning. I must not keep him longer than just to whisper that he takes far more to you than is on this paper for he carries my heart. Edith.

ALS (WP, DLC).

To the American People

To the Public: The White House, 28 May, 1915.

The American people, with characteristic generosity and an impartial spirit of brotherhood with all nations, have contributed liberally towards the relief of the appalling sufferings caused by the unprecedented war in Europe.

There has now arisen a condition of equally great suffering and need close to our own borders. Due to several years of internal disturbance, the unfortunate people of many parts of Mexico have been reduced to the verge of starvation, and unless assistance is rendered they may die in great numbers for lack of food.

The American Red Cross is ready to undertake relief work for the benefit of the Mexican people. I appeal most earnestly to our people, therefore, to contribute both money and supplies of food to mitigate the suffering and misery so close at hand. All contributions in money may be sent to the American Red Cross, Washington, or to its local treasurers. Those who are able to contribute corn, rice, beans or flour are requested to communicate with the American Red Cross headquarters, Washington, for instructions.   Woodrow Wilson.

T MS (WP, DLC).

From William Jennings Bryan

My dear Mr. President: Washington May 28th, 1915.

I am sending you a flimsy of an important telegram just received from Fuller.[1] He has been successful in securing what seems to me to be a very satisfactory treaty. It is drawn in the language which we ourselves suggested and covers everything that we asked. The only question raised by Fuller is as to whether the President's agreement to follow the advice given by our Minister should be stated in a *whereas* or later as one of the articles of the agreement. Mr. Fuller says:

"Please observe that guarantee of efficiency and honesty and agreement to follow advice of Minister has been put in recital form. This was done to facilitate signing and because of evident desire of President not to appear in a subservient position."

In the form of recital it reads:

"Whereas, the President of the Republic of Haiti has expressed his sincere desire and firm intention to guarantee the honest and efficient administration of a government in Haiti according to the Constitution and laws of that Republic—a government which will give expression to the will of the people of Haiti, protect their rights and interests, and

"Whereas it is the mutual desire of the high contracting parties that there shall exist between an American Minister Plenipotentiary—hereafter to be appointed—and the President of Haiti, such an intimate and confidential relationship as will enable the American Minister Plenipotentiary to advise as to such matters as affect the honest and efficient administration of the Government, the President of Haiti agreeing that he will follow the advice so given to the extent of requiring honesty and efficiency in officials and of removing those found to be dishonest and inefficient,"

I have conferred with Mr. Lansing about it and he agrees with me that the statement is so clearly and emphatically made in the *whereas* that it is unnecessary to insist upon its being repeated in the agreement. Taken in connection with the letter of instructions from which this treaty is prepared, there can be no doubt of the intention of the treaty, and I think that we are fortunate in securing so complete a compliance with the provisions as we asked them. If this meets with your approval, I will cable Fuller at once directing him to sign the treaty.

Hearing that you have a headache this morning, I am sorry to trouble you with this matter, but Fuller is awaiting instructions and as it takes some time for telegrams to pass back and forth, I have asked that this be brought to your attention *if you feel that you are able to attend to any business.*

With assurances of high respect, I am, my dear Mr. President,
Very sincerely yours,   W. J. Bryan

TLS (W. J. Bryan Papers, DLC).
¹ P. Fuller, Jr., to WJB, May 22, 1915, T telegram (SDR, RG 59, 711.38/16, DNA), conveying the text of an American-Haitian treaty that conformed substantially to the terms printed in WJB to P. Fuller, Jr., May 6, 1915, printed as an enclosure with WJB to WW, May 6, 1915 (second letter of that date).

From William Jennings Bryan, with Enclosure

My dear Mr. President: Washington May 28th, 1915.

I find that the despatch which I sent to you setting forth the agreement that has been reached in Haiti was sent from there on the 22nd and reached here on the 23rd. It did not, however, come to my attention until this morning; hence the delay in transmitting it to you. I have just received from Fuller a telegram dated yesterday, of which I enclose a copy. I do not know what letter he refers to as the letter of May 7th, unless it is one of the letters which he carried with him dated May 6th. We have sent no letters from the Department since May 6th. He probably means that since the President has found that this recognition is to be given upon a satisfactory agreement being reached, he will not sign the agreement until he is recognized. If the understanding as set forth in the agreement has been reached, I do not see that there is any objection to the recognition being first; in fact, we could not very well make a treaty with the President's Government without recognizing him. I think, however, that it might be well as a matter of precaution for Fuller to send him a note saying that if the agreement as reached is entirely satisfactory and the President is ready to sign it after recognition, that he would proceed at once to deliver the letter of recognition. It is hardly conceivable that the President would refuse to sign the treaty after recognition if he had agreed to it before, but an exchange of notes would put the matter beyond question. In view of the delay that has occurred in bringing the matter to your attention, I am sending this explanation in order to forward instructions as soon as possible.

With assurances of high respect, I am, my dear Mr. President,
Very sincerely yours,   W. J. Bryan

TLS (W. J. Bryan Papers, DLC).

E N C L O S U R E

Port au Prince. May 27, 1915.

Since receipt of copy of letter from State Department May seventh Hatien government unwilling to negotiate convention until recognized. In my opinion this decision is final. Very strong verbal assurances of Minister of Foreign Affairs of government's willingness to sign convention substantially submitted by me with clause regarding Mole St. Nicholas exactly as therein contained. Please instruct me whether or not I shall deliver to Minister of Foreign Affairs letter of recognition which in my opinion will be followed by signing of convention. Otherwise useless for me to remain here as full personal report will be necessary.
Fuller

TC telegram (W. J. Bryan Papers, DLC).

To William Jennings Bryan

My dear Mr. Secretary,   The White House. 28 May, 1915.

I cannot help being a little suspicious in this case, but no doubt you are right that we can hardly refuse to agree that recognition shall precede the signing of the treaty, provided, it is clearly understood that the signing of the treaty will follow, and understood, not orally, but in writing.[1]

Fuller has accomplished his errand admirably. We are to be congratulated on having secured his services.

I approve of the treaty as drawn, agreeing fully with the conclusion to which you and Mr. Lansing have come.

Faithfully Yours,   W.W.

WWTLI (W. J. Bryan Papers, DLC).
 [1] Instructions along these lines were sent in WJB to P. Fuller, Jr., May 28, 1915, T telegram (SDR, RG 59, 711.38/16, DNA).

To Edith Bolling Galt

Dearest Edith,   The White House   Friday, 28 May [1915].

I simply cannot write to-day. An almost sleepless night of agonizing doubts and fears is no proper preparation for the only kind of letter my tender love for you will ever let me write—a letter to comfort you and make you happy. My only message is this, For God's sake try to find out whether you really love me or not.[1] You owe it to yourself and you owe it to the great love I have given you, without stint or measure. Do not be afraid of what I am thinking, but remember that I need strength and certainty for the daily task and that I cannot walk upon quicksand. I love you with all my heart   Woodrow

ALS (WP, DLC).
 [1] Wilson, Mrs. Galt, and Helen Bones had been out motoring the night before between 9 and 10:40 P.M. The discussion in which Mrs. Galt and Wilson engaged must be left to the reader's imagination, but it is a safe assumption that they were alone in the back seat with the divider and curtains drawn.

From Edith Bolling Galt

[Washington]

My dearest One: Friday morning [May 28, 1915]

I would not try to write you last night, although my heart longed to pour itself out to you, and try to ease the pain I caused your own big, tender heart. I thought it was wiser to wait until this morning and now it is hard to put into words just what I

mean, but you are always so splendidly honest with me that I am
going to try once and forever, to let you look straight into the
depths of me, and then never again refer to this *more* than painful subject. I know you are right in every word you said last night,
and that I am asking something that is childish and impossible.
But, try as hard as I can, *now* it seems the only way. If this can
be changed it will be because you are master of my heart and
life—(and oh! you don't know how I long to make you so) but *you*
must conquer! I have promised not to raise barriers and not to
think defeat possible. I will patiently keep those promises, for
I love you, and your love for me has made the whole world new,
and when I am with you there is no fear, only happiness.

Edith.

ALS (WP, DLC).

Count Johann Heinrich von Bernstorff
to Theobald von Bethmann Hollweg[1]

Washington, den 29 Mai 1915.
(Botschaft)

A. Nr. 196. Präsident Wilson trägt sich wieder mit dem
Gedanken einer Vermittelung, welche dem europäischen Krieg
ein Ende bereiten soll. Wie ich höre aus bester Quelle glaubt Herr
Wilson, daß der Lusitania-Zwischenfall die Augen der ganzen
Welt auf die Kriegsführung zur See und deren Folgen für den
internationalen Handel gelenkt habe. Wenn sich der Lusitania-
Zwischenfall günstig erledigen läßt, so will der Präsident an die
Englische Regierung herantreten und dieselbe von der völker-
rechtswidrigen Störung des neutralen Handels abzubringen
suchen. Herr Wilson glaubt, daß, falls er eine dem Völkerrecht
entsprechende Kriegführung zur See erreichen könnte, er einen
günstigen Ausgangspunkt gefunden haben würde, um zu einer
Friedensvermittelung überzugehen. Der Präsident versucht jetzt
die neutralen Mächte zusammenzubringen und hat mit den
amerikanischen Republiken angefangen, deren Vertreter augen-
blicklich zu einem panamerikanischen Kongreß in Washington
versammelt sind. Dann will Herr Wilson auch an die europäischen
neutralen Staaten herantreten. Wenn es ihm gelingt, alle zusammenzubringen, gedenkt er einen Schritt bei den kriegführenden
Mächten zu tun und sie zu ersuchen eine Friedenskonferenz zu
beschicken. Dabei schwebt dem Präsidenten der Gedanke vor,
daß die neutralen Staaten sich verpflichten sollen, diejenigen
kriegführenden Mächte, welche sich weigern, die Konferenz zu

beschicken, von jeder Zufuhr an Lebensmitteln, Munition usw. abzuschneiden. Die Friedensbedingungen, an die gedacht wird, sind die folgenden:

1. Der status quo in Europa.[2]
2. Die Freiheit der Meere in so weitgehendem Maße, daß sie der Neutralisierung der See gleichkäme,
3. Ausgleichungen an Kolonialbesitzungen.

Herr Wilson scheint sich darüber klar zu sein, daß ein Druck auf uns nicht ausgeübt werden kann, da wir von fremder Zufuhr sowieso ziemlich ganz abgeschnitten sind. Andererseits glaubt er, daß die obigen Friedensbedingungen so günstig für uns seien, daß wir eher als unsere Feinde geneigt sein würden, sie anzunehmen. Darin dürfte der Präsident allerdings wohl recht haben, daß nur ein geschlagenes England sich auf die Freiheit der See einlassen würde. Den Ausgangspunkt für obigen Friedensplan bildet Ergebnis Gedankens, daß alle neutralen Staaten, einschließlich der amerikanischen, dem wirtschaftlichen Ruin oder zum mindesten sehr schwierigen Verhältnissen entgegengehen, wenn der Krieg noch lange andauert oder sich gar noch auf weitere Gebiete ausdehnen sollte.

Euere Exzellenz werden vielleicht über die Wilson'schen Pläne anderweitig auf schnellerem Wege informiert worden sein, da ich diese Angelegenheit mit dem schwedischen Gesandten besprochen habe. Ich nehme an, daß Herr Wilson versuchen wird, durch irgend eine neutrale Regierung oder sonstwie unter der Hand in Erfahrung zu bringen wie die Kaiserliche Regierung seinen Vermittelungsplan aufnehmen würde. Einer direkten Ablehnung will er sich nicht aussetzen, namentlich nicht von Deutschland, da er auf uns keinen Druck ausüben kann. Soweit ich die Sache von hier aus übersehen kann, dürfte es sich empfehlen, das Odium der Ablehnung auf England fallen zu lassen, das heute wohl jedenfalls noch nicht bereit ist, einen solchen Frieden anzunehmen, wie er Herrn Wilson vorschwebt.

Graf von Bernstorff.

TCL (Weltkrieg, No. 2, geheim, Vermittlungsaktionen, Vol. 8, pp. 190-191; GFO-Ar).

[1] Bernstorff sent the following dispatch by mail; it arrived in Berlin on June 26, 1915. However, as he says below, his friend, the Swedish Minister in Washington, telegraphed a shorter version to the Swedish Foreign Office, which in turn relayed it to the German Foreign Office on June 3, 1915.

Bernstorff's message has been treated variously by the historians who have taken note of it. Fritz Fischer, *Griff nach der Weltmacht* (Düsseldorff, 1961), p. 359, writes that Bernstorff himself proposed the plan of action suggested in the document; Fischer does not mention Wilson's name in connection with it. Karl E. Birnbaum, *Peace Moves and U-Boat Warfare* (Stockholm, 1958), pp. 343-45, strongly implies that Bernstorff fabricated the document in order to encourage the German government to come to friendly agreement with the United States on the submarine issue. Gerhard Ritter, *Staatskunst und Kriegs-*

handwerk (4 vols., Munich, 1954-68), III, 619, simply summarizes the dispatch, which he calls "a rather mysterious dispatch from Count Bernstorff."

There are two crucial questions that demand answer before one can pass judgment on this document.

First. Was it in fact fabricated by Bernstorff?

It seems inconceivable that this could have been the case. Bernstorff, a career diplomat of long service, was consistently a faithful and reliable reporter; indeed, we know of no instance in which he fabricated a report. Moreover, in the telegraphic report which he sent to Berlin via Stockholm, Bernstorff said emphatically that he did not wish to be understood in any way as having been the author of the proposals set forth in the document. (The Swedish Foreign Office to G. von Jagow, June 3, 1915, quoted in Birnbaum, pp. 343-44.)

Second. Who was "the most reliable source" whom Bernstorff mentions in the second sentence?

We are convinced that "the most reliable source" was Wilson himself. Our conclusion is based upon the following evidence and what we think are the reasonable inferences that can be drawn from it:

First. The White House head usher's diary discloses that Wilson "remained in room all morning" on Friday, May 28. The Executive Office appointment diary reveals that Wilson canceled a cabinet meeting scheduled for 11 A.M. that same day. As we have just learned from Bryan's first letter of May 28 and Wilson's letters to Mrs. Galt of May 28 and May 29, Wilson said that he had a headache and was ill on May 28 because of a contretemps with Mrs. Galt. That well may have been true (the White House diary indicates that Wilson had no breakfast on May 28). However, Wilson was not incapacitated, nor could whatever illness he had have been serious. He read Bryan's letters about the Haitian situation and replied promptly to them, and it does not seem likely that he would have canceled a cabinet meeting, particularly at this time, because he had a headache or was in blue spirits. He probably canceled the cabinet meeting because he had received a telephone call from Bernstorff requesting an immediate audience. That the White House diary does not mention a visit from Bernstorff is insignificant, because that diary is often silent about visits from various people. Wilson probably told Bernstorff to come to a side door of the White House, where "Ike" Hoover would meet him and take him to the President's study. Wilson could also have instructed Hoover not to enter Bernstorff's visit in the White House diary. We should add that we think that the meeting took place on Friday morning, May 28, mainly because of Wilson's somewhat mysterious behavior at that time. The meeting might have occurred on Saturday, but it does not seem likely. Wilson, fully recovered from his alleged indisposition, played golf all morning and had a busy schedule during the afternoon. The only time that he could have seen Bernstorff on Saturday afternoon was between two and five, when, according to the White House diary, he was out riding with Helen Bones.

Second. When Bernstorff said "the most reliable source," or "the highest source," he meant just that. He obviously could not mention Wilson's name in a telegram or letter that he knew might be intercepted by the British. Moreover, the very construction of Bernstorff's language indicates that he is paraphrasing or quoting Wilson. The Ambassador does not write that he has heard or believes that the President "wants" or "desires" or "has in mind" certain things. He says quite explicitly that Wilson "wants," "desires," "has in mind," and so on. Finally, it seems inconceivable that Bryan or Lansing—the two other only possible "most reliable sources" since House was then in London—would have divulged such important information to Bernstorff.

Third. Anyone who has read the documents in this volume to this point will not be surprised by what Wilson said to Bernstorff. Wilson was at this very moment attempting to arrange a *modus vivendi* between Germany and Great Britain for their observance of traditional international law at sea during wartime. He had already discussed with Lansing and Bryan the advisability of calling a conference of neutral nations for the effective protection of neutral commerce. Bernstorff sent an interesting message to the Imperial Chancellor regarding Wilson's determination. After reviewing the general situation vis-à-vis Germany and the United States, the Ambassador discussed the possibility that Wilson would move sternly against the British if the German authorities settled the *Lusitania* case on his terms. Continuing, Bernstorff wrote that Wilson had told a close friend: "If I receive a favorable answer from Germany I will see this thing through with England to the end." J. H. von Bernstorff to T. von Bethmann Hollweg, July 28, 1915, TCL (Der Weltkrieg, Unterseebootkrieg gegen England, ganz geheim, Vol. II, pp. 2-4, GFO-Ar). The words ascribed to Wilson are in English; Wilson's confidential friend was undoubtedly Colonel House. Later, during the *Arabic* crisis in August 1915, Wilson told Mrs. Galt (WW to EBG, Aug. 19-20 and 22, 1915) that, if the Germans did not meet his demands, he would break relations. However, he went on, he would not go to war (unless Germany declared war on the United States) but would call a conference of the neutral nations for the protection of neutral rights. Bernstorff's report to the German Foreign Office printed at June 2, the reliability of which no one has questioned, repeated that Wilson hoped to make a move for peace in a grand style, which he would like to get under way as the head of the neutrals. Finally, Spring Rice, who probably had an agent in the German Embassy or had tapped Bernstorff's wire, reported to Sir Edward Grey on June 3 (see the dispatch printed at that date) that the German Ambassador was said to have spoken recently of peace to the President and Secretary of State. The terms attributed to Wilson in Bernstorff's report of May 29 were repeated by Spring Rice.

There is an intriguing possibility that the above account does not tell the whole story. Francis van Gheel Gildemeester, son of a former court chaplain at The Hague and a Dutch subject, left Berlin on May 10, 1915, to convey certain messages to Wilson concerning the German internal political situation and possibilities of peace from Bethmann Hollweg and other German leaders. (See A. C. Miller to WJB, June 3, 1915, printed as an Enclosure with WJB to WW, June 3, 1915, and C. A. Spring Rice to E. Grey, June 6, 1915.) We know from Miller's letter that Gildemeester was in Washington at least by May 30. He could easily have been there on May 28, or even before.

It seems to us strongly probable that the following occurred on May 28:

Bernstorff called Wilson by telephone during the morning, told him that he had a secret emissary from the Imperial Chancellor with him, and asked if he and Gildemeester could see Wilson at once. Wilson agreed. Gildemeester's letter to Wilson of June 7, printed at that date, indicates that he had already seen Wilson, as he writes: "In no case do I wish you to feel that I am impatient." The third paragraph of this letter also indicates that Gildemeester had talked with Wilson. In this same letter, Gildemeester listed the peace terms that he said Germany would be willing to accept. Among them were three of the key terms that Wilson is alleged to have mentioned to Bernstorff—a peace based upon the *status quo ante bellum* (implied in Gildemeester's letter); a league of neutrals for the effective protection of neutral rights if one of the belligerents refused to go to the peace table; and complete neutralization of the seas. Moreover, Bernstorff, in his report of June 2, refers to Gildemeester in a way that implies that Wilson had talked to him: "Furthermore, one could then surely expect that Wilson would intervene according to the sending of Gildemeester here."

Therefore, we come to the conclusion that Bernstorff's report of May 29, confirmed by his report of June 2, embodied Wilson's overtures to Bethmann.

Much has been revealed in the documents about Wilson's search for an alternative to war, and much more will be revealed in future documents. The efforts to which he went to persuade Germany to join hands with the American government in establishing freedom of the seas for neutral vessels and noncontraband cargoes have also been amply illustrated in past documents and will be even more fully illustrated in documents yet to come.

Nothing came of Bethmann's and Wilson's efforts. The Chancellor's control over German foreign policy was so tenuous at this time, because the power of the army and navy were so great, that Bethmann did not dare to respond positively to Wilson. Indeed, only through heroic efforts was he able to obtain the minimal concessions necessary to prevent war with the United States. In addition, as Ritter points out (p. 523), Jagow (and presumably Bethmann as well) had concluded by the time that Bernstorff's letter arrived in Berlin that Italy's entry into the war precluded a peace based upon the *status quo ante bellum*. Finally, as the documents will soon reveal, by late June the German leaders had good reason to believe that the British would never consent to even partial freedom of the seas unless defeated.

2 He of course meant the *status quo ante bellum*. It was so understood by the German leaders.

T R A N S L A T I O N

Washington, May 29, 1915.

(Embassy)

No. 196. President Wilson is again entertaining the idea of a mediation that is intended to put an end to the European war. As I hear from the most reliable source, Mr. Wilson believes that the *Lusitania* affair has focused the eyes of the entire world on the conduct of the war at sea and on its consequences for international commerce. If the *Lusitania* affair can be settled favorably, the President wants to approach the English government and to attempt to dissuade it from its interference—contrary to international law—with neutral trade. Mr. Wilson believes that if he could achieve a conduct of the war at sea that was in conformity with international law, he would then have found an auspicious point of departure in order to move forward to a peace mediation. The President is endeavoring now to bring together the neutral powers and has started with the American republics, whose representatives are at present assembled for a Pan-American congress at Washington. Thereafter, Mr. Wilson wants to approach the European neutral states, too. If he succeeds in bringing all of them together, he intends to take the initiative with the belligerent powers and to ask them to participate in a peace conference. In doing this, the President has in mind that all neutral nations should commit themselves to cutting off those belligerents that declined to participate in the conference from all supplies of foodstuffs, munitions, etc. The peace conditions which he has in mind are the following:

1. Status quo in Europe.
2. The freedom of the seas to such an extent that it would be equal to a neutralization of the seas.
3. Adjustments of colonial possessions.

Mr. Wilson seems to realize that pressure cannot be applied on us, as we are almost completely cut off from foreign supplies in any case. On the other hand, he believes that the above-mentioned peace conditions are so favorable to us that we, rather than our enemies, would be inclined to accept them. In this, the President seems to be certainly right, indeed, as only a defeated England would consent to the freedom of the seas. The starting point for the above-mentioned peace plan is the assumption that all neutral states, including America, would face economic ruin or, at least, very difficult conditions if the war should continue much longer or even spread to other areas.

Your Excellency will perhaps have otherwise been informed

about Wilson's plans through faster channels, as I have talked the matter over with the Swedish Minister.[1] I suppose that Mr. Wilson, through some neutral government or otherwise, will try to ascertain informally how the Imperial government would receive his mediation plan. He does not want to expose himself to a direct rejection, particularly from Germany, because he cannot apply any pressure on us. As far as I can assess the situation from here, it seems prudent to let the odium of rejection fall on England, which, for the moment, at any rate, does not yet seem to be prepared to accept such a peace as imagined by Mr. Wilson.   Count von Bernstorff.

[1] Wilhelm August Ferdinand Ekengren.

To Edith Bolling Galt

[The White House]
My darling,   Sat. morning, 7. 29 May [1915].

After many, many hours of deep depression and exquisite suffering, which brought on a sort of illness which I could not explain to the doctor and for which he could do nothing, the light has again dawned for me and a new certitude and confidence has come to me. *I* have been blind as well as you. I have *said* that love was supreme and have feared that it was not! I have told you the truth and yet have myself acted as if *I* did not believe it. That weakness is gone. I not only believe that love is supreme but that it is *creative*, and that belief shall inform everything that I do or say henceforth. You love me—I *know* that you do—so much more than your words tells me so—your very presence is radiant with it when we are together and every touch of your dear hand has in it the sense of identification and loving intimacy: and you have invited me to make myself the master of your life and heart. The rest is now as certain as that God made us and gave us this sweet knowledge of each other—and *I shall win*, by a power not my own, a power which has never been defeated, against which no doors can be locked, least of all the doors of the heart. Henceforth we are not going to *discuss* our love, but live upon it and grow in it and let it lead us to strength and joy and peace by paths of its own. We are natural comrades. Our minds and spirits go out to meet one another with a perfect understanding and an enjoyment that makes our hearts young and light and free. We will take hands now and walk together without fear withersoever our infallible guide may lead us. And my darling will grow from beauty to beauty as the light of the rising path broadens about us. She will not wish to turn back or question where the path leads, but will, when its sweet end comes, turn to me and come to my arms and acknowledge with joy that she cannot do otherwise than be all in all to her own   Woodrow

ALS (WP, DLC).

From Helen Woodrow Bones, with Enclosure

Dear Cousin Woodrow   [The White House, May 29, 1915]

She said she wouldn't write another note to take the place of this, written before she read yours, because she thought you ought to know that you had hurt her feelings*(!), but she is coming to dinner and I feel *sure* you needn't feel miserable over this, even if it isn't what you want.   Helen

* by what you said about the quicksand.

ALS (WP, DLC).

E N C L O S U R E

From Edith Bolling Galt

[Washington]

Dear, weary Heart: Saturday 9:30 [May 29, 1915]

I have thought of you so tenderly these last hours, since I knew you were in pain, mental and physical, and felt so ashamed that I should add to the burden.

If only I could brighten this dreary day for you! but my love seems inadequate.

I have given it to you, and found such happiness in the giving, and instead of bringing joy to you, your note yesterday tells me it is only a "quicksand"

I am waiting for Helen to come, and see if you still want me to come to dinner tonight. I long to talk to you, but perhaps I would only add to your burden.

I trust you to tell me if this is so? My tenderest thoughts fly to you, seeking like birds to find a sheltered nest, and I long to know that you are better and happier today.   Edith.

ALS (WP, DLC).

Helen Woodrow Bones to Mary Allen Hulbert

The White House May 29, 15
Monday perfectly convenient   You must stop over   Will send
car[1]   Helen W Bones.

T telegram (WP, DLC).
  [1] Mrs. Hulbert arrived at the White House at 7:30 A.M. on Monday, May 31.
The White House diary reveals that she, Miss Bones, and Wilson went riding in
an automobile between 9 and 11:45 A.M. Mrs. Hulbert went with Margaret Wilson and Helen Bones to Arlington Cemetery to hear the President speak and then
departed for New York at 4 P.M.

To Edith Bolling Galt

[The White House]
My adorable Sweetheart,   Sunday afternoon 30 May [1915]
    This is just a love message (you will ask what the others have
been!) sent from a full heart. For my heart has been *very* full
since last night,—the happiest, it seems to me, of all the brief evenings we have had together. I slept with a new peace in my
heart last night—woke once and again to think of you and *consciously* love you, only to sleep again with a quiet heart—and did
not get up until it was time to go to church (of course I dr[e]ssed
first!) I wish I could find words in which to interpret to you my
love for you,—it is partly because I cannot that I am so impatient
to interpret it in acts, in life, in a daily relationship of comradeship and protection and joy worth all the beautiful words ever
written and the only adequate vehicle of loving thoughts. I
fancy that you *can feel* my surpassing love for you when you are
with me. To be with you is to be satisfied. It excites in me everything that it is most delightful to experience. My love for you
seems to be a release of everything that is best in me, and the
sense of comradeship is complete. Ah, my darling, my darling!
I can do nothing with a pen to-day. Our separation is too recent,
the room too empty—this room you sat in and illuminated last
night. I can only repeat and repeat again that I love you.
                                                    Woodrow

ALS (WP, DLC).

From Edith Bolling Galt

[Washington] Sunday night,
Dearest One: May 30th, 1915, 11:30
    It is a month ago tonight since you went to Williamstown, and
what a memorable month it will always be! And what a world has

opened to me in these four weeks! Your dear note of this afternoon is so completely happy and echoes so perfectly all that has
filled my own heart all day, that every word is a joy and makes
you nearer and dearer to me than ever before.

You made me so happy last night, and I came home with the
assurance that we both understood—far better than ever before—
and that *with* this understanding, and absolute faith in each
other, we have nothing to fear.

The house is very still, and, but for your love, would be lonely,
but such is the magic of this precious thing you have given me,
I do not feel alone, but encircled by your dear arms. So, goodnight, my Lord, and may the morrow bring you all that I am
wishing for you.   Edith.

P.S. I shall not be able to go to Arlington tomorrow, for I have
some stupid people on my hands from Philadelphia, for lunchen,
but I shall be with you in spirit and hope you won't be very tired.
I will try to get this to you during the morning, though Mr. Wilson
is coming to see me at ten, and I will be anxious to hear what he
says, as he has been out of town ever since we got home from
New York.

Also, I meant last night to tell you a little regarding this small
sister of mine,[1] for whose benefit you are willing to test your his-
trionic ability. Please be very tender in your judgment of her. She
is so devoted to me that she is apt to be jealous of anyone I care
for, but it is only because her own empty little heart has been
cheated and starved of that which she deserves, and the lack has
made her narrow and terribly sensative. Out of the abundance
of the glory of your love, I can see the pitifulness of her depriva-
tion and oh! Sweetheart, I am so radiantly happy I want every
one else to be.   E.

ALS (WP, DLC).
  [1] Bertha Bolling.

Reflections on Memorial Day[1]

[May 31, 1915]

Fellow citizens: I have not come here today to deliver an
address, but merely reverently to take part in expressing the sentiment of this impressive day. It is necessarily a day of reminiscences. Reminiscence is not always a profitable exercise. It generally belongs to those, appropriately to those only, who have
left the active stage of life and have nothing to think about except the things that are gone and dead. It does not behoove a
nation to walk with its eyes over its shoulder. Its business is

constantly in the years that lie ahead of it and in the present that challenges it to the display of its power. But there are reminiscences which are stimulating and wholesome, and among those reminiscences are chiefly to be ranked the recollections of days of heroism, days when great nations found it possible to express the best that was in them by the ardent exercise of every power that was in them.

That is what gives dignity to a day like this. It is not a day of regret. It is not a day of weakening memory. It is a day of stimulation. But, my friends, these stimulating memories we are sometimes apt to minimize, because we do not see the full significance of them. We are constantly speaking of the great war of which we think today as a war which saved the Union, and it did indeed save the Union, but it was a war that did a great deal more than that. It created in this country what had never existed before—a national consciousness. It was not the salvation of the Union; it was the rebirth of the Union. It was the time when America for the first time realized its unity and saw the vision of its united destiny.

The solemn lesson of these memories for us is not that we must be ready to save the Union again, for there is none among us who threaten its life, but that we must see to it that the unity then realized, the vision then seen, is exemplified in us and in the things that we do. There is no stimulation in any lesson unless it be the stimulation to duty. There is no stimulation in any occasion if it be merely the pleasure of recollection; it must also be the ardor and courage of hope. Greater days lie before this nation than it has ever seen yet; and the solemn consciousness of those who bear office in this time is that they must make their best endeavor to embody in what they do and say and are, the best things in the United States.

It does not do to talk too much about one's self, and I do not think that it is wholesome for the United States to talk too much about itself. I do not want to know what you are today so much as I want to know what you are going to do tomorrow. The only test I know of that is competent to determine what you are is the test of what you do. Let us not think of our characters; let us think of our duties and of the actions that lie before us. I have always maintained that the man who lives to cultivate his own character will result only in cultivating an intolerable prig, because his object will be himself. Character, my friends, is a byproduct; it is produced in the great manufacture of daily duty. Duty is not easy to determine. Duty for a nation is made up of so many complicated elements that no man can determine it. No

group of men without wide common counsel can possibly determine what the duty of the day is. That is the strength of
a democracy, because there daily rises in the great body of a
democracy the expression of an untrammeled opinion which
seems to fill the air with its suggestions of duty. And those who
stand at the head of affairs have it as their bounden obligation to
endeavor to express in their own actions those things that seem
to rise out of the conscience and hope and purpose of the great
body of the people themselves.

America, I have said, was reborn by the struggle of the Civil
War, but America is reborn every day of her life by the purposes
we form, the conceptions we entertain, the hopes that we cherish.
We live in our visions. We live in the things that we see. We live,
and hope abounds in us as we live, in the things that we purpose.
Let us go away from this place renewed in our devotion to daily
duty and to those ideals which keep a nation young, keep it noble,
keep it rich in enterprise and achievement; make it to lead the
nations of the world in those things that make for hope and for
the benefit of mankind.[2]

Printed in *Address of President Wilson at Arlington* . . . (Washington, 1915).
[1] At exercises held at Arlington National Cemetery. The other speakers included Bryan, Daniels, and Governor Frank Bartlette Willis of Ohio.
[2] There is a WWsh outline of these remarks, dated May 30, 1915, in WP, DLC.

To Edith Bolling Galt

[The White House] Monday morning,
My sweet darling,   31 May [1915]

A day when I neither see you nor get a message from you is a
blank on the calendar! I went to bed (early) feeling very lonely
indeed last night. You have become indispensable to me, my
sweet one, and it is *so* far from here to 1308. My thoughts run
back and forth across the distance every minute of the day and
my heart knows nothing of it: it is always with you, never here
while you are away; but I miss your *presence* so, my Love! You
are so vivid. You have such a wonderful personal charm, you
carry such an atmosphere of sweetness and intelligence and
power to comprehend and sympathize and love, if you will, that
you make any place in which you are radiant with your presence,
full of the sweet charm and dominance of you! I wonder if you
can possibly realize how your whole personality suggests love and
the very impersonation of all that is loveliest in womanhood?
Not that you wear love on your sleeve. I do not mean that. On
the contrary there is an extraordinary suggestion of dignity and

reserve about you at *all* times. One knows instinctively that you *give* the sweet things in you only when you think the gift is worthily bestowed. But one cannot look at you without feeling that he is in the presence of a noble woman to whom belong all the greatest gifts of tenderness and love. And these wonderful qualities are so nobly housed! You are so beautiful! Your beauty is of the noblest type. You might pose for any one of the great women the world has loved and been ennobled by and everyone wonder where the artist had found a mate for his original. My Love, my Lady, I love to lay these tributes of my praise at your feet. I love to *try* to put into words, no matter how imperfectly I succeed, my unbounded admiration of you. I would be happy if I could somehow immortalize you. I will not cheat my heart by holding anything back. You are entitled to know the place you hold in my mind and heart. Throughout years to come I shall let you know by something better and greater than words.

Woodrow

ALS (WP, DLC).

From Edith Bolling Galt

[Washington]

My beloved one: Monday night May 31st, 1915

How I want to come to you tonight and have you tell me all the problems that weigh so heavily, and try just by my great love and comprehension to lighten the burden. It is now 8:30 and I have just talked to our beloved Helen on the phone. I wanted so to ask her where you were, and what you were doing, but, of course, I could not. But I feel you are working, either at your desk (where I was so happy Saturday night) or else in your own room—thinking out the problems the answer from Germany makes so difficult.[1] Dearest, do you feel my arms about you and know that my whole being is in tune with yours?

Your exquisite notes of this morning and yesterday are by me, and I love every word although I feel and know my unworthiness of all your love sees in me. Still, I am happy in your belief in me, and will try to make *some* of it, at least, true.

Oh! This morning I wished so for you to listen to the tender and ernest counsel of dear old Mr. Wilson in regard to the wonderful opportunity before me in *knowing you.* He said he could not think of anything more unique in the history of the world than that *I* (whom he, bless his heart, had always believed in, and admired) and yet who lived so apart from other people—like a nun in a convent—should suddenly come in contact with

a man who occupies now the most important place in the conduct of affairs in the entire world—a man whose personality is so
striking that it dominates everyone with whom it comes in touch,
whose intellect is so profound that the whole world pauses to
listen when he spoke.

And what was I doing with this great privilege? Was I strong
enough to hold your interest permanently, or was I, of my own
indifference, and failure to fit myself to hold you, going to let
it be a mere incident of life—something that you would tire of
because of no depth in me.

As he put it, my sympathy and responsiveness and charm
would not hold such a friendship as yours without something
more tangible—of which he was pleased to say, I was capable
if I applied myself.

Otherwise I would disappoint you, ultimately. To use his illustration, which is a very good one, I would be one of two things
(a term used in regard to mines) *surface* right, which means
only picking up the bits of rock in which there is gold, or the
permanent right, which permits going down, down into the heart
of the earth until the vein of gold is found, which is the real
wealth, and which, if properly followed produces abundantly. It
is too long a conversation to write faithfully, but just to touch
on is enough to let you see, and follow. He then said if I claimed
you as a friend, he hoped you would be able to do for me what
he had failed in—that is awake some *permanent interest*, either
in some person or something—that I was too dead—that I had no
emotions—and that to his thinking all the pleasures of the world
done in an automatic way were as nothing compared to some person or happening that stir[r]ed one to the depths for either pain
or pleasure, that it was far better to suffer, even acutely, than not
to feel, and that to have all the emotions awake and pulsing was
the opening of a new world. Then he said, Why don't you ask him
to direct your life? I mean by that help you chart your course in
the waters. It would be wonderfully interesting, and by so doing
you could not fail to draw inspiration from the fountains that well
up *in this most unusual personality.*

I wish I could express this as charmingly as he did—these are
my own words which feebly explain his ideas—but I would write
more than you will have time to read if I finished this, so will wait
until tomorrow night when I can talk to you instead. I was interrupted and it is now midnight. So just a word more. I am so
happy that you miss me. It is sweet to feel I hold your heart but
that your thoughts fly back and forth between us. God keep you
always for me,   Edith

ALS (WP, DLC).

¹ J. W. Gerard to WJB, May 29, 1915, printed in *FR-WWS 1915*, pp. 419-21. About half of the German note, delivered to Gerard on May 28, was devoted to the *Cushing, Gulflight*, and *Falaba* cases. Regarding the first two, it declared that the German government would make full amends if the investigation then in progress indicated that a German submarine and aircraft had been responsible for the incidents. In the *Falaba* case, the submarine commander had intended to give passengers and crew an opportunity to save themselves; he had been unable to do so because the ship's captain had attempted to escape after being warned and had sent up rocket signals for help; even then he had waited twenty-three minutes before firing a torpedo.

As for *Lusitania*, the German government had already expressed its regret to neutral governments for the loss of their citizens' lives on that vessel. However, certain important points had to be cleared up before the United States and Germany could come to any understanding on the case. The note charged that *Lusitania* had been armed, that it proceeded under orders from the British Admiralty to use neutral flags and to ram enemy submarines, and that it had carried both Canadian soldiers and a large cargo of munitions. By carrying explosives and passengers on the same vessel in direct contravention of American law, the Cunard Company actually had been responsible for the death of American citizens on the liner. These were facts sufficiently important to merit a careful investigation by the American government. "The Imperial Government," the note concluded, "begs to reserve a final statement of its position with regard to the demands made in connection with the sinking of the *Lusitania* until a reply is received from the American government."

Wilson received an official text of the note about noon on May 31, just before he started for Arlington National Cemetery. *New York Times*, June 1, 1915.

Remarks at a Press Conference

June 1, 1915

We are waiting for you to begin this morning, Mr. President, because the situation is one which will not permit of very close questions.

I would tell you anything that I could, gentlemen, but, of course, you are all thinking of the German note. I got the text of that only yesterday, and I don't feel that it is wise to discuss it today. I know you appreciate the reasons why. And let me ask again that you will refrain from conjecturing what the reply is going to be, because some of the conjectures, as you know, are sent across the water and are accepted as an authoritative forecast, and it is very embarrassing to the government to have those things take place. I hope that our reply will not be many days delayed and, therefore, there will be the less temptation to conjecture what it will contain.

Are you prepared, Mr. President, to present a draft of your reply to the cabinet today?

No, I am not. I want to have a thorough discussion of it first.

What is the status of the Mexican note, Mr. President? When are you likely to give it out?

I am going to discuss that with the cabinet this morning;
and I hope it will be ready tomorrow morning.
For the morning papers?
Probably for the afternoon papers.
Thank you! (Laughter)
Mr. President, Senator Kern was suggesting the other day an
extra session of Congress in October, to take up the question of
amending the rules—

An extra session of the Senate, you mean. That has been
several times suggested, but no conclusion has been arrived
at about it. I am going to see Senator Kern this afternoon.
Is it likely, Mr. President, that the matter will be determined
shortly?

Probably not shortly, because, you see, there is plenty of
time, and in these days, when something turns up every
morning, one naturally waits to form conclusions of that
sort.
But the matter will be under consideration then?

Yes, sir, necessarily.
Mr. President, can you tell us anything about the future work of
Mr. Duval West?

No, sir, I cannot. His errand in Mexico is concluded.
He will not go back, Mr. President?

Not so far as appears now. But please don't state that as
a fact, because I haven't asked Mr. West whether there is
anything he would like to go back and conclude. I wouldn't
like to seem to end the matter, because he has done admirable service there. That is just for your information.
Mr. President, may I ask whether you had heard any considerable expression of opinion from various parts of the country
regarding either the German situation or the Mexican situation,
and whether those expressions give any indication as to the general tenor of public opinion?

There has been a very general expression of opinion in the
newspapers about the German matter; not much has come
to my attention about the Mexican matter.
I referred more, Mr. President, to the expressions aside from
newspapers.

Not a great many. Of course, my correspondence every
morning contains a certain number but not an unusual
number. . . .
Have you in mind, perhaps as the outgrowth of the meeting of
the Pan-American Financial Conference, to renew your recommendation for governmental purchase of ships?

I haven't had a chance to have a conference with the men who were conducting that conference as to what they conceived to be the right inferences to draw from it; so that I haven't formed a judgment about that.

Have you formed any judgment at all as to the practical results of that conference?

Only this judgment—that there was an extraordinary cordiality and readiness to cooperate with the industrialists and financiers of the United States in developing trade and intercourse between the two continents. And I think I am not wrong in saying that an entirely new spirit has arisen between the two continents—of friendship and mutual confidence.

That is sentimental rather than practical, however, isn't it?

I am speaking merely of the impressions of my mind because I haven't had time to go over the discussions of the conference and get the practical inferences from them.

Our government has no very definite idea of establishing a federal bank for South American business, has it, Mr. President?

That is a perfectly novel idea and, therefore, necessarily in inchoate form. I haven't discussed it with anyone.

T MS (C. L. Swem Coll., NjP).

A Memorandum by Lindley Miller Garrison

Cabinet June 1. 1915. All present excepting Redfield. Mexican problem taken up first.

At last meeting (May 25) we discussed question and it was agreed that the Pres. should make a statement showing that present condition was intolerable, warning all factions they must get together and that a Constitutional Govt must be established and if not U. S. would have to do whatever it might find necessary to produce that result. At this meeting (June 1) Pres. read a note he had prepared which in addition to stating intolerable conditions &c stated we would have question settled by agencies within Mexico & would give moral aid to man or group of men &c[1]

I recalled agreement of previous meeting which definitely proceeded on idea we should leave ourselves absolutely free by not stating what we intended doing &c &c Pres. at previous meeting said we might eventually have to use force & advanced the same possibility again. I thot & said that in view of this I thot present note as prepared should not be published. As prepared it simply said we were going to back another one. We have already backed Carr. & Villa & now we were going to pick another. I thot this a feeble & unnecessary statement. If we said nothing about what we were going to do, we could do whatever was wisest. If we wanted merely to back another man we need not send out any note at all. Houston agreed with me. Daniels also altho. for a different reason. Burleson was in favor of note practically as written. So was Lane. Bryan (who wanted one word eliminated because he feared it might mean intervention or inability to be free to recognize Carranza. He had a brief by Douglas Carranza's atty—the word elsewhere.[2] (We would seek suggestions elsewhere &c) W B Wilson, &c &c.

I very strong against note as written   Seems to me it does not help & will probably hurt & place us in an impossible position, i.e. it announces a policy, i.e. a new policy & behold it is a continuation of same old policy.

I fear Pres. will send note tinkered up but to same general intent as written.

This matter took up the time until 12:30. Next Pres. read an editorial from an El Paso paper summing up the editorial comment of the country on the German note of May 29th.

There was some slight discussion as to whether that reply wasn't insincere quibble & evasive. Bryan & Burleson thought note opportunity in order to enter a discussion of Germany's position with Germany. I gave Pres. a copy of my suggestions[3] (included herewith) & in course of discussion briefly stated my views. No one had anything to suggest. Pres. suggested that they had repudiated doctrine & pointed out place in note. I pointed out that it was not clear, only inferential, & that we must have a clear statement as to action & to principle. If they ack. prin. one thing was proper. If not then another. Pres. indicated disapproval of Germany's reply but did not indicate how he would treat it. He took my mem. with him.[4]

Hw memorandum (received from Harvey Mortimer).

[1] The WWT draft that Wilson read is in the C. L. Swem Coll., NjP. The statement is printed as an Enclosure with WW to WJB, June 2, 1915 (first letter of that date).

[2] The brief by Charles Alexander Douglas is missing. However, see WJB to WW, June 2, 1915 (first letter of that date).

[3] L. M. Garrison, CC draft note dated June 1, 1915 (received from Harvey Mortimer). The T draft is in WP, DLC. It stated bluntly that the German note of May 28 ignored the main thrust of the American note of May 13. The American note had cited an "elemental principle" of international law, which "absolutely insured the safety of neutrals on unresisting merchant vessels of any nationality, by the requirement of visitation before action should be taken against the vessel, and of salvage of noncombatants before the destruction of the vessel." Garrison's note demanded that the German government state explicitly where it stood in regard to this principle. This was a necessary prelude to discussion of the cases at issue between the two nations.

⁴ David F. Houston later recalled a much more extensive discussion of the German note and the appropriate American response than Garrison indicates here. One unnamed cabinet member asked what was to be done about England's interference with American trade. Bryan, who had "seemed to be labouring under a great strain and [had] sat back in his chair most of the time with his eyes closed," now became excited. "He said," Houston remembered, "that he had all along insisted on a note to England; that she was illegally preventing our exports from going where we had a right to send them; and that the Cabinet seemed to be pro-Ally. . . . The President sharply rebuked Bryan, saying that his remarks were unfair and unjust. He had no right to say that any one was pro-Ally or pro-German. Each one was merely trying to be a good American. We had lodged a protest with England and might do so again at the proper time, but this would be a singularly inappropriate time to take up such a matter with her. Furthermore, he had had indications that the control of shipping would be taken out of the hands of the Admiralty. . . , that there would be Cabinet changes, and that our reasonable demands would be met. Certainly, in any event, when we had before us a grave issue with the Germans, it would be folly to force an issue of such character with England. We were merely trying to look at our duty and all our problems objectively. He added that certain things were clear and that as to them his mind was made up." David F. Houston, *Eight Years with Wilson's Cabinet, 1913 to 1920* (2 vols., Garden City, N. Y., 1926), I, 132-33, 137. In his narrative of this meeting, Houston errs by saying that Wilson read a draft of a new note to Berlin; otherwise his account seems reliable and is based on contemporary material.

From Robert Lansing, with Enclosure

Dear Mr. President: Washington June 1, 1915.

I send you herewith a telegram which I have just received from Daniel F. Kellogg of New York,¹ whom I have known for the past thirty years, and who was a few years ago the City Editor of the New York Sun. I cannot say that I agree with the suggestions contained in the telegram; but, in view of Mr. Kellogg's standing, I think that his telegram is worthy of consideration as an expression of opinion by certain influential Americans.

Very sincerely yours,   Robert Lansing.

TLS (WP, DLC).
¹ Daniel Fiske Kellogg, most recently associated with J. P. Morgan & Co., in charge of publicity. He and Lansing were classmates at Amherst College.

E N C L O S U R E

PERSONAL

New York June 1 1915

I have not the pleasure of knowing the President personally and have not means of getting this telegram to his personal notice unless you will do me the great favor of seeing that it gets to him   I believe it is worthy of his attention   I am now wholly out of business and in the last forty eight hours have talked with nearly fifty of the best people in New York City including one who has recently retired from the chief justiceship of the Court of Appeals of our state upon the Lusitania incident. The sentiment is almost universal to the effect that while the German reply is evasive and quibbling the Government of the United States will yet not be justified in proceeding upon the assumption that the contentions raised by the Germans are either insincere or dishonest or both Even a pettifogger must be allowed to have his day in court The German contentions are these, chiefly, that the Lusitania was in fact an armed cruiser carrying concealed guns, and secondly that the action of the British government in suggesting to its merchant vessels that they should arm themselves and attack submarines qualified the privileges otherwise enjoyed by these vessels under international law as undefended property. It is universally thought here that the first contention can easily be disapproved in any competent judical investigation It is also thought by intelligent people that something of merit does attach to the second contention and that the British government in making this suggestion has complicated the otherwise clear path of international law in much the same manner that the German government has done by its action in commandeering food stuffs for the use of the military. At any rate our government will not be justified in proceeding upon the assumption that its understanding of the matter is absolutely sound and justified without any judicial investigation whatever. What is the matter with suggesting to the German government that all these questions should be submitted to some sort of speedy investigation or arbitration and that pending this there should be no repetition of the Lusitania incident You may rely upon it that this is the opinion of the best people in New York City and that people here would be strongly adverse to any government action that would make war possible on any grounds that have been disclosed to date.

Daniel F Kellogg

T telegram (SDR, RG 59, 763.72/1780½, DNA).

From James Watson Gerard

Dear Mr. President: [Berlin] June 1, 1915.

Here are some general and rather disjointed thoughts and observations and gossip.

I supposed that because I had some acquaintance with German watering-places and German-Americans that I knew a little about Germany. I was wrong. No casual traveller ever gets to know the military caste nor do the members of that caste travel except on "business."

A century and a quarter ago Mirabeau said that "war was the national industry of Prussia." Since then, Prussia, by wars of conquest, has increased her territory and has imposed her leadership and ideas on all Germany. The members of the military caste live like Spartans, and are rewarded by the fact that they rule the country and look down on the merchant class; they feel that they have created a modern industrial Germany in the same way that they would order a Krupp gun. As Prince Donnersmarck, the third richest person in Germany, told me, —"he had advised the Government that they must have a farmer class to furnish soldiers and an industrial class to pay and equip them." Hence the protection of both agriculture and manufactures. Prince Donnersmarck is a marvellous man, eighty-nine years old, successful in all his undertakings; he was governor of Lorraine during the war of 1870. The military caste (of which the naval and all Government bureaus are branches) has organized the nation for war with the efficiency of the managers of a great American corporation. The Government is an absolutism. Some tame professors are paid by the State to give an impression of "Kultur." No Jew can become an officer; officers of crack regiments do not go to the houses of persons in any kind of business; a business man is called a "kaufmann" as we speak of a housepainter. This disquisition is written to try to give you the atmosphere here.

This war is now a war for conquest or money. All people tell me that—"we must have pay for so much blood," "if we don't keep Belgium there will be a revolution," "who is to pay for the war?" etc. A Socialist who referred yesterday, in the Reichstag, to the Kaiser's speech at the beginning of the war, which stated that this was not a war to get territory, was well sat upon. Even the Socialists are all for war against Italy. None of the German colonies are fit for Europeans. Germany last year proposed joint intervention in Mexico to England.[1] If successful, Germany will try to get a foothold in the Western Hemisphere; the Monroe doctrine is like a red rag to a bull to every German. My relations with members of the Government are quite agree-

[1] Gerard was repeating a persistent rumor to the effect that a personal emissary of William II had, in July 1914, informally proposed to British officials some form of joint intervention in Mexico. It is commonly assumed that the person was Albert Ballin, who was in fact sent to England by Chancellor von Bethmann Hollweg and Foreign Minister von Jagow in late July 1914 in an attempt to preserve the peace between England and Germany. However, there is no documentary evidence in either German or British archives indicating that Ballin or anyone else spoke of Mexico to British officials at this time. See Friedrich Katz, Deutschland, Diaz und die mexikanische Revolution. . . . (Berlin, 1964), pp. 315-16, and Lamar Cecil, Albert Ballin: Business and Politics in Imperial Germany, 1888-1918 (Princeton, N. J., 1967), pp. 205-210.

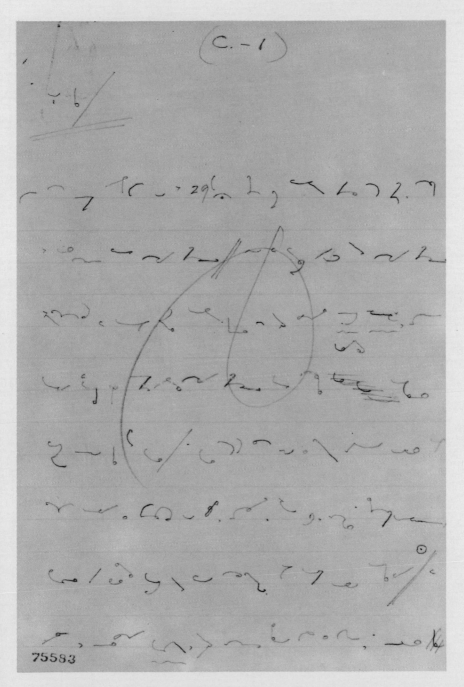

Wilson's shorthand draft of the second *Lusitania* note

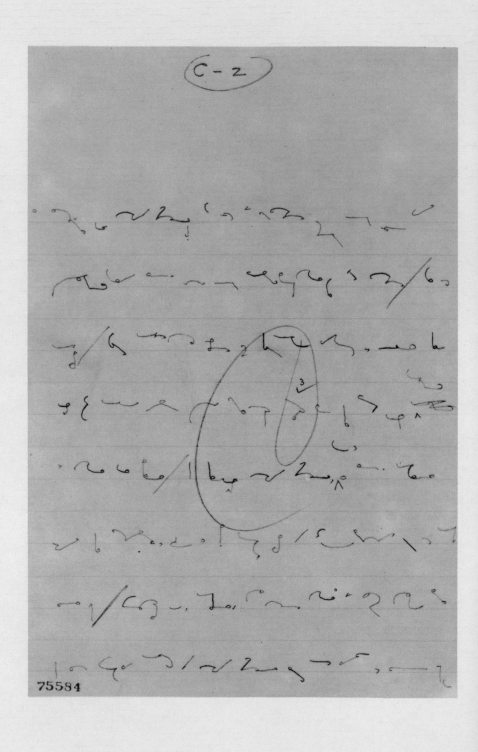

(3)

75585

(5)

75587

William Jennings Bryan

Edith Bolling Galt

able,—but there is no effective Government at present. The Chancellor will take no decisive action and leaves matters to department heads, who fight with other department heads. The Emperor saw fit to follow the traditions of 1870 and go to the field, taking the Chancellor and heads of many departments with him; hence great governmental confusion, but this does not affect military organization. He is bored by the Chancellor,—a good man but not of action or decision. Von Falkenheyn is the Emperor's favorite; he is Chief of the General Staff. Von Tirpitz and von Müller[2] (also naval) have great influence. The Kaiser is thus surrounded by military influences. Enclosed are specimens of the news published by the General Staff and given to the Emperor to read.[3] You will see that he gets only German-American news from America and no bad news from anywhere. On the "Lusitania" case there is a disposition to think because we were not warlike over Mexico that we will stand anything. The Kaiser will not see me because of the delivery of arms by Americans to the Allies, and has so stated.

There is no shortage of food supply. I was told yesterday they did not need our Polish Relief Committee[4] for German Poland as Germany can take care of that alone. The hate of Americans is intense. But this hate can be turned off and on by the Government. The people believe anything they see in the papers. The monetary situation is not bad. All the money for war supplies has been spent in Germany except perhaps for a few horses etc., from Scandanavia.

About 500 women demonstrated, in front of the Reichstag two days ago, against war. They were promptly suppressed by the police and no word was printed in any newspaper. These women were rather vague, they called von Bülow (for his failure in Italy) "an old fathead" and complained that the whipped cream (without which a German meal is a failure) was not as good as before the war. There was also some talk of high prices for food, and many said they wanted their "men" back from the trenches. But so far these cases of protest are isolated, and *the nation, as a whole, is determined on a finish fight.*

There are three thousand Americans left in Germany; only a small proportion are in business. The remainder, German-Amer-

2 Georg Alexander von Müller, chief of the naval cabinet, whose *Regierte der Kaiser?* . . . , ed. Walter Görlitz (Göttingen, 1959), is a major source for this period.

3 These enclosures are missing.

4 It had been recently organized by Gerard and others with the help of the Rockefeller Foundation. Gerard describes the organization of the commission and the obstacles that it subsequently encountered in his *My Four Years in Germany* (New York, 1917), pp. 297-300.

icans, women song-birds, piano-players and students. I have no sympathy with any but the business men, if all are caught by war. An example,—we advised a woman and her daughter to leave in August. They stayed and ran up bills of over ten thousand marks, and, as arrest for debt exists here, could not leave when they finally decided to go home. We had to raise money by subscription in the Embassy to pay their most pressing bills and get them out of the country, leaving an added prejudice against Americans behind.

Two or three froward German-Americans have attacked you, Secretary Bryan, and our Government,—some publicly. I have ordered their passports taken away and hope you will sustain me in this; allowing them longer to poison the air without rebuke was taken as a sign of weakness here. No one who abuses his own country, its Government or its chief is entitled to protection from that country.

We have the British prisoners in good shape now that the prohibition, put on visiting and inspecting camps by the State Department in November last, has been done away with by the "treaty," which I arranged between England and Germany in March. It was not until March 29th that we finally got passes to visit camps under the "treaty." The prisoners are perhaps badly treated when they are first captured; we only know of their treatment when they have been placed in detention camps. I do not believe all the atrocity stories; but one of our servants, in this house, came back from the East front recently and said the orders were to kill all Cossacks; our washerwoman reports that her son was ordered to shoot a woman in Belgium, and I myself have heard an officer calmly describe the shooting of a seven year old Belgian girl child, the excuse being that she had fired at an officer. . . .

Jane Addams came here and I arranged that she meet the Foreign Minister and Chancellor. Of course political women are not looked on with favor here but she is an exception. . . .

I fear that Germany will not give up its present method of submarine warfare. Each month new and more powerful submarines are added and England will eventually be cut off. Better to allow food, forage, copper, cotton and rubber and all raw materials, not directly used in the manufacture of munitions of war to enter Germany. In this case Germany will stop torpedoing without notice. Good for us too.

Another solution is that if Americans insist on claiming vested right to travel on belligerent vessels that we certify those vessels as not carrying munitions of war and as not being armed and the belligerents to order vessels carrying passengers not to try to ram or fire on submarines; the vessel to go to a designated port and carry a designated flag or its name prominently displayed. Possibly the Germans might agree not to torpedo such vessels without notice.

Please let me know if you want information on any particular point, and I shall try to furnish the information.

Best wishes for a solution of all the great difficulties you are called on to meet.   Ever Yours   James W. Gerard.

TLS (WP, DLC).

To Edith Bolling Galt

My lovely Sweetheart,
[The White House] Tuesday morning, 7 o'cl. 1 June, 1915.

I find I am getting to look forward to these quiet morning hours alone with my darling, when I can sit here and, without fear of interruption or thought of the outside world, say to her what I would whisper into her ear could I but hold her close in my arms and forget everything but our love. There is no one else in the world for me now—there is nothing worth while but love. Nothing else gives life, or confidence, or joy in action. A man is not sufficient by himself, whatever his strength and courage. He is maimed and incomplete without his mate, his heart's companion, the dear one to whom he is lover and comrade. Oh, it was sweet of you to come to me in my need! I love to think how you walked out of the great world into my little circle here, almost as if by chance, but really by gracious beckoning of Providence, and met me face to face with those dear frank eyes of yours and that wonderful smile of friendly greeting, giving me a thrill at the very first touch of your hand, and how immediately, when we had the chance, we found one another, found that we were meant for comrades, that it gave our spirits a happy pleasure to be together and walk the same path of intimate intercourse together. And then,—ah, it was inevitable, Sweetheart! I could but love you when once I had found you,—I could but tell you (we could keep nothing from one another) that never-to-be-forgotten night only four weeks ago! And now—oh, what joy it gives me to write it! —*you love me*! And to-night we shall say it all over again to one another, with nothing *but* joy and hope and confidence in the sweet repetition. You have brought me into the light, my Darling. God bless you! The day's very solemn duties will presently invade this quiet place where I sit now with no thoughts but thoughts of you. The German note must be answered and answered very soon. But when I see your eyes alight to-night with the sweetest, holiest thing in all the world, and hold you close in my arms and kiss you, with pledges as deep as my soul, I shall be made fit for that and more.   Woodrow

ALS (WP, DLC).

From Edith Bolling Galt

                                                    [Washington]
My best Beloved: June 1st, 1915   11:30 P.M.

I am so happy that I cannot go to sleep until I tell you—What a sort of dream-evening this has been, so radiant were the hours, and how completely you filled them!

This first June day has been so crowded with joy that my heart can hold no more, and I must talk to you, and make you feel how splendidly I love you. Each time we are together, Dearest, you seem more completely to fill my need and to stimulate and awaken every emotion.

While I write there is a gleam of the magic circle on my finger[1] that warms my heart with its *more than precious* message from you. At night I usually take off my rings but this one will stay where I can feel it, even in my dreams. And it brings me the most exquisite pleasure.

Goodnight, and may sleep fall over you as "feathers, dropped from angel's wings" and may your first waking thought be, Woodrow: She *loves* me, and *she* is as happy as a child, who asks no questions of Fate, but trusts her, and knows the future will be kind. Thank you again for the orchids, they are really *poems* in the literature of flowers, and no pen can find the prose word with which to express the delight with which I hold them. My heart goes with this back to your keeping, and I am longing for you   Edith

ALS (WP, DLC).
[1] It was not an engagement ring.

To William Jennings Bryan, with Enclosure

My dear Mr. Secretary,   The White House. 2 June, 1915.

Here is the Mexican statement recast in a way which I hope meets entirely the views you expressed yesterday.

If it meets with your approval, will you not be kind enough to let Tumulty know by telephone, so that he may release it for the afternoon papers? I rather led them to expect it yesterday when I saw them.

And will you not see that correct copies are sent (they can be sent plain in the circumstances) to our several representatives near the principal factional chiefs, so that this may serve as a direct and personal reminder to them?

Cordially and faithfully,   W.W.

WWTLI (W. J. Bryan Papers, DNA).

E N C L O S U R E

Mexico: [June 2, 1915]

For more than two years revolutionary conditions have esisted [existed] in Mexico. The purpose of the revolution was to rid Mexico of men who ignored the constitution of the Republic and used their power in contempt of the rights of its people; and with these purposes the people of the United States instinctively and generously sympathized. But the leaders of the revolution, in the very hour of their success, have disagreed and turned their arms against one another. All professing the same objects, they are nevertheless unable or unwilling to cooperate. A central authority at Mexico City is no sooner set up than it is undermined and its authority denied by those who were expected to support it. Mexico is apparently no nearer a solution of her tragical troubles than she was when the revolution was first kindled. And she has been swept by civil war as if by fire. Her crops are destroyed, her fields lie unseeded, her work cattle are confiscated for the use of the armed factions, her people flee to the mountains to escape being drawn into unavailing bloodshed, and no man seems to see or lead the way to peace and settled order. There is no proper protection either for her own citizens or for the citizens of other nations resident and at work within her territory. Mexico is starving and without a government.

In these circumstances the people and government of the United States cannot stand indifferently by and do nothing to serve their neighbor. They want nothing for themselves in Mexico. Least of all do they desire to settle her affairs for her, or claim any right to do so. But neither do they wish to see utter ruin come upon her, and they deem it their duty as friends and neighbors to lend any aid they properly can to any instrumentality which promises to be effective in bringing about a settlement which will embody the real objects of the revolution,—constitutional government and the rights of the people. Patriotic Mexicans are sick at heart and cry out for peace and for every self-sacrifice that may be necessary to procure it. Their people cry out for food and will presently hate as much as they fear every man, in their country or out of it, who stands between them and their daily bread.

It is time, therefore, that the Government of the United States should frankly state the policy which in these extraordinary circumstances it becomes its duty to adopt. It must presently do what it has not hitherto done or felt at liberty to do, lend its active moral support to some man or group of men, if such may be found, who can rally the suffering people of Mexico to their support in an effort to ignore, if they cannot unite, the warring factions of the country, return to the constitution of the Republic so long in abeyance, and set up a government at Mexico City which the great powers of the world can recognize and deal with, a government with whom the programme of the revolution will be a business and not merely a platform. I, therefore, publicly and very solemnly, call upon the leaders of faction in Mexico to act, to act together, and to act promptly for the relief and redemption of their prostrate country. I feel it to be my duty to tell them that, if they cannot accommodate their differences and unite for this great purpose within a very short time, this Government will be constrained to decide what means should be employed by the United States in order to help Mexico save herself and serve her people.[1]

T MS (WP, DLC).
[1] There is a WWsh draft of this statement in WP, DLC. In his WWT draft, Wilson had written in conclusion: "I feel it to be my duty to tell them that, if they cannot accommodate their differences and unite for this great purpose within a very short time, this Government will be constrained to turn elsewhere for suggestions as to how the United States can help Mexico save herself and serve her people." This was the sentence to which Bryan had objected.

Two Letters from William Jennings Bryan

My Dear Mr. President: Washington June 2, 1915

I am just in receipt of your Mexican statement which you were kind enough to send over. I think the amendments you have made have improved it, although, as you remember, it was quite satisfactory to me yesterday with the exception of one word.

However, as you ask for 'suggestions, permit me to inquire whether, on the first page, about one-third of the way down, it would not be wise to substitute the words "its authority denied" instead of "robbed of authority." This is merely a suggestion intended to avoid use of the word "rob." It is not, however, a material change.

In the last sentence I notice you have substituted the words "for other means" for the word "elsewhere" which was under discussion. My object in calling attention to the word "elsewhere" yesterday was that it did not express what I understood to be your intention, namely, to leave yourself free to decide what to do. The change which you have made removes the suggestion that you would *necessarilly* turn to other persons than the present leaders in Mexico and to that extent corrects the commitment which might have been understood from the use of the word "elsewhere." The phrase "look for other means" does not quite express your thought as I understood it although it comes nearer to it than the word "elsewhere,["] if I understand your point of view.

What I fear is that the papers will attempt to put a construction upon it which will exclude the possibility of recognizing either one of the factions if, upon investigation, you should find it better to recognize one of those factions than to invite the organization of a new faction. It is possible that by the time you are ready to act Carranza might exert an influence that would justify his recognition. It is possible that it might be wise to encourage Angeles if he could show sufficient support.

I think the words "to decide what means should be employed" would leave us more latitude than the words "look for other means." However, this is merely a suggestion as you know your own wishes in the matter. It is merely submitted out of a desire to render you any assistance that I can.

I shall ask to have this note sent you at once and you can advise Mr. Tumulty as to the release of the statement. If he will then advise me when it is released, as it is, or with such changes as you may desire, I will have it sent to Mexico City, to Carrothers and to Silliman.

I am, my dear Mr. President,

Very truly yours,   W. J. Bryan

Will you please indicate on enclosed copy "no changes" or such changes as you make.

TLS (WP, DLC).

My dear Mr. President: Washington June 2nd, 1915.

Ambassador Náon called to express very cordial approval of the Mexican statement and to say that when you are ready to recognize anyone, he thinks it would be wise for the ABC countries to recognize at the same time. In fact, he reminds me that this was contemplated in the agreement at Nicaragua [Niagara] and he has brought it to my attention since. I told him that I thought it would be very nice to have the ABC countries to recognize at the same time, and that it might be advisable also to notify all the other Latin-American countries having representatives in Mexico so that all could act simultaneously, and I know of no reason why the European countries might not be notified also, because the more complete the recognition the stronger the moral force of the government recognized.

You may be interested to know that Mr. Lansing came into the room just after I had dictated my letter to you in regard to the two suggested changes this morning. I showed him the statement and he read it through, stopping on the last sentence to suggest the very change which I had a few moments before mentioned in my letter. He even used exactly the same words, namely, "what means should be employed." I thought you might be interested to know that his judgment supports the change.

With assurances of high respect, I am, my dear Mr. President,   Very sincerely yours,   W. J. Bryan

TLS (W. J. Bryan Papers, DNA).

Two Letters to William Jennings Bryan

My dear Mr. Secretary,   The White House. 2 June, 1915.

I like these suggestions very much indeed, and hope that when the proper time comes you will act on them.

Faithfully Yours,   W.W.

P.S. It is very interesting that Lansing should have made the same suggestions about the closing words of the statement. It furnished me with exactly what I was looking for.   W.W.[1]

[1] The revised statement was given to the press immediately after this exchange.

My dear Mr. Secretary,   The White House. 2 June, 1915.

I have no doubt that this letter of Belt's[1] gives us in detail a very clear view of what we have all along known or inferred, and it ought still further to put us on our guard. I am very much obliged to you for having let me see it.

Faithfully Yours,   W.W.

WWTLI (W. J. Bryan Papers, DNA).
[1] J. W. Belt to W. J. Bryan, May 21, 1915, TLS (W. J. Bryan Papers, DNA).

In this lengthy letter, John W. Belt, a Spanish-speaking assistant to United States Consul John Reid Silliman, discussed the activities of an "International Committee" of American and other foreign businessmen based in Mexico City. He asserted that their objective was to bring about intervention by the United States in Mexico and that, to attain this end, they were carrying on an active propaganda campaign in the United States, as well as getting into contact with American political leaders, such as Theodore Roosevelt, who opposed the administration's Mexican policy. He also reported on continuing serious shortages of food in the areas of Mexico that he had visited.

From Eliseo Arredondo

Mr. President: Washington, D. C. June 2, 1915.

I have the honor to include hereinafter, for Your Excellency's information, a cablegram I have received from Mr. V. Carranza, reading as follows:

"Veracruz, June 1st, 1915.

Eliseo Arredondo, Esquire,
     Mexican Embassy,
          Washington, D. C.

Our recent military successes make the triumph of our cause a palpable fact, and I have, therefore decreed the free importation of all kinds of food supplies for the City of Mexico. Affectionate regards.

V. Carranza."

I have hastened to bring this matter to Your Excellency's attention aiming to allay the excitement caused here by reports regarding the precarious conditions alleged to be raging in the City of Mexico.

Mr. Carranza, the only Mexican official who had the courage to protest against Huerta's usurpation and to oppose him by the force of arms, because he loved his people and their institutions, has today given a new proof of his kindness by inclining to the necessities and privations of the inhabitants of the Capital, renouncing the rights of war, at the risk of sacrificing the success of military operations near that city, and going perhaps to the extent of aiding his enemies, the Zapatistas, who are still in control of it, has directed General Pablo Gonzales, Chief of Operations, to permit the free entry of all kinds of food stuffs into the Capital to allay the conditions of the suffering poor.

I beg to invite Your Excellency's attention to the fact that Mr. Carranza's action is a severe denial of all the calumnies preferred against him by his enemies, and that subservient to the sentiments of humanity inspiring him, he has once more shown to the world all the force of his character and the loftiness of his aims, by postponing political necessities to the supreme exigencies of the people.

I trust that the attitude of Mr. Carranza may be justly appreciated by Your Excellency, who has shown so much interest in the betterment of the masses, and it affords me great pleasure in reiterating to Your Excellency the assurance of my highest consideration.   E. Arredondo

TLS (WP, DLC).

From William Jennings Bryan

My dear Mr. President: Washington June 2nd, 1915.

I am sending you a map which was sent me by the Constitutionalists here in the city.[1] It gives the military situation *as they announce it*. It is to be expected, of course, that it will state the maximum of their claims and I do not mean to endorse its accuracy. I am only sending it to you that you may see the extent of their claims. I hope you will understand that I am not advising the recognition of Carranza in what I have said; my only purpose was to leave the matter open so that you could act according to the light which you had when the time came for action. I shall be pleased to send you from time to time any information which would contribute to an understanding of the situation.

With assurances of high respect, I am, my dear Mr. President,
Very sincerely yours,   W. J. Bryan

TLS (W. J. Bryan Papers, DNA).
[1] This enclosure is missing.

Three Letters to William Jennings Bryan

My dear Mr. Secretary,   Washington. 2 June, 1915.

Thank you for letting me see these papers.[1] I am entirely open to anything that events may open to us, even the recognition of Carranza if he should develop the necessary influence and begin to bring real order out of chaos. But I think our statement ought to precipitate things (in the chemical sense) and open up either this or some other channel of action.

Faithfully Yours,   W.W.

WWTLI (W. J. Bryan Papers, DNA).
[1] RL to JPT, May 25, 1915, TLS (WP, DLC), enclosing V. Carranza to his generals, May 3, 1915, T translation of memorandum (WP, DLC). Carranza declared that finally, after much vacillation, the United States Government was beginning to accept the Constitutionalists as the best hope for the Mexican people. In order to enhance the possibility of American recognition, Carranza went on, he was contemplating issuing a proclamation, which he outlined to his generals for their consideration. It provided for guarantees to foreigners of

their lives, liberty, and property rights; the restoration of law and order; religious freedom and separation of church and state; an equitable distribution of land; the promotion of both public and private education; and the holding of both local and national elections, as previously pledged by the Constitutionalists. These pledges, said Carranza, "form part of the revolution and constitute an obligation contracted with the country, which the Constitutionalist Government will not fail to comply with." He closed with the additional comment: "I communicate the above to you to give you an exact idea of the international situation, which has assumed transcendental importance."

Carranza issued this proclamation, entitled, "Declaration to the Nation. . . ," on June 11, 1915. It is cited and summarized in n. 1 to the remarks at a press conference printed at June 15, 1915.

My dear Mr. Secretary,   The White House. 2 June, 1915.

Would you be kind enough to let me have, for the guidance of my thought on this anxious matter, an outline of the answer you think we should make to the German reply to our note? I feel that I very much need all the counsel I can get, and I shall, of course, chiefly value yours. I meant to ask you this yesterday.

I would like very much to have also a similar memorandum from Mr. Lansing, if he will be kind enough to prepare one for me.

With warmest regard,
                          Faithfully Yours,   Woodrow Wilson

WWTLS (CLO)

My dear Mr. Secretary,   The White House. 2 June, 1915.

Will you be kind enough to lay before Mr. Lansing, for me, the following questions.

Am I justified in assuming that the action of the commander of the *Falaba* in seeking to escape and in signalling for help did not at all alter the duty of the commander of the submarine in regard to the treatment to which her passengers and crew were entitled?

Am I right in holding that international law has never recognized the right on the part of any nation to establish a prohibited or, so to say "posted," danger zone on the high seas and demand that it be cleared for her operations or that it be admitted that neutral vessels enter it at their own risk?

                          Faithfully Yours,   W.W.

WWTLI (SDR, RG 59, 841.857 L 97/88, DNA).

From William Jennings Bryan, with Enclosures

My dear Mr. President: Washington June 2, 1915.

Responding to your generous request for suggestions as to the reply to be made to the German note, I beg to enclose some suggestions submitted by Mr. Lansing. I have asked him to amplify his statement by giving his opinion as to the points raised in the German note and will send that with comments when it is ready.

You will notice that in proposition one of his note, he leaves out the word "unarmed." You will remember that he suggested the word "unresisting" in place of "unarmed." I have asked him to give such authority as he can find on the distinction between "unarmed" and "unresisting." He has given me a memorandum, dated June 2nd, which I enclose, but he will not be able to prepare today an opinion on the different propositions. I am asking, therefore, that you will allow me to submit a few suggestions this evening and then tonight I will take time to go over the answer and send you a memorandum tomorrow covering all the points raised. I think that Mr. Lansing will by that time be able to complete the memorandum which he has in mind.

There are two thoughts which I beg to submit at this time: First, that we should not feel it necessary to make an immediate answer: (a) because it is more important that the answer should be wisely drawn than that it should be speedily sent; (b) that time itself is a factor of no mean importance. In our peace plan we have emphasized the advantage of time for investigation and deliberation. The matter with which we are dealing is one of the first magnitude. It involves questions, which have in times past, furnished an excuse if not a cause for armed conflict. Our note to Germany, while unequivocally stating this Government's position, was couched in friendly language and the German reply is in the same tone. There is apparently no desire on either side for war; and there is always hope of an amicable adjustment where neither side desires war. So much on the subject of time.

Second: It seems to me that the note can properly be subjected to legal treatment—that is, we can take up the different points raised by the German Government and, assuming that they are presented in good faith, treat them as we would if it were a case in court, drawing a distinction between material and immaterial propositions. In court, facts which are not material are met by a demurrer, which means that even if the proposition stated is true, it does not effect the issue. If the proposition presents a fact, something which if a fact would materially effect the issue, we can then answer the proposition if we believe the statement of fact to be erroneous, or investigate it if we are not in position to deny it. The above is merely a brief suggestion to accompany Mr. Lansing's suggestion.

I do not agree with Mr. Lansing as to the propriety of using the word "unresisting" instead of "unarmed." It seems to me that the character of the vessel is determined, not by whether she resists or not, but by whether she is armed or not. Take, for instance, the crusier; the fact that she is armed raises the presumption that she will use her arms and, therefore, she is not entitled to the same treatment as the unarmed vessel. If we use the word "unresisting," the attacking party would not be entitled to employ force until after the vessel had actually used her arms, which would give the vessel attacked a great advantage over the vessel attacking.

Neither do I agree with him as to the advisability of requiring the German Government to first agree to the principals involved before we discuss the facts of this particular case. It is the custom of the State Department to investigate the facts before taking a position. In the case of the Lusitania we stated our position upon *a state of facts as we understood them.* If a question is raised as to the correctness of the assumed facts, I can see no reason why we should refuse to consider the question of facts. For instance, suppose the German Government had replied that our note was based upon the assumption that certain American[s] were drowned by the sinking of the vessel, but that it was Germany's understanding that no Americans were on the vessel and, therefore, none could have been drowned. If that was the fact questioned is there any reason why we should answer "you must first tell us what you would do in case American citizens were drowned and then we will discuss whether they were drowned or not?" If the facts which they set up are not material, that is if we could demur to them, we can so state, but I do not see how we could reasonably refuse to consider a question of fact when it is properly raised.

This I am writing in a hurry and I am simply thinking out loud. I want to go over the note carefully and take it up point by point, and then I shall be pleased to lay before you a more matured suggestion as to its treatment.

With assurances of high respect, I am, my dear Mr. President,
Very sincerely yours,   W. J. Bryan

P.S. I suppose the German Ambassador brought before you the suggestion which he made to me, namely, that this question of fact is raised in order to give the German Government a plausible excuse for accepting our position if the grounds upon which its action was based proved to be erroneous. If Germany is really looking for a way out we cannot do otherwise than assist her. This might not be to the advantage of sensational newspapers, but I am sure that it would meet with unanimous approval throughout the country.

TLS (WP, DLC).

E N C L O S U R E   I

Robert Lansing to William Jennings Bryan

Dear Mr. Secretary: [Washington] June 1, 1915.

The American note of May 13th was founded on the following principles of law and humanity:

1. Citizens of neutral nationality are entitled to traverse the high seas in merchant vessels of any nationality.

2. They are entitled to be protected from danger to life by the exercise of the belligerent right of visit and by the performance of the belligerent duty of placing passengers and crew of an enemy or neutral merchant vessel in safety in the event that the vessel is destroyed.

3. To destroy a merchant vessel without safeguarding the lives of the persons on board is inhuman and morally wrong.

The German note of May 28th does not admit, deny or even discuss these principles which affect the future as well as the past conduct of the German naval authorities. The note reviews the facts and seeks to raise doubts as to the correctness of those on which this Government relies.

The essential issue between the Governments is one of principle and not of fact. I can see no benefit to be derived from disputing as to the invasion of a right unless both parties agree that the right exists.

The German note appears to have been drafted with the design of drawing this Government into a controversy as to the facts and avoiding the questions of the principles involved.

In my opinion the reply to the German note should state that a discussion of the facts of specific cases would be premature before the rights asserted in the American note had been admitted and assurance given that in future those rights would not be violated; that upon receiving such admission and assurance this Government would consider the conflicting evidence as to the facts; and that the question of liability depends primarily on the principles applicable to the cases which have arisen.

The German note is not expressed in language which evinces

a friendly sentiment for the United States. It shows an inflexible purpose to continue a course of action which this Government has frankly asserted to be illegal and inhuman. In view of the tone of the German note I do not think that the reply should be less firm or should repeat the friendly expressions of the note of May 13th, which have been, with apparent intention, ignored by the German Government.

Faithfully yours,   Robert Lansing.

ENCLOSURE   II

Robert Lansing to William Jennings Bryan

Dear Mr. Secretary: [Washington] June 2, 1915.

In drafting the note of May 13th you will recall that I suggested that the word "unarmed" be changed to "unresisting." There were two reasons for the suggestion.

First. It is entirely legal for a merchant vessel to carry a defensive armament without losing her character of a vessel of commerce. The Department issued a statement to this effect last September,[1] as the law was well settled on that point. The use of the adjective "unarmed," therefore, implied that if *armed* a vessel changed her status and was subject to different treatment, which practically contradicted the Department's statement.

Second. The adjective "unresisting" appeared broader in application in that it covered not only an armament of the vessel but any use of small arms against a boarding party and any attempt to ram a submarine which had signalled a vessel to stop.

As you will recall you thought the word "unarmed" should be retained, and I think that I was at fault in not explaining my reasons more fully.

The German Government has seized the opportunity in its last note to build up an argument on the allegation that the LUSITANIA was armed and the German Ambassador has sent to the Department several affidavits to support the allegation. While I do not think that these affidavits, if true (which is doubtful) constitute a substantial argument for Germany since they do not show that the German Government knew of the armament on the LUSITANIA before the vessel was sunk, I believe, if opportunity offers, the idea of "unresisting" should be emphasized as the only legitimate reason for attack without visit.

Faithfully yours,   Robert Lansing.

TLS (WP, DLC).
[1] See WW to RL, Sept. 17, 1914 (second letter of that date), n. 1, Vol. 31.

To William Jennings Bryan

My dear Mr. Secretary,   The White House. 2 June, 1915.

I am very much obliged to you for the suggestions you have sent me about the note we are to send to Germany, and will welcome anything further you may be good enough to send.

I think that time (though of course not haste) is of the essence in this matter in order that the German Government should be made to feel that we regard it as pressing; for they show not the least inclination or purpose to change their methods even pending this interchange of views.

Faithfully Yours,   W.W.

WWTLI (W. J. Bryan Papers, DNA).

To Juliet Barrett Rublee

My dear Mrs. Rublee: .   [The White House] June 2, 1915

I thank you sincerely for your very interesting and informing letter of June first.¹ Its contents interest me deeply.

I followed as best I could the action of the women at the Hague and the other day read the resolutions adopted with the greatest interest and admiration.²

Cordially and sincerely yours,   Woodrow Wilson

TLS (Letterpress Books, WP, DLC).
    ¹ Her letter is missing. She had recently returned from the International Congress of Women at The Hague, where she represented the Washington branch of the Woman's Peace party.
    ² The International Congress of Women had passed twenty resolutions about ending the war and building a "permanent peace." Compiled from the recommendations of various peace organizations, the women's program endorsed international arbitration, a society of nations, and the democratic conduct of foreign policy, including participation by women. It also recommended principles of territorial integrity that should be applied in the peace settlement. In what was to become their most controversial resolution, the delegates accepted the plans offered by Julia Grace Wales and Rosika Schwimmer, delegates from the United States and Hungary, respectively, for a conference of neutrals which would "without delay offer continuous mediation." The conference would provide a forum for diplomatic relations between the belligerents by inviting "suggestions for settlement from each of the belligerent nations" and submitting to all of them simultaneously "reasonable proposals as a basis of peace." At the end of its meetings, the congress agreed, over considerable opposition, to send envoys to the capitals of Europe and to Washington to carry the resolutions to world leaders and urge an end to the war. International Congress of Women, *Report* (Amsterdam, n.d.), pp. 35-41.

To Edith Bolling Galt

[The White House]
My own Darling,   Wed., 7 A.M., 2 June, '15

How your presence fills this work-a-day room this morning! The chairs stand just as we left them, and the deep happiness and charm of all the pretty, ineffably sweet things you said and did last night seems still to transform everything about me! Outside it rains dismally and a cold mist half blots the landscape out, but within the room is radiant, because Love has been in it,—is still in it—presides over and blesses it and makes it a place where work may be happily done and strongly, with stout heart and clear purpose. Ah, my dear one, my dear One, it grows harder each time to let you go—you seem so to belong to me and I need you so, you give me such joy and strength—and yet each time you are here you seem to leave more of your sweet spirit here,—the great house seems less empty because you have been in it and have brought love with you. You are so great and potent a spirit, my wonderful Darling. I think of you very much as Mr. Wilson does,—as a wonderful woman whose gifts of heart and mind have never yet been realized (even by herself) or developed in use. But he mistakes the means by which you are to discover yourself and be at your best, for the service and glorification of the things you believe in and the persons (the man) you love. It is not to be by study or by any formal preparation. Study is always incidental, anyway, when it is real and accomplishes its only genuine object. It is to be by the time-old illumination of Love: by throwing your whole sweet nature open to its dominion—as I have seen you do. That's the path of light not only but of power. It quickens and enhances every gift. It removes every barrier to vision. And, oh, how wonderful it is to see my darling tread it! She grows daily more radiant and more inspired, as if with a new and strange life. Her eyes are wells of gladness as she looks out upon what she never saw before. And, as I witness the transformation, a sort of awe comes over me, that *I* should have played a part in it, that *I* should have spoken to her and called her to life and shown her joy and freedom and all the sweet domain of a woman's happiness. God bless her and keep her and make me worthy of this great trust!

Your own   Woodrow

ALS (WP, DLC).

From Edith Bolling Galt

[Washington]

My precious One: Wednesday morning [June 2, 1915].

Please don't think me silly or afraid. I admit I am a coward when I think any harm might come to you. So please don't see von Bernstorff *alone*. I have just read in the Post that he is coming to see you today and it gave me a sudden panic.

I never realized so fully before how I love you. The world would be a blank without you   Edith

ALS (WP, DLC).

Count Johann Heinrich von Bernstorff to the German Foreign Office[1]

Nr. 614.   Washington, den 2. Juni 1915.

Der Ernst der hiesigen Situation veranlaßte mich, Audienz beim Präsidenten Wilson nachzusuchen. In einer außerordentlich freundschaftlichen Unterredung, in der wiederholt der beiderseitige Wunsch betont wurde, einen Ausweg aus den gegenwärtigen Schwierigkeiten zu finden, kam Wilson immer wieder darauf zurück, daß es ihm nur auf die Humanitätsseite der Frage ankomme, der gegenüber der Schadensersatz für die auf der Lusitania umgekommenen Amerikaner zurücktrete. Sein Bestreben gehe auf gänzliche Aufhebung des Unterseebootskrieges. Gegenüber diesem Endziel würden geringere Konzessionen unsererseits nur ein Kompromiß sein. Wir sollten durch Aufgabe des Unterseebootskrieges einen Apell an die Moral richten, da nur durch eine Verständigung, nicht mehr durch die Waffen, der Krieg endgültig entschieden werden könne. Würden wir den Unterseebootskrieg aufgeben, so werde er dann auf Aufhebung der englischen Aushungerungspolitik dringen. Nach bestimmten Nachrichten aus London werde das gegenwärtige Kabinet darauf eingehen. Wilson hofft, dass damit ein Anfang gemacht würde, für eine Friedensaktion im großen Stile, welche er an der Spitze der Neutralen in die Wege leiten möchte.

Die amerikanische Antwortnote wird wahrscheinlich die ganze juristische Seite bei Seite schieben und nur die humane betonen, letztere sehr stark, aber, wie Wilson mir sagte, in scharfer Form.

Präsident betonte, dass der Punkt, indem wir uns vereinigen könnten, der wäre, dass Deutschland und Vereinigte Staaten von Amerika immer für die Freiheit der Meere eingetreten seien.

*Gruppe fehlt.

Die sehr freundschaftlich verlaufene . . . .* darf nicht über Ernst der Lage täuschen. Wenn uns nicht gelingt, in der nächsten Note zu beruhigen, wird Wilson an Abbruch der Beziehungen nicht vorbeikommen. Empfehle dringend, dies zu vermeiden wegen moralischer Wirkung und unmittelbarer Steigerung der Waffenausfuhr ins Ungemessene sowie Gefahr umfassender finanzieller Stützung der Gegner. Für den Fall einer Verständigung aber besteht Aussicht, dass vorhandene Strömung auf Waffenausfuhrverbot obsiegt. Ferner ist dann Eingreifen

Wilsons im Sinne der Entsendung Gildemeister hierher sicher zu
erwarten. Entscheidend für Erfolg, ob unsere Note richtigen Ton
trifft für öffentliche Meinung, die hier ausschlaggebender Macht-
faktor. Dazu erforderlich Beiseitelassung juristischer Einzel-
heiten und Erörterung auf Basis des Gesichtspunktes der
Humanität. Um richtigen Eindruck in Berlin zu geben, abreist
Meyer-Gerhard[2] als Rote-Kreuz-Delegierter morgen nach
Deutschland,[3] bis zu dessen Eintreffen unsere Antwort . . . .
. . .*) zu verschieben. Hiermit Wilson einverstanden.

Hiernach[4] Gedankengang für unsere Note etwa folgender:
Deutschland bereit Frage des Schutzes Amerikanischer Menschenleben und amerikanischer Schiffe unter Gesichtspunkt der
Humanität zu prüfen. Anerkennt, dass Vereinigte Staaten immer
für Freiheit der See ebenso wie Deutschland eingetreten.
Amerika hat zur Fortbildung internationalen Rechts im Sinne
größter Humanität wesentlich beigetragen. Mit Dank zu begrü-
ßen, dass größte neutrale Macht auch jetzt für Humanität ein-
tritt. Deutschland bietet hierzu gern die Hand in dem Vertrauen,
daß Vereinigte Staaten auch auf andere Macht in gleichem Sinne
einwirken werden.

Unter diesem Gesichtspunkte zunächst die bekannte Zusich-
erung für neutrale unbewaffnete Handelsschiffe, schwierig ist
Frage der Sicherung amerikanischer Menschenleben. Garantie,
wenn auf neutralen Schiffen. Wenn auf feindlichem Schiff, was
ist dann Gebot der Menschlichkeit falls Munition an Bord?
Tragischer Gewissenskonflikt für Kommandanten des Untersee-
boots. Passieren lassen unmenschlich gegen viele Tausend eigene
Landsleute, Torpedieren gefährdet Nichtkombattanten, Warnung
unmöglich wegen eigener Sicherheit und Erfolg der Vernich-
tung von Munition. Größte Forderung der Menschlichkeit für
ihn Schutz seiner Landsleute, darum keine Munition, Explo-
sivstoffe und Kriegsmaterialien an Bord. Deutschland bereit
reine Passagierschiffe zu respektieren, vertrauend, dass amerikanische Regierung nicht gestattet, daß Gegner hiervon Vorteil
zieht behufs Munitions, pp. Beförderung.

Alles bis auf weiteres. Darüber hinaus Aufgabe des Unterseebootskrieges, wenn England Londoner Deklaration wieder-
herstellt bezüglich Begriff der Konterbande, Blokade, Aushung-
erungstheorie. Gegenwärtige Situation als günstigster Moment
für Umschwung in Haltung der Vereinigten Staaten von
Amerika sollte nicht verpaßt werden. Wenn getragen von
großen Humanitätserwägungen und Ausdrücken, halte ich
folgende Mindestkonzessionen für nötig und ausreichend:[5]

1. Neutrale unbewaffnete Handelsschiffe werden nach Londoner Deklaration behandelt wie bereits zugesagt.

2. Amerikanische Menschenleben sicher auf neutralen Schiffen sowie auf feindlichen Schiffen, wenn letztere reine unbewaffnete Passagierschiffe ohne absolute Konterbande an Bord.

Alles dies unter Wahrung grundsätzlichen Standpunktes und nur bis auf weiteres um Vereinigten Staaten Chance für Vermittelung zu geben.

Selbstverständlich habe ich in Unterredung mit Wilson unseren Standpunkt eingehend verteidigt, was ich der Kürze wegen oben fortließ.   Bernstorff.

T telegram (Der Weltkrieg, ganz geheim, No. 18a, Unterseebootkrieg gegen England, Vol. 3, pp. 103-104, GFO-Ar).
  ¹ The following telegram was sent in German diplomatic code over the State Department's wire to Berlin with Wilson's and Bryan's permission.
  ² Anton Meyer Gerhard, representative of the German Red Cross in New York.
  ³ Wilson arranged for safe passage for Meyer Gerhard. About his role in the subsequent negotiations, see Link, *Struggle for Neutrality*, pp. 433-36.
  ⁴ This could be translated, in this context, "according to Wilson." In any event, Bernstorff was probably paraphrasing Wilson in this and the two following paragraphs.
  ⁵ Reading the first sentence in the last paragraph, it seems almost certain that Wilson suggested the following minimal concessions.

T R A N S L A T I O N

Washington, 2 June 1915.

No. 614. The seriousness of the present situation here prompted me to seek an audience with President Wilson. In an extraordinarily friendly exchange of views, in which it was repeatedly expressed that both sides wished to find a way out of the present difficulties, Wilson again and again came back to the point that for him only the humanitarian aspects of the question are important, compared to which the indemnity for Americans who had been killed on the *Lusitania* was of secondary importance. His efforts [he said] are directed to the complete cessation of submarine warfare. Compared to this final objective, lesser concessions from our side would only be a compromise. We should [he said] signal a recognition of moral standards by giving up submarine warfare, because the war [he said] could be decided finally only by a peaceful understanding and not by the continued use of arms. If we would give up the submarine war, he then would [he said] press for the ending of the English hunger blockade policy. According to reliable news from London, the present cabinet there would [he said] be willing to go along with that. Wilson hopes that thus a beginning would be made for a peace move in grand style, which he would like to get under way as the head of the neutrals.

The American note of reply will probably put aside the whole legal aspect and stress only the humanitarian one very strongly, but, as Wilson told me, in a clear form.

The President emphasized that the point upon which we could unite is that Germany and the United States have always stood for the freedom of the seas.

The cordial nature of the [conversation], however, must not blind us to the seriousness of the situation. If we do not succeed in calming it down in our next note, Wilson will not be able to prevent a break in diplomatic relations. I advise you urgently to avoid this, because of the moral impact and the immediate increase of the export of arms in immeasurable quantities, as well as the danger of comprehensive financial support for our enemies. But in the event of an understanding, there is a prospect that the present movement for an arms embargo would succeed. Furthermore, one could then surely expect that Wilson would intervene according to the sending of Gildemeester here. Decisive for success is whether our note strikes the right chord with regard to public opinion, which is the decisive power factor here. To achieve this, it will be necessary to put aside legal details and haggling, only a discussion on the basis of humanitarian aspects. To give the right impression in Berlin, Meyer-Gerhardt will leave for Germany tomorrow as a Red Cross representative. Until his arrival, our answer [should be] delayed. With this, Wilson is in agreement.

In view of this, the line of thought of our note should be approximately as follows: Germany prepared to investigate question of protection of American lives and American vessels from the viewpoint of humanitarian aspects. Acknowledges that United States as well as Germany has always supported freedom of the seas. America contributed significantly to the development of international law to make it as humane as possible. Germany notes with gratitude that the largest neutral power supports humanity even now. Germany willingly offers her hand, trusting that the United States will exert its influence in the same sense on the other power.

According to this point of view, first of all, the well-known assurance for neutral unarmed merchant vessels. Difficulty is the question of the protection of American lives. Guarantee if on neutral vessels. If on enemy vessels, what then is the command of humanity in case ammunition on board? Tragic conflict of conscience for submarine commander. To let pass inhuman toward many thousands of own countrymen. Torpedoing endangers noncombatants. Warning impossible because of own security and success of destruction of ammunition. The greatest demand of humanity for him protection of his countrymen, thus no ammunition, explosives, and war materials on board. Germany prepared to respect innocent passenger ships, trusting that American government will not permit our enemies to benefit hereby in the munitions trade.

This is all until new arrangements. Furthermore, giving up of submarine war if England again agrees to respect Declaration of London concerning the rules of contraband, blockade, and starvation policy. The present situation is favorable. The moment for reversal of the attitude of the United States of America should not be missed. If characterized by great humanitarian ideas and phrases, I deem following minimal concessions necessary and sufficient:

1. Neutral unarmed merchant vessels will be treated according to the Declaration of London, as already assured.

2. American lives secure on neutral vessels, as well as on enemy vessels, if the latter innocent unarmed passenger ships without absolute contraband on board.

All this by adhering to our principal point of view and only for the time being to give United States a chance for negotiation.

Of course I defended in great detail our position during the exchange with Wilson, but omitted this in the above for the sake of brevity.   Bernstorff.

To Frank Irving Cobb

Personal.   The White House June 3, 1915
My dear Mr. Cobb:

I have been a long time acknowledging your letter of May twenty-first about your conversation with Captain von Papen, but I beg that you will not judge from that that I was ungrateful. On the contrary, I appreciated the letter very much indeed and read it with keen interest.

Intimations of a similar sort have been conveyed to me through various sources, but the trouble is that there is always in the background a desire to propose terms of accommodation which it is perfectly clear that the Allies would not for a moment consider. I have tried to enter every door that was opened even by a mere crack but have always found that somebody had his back against it on the other side.

With warmest regard,
        Cordially and faithfully yours,   Woodrow Wilson

TLS (received from Brian Corrigan).

From Edward Mandell House

[London, June 3, 1915]

Within the past few days I have seen almost every important member of the new ministry and have urged them to meet your request in regard to interference with our legitimate rights at sea. I have told them that if our differences with Germany should be composed your request would probably be turned into a demand. Sir Edward Grey has gone for a long rest, but his temporary successor has promised to facilitate everything. I asked him to please have the long-delayed reply to your note ready to transmit at a day's notice, saying that notice would probably be given to him as soon as the controversy with Germany was concluded. He promised that it should be ready when asked for. They are concerned about Mexico and are hoping you will not intervene. It has been suggested that such action would play into Germany's hand and that that would give many thousands of Germans in the Americas a chance to go to Mexico and fight in her army in the event of war with Germany. I would suggest an address to Congress placing the blame of this fearful conflict upon Kaiser and his military entourage and I would exonerate the great body of German citizenship stating that we were fighting for their deliverance as well as the deliverance of Europe. This should have a fine effect upon German Americans. We are sailing on the St. Paul Saturday.

T transcript of WWsh decode (WP, DLC) of T telegram (WP, DLC).

From William Jennings Bryan

Washington
My Dear Mr. President: Forenoon June 3, 1915.

I have gone over the note carefully[1] and beg to submit the following suggestions. The first paragraph of the note, after the one expressing a desire to contribute to the clearing up of the misunderstanding, takes up the cases of the CUSHING and GULFLIGHT and explains that there is no intention to injure neutral vessels and that an apology will be offered and reparation made for any injury done by mistake. The suggestion is then made that the investigations made by the parties may be supplemented by the investigation provided for in The Hague Convention. Where they disavow any intention to attack a neutral vessel and offer apology and reparation, it seems to me that

[1] The German note of May 28.

we are justified in accepting such an answer, except where life is lost. In our note we specifically assert this principal. In the case of the CUSHING no lives were lost. In the case of GULFLIGHT two of the crew jumped overboard and drowned. I presume that the manner of death would not change the rule, since the men jumped with a view to saving their lives and may be supposed to have acted upon what to them seemed the best means of escape after the ship was struck.

In the case of the GULFLIGHT it may be necessary to consider the fact that the ship contained contraband of war and was being convoyed by two British vessels. The German Government reports that the commander of the submarine did not see the flag until after the order was given to fire the torpedo. Under all the circumstances, it seems to me, that in this case we can afford to continue investigation with a view to securing suitable reparation.

The sinking of the FABALA presents a different issue. The sinking of the steamer was intentional and the German Government affirms that the commander had the intention of allowing the passengers and crew "ample opportunity to save themselves." This indicates a recognition of the rule in regard to dealing with prize ships. It is asserted that ten minutes were given and that the time was extended to twenty-three, and then as an excuse for not giving more time, it is stated that "suspicious steamers were hurrying to the aid of the FABALA." The question raised here is whether the coming of steamers to the rescue relieved the submarine commander of the obligation to give sufficient time for the crew to escape. In other words, is the sinking of the ship a matter of greater importance than the rescue of the passengers? I shall ask Mr. Lansing to look up the authorities for this question must often have been raised. As the taking of prizes is an old custom, it must frequently have occurred that ships have come to the rescue of a merchantman that has been overtaken. In such case has the attacking ship the right to *sink* the vessel, passengers and all, rather than allow the prize to escape? As we have no information as to the approach of the "suspicious steamers," might it not be well to ask further information on this subject, and in so doing, ask whether we are to understand that the German Government asserts as a rule of international law, that the right to sink the prize is paramount to the obligation to allow the passengers time to escape—that being the real issue presented in the FABALA case. If, on investigation of authorities, we find that the approach of rescuing vessels does not justify sinking prize we can so state, an investigation of the facts being in that case unnecessary.

We cannot well object to arbitration where arbitration is possible. Neither can we object to investigation in any case. Our thirty treaties commit us to the doctrine of investigation *in all cases* and since this form of treaty was offered to Germany and the principal accepted by her, (Germany was the twelfth nation to accept the principal) we could not consistently refuse to apply this document to all questions that may arise between us. It seems to me that these treaties not only furnish us the most plausible excuse that we can find for investigation, but leave us no valid excuse for not resorting to the plan. Nothing could more forcibly emphasize the value of this peace plan than the employment of it in this case, and now that we have stated our position and received Germany's reply, the objections urged against making the statement at the time the note was sent would not seem to apply. The use of this idea at this time might even exert a profound influence upon the making of the treaty between belligerent nations at the end of the war. The plan for investigation of all difficulties is the simplest plan that can be found for dealing with disputed questions and, though simple, gives the greatest promise of effectiveness.

When Mr. Lansing finishes his suggestions in regard to the excuses given for the sinking of the LUSITANIA, I will prepare a comment on each one of the excuses. In dealing with the LUSITANIA, it is, in my judgment, necessary to bear in mind that our only concern is with the protection of the rights of our people. We have not felt called upon to express an opinion on submarine warfare when other vessels not bearing Americans have been sunk. Whatever views we may have as to the moral character of the means employed by the belligerents, we do not feel it our duty to express opinions merely for the purpose of announcing our views. We could, of course, contribute something towards the formation of public opinion against the belligerent which employs methods which we might denounce and in favor of the belligerent which was the victim of the methods so denounced, but even the most biased among our citizens would hardly feel justified in asking us to take any position merely for the purpose of helping one side or the other.

It seems to me that, having stated our position without equivocation, we are not only justified but compelled by duty to do what we can to prevent our citizens incurring unnecessary risks. The precedents for this are abundent. Take the case of a riot for instance, the authorities not only endeavor to prevent shooting upon the street, but they order all citizens to remain at home in order to avoid the dangers necessarily incurred on the street. The authorities are not absolved from the duty of enforcing order and of punishing those guilty of violence, but as a matter of precaution, they restrain citizens from the exercise of their rights in order to prevent injuries that might otherwise be inflicted unintentionally. The bystander is always in danger when there is shooting upon the street and no government would feel justified in refusing to warn noncombatants away from the dangerous place, merely because the citizens ordinarily have the right to go upon the streets.

For the same reason we advised all American citizens to leave Mexico, not because they did not have a right to stay there, but because we thought it unwise for them to incur the risks involved in staying. We went to the expense of bringing out those who were not able to pay their own way. We did not refuse to give such protection as was possible to those who remained, but we warned them of the extraordinary danger involved in remaining. It seems to me that we cannot well justify a failure to warn American citizens against going into the danger zone on foreign ships —especially on ships which, by carrying ammunition, invite extraordinary risks. It is not sufficient to say that, according to international law, American citizens have a right to go anywhere and that the Government's protection will follow them, no matter what risks they take. If the authorities of a city are justified in warning people off the streets of the city in which they reside, surely a nation is justified in warning its citizens off of the water highways which belong to no nation alone, but to all the nations in common.

The German Government pleads as one reason for the attack upon the LUSITANIA that it was carrying 5,400 cases of ammunition "destined for the destruction of brave German soldiers, etc." This ammunition was valued at about $150,000. We have clearly stated the Government's position in regard to the rights of Americans and if it is thought desirable, this right can be restated in language specifically asserting that, according to this Government's view of international law, citizens have a right to travel with contraband and that their rights cannot be violated merely because the vessel carries contraband. Still it is not only consistent, but, in my judgment, a matter of imperative duty to not only warn our citizens against the exercise of this right at this time, but to do whatever lies in our power to prevent the incurring of such risks. Would it not be advisable to reverse the rule by which passenger ships are permitted to carry ammunition? The law says that no ship shall carry gun powder without a license. This has been interpreted by a department order not to apply to gun powder contained in small ammunition. If that order was invoked and it was interpreted to exclude all ammunition, it would add to the security of passengers.

I believe that Germany is looking for a way out and that, having stated our position unequivocally on the subject of the use of submarines against merchantmen, we would be justified in taking all the precaution possible to prevent our citizens taking risks. If—not for the benefit of Germany but for the benefit of our own people—we announce that passenger ships will not hereafter be allowed to carry ammunition, I think Germany would be very likely to say that no passenger ship would be attacked if assurances were given that it did not carry ammunition. This we could do without invoking any new legislation. In my judgment, you would be justified in going even further and saying that Congress would be asked for legislation authorizing the refusal of clearance to passenger ships carrying contraband. If such a rule was adopted, contraband would be carried on ships without passengers and thus the safety of passenger ships would be assured. But even if you do not feel justified in going so far as to advise the legislation suggested, forbidding the carrying of contraband on passenger ships, I believe the order in regard to ammunition would have a powerful influence upon Germany just at this time, and I feel sure that it would be approved in this country. A person would have to be very much biased in favor of the Allies to insist that ammunition intended for one of the belligerents should be safe-guarded in transit by the lives of American citizens or, for that matter, by the lives of citizens of any country.

I hope you will pardon the length of this note, but I am sincerely anxious to render you any service I can in the solution of the difficult problem presented by the LUSITANIA disaster. I recognize, of course, that the responsibility rests upon you and that in the final decision your judgment and your conscience are the only guides upon which you are justified in relying. Those of us who have been honored by being selected as advisors are in duty bound to give you, when desired, the benefit of our judgment and conscience, but none of your associates realize more fully than I that we can only assist insofar as the reasons which support our conclusions appeal to you. I know of no other way of discharging the duty of an advisor than to outline the course that I would pursue if the responsibility for action were upon me. The earnestness with which I have spoken in the discussion of these questions measures the depth of my solicitude and the sincerety of my desire that your decisions may, by safeguarding our

country's wellfare, redoun[d] to your own personal credit and
to the advantage of our party.

    With assurances of high respect, I am, my dear Mr. President,
                Very sincerely yours,   W. J. Bryan

TLS (WP, DLC).

From William Jennings Bryan, with Enclosure

                                        Washington
My Dear Mr. President: Afternoon June 3, 1915.

    I am sending you the memorandum prepared by Mr. Lansing.
I have not, of course, had an opportunity to examine the authorities upon which he bases his opinion, but the arguments which
he presents seem, for the most part, reasonable.

    The objection based upon the fact that the LUSITANIA was
built by the aid of the Government and is subject to being called
into the Government use˙ is, it seems to me, quite effectively
answered. I am not sure, however, that I would go as far as he
does when he says that if the vessel were entirely owned by the
British Government and yet put in trade as a merchant vessel, it
would occupy exactly the same character as a privately owned
merchant vessel.

    As to the second argument, namely, that the LUSITANIA had
guns on board: It seems to me that that fact would be material if
she had any guns other than those made known to us. We have
regulations in regard to the size of the guns that can be taken on
a merchant vessel. If it could be shown that the LUSITANIA had
concealed guns which were not made known to our authorities,
and that the fact was made to the German Government, it seems
to me that it might properly have some bearing, unless we take
the position that it is the *unresisting* ship and not the *unarmed*
ship that is entitled to protection. I think that it might be well
for us to state the facts as we understand them and express a
willingness to hear any arguments that contradicts this position.

    While, as you know, I have felt that we ought to do something
to protect our flag from use by belligerents, I do not see that the
question of using neutral flags can be raised in this case, because
there is no doubt that the LUSITANIA was flying a belligerent flag.
What Mr. Lansing says about the impossibility of ram[m]ing a
submarine with a ship the size of the LUSITANIA would seem to
be quite conclusive, although, if it is true that secret instructions
have been issued instructing merchant vessels to adopt, in regard
to submarines, a course different from that occupied by mer-

chant vessels in resisting the attack of armed crusiers, that fact ought to be taken into consideration. In other words, if a submarine is to be bound by the rules applicable to merchantment, then the merchantmen ought also be bound by the rules applicable when the merchantmen are attacked by a crusier.

It seems to me that the question of ammunition is the most serious one raised and I do not share Mr. Lansing's view that we can ignore entirely the question raised as to whether our law was violated. Even if we say that the enforcement of our laws must be entrusted to our own officials and not to commanders of submarines of belligerents, still we must consider the moral effect of a position which would make us seem to acquiesce in the carrying of American citizens with ammunition in violation of law. I feel that our position would be very much strengthened by affirmative action which would for the future prevent the carrying of ammunition by passenger ships, and, as I said in my note of this morning, which accompanies this, I believe it would have a very beneficial influence, both on public opinion in this country and on the German Government, if we took action at once in regard to the carrying of ammunition.

With assurances of high respect, I am, my dear Mr. President,
Very sincerely yours,   W. J. Bryan

TLS (WP, DLC).

ENCLOSURE

Robert Lansing to William Jennings Bryan

Dear Mr. Secretary: [Washington] June 3, 1915.

I am submitting a memorandum on the allegations of facts contained in the German note of May 28th.[1] If I had more time, it could be very much abbreviated.

It seems to me that only two of the allegations are relevant to the German defense, namely:

(1) That the LUSITANIA was armed, and

(2) That the commander of the submarine feared the LUSITANIA would ram him.

There is no evidence that the German Government had information that the vessel was armed or information sufficient to found a belief to that effect.

As to the second allegation, the danger of the LUSITANIA, a vessel of over 31000 tons burden, being able to maneuver so as to ram a small swift moving craft like a submarine is too remote to warrant serious consideration. That the commander actually feared being rammed I believe to be false.

The remaining allegations are irrelevant to the defense that the submarine was justified in torpedoing the LUSITANIA without visiting her and without putting her crew and passengers in a place of safety. If the vessel was laden with war supplies, if she flew a neutral flag, if she had Canadian soldiers on board, and if she violated several laws of the United States as to her cargo, these facts in no way affect the question.

While the memorandum reviews these facts, I think that it would be unwise to controvert or discuss them.

Faithfully yours,   Robert Lansing.

TLS (WP, DLC).
    1 RL, "GERMAN ALLEGATIONS REGARDING LUSITANIA," TS memorandum dated June 2, 1915 (WP, DLC). This nineteen-page memorandum answering the German allegations is well summarized in both Bryan's and Lansing's letters.

The First Draft of the Second Lusitania Note[1]

[June 3, 1915]

Allow me to acknowledge the receipt of your note of the twenty-ninth of May, transmitted through the Honorable James W. Gerard, Ambassador of the United States of America near the Imperial German Government, in answer to the note I had the honour to address to the Imperial German Government on the thirteenth of May. *on behalf of the Government of the United States*.

The Government of the United States notes with pleasure that in speaking of the attacks made upon the steamers *Cushing* and *Gulflight* the ⟨full⟩ recognition by the Imperial German Government of the principle of the freedom of the seas to all neutral ships and looks forward with confidence to a satisfactory acknowledgment of the responsibility of the Imperial German Government for the mistakes of its officers in those cases when it shall have acquainted itself with all the facts. The facts are of so simple a nature as probably to render unnecessary any such formal inquiry as Your Excellency's note suggests, and will serve, I feel sure, to emphasize the extreme danger of neglecting the safeguards which centuries of experience have shown to be the only means of preventing intolerable injury to the innocent in times of war.

    1 Words in angle brackets were deleted by Wilson from this WWT draft. Words in italics were added by him. There is a WWsh outline and a WWsh draft of this note in WP, DLC. There is a WWsh draft of certain portions of the first draft with additions to that draft in WP, DLC. Wilson incorporated these changes and additions into what he called the third draft. It is printed as Enclosure II with WJB to WW, June 7, 1915.

The Government of the United States would, in this connection, again ⟨very respectfully but⟩ very earnestly call the attention of the Imperial German Government to the ⟨fate⟩ fact that the policy of the Imperial German Government in seeking to establish a war zone free for its operations on the high seas, ⟨from⟩ which neutral vessels are warned that they will enter at their peril, itself constitutes a very grave and quite unprecedented infringement upon the freedom of the seas and the rights of neutral nations and is sure to be fruitful of fatal and tragical mistakes such as were made in the cases of these two steamers; and urges upon the Imperial German Government the necessity for a reconsideration of the whole situation. The freedom of the seas, for which the Imperial German Government contends, cannot be vindicated by any violation of that freedom.

With regard to the case of the steamer *Falaba*, upon which an American citizen lost his life, the Government of the United States is surprised to find the Imperial German Government contending that an effort on the part of a merchantman to escape capture and secure assistance alters the obligations of the officer seeking to make the capture in respect of the safety of the lives of those on board the merchantman. These are not new circumstances. They have been in the minds of statesmen and of international lawyers throughout the development of naval warfare, and the Government of the United States does not understand that they have ever been held to alter ⟨in any degree⟩ the principles of humanity upon which it has felt itself obliged to insist for the protection of the rights and the lives of its citizens. It does not understand the Imperial German Government, however, as seeking in this case to relieve itself of responsibility, but only as setting forth the circumstances which led the commander of the submarine to be hurried into the course he took.

Your Excellency's note, in discussing the loss of American lives on the steamship *Lusitania*, speaks at some length of certain information which the Imperial German Government has received with regard to the character and outfit of the vessel which Your Excellency fears may not have been brought to the attention of the Government of the United States. It speaks of the *Lusitania* as equipped with masked guns, supplied with trained gunners and special ammunition, transporting troops from Canada, carrying a cargo not permitted under the laws of the United States to a vessel *also* carrying passengers, and in virtual effect acting as ⟨a subsidiary⟩ *an auxiliary* to the armed naval forces of Great Britain; but it makes no reference to the grave implications of these statements with regard to the responsibilities of the United States. Perhaps those implications were not thought of when the note was drafted. It would have been an inexcusable breach of neutrality on the part of the Government of the United States to permit a vessel of such a character and so equipped to leave its ports. It was its duty to see to it that the vessel was not armed, that it was not serving as a transport, that it did not carry a cargo prohibited by the laws of the United States, and that, if in fact in the service of the navy of Great Britain, it should not receive clearance papers as a merchantman; and of course it performed that duty with scrupulous vigilance, through its regularly constituted officials. The Imperial German Government has been misinformed.

But the sinking of this passenger ship involves principles of humanity which throw into the background any special circumstances of detail that may have surrounded the case, principles which lift it, as the Imperial German Government will no doubt be quick to recognize and acknowledge, out of the class of ordinary ⟨subjegts⟩ *subjects* of diplomacy. Whatever be the other facts, the ⟨great⟩ *principal* fact is that a great steamer, primarily and chiefly a conveyance for passengers, and carrying more than a thousand souls who had no part or lot in the conduct of the war, was sent to the bottom without so much as a challenge or *a* warning and that men, women, and children were sent to their death in circumstances unparalleled in modern warfare. The fact that more than one hundred Americans were among those who perished makes it the duty of the Government of the United States to speak of these things and to call the attention of the Imperial German Government to the grave responsibility which the Government of the United States conceives it to have incurred in this tragic occurence. It is the opinion and contention of the United States that there is here demonstrated the full case against the use of submarines against merchantmen where visit and search are impracticable and where the humane principles of international law are impossible of application.

Your Excellency's note closes ⟨, my Government is happy to observe,⟩ with the intimation that the Imperial German Government is willing, now as before, to accept the good offices of the United States in an attempt to come to an understanding with the Government of Great Britain by which the conditions and character of the war upon the sea may be changed. The Government of the United States does not understand the Imperial German Government as seeking to make the responsibility of the Imperial German Government for any wrongs done the people or Government of the United States by its representatives or com-

manders in any way contingent upon the willingness of Great
Britain to discuss with the Imperial German Government these
matters which in fact affect the whole world. It is the more ready,
therefore, again to offer its good offices in this or any other matter
⟨that⟩ that may afford promise of even a partial accommodation
between the parties to the present war *or of any mitigation of
its terrors.* It stands ready at any time to convey to either government any intimation the other may be willing to have it convey,
and covets the opportunity thus to serve its friends and the world.

In the meantime, welcoming though it does the opportunity
to clear up any question connected with the matters it has felt
it its duty to present to the Imperial German Government, it confidently looks to see the justice of that great Government vindicated in ⟨those⟩ cases where Americans have been drawn into
what is no quarrel of theirs, and the humanity of that great Government, as well, made secure against the future, whatever in
⟨its⟩ *the opinion of the Imperial German Government* may have
been the provocation or the circumstantial justification for the
past action of its commanders at sea. The Government of the
United States, therefore, very earnestly renews the representations of its note of the thirteenth of May, and relies in these
representations not only upon the general principles of international law hitherto recognized among nations but also upon
the solemn covenants of the treaty of 1828 between the United
States and the Kingfom of Prussia.

WWT MS (WP, DLC).

From William Jennings Bryan, with Enclosure

My Dear Mr. President: Washington June 3, 1915.

I am sending you a letter from Mr. Miller of the Reserve Board,
in explanation of a letter which he has received from a Hollander
who has recently had a talk with one of the German Cabinet.
The man is vouched for by Jane Addams' Secretary[1] and has, I
think, been in touch with the German Embassy since he arrived
here.

With assurances of high respect, I am, my dear Mr. President,
                    Very sincerely yours,   W. J. Bryan

TLS (W. J. Bryan Papers, DNA).
[1] Miss Addams did not have a secretary; it is impossible to conjecture about
which of her associates had been in touch with Bryan.

ENCLOSURE

Adolph Caspar Miller to William Jennings Bryan

My dear Mr. Secretary: Washington June 3, 1915.

In sending you the enclosed letter from Mr. F. von Gheel Gildermeester,[1] which I believe will be of some interest to you, I want to make a brief statement in explanation.

I met Mr. Gildermeester last Sunday for the first time. He is from Holland and has just come by way of his country from a visit to Germany where he had an opportunity to meet some high officials of the government and to acquaint himself with the state of sentiment in certain sections of the German public which he believed to be of such interest and importance as to merit being brought to the attention of our government. Mr. Gildermeester makes upon me the impression of being a candid, straightforward, intelligent man without ulterior or selfish, much less sinister purposes. He represents that there is a sharp cleavage between the militarist or war party in Germany and the moderate or peace party, and believes that this Government should consider the bearing of any steps it may take in negotiating with Germany on the status of the peace movement there which he represents is already strong and gaining in strength. My interpretation of the recent German note which invites an investigation of the "facts," after talking with him, is that this may be done largely for the purpose of saving the face of the militarist element in the Government with the German people who have not had the full information regarding the incident, the censorship of the press being in the hands of the militarist party. He thinks a hard and unyielding attitude on our part at this time would strengthen the grasp of the militarist element and that thereby the war would be greatly prolonged and the opportunity of this country in the restoration of peace would be diminished.

I have learned from other sources that Mr. Gildermeester has come here with the knowledge of Minister Delbruck[2] and, I believe, others in the German Government who had sufficient confidence in his high purposes that they were willing to avail themselves of his proffered services to communicate an indication of their attitude to the Government and people of this country, and Mr. Gildermeester is ready to do anything that he can, of a similar nature, for this Government, his interest being that of an early restoration of peace.

I give you his letter and this statement for what you may

judge it to be worth and in the discharge of an obligation which I felt was mine after meeting Mr. Gildermeester and satisfying myself of his genuineness.

I have the honor to remain, with high esteem,

Yours very sincerely,   A. C. Miller.

TLS (W. J. Bryan Papers, DNA).
1 This letter from Gildemeester to Miller is missing.
2 Clemens Delbrück, Minister of the Interior.

From William Jennings Bryan

My Dear Mr. President: Washington June 3, 1915.

Ambassador Bernstorff brought over his cipher telegram to be sent to his Government through our Embassy. He suggested that he could give me a paraphrase of it if I desired. I told him that that might enable us to be sure that he properly interpreted your views in the conversation which his telegram reports. I reminded him that I was a little embarrassed by a misconstruction which was placed upon the telegram sent by Ambassador Dumba. He said he would send over the paraphrase and we have been holding the message waiting for the paraphrase.

For fear I may not be directly interpreting your wishes in the matter, I write to ask whether you think it better to send the telegram on without waiting for the paraphrase? If you will telephone to my house tonight, I can have the message forwarded, if you think we had better not wait for the paraphrase.

With assurances of high respect, I am, my dear Mr. President,   Very sincerely yours,   W. J. Bryan

TLS (W. J. Bryan Papers, DNA).

Sir Cecil Arthur Spring Rice to Sir Edward Grey

Washn. 3 June 1915

German Amb. is said to have spoken of peace to President and S of S. The terms he mentions are restoration of Kingdom of Poland "freedom of seas" and increase of German colonies. Straus also came from N Y to interview S of S.

German agents give out that there will be peace in three months, and Hamburg America line is making arrangements accordingly. "Freedom of Seas" of which German agents always talk means prohibition of interference with private trade in war time and is supposed to have great attractions for President

who may propose a "peace league" with that object. Negotiations
as to this may possibly arise out of present crisis.

Hw telegram (FO 115/1920, p. 243, PRO).

To Edith Bolling Galt

[The White House]
My precious Darling,   Thursday, 3 June, 1915 7 A.M.

Good morning! How I wish I could hold you in my arms and
give you the morning greeting that is in my heart! For the hours
are full of you and my heart sings all day long of the love you
give it. The rain pours down outside and nature seems in her
dullest, dreariest mood, but the light that shines in my heart
is not affected. Its source is in the love of a radiant lady who in
the greatness of her heart has come to me with all the sweet gifts
that a man's heart could desire. Love has set me free from all
real distress. I smiled, my darling Sweetheart, at your little
panic about Bernstorff yesterday, but it was a very, very tender
smile and a very happy smile, and how my heart leaped at the
revelation of that sweet little pencilled postscript! God bless
you! As a matter of fact, the poor distressed man came to ask
how he could assist to bring his crass government to its senses,
for he sees the blunders it is making. I liked him for the first
time. He dropped the Prussian and became the man. The
weather of course kept me indoors, and I did a jolly lot of work.
Now that my heart is at ease I can do my work again—and
much better than before—and yet not for a moment lose touch
of you and the inspiration your sweet, wonderful love gives me.
Margaret and Helen and I went over to see Nell and the baby
(and incidentally Mac.) after lunch and when we came back
to the house I indulged myself in a two-hour nap (necessary
before seeing Miss Boardman for half an hour about Red Cross
relief in Mexico!); but, for the rest, it was work, work, work
till bed time, including getting all the things straight in my
head which I must include, either explicitly or by implication,
in the note to Germany which I am going to try to draft to-day.
It is a different thing working here at this desk now that you
preside over it. While I sit in my chair, I am all the time conscious of the sweet lady who has stood there bending over me.
I feel her gentle caresses and the precious kisses she gave me,
and everything is made easy—I am strong and happy because
I am her own   Woodrow

ALS (WP, DLC).

From Edith Bolling Galt

[Washington]

My precious One: Thursday night June 3rd, 1915

I have read Washington's "Farewell Address" and your note to Germany, and it is now so awfully late that I can only talk to you a minute.

I was so genuinely pleased when you said you wanted to read me your answer to Germany. And it was the greatest delight to be in your chair, surrounded by all the work-a-day things that come in such daily touch with you. And have you there opposite me, reading, what is to be such pregnant history, and letting me share the vital things that are making you famous. My Darling I am not quite clear as to what I said, and the reply from any pen but yours would be a strong one. But, I think, to me there was nothing of *you*, yourself, in it and therefore it seemed flat and lacking color.

I know how hard it is to *answer* everything, in comparison to the freedom of choosing what you feel to write. And therefore I am conscious how much you are circumscribed, and it is all because of my love for you that I am hard to satisfy. The note to Germany[1]—as I have just reread it—is so splendid that it will go ringing down the ages. And this new one must be an echo, only in reiteration of principles. And you must put some little of your *splendid* incomparable self in it.

Goodnight, or rather good morning my beloved one—and always remember I love you,   Edith

ALS (WP, DLC).
[1] She meant the first *Lusitania* note.

To William Jennings Bryan

My dear Mr. Secretary,   The White House. 4 June, 1915.

I was out last night and did not see this letter until bedtime.

I think that the sooner Bernstorff's despatch to his government gets off the better, and perhaps, since his paraphrase is delayed we had better not wait for it but send the despatch at once. It is hardly possible that he can have misunderstood what I said to him, and he has the experience of Dumba's mistake in mind.

Faithfully Yours,   W.W.

WWTLI (W. J. Bryan Papers, DNA).

To William Jennings Bryan, with Enclosure

My dear Mr. Secretary,   The White House. 4 June, 1915.

I have read these[1] with a great deal of interest. I have no doubt that the opinions of Mr. Moorehead are those of a very large proportion of our fellow countrymen, as they are of course our own.   Faithfully Yours,   W.W.

WWTLI (W. J. Bryan Papers, DNA).
  [1] The other enclosures are missing. Or perhaps Wilson meant to write "this" instead of "these."

E N C L O S U R E

John Henry Morehead[1] to William Jennings Bryan

My dear Mr. Bryan: Lincoln Nebraska May 18th, 1915

It is very easy for us to object to other men's actions, without even thinking of it.

This letter is to say that as nearly as I can learn, the people of Nebraska are very much in sympathy with your course in the recent unfortunate affair of the sinking of the Lusitania by the Germans. Being quite an old resident of the State, and having watched the sentiments of the people on different questions, I feel somewhat qualified to speak in regard to the public feeling at this time.

I realize that we must maintain the dignity of our country, but to enter into any long drawn out war would sacrifice millions of lives, and it has, for many years, appealed to me as something in the nature of a fist fight, which at one time was more popular than today.

I believe that I am correct in saying that 90% of the people of Nebraska are strongly in favor of adjusting these differences by arbitration and by civilized and intelligent methods. Every day, men are in my office from different parts of the State, and I have a splendid opportunity to find out the sentiment; and as stated, I feel sure that a large percentage of the people of Nebraska, are heartily in sympathy with you and President Wilson, and your method of handling the matter.

I realize that this comes without solicitation, and I have not, in a single instance allowed myself to be quoted by any of the newspapers, feeling that what I said might be misconstrued. I only write this to give you my ideas of the sentiment of the people of Nebraska.

Crop prospects in Nebraska are splendid; money matters are easy and I feel that we have many things to congratulate ourselves on. The State Bank Report is the largest in the history of the State.

Hoping that this will find yourself and wife in the best of health, and assuring you of my best wishes, I am
Yours truly,   John H. Morehead

TLS (W. J. Bryan Papers, DNA).
  ¹ Governor of Nebraska.

Two Letters from William Jennings Bryan

My dear Mr. President: Washington June 4th, 1915.

Senator Martin of Virginia and Congressman Flood called this afternoon and asked me to communicate to you the reason of their call. Senator Martin was the spokesman but Mr. Flood concurred in what he said. The Senator spoke with great earnestness to the effect that this country does not want war with Germany and that it expects you to find a way out that will not involve hostilities. He spoke of the question of passports and expressed the opinion that while the demand for or giving of passports is not necessarily an act of war, that it is so near it that it involves risks that ought not to be taken. He said that he had talked with three senators whom he had found in town and that they were all of the same opinion as he is and would vote against a declaration of war, if the subject were presented. Mr. Flood made the same remark in regard to the House—that he was sure that they would vote against such a declaration. They both expressed themselves as believing that the Lusitania case did not jsutify [justify] a resort to hostilities and that they felt sure the country did not regard the matter as one that would justify war. I asked them to put their views in writing, that I might be sure to submit them accurately and they said they would, but as they may not have time to send me the letter this evening, I am writing you the substance of their conversation from memory.

With assurances of high respect, I am, my dear Mr. President,
Very sincerely yours,   W. J. Bryan

My dear Mr. President: Washington June 4th, 1915.

Mr. B. Howell Griswold, Junior, called, as you will remember, with Dr. Goodnow and asked for a letter expressing approval in the matter of a loan. I told him and Dr. Goodnow that if they would write such a letter as they desired you to sign I would submit it to you and let you make such changes in it as were necessary to bring it into conformity with your views as to what was proper. I sent the draft to you on May 3rd. Will you please make such changes in it as you desire.

With assurances of high respect, I am, my dear Mr. President,

Very sincerely yours,   W. J. Bryan

TLS (W. J. Bryan Papers, DNA).

From Sir Horace Plunkett

Dear Mr. President,   Dublin. June 4th. 1915.

Although a citizen of the British Empire, I have been for five and thirty years a sympathetic observer of men and things in the United States. I have witnessed many changes in the mutual regard of the two branches of the English-speaking race, and have noted a marked and accelerating progress towards a right understanding of their respective points of view.

I had cherished the hope that your administration would inaugurate that subordination of competition to co-operation between the two peoples upon which the firm establishment of the world's peace has long seemed to me ultimately to rest, and in the rude shock our common civilisation has sustained, I do not abandon this hope. These observations are merely a preface to the one thing I wish, from my inconspicuous position, to say to one who in other times and upon matters of less moment has honoured me with an invitation to speak.

Colonel House, in his own quiet, tactful and marvellously persuasive way, has, to my certain knowledge, rendered an inestimable service to the Government of this country by his counsel and advice in regard to its attitude to the United States in this crisis. What similar service he may have rendered to you and to his people in other European countries you will know. He sails to-morrow and I can well believe that, as he cannot be in Europe and America at the same time, it may be better that he should now be at your side. As I have had the privilege of introducing him to some people he wished to meet over here, and of explaining to them some aspects of American public life which it was necessary for them to know in order to appreciate the value of Colonel House's help, I have offered to be of any assistance in my power should misunderstandings arise in his absence which informed, unofficial intervention may be best qualified to remove. I have also offered to keep him advised of any events or movements of opinion, which, from the possession of his confidence, I feel he ought to know. I merely wish to assure you, Mr. President, that something will be done to minimise the loss to us over here which must be set against the gain to you and to the United States in having Colonel House at Washington.

I am, with deep respect,

Yours sincerely,   Horace Plunkett.

TLS (WP, DLC).

From Edith Bolling Galt

Dearest and Best: [Washington] June 3rd [4th] 1915.

In your dreams do you feel my thoughts and love surrounding you? for now it is one oclock and I have put on a blue dressing gown and let my hair down, and come back to my desk for a minute with you before I go to bed. Dr. Grayson came in right late to call, and we sat here talking until midnight—neither of us remembering the lateness of the hour.

Don't be shocked—for he was reading me his speeches, and telling me of his hopes and fears in another direction[1]—and—incidentally—saying such beautiful things about you, that my heart expanded and glowed.

I have just reread your loved note of this morning. Could any one, any *woman* fail to respond to such wooing? You love, as you do everything else, in such a royal way, and I find myself drinking in your words, trying to feed my hungry heart with them. For, now that it is awake, it tugs at restraint and longs to come and seek its lord and master!

Goodnight, and thank you for your dear thought in getting Helen to phone me in regard to your interview. It *was* such a comfort to know you would not see him alone, and it was like you to remember my anxiety and try to lessen it.

Have you been happy today, Woodrow? and is the world as beautiful to you as the world your love has created for me?

Edith.

ALS (WP, DLC).
[1] His courtship of Alice Gertrude Gordon.

To Edith Bolling Galt

[The White House]

My darling Sweetheart,   Friday, 4 June, 1915 7 A.M.

No, indeed,—it is no dream! It *was* a dream, *my* dream, but it came true,—and how completely and gloriously! It is a calendar month to-day since I told you of my love for you,—told you because it had taken complete possession of me and I *could* not hold it back,—and now! It *is* almost incredible that such a wonderful and ideal thing could happen in a single month,—but it was the lovers' month, the happy month of May, when many wonders come to pass and everything is recreated. Now you love me and are all the world to me! I lack nothing but to be with you always. Ah, my sweet One, it is more delicious and satisfying to be together each time that I see you than it ever was before— and more exquisitely painful to part; and yet happiness is more possible than ever, too, while we are separated,—indeed I cannot be really *un*happy even when you are away from me because of the deep, the blessed realization of your wonderful love that remains with me and makes every day bright and full of strength. Oh, it was sweet to hear my darling whisper last night that she could not be happy away from me, and my heart knows to the full what the pain is she was thinking of. But there is something wonderfully sweet that sustains me and that shines also in her letters when we are apart,—the certitude of love, the glory of it, the sustaining power of it, and the confident hope of fulfilment! I dread to have June end and have you go away from Washington (I have no love for the place and when you are out of it it will be empty of *all* that redeems it!) but, oh, it will be delightful, my precious one, my own darling, to think, to know, that you are *at my home* and that when I go there I shall find *you*! Wherever you are will henceforth be my only real home, the only home of my heart, the only place where I can be really happy and at ease. Ah, sweetheart, as I dream here in this quiet room you seem still to be in my arms and I seem still to feel on my lips those sweet kisses by which you gave me leave to seal myself

Your own   Woodrow

My love is so much greater than anything I can write!

ALS (WP, DLC).

From Edith Bolling Galt

My precious One: [Washington] June 4th, 1915

You are a perfect wonder! Never have I seen so finished an actor, and you have charmed my small sister so that she can talk of nothing else. All the way home after we left you she plied me with questions such as these—"Hasn't he the most wonderful eyes you ever saw? and such an exquisitely modulated voice—did you notice how beautifully he expresses himself, and yet so simply and naturally? Do you think he liked me? and, I hope you don't think I was too absorbed in him, and did not pay enough attention to Miss Wilson—but he is so fascinating I could not help it—" etc etc. until I almost forgot my own part and answered just the way I felt, but caught myself in time to be mildly enthusiastic about you and do a lot of raving over Helen and Margaret.

You were splendid to do this for me, and so far she has not even mentioned that you knew I was one of the party. So the object has been a success!

Really, Sweetheart, you *were* so splendidly indifferent to me that I had to get your note of this morning and read it the minute I came home to reassure myself that it "isnt a dream." All the time you were sitting in the big chair (making tea so gracefully) my thoughts were flying back to this date a month ago —wondering how so much radiance could have been crowded into thirty days—asking myself if it is possible you and I are the same people we were then—if the world was really so perfect a place, and only I asleep, and unable to see its glory until you, the fairy prince, came and kissed my eyes and waked me to the realization of the exquisite beauty around me. When they were asking for a definition of the word "charm," I found it so hard not to say in *two words* the most perfect definition that could be given—Woodrow Wilson, and I leave it to any lexicographer to find a more concise or convincing one if he thought a thousand years.

I am so touched by all you say about my going to *your home* and it thrills me beyond anything words can utter to have you feel that wherever I am henceforth will be *"home"* for you— the only place you can be "happy and at ease." Precious One, if I can always fulfill this mission—making you *happy and at ease* then indeed will the awaking of my own spirit be justified, and it will be a glory to have lived. No wonder I am afraid of Bernstorff and such people, for the pent-up feeling of dead years seems so terribly awake that it frightens me with its very fierceness. Oh! I want to talk to you—I can't write.

Did you—as the paper tonight says—finish the reply to Germany today, and will it go forward tomorrow? I hope for your dear sake, it is over, for you will then have a freer weekend holiday with that, at least, temporarily off your mind.

12:30

I wrote the foregoing right after dinner, but did not finish it before being interrupted.

There is just room on this page for a long goodnight. I hope you are already in the land of dreams and that the morrow will bring you happiness.   Edith.

ALS (WP, DLC).

From William Jennings Bryan

My Dear Mr President   Washington June 5 1915

The fact that the note to Germany has not yet been completed encourages me to trespass upon your time for a moment to present again three matters which, to my mind, are necessary to insure us against war with Germany.

1st A reference to the plan embodied in our 30 treaties—the principle of which has been accepted by Germany. Her mention of arbitration opens the way and makes the suggestion easy, if it does not in fact compel the suggestion. It will insure a peaceful settlement of this controversy, and we can not forget that the peace plan for investigation in *all* cases was endorsed by the Senate and is *now in force* with Great Britain France & Russia.

Second.   Steps to prevent passenger ships from carrying ammunition. This is also referred to by Germany. Action ought, in my judgment, to be taken before the reply is sent.

3rd   Before we send another note to Germany I think we should make a renewed protest to Great Britain against interference with our trade with neutrals. These three propositions have been under consideration before. The first was decided upon—that is the idea was to be given to the public and communicated to Germany but you were dissuaded by some thing that you heard. The second is thought by the Atty Gen to be possible—and even if it could not be accomplished as a matter of fact, the same end could be reached almost as well by advice, such as was given to Americans in Mexico.

The third suggestion was about to be carried out but you were dissuaded by a message from Mr House.

I beg to renew the suggestions most urgently believing, as I do, that without them the note as you outlined it at the cabinet meeting would be likely to cause a rupture of diplomatic relations, and this might rush us into war in spite of anything we could do. If the ini[ti]ative were with us, I would not fear war for I am sure you do not want it, but when the note is sent it will be Germany's next move. If the note causes her to act in an unfriendly way it may cause conditions here that will increase the difficulties of our position. This may be our last chance to speak for peace, for it will be much harder to propose investigation *after* some unfriendly act than *now*.

Pardon me for presenting these suggestions so earnestly but I am sure that the sober judgment of the people will not sustain any word or act that *provokes* war. They will support you *if war comes* but they will do all in their power to prevent war and I fully share their desire and purpose in this respect.

With assurances of high respect I am my dear Mr President
Very truly yours   W. J. Bryan

ALS (WP, DLC).

To William Jennings Bryan

My dear Mr. Secretary,   The White House. 5 June, 1915.

I hope that you realize how hard it goes with me to differ with you in judgment about such grave matters as we are now handling. You always have such weight of reason, as well as such high motives, behind what you urge that it is with deep misgiving that I turn away from what you press upon me.

I am inclined to think that we ought to take steps, as you suggest, to prevent our citizens from travelling on ships carrying munitions of war, and I shall seek to find the legal way to do it. I fear that, whatever it may be best to do about that, it is clearly impossible to act before the new note goes to Germany.

I am sorry to say that, study as I may the way to do it without hopelessly weakening our protest, I cannot find a way to embody in our note the principle of long discussion of a very simple state of facts; and I think that our object with England can be gained better by not sending a note in connection with this one than by sending it; and, after all, it is our object and the relief of our trade that we wish to accomplish.

I recast the note last night. I hope you will think a little better of it.

I would be very much obliged if you would go over it for substance, making any suggestions that may occur to you, and that you will ask Mr. Lansing to go over it for form and validity of statement and claim.

With the warmest regard, and with a very solemn and by no means self-confident sense of deep responsibility,

Cordialyy and faithfully Yrs.,   Woodrow Wilson

WWTLS (CLO).

From William Jennings Bryan

My Dear Mr. President: Washington June 5, 1915.

You have probably seen the enclosed flimsy,[1] but notwithstanding this probability, I am sending you a copy of this despatch from Garza. It is the first echo and it is certainly along the right line and well expressed.

We are sending to Carranza the message intended for him and to Villa the telegram addressed to him.[2] It looks like your appeal may bear fruit.

With assurances of high respect, I am, my dear Mr. President,
Very sincerely yours,   W. J. Bryan

TLS (W. J. Bryan Papers, DLC).

[1] J. M. Cardoso de Oliveira to WJB, June 4, 1915, T telegram (W. J. Bryan Papers, DLC), printed in *FR 1915*, p. 697. This telegram consisted of separate messages from Roque González Garza to Venustiano Carranza and Francisco Villa, which González Garza requested the Secretary of State to forward to the intended recipients. In both, he called attention to President Wilson's statement and warning to Mexico of June 2 and requested that they consider it and inform him of their opinions in regard to it. In the message to Carranza, González Garza declared that, in his own revolutionary faction, there existed a strong belief that it was "necessary to arrive at a unification of the revolutionary elements as the revolution has triumphed and there obly [only] exists for the realization of its ideals, the extirpation of useless and unpatriotic personalisms." To this end, he declared his willingness to give up his executive power as president of the revolutionary convention "within twelve hours to the Provisional President who may be nominated by the revolutionists united."

[2] That is, the messages communicated by Cardoso de Oliveira in the telegram discussed in n. 1.

From Robert Lansing, with Enclosure

Confidential

Dear Mr. President: Washington June 5, 1915.

Since I wrote the enclosed letter to Secretary Bryan I found that he had gone to Secretary McAdoo's house. I therefore telephoned him the substance, and he requested me to send the letter to you.   Very sincerely yours,   Robert Lansing.

TLS (WP, DLC).

E N C L O S U R E

Robert Lansing to William Jennings Bryan

Dear Mr. Secretary: [Washington] June 5, 1915.

I have received the draft of the note to Germany, prepared by the President, and also your statement of his request that I should go over the note for form and validity of statement and claim.

This note is of such grave importance to this country that I do not feel I can comply with the President's request properly at the Department, or within a short time. I desire to take the draft home with me and study it tonight and tomorrow, unless the President is desirous that it should be sent tomorrow. I think, in justice to myself, as well as to my duty to you, that I should have this time for consideration of the matters submitted to me by the President.   Faithfully yours,   Robert Lansing.

TLS (WP, DLC).

To Edith Bolling Galt

[The White House]

My Darling, my Darling,   Saturday, 5 June, 1915 6.55 A.M.

If ever again I have to be with you for an hour and a half with only two stolen glances to express my all but irresistible desire to take you in my arms and smother you with kisses, I am sure I shall crack an artery! I schooled myself beforehand for the task with this poem of one of the old Elizabethans

"Eyes, hide my love, and do not show

To any but to her my notes,

Who only doth that cipher know

Wherewith we pass our secret thoughts:

Belie your looks in others' sight,

And wrong yourselves to do her right."[1]

It was fun, in a way, while it lasted, and done with zest because you had bidden it, but, ah, after it was over, your lover was very sad, to have missed all the sweet talk he might have had with the lady he adores,—who was dressed bewitchingly, looking her very best, and too tempting for words. Phew! please do not exact it again!

I liked your sister so much, my Darling. She is good fun; she knows how to talk and she can talk about interesting things and not be dull. I am sure that, if she gives me a chance, we shall be good friends. I hope she liked me as much as I liked her. We shall find a great deal in common.

And I worked for you all last evening, too, till late bed-time; —revising the reply to Germany. I have simplified it and, I believe, strengthened it in many ways, and hope that I have brought it nearer to the standard my precious Sweetheart, out of her great love, exacts of me. Bless your heart! How fine you are and how deeply I admire you,—and my love surpasses words,—as I shall try to tell you this blessed night when I shall be happy again with you.   Your own   Woodrow

ALS (WP, DLC).
[1] Samuel Daniel (1562-1619), *Hymen's Triumph* (London, 1615).

From Edith Bolling Galt

[Washington]

My precious One: May [June] 5th & 6th, 1915

The clock is just tolling out the midnight hour, and, at last, I can feel I am alone with you, away from that deadly telephone, which has kept up a continual ringing ever since I got home.

First it was Dr. Grayson, who sounded really sick, and who poured out his heartache to me, as much in his *tone* as in what he said. I do feel so sorry for him, and the long agony of uncertainty he has been through. Unless you really need him, Sweetheart, make him stay away next week and take a few days complete rest. After talking to him, and to Helen (who was sweet enough to call and ask me if I was safe and sound) my sister telephoned, and asked a thousand questions about you—*what we talked about*, if I thought you really liked her, and *if* I enjoyed being there! I answered these as well as I could, and now I instinctively turn to you before I go to sleep: ☉ Do you know what that round thing stands for? Well, it is a bad word, for I had to stop again to answer the telephone, and it is now nearly one oclock and it does not seem quite proper to be talking to a gentleman at such an hour. However at this long distance I will disregard conventions and go on talking to you because—I can't help it!

What great fun it is to be together, and just the content that fills my heart keeps me from talking, or telling you so many things I think of when I am away.

I am so pleased that you "worked for *me* on the German reply." I am more than honored, and wish I could have heard the finished document. Then, I did want to ask you more about the resignation of "W.J.B." but saw the subject troubled you so would not let myself discuss it. I think it will be a blessing to get rid of him and might as well frankly say I would like to be appointed in his place, for then I should have to have daily conferences with you. And I faithfully promise not to interfere in any way with your continuing to do all the work!

I know how you feel about being loyal to this person, but if he deserts you now he is entitled to small courtesy or consideration, and I would not hesitate to put myself on record if he does so scurvy a thing.

Remember, when you are sitting silent and with Presidential, Presbyterian air in church tomorrow, that just a few squares away there is someone who loves you, who says a fervant amen to the prayer for "all those in authority," and who longs to have you with her where she can turn to find, in your dear eyes, the answer to so much that is in her heart.

I think I will go to lunch at Mother's tomorrow, so am afraid I will be out if you send me a note. But I will try to get this to you before the day is over.

I have had such a happy evening, dearest one, and please forget all I said that troubled you. Goodnight, and "God bless you all the day, and God keep you all the night."

Always   Edith.

ALS (WP, DLC).

Sir Cecil Arthur Spring Rice to Sir Edward Grey

Private   Washington 6 June 1915

I am told that a Netherlands subject van Gheel Gildemeester whose father was court chaplain at the Hague arrived here on Friday with letters showing that he was charged with message from German Chancellor to U S Govt. He was introduced to Members of Cabinet by a German American member of the Federal Reserve board.[1]

Terms of peace with which he is charged are similar to those announced by German Ambassador namely freedom of seas, Poland restored, increase of German colonies (but not restoration of Tsing tau) Evacuation of conquered territory annexation of Luxemburg & cession of part of Alsace to France. He has been in communication with a press writer of German extraction who is acting as German Ambassador's agent[2] although the paper for which he writes is anti-Prussian.

President has received this message and as you will have gathered from language held in London by a personal friend of the President's the idea of "freedom of the seas" is viewed by him sympathetically.

President is believed to nurse the hope that he will be accepted as mediator on the basis of "freedom of seas" as proposed by U S at Hague Conference.

The object of Germany is thought to be to make immediate peace and at once commence preparations for war with England depriving her in advance by a concert of the powers of England's principal arm against Germany. This country will no doubt at first accept the idea with enthusiasm in spite of the warnings of experts and the President's mind is probably prepared in advance.

Indications are that German circles here believe peace will take place in three months.

The character of the person named above is not good and he has been under arrest. He could be easily repudiated. The official Dutch Minister is merely a tool of German Ambassador.

Hw telegram (FO 115/1920, pp. 259-60, PRO).
  1 That is, Adolph C. Miller.
  2 Oswald Garrison Villard.

To Edith Bolling Galt

[The White House]
Sunday, 6 June, 1915 10.20 A.M.

Good morning, my precious Darling. Last evening made me over again, by the magic your dear love works upon me. And every time I am with you a delightful thing happens,—*I fall in love with you all over again*,— or is it that I just fall deeper in? There seems to be no end or limit to the sweet experience. I seem each time never to have seen the full sweetness and various womanly depths of my incomparable sweetheart. You asked me last night if I thought it was *unwomanly* in you to come here as you do at my earnest prayer! I think it is triumphantly womanly, the triumph of a really great woman's generous heart over everything—every petty thing—that threatened to stand in the way. The most striking and one of the most noble things about you is the fearless frankness of your heart. You are not frank merely as a man is frank (when he *is*). You are frank with your heart,—he is frank with his mind. And you love royally, like the noble creature you are, giving the best that is in you and not counting the cost. Unwomanly indeed! It is the most beautifully womanly thing I ever knew of. The man you love cannot come to you, because of circumstances over which he has no control and to which he yields for your sake: therefore you come to him, like the princess you are, and give him joy and life itself, and leave him with an admiration, an adoration in his heart which transcends ordinary love by the very measure of *your own greatness*. My heart followed you last night like a courtier. It attends you all day with delight that it is permitted such a service and as long I live I shall feel that I have an incalculable debt to pay for what you are now doing for me. And, God helping me, I will pay it, with interest. I love you beyond all words—only deeds of love can show how much, my Darling. The happiest circumstance of my life is that I am   Your own   Woodrow

ALS (WP, DLC).

To Robert Lansing

My dear Lansing: The White House June 7, 1915

Thank you for letting me see this.[1] I have no doubt that it interprets a very large element of opinion in the country, but I do not think that anything that we are doing would exclude temperate action.   Faithfully yours,   Woodrow Wilson

TLS (SDR, RG 59, 763.72/1780½, DNA).
  [1] D. F. Kellogg to RL, June 1, 1915, printed as an Enclosure with RL to WW, June 1, 1915.

Two Letters to William Jennings Bryan

My dear Mr. Secretary,   The White House. 7 June, 1915.

This expression of the views of Senator Martin and Representative Flood has made a deep impression on me, and I have no doubt echoes a great part of public opinion. I wish with all my heart that I saw a way to carry out the double wish of our people, to maintain a firm front in respect of what we demand of Germany and yet do nothing that might by any possibility involve us in the war.   Faithfully Yours,   W.W.

WWTLI (W. J. Bryan Papers, DNA).

My dear Mr. Secretary,   The White House. 7 June, 1915.

In all our dealings with Garza he has shown himself reasonable and capable of seeing a little beyond his nose. This utterance and action of his is wholly creditable, and is certainly, as you say, a ray of hope out of the darkness down there.
                        Faithfully Yours,   W.W.

WWTLI (W. J. Bryan Papers, DLC).

To William Jennings Bryan, with Enclosure

My dear Mr. Secretary: The White House June 7, 1915

Here is the letter to Mr. Griswold, which I have revised, and I sincerely hope it will be acceptable to the gentlemen in Baltimore.

Replying to the suggestions in your letter of May thirty-first accompanying Mr. Griswold's letter,[1] I quite agree with you that all reference to the six-Power group should be omitted.

I am also willing to leave to them the question of when and how these plans shall be communicated to the public.
     Always   Faithfully yours,   Woodrow Wilson

TLS (Letterpress Books, WP, DLC).

¹ As Swem's shorthand notebooks reveal, Wilson dictated "May 3rd," that is, WJB to WW, May 3, 1915. "Griswold's letter" is the draft which Wilson revised in the enclosure printed below.

E N C L O S U R E¹

PROPOSED LETTER FROM THE PRESIDENT TO MR. GRISWOLD

Dear Mr. Griswold:

⟨PROPOSED CHINESE LOAN⟩

Referring to your letter of the 10th ultimo,² I am writing to express to you the attitude of the Administration with respect to the proposed loan. ⟨The suggestion of the loan in the form in which you have made it, is substantially different from the request made of us by bankers representing the "Six Power Group" which required the direct sanction of this government to an agreement with bankers of foreign nations and imposed upon the Chinese a lien upon an obsolete salt tax.⟩

The loan in the form proposed in your letter is not objectionable to this government. On the contrary, the Administration ⟨, pursuing its policy of supporting⟩ *will always seek to support citizens of the* United States citizens in *all* legitimate enterprises abroad; ⟨will⟩ *and it would* welcome action by American bankers which ⟨should⟩ *would* be of benefit to the Chinese people and *tend to* increase the⟨ir⟩ friendly ⟨feeling toward Americans.⟩ *relations between the two peoples.* The Administration does not consider that there is anything in ⟨the⟩ *its* present ⟨condition of its⟩ relations with foreign countries which ⟨makes⟩ *would make* it ⟨, from the standpoint of the government,⟩ inexpedient that negotiations for such a loan should be undertaken by American bankers at the present time.

There is a suggestion which I should like to make. If the loan is agreed upon, the offering should be so arranged that an opportunity to participate in the underwriting will be given, so far as practical, to American bankers of credit and standing generally, *and the loan made in effect a popular one.* At all events, I should like to see the field of underwriting a very large one. I understand the difficulties of making a general offering ⟨and appreciate the necessity of explaining⟩ , *but it may be explained* to the bankers that the offering has been ⟨so⟩ made ⟨at⟩ *in this way at* the request of the ⟨United States⟩ Government. ⟨As at present advised, I think the Government would make this request.⟩

If the loan can follow substantially the lines indicated above, the Administration will give the bankers every reasonable encouragement. It is contrary to our policy to make our government the collector of debts for its citizens⟨. We will not commit⟩ , *and we must not be understood as committing* the government to the use of physical force for this purpose; but all ⟨other⟩ legitimate assistance will be rendered.

This letter is personal and confidential. You may state to other bankers the attitude of the Administration as expressed herein, but I should prefer that the letter itself should not be used except *confidentially* in the course of your negotiations ⟨with those who are to be more closely associated with you in the inauguration of the business⟩.   Very truly yours,[3]

T MS (W. J. Bryan Papers, DNA).
  [1] Words in angle brackets deleted by Wilson; words in italics added by him.
  [2] That is, B. H. Griswold to WW, April 10, 1915, Vol. 32. When Griswold drafted this proposed letter in early May, the "10th ultimo," of course, was April 10. This phrase remained as written above in the letter cited in n. 3 below.
  [3] This letter was sent with corrections as WW to B. H. Griswold, June 10, 1915, TLS (B. H. Griswold Papers, MdHi).

From William Jennings Bryan, with Enclosures

My Dear Mr. President: Washington June 7, 1915.

I am sending you the suggestions made by Mr. Lansing in the form of a re-draft of the note, together with a letter from Mr. Lansing explaining the changes so that the re-draft can be intelligently read. While I have expressed to you orally and in former communications my views as to the line that should be followed, I feel that I owe it to you to offer some suggestions in regard to the text as you desire it to be. In the paragraph beginning near the top of page, you use the CUSHING and GULFLIGHT incidents as a justification for condemning the establishment of a war zone. It seems to me that, in view of the fact that we accept the offer made by the German Government and accept apologies and reparation in case of attack of neutral vessels by mistake, it is an unnecessary enlargement of our demand which really weakens the demand itself. Our interest in the war zone ceases to be acute if the right for which we ask, namely, that time will be allowed for passengers to escape, is recognized. While there is force in the suggestion that they should avoid the the [sic] setting apart of a zone because mistakes are liable to occur, still, what we are really demanding of them is that everywhere, whether in any particular zone or upon the seas generally, they shall not sink a merchantman without giving the crew and passengers time to escape.

2)[1]   Second; the sentence beginning near the bottom of the third page and concluding on the second line of the fourth page states that there is no adequate compensation for the lives of the two seamen lost on the GULFLIGHT. I suggest that that sentence raises a question which is nowhere answered in the note. If there can be no adequate compensation for the loss of life of these two seamen, how are we to settle this particular case? Would it not be well to indicate the manner in which this claim can be adjusted? Do you mean that *although* a pecuniary compensation is accepted, it cannot be adequate for the loss of life? This would indicate that in this particular case damages will be accepted– the vessel having been attacked without intention. If, however, you mean that money cannot be accepted in such cases, then what other compensation have you in mind? The punishment of the officer or the physical punishment of the government responsible for it? It would, in my judgment, be unfortunate to raise an inquiry upon the subject and then leave it a matter of doubt as to what would be acceptable or to leave the impression that nothing whatever can be done to atone for this mistake.

3)   Third; the next sentence following, that is the sentence beginning on the second line of the fourth page, would seem to be not only a surplusage, but a surplusage that is calculated to offend. It evidently refers to the argument which is made by Germans not in their notes to us, but in their interviews in favor of the freedom of the seas, and, it seems to me, that it detracts from the dignity of the paper to turn aside from the main discussion to answer an argument that is not involved in the controversy. I think that in discussing the FALABA, some attention should be paid to the assertion that the failure to give sufficient time for the passengers and crew to escape was due to the alleged fact that "suspicious steamers were hurrying to the aid of the FALABA." This statement raises two questions, one of law and one of fact. In the first place we do not have any other evidence except that contained in this note that suspicious steamers were hurr[y]ing to the rescue, but if that is a fact and a material fact, it cannot be overlooked. The second point raised is whether if it were true it would be a justification for the sinking of the vessel. I feel sure that there must be precedents on this point and I have asked Mr. Lansing to investigate. I would not feel like answering from intuition and I could not answer it on information without knowing what the precedents are. It seems to me that many cases of this kind must have arisen during the operation of the rules in regard to prizes. It must often have occurred that vessels have hurried to the rescue of a prize ship before the

passengers and crew could have been taken off. What is the rule in such a case? Must the attacking vessel withdraw and leave the prize ship or is it justified in sinking the prize ship, crew and all? If a merchantman, instead of stopping when ordered to stop, continued its efforts to escape, it can be sunk. Its refusal to stop changes to that extent the character of the vessel. Does the effort of another vessel to rescue it have the same effect as a continued effort to escape, or must the attacking vessel withdraw, if it sees a vessel of superior force approaching before it is able to rescue the passengers?

I am inclined to think that the use of the phrase "is surprised to find" might be softened by the use of some milder phrase like "the United States is sure that upon more complete investigation" or that "upon more complete consideration, the Imperial German Government will not contend etc," or something like that.

In the discussion of the LUSITANIA on pages six and seven the note speaks as if our statement of the facts foreclosed further discussion. I do not understand that either side has a right to assert a statement of facts and then act upon the theory that there can be no further dispute. We think that the facts assumed to be true by the German Government are in fact erroneous, but the real facts are the things that must decide, not the facts as assumed by either side. And right here, it seems to me, is not only an opening for the suggestion which I have had the honor to submit to you, but a condition that really requires the thing suggested. If, in our reply, we say, as the note seems to say, "all of these things alleged or assumed by you to be facts and upon which you acted are without foundation, and, therefore, there is nothing further for you to do but to accept our view of the law as applied to the facts as we state them," we shall, it seems to me, foreclose any further discussion of the facts and make ourselves the final judges. We would not, however, regard Germany as justified in saying to us "we have investigated this matter and we regret to inform you that all the facts upon which you rested your claim are erroneous, and, therefore, we expect you to withdraw the claim." Would it not be proper here to say something like this: "we have stated the facts as we believe them to exist and this statement, if true, would seem to remove the grounds upon which Germany bases her departute [departure] from the rules covering prizes. If she is satisfied that these assumed facts are erroneous, we feel sure that she will be pleased to acknowledge that a grave mistake was made. If, on the contrary, she feels that she has reason to question the facts

[facts] as we have stated them, we respectfully suggest a joint investigation in order that the true facts may be arrived at, since the real facts must determine the principal to be applied." I think that if you are inclined to favor such a statement, it would be still further emphasized by the suggestion that the treaties which we have made with thirty countries, the principal of which Germany has approved, would indicate a means by which these facts might be arrived at.

I agree with Mr. Lansing in the reference which he makes in Section K, page 3 of his explanations to the Treaty of 1828. It does not seem to apply to this case. I do not agree with Mr. Lansing, however, in his view of the words "with honor" in the third line on page ten. I think a softer word would be better, for instance, "no Government is justified in resigning"—"with honor" might be regarded as offensive. I do not agree with him either in advising the omission of the paragraph covering the first half of page twelve—I believe that is a very important part of your statement and not only adds strength to it, but indicates that the note is written in the language of a friend.

I think the reference to our willingness to be the means of bringing the two governments together on some concessions is a very important part of the note. The only trouble is that the first part of the note will, in my judgment, make it unnecessary as it now stands, for Great Britain to make any concessions. If we undertake the task of protecting her passenger ships from submarines she will not have as much of an incentive as she otherwise would to agree upon concessions that would be valuable to neutrals. The effect of what you would say to Germany is more than counterbalanced by the encouragement which is given to Great Britain *not to make any concessions at all*, that is to refuse the concessions which are so important to our wellfare. In saying that Great Britain will be encouraged to refuse concessions, I am only saying that she, like other belligerent nations, will view the matter from the standpoint of her own interests and not from our unbiased point of view.

It is not pertinent to this discussion of this note to reiterate what I have said in regard to the wisdom of making at the same time representations to Great Britain in regard to the interference with our ships, but I will venture to repeat that I believe the reception of this note and the action likely to follow would be much more favorable to us if, before the note was sent, you announced that, pending negotiations with Germany as to the use of submarines and without any surrender of any of our rights, you felt impelled to refuse clearance to belligerent ships carrying American passengers and to refuse clearance to American passenger ships carrying ammunition. I believe that the moral effect of such an announcement, coupled with the suggestion in regard to investigation, would, without in the least subtracting from the strength of the note, relieve the tention, deny to the jingoes foundation for their alarming statements and win the approval of our people, who, while firm in insisting upon the respect for our rights, will be quick to recognize the christian forbearance exhibited at a time when the exigincies of war make it difficult, if not impossible, for Germany to consider this question upon its merits and apart from its connection with the war in which she is engaged.

With assurances of high respect, I am, my dear Mr. President,
Very sincerely yours,   W. J. Bryan

TLS (WP, DLC).
[1] This and other marginal notations WWhw.

E N C L O S U R E   I

Robert Lansing to William Jennings Bryan

Dear Mr. Secretary: [Washington] June 7, 1915.

I enclose herewith the President's draft of a note to Germany with suggested changes indicated by underlining and parentheses. The underlined portions indicate new matter or changed phraseology, and portions within parentheses indicate suggested omissions. I enclose also a memorandum on certain of the suggestions which require explanation.[1]

Faithfully yours,   Robert Lansing.

TLS (WP, DLC).
[1] RL, TS memorandum dated June 6, 1915 (WP, DLC), commenting on the changes that he had made in Wilson's draft and explaining that most of them had been made in an attempt to insure against any possible loss of meaning when the note was translated into German at the German Foreign Office.

E N C L O S U R E   I I[1]

American Ambassador, Berlin.   Robert Lansing.

You are instructed to deliver textually the following note of the Minister of Foreign Affairs.

In compliance with Your Excellency's request I did not fail to

[1] In order to show Lansing's changes, we have retained his new text in italics and his excisions from Wilson's so-called third draft in square brackets (Lansing actually used them, not parentheses).

transmit to my Government immediately upon their receipt your note of May 28th in reply to my note of May 15th[2] and your supplementary note of June 1st setting forth the conclusions so far as reached by the Imperial German Government concerning the attacks on the American steamers CUSHING *and* GULF-LIGHT. *I am now instructed by my Government to communicate the following in reply:*

⟨[Allow me to acknowledge the receipt of your note of the twenty-eighth of May, transmitted through the Honourable James W. Gerard, Ambassador of the United States of America near the Imperial German Government, in answer to the note I had the honour to address to the Imperial German Government on the thirteenth of May on behalf of the Government of the United States, and also the receipt of your supplementary note of the first of June communicating the conclusions of the Imperial German Government, so far as arrived at, concerning the attacks on the steamers CUSHING and GULFLIGHT.]⟩

The Government of the United States notes with gratification the full recognition by the Imperial German Government, in discussing the cases of ⟨these two steamers,⟩ [[the *Cushing* and the *Gulflight*,]] of the principle of the freedom of all parts of the open sea to neutral ships and the frank willingness of the Imperial German Government to acknowledge and meet its liability where the fact of attack upon neutral ships *"which have not been guilty of any hostile act"* by ⟨[those in control of its]⟩ *German* aircraft or vessels of war is satisfactorily established; and the Government of the United States will ⟨[of]⟩ *in due* course lay before the Imperial German Government, as it requests, full information concerning the attack on the steamer CUSHING.

⟨The Government of the United States cannot turn away from the discussion of these cases without again very earnestly calling the attention of the Imperial German Government to the fact, that *its attempt* [the policy of the Imperial German Government in seeking] to establish a war zone upon the high seas which neutral vessels are warned that they will enter at their peril, itself constitutes a very grave and [quite] unprecedented infringement upon the freedom of the seas and the rights of neutral nations *and their citizens*, and, [is sure] if persisted in, *will* [to] continue to be fruitful of fatal and tragical mistakes such as

---

Wilson next emended Lansing's revision to produce the final draft. Wilson's deletions are printed in angle brackets; his new text is printed in double square brackets. Angle brackets followed by square brackets indicate that Wilson accepted Lansing's deletions.

[2] He meant transmitted on May 15.

these *of the* GULFLIGHT *and* CUSHING. *This Government* [It] therefore urges upon the Imperial German Government the necessity for a reconsideration of the whole situation. The submarine attack upon the steamer GULFLIGHT resulted not merely in damage to the vessel but also in the loss of the *lives* [life] of two of her seamen, and for [such] loss of life *in such circumstances* no adequate compensation is possible. The freedom of the seas, for which the Imperial German Government is contending, cannot be vindicated by [a] violations of that freedom on the part of that great Government [itself].⟩

With regard to the ⟨[case]⟩ *sinking* of the steamer FALABA, ⟨[upon]⟩ *by* which an American citizen lost his life, the Government of the United States is surprised to find the Imperial German Government contending that an effort on the part of a merchantman to escape capture and secure assistance alters the obligation of the officer seeking to make the capture in respect of the safety of the lives of those on board the merchantman *although the vessel had ceased her attempt to escape when torpedoed.* These are not new circumstances. They have been in the minds of statesmen and of international ⟨[lawyers]⟩ *jurists* throughout the development of naval warfare, and the Government of the United States does not understand that they have ever been held to alter the principles of humanity upon which it has insisted. Nothing but actual forcible resistance *or continued efforts to escape by flight when ordered to stop for the purpose of visit* on the part of the merchantman has ever been held to forfeit the lives of her passengers or crew. The Government of the United States, however, does not understand *that* the Imperial German Government ⟨[as]⟩ *is* seeking in this case to relieve itself of liability but only ⟨[as setting]⟩ *intends to set* forth the circumstances which led the commander of the submarine to allow himself to be hurried into the course which he took.

Your Excellency's note, in discussing the loss of American lives ⟨[on]⟩ *resulting from the sinking of* the steamship LUSITANIA, ⟨[speaks]⟩ *adverts* at some length ⟨[of]⟩ *to* certain information which the Imperial German Government has received with regard to the character and outfit of that vessel, ⟨[which]⟩ *and* Your Excellency ⟨[fears]⟩ *expresses the fear that this information* may not have been brought to the attention of the Government of the United States. It *is* ⟨*asserted*⟩ [[stated]] *in the note that* ⟨[speaks of]⟩ the LUSITANIA ⟨[as having been]⟩ *was undoubtedly* equipped with masked guns, supplied with trained gunners and special ammunition, transporting troops from

Canada, carrying a cargo not permitted under the laws of the United States to a vessel also carrying passengers, and serving, in virtual effect, as an auxiliary to the ⟨[armed]⟩ naval forces of Great Britain. Fortunately these are matters concerning which the Government of the United States is in a position to give the Imperial German Government ⟨authoritative⟩ [[official]] information. ⟨[Such]⟩*Of the* facts ⟨*asserted*⟩ [[alleged]] *in Your Excellency's note*, if true, the Government of the United ⟨[is]⟩ *would have been* bound to take official cognizance ⟨[of]⟩ in performing its recognized duty as a neutral power *and* in enforcing its national laws. It was its duty to see to it that the LUSITANIA was not armed for offensive action, that she was not serving as a transport, that she did not carry a cargo prohibited by the ⟨[laws]⟩ *statutes* of the United States, and that, if in fact ⟨[in the service of the navy]⟩ *she was a naval vessel* of Great Britain, she should not receive clearance ⟨[papers]⟩ as a merchantman; and ⟨of course⟩ it performed that duty *and enforced its statutes* with scrupulous vigilance through its regularly constituted officials. It is able, therefore, to assure the Imperial German Government that it has been misinformed. [[If the Imperial German Government should deem itself to be in possession of convincing evidence that the officials of the Government of the U. S. did not perform these duties with thoroughness the Government of the U. S. sincerely hopes that it will submit that evidence for consideration.]]

Whatever may be the contentions of the Imperial German Government regarding the carriage of contraband of war on board the LUSITANIA *or regarding the explosion of that material by the torpedo, it need only be said that* [[in the view of this Government]] *these contentions are irrelevant to the question of the legality of the methods used by the German naval authorities in sinking the vessel.*

But the sinking of ⟨*these* [this]⟩ passenger ships involves principles of humanity which throw into the background any special circumstances of detail that may be thought to ⟨[have affected]⟩ *affect* the cases, principles which lift it, as the Imperial German Government will no doubt be quick to recognize and acknowledge, out of the class of ordinary subjects of ⟨[diplomacy]⟩ *diplomatic discussion* or of international ⟨[obligation]⟩ *controversy.* Whatever be the other facts [[regarding the *Lusitania,*]] the principal fact is that a great steamer, primarily and chiefly a conveyance for passengers, and carrying more than a thousand souls who had no part or lot in the conduct of the war, was ⟨[sent to the bottom]⟩ *torpedoed and sunk* without so much as a challenge or a warning, and that men, women, and children were sent to their death in circumstances unparalleled in modern warfare. The fact that more than one hundred American citizens were among those who perished ⟨makes⟩ [[made]] it the duty of the Government of the United States to speak of these things and once more, with solemn emphasis, to call the attention of the Imperial German Government to the grave responsibility which the Government of the United States conceives ⟨[it to have]⟩ *that it has* incurred in this tragic occurrence and *to* the indisputable principle upon which ⟨[it]⟩ *that responsibility* rests. ⟨[It conceives that it]⟩ *The Government of the United States* is contending for something much greater than mere rights of property or privileges of commerce. It is contending for nothing less high and sacred than the rights of humanity, which every ⟨[nation]⟩ *government* honours itself in respecting and which no *government* ⟨[nation] can *with honour* resign on⟩ [[is justified in resigning on]] behalf of those under its care and authority. ⟨No case could more vividly or thoroughly demonstrate than does this case of the LUSITANIA the overwhelming argument against the use of submarines against merchantmen where visit and search are impracticable and where the humane *rules* [principles] of international law are impossible of application.⟩ *Only her actual resistance to capture or refusal to stop when ordered to do so for the purpose of visit could have afforded the commander of the submarine any justification for so much as putting the lives of those on board the ship in jeopardy. This principle the Government of the United States understands the explicit instructions issued on August 3, 1914 by ⟨[of]⟩ the Imperial German Admiralty to its commanders at sea to have recognized and embodied, as do the naval codes of all other nations, and upon it every traveller and seaman had a right to depend.* It is upon this principle of humanity as well as ⟨of⟩ [[upon the]] law *founded upon this principle* that the United States must stand. ⟨and stand without compromise or abatement of its rights.⟩

The Government of the United States is happy to observe that Your Excellency's note closes with the intimation that the Imperial German Government is willing, now as before, to accept the good offices of the United States in an attempt to come to an understanding with the Government of Great Britain by which the character and conditions of the war upon the sea may be changed. The Government of the United States would consider it a privilege thus to serve its friends and the world. It stands ready at any time to convey to either government any intimation or suggestion the other may be willing to have it convey and cordially invites the Imperial German Government to make use of its services in this way at its convenience. The whole

world is concerned in anything that may bring about even a
partial accommodation of interests or in any way mitigate the
terrors of the present distressing conflict.

[In the meantime, whatever *arrangement* ⟨[action]⟩ may happily be *made* ⟨[taken as]⟩ between the parties to the war, and
whatever may in the opinion of the Imperial German Government have been the provocation or the cirsumstantial justification for the past acts of its commanders at sea, the Government
of the United States confidently looks to see the justice and
humanity of the Government of Germany vindicated in all cases
where Americans have been wronged or their rights as neutrals
invaded.][3]

The Government of the United States therefore very earnestly
and very solemnly renews the representations of its note *transmitted to the Imperial German Government on the fifteenth*
⟨[of the thirteenth]⟩ of M'ay, and relies in these representations
⟨[not only]⟩ upon *the principles of humanity, ⟨and⟩* the universally recognized understandings of international law, ⟨[but also
upon the explicit covenants of the treaty of 1828 between the
United States and the Kingdom of Prussia.]⟩ [[and the ancient
friendship of the German nation.]]

[[The Government of the United States cannot admit that the
proclamation of a war zone from which neutral ships have been
warned to keep away may be made to operate as in any degree
an abbreviation of the rights either of American shipmasters or
of American citizens bound on lawful errands as passengers
on merchant ships of belligerent nationality. It does not understand the Imperial German Government to question those
rights. It understands it, also, to accept as established beyond
question the principle that the lives of non-combatants cannot
lawful or rightfully be put in jeopardy by the capture or destruction of an unresisting merchantman, and to recognize the
obligation to take sufficient precaution to ascertain whether a
suspected merchantman is in fact of belligerent nationality or
is in fact carrying contraband of war under a neutral flag. The
Government of the United States therefore deems it reasonable
to expect that the Imperial German Government will adopt the
measures necessary to put these principles into practice in
respect of the safeguarding of American lives and American
ships, and asks for assuranc̦es that this will be done.]]

TS MS (SDR, RG 59, 763.72/1830, DNA).
  [3] Wilson restored this paragraph as emended by Lansing. The typographical
error "cirsumstantial" was corrected when this note was sent to Berlin on June
9. It is printed in *FR-WWS 1915*, pp. 436-38.

From Francis van Gheel Gildemeester

Sir: New York June 7, 1915

In no case do I wish you to feel that I am impatient or presuming to intrude myself upon your valuable time in the matter of the negotiations now pending between the United States Government and the Government of Germany; but I have some views that I believe it would be well to bring to your attention.

This morning I had an interview with Mr Herman L Ridder of the New York Staats Zeitung, and during the course of that interview took occasion to suggest to him that he should modify his utterances and views of his paper on the subject of the present negotiations; and Mr Ridder graciously consented to preserve a perfectly fair and neutral attitude, and in addition has kindly furnished me with personal letters to Mr Herman L Brand of the Illinois Staats Zeitung and Mr Miller[1] of the Abendpost of Chicago. Each of these letters is in the same tenor, suggesting that all articles of these papers be in a tone of strict neutrality and in harmony with the working and attitude of the administration at Washington.

You appreciate, Mr President, that Sir Edward Grey is willing to commence negotiations for peace. You know also that Professor Delbruck in Germany told me personally that they were willing to come to negotiations if a real neutral would help. I quote from Professor Delbruck:

"We the diplomats in Germany are very sorry for what you Hollanders suffer and I can tell you that we are willing to come into negotiations if a real neutral, with a neutral point of view will help us. I can assure you that we will leave Belgium the moment that peace negotiations are entered into."

I give you herewith a scant outline of the point of view, or some of the principles upon which a peace settlement might be based, with which I know that Germany would concur and be willing to act in harmony with.

(1) There should be no apportionment of the blame for this war; the past must be forgotten and only the future faced.

(2) A conference with belligerents and neutrals under the lead of the President of Switzerland must meet to frame the peace settlement in such a way as to make for a permanent peace.

(3) Belgium must be restored.

(4) The seas must be neutralized.

(5) The neutral nations must unite in agreeing not to furnish any supplies, ammunition or help of any kind, direct or

indirect to any belligerent which refuses to enter into peace negotiations.

(6) All proposals for the settlement of the war and establishment of peace must be submitted to the President of the United States.

Of course, you appreciate, Mr President that peace negotiations commenced at this time will save many thousands of lives and millions of property. Numberless communications looking to this end are arriving every day, and I am sure that at the moment, your proposal to the belligerent countries looking to a permanent peace would be received, a common willingness to negotiate would be manifested by the various countries now at war.

In conclusion I cannot do better than to quote from a paragraph of a letter written to the Honorable Secretary of State on the 5th inst, carrying the same import.

"I pray, therefore, that you may have the wisdom to know how to act in harmony with the wishes and heartfelt desires of the many millions throughout Europe who are today looking to the American Government as the only one who can give them relief."

Believe me with sincere regards,

Your humble servant,   F. v. Gheel Gildemeester[2]

.TLS (WP, DLC).
  [1] Paul Ferdinand Mueller.
  [2] Wilson attached the following note to this letter: "Please acknowledge this and say that I have read it with attention and appreciation."

Sir Cecil Arthur Spring Rice to Sir Edward Grey

Private.   Washington, June 7, 1915.

My tel. of June 6.

I hear person named[1] has letter from Queen of Holland and has seen President and S of S.

The German plan seems to be to hold out inducement of American mediation on basis of immunity of private property from seizure at sea and withdrawal of Germany from conquered territory. On L. question conciliatory answer from President is hoped for which after Gerhard's arrival in Berlin Germany could answer promising to suspend submarine warfare if England suspends blockade. U S note would then be addressed to us complaining of departure from international usage. Meanwhile mediation proposals could be worked out and submitted. If refused by allies blame would be laid on them. In next month striking German successes appear to be expected resulting in improved German position for further negotiations if necessary.

German proposals are designed to cause trouble between France and England if England refuses to surrender colonies as consideration for evacuation of French territory and also to detach Poles in Europe and here from Russia.

Hw telegram (FO 115/1920, p. 266, PRO).
  1 That is, Gildemeester.

Two Letters to Edith Bolling Galt

[The White House] Monday,
My precious Darling,   7 June, 1915 6.35 A.M.

I waked up earlier than usual this morning—came suddenly *wide* awake—and for a few moments could not think what was the matter with me. Then I knew. It was that you had thought of letting Miss Gordon live with you next winter and monopolize you to the inevitable exclusion of the man who loves you as, I believe, few women were ever loved before! That danger is gone now, I know, but the keen pang it had cost me last night had left its touch on my heart and I waked as I do only when something has disturbed me. For that disturbed me much more than has the circumstance of W.J.B's threatened resignation. You cannot criticise me for any length of loyalty after this, my Quixotic Darling! Remember, Sweetheart, that what I told you Friday night is literally true: you have my happiness in your keeping. Please, as you love me, include me in all your future plans—as I do you in all of mine!

Oh, but it was sweet to be with you last night! That pretty little gesture you made towards me when you saw me yesterday in the motor at the Circle was my undoing. I could not bear to end the day without even a touch of your hand! The way you let your hand rest in mine, my bewitching Sweetheart, fills me with happiness. It is the perfection of confiding love. Everything you do, the little unconscious, instinctive things in particular, charms me and increases my sense of nearness to you, identification with you, till my heart is full to overflowing. It is such a *pleasure* to love you,—such *fun* to love you! It so *lightens* my heart. It fills me with a sort of buoyancy that is life itself. In brief, my whole heart and my life itself—everything that is of the present or future—are wrapped up in you. And your love for me, my Darling! It seems to me the expression of everything that is adorable in a woman. You love as prettily, as charmingly, as you do everything else, and with an appealing sweetness that brings tears of joy to my eyes when I think of it, and when I *see* it makes me the happiest man in the world. How I love to make love to you! It is the delight of trying to express everything that is fine and true in me to the one woman who seems worthy of it all. My Sweetheart, my delectable comrade,—dear chum of my mind and my heart, please remember this sacred partnership when you plan, and prefer no one to

Your own   Woodrow

Sweetheart,   [The White House] 7 June, 1915.

Here are the books I was speaking of the other night at dinner. I know that you will enjoy them.

What a delightfully long way we have gone since I wrote you my first note, with Hamerton's "Round My House" and you so sweetly replied that it would always be a red letter day on your calendar because I had pledged you my friendship!

I love to think that these books will give you pleasure and also serve to remind you of   Woodrow

ALS (WP, DLC).

From Edith Bolling Galt

[Washington, June 7, 1915]

Thank you, dearest One, for calling me up to tell me of your ready and tender sympathy which I knew I could always claim.

I am quite content with the paper as it now stands, and reading it myself I am able better to follow the things that sounded involved before. You don't know how much I treasure your confidence in me, and your splendid acceptance of what was really ignorant criticism.

As regards "W.J.B." Of course I am not glad if it puts any additional burden on you, but I believe it will work out for your ultimate good, and your own loyalty is unmatched by his. Forgive this hurried line. I could not read the paper until now as Altrude[1] came immediately after it did, and I had to wait.

Don't worry over next winter. I am sorry if I caused you pain. I never want to do that. Goodby until tonight when I will answer your dear notes   Edith

ALS (WP, DLC).
[1] The nickname of Alice Gertrude Gordon.

To Edith Bolling Galt

[The White House] Monday afternoon,
My precious One,   7 June, '15 5.20.

My heart is so heavy with your grief[1] that I cannot wait till
to-morrow to say more than I could say over the telephone. I had
to try to keep out of my voice the tenderness that was in my
heart. Any sorrow or anxiety of yours is mine also, my Darling.
It is my privilege to share it and a privilege I covet, if by sharing
it I can lighten it. If there is any counsel I can give or anything
of any kind that I can do, I know that you will tell me. If there
is not, you can at least ease your heart, to-morrow evening, by
telling me, and give yourself the luxury you denied yourself the
other evening of pouring out to me, close in my arms, everything,
big or little, sweet or sad, that is in your heart. Meantime, Sweetheart, I am with you every minute in my thoughts. My heart is
full of you and follows every movement or thought it can divine
here where I cannot hear your dear voice or look into your speaking eyes. I love you with every thought of every hour of the day,
yearn to be with you when you are sad or perplexed and help you,
if in no other way, by spoken love and a touch of the hand or a
kiss on your tired eyes and your sweet lips. My Darling, my
Darling, I do not know what to say, because I can only conjecture the trouble, but this is only sent as a caress and to tell you
once more of my unspeakable love for you. It is only my arms
stretched out to you across the spaces that will not let me speak
to you or touch you.   Your own   Woodrow

I am so glad you like the "note" as it now stands.

ALS (WP, DLC).
[1] It was a crisis in the Bolling family, the details about which begin to
unfold in EBG to WW, Aug. 7, 1915.

Two Letters from Edith Bolling Galt

Dearest One: [Washington] June 7, 1915

I am so sorry I told you that I was troubled, for you already
have too heavy a burden, and I never want to add to it. I will tell
you and will love to tell you, everything—and it will ease the pain
to talk to you.

But, until I *can* talk to you please do not let my shadows touch
you. Things will be brighter with you to share them. Thank you
with all my heart. I am going to try to get to bed fairly early as

I got no sleep that night. Please do the same for you too have had a hard day.

                                        Always   Edith

ALS (WP, DLC).

Dearest: [Washington] June 7th [8th] [1915] 3 A.M

I cannot write tonight, or rather this morning, for I have a very heavy heart, but I know you will be disappointed not to have a word. So this is just to tell you that my thoughts will be with you, and I hope "W.J.B." will prove himself worthy of your trust and confidence, and you can get him to do the wise thing.

Don't worry over my sadness—it is nothing about you—and your love seems all the more a haven. I will tell you of it when I see you, and in the meantime I must think out what is my duty. Perhaps it will mean a shorter stay at Cornish, but, at least, we will have your first visit there over the 4th. Then I may have to join my mother & sister. God keep and bless you always

                                        Edith.

ALS (WP, DLC).

To Edith Bolling Galt

                              [The White House] Tuesday morning,
My precious Darling,   8 June, '15 7 o'cl.

Yesterday was a day of intense anxiety for me, but one blessed thing came out of it,—a fuller consciousness than ever before of what your sweet love means to me. All day long, back of the deep perplexities, lay the joy of what you have given me, of what you have become to me. In the midst of it all my heart could hum a little song of happiness, and, but for the ache there was there *for* you, because *you* were sad and anxious about your own dear ones, and I could not help except dumbly, the comfort and deep content of it would have conquered everything else in my thoughts. I am afraid, my dear One, that many consequences will spring out of Mr. B's action which will be very serious to the country and to the administration,—for the newspapers do not express the real feeling of the country for that strange man, and he is evidently going to make a determined effort to direct public opinion in this German matter. He suffers from a singular sort of moral blindness and is as passionate in error as in the right courses he has taken. There are deeper waters than ever ahead of us. To me personally it is, of course, a matter of indifference, but it may mean serious things for the country, and the country I love with a deep passion. But with your hand in mine, your life linked with mine, my incomparable Darling, *nothing* will hurt me *too* deeply. I am fortified now against anything that *can* happen, *for you love me*,—I can turn to you for the things that instantly heal and restore and make the heart glad. You have given me the *fullness* of life by giving me the deep joy and content that are its fountains. I wish I knew how to put into words what you are to me, my Sweetheart. You *fill* my heart. Your sweet love awakens in me everything that is sweet like itself, and everything that is strong. How many people you comfort and sustain and give joy to, my Darling, ministering to them the sympathy and help that gives life; and to me you have given all,—that royal *heart* of yours! What can hurt me *now*, what dismay me or turn me aside? When I take you in my arms to-night nothing but sheer joy can come near me. I am safe and happy because I am   Your own   Woodrow.

ALS (WP, DLC).

From Edith Bolling Galt

Dearest One: [Washington] Tuesday [June 8, 1915], 9.45

Your tender note has just come and I am full of the comfort of it, but so sorry you think this resignation means deeper waters for you.

Bless your dear heart! How happy it makes me to feel that I can lighten the burden.

I meant to write you a long answer to your *three* notes of yesterday, but I was just so tired, I could not last night, so will wait and tell you tonight.

I feel much better today and very rested.

I will think of you in the Cabinet meeting and be bending over your chair to comfort you.

Goodby. For a few hours go out and play golf this afternoon, for you will need to be braced up   I mean after the session this morning not before seeing *me*!   Always,   Edith.

ALS (WP, DLC).

Remarks at a Press Conference

June 8, 1915

Mr. President, has the government any intimation of a [possibility] of peace between the fighting nations and the govern-

ment as a government, as more individuals connected with it
have? Any significance?

> None that I know of. Of course, being readers of the news-
> papers, we know what everybody else knows. I say that so
> that you won't think that we are secluded and uninformed.

Mr. President, was the discussed delay in the dispatch of the
note to Germany caused by any suggestions that were made
after the note had been prepared?

> There hasn't been any delay. That is the interesting part of
> the whole thing. It just happens that we can't write a note
> as rapidly as the newspapers can, and, having to be care-
> ful, we have been careful. There hasn't been any delay. No-
> body has held it up. It is going just as soon as it is finished.

Has there been a subsequent suggestion, Mr. President, as is
printed in some of the papers this morning, that Mr. Bryan
has sought a different solution of the problem than the one that
is to be found in your note?

> Well, I brought the note, or rather the rough sketch of it,
> before the cabinet. There were all sorts of suggestions there,
> but nothing has modified the general character of it.

The note as it stands today meets with the approval of the full
cabinet?

> I think so, sir.

You really admit, then, Mr. President, that the newspapers have
been a little rapid on this proposition?

> I do, most decidedly. I mean it. And they have embarrassed
> me infinitely again, on my request and prayers that the gov-
> ernment should not be forestalled. They have created an
> initial impression on the other side of the water that will be
> permanent.

Isn't it a fact, though, Mr. President, that these speculations
have appeared in the papers that, generally speaking, are foreign
to the administration?

> That may be, sir, but the speculations are not foreign.

Mr. President, have you any information that you can give us
regarding the situation in Mexico?

> No, sir, none that hasn't appeared in the newspapers. We
> haven't any additional information.

Mr. President, has the government offered any direct encouragement to this League of Peace meeting that is to be held in Philadelphia on June 17?[1]

---

[1] The organizational meeting of the League to Enforce Peace. About the
origins of this organization, see Ruhl J. Bartlett, *The League to Enforce Peace*
(Chapel Hill, N. C., 1944), pp. 25-42, and Warren F. Kuehl, *Seeking World*

No, sir. We haven't had anything to do with it one way or the other. I didn't ask for our [participation].

Has any other government offered encouragement, so far as you know?

Well, frankly, I don't know anything about it except what everybody knows in the newspapers.

Can you indicate yet, Mr. President, when the note will go forward?

I think very shortly, indeed. I think it is practically completed.

Will it go before the cabinet today again?

Yes, for the last revisions, last suggestions, I mean.

Do you know whether the Allies have given their guarantee of the safety of Mr. Dernburg back to Germany?

I hadn't inquired about that. I don't know.

Have you gotten any report, Mr. President, on the *Nebraskan* case?[2]

Only a very partial report. Just a preliminary report.[3] It had nothing in it that was not generally known.

Mr. President, is Mr. Lind in any official capacity in the Mexican matter at this time?

No, sir.

Mr. President, can you say anything about the German reply on the *Gulflight* and *Cushing* cases?

In what manner do you mean?

As to their reply to you? Nothing has been said about that. I wondered if that was covered in the negotiations?

Well, the reply speaks for itself. I don't see anything else to say.

May I ask, is the reply satisfactory to this government in the *Gulflight* and *Cushing* cases?

You will notice that the German government admits liability in the case of the *Gulflight* and asks for further information as to the *Cushing*.

Mr. President, does that mean that the German government

Order: *The United States and International Organization to 1920* (Nashville, Tenn., 1969), pp. 181-92.

[2] The American cargo steamer *Nebraskan*, sailing in ballast from Liverpool bound for Delaware Breakwater, was torpedoed off the south coast of Ireland on May 25. There were no injuries but the crew abandoned ship briefly until it became clear that the vessel was not severely damaged. The ship returned to Liverpool under her own power but with several of her compartments flooded. *New York Times*, May 27-31, 1915.

[3] J. W. Gerard to WJB, June 4, 1915, *FR-WWS 1915*, pp. 432-33, reported only that, when he asked the Foreign Minister for a report on the *Nebraskan*, Jagow replied that he knew of none but would ask the Navy Department about the incident. Gerard was unable to transmit a report until July 12 (*ibid.*, pp. 468-69).

admits liability, which means that it will go to its prize court without any [protest] of this government?

> I don't know what the formal method of it will be. They don't suggest that it will go to the prize court in their communication.

It would seem to be an impression under their ruling. They say it was necessary just as a matter of routine.

> It may be. I don't know.

In that connection, Mr. President, the suggestion was made sometime ago by the State Department that the German government had the case of the *Frye* demand adjusted through the embassy here. Do you know whether that has gone any further?

> I haven't followed that.

T transcript (WC, NjP) of CLSsh (C. L. Swem Coll., NjP).

To Joseph Patrick Tumulty

Dear Tumulty: [The White House, c. June 8, 1915]

My Fourth of July ammunition is entirely given out and there is no foreign source of supply to call on. Will you not be kind enough to beg me off from Mr. Battle[1] by telling him that I really and sincerely feel disqualified for writing letters which would be worth reading on such occasions?

The President.   C.L.S.

TL (WP, DLC).
  [1] George Gordon Battle, who had asked Wilson to deliver an address or send a message to be read at a public meeting in New York on July 4. G. G. Battle to JPT, June 7, 1915, T telegram (WP, DLC).

From William Jennings Bryan

My Dear Mr President   Washington [June 8, 1915]

You suggested giving resignation & acceptance to the press tonight for tomorrow morning papers.[1] I thought it might be better to give them to the press when the resignation takes effect, namely, when the note is sent. But the papers are now reporting "dissention in cabinet" and it may be just as well to give the facts to the papers *at once*. I am willing & leave it entirely to your discretion.

With assurances of respect I am my dear Mr President
Yours truly   W. J. Bryan

JUNE 8, 1915 371

ALS (WP, DLC).
1 Bryan had made his decision to resign on June 5. For details of his resignation, see Link, *Struggle for Neutrality*, pp. 419-27; Paolo E. Coletta, *William Jennings Bryan* (3 vols., Lincoln, Neb., 1964-69), II, 336-57; and Lawrence W. Levine, *Defender of the Faith, William Jennings Bryan: The Last Decade, 1915-1925* (New York, 1965), pp. 3-25.

From James Watson Gerard

My dear Mr. President,   Berlin June 8, 1915.

Lincoln never passed through a crisis greater than that with which you are contending. You are fighting first for humanity and some decency in war and second determining whether a European Emperor shall or shall not dictate their political attitude to certain of our citizens.

It is regrettable to be compelled to think that the German nation knows no treaty or law except the limit of its own desires.

We are still awaiting your second "Lusitania" note and I fear that Germany will never consent to abandon its present hideous method of submarine war; it is extraordinary to hear Germans of all classes extol mere brute force as the only rule of international life; it is a warning to us to create an army and increase our fleet and coast defenses.

The Germans fear only *war* with us—but state frankly that they do not believe we dare to declare it, call us cowardly bluffers and say our notes are worse than waste paper. Breaking diplomatic relations means nothing to them.

Von Wiegand is just back from Przemysl and says that the Russians were defeated by woful want of artillery and ammunition. Their power of offense is broken for many months. From the West I hear the French are rather discouraged—there is no sign of faltering here and 300,000 Bavarians will soon invade Italy .

Germany has ample food and gets all copper etc. necessary for war purposes through *Sweden* in exchange for potash and other commodities. . . .

The King of Bavaria[1] yesterday announced in a speech that Germany's frontiers must be extended by this war. Both von Jagow & Zimmermann have recently told me that Germany intends to keep Belgium, for the rather novel reason that the hate of Germany is so intense in Belgium, that after the war Belgium would be an outpost of England, if again allowed to become an independent country.

We have been five weeks without rain—and there is already some worrying about the crops in consequence.

The Emperor has refused to see me for eight months on the sole ground that I am an *American*. I hope, therefore, that you will notify Count Bernstorff that you will not see him again.

Very respectfully   James W Gerard.

TLS (WP, DLC).
1 Ludwig III.

Sir Edward Grey to Sir Cecil Arthur Spring Rice[1]

PERSONAL & MOST SECRET.   [London] June [c.8] 1915.

Your telegram, Private, of June 7.

Freedom of the seas.

My personal view is that, if there were really a great League of Peace, which made aggression practically impossible, we might agree that, in time of war, all merchant shipping should be immune from capture, provided that other countries, such as the United States, would enter into an engagement that, if this immunity was violated by any Power, they would go to war against that Power. We have long said that we might give up the right to interfere with merchant shipping if, by so doing, we could secure a great reduction in the expenditure on armaments, and diminish to vanishing point the risk of war. If such an arrangement were agreed to, it would be clear that the British Navy could not possibly be used as an aggressive force.

If, however, by freedom of the seas Germany means that her commerce is to go free upon the sea in time of war, while she remains free to make war upon other nations at will, it is not a fair proposition. If, on the other hand, Germany would enter after this war some League of Nations where she would give and accept the same security that other nations gave and accepted against war breaking out between them, then expenditure on armaments might be reduced and new rules to secure freedom of the seas made.

The sea is free in time of peace, anyhow.

I expressed these personal views to the President's friend, and there can be no objection to your making use of them as a personal expression of your own opinions.

T telegram (FO 800/95, p. 73, PRO).
1 There is no copy of this telegram in the British Washington legation files (FO 115, PRO). However, there is no reason to believe that it was not sent; Spring Rice probably destroyed his encoded copy. Grey wrote to Lord Crewe on June 14 about the subject matter of this telegram and asked Crewe to show his letter to Prime Minister Asquith. See Stephen A. Oxman, "British Response to President Wilson's Peace Efforts, 1914-1917" (D. Phil. dissertation, Oxford University, 1973), pp. 193-95.
Moreover, it is significant that Grey said that he had expressed the views reported in the telegram to House and that Spring Rice might make use of them as a personal expression of his own views.

From Edith Bolling Galt

Dearest One: [Washington] June 8th, 1915

It is just an hour since we were together, and already I have thought of so many things I wanted to say to you, and am furious with myself for failing to make wise use of the brief hours we are together.

Almost as soon as I got home Gertrude Gordon called me on the phone and we have talked over the one topic that interests her until there is nothing else to say. All of which reminds me that I did not thank you, as I meant to do, for what you said to Dr. Grayson about staying away. He was so touched by it and told me of it last night with tears in his voice.

Then he added, "I would rather have this assurance from the President than anything I know of for, as busy as he is, and as much as he has on his mind, to think this much about me means an *awful lot.*" But I must not take up all my note with other people, for I must tell you something far more important. It is that I love you, and that I am just as ashamed of myself as you are of me for my "fit," but feel lots better, and oh! so much happier for seeing you and being with you.

I feel that I failed you tonight when you needed diversion, and something deeper than that, so if this little goodnight talk fulfills its mission it will bring you the happiness I failed in and whisper that with wires crossed, or straight you are the centre of my thoughts—they turn to you as a humming bird to its nest, and that only by the emptiness of the world when I leave you do I realize how exquisitely you fill and make radiant my life.

Do you know this little poem of Mrs. Brownings?[1] I have always thought it sweet, but now I know it means *she* loves, and knew she was awake!

Please, my Lord, be happy, and forget even a passing sense of pain, and know that I cannot really "count the ways." They are too many and too subtle. Goodnight and remember I am *always* Edith, even though instead of just *plain Edith* I *might* become   *Your own*   Edith.

ALS (WP, DLC).
[1] She enclosed a printed copy of "How do I love thee?"

Edward Thomas Brown
to Mary Celestine Mitchell Brown

Dearest Sweetheart: The White House June 8th, 15.

You will know this morning of the dramatic events which occurred today.

The President's final decision on his second note to Germany and Mr. Bryan's resignation. The news was not released until six oclock to-night and then the town was in a feverish uproar, with extras flying every few minutes.

I did not reach here from N. Y. until this morning (having stopped over in Baltimore for a day) and just had time to reach "The House" in time for lunch. The President seemed just as usual if anything looking better than he did on my last visit. After lunch he said we would not start for the *links* until three, that he was going to have Mrs. Coon, of whom he is always making funny remarks as to her efforts to preserve his "remaining thin locks," which by the way you know is not at all true (except in spots).

When we reached the Virginia course, he started off badly and I began with a rush. I won the first, second third & fourth holes and then when we were rather close to-gether & the caddies some little distance away he remarked I will tell you what's the matter with my golf, but don't say anything about it, "Mr. Bryan has resigned."

For a moment it almost took my breath away, for I knew it was over the German note and I couldn't imagine a desertion by anyone at this crisis.

And then a curious thing happened to our game. Play as hard as I could, the President *won* the next *four* holes straight making us even, which we kept up until the seventeenth hole & on the 18 I took by a scratch. The question is did the fact of simply communicating what was up[p]ermost on his mind, so steady his nerves as to enable him to get back on his usual game, or did such a startling piece of news so affect my nerves as to put me entirely off my game.

When we were laughing over the game at the dinner table to-night, I told him he had deliberately told me for the purpose of knocking me off the wonderful stride I was making and it simply proved what I had always known, "he was the most resourceful man I have ever known."

He laughingly replyed "there might have been a tinge of method in his madness."

He was perfectly delightful all the evening—never talked more brilliantly and never seemed better or looked better.

I forgot to mention after I had caught my breath, and could digest the news a little bit—"Well Governor it shouldn't worry you, it would make no difference if the whole d.- - - shoot match were to resign, the people are behind you and the Country will uphold you." He said he was not thinking of the effect at home, but what might be the effect abroad. I told him in my opinion, it would have the opposite of what he was thinking for it would show the world that he meant what he said in his first note & everyone would soon realize that the entire country was backing him up. . . .

I wish you were here,   Your own   Edward

ALS (RSB Coll., DLC).

To William Jennings Bryan

My dear Mr. Secretary: The White House June 9, 1915

It was very thoughtful of you to send me your note of yesterday afternoon about the release of the letters and I was glad to take advantage of it to avoid misunderstandings.

The note is now finished and will go forward probably this afternoon, as soon as it can be put into cipher. I need not tell you again how sincerely I deplore what is to accompany its dispatch.

I am sending to Mr. Lansing today, according to what I understand is the custom of the department, a letter designating him Secretary of State *ad interim*, so that he may sign the instructions to Gerard.

With warmest regard,
    Cordially and faithfully yours,   Woodrow Wilson

TLS (W. J. Bryan Papers, DLC).

From William Jennings Bryan

My Dear Mr President: Washington June 9th, 1915

It is with sincere regret that I have reached the conclusion that I should return to you the commission of Secretary of State with which you honored me at the beginning of your administration.

Obedient to your sense of duty, and actuated by the highest motives, you have prepared for transmission to the German Government a note in which I can not join without violating what I deem to be an obligation to my country, and the issue involved is of such moment that to remain a member of the cabinet would be as unfair to you as it would be to the cause which is nearest my heart, namely, the prevention of war.

I, therefore, respectfully tender my resignation, to take effect when the note is sent unless you prefer an earlier hour. Alike desirous of reaching a peaceful solution of the problems arising

out of the use of submarines against merchantmen we find ourselves differing irreconcilably as to the methods which should
be employed.

It falls to your lot to speak officially for the nation: I consider
it to be none the less my duty to endeavor as a private citizen
to promote the end which you have in view by means which you
do not feel at liberty to use.

In severing the intimate and pleasant relations which have
existed between us during the past two years permit me to
acknowledge the profound satisfaction which it has given me to
be associated with you in the important work which has come
before the State Department, and to thank you for the courtesies
extended. With the heartiest good wishes for your personal welfare and for the success of your administration I am my dear
Mr President,   Very truly yours   W. J. Bryan

ALS (WP, DLC).

To William Jennings Bryan

My dear Mr. Bryan: The White House June 9, 1915.

I accept your resignation only because you insist upon its acceptance; and I accept it with much more than deep regret, with
a feeling of personal sorrow. Our two years of close association have been very delightful to me. Our judgments have accorded in practically every matter of official duty and of public
policy until now; your support of the work and purposes of the
administration has been generous and loyal beyond praise; your
devotion to the duties of your great office and your eagerness
to take advantage of every great opportunity for service it offered
have been an example to the rest of us; you have earned our
affectionate admiration and friendship. Even now we are not
separated in the object we seek but only in the method by which
we seek it.

It is for these reasons that my feeling about your retirement
from the Secretaryship of State goes so much deeper than regret.
I sincerely deplore it. Our objects are the same and we ought to
pursue them together. I yield to your desire only because I must
and wish to bid you Godspeed in the parting. We shall continue
to work for the same causes even when we do not work in the
same way.

With affectionate regard,
                Sincerely yours,   Woodrow Wilson[1]

TLS (CLO).
[1] There is a WWsh draft of this letter, dated June 8, 1915, in WP, DLC.

From Franklin Delano Roosevelt

My dear Mr. President   Washington. June 9th 1915

I want to tell you simply that you have been in my thoughts during these days and that I realize to the full all that you have had to go through. I need not repeat to you my own entire loyalty and devotion—that I hope you know. But I feel most strongly that the Nation approves and sustains your course and that it is *American* in the highest sense.

Always faithfully yours   Franklin D Roosevelt

ALS (WP, DLC).

To Edith Bolling Galt

[The White House]
My precious Darling,   Wednesday, 9 June, 1915.

I suppose the papers will be very interesting reading this morning, but I think I shall allow myself the usual indulgence of not reading them. I know so well what they are going to say that I could almost write their editorials for them. What a bore that would be! Comment does not help when difficult things are to be *done.* I always prefer to skip the buzz of the first week or two after a striking or really important thing has happened and be guided by the later opinions, the second thought, of the country, the permanent after impression—and to wait for my own second thought, too. The impression upon my mind of Mr. Bryan's retirement is a very painful one *now.* It is always painful to feel that any thinking man of disinterested motive, who has been your comrade and confidant, has turned away from you and set his hand against you; and it is hard to be fair and not think that the motive is something sinister. But I shall *wait* to think about *him* and put things to be *done* in the foreground. I have been deserted before. The wound does not heal, with me, but neither does it cripple. My thought this morning, therefore, is that there is now a chance to do a great deal of *constructive* work in the State Department for which Mr. Bryan had no gift or aptitude,—if only I can find the right man for the place, or, rather, if only I am free to *take* the best man for the place. Fortunately the chief characteristic of my mind is that it always at once moves on *to the next thing.* All this, dear Heart, just to relieve any anxious thought you might have about me this morning,—any fear that I was at all touched with discouragement. Mr. B. can do a lot of mischief, but he cannot alter anything essential, and my personal fortunes are neither here nor there.

This is not a tube-rose letter, my strange, lovely Sweetheart. Tube-roses do not grow in my garden. I abominate them. But blood-red real roses grow there, whose perfume ought to make any heart seem full of the very spirit of life; and this is a bunch of blood-red roses which I hope that you will wear at your heart to warm you with the devoted love of

Your own   Woodrow

ALS (WP, DLC).

Two Letters from Edith Bolling Galt

[Washington] Wednesday, A.M [June 9, 1915]

Hurrah! old Bryan is out!

This editorial in the Post[1] does my heart good, and I know it is going to be the greatest possible relief to you to be rid of him. Your letter is *much* too nice, and I see why *I* was not allowed to see it before publication.

I could shout and sing that at last the world will *know* just what he is.

All my "fits" are gone this morning, and if you could see me you would not recognize the "Lady of Vapors."

I hope dearest One you slept and feel rested and refreshed this brilliant morning.

Please let me see the editorials, if there are any possible ones, in *favor* of "W.B.J."—and I shouldn't *mind* reading others about an *adorable* person if they are interesting.

Your *penitent*, and worshiping,   Edith.

[1] "Mr. Bryan's Resignation," *Washington Post*, June 9, 1915. This editorial suggested that Bryan had long been considering departure from office since the secretaryship of state had not been congenial to him, and he had been "more and more inclined to turn from politics to the field of religion and temperance." "Mr. Bryan," it continued, "is capable of doing great good as a moral teacher." He would now be free to speak his mind on such questions. However, he would speak in the future as a private citizen rather than as the leader of a party in or out of power. Meanwhile, the secretaryship would probably be filled by a man better qualified by temperament and training to fulfiill its exacting duties. The editorial also noted approvingly that the published correspondence between Wilson and Bryan indicated that the new note to Germany would be "strong and uncompromising." "That is what the country expects," it declared. "The people will support the President as against Mr. Bryan or any other man who proposes an ineffectual method of enforcing American rights."

[Washington] June 9th, 1915, 2:15 P.M.

You are a very subtle, and a very adorable person. I hate to admit that the "blood-red roses" not only do glow with color, and do warm my heart with their sweetness but also prick with a tiny thorn—which, to be perfectly honest, is exquisite pleasure.

You are a fencer so worthy of anyones steel that fencing becomes a delight, and I just glow when you beat me at my own game.

I don't know how many times I will try to parry your thrusts before you get entirely under my guard (and, I warn you that I am a good fighter, and stubborn beyond measure) but you have my heart on your side, which is a tremendous handicap to me. And I promise to be a good sport and acknowledge if I am beaten.

I have just had another call from Mr. Wilson and think that, in spite of all his imaginings, I have convinced him *you* are above suspicion as far as falling in love with me goes. He talked on and on about you, and the *crisis* in my life coming out of your friendship for me—that by September he expected to hear that I had come to some fixed and definite plan for my future. That no responsive person with such quick sympathies as mine could come in touch with such a personality as yours without having the deepest emotions awakened and stirred to the depths, etc. etc. When I said "Please be more direct in what you expect of me. You give me the impression that you are warning me against something, and I can't quite determine what." At last he said, "Well, to sum it all up, I don't mean it as a *warning*, that is not the word, but I might say as a prophesy. He is a man, and you are a woman—each, most attractive. Why shouldn't you attract each other, or at least *one* attract *the* other?" You should have heard me laugh, as I answered, "Oh! I see. You know the President's charm and what you term the *glamour* of the White House and you are afraid I will get my silly little head turned by their charming hospitalities to me as Miss Bones' friend, and end by falling in love with the President. I, who pride myself on my coldness and unresponsiveness!"

Whereupon, the dear old gentleman said, No, I don't mean that exactly but we could not expect him, as burdened as he is, to have time or thought for such things himself, although he may rest in your sympathy and companionship, which would be the foundations for stronger emotions, if he were circumstanced as private individuals are, and which in the future, with more leisure, might develope into love. But with you it is different. You have lived apart from the world so long—that to be thrown suddenly so intensely into the strong light that beats upon the thrown [throne], and come in touch with a man who holds the centre of the stage, not only by position, but attainments, is enough to create any sort of intense feeling in you, who were made for warmth and life in its deepest fulfillment. So, my Lord, *I* am the suspicious person, and you, wrapped in the robes of state and serious meditation, could never be thought of as a lover or a person in whose garden grow deep red roses—roses that bring sweetness and light to the heart that beats under their fragrant petals when they are sent, fresh cut, from their living stem.

I am so happy that you are not letting Mr. B's act really depress or trouble you. It must come right, and cannot add to your burden, save for the moment until things and people readjust.

How I want you this afternoon! It is a just punishment that now I must wait for days before I can see you. The sands of the precious hours we were together last night ran low before I *found myself*, and your dear note tells me you can "turn to the next thing" and not even bend gracefully that rod of iron inside. Well! I can't. I am *homesick* for you, and want your arms about me   Edith.

ALS (WP, DLC).

Two Letters to Edith Bolling Galt

[The White House]
My adorable Sweetheart,   Thursday morning, 10 June, 1915.

You make royal amends when you have been bad! That poem of Mrs. Browning's has always seemed to me one of the most perfect expressions in our language of what is sweetest and best and deepest in a woman's love, but your letter, my wonderful Darling, *added* to the poem, gave me glimpses of things deeper yet and sweeter. The great deeps in you, my Edith, are breaking up, and when their great tides begin to run without let or hindrance you will be the happiest woman in the world and I the happiest man! You will be more than happy: you will be one of the noblest women in the world, for utter allegiance to Love will have transformed you. Ah, Dearest, I have tried to grow bigger and truer and better as the years have gone by, have tried myself to learn the lesson I speak so inadequately in that little essay about how a man comes to himself,[1] and I can testify that the only power that has ever helped me in the least is Love. And my love for you has come to me in these days, when I seem to be put to the supreme tests of my life, like a new youth, its enthusiasm and romance seeming to make duty itself clearer and easier and more worthy of the best that is in me. Your love for me has given me life not only, but has also brought me back gayety and elasticity and ease of action. I love you with an infinite tenderness, my own Darling, but with something also that goes much deeper and stirs me more than mere tenderness, —with a sort of fierce devotion compounded of every masculine force in me and drawn out by your own strength. You have never realized the splendid strength that is in you because you have never before given it the right direction; but you are finding it now. You are, oh, so *fit* a mate for a strong man! Love has come to you now like a challenge, and all that is loveliest in you is coming out like a new glory. And I adore you. My heart is full of light and joy because of you. It is such a delight to love you! You do not yet know the force or depth of it, but you shall know to the utmost what I mean when I say that I am

Your own   Woodrow.

ALS (WP, DLC).
1 "When a Man Comes to Himself," printed at Nov. 1, 1899, Vol. 11.

The White House [June 10, 1915]

I will send you all the editorials when they have been collected. What a dear partisan you are!   W.

ALI (WP, DLC).

From Edith Bolling Galt

[Washington] June 10th/ 1915   11:45 P.M.

It just broke my heart, my precious One, to hear you say how lonely and unaided you feel in this great work you are doing so splendidly.

Of course I knew that it was so, but fondly hoped you were unconscious of the way you carry all the burden on your own dear shoulders and what figure heads most people are! Oh! how I longed to put both my arms 'round your neck, and beg you to let me take part of the weariness, part of the responsibility, and try to make you forget everything else in the assurance of the love and loyalty that fires my heart.

Please try to feel it enfolding you my Beloved One, wrapping you up as a garment, a shield, and a very present help. Only thus can I be worthy of the great love you have given to my keeping, and only thus can I feel I am serving my Lord and Master.

This has been such a happy evening together and I did not once catch sight of the rod of iron inside—so flexible and easy to adjust does it seem.

Tomorrow is another old Cabinet meeting day which means you will be tired out. I am so sorry!

Goodnight, and may the morning bring you new strength and comfort.   Edith.

Friday—10 a.m.

I cannot let this go, since reading your dear note without telling you how perfectly I sensed your mood last night. I felt it all through the hours that have intervened and sent my spirit out into the starlit darkness to seek and find yours and tell you I was keeping the vigil with you, and feeling the hurt of your betrayal. Of course, coupled with this feeling in me is the one of joy that at last you are rid of this awful creature, and that the whole world is with you in sympathy and understanding. But I know you are too generous and loyal to what you think he has done for you to be able to see this side, and can only quiver at the hurt, while you keep an undisturbed face toward the world.

Let me help you my Darling. Draw on all that is in me in your need and may I never fail or disappoint you is the prayer of your own   Edith

ALS (WP, DLC).

From Mary Allen Hulbert

Dearest, dearest friend: [Boston, c. June 10, 1915]

You know how we hold you in our thought. God bless you! I have written to Helen perhaps she will find a moment when you can hear of my plans. An old friend of mine Mr. Grant Squires[1] recently returned from abroad is to be in W. the 15th. Can you see him? He will send his address and you must act as you think best.

He married Sallie Jenkins the daughter of our old clergyman in Pittsfield. Allen has asked me to send $7500.00, which takes our all. He feels sure of large returns from this, but—I have my ticket to California and am sure all will go well. It must.

I am well, and still feel the tonic of that one day of happiness.[2] Write me, if you ever have a time of freedom. I will let you know where and how I am.

And you know I am, always

Your devoted friend   Mary Allen Hulbert.

Do you know?

ALS (WP, DLC).

[1] Squires, who married Sarah Eaton Jenkins, practiced law in New York and handled some of Mrs. Hulbert's financial affairs. He had recently returned from serving with the Commission for Relief in Belgium.

[2] When she visited the White House on May 31.

From Cleveland Hoadley Dodge

My dear President   New York June 11th 1915

You have done so many wonderful things since I saw you last month, that I have felt like writing at least twice a week to tell you what I thought of you, but have nobly refrained.

I cannot however hold in any longer, & must tell you how strongly I approve of the position you have taken, in the last note to Germany. How good Mr. Bryan after signing the previous notes, could object to the substance or tone of this last one, nobody can understand. Whether to congratulate you, or condole you, on his resignation, I do not feel sure, though if I were in your place, I think that I could stand being congratulated. It must be a relief & it hardly seems possible that Bryan can injure the great purposes for which you are striving, and, thank God, that you are not the man to worry over any effects on your own political future

What you have done regarding Mexico is just right. Knowing Mexico so well, I have followed your policy with keen interest & approval & have admired your great patience & wisdom, but I feel sure that you waited long enough & made your strong protest at just the right time. With a little more patience & firmness, I think that you will accomplish what you want.

I sincerely trust & pray that the strain of the past few weeks has not been too much for you. One can hardly wonder that Bryan's importunities have given you headaches. Please remember that there is always a haven of refuge for you at Riverdale or on Corona & when your stern trainer Dr Grayson commands a change, tell him to telephone me & make all the necessary arrangements—if not immediately, at least sometime this Summer.

A Dios, great friend

Ever devotedly your's   Cleveland H. Dodge

ALS (WP, DLC).

To Edith Bolling Galt

[The White House] Friday morning

My own Darling,   I wont say what hour. 11 June, 1915

That ride last night was a very searching experience to me. From beginning to end it seemed to me like an epitome of my own life,—as I was trying to tell you in broken sentences,—a ride through the night, clinging to love, *personal* love, the one thing a man's heart cannot live without,—and all the while your face only half disclosed in the changing light, and yet at last, as we neared home (you and I who live apart and yet have the same home) wholly revealed to me, in the full light, radiant with tender love, too deep for words. It seems to me that this is the way I see you always: first through a half light full of shadows in which you elude me, and then with a final revelation full of perfect solace and hope and joy. And above us all the while, not the staring day, but heavens full of stars, immense, calm, eternal, filled with peace and certainty and the reassurance that there is no chance but fixed laws of God to which all the world moves obedient, not least the fortunes and hearts of men. I started out on the ride disturbed and unhappy, but I came back, though very solemn and a bit sad, yet sustained by a new sense of strength and a new confidence that God's in his Heaven and all's well. Days like these certainly try men's souls,—when loyalty and devotion and the things that spring from the very heart are being tried out, and the real standards by which we are to be judged made clear. How instantly the country hit upon the heart of the matter in condemning Mr. Bryan: how quick and clear it was in saying that that is not loyalty or true fealty that is given *upon terms*. How instinctively the larger things are seen, and true self-forgetfulness demanded of those who serve, and profess to serve, not for themselves, but for love! Sadness *will* creep in when the test fails. I have to admit (to the dear one I love most in all the world) that the defection touched me to the quick and the week has been one of the hardest in these hard years which have exacted such a tribute of sorrow; but I have not for a moment lost hold of myself and love has been my sufficient salvation,—the love that *will* not fail and that will not stop to count the cost!   Your own   Woodrow

ALS (WP, DLC).

From Edith Bolling Galt

                                                      [Washington.]
Dearest and Best: June 11, 1915   10:40 P.M

I have just read over again your sad little note written this morning at an unknown hour, and my heart yearns to tell you again of all the love and tenderness that wells up in it. I have been very near you today, and tried to compel your spirit to feel mine near—and to bring you abiding assurance of "the one thing a man's heart cannot live without."

Did you feel it, and were you happier because of it?

Helen and I had such a good time together today, and I hope

you did not miss her too much. How I wished you could have been with us!

After we got back—at 2:30—I went out to Cleveland Park to play "Auction" with eight very nice people. (I should have said *seven* as I was the other fellow) and there I heard a most interesting history of Gen. Lee's birthplace—where we had such a happy time! Or rather the history is more of the present owners and who they are.

I will tell you about it when I see you. I stayed there until Six, when I took one of the guests home. She lives in a quaint old house in Georgetown, and the grounds are filled with splendid old forest trees, in and out of whose friendly branches darted red birds like tongues of flame. And over all the fences ran a riot of "Dorothy Perkins'" roses. It is a restful, sweet old place, and I felt refreshed by lingering a minute while she cut sprays of roses for me; which I took to mother, because someone else, who has a garden, had sent me a great box of "lovesome" blossoms, which make my room fragrant while I write.

You see you asked me to tell you of what I do, so this is a history of a day. I took dinner with mother, after which I took Randolph, my brother,[1] for a ride. We went down by the Potomac, but the call of Va. was strong so I crossed the bridge and went to Arlington. We were caught in a shower, so I came home at 9:30 and am going to bed as soon as I finish this.

Always yours,   Edith.

Forgive abrupt ending—I was interrupted.

ALS (WP, DLC).
[1] John Randolph Bolling, the eighth child of William Holcombe and Sallie White Bolling, lived with his mother in Washington, D. C., where he held various jobs in business.

From Robert Lansing, with Enclosures

Confidential.

Dear Mr. President: Washington June 12, 1915.

I am sending you a proposed telegram to our Embassy at London, which, if it meets with your approval, will you please return to the Telegraph Room of the Department for transmission.

I would not trouble you with this matter, except that it bears directly upon the policy of our sending a note to Great Britain at this time. Briefly, the situation is this: Great Britain has prepared a reply to our note of March 30th. From the confidential information obtained here as to the contents of the note, it would appear to be largely a defense of retaliation against Germany, based upon further alleged violations of the laws of war and humanity by the German Government. If our information is correct, and I have reason to believe that it is so, it seems to me that such an answer at this time would complicate matters and have an undesirable effect upon Germany. I do not think, therefore, that it would be good policy to encourage the sending of such a reply at the present time.

Of course, knowing that Great Britain has a reply prepared and is only withholding it out of consideration to this Government, in view of the controversy with Germany, we could not in fairness, except in extreme cases, send another note of complaint to Great Britain, until that Government had an opportunity to answer our note of March 30th.

It is on account of this situation that the telegram sent to you for approval is drafted.

I am, with great respect,

Very sincerely yours,   Robert Lansing.

TLS (SDR, RG 59, 763.72112/1241, DNA).

E N C L O S U R E   I

London June 10, 1915.

2258. Confidential. I have again taken up in extenso with Lord Crewe, temporary in charge of the Foreign Office, our troubles about stopped cotton cargoes. After making urgent requests for early answers in a number of specific cases which are of an imperative nature, I expressed the hope on my own account that the British answer to our note on the blockade would not be longer delayed. He confessed confidentially that it was ready and he implied that it was held till our correspondence with Germany should be out of the way. I suggested that if the contents of the reply were satisfactory to us this was a peculiarly good time to send it especially if the British government should see its way to settle these cotton controversies promptly by acceding to our requests. I reminded him that it is a very good time now to clean up our whole docket.

He expressed agreement with me. Such an attitude of the First Secretary is one thing. Action by the Admiralty and by committees on shipping is sometimes another thing. I am informally making renewed urgent representations also to the new members of the Admiralty and of the cabinet committees.

American Ambassador, London

T telegram (SDR, RG 59, 763.72112/1241, DNA).

ENCLOSURE II

STRICTLY CONFIDENTIAL.   Washington, June 12, 1915.

Your 2258 tenth. If British reply to Department's note March thirtieth acquiesces in United States position therein taken, Department would be glad to receive it promptly, but if it makes no concession to American views and is calculated merely to aggravate situation, perhaps wiser to withhold it in hope that some practical solution of differences may be found through more intelligent exercise by British Goverment of discretionary powers reserved under order in council, and greater effort on their part to avoid repetition of present difficulties.

Department has been confidentially informed of contents proposed British note as first drafted, and if this information is correct, transmission of note in that form might bring to a climax increasing agitation against British interference with neutral shipping, which in any event will break out soon, if British authorities continue in their present course, and then it will be more difficult to find a solution.

You may use this orally and unofficially.   Lansing.

T telegram (SDR, RG 59, 763.721112/1241, DNA).

From Walter Hines Page

Dear Mr. President: London. 12, June 1915

I cannot refrain from sending you my sympathetic congratulations, nor can I for one moment doubt the swift rally to your support of all American opinion that is worth having. I think I value Mr. Bryan's good qualities at their full value: he himself prevents right-thinking men from forgetting his unfortunate deficiencies. When he might decorously and loyally have gone off and kept quiet, he must needs go and hang himself in public —that's all it will come to. And that's all he deserves.

His addressing the public in opposition to your method condemns him simply to ignominy here, where such a breach of good manners wd. be instantly fatal to any man in public life. My only fear is that he will so encourage the Germans in Germany as to make it impossible to deal with them—an impossibility that I have feared all the time, now made certain. He plays right into their hands.

For a man who is not an avowed executioner you are doing nobly in making a death-roll for the public good—Clark, Roose-

velt, Bryan, not to mention minor persons who have conven-
iently succumbed.*

Always heartily yours,   Walter H. Page

  * And there are more who will die of the free and open air,
which is your atmosphere.

ALS (WP, DLC).

To Edith Bolling Galt

[The White House]

My own Darling,   Saturday morning 12 June, 1915.

    I turned in at half past nine last night, as tired a chap as ever
you saw, and got about nine hours sleep—and am still sleepy!
But, though I am even yet not quite awake, I feel greatly rested
and know that I shall feel very differently to-day. Yesterday I
was pretty well played out. And how I did miss that sweet ally
of ours, that darling cousin of mine, dear Helen. She went out
at eleven in the forenoon to be with you and did not turn up again
until seven! I envied her with all my heart when I found that she
had been with you for lunch. For my need of you, my precious
Sweetheart, seems to increase with each day,—each day that I
know you better and that we are drawn closer to one another by
some common experience. I feel, and rejoice to feel, that this
desertion of Mr. B's was an experience we went through *together* and which has bound us together by a new and more
intimate sympathy and sense of identification. How little the
public knows of *all* that it has meant to me, and of the sweet
solace it has brought me, in my dear Love's sympathy and loyalty! And, speaking of how little others know of the joy that has
come to *us* in these trying days, I am reminded of your last
conversation with Mr. Wilson (I was reading your account of
it over again last night just before I went to sleep) and my half
ashamed feeling that *I* should *not* be suspected! He knows what
an adorable person you are. He must know that, unless I am
something less than human, I *must* fall in love with you! Indeed
he does know that I will some day when I begin to take notice.
With the feeling about you that I have, and that he evidently has
in a different way, I hate to have him think that I have not *already* rendered you my homage, my Queen. I am not so slow as
he thinks and you are irresistible. Above all, I do not *like* to
have him think that you would fall in love with me before you
knew that I had fallen in love with you. Why not tell him, and

set him right about both of us? I am so proud and happy about it all that I would love to tell it to everybody who really knows either of us,—for it is the best part of my life now that I am

Your own   Woodrow

ALS (WP, DLC).

From Edith Bolling Galt

[Washington] June 12, 1915

For a real *out and out quitter* commend me to the modest person who calls himself the "most enchanting sweetheart he ever saw!" After giving you my hand on the promise that if you came home with me it was "for keeps," you sweetly shook hands with me at the door and handed me into the car in your most disinterested and Presidential way!!!

Well, fortunately the night air was deliciously cool and so calmed my beating heart and cooled my burning cheeks. I wanted to ride on and on in the night and think over the many things that filled my thoughts, and made these last few hours so full, so rich. But instead in less than an hour from the time we were together in the Oval Room, I am here at my desk, trying to bring you vividly before me, and make you as real as you were the 60 minutes away, when I could put out my arms and fold you close and find your splendid eyes looking straight into mine.

I hope you were happy, dear Heart, and that you are already in the land of dreams where all that is vague and uncertain is made real and there is nothing to disturb or trouble you. It has been such a happy evening, and I am still full of the joy of it. I intended bringing the pictures back with me, but forgot them in the pure joy of being with you. Don't bother to send them until I see which you want to keep, and tell me if you agree with me that at last we have Mr. Wilson on a false trail. And now I am sleepy, so good night my Lord, and sweetest dreams attend you. If I can I will come to Arlington tomorrow, for I would love to watch you. But if not remember I am thinking of you there and remembering "The birds sing nowhere quite so sweet, and nowhere hearts so lightly beat, for heaven and earth both seem to meet *Down in Virginia*![")]

Your own   Edith.

ALS (WP, DLC).

To Edith Bolling Galt

[The White House]

My adorable Sweetheart,   Sunday morning 13 June, 1915

The delight of last evening is still upon me so strongly that [it] is almost as if I were still looking deep into your eyes and reading there the whole sweet secret of my happiness. I think you do not know how much of yourself you unconsciously reveal, —you *certainly* do not know what a heart-full of beauty you show and of a tenderness that surpasses beauty, even surpasses the charm that makes you always irresistible. Little as Mr. Wilson knows about *Woodrow* Wilson he knows you, for he describes exactly what has been pent up and hoarded in you and what will happen when you wake and *find* yourself. He does not know that it *has* happened. He only suspects it. He sees a great change in you and is seeking to understand it, and, knowing and affectionately admiring you, as he does, he is so afraid that what he suspects has *not* happened to you—that you have not heard the call of supreme love and responded—to become the perfect woman he knows it would make you—and I know it has made you, often as you try to draw back into your smaller, your prison self and deny the miracle and mystery. Seeing you as I saw you last night, my radiant, wonderful Darling, is like witnessing some deep and glorious mystery, like being present while life is created. There are moments when I feel the *awe* of it and wonder why *I* was permitted to be the instrument of it. And the beauty and joy of it is unspeakable. I love you with an intensity that *hurts* because it can have no adequate expression. And, oh, my precious Queen, how empty the house is without you—how empty my arms are, and my lips can speak nothing worth while all day long for lack of your kisses. I am infinitely homesick for my Darling—and shall always be when she is not with me, to share every experience and every thought and every turn of life and fill it with the love without which it can contain neither happiness nor inspiration. The holiday of yesterday and that blessed talk with you last night have cleared all the cobwebs away from my brain, my sweet One, and I am feeling wholly fit this morning because I am   Your own   Woodrow

ALS (WP, DLC).

From Edith Bolling Galt

Dearest One: [Washington] June 13th, 1915

It seems so natural a thing to be with you now instead of anyone else that I find myself always expecting you, and yet I was
so surprised to find you at my threshold when I opened the door
tonight. I wonder if it pleased you as much as it does me that
the first time you *asked* for admission to my home, I myself
answered your call and threw the door wide to bid you welcome.
Of course you did not come in, only took my hand in yours for
a moment, and gave me one of your deep looks from those wonderful eyes and—I followed you into the night!

Does it not mean something that at first it was dark, with rain
falling softly, like happy tears, and then the sky cleared
and thousands of stars came out to smile down on us, and we
went on and on over old roads that seemed new because we
were together? I like to think it does mean something, and to follow it out still further is to believe that as soon as we *parted* the
clouds gathered, and the pouring rain, that beats against the
windows as I write, came down in torrents, and the house seems
lonely and empty without you.

I wish I could have helped you with tomorrow's speech, but
I can never quite believe you when you say you don't know *what*
to say. I know you will say something that no one else could ever
say, and it will be something I shall glory in. Wish I could hear it
as you utter it, but I will read it in the papers and try to picture
how you look when you say it. My sister told me to tell you she
had made up a riddle concerning "W.J.B.," and she will tell it to
you when she sees you and see if you can give her the answer.
Thank you for all the lovely, sweet things you said to me in your
note today that had to be hidden for so many hours before I could
know them. Goodnight   Always yours,   Edith

ALS (WP, DLC).

A Flag Day Address[1]

June 14, 1915.

Mr. Secretary,[2] friends and fellow citizens: I know of nothing
more difficult than to render an adequate tribute to the emblem
of our nation. For those of us who have shared that nation's
life and felt the beat of its pulse, it must be considered a matter
of impossibility to express the great things which that emblem
embodies. I venture to say that a great many things are said
about the flag which very few people stop to analyze. For me, the

flag does not express a mere body of vague sentiment. The flag of the United States has not been created by rhetorical sentences in declarations of independence and in bills of rights. It has been created by the experience of a great people, and nothing is written upon it that has not been written by their life. It is the embodiment, not of a sentiment, but of a history, and no man can rightly serve under that flag who has not caught some of the meaning of that history.

Experience, ladies and gentlemen, is made by men and women. National experience is the product of those who do the living under that flag. It is their living that has created its significance. You do not create the meaning of a national life by any literary exposition of it, but by the actual daily endeavors of a great people to do the tasks of the day and live up to the ideals of honesty and righteousness and just conduct. And, as we think of these things, our tribute is to those men who have created this experience. Many of them are known by name to all the world—statesmen, soldiers, merchants, masters of industry, men of letters and of thought, who have coined our hearts into action or into words. Of these men we feel that they have shown us the way. They have not been afraid to go before. They have known that they were speaking the thoughts of a great people when they led that great people along the paths of achievement. There was not a single swashbuckler among them. They were men of sober, quiet thought, the more effective because there was no bluster in it. They were men who thought along the lines of duty, not along the lines of self-aggrandizement. They were men, in short, who thought of the people whom they served, and not of themselves.

But while we think of these men, and do honor to them as to those who have shown us the way, let us not forget that the real experience and life of a nation lies with the great multitude of unknown men. It lies with those men whose names are never in the headlines of newspapers, those men who know the heat and pain and desperate loss of hope that sometimes comes in the great struggle of daily life; not the men who stand on the side and comment, not the men who merely try to interpret the great struggle, but the men who are engaged in the struggle. They constitute the body of the nation. This flag is the essence of their daily endeavors. This flag does not express any more than what they are and what they desire to be.

As I think of the life of this great nation, it seems to me that we sometimes look to the wrong places for its sources. We look to the noisy places, where men are talking in the marketplace;

we look to where men are expressing their individual opinions; we look to where partisans are expressing passion instead of trying to attune our ears to that voiceless mass of men who merely go about their daily tasks, trying to be honorable, trying to serve the people they love, trying to live worthy of the great communities to which they belong. These are the breath of the nation's nostrils; these are the sinews of its might.

How can any man presume to interpret the emblem of the United States, the emblem of what we would fain be among the family of nations and find it incumbent upon us to be in the daily round of routine duty? This is Flag Day, but that only means that it is a day when we are to recall the things which we should do every day of our lives. There are no days of special patriotism. There are no days when we should be more patriotic than on other days. We celebrate the fourth of July merely because the great enterprise of liberty was started on the fourth of July in America. But the great enterprise of liberty was not begun in America. It is illustrated by the blood of thousands of martyrs who lived and died before the great experiment on this side of the water. The fourth of July merely marks the day when we consecrated ourselves as a nation to this high thing which we pretend to serve. The benefit of a day like this is merely in turning away from the things that distract us, turning away from the things that touch us personally and absorb our interest in the hours of daily work. We remind ourselves of those things that are greater than we are, of those principles by which we believe our hearts to be elevated, of the more difficult things that we must undertake in these days of perplexity when a man's judgment is safest only when it follows the line of principle.

I am solemnized in the presence of such a day. I would not undertake to speak your thoughts. You must interpret them for me. But I do feel that, back, not only of every public official, but of every man and woman of the United States, there marches that great host which has brought us to the present day—the host that has never forgotten the vision which it saw at the birth of the nation; the host which always responds to the dictates of humanity and of liberty; the host that will always constitute the strength and the great body of friends of every man who does his duty to the United States.

I am sorry that you do not wear a little flag of the Union every day instead of some days. I can only ask you, if you lose the physical emblem, to be sure that you wear it in your heart, and the heart of America shall interpret the heart of the world.[3]

T MS (C. L. Swem Coll., NjP), with a few WWhw emendations and editorial corrections.
  [1] Delivered at Flag Day exercises at the Treasury Department.
  [2] W. G. McAdoo.
  [3] There is a WWT outline, dated June 14, 1915, of these remarks in WP, DLC.

To Robert Lansing

My dear Mr. Secretary,   The White House. 14 June, 1915.

I think that this despatch ought to be sent. Every word of it is true.

But Colonel House, who comes direct from London, landed in New York yesterday from the Saint Paul; and, if a delay of a day or two would not be imprudent, I think we had better wait to get his advice. He is well informed, I happen to know on these very matters and has himself been advising the British Foreign Office of our attitude.   Cordially Yours,   W.W.

WWTLI (SDR, RG 59, 763.72112/1258½, DNA).

To Franklin Delano Roosevelt

My dear Mr. Roosevelt: The White House June 14, 1915

Your letter of June ninth touched me very much and I thank you for it with all my heart. Such messages make the performance of duty worth while, because, after all, the people who are nearest are those whose judgment we most value and most need to be supported by.

With the warmest regard and appreciation,

      Cordially and sincerely yours,   Woodrow Wilson

TLS (F. D. Roosevelt Papers, NHpR).

To Joseph Rucker Lamar

My dear Lamar: [The White House] June 14, 1915

You always write me just when I need such letters as you are generous enough to send, and I want you to know how genuinely grateful I am for your judgment of me and for the affectionate friendship you are good enough to give me.[1] I appreciate it with all my heart.

      Cordially and sincerely yours,   Woodrow Wilson

TLS (Letterpress Books, WP, DLC).
  [1] J. R. Lamar to WW, June 11, 1915, ALS (WP, DLC).

To Ellen Duane Davis

My dear Mrs. Davis: [The White House] June 14, 1915

Your letter of the eighth[1] gave me a great deal of deep pleasure and the little present you sent for the baby delighted Nellie very greatly indeed. She wants me to send you her love and dearest thanks.

I do not think that either you or E.P. can realize how much strength as well as pleasure it gives me to have friends who are thinking about me with the generous affection that you two bestow, and my heart is deeply grateful.

I am very sorry indeed to hear that you are not going to have any summer vacation. I pray the more earnestly that the summer may be mild.

The eggs continue to be delightfully fresh and do me a lot of good, but not so much as the thought that prompts their sending.   Cordially and faithfully yours,   Woodrow Wilson

TLS (Letterpress Books, WP, DLC).
[1] This letter is missing.

To Cleveland Hoadley Dodge

Personal.

My dear Cleve: The White House June 14, 1915

Your letter of June eleventh expresses my own feelings about what has been happening recently as clearly as I could express them myself, though I could not venture to say this to many persons. Mr. Bryan has been singularly loyal during these two years and I must admit a certain degree of amazement at his present action, but I suppose that it was inevitable that it should come.

Such letters as this of yours make all burdens easy to carry. What a man needs more than anything else, I find, is the confidence of the people he loves and believes in, and you give these things in such measure that I am deeply your debtor, my dear fellow.

Always   Affectionately yours,   Woodrow Wilson

TLS (WC, NjP).

From Robert Lansing

Dear Mr. President: Washington June 14, 1915.

The Department has to-day received a telegram from Mr. Paul Fuller, Junior, mentioning his return from Haiti, and stating that

his full written report will be ready by Wednesday.¹ He adds
that in the meantime he is ready to make such oral report as the
Department or yourself may desire before that date. I do not
know any reason why Mr. Fuller should make an oral report
prior to the presentation of his written report, and personally I
feel that a talk with Mr. Fuller would be advantageous after reading and considering his written report.

    As you may, however, have some reason for desiring to talk
with Mr. Fuller immediately, I will defer answering his telegram
until I learn your wishes in the matter.

Very sincerely yours,   Robert Lansing

TLS (SDR, RG 59, 838.00/1197, DNA).
  ¹ It is P. Fuller, Jr., to the Secretary of State, June 14, 1915, TLS (SDR,
RG 59, 838.00/1197, DNA), a thirty-six page report. It is summarized in n. 1
to WW to RL, July 2, 1915 (fourth letter of that date).

Two Letters to Edith Bolling Galt

[The White House]
Monday morning 14 June, 1915

    Oh, Sweetheart, Sweetheart, what a happy ride that was! The
delight of it is still strong upon me. I woke up with an exquisite
sense of comfort and happiness. We came back to an empty
house, of course, because we had left you at what is really not
your home, and my heart ached at the parting (each time we
separate it seems to me to be more nearly intolerable to let you
go than it seemed the time before, and I do not know how much
longer I can stand the growing pain!), but those brief hours
together had been so *perfect* in their joy of love and companionship that I could not feel really lonely or sad. You exquisite
Darling! I am *so* happy when I am with you! And you were so
perfectly delightful last night, in whatever mood, playful or
serious, talking of affairs or yielding to love. I feel nearer to you
and am more perfectly in love with you each time we see one
another. There is always some new charm to discover in you!
How can a man think up a speech when he has something so
engrossing as you to think about? It is so uninteresting to think
about anything else. I shall be proud of myself if I can do any
work at all at Cornish. I think I shall have to send a confidential
personal message to the Kaiser telling him why I should like the
German reply held back until about the tenth of July. If he is
really human and has any heart in him he will understand and
give me time to be with my Love. Ah, Sweetheart, the colour
and zest had gone out of my life when you came into it to restore

them. I was trading on old capital and making shift to live and work without any real interest in my own life, just a tool of duty. And was not my dear, dear Sweetheart in very much the same condition (only used to it and fancying her self content with emptiness) and is it not infinitely sweet to find our lives full again, romantically full, of everything that stirs our hearts and justifies joy? If I have brought to you, my Love, what you have brought to me, I am indeed happy, and fortunate beyond all other men. My pride in your love exceeds the strain of my daily tasks by so much that they are made easy to carry and joy is stronger than anxiety or fatigue.   Your own   Woodrow.

Dear Love,   [The White House, June 14, 1915]
    What do you think of ladies writing me such letters as this?[1]
    Your note of last night is the sweetest poetry of love I ever read. My incomparable Darling!   Your own   Woodrow

ALS (WP, DLC).
    [1] The enclosure is missing.

From the Diary of Colonel House

[Roslyn, L. I.] June 14, 1915.
    I went to New York at eight o'vlock [clock] to meet McAdoo and had a two hour conference with him. The President asked him to tell me what he had in mind concerning Mr. Bryan's successor. In the event I would not consider it, which he regarded as certain, he wished to know what I thought of Thomas Jones of Chicago or Secretary Houston. He sent many affectionate messages and hoped the weather would soon permit me to come to Washington.
    I asked McAdoo why the President did not consider Lansing. He replied that he did not think he was big enough. I told McAdoo to say to the President that, in my opinion, it would be better to have a man with not too many ideas of his own.

T MS (E. M. House Papers, CtY).

Remarks at a Press Conference

June 15, 1915
Mr. President, can you tell us anything now with regard to plans for the Mexican situation?

No, I can't. It's too inchoate yet. I think it's taking shape.
You have had both the Carranza and the Villa statements?[1]

Yes. I haven't had time to study them carefully.

Mr. President, would you care to tell us what change, if any, was made in your note to Germany, after Mr. Bryan resigned and before it took effect?[2]

I think it would be wise not to discuss anything connected with the resignation. That is my instantaneous feeling about it.

I thought perhaps if we confined our suggestions to that one point?

I would have no objection to discussing it with the utmost freedom, but I think perhaps it would be better not to, sir.

Is it true, as was stated in some South American paper, that South American diplomats were conferred with and consulted before the note went forward?

No, sir. And I would, I hope that you all will say No. Just among ourselves, that is not true.

Referring to another newspaper publication, Mr. President, has the United States had any opportunity to lead or to encourage a number of neutral nations looking toward a conference for peace?

No more than has appeared—what everybody knows.

There is a statement to the effect that we are the only nation that didn't encourage that, which is not based on fact?

No, sir. We have encouraged everything of that sort, so far as we legitimately could—I mean, everything that was for peace and accommodation.

Mr. President, it has been printed that you sent for Colonel House to return to Washington?

No, sir, I didn't. Colonel House is not an errand boy.

Do you know whether he will be in Washington soon?

I hope so, yes. He is at present, I think, with either of his daughters.

Has Mr. West returned from Texas?

No, not that I know of.

He is expected back this week, I understood.

Is he? I didn't know that.

Can you say anything as to the attitude of the administration with regard to trust prosecution suits, in view of the decision of the Supreme Court yesterday in the Cash Register case?[3]

I am afraid I haven't heard of that.

The Supreme Court refused to review the judgment of the circuit court in the case of the officials of the Cash Register Company who were convicted under the antitrust act.

In other words, it confirmed the convictions so far as it was—

It reversed it.

It reversed it?

There will be a great deal of speculation as to whether the administration will push cases of that sort.

This is the first I have heard of it.

Mr. President, have you any information or comment to make upon the economic conditions of the country—the question of our crops, the prospects for large crops of foodstuffs?

No, sir. I understood that the prospects are unusually fine; but, to tell the truth, I haven't been able to study economic questions recently.

JRT transcript (WC, NjP) of CLSsh (C. L. Swem Coll., NjP).

1 V. Carranza, "Declaration to the Nation by the First Chief of the Constitutionalist Government of Mexico and Depository of the Executive Power of the Republic," June 11, 1915, T MS (WP, DLC), and F. Villa and Miguel Díaz Lombardo, memorandum, June 10, 1915, T MS (SDR, RG 59, 812.00/15389, DNA), answered Wilson's statement and warning printed at June 2, 1915. Carranza reviewed his legitimate descent from the revolution of Madero and measured his success against the forces of rebellion: "The Constitutionalist Government has control of over seven eighths of the national territory," and "nine tenths of the total population of the Republic, are governed by the administration I preside." Recent military victories, he declared, made it possible to increase his humanitarian work to relieve the Mexican people from the ravages of war, but until he gained recognition as the leader of Mexico, he could not correct the misinformation governing other nations' attitudes toward his administration. He insisted that he met the conditions for recognition, "because the Constitutionalist Government is now in fact in definite possession of the sovereignty of the country; and the legitimate army of sovereignty is the essencial condition to be borne in mind when deciding upon the recognition of a government." He appealed to other factions to submit to his authority and repeated the "programme of social reform" set forth in December 1914: protection of foreigners and their interests, civil order, separation of church and state, no confiscation of property to settle the agrarian question, respect for private property, and public education.

Villa described the "anarchy" in Mexico as the result of differences between "the leaders who believed it to be impossible, within the Constitution, to make the revolutionary principles effective" and those, like himself, who "thought that constitutional reforms should be made by a congress, elected by the people." He then took issue with Wilson's assessment of conditions in Mexico, blamed Carranza for renouncing plans for central authority, cited Duval West and C. A. Spring Rice on the protection afforded foreigners in areas controlled by Villa's forces, and emphasized the remarkable advances made in civil programs under conditions of war. "We have not arrived at such a state of misery and despair that we require help from abroad," he insisted. Insofar as Carranza would accept the aim of free elections, Villa would, "in the light of possible intervention in our national problems, by a foreign power," unite with him to realize the principles of the revolution, "especially the agrarian question, and the development of instruction for the masses."

2 See the entry from the House Diary printed at June 20, 1915.

3 United States v. Patterson, 238 U.S. 635 (1915). The Supreme Court denied certiorari in the government's case, alleging criminal violations of the Sherman Antitrust Act, against twenty-seven officers of the National Cash Register Co. In one of the few cases brought against corporate officials under the criminal clauses of the Act, the indictments, obtained in June 1912, were overturned by the Circuit Court of Appeals, Sixth Circuit, in March 1915. See 201 Federal Reporter 697 (1912) and 222 Federal Reporter 599 (1915).

To Robert Lansing

My dear Mr. Secretary,   The White House. 15 June, 1915.

I quite agree with your judgment in this. I think it would be well to have Mr. Fuller's written report first and discuss the situation disclosed by it afterwards, orally.

Cordially Yours,   W.W.

WWTLI (SDR, RG 59, 838.00/1203½, DNA).

Two Letters from Robert Lansing

Dear Mr. President: Washington June 15, 1915.

I enclose herewith a memorandum and its translation from General Villa,[1] which was handed to me yesterday afternoon by Señors Bonilla and Llorente,[2] the Villista representatives here. I told them that I would receive the documents personally and unofficially.

I thought you might desire to look them over before the Cabinet meeting this morning, so I am sending them at this time.

Very sincerely yours,   Robert Lansing.

TLS (SDR, RG 59, 812.00/15389, DNA).
  [1] Lansing enclosed F. Villa and M. Díaz Lombardo, memorandum, June 10, 1915, summarized in n. 1 to remarks at a press conference just printed.
  [2] Enrique C. Llorente, Villa's regular agent in Washington.

Dear Mr. President: [Washington] June 15, 1915.

The British Ambassador, during an interview this afternoon, spoke very strongly (I believe under instructions) about the indifference of this Government and the American press to the recent Zeppelin attack on London. He said in brief that London was an undefended city, that many Americans resident there were in imminent danger if the attacks were repeated, and that he considered it our manifest duty to protest against acts which could have no military advantage to excuse them. He grew rather excited and closed with "I must officially inform you that we cannot protect American citizens or your Embassy in London from these outrages."

I replied that I appreciated the point of view of his Government and would consider the subject.

He then asked me to submit the matter to you and I have adopted this method of complying with his request.

I am, Sir, with great respect,

Very sincerely yours,   Robert Lansing

CCL (SDR, RG 59, 763.72/1868½A, DNA).

From David Benton Jones

My dear Mr. President: Chicago June 15, 1915.

Last week a man from Nebraska, of trained mind and strong personality, came to our luncheon table and gave us an intimate appreciation of Mr. Bryan. Very briefly it was that under his evangelical garb there is the monumental egoist and the man greedy for gain. Recognizing the inevitableness of his withdrawal, he chose the most dramatic moment for his exit, regardless of consequences to his party or to the nation. His greedy eye saw only the box office receipts and the senator-ship from Nebraska.

The speaker has known him from youth. He spoke with a detachment and an absence of feeling which we could not share.

It is likely that Mr. Bryan has added to the German government's inability to see that the core of your contention is not debatable. It is also likely, I think, that nothing will enlighten it but the final declaration that this government will regard another occurence as a "hostile act." I believe the feeling of the country is fully prepared for that final word.

Any movement in favor of peace at the present time would in its nature be like lancing an abcess prematurely, which as you know is a very dangerous operation. I have personally known of one death to result from such an operation. Hideous and destructive as the war is, it ought not to end before it has burned into the soul of the German people the truth that might does not make right. I have no wish to see the German people crushed, but it is very important indeed for them to have that truth established once and for all.

During this partial respite I thought you would appreciate the picture drawn of Mr. Bryan by a very able man who has known him well; and I could not resist the temptation of adding what I have said about any movement for peace at the present time.

In our anxious watching of your course the words of the prophet have more than once occurred to my mind: "In quietness and in confidence shall be your strength." The recognition and response of the country has left nothing to be desired.

Very sincerely yours,   David B. Jones.

TLS (WP, DLC).

From Edith Bolling Galt

[Washington] June 14 [15], 1915.
Dearest One,   40 minutes after midnight

I can only send you a message of love tonight for I am dreadfully tired. It was such fun watching you today, and hearing all the people around me say lovely things about you. Of course it was a disappointment not to *hear* your speech, but I could, at least, see your eloquent back, and get an occasional tone of the dear familiar voice that would send a thrill all through me. Then I have read the speech in the paper and think it is strong and interesting and quite distinct from the usual, commonplace, poetical effusions we are weary of the repetition of.

On the whole, my Lord, I am quite proud of it, and more than proud of you. And really I can't blame this lady, whoes note you sent me, for her adoration, though I do object to her modest claim of "Dear *My* President" Even I would not dare so much, and you know me for a courageous person. I think the "alliance with the stars" a wonderfully interesting point of view and hope you will keep it, for it rings so true. I love the closing sentence and feel its honesty.

I have wanted you, particularly, tonight and it was a real test of character not to come in today when I brought Helen back. But I knew it was wiser not to. So I made myself go and work—*really* work today. I wonder if you ever think of me as a business woman, going over ledgers, notes, and interest due in Banks, safeguarding credits etc. etc. Well, I will tell you a secret I simply *hate* it and know almost nothing about it but have to put up a sort of bluff, not only about the practical side, but assume an interest in things that bore me more than they are worth. But for the moral responsibility felt toward the men who have been employed for years, and who now are old in service, and the manager,[1] who is devoted to me and serves me with absolute singleness of purpose, I would be happy to get rid of the whole thing at any sort of financial loss. But I cannot, and must not think of my own preferences in the face of such real sacrifice on the part of this man who is of such plain origin and yet whose heart is pure gold, and whose sympathies are as tender as a womans, and who would, I believe, unquestioningly lay down his life for me. I sometimes hate myself when I feel that he is ordinary and uneducated, for he is so much finer inside than I am. And after all as you say our *cases* don't amount to much, if they are not filled with worthy things. I don't know why I have written you of this, but that it is one of my responsibilities, and it helps me to talk to you about everything. I stayed down town until nearly five, going over the whole situation and came home too tired to do anything more. Goodnight. I hope all the happiness of last night has not faded and that you are still in the same delicious mood I left you in.

Yours with my whole heart,   Edith.

ALS (WP, DLC).
¹ Henry Christian Bergheimer.

To Edith Bolling Galt

[The White House]

My own Darling,   Tuesday morning, 15 June, 1915.

What a long, long, barren day yesterday was without you, without so much as a touch of your dear hand. It was lovely to *see* you (and to catch a glimpse of a sweet soft light in your eyes, in spite of your strictly non-commital, public-audience expression of disengaged interest) and the hardest task of the day was to keep my eyes away from you, but I was disturbed when I had that pleasure, because I was afraid you were going to hear a poor speech from a man who would be deeply unhappy if you could not admire him and who wishes above all things to live up to your standard for him, and also because you and Helen were so badly placed and I could not come and claim you and say to everybody, "This beautiful lady is my own love and belongs in the seat nearest me." And you did look so stunning, my lovely Sweetheart! The word is Helen's in speaking of you afterwards when I asked every question a lover would ask about you. When I looked at you it was hard to keep tears out of my eyes,—tears of happiness, because my heart was so full of the words of that wonderful note you wrote after our last ride,—it gave such *perfect* expression to the deepest things that were in my heart that night and I did not know how to express. If love has made a poet of me, my sweet One, it has no less made a poet of you,—and the wells the poetry in you comes from are so deep and pure! It is *so* natural for us to be together, my Love, (as you say in that sweet note) and it makes me happy beyond all words to realize how all our thoughts and hopes and purposes are becoming interwined and knit together in a new life that is shaping itself in our hearts, how we are coming each day to understand and love one another more and more easily, more and more as a matter of course, and how, as the dear understandings and intimacies grow more and more natural, their meaning deepens and they grow more and more wonderful, more and more romantic, with the romance that comes with the complete and gloryfying vision of love. Ah, Sweetheart, nothing can ever sever or weaken the ties that bind us to one another, and as they are drawn closer and closer the world will brighten about us; and then will come the perfect days when we shall never be separated! My Darling! Good-bye until to-night.   Your own   Woodrow.

ALS (WP, DLC).

From Edith Bolling Galt

My precious One: [Washington] June 15, 1915.

Just a line to say goodnight all over again and tell you what a balm this evening has been to me. I can still feel your dear, mesmeric fingers on my brow, and the pain grows less through my eyes, because my heart is so at rest.

It is such unspeakable comfort and joy to have you take care of me. I had so schooled myself to depend only on myself, that I *thought* it satisfied! Now, I know that it does not, and from the way in which I gave up my much-heralded independence of sympathy or help, and clung to you for both, I fear my best friend would never know me.

But, personally, I like my *new* self much better than the old.

You said tonight, Dearest, that you loved to feel you could help me. Don't you see you are helping me every day, every hour of the day, helping me to find myself—and you are such a fascinating person to go on a voyage of discovery with. I found this little quotation the other day and while not beautiful it expressed something I felt very strongly yesterday—

"The longest day, is in June they say.
    The shortest, in December.
But they never came to me that way;
    The shortest I remember
You came a day with me to stay
    And filled my heart with laughter.
The longest day, you went away,
    'Twas the very next day after."[1]

                          Goodnight your own   Edith.

ALS (WP, DLC).
[1] "Shortest and Longest," George Birdseye.

To Robert Lansing

My dear Mr. Secretary,   The White House. 16 June, 1915.

I have read these papers[1] through with close attention, and thank you for handing them to me.

As I said to you yesterday, I am, and have long been, deeply interested in the purchase of the Danish West Indies. I hope that you will take the matter up very seriously and that it may be possible to have a concrete proposal, if possible in the form of a treaty, to lay before the Senate at its next session.

Cordially and Sincerely,   W.W.

WWTLI (SDR, RG 59, 711.5914/30½, DNA).
[1] A group of background papers on the proposed purchase of the Danish West Indies, included among those printed in *FR 1917*, pp. 457-591.

From Edward Mandell House, with Enclosures

Dear Governor: Roslyn, Long Island. June 16th, 1915.

I have been thinking every day that the weather would turn cool so I might go to Washington. I am beginning to fear that the cool spells are over for the summer and I am sending you this letter in order to say some of the things which I hoped to say in person.

The situation as far as the Allies go is not encouraging. Much to their disappointment and to the surprise of the Germans they have not been able to make the progress which they thought the spring and summer weather would bring about. They have made two cardinal errors. One was the attempt to force the Dardanelles by sea only. They found this was impossible and before they could send a land force to cooperate with the fleet, the Turks, under the direction of German officers, had time to make the Straits almost impregnable. They will finally get through, but at a terrible cost.

The second mistake was in not accelerating during the winter months the manufacture of high explosives. When the spring campaign opened and they attempted to storm the German trenches, they found that they not only had insufficient ammunition, but what they had was of the wrong kind. This mistake was more largely made by the English than by the French.

The Germans, through their espionage system, evidently knew the weakness of the Allies, consequently their great concern regarding the munitions of war coming from America. When I was in Berlin in March it seemed to me that they were talking nonsense when they said that if we would stop the shipment of munitions, the war would end within a short time.

The English have been unable to do more than hold their ground, and the Russians have been utterly unable to withstand the German onslaught for the reasons that they have neither sufficient arms nor ammunition. It has resolved itself into a war of munitions rather than one of men.

Germany was much more willing for peace in the Autumn than she has been since. I am enclosing you a letter from Gerard bearing up this phase.

There was the greatest possible concern in England when I left, although they are confident of ultimate victory if the Allies hold together, but it will be delayed longer than anticipated, and perhaps it would not come at all if their American supplies were for any reason shut off.

I need not tell you that if the Allies fail to win it must necessarily mean a reversal of our entire policy.

The sinking of the Lusitania, the use of poisonous gases and other breaches of international laws made it impossible for me to continue the discussion in England of the freedom of the seas or the tentative formation of a peace covenant. If these things had not happened, I could have gone along and by mid-summer we would have had the belligerents discussing through you the peace terms.

The difficulty is not with the German Civil Authorities but with the Military and Naval as represented by the Kaiser, von Tirpitz and Falkenhayn. The feeling is not good between the Foreign Office and von Tirpitz for their differences are irreconcilable. In my opinion, von Tirpitz will continue his submarine policy leaving the Foreign Office to make explanations for any "unfortunate incidents" as best they may.

I think we will find ourselves drifting into war with Germany for there is a large element in the German Naval and Military factions that consider it would be a good rather than a bad thing for Germany.

Regretable as this would be, there would be compensations. The war would be more speedily ended and we would be in a strong position to aid the other great democracies in turning the world into the right paths. It is something that we have to face with fortitude being consoled by the thought that no matter what sacrifices we make, the end will justify them.

You may be assured that the situation as far as you are concerned and the influence of America could not be in better con-

dition. I am certain, unless a change comes, you will be the foremost figure in the final adjustment.

Affectionately yours,   E. M. House

I am also inclosing copies of letters from Sir Edward Grey and
Bernstorff[1] which may be of interest.

TLS (WP, DLC).
  [1] J. H. von Bernstorff to EMH, June 12, 1915, TCL (WP, DLC), welcoming
House home and saying that he hoped to see House soon.

E N C L O S U R E   I

James Watson Gerard to Edward Mandell House

My dear Colonel: Berlin, June 1st, 1915.

I am afraid also that we are in for grave consequences. This
country, I fear, will not give up the torpedoing without notice of
merchant and passenger steamers, and their recent victories over
the Russians have given them great confidence here. They seem
also to be holding the Dardanelles and their lines in France and
Belgium with ease, and probably Italy will be defeated.

The only thing that can gain the war for the Allies is universal
service in England and the throwing into the balance of at least
two million more English troops. If the English knew what the
Germans have in store for England in case of success, the very
dead in the graveyards would volunteer for the war.

It is the German hope to keep the "Lusitania" matter "jollied"
along until the American papers get excited about baseball or a
new scandal and forget. Meantime the hate of America grows
daily.

As to food and even raw materials the Germans have enough
for war purposes. They need raw materials for trades, but have
everything needed for the manufacture of munitions: and as
they are spending all the money for war supplies in their own
country, their financial situation is good for the present. They
expect some other country to pay the cost of the war.

In Governmental circles there is now no talk of giving up
Belgium. They want to keep it and exact great indemnities from
other countries.

They are building new and great submarines (2800 tons) and
are putting so many in the water that I think they will soon become a serious menace to England. That is why a great land
army is necessary.

There was a small womans demonstration for peace in front
of the Reichstag the other day, promptly suppressed and reported
in no newspaper, but I hear or see no other signs of dissatisfaction with the war: even the Socialists are against Italy.

If England will not compromise the submarine matter by letting raw materials pass, then the only possible solution is that if
Americans claim a vested right to travel on British ships that we
shall certify that such ships have no munitions on board, are not
armed, and will not ram submarines—in which case such ships
would be carefully protected by their name prominently displayed and a particular flag. (Like the ships of the Belgian Relief
Commission) Or we might threaten an embargo on arms etc.
unless England let raw materials through.

Will cable if anything comes up. Best wishes to Mrs. House.

Yours as ever,   James W. Gerard.

E N C L O S U R E   I I

Sir Edward Grey to Edward Mandell House

Fallodon, Northumberland.

Dear Colonel House: June 2, 1915.

I shall miss you very much when I return to London, but I
agree that the relations between the United States and Germany
can or may soon become critical, and if so you need to be with
the President.

The more I consider this war the more I feel that your Government must take a hand in the larger aspects of the peace, if
humane ideals are to get and keep the ascendancy over material
militarism and political ambition. Germany is the peril today, but
the peril will recur every century in Europe if Europe is left to
itself. And the peril now cannot be confined to one continent—
the world is too closely knit together by modern inventions and
conditions.

It will in my opinion be downright folly on the part of Germany, if she forces the United States into war and unless they
can force your people [they] will naturally wish to keep out of the
war. But it seems to me that Providence often chooses to wreak
brute force by the faults it generates in itself and it is possible
that over confidence may lead Germany to be reckless enough to
push you into war.

One probable course of events will be more apparent when I
come back to work at the end of the month.

I hope someday you will be in England, when you can spend

a few days with me here and review the memory of the present troublous times in the light of happier days and leisure and perhaps I may have an opportunity of meeting the President then too, when his spell of office is over.

Yours very sincerely,   Edward Grey.

TCL (WP, DLC).

From Edward Mandell House

Dear Governor: Roslyn, Long Island, June 16th, 1915.

McAdoo has been talking to me concerning Mr. Bryan's successor and has told me what was in your mind.

I have a feeling that if Lansing is at all acceptable to you that he could be used to better advantage than a stronger man. It seems to me that the whole office should be reorganized, a very efficient man being placed as First Secretary and another one as Second Secretary. These with Lansing should be able to do the details intelligently, and you could direct as heretofore and without half the annoyance and a[n]xiety that you have been under.

The First Secretary should be able to write a note that could be sent to any government without revision by you. You could also get a good Counsellor to aid in the work.

I think the most important thing is to get a man with not too many ideas of his own and one that will be entirely guided by you without unnecessary argument, and this, it seems to me, you would find in Lansing. I only met him once and then for a few minutes only, and while his mentality did not impress me unduly, at the same time, I hope that you have found him able enough to answer the purpose indicated.

Affectionately yours,   E. M. House

TLS (WP, DLC).

From David Lawrence

PERSONAL and Confidential.   [Washington]

Dear Mr. President: Wednesday June 16th [1915]

I had a long confidential talk today with Charles A. Douglas who is legal adviser to Carranza here. He plans to start for Vera Cruz the forepart of next week and has urged Carranza to make no reply to the Villa overtures until he can talk over the situation with him. Carranza's impulse has been to treat the overtures made by his adversaries with defiance, pressing his military

campaign but Douglas apparently has dissuaded him from making any public utterance on the subject for the time being.

I asked Douglas what he would advise Carranza to do and he
said he was undecided—that he could not understand just what
would be the policy of the United States. He seemed to have this
view of it: If the United States remains passive in the situation, Carranza should press his campaign vigorously and after
taking Mexico City and driving the Villa forces north to Torreon,
formally ask for recognition and moral support. On the other
hand, if the United States intends to insist on a coalition of the
factions, and will "require such a settlement," he (Douglas)
would like to be informed in some definite way so that a course
could be pursued which would conserve the interests of Carranza and his followers. He says Carranza realizes that without
the approval of the United States no government can stand in
Mexico and while there will be resentment over any outside
insistence, it will be accepted and the best made of it. I suggested
to him that if the provisional president agreed upon were pledged
to conduct an election with bi-partisan watches and inspectors,
with a machinery that would carry conviction to Mexicans as
well as outside governments of the fairness of the ballot, Carranza ought to be willing to submit his candidacy to the Mexican
people rather than to insist upon his arbitrary selection at this
time as president ad interim. Douglas seemed impressed with the
idea that if there were some agreement or assurance ahead of
time as to the method of conducting the election, the problem
of setting up a provisional government would be more easily approached.

Douglas will have much influence with Carranza. He says that
irrespective of what his own opinion might be of how the United
States should deal with the situation, he believes in giving Carranza the facts of American policy so that he may know how to
act. He asked me if I heard anything in official quarters as to
what our policy might be to let him know before he goes. I suggested that he call at the State Department before he goes. If no
other means presents itself and I can be of service in conveying
any impression to him, I will be glad to do it. Douglas would not
inquire as to its source but would accept it as an accurate statement of the official view if I told him I had it "on good authority."
I would prefer to talk with you, however, in the latter event.[1]

Sincerely,   David Lawrence

TLS (WP, DLC).
  [1] The White House appointment books do not note any meeting between
Wilson and Lawrence during this period. However, Wilson's letter to Lansing
of June 17, 1915 (second letter of that date) was almost certainly a product
of a conversation with Lawrence.

To Nancy Saunders Toy

Dearest Friend,   The White House. 16 June, 1915.

I am sure that you understand why I do not write more often, to tell you at least of our enjoyment of your own letters[1] and our gratitude at being so thought of, but all the same I feel ashamed that I can only send you, once in a long while, a few lines of acknowledgement and affectionate appreciation. All the sort of spirit that ought to go into personal letters seems to have gone out of me for the time being. But not the feeling that would prompt them. I value my friends more than ever and I think my thoughts turn to them more constantly and with deeper appreciation of what their generous confidence and thoughtfulness mean to me.

I am sincerely obliged to you for having let me see the enclosed.

In haste, with warmest messages from us all and sincere regards to Mr. Toy,

Always   Your true friend,   Woodrow Wilson

WWTLS (WP, DLC).
[1] They are missing.

To Edith Bolling Galt

[The White House]
My precious Darling,   Wednesday morning 16 June, 1915

Last evening brought me a new and exquisite happiness, the happiness of taking care of you and comforting you. When I was trying to soothe and relieve your dear head my heart was too full for words with the joy of rendering you a little tender service, with love in every touch of my fingers, and when the tears came and you came into my arms as to a home and haven, I could have wept with you for the sheer joy of it. And your simplicity and sweetness in it all were beyond measure touching and beautiful, my adorable Sweetheart. I hope some tithe at least of the happiness it gave me came to you also. I wandered about my room for a good while after you left, trying to quiet the pain of parting with you, and then, when I could not do that, went to bed to lie awake whispering endearments to you until the comfort and joy came back and I slept like one to whom hope has pledged fulfilment by bonds that cannot be forfeited. I think your dear heart must have come back to me and touched me with some sweet embrace, for I somehow knew that you were near me. And this morning the joy and deep abiding happiness of your exquisite love is still like a glory about me, and I seem to have a new life.

I could not long lie still and murmur sweet names to my Love, I just had to hurry here to the study and write a message that would a bit take the strain off my heart that it must always feel until we are separated no more. My wonderful Sweetheart! Your sweetness last night, and your utter loveliness in it all, filled me with unutterable longings and delights,—longings to *satisfy* you, and delight that I should be the object of it. And the singular *dignity* of it! Not a touch of weakness,—just the self-revelation of a tender and noble woman whose heart has been pent up and kept proudly aloof, and who now turns to her lover and throws the gates wide,—no, not quite wide yet, but wide enough to show him the sweet and holy places where her true spirit lives. And he *knows* they are holy, takes the shoes off his feet, and stands with worshipping eyes to see his sovereign lady in all her perfect purity and beauty, knowing that he is blessed beyond all other men and has seen his own happiness in the sweet revelation! With my whole heart and spirit.

Your own   Woodrow.

ALS (WP, DLC).

From Mary Allen Hulbert

Hotel Manhattan

Dearest Friend,   [New York] June 16th [1915].

I am sorry you were caught in the rain yesterday. So was I, and wasn't it a storm! I had no motor to dash to, or in, but hurried with the scurrying crowd up Fifth Ave. to this hotel, where I have been since yesterday morning.

There is no peace for my old bones this side the grave. Allen must have $6000.00 by June 25th, or he feels his efforts in business life will be in vain, the great *opportunity* gone. So, failing to negociate the three very excellent Bronx mortgages for six, and nine (4500 each) thousand respectively, I threw some things in a bag and came by Fall River boat to try my luck here. I have journeyed to lower Broadway by subway that I loathe. I have spoiled a good hat. I have a blistered toe, and, as yet, I have not succeeded. As these mortgages are all we have left— outside the cottage at Nantucket—"me heart" is heavy—(that weak heart!) but this is the *last*. I shall hold fast to the balance to buy bread. In the back of my mind too, there always lurks the recollection of a loan of $600.00 due a friend. I saw my real estate agent in Pittsfield who gave me no hope, in the present war conditions of a sale of that property, but it is rented until a year from July thank goodness, for enough to carry the place. I never even smell the check. In your idle moments—if you hear anyone longing for a place of rest and quiet comfort for the summer—just mention "Sandanwede," will you?

I have walked my feet off with that book of recipes. No publisher seems to yearn for it, although my friends do. Its illuminating to see the cold shoulders a woman encounters when she enters the province of the business world. Charm is not marketable, if one has it. In the morning it is an interesting experience. At night, alone in my room, with bruises aching, it wears a less interesting aspect. I think of you, and try to belittle my own affairs by comparing them with your stupendous ones, and so comfort myself. If it were not that I can thank God, humbly for such a friend, it would be cold comfort at times, so selfish are we, am I, rather. Allen transferred the mortgages to me, and wouldn't you think that good safe investments bearing 6% would be desirable to buy, or loan the amount on? I go to see a Jew gentleman today an expert in the Bronx real estate, and if I am successful, I leave tonight at six on the Fall River boat, thence to Nantucket, by way of rail (changing at Myricks at 7 a.m.) to New Bedford for the Nan. boat. I shall pack as quickly as possible and leave from *here* for California about the last week in this month. The New Bedford boats run after the 18th, and one comes more directly and cheaply from Nantucket here, than to Boston. If it were not that Allen is at the end of the journey, I would dread it, alone. I seem destined for lonliness. I who love companionship, and dearly like to talk. *Do* you *know*—I do—oh! so *dearly*.

This isn't a letter, its just a little talk. Read it when you have time. Nantucket will be my address until further notice. I can not get the amount by mortgaging the Nan. Cottage, as the bank there has loans out to its limit. A nasty spiteful mason, named Ring, who would like to be P. Master, sued us for work done, *unsatisfactorily*, on chimney, and I settled by the advice of lawyer. Money seems quite important doesn't it? I think I may go into house decoration in Los Angeles, if there is any really good opportunity. Of course you know I only think in black & white to you. And its such a comfort that you understand my conflicting statements not to be naughty lies.

God bless you, M.A.H.

ALI (WP, DLC).

Two Letters to Robert Lansing

My dear Mr. Secretary,   The White House. 17 June, 1915.

Of course we understand that the British Government cannot defend our people or our Embassy against these air raids; but we also understand, as Sir Cecil does not when he is under great excitement, that it is none of our business to protest against these methods of "warfare," no matter what our opinion of them may be.

I feel a great deal of sympathy with the Ambassador, and am quite willing to let these incidents pass with a complete understanding of how they occur.   Cordially Yours,   W.W.

WWTLI (SDR, RG 59, 763.72/1869½, DNA).

My dear Mr. Secretary,   The White House, 17 June, 1915.

I have been feeling, the past [t]wenty-four hours or so, that it was possible we were not using all the influences we might use in Mexico to guide what is taking place there.

Would it be possible to find some direct but unofficial channel through which we could convey to General Carranza this impression:

That it was within the possibilities that we might recognize him, as things are now apparently shaping themselves,—at any rate that that possibility was not excluded by anything we had yet determined upon,—but that he need not expect us to consider that course seriously unless he went the full length of conciliation and conference with all factions with a view to the accommodation upon which the opinion of the whole world now insists. He cannot in our view afford to insist upon establishing his own dominion unless he first makes a genuine effort to unite all groups and parties.   Cordially Yours,   W.W.

WWTLI (SDR, RG 59, 812.00/15285½, DNA).

To Sir Horace Plunkett

My dear Sir Horace: [The White House] June 17, 1915

Your letter of June fourth brought me a great deal of deep gratification, both because of its generous expressions of confidence and because of its confirmation of my own feeling and judgment about Colonel House.

It is fine to know that you are so generously willing to play the part you suggest and you may be sure that there would never be the slightest hesitation on my part about resorting to you in any possible contingency. I thank you most warmly and send you my warmest personal regards.

In haste   Faithfully yours,   Woodrow Wilson

TLS (Letterpress Books, WP, DLC).

From Robert Lansing, with Enclosure

My dear Mr. President: Washington June 17, 1915.

In compliance with the suggestion contained in your note to me today I have drafted a confidential telegram to Consul Silliman, which I herewith enclose.

I do not know any unofficial channel by which this could be conveyed to General Carranza. Mr. Silliman is, I think, discreet enough to understand the purpose of communicating the substance of the telegram to General Carranza in a personal way.

Faithfully yours,   Robert Lansing.

TLS (SDR, RG 59, 812.00/152851½, DNA).

E N C L O S U R E

Proposed confidential dispatch to Consul Silliman.

American Consul, Vera Cruz.

To be deciphered by Silliman.

When an early opportunity permits, please say to General Carranza casually and in an unofficial and personal way that the Government of the United States is watching with the greatest earnestness for indications that the leaders of the principal factions in Mexico are assuming a conciliatory attitude toward each other with the view to finding in the near future some common basis for an understanding which will result in peace, order and reconstruction in the strife-ridden Republic. Emphasize determination of United States to adopt such measures as may be expedient to preserve Mexico for herself and the world. Intimate cautiously that it is within the possibilities to this end that the United States might recognize General Carranza in view of the way in which things appear to be shaping themselves—at any rate, the possibility of such recognition is not excluded by the policy of this Government, but that if General Carranza does not go the full length of conciliation and conference with all the principal factions, with the aim of adjusting differences and restoring peaceful conditions which the opinion of the whole world demands, the situation thus created may prevent the possible consideration of recognizing General Carranza, who need not in that event expect the Government to consider that course, much less adopt it. Impress upon him the utmost interest which the United States Government and the people generally throughout this country have in the early termination of personal jealousies and factional quarrels. They hope for and expect a unity of purpose on the part of the leaders to sink personal pride and aggrandizement, and patriotically unite in an effort to rescue the Republic from the present conditions, which are causing poverty and famine at home and discrediting the Mexican people throughout the world. If the leaders are inspired with these motives the United States is hopeful that a new state of affairs may result, which will pave the way for synpathetic understanding and mutual confidence between the two great neighboring Republics. In this view General Carranza cannot overlook the advantage and possible duty of not insisting upon the establishment of his own dominion over Mexico, until he has exhausted all reasonable means to unite the contending parties in a common movement which will bring peace and order to the entire Republic.

T telegram (SDR, RG 59, 812.00/15285½, DNA).

To Mary Allen Hulbert

Dearest Friend,   [The White House] 17 June, 1915.

Your letter from New York shows you in real perplexity and distress and disturbs me. Please let me know whether you succeeded in your mission at last and what the character of the mortgages is: what sort of property they are on, in what condition, etc. I hope most fervently that Allen knows what he is about in parting with these last assets.

I judge that you are well and rejoice in that at least.

In great haste,
                    Your devoted friend,   Woodrow Wilson

WWTLS (WP, DLC).

Robert Lansing to Joseph Patrick Tumulty

My dear Mr. Tumulty: Washington June 17, 1915.

The Department has received from the local representative[1] of the so-called Constitutionalist Government of Mexico a letter

dated June 12, transmitting a copy of a declaration to the people
of Mexico by Mr. Venustiano Carranza, which I enclose herewith,
and asking that its contents be made known to the President.[2]

I am, my dear Mr. Tumulty,

Very truly yours,   Robert Lansing

TLS (WP, DLC).
[1] Eliseo Arredondo.
[2] Lansing enclosed a translation of Carranza's "Declaration to the Nation
by the First Chief of the Constitutionalist Government of Mexico and Depository
of the Executive Power of the Republic," about which see n. 1 to remarks at a
press conference printed at June 15, 1915.

To Edith Bolling Galt

[The White House]

My precious Darling,   Thursday morning 17 June, 1915

Another long, long day of separation has gone by,—it was *very*
long, for my Darling becomes more and more indispensable to
me every day. Every day seems to reveal her loveliness more and
more clearly to me and my heart is more and more deeply
involved; for it is true, my Beloved One, as you say in that sweet
note written Tuesday night, that you are every day more and
more finding yourself,—your *true* self, so long buried and denied,
and I am the happiest man alive to be your companion (your
inspiration?) in the sweet discovery. I wish I could tell you, Dearest, (I wish there were some special language of the heart
adequate to tell you) my emotions in witnessing the sweet
miracle. To see the clouds clear away from that great heart, to see
the fountains of tender womanhood stirred within it and begin
to yield their life-giving powers, to see the happiness of surrender
begin to dawn, and be myself the proud conqueror, has brought
me a happiness, a sense of privilege, a full confidence of delightful hope beyond all words except those of the heart, which are
not words at all but acts of gratitude and tenderness and love.
My heart bursts with joy to think of it. I have helped you, I have
helped you to the sweetest discoveries of life!—that's enough to
make any man strong with hope and happiness for the rest of his
life. And I am *so* glad you *like* your new self better than your
old self. *Of course you do!* The old self could find no real happiness: this new self stands and drinks at the inexhaustible
sources of it! It brings tears of joy to my eyes to know that henceforth, my precious One, we shall drink always together there! I
seem to have those two selves visibly before me here as I write, in
two photographs propped up against the stand on my table (the
door is locked), the one infinitely sweet but a little sad and wist-

ful, the other breaking into a bewitching smile and with eyes alight with a look in which lies every delightful thing, and over them both, in every line and light, the glory of my Darling, whom I adore! Good morning, Sweetheart.

                                    Your own   Woodrow

ALS (WP, DLC).

Two Letters from Edith Bolling Galt

Dearest One: [Washington] Thursday, June 17, 1915

I could not write last night, and this morning I must hurry as the boy is waiting.

I have read and read again your dear note, and will answer it more fully tonight. I am so glad you are happy.

I will be with you in my thoughts all day, and this tells you—

                                    I love you,   Edith

Dearest One: [Washington] June 17th, 1915

You have just left me and, while you are speeding toward the "Maison Blanche," I am easing my heart by writing some of the things I cannot speak—even before our blessed little Helen.

But before I tell you about yesterday I must thank you again for this great box of radiant roses   I came in this noon, from out the glare of the street, to rest my eyes on cool masses of fern and a dewy cluster of these exquisite blossoms.

But, aside from their own lovliness, they brought me joy—joy unspeakable—for they told me of you and that you were thinking of me. So I love to wear them over my heart, where they whisper all the day the things I love to hear. I promised to tell you concerning the ride yesterday. Well! *I* felt I must see you—must make you feel my need, and suddenly I seemed to have, as though photographed on my brain, a vision of yourself, and the assurance that I *would* see you before I went home.

When, suddenly, as I took the curve winding toward the right, I looked and saw you coming—way off—so far I could *feel*, more than see, you. For a second the impulse to turn 'round and go to meet you was *almost* fatal. But I feared it would look pointed so I kept on and watched you across the green that seperated us— hoping, yes (as unwomanly as it sounds) hoping you would see and follow me—but alas! The stately car moved on to its haven beyond the Bridge (with apologies to the poet) and I found the road *closed* where I had gone so after all I had to turn 'round and follow you across the Bridge. But it was too late. You were out of sight. And so I lingered, longing to go 'round and meet you on the new road and yet too proud to let anyone else suspect.

So, resolutely, I turned my face homeward. I had *seen* you, and I must be content!

I am so sleepy I must stop and go to bed. Could you feel how perfectly happy I was on the ride tonight, how content, how satisfied. Goodnight my Precious One.

Always your own,   Edith.

ALS (WP, DLC).

To Robert Lansing

My dear Mr. Secretary,   The White House. 18 June, 1915.

This telegram has my approval. Silliman, however, is not the best channel through which to make an impression. I fear he rather bores and irritates Carranza, from what I have learned. I think, therefore, that we had better seek others, in addition.

I understand that Judge Douglas is going to start for Vera Cruz on Monday. Would it not be well to have a talk with him (not at your office, but at your house and as privately, as much away from the newspapers, as possible) and let him go down with a full understanding of our position, namely that Carranza must meet every honest advance half way if he expects to win our confidence, and that he must win our confidence, at least in some degree, if he hopes for ultimate recognition.

There is another matter which it might be well to add to the despatch to Silliman today and in your talk with D., namely the *very* bad impression that is being made by the exportation of food from Vera Cruz at the very time we are sending food in to the starving.[1] It ought to be stopped at once.

Cordially Yours,   W.W.

WWTLI (SDR, RG 59, 812.00/15286½, DNA).
[1] The revised telegram was sent as RL to J. R. Silliman, June 18, 1915, T telegram (SDR, RG 59, 812.00/15261a, DNA).

Two Letters to Edith Bolling Galt

[The White House]

My beloved Sweetheart,   Friday morning, 18 June, 1915.

The exquisite sweetness of being with you is the most delicious combination of stimulation, comfort, and sheer enjoyment that a man's heart and mind could desire! I am still conscious of it in every fibre of me, and I *know* that you are all the world to me. The world seems a good place to live in because you are in it and because you love me. And the luxury of keeping nothing back, of letting both my mind and my heart speak out loud whatever is in them, as if I were speaking to another, better self: the intimacy and confidence and security of it fills my heart with a deep, unspeakable gladness. And the best of it all is to feel your happiness in it, my Darling. *That* is the real reward—to know that I *give* something as well as take all that my heart desires and to see the radiance in your wonderful face, to feel the tenderness and confidence of your gentle caresses. You are adorable, and to enable you to *find* yourself is to witness the most beautiful transformation a man was ever permitted to see. I shall turn to my duties to-day with a new zest, for I am renewed every time I am with you. There is not only a great deal to do but this is the time to do it, when (and while) the country is back of me with enthusiasm and something like unanimity,—while it believes implicitly in my judgment and is ready to think me right in everything I do—for there's no telling how long it will last, and some of the things waiting to be done are very delicate and ticklish. For example, there is not only the Mexican situation, which has to be handled with velvet gloves, and in which I am dealing with an incredibly volatile people, but also some intimate political matters like the chairmanship of the National Democratic Committee and the outlining of plans (including getting money) for the next campaign. McCombs, the present chairman, has turned out the most unconscionably jealous and faithless and generally impossible person, and nobody is any longer willing to work with him—and he ascribes his failure to me! But all these things* have grown easy because I am   Your own   Woodrow.

    * I will tell you all about them when we are together.

My precious Darling,   Friday, 2.30 [June 18, 1915]

    Here are the books. I will not write in them until I can write what my heart dictates.

    Your note written last night has made me deeply, deeply happy.

    With a heart full to overflowing with devoted love,
                                        Your own   Woodrow

ALS (WP, DLC).

Two Letters from Edith Bolling Galt

Dearest: [Washington] June 18, 1915

Thank you more than I can say for the books. They will always be a treasured possession, and I almost wish you had written in them.

I think the "Dedication" to your father[1] is one of the most beautiful tributes I ever read, and so like you in every word. I hope he was still living when you wrote it, for it would mean such infinite things to him.

I was out when Mr Hoover brought the package and I can't resist sending a line to thank you for the note as well as the books. Yours always Edith.

[1] In *Congressional Government*.

[Washington] Sunday night 11:30
Dearest One: June 18th, 1915

Much as I love your delicious love letters, that would make any woman proud and happy, I believe I enjoy even more the ones in which you tell me (as you did this morning) of what you are working on—the things that fill your thoughts and demand your best effort, for then I feel I am *sharing* your work and being taken into partnership as it were.

I know there are many things you don't care to put on paper, for fear it might fall into other hands, and therefore it is difficult to share your work. But I feel so close when I know what you are doing, and all day I have been made happy by your confidence. Please don't forget to tell me about the Democratic Committee matter "when we are together."

We missed you so this afternoon, and even tea as strong as Samson would have seemed good if made by certain, strong, capable hands. But, I suppose, it was wise the way it happened —but, oh dear!

Helen whispered to me you had gone to call on that awful Deserter.[1] If anything could make me hate him worse than I did before, this would accomplish it. And I will be glad when he expires from an overdose of peace or grape juice and I never hear of him again.

You will think me in a horrible humor if I dont stop. So goodnight and happy dreams my Lord. And thank you again for your books. I am *so* happy to own them

Always yours, Edith

ALS (WP, DLC).
¹ Wilson paid a call on Bryan at his Washington home at 4:45 P.M. on June 18.

To Edith Bolling Galt

[The White House]
My beloved Sweetheart,   Saturday morning, 19 June, 1915.

How perfectly bewitching you looked yesterday in that lovely pink hat as you sat on the south portico, laughing gaily at something I could not hear,—something, I think, that your sister was saying. I had not been invited to the tea, indeed I had been carefully kept in ignorance of who was coming not only but of the fact that anybody was coming, and I know (occasionally) how to take a hint; but I had not been forbidden to *peep* at the lady I adore. I slipped quietly into the green room and there, from behind the lace curtains, feasted my eyes on the loveliest person in the world,—with, oh, such a longing to go to her and take her in my arms and cover her with kisses, whispering in her ear every sweet secret of deepest love! And then I forced myself to turn away and go off for a ride through alternate rain and sunshine. It was sweet of you to choose the seat you did. You must have known that only there could your lover manage to see you without being seen. I wonder if you will chide me for what I did yesterday afternoon,—for calling on W.J.B. to say goodbye? The only thing that made me feel uneasy about it was that I could not do it with genuine cordiality; but I did it on the best political advice! If we treat him with perfect generosity (and in the midst of it all he is praising me, you know, very generously indeed) the least bit of reaction against us on the part of his friends (whose name is legion) is prevented and absolutely all his guns are spiked. He looked amazingly well and refreshed! No stranger man ever lived, and his naivete takes my breath away. I will tell you about our conversation (or, rather, about what he said, for I let him do all the talking) this evening. Mrs. Bryan, I thought, was constrained and uneasy, but not he! He was full of enthusiasm about what he was doing for peace and about what he was going to do, and perfectly at his ease. I made the excuse of a clap of thunder to get away. It was after that that I went back to the "Maison Blanche" and got a glimpse of a *perfectly* enchanting lady and thereby blotted out every impression but that of loveliness and sweetness and charm—forgot that there were dangers and enemies and remembered only that I am

Your own   Woodrow

ALS (WP, DLC).

From Edith Bolling Galt

[Washington] Saturday, June 19th, 1915.

How perfectly you comprehend things, my precious One, and what a joy it is to talk to you and tell you some of the things that make my heart heavy. Thank you for your patience in waiting for me to unwind so long a thread—and for your instant sympathy.

Have you looked out of your window at the moon? It is perfectly beautiful, and I told Helen over the phone a moment ago I want to get my "perambulator"[1] and go for a ride. She declines to go with me, so, unless you will volunteer, I have to go alone!!

I am so glad that I can really bring you happiness Sweetheart, and writing that brings back the words in the first note you ever wrote me. Do you remember it? You said, "I covet nothing more than to give you happiness, you have given me so much." My sincerest prayer is that you can always feel and say that, for then my happiness will be assured.

How strange it will seem not to begin each day with a written Love Song from you, and end it with a goodnight note to go to you early next day. I shall miss them more than I let myself think, and it was such grim fun to have you say you were blue because I am going away. To tell you the truth I have felt for days as though something dreadful was hanging over me. And, in spite of the happiness of being together at Cornish, it is so sad, because it is the closing of our first chapter that began May 4th and, though the second chapter may go further into the story, still the *beginning* belongs to the first, and therefore it is hard to end it and give up our happy chance meetings, and feel that until the summer is gone we cannot establish the same conditions under which such a miracle has come to pass. I wonder if you will to go church tomorrow? If you do get a long—Just here I had to answer the phone and I can't remember what I was writing, so forgive unfinished sentence. Goodnight.

Always yours   Edith.

ALS (WP, DLC).

[1] Her electric runabout. She is said to have been the first woman in Washington to drive her own car.

To Edward Mandell House

The White House, June 20, 1915

Would it be possible and convenient for you to remain in

Roslyn until Thursday next and let me spend that day there
with you   Woodrow Wilson.

Hw telegram (E. M. House Papers, CtY).

From Mary Allen Hulbert

Nantucket,
Dearest Friend: Massachusetts, June 20th [1915].

I *am* disturbed, but thought I had concealed the fact. Please
do not worry about me. I shall go doggedly on, taking whatever comes, and do my best to keep the hope alive that is in me.
The mortgages are in the Bronx, N. Y.   bear 6%   And I go to
N. Y. again tomorrow to complete the sale, at least I think they
are sold, although the decisive word has not yet been said. I
am sending the money· Allen wants because I feel he would
perhaps blame me for frustrating his plans. It is *his* money,
and I would send it if it were mine for I *must* have faith in him.
He has a little apartment. And we shall have no servant, but we
shall be *together* and its better than eating my heart out in this
lonliness. Again, do not worry about me. You have enough. The
knowledge of your friendship is comfort and strength to me.
I shall be at the Manhattan only from six to 5.30 on Tuesday,
if I can complete the business in one day. If not, until Wednesday at 5.30, when I take the New Bedford boat back. I'm tired
of rushing about but am getting into the "drummer" frame of
mind, that any place to lay my head is privilege.
                                God bless you   M.A.H.

I expect to leave for L. A. about the 29th, if I am not too tired
to travel. If I am, will wait two or three days, or until I can get
accommodations.

ALI (WP, DLC).

From the Diary of Colonel House

[Roslyn, L.I.] June 20, 1915.

Attorney General Gregory arrived on the ten o'clock train this
morning. He told me practically everything of importance that
has happened in the Cabinet since I have been away, more
especially concerning the two notes to Germany and Mr. Bryan's
resignation.

He said the President read my cable of May 9th to the Cabinet
on Tuesday May 11th. He opened his remarks by stating that

he wished them to hear my views as to the answer which should be made to Germany, and they knew the confidence he had in my judgment and ability to see a situation clearly. The cable was then read and favorably commented on.

Mr. Bryan told Gregory later that the only objection he had was that the cable was read to the Cabinet before he, Bryan, had seen it. He thought the President should have read it to him first and given him an opportunity of discussing it before it was submitted to the Cabinet.

After reading my cable, the President read them a memorandum he had made and which embodied the note as it was finally sent to Germany. While the discussion was going on, Bryan showed some heat and said there were some members of the Cabinet who were not neutral. The President turned to him and said, with a steely glitter in his eyes, "Mr. Bryan you are now [not] warranted in making such an assertion. We all doubtless have our opinions in this matter, but there are none of us who can justly be accused of being unfair." Mr. Bryan apologized and the incident passed.

Gregory said this was the second time since he had been in the Cabinet that the President had set his jaw so firmly. The other time was when Redfield had in some way transgressed the proprieties.

Bryan did not attend the Cabinet meeting the day he offered his resignation, but the President suggested that he be invited and all the Cabinet welcomed the suggestion. Mr. Bryan told Gregory after he had resigned that there had been inserted in the note a sentence which he, Bryan, had written, and which had been originally eliminated.[1] After the resignation and before the note was published, Bryan said the sentence was reincorporated in it. Gregory said, however, Mr. Bryan was mistaken, and the sentence was discussed at the Cabinet meeting when his resignation was offered, and at which Mr. Bryan was present. They had been discussing the note for some minutes before Mr. Bryan appeared and whether that sentence had been covered before or after Mr. Bryan came in is not of importance for the reason that the entire message was upon the table and was handed Mr. Bryan to read. This is also the President's recollection. Mr. Bryan evidently wishes it to appear that he resigned because the President refused to include a certain sentence modifying the note, and after he resigned, the sentence was used.

Another interesting incident Gregory told and which I was able to corroberate by a despatch sent me by Gerard, was that Mr. Bryan prepared a letter after the first note was sent to the Ger-

man Government to the effect that they should not consider
the note seriously, that it was meant in a "Pickwickian sense."
The President refused to sign this letter. Gregory enlarged upon
the stupidity of such a suggestion. I agree that it would have
ruined the President. It would have been saying to the American
public, "We are standing firm in demanding our rights," and
behind their backs it would be saying to the German Government "We merely send this note to deceive the American people and do not mean what we say." It occured to both of us that
if the President had consented to do this, it would have been
akin to treachery.

1 Bryan's biographer tells essentially the same story: Coletta, *William Jennings Bryan*, II, 344-45. Bryan referred to the sentence which Wilson added to
allow the German government to submit new evidence in the *Lusitania* case:
"If the Imperial German Government should deem itself to be in possession
of convincing evidence that the officials of the Government of the United
States did not perform these duties with thoroughness, the Government of
the United States sincerely hopes that it will submit that evidence for consideration." Bryan, citing the precedent of the "cooling off" treaties, had consistently
argued for such a statement, against the objections of both Wilson and Lansing.
Wilson added the sentence sometime between June 7 and June 9, when he sent
the final version of the note to the State Department. It is impossible to determine
whether he added the sentence before or after the cabinet meeting on June 8.

From Edith Bolling Galt

[Washington] Sunday morning, very early.
My precious One: June 20th, 1915

When this is in your dear hands I will have started on the
"Broad highway" that will lead to your home! And how much
more than a tiny piece of paper I am leaving with you.

Can you feel it throb and beat as you hold it, and will you
let it whisper, all these intervening days before you come, I love
you. Will you let it nestle close next your own heart and leave
no room between for loneliness or sadness?

When the house seems empty will you go to your window and
look out to the great out of doors and feel that I am there, calling back to you—signalling to you to hurry and come—that you,
and only you make my world complete.

You will not be alone my loved Lord for you will feel my
spirit so near that you have but to whisper to summon it, and
I will come and fold you in my arms.

I have been awake a long time and thinking over the things
you told me last night. I am afraid I was not a speck of help
to you about even a suggestion regarding the Chairmanship. It
is such a burden for you to carry all alone, and I was thinking
of that side of it so that I did not realize how unresponsive I

must have seemed. How I wish I could *really* help you—I mean in a practical way—but that is where I am so useless.

All I can do is to love you—and be a refuge when you are weary or disheartened.

The paper this morning does my heart good for it tells such admiration of all the people for you. I have read pages of how the whole country is standing for you—and our Va. "Glass" says—Mr. B's act has made you 50 percent stronger in the South and Middle West.

I wish you could feel the thrills of pride run like fire through your veins that I feel when people appreciate you. It is such exquisite pleasure, for it is always followed by the wonderful thought that you love *me*!

Please don't work too hard these three days and a half. Stay out, take long rides, and play golf. And sleep and sleep and sleep, so you will be ready to talk to some one who is longing for the music of your voice.

And now good by again Sweetheart. And God watch between thee and me, and keep us when we are absent one from the other.   Your own   Edith.

ALS (WP, DLC).

Two Letters to Edith Bolling Galt

                                         [The White House]
My Darling,   Sunday morning 20 June, 1915

I tried to sleep late this morning, but could not for thinking of you! It was very blissful thinking and much more refreshing than sleep. I lay in bed a long while, resting luxuriously, but presently had no desire to sleep again because it would have been to lose you in that vague country and so lose the deep happiness that I at once became conscious of when I woke. For I had had a new vision of my Darling last night, a fuller revelation of the heart, the soul, that has awakened in her, the passionate, revealing love that has disclosed *herself* and all the world of loving passion to her. I had held this sweet awakened woman in my arms while she was shaken with the consciousness of it all, —had held her close to me with an ecstacy of sympathy, of comprehension, of love that was a sort of worship, full of reverence for the sacred things that were being laid open to me; and had felt that it was nothing less than the marriage of our spirits. And for a little she was afraid! Ah, my Darling, I love you utterly. There can be nothing to fear in love which increases

alike in depth and tenderness with each revelation of yourself
to your lover. For it does. When we parted last night I was conscious of loving you with a love more intimate, more comprehending, more tender and devoted than ever,—and the sweetness of it has filled me with a deepened happiness ever since.
I soon found that I *could* not lie in bed indefinitely. I simply
had to get up and come to the study here and pour out to you
so much of what was in my heart as I could find words for. Most
of it is too deep, too near the sources of life, to find expression in
speech. It has become part of me,—the best and purest part of
me! As I look back on last evening, my precious One, it seems
to me that I so lamentably failed to make you realize how completely I understood, comprehended, and how perfectly I sympathized. It seemed to me as if we were but *one* mind and heart,
seeing the world and each other with the same eyes, the same
emotions, the same yearnings, and with an insight that
penetrated to the heart of things, and that our love for each
other was proved and made perfect in the wonderful light that
shone about us. I love you as I never did before and am with a
new passion   Your own   Woodrow

                                          [The White House]
My precious Darling,   Sunday evening 20 June, '15
    Good-bye! It breaks my heart to write the words,—and you
would understand so much more perfectly what they mean to me
if I could hold you close in my arms and whisper them to you
between kisses. But you *will* know what they mean: your own
dear heart will echo the meaning,—of our first parting since
our hearts came together in perfect understanding. Perhaps,
as you say, this is the close of the first chapter of our happy,
happy romance, my Sweetheart, but there will be no break in
the lovely story and the meaning of it will grow deeper and
sweet and more wonderful to the end,—a story of deepening
comprehension of the wonderful and beautiful thing that has
happened to us, of a love daily made more true and serene and
perfect. Its most wonderful and inspiring passages are yet to
come. I look forward to them with such eagerness and such
happy confidence and with such unspeakable joy—to the constant and unbroken companionship and intimate partnership of
a life made bright by love,—a love which has come to us with the
slow and steady revelation as of a thing predestined and
inevitable and which will go on from revelation to revelation
until we stand in the full light of a perfect joy. In this very

moment of sadness (more poignant than I had deemed possible) I feel the elation of a man who is moving steadily towards
the most rewarding and the sweetest experiences of his life. My
discovery of you has *moved* me so, my adorable Sweetheart, and
it is pure joy, without touch of either fear or misgiving. Let us
both think of the future and plan to make this second chapter
more wonderful than the first. It is only an imaginary division
in the story. Every morning I am going to write to my Darling
as before. What are time and space to us more than mere teas-
ing inconveniences? They are only for a little while and we
shall win a victory over them—laugh as we look back on them
and see how they served only to confirm our love and make us
realize more perfectly than ever before how dependent we are
and must always be upon one another. I shall carry you in my
heart every minute of the day. I shall be lonely, oh, so lonely,
without you during every day during which we must be separated
this dreary summer. But it need never happen again,—it *shall*
never happen again,—and how sweet it will be to *know* one
another's thoughts, to be conscious all the long days and nights
through that we belong to one another, that we live for one
another, that there are a new heaven and a new earth about
us because love has made us free and made us complete. There
are no words in which to express what is in my heart at this
good-bye. But you will know. These lines are written only to
keep you company on the journey and to bid you coin *any*
and *every* love message your heart desires for your comfort and
refreshment as from your lover. For there is no sort or degree
of love your heart *can* long for that my heart does not contain
for my own Darling. I am altogether and always

Your own   Woodrow

ALS (WP, DLC).

From Charlotte Everett Wise Hopkins[1]

My dear Mr. President: [Washington] June 21, 1915.

I have wanted for weeks to ask permission to see you for a few
minutes about the Ellen Wilson Memorial, but with the crushing burdens that you have been carrying I have felt that it would
be an intrusion and a privilege that I had no right to claim. So,
instead of trying to see you, I am going to try as briefly as possible to get the advice and help I need.

When you returned the plans you very kindly said that you
would write any note of approval that I wanted. I do want some-

thing that you would be perfectly willing that I should publish, giving the plan your official and personal approval; not, of course, as a memorial to your dear wife, for that you have already most graciously expressed, but on the broad ground of improved housing, not only for Washington, which sadly needs it, but as an object lesson for the whole country. This is what I am planning to make it.

The reason I feel so strongly about your indorsement is because, confidentially, I have met in many directions, and particularly among the Southern element, with opposition because this first block is to be for colored people. In every instance I have replied that Mrs. Wilson understood the general situation, grasping at a glance the fact that with 96,000 negroes, a third of the population, the great crying need was improved living conditions, as, partly from poverty and partly from a certain unwritten law that they cannot live in the better parts of the town, and also because the landlords of colored sections keep only just within the law as to repairs, in most instances furnishing no water and no plumbing, the negroes live under the most insanitary conditions, physical and moral. All of this reacts on the white population. Mrs. Wilson never made any secret to any of the men she took in the alleys that the work she was trying to do in passing the bill was to improve the conditions of the negroes. Only 2,000 whites live in these alleys. She was, perhaps as you know, a stockholder in the Sanitary Housing Company.[2] She went to the Colored Social Settlement and gave them money and in all her work her interest centered in what she saw was to improve the living conditions of the negro. I have tried my best to make this clear to the various Southern people who have criticised this work because it is for negroes and if you could in any way make that clear in your note of approval it would be a great help.

My hope is, in fact my faith is, that once this block is built, similar blocks will rise up all over the country for all races, black and white, Americans and foreigners. The plans have already attracted much attention. The Los Angeles Board of Health and the Salem Rebuilding Fund have sent for them and, greatest compliment of all, the Department of Social Ethics of Harvard University, Dr. James Ford, Director, says they are the best housing proposition that has been submitted to Harvard for its permanent housing exhibit.

Since the act of incorporation has passed the incorporators have met and chosen the directors. I enclose a list of them and the advisory board.[3] I have had given me $5,180 so far, which is drawing 3 per cent interest. I am now in treaty for the block in the southwest, one which Mrs. Wilson spoke of as being ideal for future housing, and I have just had a proposition made me from the General Film Company, whose manager, Mr. Koepfel,[4] says he was the person who showed "The Birth of a Nation" in the White House. Their proposition is to make a film of alley conditions, with a thread of a story about the pathetic family who lived in the alley and then kindly people showed them how much better off they would be in some of these sanitary houses, where they are taken and develop into a family with some hope and some future in the charming homes of the Memorial, the children getting the benefits of playgrounds, kindergartens, library facilities; the mothers and fathers enjoying the library and the settlement house features, the women using the laundry to get their washing out of their own smaller quarters, the co-operative shops furnishing the food—in fact, the whole story as it is now planned on paper. The most of its features I talked over with Mrs. Wilson, not for one instant dreaming that I should have to do it alone and in memory of her whose helpfulness and sympathy were so valuable.[5]

For this film the company tell me they would want your co-operation, of course in the simplest way, and nothing that would be any lack of dignity in your position—only if you should sit for a picture to show you signing the act of Congress abolishing the alleys and the act of Congress incorporating the Memorial,[6] possibly with a picture of Mrs. Wilson on the desk.

I have hesitated to ask you this and I, of course, shall do absolutely nothing further if you feel either that you do not want to do it or that you would not like to have the film shown. The few people who know about it think it is a great idea. The film company tell me that they think it would bring in possibly twenty-five or thirty thousand dollars. It is simply a question as to whether you are willing to help in this way. You will of course believe me that I would have nothing done that would not be absolutely dignified and in keeping not only with your great position but with the sweet woman in whose honor I am trying to do it.

It will be necessary to raise $20,000 before we can begin to do anything and were I able to announce that the land had been secured, which I trust I may be able to do by the first of August, and also your consent to this film idea, I think the money would come in rapidly. The Georgia D.A.R.'s made a State-wide appeal on Flag Day. I have not yet heard the result. One of the Chautauqua lecture routes is using the story to improve housing through the Middle West.

Pray pardon me for sending you such a volume but it is almost

impossible to condense my story. May I trespass for a minute
more to tell you how I have followed with the deepest interest
all you have done these last weeks in the most difficult position that probably any President except Lincoln ever was placed,
and how splendidly we feel you have fulfilled your great trust?
I can only hope that you will at least have a few weeks' respite
to rally from the overwhelming fatigue of your life.

    Believe me,
       Very respectfully yours,   Charlotte Everett Hopkins[7]

TLS (WP, DLC).
  [1] Mrs. Archibald Hopkins, chairman of the District of Columbia section of
the woman's department of the National Civic Federation and social activist.
She had become a friend of Mrs. Wilson while lobbying for the rehabilitation
of alleys in the District of Columbia; they had together also laid plans for model
housing.
  [2] This "business philanthropy" was founded in 1904, during an earlier wave
of interest in District of Columbia housing conditions, and built low-income
apartments to replace alley dwellings. See Constance McLaughlin Green, *Washington: A History of the Capital, 1800-1950* (2 vols., Princeton, N. J., 1962),
II, 152-56, 161-63; and Appleton P. Chandler, Jr., "Philanthropy that Pays
Dividends," *The Nation's Business*, XXVI (March 1938), 20-22, 90.
  [3] The list of incorporators and directors included many of the prominent
philanthropists and social workers in the country. The advisory board included
many cabinet members, the Vice-President, the William Howard Tafts, etc.
  [4] Unidentified.
  [5] The Editors have found no evidence that this film was ever made; indeed,
it seems unlikely that it was.
  [6] Wilson had signed a bill to incorporate the Ellen Wilson Memorial Homes
on March 3, 1915. It empowered the incorporators to build "one or more blocks
of sanitary houses for the working classes" and to rent them at rates low
enough "to cause the abandonment of dilapidated and insanitary houses, as
an object lesson in the housing of the working classes under good conditions."
Cong. Record, 63d Cong., 3d sess., p. 4911. Congress dissolved the corporation
in 1934 at the behest of the directors because the funds had not yet reached
the minimum $25,000 that the charter required before land could be acquired
or buildings begun. Mrs. Hopkins explained that, after the start of a subscription campaign, "the United States entered the war and all our thoughts and
energies were diverted." House Report No. 1762, 73d Cong., 2d sess. (Washington, 1934).
  [7] Wilson's reply is WW to Charlotte E. W. Hopkins, July 23, 1915.

From *The Princeton Alumni Weekly*

Dear Sir: Princeton, New Jersey, June 21, 1915

    We are in receipt of your note of June 18th relative to your
discontinuing your subscription to the Princeton Alumni Weekly,
and in reply would state that on March 8, 1915, we received a
check for $3.00 in payment of your subscription for the Weekly
for the year ending March 29, 1916. We presume that it will
be satisfactory to you to keep your name on our mailing list until
the expiration of your subscription.

        Yours very truly,   Princeton Alumni Weekly.
                                   per Roy[1]

TLS (WP, DLC).

¹ Wilson's instructions, written on this letter, were: "W'd prefer to have it taken off now." Perhaps he had been annoyed by President John Grier Hibben's speech at the Annual Lake Mohonk Conference on International Cooperation, on May 18, 1915 (printed in the *Princeton Alumni Weekly*, xv [May 26, 1915], 813-15). Hibben strongly attacked pacifists; indeed, Wilson might well have interpreted Hibben's speech as a highly critical commentary on his "too proud to fight" speech of May 10.

To Edith Bolling Galt

[The White House]

My Beloved, my Beloved!   Monday morning, 21 June, 1915

What shall I say to you this morning? Here I sit at my desk; the hour is the same that finds me every morning pouring my heart out to you,—but, oh, the difference! The House is empty, the town is empty! My Sweetheart, my darling is gone, and I sit here with a longing at my heart which I can hardly endure. But I have just read that tender, that wonderful good-bye letter you handed me last night and my eyes are still dim with the tears it brought into them, tears of deep and exquisite happiness be-cause of your love. The letter is a vision of yourself, my lovely Darling, and it has brought me what you always bring me—what you brought me last night. I loved your gayety then, Sweetheart. I understood it. I felt the keen charm of it. I struggled to free myself and share it. And then, seeing, as you always do, what I was suffering, what I needed, you turned to me with a tender-ness and love which are surely the most winning and adorable any man was ever permitted to see, and the weight was lifted from my heart, I lived again, and was inexpressibly happy. And I am happy this morning, my sweet One, in spite of the lump in my throat. For this wonderful love you have given me fills all the world with peace for me, fills this otherwise empty house with your presence, fills my heart and all my thoughts and makes me proof against weakness, proof against real sadness, even now. I am complete in you, and nothing can really hurt me while you love me. I know, to use your own dear words, that I am *not* alone, that your spirit is near me all the while, and that I have but to whisper to summon it. My heart will turn to you every min-ute for that sweet comfort. I wonder if the people about me here will realize that I am not really here at all—that my thoughts are away? For they will be. Where you are will always henceforth be where I am, in heart and thought and spirit. And being with you will be life and joy to me always. Don't think, dearest, that you did nothing to help me when I talked of the chairmanship —you did everything. You comprehended and sympathized and were the true comrade of all my thoughts. You were my own incomparable mate, who have completed my strength by your love and brought every perfect blessing to

                                   Your own   Woodrow.

When you are shopping buy for Helen something she wants –for me–please

ALS (WP, DLC).

From Edith Bolling Galt

Dearest One: New York June 21st, 1915 10:25 P.M.

I do hope the day has not seemed very long, and that you got the telegram we sent from Philadelphia when you got back from golf. *Helen* sent you another from here and we thought of calling you on the phone, but decided it was better not, though the man at the desk has just told us the White House called to know if we had arrived, and that has worried our blessed little chaperone lest her message seem long in reaching you–bless her heart! What do you suppose she brought and put on my dressing table? Your picture–such a lovely one that I have only to lift my eyes to find yours–and oh! it is such a comfort.

I have such a lot to tell you that I must hurry to get this in the mail so you will have it in the morning. I will begin with our start.

We got off in five minutes after I phoned Mr. Hoover and had a beautiful run over the most perfect roads. The only thing to mar the happiness was that you were not there to share it. And we missed you so.

We got to Phil. about 2, and as White wanted gas for the car, we went to Wanamakers where we sent you the telegram. We started again at 2:30 and went through Trenton where we saw the State House and thought of the many hours you had spent there and caught a glimpse of your old colored messenger.[1] Then we went direct to Princeton, which I think is perfectly charming.

Helen and I got out and walked through the grounds, and she told me [about] so many interesting landmarks. Of course my chief interest was you and where you had been, had lived, had worked, all of which this dear little guide anticipated and told me–all she knew. Then we went to see your portrait, which I think is perfectly awful![2]

If you looked like that I could not love you, but it serves to emphasize your splendid intellect and strength which is so lacking in the picture that it makes it a burlesque. Only the hands are good, not so much as replicas of yours as that they express vigor and purpose and individuality.

We left Princeton, after having Tea at the Inn, about 6:30 and had to make 2 detours before coming to Jersey City, but the roads all the way were firm and almost no dust.

The lights in the water reflected from the thousands in the city were exquisitely lovely as we neared the ferry. And we are not one bit tired. Mr. Jervis and White took such splendid care of us that we did not have to think for ourselves.

All this is but a sketch of the day to tell you how completely I realize that these more than delightful things have all come to me through you and your dear love. Never for a moment can I forget your thought and tender solicitude and be happy because of its eloquent assurance of your love

This time last night we were together, but only Tuesday, Wednesday, Thursday, and we will be together again, and I will whisper all I want you to know. Helen and I laughed so at the way the telegraph operator read her writing in the message she sent from Philadelphia. It was "The Pres. The White House," but he read it *Wm* President, The White *Home*, and could not read the last word at all. It was *Love*—poor man! Perhaps he does not know the meaning of it. Now I must stop. Thank you for your blessed note of last night. I am going to have a fine time directly reading it all over again. My tender love,

Always yours   Edith.

P.S. This is literally the longest day in the year!

ALS (WP, DLC).
  [1] Sam Gordon.
  [2] The portrait by Frederic Yates, reproduced in Vol. 16 of this series.

A Press Conference

June 22, 1915

Have you anything about Mexico this morning, Mr. President?
  Not a thing that is new.
Have you had any word that General [Huerta] is coming?
  No word, other than what the public knows. I have read the rumors, but I don't know anything about it.
Mr. President, have the resolutions that were adopted by the League to Enforce Peace, American Branch,[1] been submitted to you for your approval?
  They haven't come to me, no.

Do you know in a general way what they are? Have you given them your approval, or do you approve of them?

> I must confess that I supposed they would come to me, and I haven't read them. Perhaps a mortifying confession, but I have been very busy.

Are you making any renewed efforts, Mr. President, to submit offers for the good offices of the United States to the warring powers?

> All the offers of that sort that I have made have been made publicly or semi-publicly. You know all I know about it. I think it is generally understood that this government would be more than glad to do anything that was possible.

Mr. President, are you ready to take the country into your confidence on the Secretary of State?

> No, sir. I haven't taken myself in yet.

Have you had a chance to consider, Mr. President, the suggestion of sending a delegation to a continuous conference of neutrals to make suggestions for peace? Some women made a resolution before you.

> I haven't had an opportunity to consider that. . . .

Will the note to Germany on the *Frye* case be ready to go before you leave Washington?

> I don't know whether it will or not. Mr. Lansing is temporarily out of town, and I shan't see him until tomorrow afternoon, and I don't know what the state of the proceedings is.

Mr. President, have you had any word when the German note might be expected?

> No, not any at all. I saw a dispatch from Mr. Gerard only yesterday, but I didn't seem able to form any conjecture.

Mr. President, last week I think you said that things in Mexico were shaping up somewhat. Have they taken any more definite form?

> They have been, apparently, shaping down since then. There is another interrogation point thrown into the machinery.[2]

JRT transcript (WC, NjP) of CLSsh (C. L. Swem Coll., NjP).
 [1] The League to Enforce Peace supported American entry into a league of nations binding members to submit disputes to a judicial tribunal and a council of conciliation and to hold regular conferences for the purpose of settling issues of international law to guide these bodies. It also proposed that member states combine military and economic forces against any state making war on a member nation *before* submitting questions for adjudication or concilation. "LEAGUE TO ENFORCE PEACE   AMERICAN BRANCH," CC MS (A. L. Lowell Papers, MH-Ar). Lowell sent this document to Wilson on June 30, 1915.
 [2] Wilson no doubt referred to the message sent to Carranza suggesting conditions for recognition, enclosed in RL to WW, June 17, 1915, to which no

reply had been given, and to negotiations between authorities in Mexico City and the *Carrancista* General Pablo Gonzáles. During the previous week, Gonzáles had threatened to invade Mexico City, and supporters of the Convention, who controlled the city, proposed a ceasefire and a transitional coalition government. To this Carranza replied: "No responsibility assumed for consequences of resistance by forces occupying city or for disorder or depredations attending evacuation." J. M. Cardoso de Oliveira to RL, June 14; June 15, noon; June 15, 5 P.M.; and June 17, 6 P.M., 1915; RL to J. M. Cardoso de Oliveira, June 15, 6 P.M. and June 16, 7 P.M., 1915; J. R. Silliman to RL, June 15 and 21, 1915; and RL to J. R. Silliman, June 15 and June 19, 1915, *FR 1915*, pp. 708-18.

Insofar as is known, this was Wilson's last press conference until September 29, 1916. Wilson left for Cornish for a vacation on June 23. He returned to Washington on July 19 on account of the convergence of a number of urgent problems. Presumably, he did not resume his press conferences because he could not find the time for them.

To Edward Mandell House

The White House 6/22 1915

Expect to reach Roslyn at nine Thursday morning   shall have had breakfast   must leave at seven   Woodrow Wilson

Hw telegram (E. M. House Papers, CtY).

To Robert Lansing

My dear Mr. Secretary,   The White House. 22 June, 1915.

I am very anxious to have the foundations laid at once for the course with regard to Mexico which we outlined, or, rather, indicated, very briefly in conversation the other day. Do you not think it would be well to see the A.B.C. men now to ascertain whether they would be willing (that is, whether their governments would be willing) to cooperate with us in advice and political action (recognition and the like) in bringing order out of chaos there?

I do not feel particularly cordial to the Chilean administration just now because they have been making so many selfish difficulties about the general political understandings we have been trying for some months to establish in formal fashion between ourselves and Latin America; but of course it would be a mistake to leave them out in this Mexican business.

Our idea was, you remember, to include in the coöperative conference also, the three ranking ministers next after them in the Latin American group; but it would be well to sound out the beginning of the alphabet first.

Cordially Yours,   Woodrow Wilson

WWTLS (SDR, RG 59, 812.00/15338½, DNA).

To William Gibbs McAdoo, with Enclosure

My dear Mac: The White House June 22, 1915

I have read the enclosed letter with a great deal of attention and you may be sure fully credit the motive Mr. Untermyer had in writing it. My great trouble is this: I do not see how it is going to be possible to allow the private interests most concerned in Mexico to finance her government without putting that government virtually under their control, and I fear that, whatever the understanding might be, the country would feel most uneasy about it. Do you see any way of working it out?

Faithfully yours,   Woodrow Wilson

TLS (W. G. McAdoo Papers, DLC).

E N C L O S U R E

Samuel Untermyer to William Gibbs McAdoo

PERSONAL.

Dear Mr. Secretary: New York June 19th, 1915.

Following our Wednesday's discussion, I have been further investigating and considering the Mexican situation from the viewpoint of the possibility of achieving prompt practical results. My interest in the subject is prompted solely by the conviction that this is the psychological moment to accomplish a substantial public service. The hope of being a factor in the solution of so big and vexatious a problem may well stir the patriotism and ambition of the most unemotional citizen and the service is one in which I should be proud to be a volunteer.

I realize that the subject is commanding the best thought of the country at the hands of men who are vastly more familiar with this complicated situation and it is therefore with hesitation that I am venturing to put forward my point of view. I am doing so only because my relations with some of the business interests that are most largely concerned in the restoration of peace and order have enabled me to obtain a fair understanding of the difficulties that surround the situation and to approach the subject from a purely disinterested and public-spirited standpoint.

From the beginning I have been and still am in thorough sympathy with the Administration policy of non-intervention; but the time has arrived when it is essential that we put forth a helping hand insofar as it can be done without becoming embroiled in the troubles of our sister republic and without arousing the animosity or suspicion of those whom we are unselfishly anxious to befriend.

I realize also that there can be no just or permanent solution that does not primarily involve the settlement of the land problem in a way that will open up the ownership of the land to the people.

No plan is feasible that does not provide for a substantial Government loan of from $25,000,000 to $35,000,000 (gold) and no loan is possible unless accompanied by recognition or promise of recognition by us of the Government that applies for the loan. The money is needed primarily to organize and equip an army of at least 100,000 men to establish Constitutional government, restore and maintain order, and to assure the stability of the new Government. A small part of it could and doubtless would be used to get the bandit leaders out of the country, by way of insurance against renewed insurrections during the formative period of the new Government and to enable it undisturbed to work out the necessary land reforms.

I am assured by men who are familiar with the conditions in Mexico that it is comparatively easy at this time to effect such arrangements but those are things with which our Government would and could have no direct concern. They would have to be worked out between the lenders and the newly-constituted Mexican authorities.

The loan is not attractive on its merits as a banking proposition, especially at this time. No independent financial interest would either now or in the near future undertake it, even at a high rate of interest, during these extraordinary times of world cataclysm, when the great financial interests that are in command of money are holding on to their resources like grim death in the confident and wellfounded expectation that the requirements and readjustments following the European War will give to money unprecedented value and returns. It would be impossible to put up a proposition for a Mexican Government loan that would attract capital on its merits.

This loan must and can be assured through the efforts and largely upon the credit of the men whose interests are already in Mexico and which can be rescued only by this further investment. From or through them it can be had on reasonable terms, provided the new money is made secure. It is a mere bagatelle as compared with what they have at stake.

To assure the investment involves (1) eventual recognition of the borrowing Government; (2) pledging of the Customs receipts to the extent to which they are still unpledged (the bulk of them are already appropriated); (3) the administration of the revenue under the direction of our Government or through the medium of a Commission appointed by us, as we are doing in San Domingo and are about to do in Hayti.

Such an arrangement would secure the practical results of intervention without involving any of its attendant hatred, dangers and responsibilities, all of which it should be our purpose to avoid.

Our Government will of course have to be satisfied with the new executive and officials and that they are qualified to carry out the reforms to which we are committed as best calculated to bring about permanent peace and Constitutional government. However much we may deplore the fact, it is in my judgment a mere irridiscent dream ever to expect the solution of this problem without this money power back of the agency selected to bring about the desired result. Even with the present contending forces eliminated by arrangement, others will take their place and there will be years of guerrila warfare and consequent instability unless the Government in power has a substantial, well-equipped army to back up its recognition by the United States— and it takes money to maintain such an army.

I am conscious of the hopeless inadequacy of any attempt to outline within the brief compass of a letter anything that can be dignified by the name of a "plan." If these suggestions convey to you the general idea I have in mind and you think it worth while to place them before the President, I will be pleased to elaborate and discuss the matter if thought worth while. If it appeals to the President I have reason to believe it can be worked out, but have no commitment from anyone to that effect and am representing no particular interest in putting forward these suggestions.

Please understand that so far as I am concerned there is no element of private or business relation or of any form of commercialism connected with the proposal and that my only relation to it would be that of a willing volunteer who would have no obligation to any private interest and would feel honored to be concerned in the performance of so exalted a public service.

I have tentatively arranged to leave here on Sunday the 27th with my family for a trip through the Yellowstone Park and over the Canadian Pacific to the Pacific Coast, but would cancel that arrangement and change my plans if it is considered of sufficient importance for me to do so.

With kind regards believe me

                    Sincerely yours   Saml. Untermyer.

TLS (W. G. McAdoo Papers, DLC).

From Charles Richard Crane

Dear Mr President   [New York, c. June 22, 1915]

I had a nice little visit with Colonel House last Saturday. He was looking well but thin and very glad to be on this side of the Atlantic. He is enthusiastic about the way our Representatives are carrying their heavy burdens and quite confirmed the observations of that very keen young man—Henry James Jr.—who has just returned from a careful survey of conditions for the Rockefeller work.[1]

The old European method of developing a Diplomatic corps may be good enough for routine purposes but, in such a situation as the present one—a great emergency—it is a fine thing to have at important posts men desciplined by the American habit of action—of taking initiative and not being afraid of responsability, not too much controlled by tradition and precedent. We all thank the Good Lord that you discovered Colonel House and Mrs House seems to be up to the standard apparently required of the wives of your aids—the highest standard I have known since I first found Washington, many years ago.

This is introductory to a few words about another valuable aid, with also the finest kind of a wife,[2] Mr Fred Delano. I merely write about him in case you feel obliged to add another member to your cabinet. Mr Delano is nominally a Republican but has never taken an active part in party politics. Although he has been one of the most useful citizens of Chicago in everything leading to civic betterment and, although I have worked with him for years, I did not until the other day know that he was a nominal Republican. He is one of the finest men in the country, of wide experience, calm judgment and firm principles and would contribute to the cabinet councils a point of view that would be different from any other member and of great value. He comes from one of best old New England families and in many ways could represent what is best there. He could also express the best from the side of property, while he is absolutely trusted by progressives of the Brandeis kind.

Although born and brought up in New England and a graduate of Harvard he was for a long time in active service of both the Burlington and the Union Pacific roads and knows our agriculture and economic life very well. If this picture should require any filling in I shall be glad to come down to Washington with my brushes and paint pot.

Mrs Crane[3] has just been going through a rather serious siege at the Presbyterian Hospital here. She is happily doing well and the doctors feel that she will be much improved in health by the

visit among them. She does not ask for much else than news of
you. Fortunately I have been able to assure her of your serenity
and the wide and rapid growth of sympathy and appreciation of
you during the last trying three months.

With warm greetings to the rare dear ladies who help you
look out on your lovely lawn, I am

Yours very faithfully   Charles R. Crane

ALS (WP, DLC).
  1 Henry James, son of the psychologist, William James, and business manager of the Rockefeller Institute for Medical Research. James had served on
the Rockefeller Foundation's commission to investigate the organization of
relief for noncombatants in Europe.
  2 Matilda Annis Peasley Delano.
  3 Cornelia Workman Smith Crane.

To Edith Bolling Galt

[The White House]

My precious Darling,   Tuesday morning, 7 o'cl. 22 June, 1915

Now I *know* that the twenty-first of June is the longest day in
the year! I did everything I could think of to fill it up, but it
remained hopelessly empty and quite interminable. There did
not seem (for once) to be work enough to fill the morning
till noon when I had an engagement to see McAdoo and "our
Virginia Glass" about rural credits legislation at the next session
of Congress; and when they came they actually did not stay
their full half hour (I never knew such a thing to happen before!). At 12:30 I shook hands with several hundred veterans of
Something,[1] but they would not string out till one,—so I came
upstairs and threw myself on the lounge in my bed-room for a
few minutes, and then a very lovely thing happened, which put
me in spirits for the day! As I lay between sleeping and waking
you came and nestled close to me. I could feel your breath on
my cheek, our lips touched, and there was all about me the sweet
atmosphere that my Darling always carries with her. I dared
not open my eyes. I lay there like one entranced and blessed and
rose more than rested,—refreshed, renewed, and happy. My
Darling had come to me and the day was redeemed! Grayson
came in to lunch and—another. Tell Helen that she just missed
her favourite cousin. She had hardly gone before in walked Fitz
William Woodrow,* come back to seek a job for the summer
which he thought he could get. And so I sat down to lunch with
the two men, not thinking of them at all, but of two lovely ladies
speeding over the highways, and wondered if my face showed
the sweet vision I had had as I rested in the room overhead. At

two I had another interview, with the editor of a St. Louis newspaper[2] whom I have known for a long time. At half past two I
went to the dentist's (you see I had planned the day to suit my
humour and provide abundant diversion) and let him stand
with both feet on a nerve or two for the space of an hour or so.
After that I took a ride all by my lee lane and there were not
rides enough to last till Margaret's train time. When her train
time came she did not: her train was an hour late. There were
the same gentlemen for dinner. I worked until I was so sleepy
I could not see, waiting to hear that the dear lady who had taken
her departure that morning and taken my heart with her was
safe, with "our blessed little Helen," in New York. You should
have seen me walking fiercely up and down the hallway upstairs here while the office was trying, about ten, to get the Hotel
Wolcott and quiet me. No message had come except the one of
the afternoon[3] which relieved my anxiety about Helen's neck!**
And so at last the day ended. I knew my precious one was safe
and my heart was quiet enough to let me go to bed. Ah, my
Beloved, each day some new turn of experience makes me realize
more fully than ever how deeply I love you. I dare not try to
write you a love letter this morning. It *hurts* too much, because
you are away. I know I could not see the page before me through
the tears of happiness and loneliness that would blind me—are
blinding me now. Suffice it to say I love you with the whole passion of my life and am altogether   Your own   Woodrow

Dearest love to Helen.
* He is to lodge here for the present.
** The telegram from N. Y.[4] did not reach me till this
moment. Bless you both. 9.15 a.m.

ALS (WP, DLC).
1 The Veteran Employees Association of the Schuylkill Division of the Penn-
sylvania Railroad. There were 275 of them.
2 George Sibley Johns.
3 Helen W. Bones to WW, June 21, 1915, 2:40 P.M., T telegram, WP, DLC.
4 Helen W. Bones to WW, June 21, 1915, T telegram, WP, DLC.

From Edith Bolling Galt

The Wolcott   New York
Dearest One: June 22, 1915 5 P.M

I wonder if you really *have* felt my thoughts and spirit with
you, as they have been, all day. Your dear note, written yesterday just as we were leaving, came up with our breakfast tray
this morning, and I could not pay attention to coffee and rolls
with such a delicious love song in my keeping.

I am so sorry you were so lonely my precious Lord and hope the rest of the day you were too busy to feel our absence.

I wrote you last night and hope it came to you promptly and told you of our happy comfortable journey. After I finished my letter we got to bed, and before I went to sleep I read over again the dear messenger Helen brought me. I slept pretty well, but woke very early this morning with *you* as my first conscious thought, and the hope that you were well and happy. We had breakfast upstairs, and went out in the car about ten. It is almost cold, and while not raining has been a gray sort of day. Helen wanted to see a friend, whom she took riding and we all enjoyed it and drove way out Riverside.

Then we left the friend and went shopping. I got a little white dress for you to give Helen which she was crazy for. I hope you will like it, and she is so overcome by your thought of her you would be touched if you could have seen her pleasure and appreciation. She had gotten one dress for herself and said she thought this other one was lovely, but she must not get it. So then I told her of what you wrote me, and that I was going to get it for you to give her and she almost cried. The dress was ten dollars and ninety five cents, and I hope you meant for me to get something like that.

We went to the Holland House for lunch and then took a walk up 5th Ave, which we both love, and looked at a lot of new things & have just gotten home and Helen is resting. We are going to the theatre tonight, and how I wish you were with us.

This is my night to come to dinner with you. I wonder if you will think of it and miss me? Well, I *am* thinking of it and missing you and will come in my thoughts and sit at your right and tell you how glad I am to be back again with my Beloved.

I hope you have been interested in this detailed account of what we have done. We are going to leave about ten tomorrow morning—I think—and I will not try to write to you again for you will leave tomorrow, and I wont know where to reach you.

So this is goodby until you come to Cornish. It will be three days, but there is no help for it. You will know I am holding you close in my thoughts and that I will count the hours until your coming!

Helen sends you her love, and she is a perfect dear.

I am going to rest now a little while before dinner. We will be a[t] Springfield tomorrow night. And wherever you are my thoughts will follow you and tell you, I love you, always,

Edith.

ALS (WP, DLC).

To Helen Woodrow Bones

White House June 23 1915   8 50 PM

Lansing appointed Secretary of State. All well and send love. Hope second days ride had been as enjoyable as first Letter sent to Springfield   Woodrow Wilson

T telegram (WP, DLC).

To Charles Richard Crane

My dear Friend: [The White House] June 23, 1915

Thank you with all my heart for your recent letter after seeing House. It is full of things that interest me and help me. I read with especial interest what you had to say about Mr. and Mrs. Delano.

I am getting off tonight to see House and go off to a little breathing spell at Cornish, and this is just an affectionate message.

I am so glad that Mrs. Crane is feeling so much better. Please give her my warmest regards and my congratulations.

Always

Cordially and affectionately yours,   Woodrow Wilson

TLS (Letterpress Books, WP, DLC).

From Robert Lansing

Dear Mr. President: Washington June 23, 1915.

I enclose herewith a printed copy of the memorandum which we received to-day from London, covering certain features of our note of March 30th.[1] I thought you might wish to take the copy with you.   Faithfully yours,   Robert Lansing.

TLS (WP, DLC).

[1] The memorandum reviewed Great Britain's concessions to American trade, especially with regard to cotton exports. After reviewing the agreements reached with representatives of American cotton interests—permitting shipments contracted for before March 2 and shipped before March 31—and repeating American assurances that the agreements conceded all that cotton interests could ask, the memorandum contended that no arbitrary interference with the cotton trade had occurred. Most delays in handling cotton and other cargoes resulted from actions of the shippers, not from British regulations. For the future, the British offered to allow shipments sold before June 15, even if shipped later than that date, and to give special consideration to certain kinds of cargoes sold to neutral nations. However, the British refused otherwise to consider special cases through diplomatic channels. WHP to RL, June 22, 1915, printed telegram, WP, DLC; printed in *FR-WWS 1915*, pp. 443-46.

To Edith Bolling Galt

[The White House]

My precious Darling,   Wednesday morning 23 June, 1915

I am sure you must feel, without my telling you, how constantly and lovingly my thoughts have followed you ever since you left; and you came to me again last night, bless your heart, just as I was falling asleep,—came with infinite tenderness and charm. You are never so bewitching as when you make love! I shall be tempted, till I come to you, to be always dozing. I love you beyond all words, my adorable Sweetheart, and your love is my life. With what delight did I seize and devour your dear letter, written Tuesday night. I am so glad you saw Princeton, after all (though I coveted being your guide there myself) and thought it attractive. We must go back there some day and really see all of its charms. It is too various for a mere casual visit. What you said so sweetly in that letter, my Darling, about my thought for your comfort and pleasure made me more keenly conscious than I have been before of the deep longing in me for the privilege of constantly taking thought for you. The sweetest part of my love for you is that I may devote myself to your happiness. It is so delightful to think of taking thought for you all the day long!

The chronicle of yesterday was very simple with us: just desk work, a short cabinet meeting; a talk with Mac. in which he benevolently and with the best intentions sought to render assistance in Mexican and other foreign matters which are none of his business; golf, and a long ride with dear Margaret. Margaret is the only member of the family who had any adventure. She went riding with a young Princeton man who is one of Commissioner Daniels' assistants,[1] and, to her keen mortification, was thrown from her horse by his sudden shying. She rolled directly under him, but he stepped carefully over her. Young Woodward sprang from his horse to her assistance and, in his haste and excitement, released his horse entirely. Both horses ran away and the two bored riders had to hunt them till they found them at a nearby farm where fortunately they had run into a paddock and could be cornered and caught. Margaret was of course bruised and a little strained but I think not hurt, except in her pride. She went for a long drive with me last night and said she was not even tired—only a little stiff. Horse-back riding is certainly the sport for adventure.

To-night I get away, and, though I shall stop all day to-morrow with Mr. House at Roslyn (Long Island), it will be at least start-

ing for Cornish and the sweet, incomparable lady who is all the world to me. And this is my last letter till I see her. This will reach you to-morrow, and the next day I shall come in person to say what no letter can say—what a lover whose love goes too deep for words, is too tender to express in anything but acts of devotion, can say only with his eyes, with the tones of his voice, with kisses and caresses, and the sweet syllables he can whisper into his Sweetheart's ears. Ah, my Love, my Love, how unspeakably eager I am to see you, to be close beside you, to hold you in my arms and feel myself full of the life and joy of existence which only you can give me. And how, after once having had you in my home shall I ever have the strength to give you up again, even for a little while!

Good-bye, my Darling. How it will brighten all the world to see you again,   Your own   Woodrow

Love, no end of love, to darling Helen,—and to Jessie.   W.
                                                          8.40.

Your dear letter of yesterday afternoon has just been handed me, you Darling. You perfectly interpret my wishes. I wanted a detailed account of your day—and the love that runs all through this precious letter will make the day easy for me. Thank you for the purchase you made for Helen. You did it in just the right way—just the way I wanted it done. It gives me such pleasure to make her happy—and to do it through you, my other, dearer self, more than doubles the pleasure. My Darling! God keep you. I love you with all my heart!   W.

ALS (WP, DLC).
¹ Thomas Mullen Woodward, A.B. Princeton 1906, an attorney with the Interstate Commerce Commission.

From Robert Lansing, with Enclosure

Dear Mr. President: Washington June 24, 1915.

I enclose herewith a copy of a telegram received by the Red Cross today. The underscored sentence indicates, to my mind, that Carranza intends to use the food supply of Mexico for purposes of revenue, which is very disquieting in view of the famine conditions which are daily growing worse.

Faithfully yours,   Robert Lansing.

TLS (SDR, RG 59, 812.00/15338½A, DNA).

E N C L O S U R E

Telephoned to Mr. Canova by Miss Boardman, June 24, 1915.

Telegram from O'Connor,[1] Red Cross Representative.

Arrived yesterday; conferred with Shanklin, Silliman and Carranza. <u>Latter refuses allow purchase supplies in Mexico.</u> Guarantees protection supplies imported. Offers safe conduct Shanklin and self to front with medical supplies received for hospital, Mexico City. No arrangement yet from City account interruption communication. Best for us to wait to reach city and learn possibilities of purchase then.

T MS (SDR, RG 59, 812.00/15338½A, DNA).
[1] Charles James O'Connor, Director of the Pacific Division of the Red Cross.

From the Diary of Colonel House

June 24, 1915.

This morning Gordon and I went to the Roslyn station at 8.45 to meet the President. There were some decorations and a number of people had gathered to greet him. He came out by special train and received three rousing cheers when he stepped upon the platform. He greeted me with warmth and affection, placing both hands over mine. We drove to Gordon's cottage and after remaining in the house a minute, went on the terrace and began one of our most intimate conversations.

I did most of the talking for it was for me to elaborate upon the various reports I had made to him by cable and by letter. He seemed delighted with the work done and the good relations established in the different capitals. He referred to Sir Horace Plunkett's letter, repeating that part of it verbatim in which Sir Horace speaks of my service in England in setting the Government straight in their attitude toward America.

I shall not go into detail of my conversation regarding European affairs because they have been stated at various times in the diary. I told him I had left matters in such shape that there were people in each of the belligerent countries ready to notify me when it was thought I had best return. After receiving these notifications, we could consider whether it was worth while to heed them. He replied, "That is a matter for you to determine. I want you to go whenever you consider the time propitious."

I explained why I had come back, and he fully approved, believing it was the wise course to pursue. He cuncurs that our Ambassadors should return home at least once a year and get in touch with our people so as to retain their American viewpoint rather than to acquire that of the countries to which they are accredited.

We discussed the possible appointment of Lansing. He had understood from McAdoo and my letter that I approved of the appointment, and he had come to believe it was best for the reasons I had mentioned. That is, he is practically his own Secretary of State and Lansing would not be troublesome by obtruding or injecting his own views.

He said when Mr. Bryan informed him of his intention to resign he had remarked with a quiver in his voice and of his lips "Colonel House has been Secretary of State, not I, and I have never had your full confidence." The President tried to minimize what I had done, but was not very successful for facts were against him, although Mr. Bryan knew but a small part of my work. The President said he had only shown him a few of my messages, and excused himself for this by saying how utterly impossible it would be to let Mr. Bryan know his whole mind.

He mentioned the South American proposal which I had formulated and started and said it was just where I left it, Mr. Bryan being unable to move it further. He said he would now like to push it to a conclusion and he hoped we would be able to do so. I replied that Mr. Bryan had never done any serious work in his life; that he was essentially a talker, and I believed if he had remained in the State Department two years longer and had been suppressed as he has been during the past two years, it would have killed him. The President had noticed a change for the better even in the short time he had been out.

I do not minimize the good Mr. Bryan has accomplished during his eventful life, but he has done it largely through suggestions which others have carried out, and which he could not have done himself. He has imagination and has genius in certain directions, but he lacks the kind of ability necessary to carry out his ideas.

When I told the President about Burleson and Gregory offering to resign so as to leave me free to accept the Secretaryship of State without embarrassment to him, he was deeply touched at this evidence of loyalty and said, "I am glad you told me for it is something I shall always remember with Pleasure." He added, "Of course you know how glad I would have been to have had you accept the office."

We took up Mexican affairs and he is to try the plan of getting the A.B.C. Powers and perhaps two others of the larger South American Republics to insist upon the different factions in Mexico getting together. He wondered if they would undertake this work. I was sure they would. And if they once get a government in Mexico started, he should throw all the moral and financial weight of the United States back of it, and insist upon there being no change until peace and order reigned.

He then said, I have an intimate personal matter to discuss with you. You are the only person in the world with whom I can discuss everything. There are some I can tell one thing and to others another, but you are the only one to whom I can make an entire clearance of mind. What would you think of my getting married again? Since you left I have met a delightful woman and I am thinking of asking her to marry me. Do you believe I would lessen my influence with the American people by taking such a step? And when do you think I could do it? I have led such a lonely life that I feel it is necessary for me to have companionship of that sort, and my dear dead wife would be the first to approve if she could know, for she has talked to me about it and I am sure I would be following her wishes.

I was moved by his confidence in me and the affection for me which led him to make such a statement. Both Grayson and Gregory had told of the rumor prevalent regarding this lady, and Grayson had said that, in his opinion, the President's affections were seriously involved and that, sooner or later, he would ask her to marry him. I did not let the President know I had any intimation of the matter, nor did I let Grayson know later when he spoke again about it that the President had taken me into his complete confidence.

The President seemed pleased that I approved his plans. I feel that his health demands it and I also feel that Woodrow Wilson today is the greatest asset the world has. If he should die or become incapacitated, it is doubtful whether a right solution of the problems involved in this terrible conflict and its aftermath would be possible.

We discussed when it would be advisable for him to take this step. I urged postponement until Spring, that is for about a year.

He spoke of Garrison, and asked whether I knew that at one time he was about to tender his resignation. I reminded him that it happened the day I left for Europe. He said Garrison was an able fellow, but had become thoroughly spoiled by adulation heaped upon him by newspapers, and he was a great nuisance in Cabinet meetings because he not only talked so much, but tried to inject his opinions into every department. The President declared he would never again try to persuade a member of his Cabinet to remain when dissatisfaction was once indicated. If

Garrison mentioned it again, he would let him go. I approve this
for it in [is] in line with what I have been telling him during his
entire administration. There is no worse policy than to let people
feel that you are dependent upon them for, as a matter of fact,
Woodrow Wilson is dependent upon no one person.

He said First Assist. Secretary of State Osborne had tendered
his resignation soon after Mr. Bryan had tendered his, but he
had declined to accept it. He thought, however, Osborne intended
to retire in the Autumn anyway, and he asked what I thought of
William Phillips for the place. I approved heartily, for this was
my suggestion to him more than a year ago. He was afraid
Phillips' present place could not be properly filled. I was sure,
now Mr. Bryan was gone and was not there to insist upon some
incompetent democrat, we could get just as good a man as
Phillips, and out of the regular service. I mentioned Laughlin of
the London Embassy, Bliss of Paris, and Grew of Berlin.

He said he had explained to Lansing our relations, and he did
not believe we would have any trouble with him. He thought it
wise however for me to have a talk with Lansing, inviting him
to Manchester for the purpose. I asked if I should tell Lansing
the whole story regarding my European work. He replied, "No,
not fully, but enough to get him to work in harmony with us."

I gave the President the plan by which I can reach Sir Edward
Grey by cable without the knowledge of anyone, explaining that
such messages need not go through the British Embassy or
through our Embassy in London. He was pleased and while we
may not wish to use it, yet it may become necessary at anytime.
Neither of us have confidence in the British Ambassador's ability
to handle situations on account of his delicate health.

Apropos of the British Ambassador, during the day a letter
came from him written in such cryptic style that neither the
President nor I could understand what he was trying to say.[1]
Finally the President laughingly remarked, "When you see him
tell him I read his letter and would like to know what it was
about."

He asked me to suggest a good man for Santo Domingo in
place of Sullivan. We agreed that care should be used in getting
rid of incompetents Mr. Bryan had put in, so as not to widen
the breach between Mr. Bryan and himself.

It was now around noon and we had been in constant conference for nearly three hours. The President becomes mentally
tired rather easily and I purposely changed the subject to less
serious topics. We strolled down the hill to call upon his old

[1] It is missing.

college friend Mr. Godwin,[2] who is a grandson of William Cullen Bryant, and who lives in the old Bryant home. When we returned to the terrace, he permitted the army of newspaper men and photographers to come up. We sat before the cameras for about ten minutes until they had their fill. The President, however, drew the line at the moving picture men who only caught a glimpse of us as we motored down the hill later in the day.

Dr. Grayson and Gordon lunched with us, and after a further talk with the President about general topics we motored to Piping Rock where he played golf with Gordon and Grayson. We returned to the cottage about six o'clock, remaining until seven when we motored to the Roslyn station. There was a large crowd assembled to see him, and when he stepped from the automobile, there was enthusiastic cheering.

In bidding him goodbye I urged him not to allow anyone to come to Cornish and to forget, as far as possible, the cares of state, and said he could place anything or anybody upon my back he pleased, and I would promise to hold it or them until his vacation was over. He laughed and said, "Will you sit on their necks?" I promised that I would. This ended one of the pleasantest days we have had together. . . .

The President said a French cruiser had gone into Haiti to protect the French bank there. He immediately despatched an American cruiser, thanked the French Government for what they had done, and told them he would relieve them. He said while Mr. Bryan was always using the "soft pedal" in negotiations with Germany, he had to restrain him when he was dealing with Santo Domingo, Haiti and such small republics.

I mentioned that Sir Edward Grey was occupying Winston Churchill's house in London, to which he quickly replied, "I am occupying his house in Cornish."[3]

When I spoke of how much depended upon him and how anxious I was that he might maintain his health and strength he said his belief was that Providence did not remove a man until his work was finished. I did not reply to this although I wanted to ask him not to let such a belief prevent him from taking every precaution to preserve his life and health.

I asked how he thought Marshall would hold down the Presidentcy in the event of his death. He replied, "The situation would hold him down and sit on his neck."

He showed considerable resentment at George Creel's article

[2] Harold Godwin.
[3] Winston Churchill, the American novelist, owned Harlakenden.

in the last Harper's Weekly[4] in which he gave Bryan credit for having passed practically all the effective legislation during this Administration. While Creel speaks kindly of the President, he thinks it was Bryan's influence with Congress that made it possible to write into law the Tariff, banking laws, etc. etc. In this he is wholly mistaken as this diary has shown. What impressed me, though, was that the President seemed to care so much what Creel said, indicating some fear lest this view might be shared by the public.

In discussing the shipping troubles with England, I remarked that the British viewpoint was that the United States should not raise an objection to their action as to cotton. They feel they would have been justified in declaring cotton contraband, following American precedent in '61-'65, and since they paid full price for all cargoes taken, they thought we should have no complaint. They [The] President replied that when they consented to make cotton non-contraband, they relinquished their right to hold it up as they are doing. I was surprised he did not see that from the standpoint of equity the English are right, and if we met them in the same spirit they have displayed to us, we should be content with their action.

Another thing he told me was he was greatly relieved now that Mr. Bryan had gone, since he had been a constant source of concern to him.

[4] George Creel, "The Commoner," *Harper's Weekly*, LX (June 26, 1915), 604-606.

From Robert Lansing, with Enclosure

Dear Mr. President: [Washington] June 25, 1915.

In order that I may be sure that you receive a copy of important telegrams, I enclose a copy of a telegram from Ambassador Gerard in relation to the reply of the German Government to our last LUSITANIA note.

Faithfully yours,   Robert Lansing

CCL (SDR, RG 59, 763.72/1903, DNA).

E N C L O S U R E

Berlin (via Copenhagen) June 24, 1915.

2501. CONFIDENTIAL. Note as at present drafted will offer security to ships usually and especially engaged in passenger traffic. There is a fight on between the peace party and the war party as to whether this offer shall be unconditional simply expressing a hope that ammunition and arms shall not be sent on these ships or as to whether this offer shall be made conditional on the fact these passenger ships shall not carry arms and ammunition. Foreign Office and the Chancellor are for the former proposition; the war von Tirpitz party for the latter. I think the feeling between America and Germany will be helped to a better understanding if you can assure me that President will come out and endeavor to secure non-shipment of arms and ammunition on these passenger ships and allow me to convey this informally to Foreign Office. The peace party is having a hard time and will receive I hope some encouragement from our side. Of course all above is informal and confidential but my information from high and good sources is confirmed by information given Conger of Associated Press.[1] A friend of mine in Foreign Office has suggested that President send me a message to give Kaiser personally. Kaiser would then have to see me which friend thinks will help as Kaiser now entirely surrounded by military and hears only war talk. Gerard, Berlin.

T telegram (SDR, RG 59, 763.72/1903, DNA).
[1] Seymour Beach Conger, director of the Berlin bureau of the Associated Press.

From Robert Lansing, with Enclosure

My dear Mr. President: Washington, June 25, 1915.

In connection with your note to me of the 22nd, relative to approaching certain of the representatives of other American States in regard to cooperating with us in advice and political action as to Mexico, I enclose a memorandum, showing the three Ambassadors and their present addresses and also the three ranking Ministers from other countries (the rank, of course, depends upon the dates of their assuming their posts in Washington).

My own impression is that the three Ministers are probably as available as any who could be selected. With Calderon and de Pena I have exceptionally intimate relations. Of course, this gives Central America but one representative. I do not know as this is an objection, but if it is, I think that the excuse that length of service in Washington has governed their selection would overcome any objection which might be made, and prevent the criticism of favoritism.

It would seem to me that Dr. Naón and Mr. da Gama should be first approached. As you know, I am going to be in New

York the night of Monday, the 28th, and I thought I might be able to arrange a meeting with Mr. da Gama there, if it met with your approval. If it does, will you please telegraph me to that effect, in order that I can arrange with the Ambassador to come to New York?   Faithfully yours,   Robert Lansing.

TLS (SDR, RG 59, 812.00/15338½, DNA).

E N C L O S U R E

June 15, 1915.

Amb. da Gama	Brazil:	Herron Hall, Long Branch, N. J.
" Naón	Argentina:	Latrobe Cottage, Buena Vista Springs, Pa.
" Suárez-Mujica	Chile:	Here.
Min. Calderon	Bolivia:	Here.
" de Pena	Uruguay:	Blue Ridge Summit, Pa.
" Méndez	Guatemala:	Here.

T MS (SDR, RG 59, 812.00/15338½, DNA).

To Mary Allen Hulbert

My dear Friend: EN ROUTE, June 25, 1915

I am very much distressed that I did not see just how to help until it was too late. Your Special Delivery letter was not handed me until after business hours on Wednesday and I was to leave that night at midnight. I did not know Allen's address and could not have telegraphed what was necessary to him without making arrangements which could not be made on the spur of the moment or through third parties.

I console myself by thinking that perhaps it was best, after all, not to strip yourself and that it may turn out that nothing real was lost, but this is poor consolation when I should have liked so much to help.

I am dictating this in haste on the train but you may be sure that I send it with deepest sympathy and with the hope that everything will come out better than you fear.

Always   Faithfully yours,   Woodrow Wilson

TLS (WP, DLC).

From Charles Richard Crane

Dear Mr President   [New York] June 26, 1915

It is very good indeed to see the practically universal approval of your act in making Mr Lansing Secretary of State. He has certainly made a fine impression during his brief career with you. Of course the real interpretation is that the country is abundantly satisfied with the way our difficult foreign problems have been met and is not disposed to take the slightest chance on any change just now. You yourself have made a great reputation as a Secretary of State and are elected to that office by the voters and votes of the whole world. Perhaps your most serious menace will be an offer soon of some enthusiastic college to give you an L.L.D.

All demand for Root, or some other brilliant republican lawyer, to go to your aid has ceased and it is now definitely recognized that there was a note in your German messages that Root could not possibly have put into them; that it was this note that made the messages "carry" and satisfy to the highest degree the Americans behind you and *really* touch the German spirit—for *that* has been done for the first time since the war began. No simply intellectual "stunt," however brilliant, could have had this double and most happy result.

Please take the best possible care of yourself and rest in the belief that "all is well."

If you would like to send one of your little notes to Mrs Crane at the Presbyterian Hospital it would make her very happy.

She is getting along wonderfully and is quite serene about the whole event and Tuesday evening the Russian choir is going to sing for her and the other patients.

Perhaps sometime this Summer I can bring them up to sing for you.   Always devotedly   Charles R. Crane

ALS (WP, DLC).

To Rudolph Forster

Windsor, Vermont, June 28, 1915.

Please transmit following message to the Attorney General:

"Have just learned of the detention of Huerta and Orozco.[1] Sincerely hope that it will be possible for you to detain them and permanently prevent⸱their entering Mexico.

Woodrow Wilson."

T telegram (EBR, RG 130, DNA).

[1] Huerta had been arrested in Newman, N. M., on June 27 by federal marshals to prevent his crossing into Mexico to lead a counterrevolution, financed and

armed with German assistance. See Michael C. Meyer, *Huerta: A Political Portrait* (Lincoln, Neb., 1972), pp. 213-26.

From John Sharp Williams

Confidential.

Benton, Mississippi,
My dear Mr. President: June 29, 1915.

I have just received a letter from Senator Hoke Smith together with a long article that he has written[1] in which he contends that Great Britain is without warrant in law or justice in destroying the South's foreign cotton market, etc.

He seems to be totally ignorant of the doctrine of "continuous voyage," which our government insisted upon during the Civil War, which the British government insisted upon during the Boer war, and which Japan insisted upon during the Japanese-Russian war.

Of course, he is right in saying that Great Britain has trenched upon our neutral rights. Of course, from the standpoint of wanting re-election in Georgia, or from the standpoint of anybody's wanting re-election in any of the cotton states, he is politically right.

I write this, though, to impress upon you the importance of not getting our hands full with Germany and Great Britain both at the same time. If Germany shall not accede to our reasonable demands, then the British situation will cure itself, because we ourselves would be compelled to stop all exportation of American products to Germany or to neutral ports *in transitu* for Germany, or to neutral ports pretendedly to stop there, but really to go on to Germany, which latter involves the doctrine of "continuous voyage." If Germany upon the contrary shall satisfactorily accede to our demands, then we can take up the matter with Great Britain and force it just as far as our rights under international law justify us in forcing it.

Senator Smith wrote me a letter asking me to read his article. I suppose you have read it. If not, I enclose it herewith.

I am personally, perhaps, very much more interested in cotton than he is, but I can see something besides cotton. I am perfectly aware also of the fact that it is dangerous to tell my constituents that I can see something else besides cotton.

I was a little astonished some time ago to see the position taken by young Webb,[2] of North Carolina—by the way, a very fine fellow—which was almost on all-fours with the position taken by Senator Smith. We can't afford to put our backs against the wall while we make demands, which are virtually ultimata, upon both Germany and the allies at the same time. There is no common sense in that. Prudence is the highest form of common sense.

I am, with every expression of regard,

Very truly yours,   John Sharp Williams[3]

TLS (WP, DLC).
[1] Smith's article had appeared in the *Atlanta Journal*, June 13, 1915. The legislature of Georgia, on June 28, adopted resolutions calling upon the President to use all means within his power, "diplomatic if possible, retaliatory if necessary," to reopen the central European market to cotton. Link, *Struggle for Neutrality*, p. 600.
[2] Edwin Yates Webb, Democratic congressman from the 9th district of North Carolina.
[3] Wilson's reply is printed as an addendum in this volume.

From Edith Bolling Galt

Cornish, New Hampshire [c. June 29, 1915]

Good morning: Do you feel like taking a walk with me this glorious day, my dearest one, or are you afraid of the damp? If you want to go, I will be ready by ten thirty.   E.

ALI (WP, DLC).

To Edith Bolling Galt

Cornish, New Hampshire [c. June 29, 1915]

Of course I do, my precious Little Girl. It will be jolly. I love you with all my heart. I will be ready   Woodrow

ALS (WP, DLC).

A Pledge

Cornish, New Hampshire June 29, 1915

I promise with all my heart absolutely to trust and accept my loved Lord, and unite my life with his without doubts or misgiving,   Edith.[1]
West Porch

ALS (WP, DLC).
[1] They had just become engaged.

From Abbott Lawrence Lowell

[Cambridge, Mass.]

My dear President Wilson: June 30, 1915

Some of us who are interested in promoting peace in the future by what seems to us rational methods, have formed an associa-

tion to further a suggestion which seems to us promising.[1] I
enclose the resolutions, which give the outline of the plan. We
have felt that whether the proposal meets with general favor or
not, it is proper to inform you of it; but to do so in such a way
as not to request any expression of opinion. I am therefore writing to you in this informal way.

Very truly yours,   A. Lawrence Lowell

CCL (A. L. Lowell Papers, MH-Ar).
 [1] Lowell enclosed the proposals adopted by the League to Enforce Peace—
American Branch, summarized in n. 1 to remarks at a press conference printed
at June 22, 1915.

William Wesley Canada to Robert Lansing

Vera Cruz, Mexico   June 30, 1915

Following from Brazilian Minister:

653, June 22, 10 A.M. "After some days of interruption of
cable communication, which I am informed by manager of Cable
Company was caused by Carrancistas at Otumba, I beg to inform you that Carrancistas under Pablo Gonzalez have been unable to occupy city within time fixed by them and that so far they
have been held back at every point by the Conventionists forces[1]
who have defended themselves with energy. It is to be feared
that present state of affairs may last several days or even weeks
with the consequent alarming lack of food and other inconveniences because even in the event that Carrancistas by shortness
of ammunition of the Conventionists should succeed in occupying the city after desperate fighting even in the streets of the city
with the utmost danger for all, a horrible state of distress and
hunger will certainly prevail for a considerable time, for if the
Conventionists should have to evacuate the town they will
besiege it, causing the same evils that the Carrancistas are now
causing and even worse. The prospects for foreigners and non-
combatants are therefore dreadful; to begin with there is no
more corn and great scarcity of (all) other staple articles in
town; this has already caused great suffering amongst all classes
and popular disturbances even against this Legation as it was
falsely reported that we had plenty of food in deposit. The movement was readily suppressed by the authorities but I am sorry
to be obliged to say that the general animosity against the United
States Government is growing very much because everybody
blames the United States for the present state of things; first
for having apparently satisfied themselves so far as they believe
with a purely negative answer from Carranza when two of the

other factions were disposed to enter into negotiations, and secondly for not having impressed upon him the absolute necessity of arranging for an armistice in the course of which the United States Government should have used its good offices for the conclusion of a peaceful settlement. This being the case, and following the insistent advice of several friends, American and Mexican, including that of a high officer of the Convention and also on account of the daily receipt of anonymous letters containing tremendous threats, was obliged to increase our American guard to eight men, which I will increase to twelve as before if necessary. To be just, I desire to emphasize the good will of the authorities, to prevent any disagreeable incidents, but do not know how far they will be able to afford the necessary protection, as if the Carrancistas should gain ground toward the occupation of the city, the Legation and foreigners specially American, will run great risk from the outrages of the mob and soldiers, who, perhaps, will not be controlled during the disorder that will precede the evacuation, as, I repeat, that the bad feeling goes to the absurd point of believing that the Carrancistas come this time under the auspices of the United States. I beg pardon if in my desire to be loyal and giving you an exact and truthful account of the situation and of the general feeling here, I have been unhappy enough to be too frank or disagreeable.

Kindly copy this and following on the situation to Brazilian Embassy.   Cardoso de Oliveira"

T telegram (WP, DLC).
1 That is, the *Zapatista-Villista* forces.

From John Eugene Osborne

Washington, June 30, 1915.

Following message just received from the Brazilian Minister at Mexico City, dated June twenty-five, six p.m., transmitted by Consul Canada, Vera Cruz. (Quote).

I confirm my 653, June 22, 10 a.m. Although cable lines are not cut Manager Cable Company has informed me that service is interrupted by Carrancista authorities and not even messages of Diplomatic Corps allowed to pass. Convention claim have been able repulse Carrancistas. However, general situation is growing worse as there is no prospect of getting any relief for the hungry. The very much feared bread riots began this morning when the mobs sacked all the markets and several grocery stores. This, of course, is only the beginning, as the city being isolated from all producing centers the hungry mobs will keep up the looting which will eventually spread to banks and private houses. The situation is considered more acute account of several Zapatistta generals who, disregarding the orders of the President of the Convention,[1] are inciting the masses to violence and pillage. The only possible relief can come from the immediate opening of railroad traffic with Vera Cruz and the bringing in of the Red Cross supplies. On account of the above Diplomatic Corps consider it imperative that cable and railway communication be opened immediately to bring necessary relief and avoid very grave complications and probably loss of life to foreigners here by violence or lack of food. Am sending this message by special messenger to Vera Cruz. (Unquote).   John E. Osborne

T telegram (SDR, RG 59, 812.00/15337, DNA).
  [1] Roque González Garza.

To Edith Bolling Galt

[Cornish, N. H., c. June 30, 1915]

Would my Sweetheart make me happy by taking another walk with me this morning? I will be at her call, and ready any time she will.

With love beyond measure   Woodrow

ALS (WP, DLC).

From Edward Mandell House, with Enclosure

Manchester,
Dear Governor: Massachusetts. July 1st, 1915.

Several days ago I received this telegram from Mrs. Harriman:

"Developements southern border make it important you should see Iturbide, leader of movement which promises most hopeful solution along lines favored by Administration. Prompt action necessary. Iturbide can go to you any day. If favorably impressed will you arrange meeting with Chief. Secretary Lane approves above and urges your cooperation."

I replied as follows:

"My own feeling is that an interview with Iturbide will add nothing to the solution of the problem and I would prefer not to discuss the matter with him unless Secretary Lansing thinks it desirable for me to do so."

Today I have the following from Mrs. Harriman:

"I have awaited Secretary Lansing's return. He is very glad to have you see the man in question. Department considers him the only loophole.[1] Ethel[2] and I will arrive with the two men on first train out of Boston Saturday afternoon. If this is not convenient will come Sunday."

I have wired Mrs. Harriman putting her off for the moment until I can hear from you. I shall be glad to follow your wishes in the matter.

I had determined not to disturb your vacation, but this seems to require an immediate answer. Will you not advise me by wire upon receipt of this.

I hope you have rested well and that your holiday has been full of benefit.

My telephone number is Manchester 329 in the event you should ever wish to reach me.

                              Affectionately yours,   E. M. House

P.S. I am enclosing you a copy of a letter from White which may interest you.

TLS (WP, DLC).
   [1] Again, see Link, *Struggle for Neutrality*, pp. 470-476.
   [2] Ethel Borden Harriman, only child of J. Borden Harriman and Florence J. H. Harriman.

E N C L O S U R E

Sir Edward Grey to Edward Mandell House

                              Fallodon, Northumberland.
Dear Colonel House: June 6th, 1915.

I was very glad to hear from Drummond,[1] my private secretary at the Foreign Office, that a cypher has been arranged which you can use with me direct, this is a most satisfactory arrangement.

If as you think likely the United States drift into war with Germany, the influence of the United States in the general aspects of the peace will be predominant and perhaps decisive, for it is the one country that can neither be beaten nor exhausted. (I mean by the general aspects of peace, those which are concerned with preserving peace in future, as distinct from local and particular conditions such as the destiny of Alsace and Lorraine, which are purely European.)

But the dilemma I foresee is that the desire of the people of the United States to keep out of war with Germany may lead to burying the Lusitania issue inconclusively, in which case Germany will disregard and the other belligerents will hope little from American influence in future and the tendancy will be to discount it.   Your sincere,   [Edward Grey]

TCL (WP, DLC).
¹ (James) Eric Drummond.

A Memorandum by Franklin Knight Lane

July 1, 1915.

MEMORANDUM.

I had a talk this morning with Mr. Llorente, the representative here of General Villa, who brought with him General Angeles. Angeles expressed the desire to pay his respects, and we chatted at some length regarding parts of Mexico with which I was familiar. He says that it had been his hope that he might speak with the President, so as to let the President know how the Mexican people felt toward him; that they regarded him as their friend and not as their enemy. I told him that I had no doubt the President would be quite anxious to know what his views were, but that they should be communicated through the Secretary of State. He said he had not yet had an interview with Mr. Lansing, but was quite anxious to have one.

I asked him what policy he thought would bring peace to Mexico, and he said the policy outlined by the President. I asked him if he thought that the various factions of the Constitutionalists could be brought together to agree upon a provisional president, and he said that they could if the United States would exercise some pressure upon Carranza, who is a very obstinate man. I asked him in what shape this pressure should be applied, and he said by letting him know quietly that if he did not agree to the compromise provisional president that the United States would put an embargo upon munitions as against him, and regard his ships as pirates. I asked him if this would not antagonize the Mexican people, and he said that if it was known that an effort had been made by the United States to adjust the differences between the factions and that Carranza had stood out against the success of such effort, that the Mexican people would be glad that the President brought pressure to bear that would secure this result. He thought that no pressure would be necessary if it was stated emphatically that such pressure would in the end be used if Carranza were obdurate. I asked him who he thought would be most likely to secure Carranza's support as well as Villa's as provisional president. He replied Vasquez Tagle,¹ a former member of Madero's Cabinet and now a practicing lawyer in the City of Mexico who had taken no part in political affairs since the Madero Cabinet went out. I asked him if Bonilla was satisfactory. He said more satisfactory to the Villa element than to the Carranza element, because Carranza had at one time put Bonilla in jail.

I asked him if it would not be necessary, not only to agree upon the provisional president, but to agree upon a program that would insure a fair election, and a Cabinet and the governors of the different states. He said he thought that the Cabinet should be a fusion cabinet, representing all elements. He did not reply as to the governors of the states.

I asked him how long the war would continue. He said he thought for a long time, unless pressure was brought to bear that would bring it to an end. I asked him as to the starvation of the people in Mexico, and he said he knew nothing about conditions in Carranza's territory, but that in Villa's territory the crops were planted and there was promise of a large crop. He did not deny that the people were in a bad way at this time.   Lane

TS MS (WP, DLC).
¹ Manuel Vázquez Tagle.

A Proclamation

[[July 2, 1915]]

A national exposition in commemoration of the achievements of the negro race during the last fifty years will be held in Richmond, Va., July 5 to 25, 1915. The occasion has been recognized as of national importance by Congress through an appropriation of $55,000 to aid in its promotion and consummation. This sum is being expended, by the terms of the appropriation, under the direction of the Governor of Virginia. The exposition is under the auspices of the Negro Historical and Industrial Association. The action of Congress in this matter indicates very happily the desire of the nation as well as of the people of Virginia to encourage the negro in his efforts to solve his industrial problem.

The National Negro Exposition is designed to demonstrate his progress in the last fifty years and to emphasize his opportunities. As President of the United States, I bespeak the active interest of the nation in the exposition and trust that every facility will be extended to the leaders whose earnest work has made the undertaking possible.

Printed in the *New York Times*, July 3, 1915.

To Robert Lansing

My dear Mr. Secretary,   [Cornish, N. H.] 2 July, 1915.

This is very gratifying to me.[1] It begins to look as if this important thing could be achieved at last.

It is very interesting that these communications should have crossed each other. I think that it will be wise to pursue the matter as diligently as it is found opportune and wise (over there) to push it.   Faithfully Yours,   W.W.

WWTLI (SDR, RG 59, 711.5914/31½, DNA).
    [1] M. F. Egan to RL, May 24, 1915, TLS (SDR, RG 59, 711.5914/27, DNA), printed in *FR 1917*, pp. 590-91. Egan reported that the Danish Foreign Minister, Erik Scavenius, in an informal conversation had indicated that the Danish government would be receptive to a proposal by the United States to purchase the Danish Antilles.

To Josephus Daniels

My dear Daniels: Cornish, N. H., July 2, 1915

Will you be kind enough to tell me whether there is anything I can properly and legitimately do to set forward Cary T. Grayson's chances of promotion? I mean any such thing as, for example, ordering him to an examination or facilitating the process by which he may qualify.

I need not say that he has not spoken to me about this and that the question has arisen in my own mind merely out of the desire to reward an uncommonly faithful and serviceable man. It would embarrass him if I were to do anything irregular and I myself would not desire to do anything of that kind, but I thought that it was possible that I might legitimately increase his opportunities in some way that would be above criticism.

    Always   Affectionately yours,   Woodrow Wilson

TLS (J. Daniels Papers, DLC).

From Joseph Patrick Tumulty

[The White House] July 2, 1915

Secretary Lansing writes me[1] in reply to your telegram[2] as follows: "I have just received your letter containing a copy of a cipher telegram from the President relative to an effort to obtain an agreement to an armistice from Carranza. I can see no objection to attempting to do so, unless possible failure would affect our influence. I myself doubt very much whether Carranza would consent to an armistice on account of the military operations which are proceeding against the City of Mexico; in fact, I doubt very much whether his generals would consent even if he were willing at the present time to cease hostilities. As you know, Shanklin with O'Connor of the Red Cross are attempting to get through a trainload of provisions to the city which may, if they succeed, in large measure relieve the situation. In view of our later dispatches the condition in Mexico does not seem to be as desperate as it has been reported to us; in fact, starvation does not exist there at the present time, though it is imminent within the next three or four weeks. If the President desires, however, telegrams can be sent to Vera Cruz and Mexico City insisting that the two factions come to an agreement as to an armistice, but there should also be included in the telegrams the grounds for our insistence which, it seems to me, are not in these circumstances easy to be defined."   Tumulty.

T telegram (WP, DLC).
  1 RL to JPT, July 2, 1915, CCL (SDR, RG 59, 812.00/15410½, DNA).
  2 Wilson's coded message was: "Do you think in view of the Brazilian Minister's telegram of June 30th from Mexico City there would be any possibility of even now obtaining some results by insisting to Carranza upon an armistice such as is suggested in that message?" Quoted in JPT to RL, July 2, 1915, TLS (SDR, RG 59, 812.00/15410½, DNA).

Four Letters to Robert Lansing

My dear Mr. Secretary,   [Cornish, N.H.] 2 July, 1915.

The policy clearly indicated here[1] is not only disappointing: it is disgusting. I thing [think] I have never known of a man more impossible to deal with on human principles that [than] this man Carranza.   Faithfully Yours,   W.W.

WWTLI (SDR, RG 59, 812.00/15409½, DNA).
  1 See the Enclosure printed with RL to WW, June 24, 1915.

My dear Mr. Secretary,   [Cornish, N. H.] 2 July, 1915.

These suggestions of Gerard's[1] seem to me entirely unwise, or, at the least, impossible of acceptance, as, I dare say, they seem to you. But if you have any thought that something might be done, I would be very much indebted to you if you would indicate it.   Faithfully Yours,   W.W.

WWTLI (SDR, RG 59, 763.72/1961½, DNA).
  1 J. W. Gerard to RL, June 24, 1915, printed as an Enclosure with RL to WW, June 25, 1915 (first letter of that date).

My dear Mr. Secretary,   [Cornish, N. H.] 2 July, 1915.

This is exceedingly interesting.[1] Evidently it will be wise to keep a vigilant eye open down there, especially in these days when everything is in solution and there is no one point of intrigue which it is sufficieyt [sufficient] to watch.

Faithfully Yours,   W.W.

WWTLI (SDR, RG 59, 894.20212/87½, DNA).
[1] L. J. Canova to RL, June 19, 1915, TLS (SDR, RG 59, 894.20212/85½, DNA), which listed attempts of certain Japanese subjects to acquire territory in the western hemisphere between 1910 and 1915. Most instances concerned individual buyers, and the State Department had failed to prove involvement by the Japanese government. Of particular moment were contacts between the Japanese and Carranza and the presence of Japanese ships off the coast of Central and South America.

My dear Mr. Secretary,   [Cornish, N. H.] 2 July, 1915.

After you have had a chance to read and reflect fully upon Mr. Fuller's report,[1] I would very much value an expression of your opinion as to what ought to be done in Haiti, and how it ought to be done. It gives me a good deal of concern. Action is evidently necessary and no doubt it would be a mistake to postpone it long.

Faithfully Yours,   W.W.

WWTLI (SDR, RG 59, 838.00/1197, DNA).
[1] Paul Fuller, Jr., to RL, June 14, 1915, TLS (SDR, RG 59, 838.00/1197, DNA). Fuller reported on his Haitian trip in minute chronological detail, from his arrival on May 14 until his departure on June 5, in order to show the difficulties of negotiating a treaty with President Sam and his Secretary of Foreign Affairs, Ulrick du Vivier. Fuller's objective was to gain consent to an agreement in principle before granting recognition, but the Haitian leaders feared that to bargain with the United States before being recognized would open them to criticism from rival factions. Furthermore, the Haitian cabinet sought certain changes in the proposed treaty. They wanted a promise that the customs service and all other offices collecting revenue would employ only Haitians. Whereas the United States offered to protect Haiti from foreign aggression and to suppress insurrection, Haitians sought to "have recourse to the aid of the American Government to suppress serious disorders" and to be able to order the removal of United States forces "upon the first formal request made by a constitutional authority." Fuller left Haiti because he could not, without consulting the State Department, accept terms that put the army and navy of the United States "in the position of lackeys to any foreign government."
In conclusion, Fuller expressed his belief that most factions would accept the terms of the treaty and that, in a short time, Sam's government would be forced to sign because of worsening conditions. If this did not occur, Fuller recommended intervention, as follows: "I feel and recommend that the United States should intervene by the landing of its marines and should take necessary steps to establish an honest and efficient administration. When this result has been accomplished, the United States should invite (and would unquestionably obtain) a Treaty along the lines of the Platt Amendment,—as preliminary to turning over the administration to the Haitians. This beneficent purpose could in my opinion be accomplished without loss of life and without loss of friendship. Only such a thorough re-organization as an American occupation would bring about, will in my opinion ever permanently change the present conditions which are destructive of freedom, of progress, of peace, and are intolerable to Haitians and foreigners alike."

From William Bauchop Wilson

My dear Mr. President: Washington July 2, 1915.

I have the honor to advise that I have today directed the arrest for deportation of Victoriano Huerta on the grounds that he is an alien unlawfully in the United States in that:

First: He has admitted the commission of a crime involving moral turpitude. This charge is based upon the theory that the arrest and incarceration of Madero and members of his cabinet was a crime involving moral turpitude and that his proclamation of February 18th, 1913, was an admission that he had committed the crime. . . .[1]

Second: He is a person who advocates or teaches the duty, necessity or propriety of the unlawful assaulting of officers of an organized government because of their official character. This charge is based upon the theory that the arrest and imprisonment of Madero and members of his cabinet and one hundred and ten deputies was an unlawful assault upon the officers of an organized government because of their official character, and that the arrest and imprisonment having been directed by Huerta constituted advocacy of the same by him.

Third: At the time of entry into the United States he was likely to become a public charge. This charge is based upon the theory that at the time of entry into the United States he was likely to engage in filibustering expeditions in violation of our neutrality laws and therefore likely to become a public charge by being imprisoned for the offence at public expense in one of our jails.

If these charges are sustained it is proposed to deport him to Spain, from whence he came to the United States.

Faithfully yours,   W B Wilson

TLS (EBR, RG 130, DNA).
[1] Wilson here gave the text of Huerta's proclamation.

From Franklin Knight Lane

Dear Mr President,   Washington [July 2, 1915]

I sent you yesterday memo. of a talk with Angeles. A duplicate was sent to Lansing. Angeles believes in the "thumb" theory.

Cordially   Franklin K. Lane

ALS (WP, DLC).

From Charles Richard Crane

Dear Mr President   [New York] July 2 1915

You made Mrs Crane very happy by your little friendly note.[1] Thank you! She is now sitting up and is to be out of the Hospital in a few days.

Mr President, wouldn't you like to ask Jane[2] to come to see you soon after she returns? The women are very proud of her and I feel that she has gotten by the very dangerous work they crowded her into with a great deal of grace and dignity.[3] Of course she is the best we have and has really been received everywhere as a spiritual messenger. Later on she and Mott may help you in a great service to the world. Added to her great spiritual power is wonderful wisdom and discretion. Every woman in the land and most men would be cheered by knowing that you and she were in conference.

I suppose that she will arrive on the St. Louis about Sunday.

This evening I am going to Wood's Hole with Secretary Houston to spend the Fourth with my children and grandchildren.

I want to get back the idea that there is something on the planet besides Germans and microbes. Just at present I feel a good deal like the astronomer at the Yerkes' observatory—ashamed of my planet. A serene Fourth to you and your family, dear Mr President!   Faithfully   Charles R. Crane

ALS (WP, DLC).
[1] WW to Cornelia W. S. Crane, June 29, 1915, TLS (Letterpress Books, WP, DLC).
[2] Jane Addams.
[3] Miss Addams had met with foreign ministers and other political leaders in The Hague, London, Berlin, Vienna, Budapest, Bern, Rome, Paris, and Le Havre as an envoy of the International Congress of Women. She reported on her experiences in a speech at Carnegie Hall on July 9, published as "The Revolt Against War," *The Survey*, XXXIV (July 17, 1915), 355-59.

A Telegram and a Letter to Edward Mandell House

Windsor Vt [July] 3/15

Advise that you should not see the man you question   I think those who are suggesting it are misled as to the facts   If you can get in touch with McAdoo he can tell you a great deal

Woodrow Wilson

T telegram (E. M. House Papers, CtY).

My dear Friend: Cornish, N. H., July 3, 1915

I am sincerely obliged to you for asking my advice about complying with Mrs. Harriman's suggestion. I think that Lane has been misled into being hopeful where there is little hope. Moreover, it has not yet been made at all clear to me what financial interests are back of Iturbide. I feel it very important that we should keep out of these things until something further is developed which will give us clear ground to walk on.

You don't know with what pleasure I look back to my little visit with you at Roslyn. It was refreshing and delightful, and rewarding, too. I hope that you and Mrs. House and all your little scattered family are well. We must get hold of each other again very soon.

Thank you for the letter from Grey. I am inclined to agree with the view he expresses.

Affectionately yours,   Woodrow Wilson

TLS (E. M. House Papers, CtY).

To Joseph Patrick Tumulty

My dear Tumulty: Cornish, N. H., July 3, 1915

I am heartily obliged to you for your telegrams. It is characteristic of you to keep my mind free by such messages. I am really having a most refreshing and rewarding time and am very thankful to get it. I hope that you are not having depressing weather in Washington and that you are finding it possible to make satisfactory arrangements for the family, so that we can have the pleasure of having you with us at the White House when I get back.

With warmest messages from us all,

Affectionately yours,   Woodrow Wilson

TLS (J. P. Tumulty Papers, DLC).

From William Bauchop Wilson

My dear Mr. President: Washington July 3, 1915.

Referring to my letter to you of yesterday, I have the honor to state that after issuing the warrant for the arrest of Huerta I had a talk with the Attorney General who informed me that the Department of Justice had the situation well in hand and that proceedings under the immigration law at this time might embarrass it in the conduct of the pending case. I therefore immediatcly gave instructions to the supervising inspector at El Paso not to serve the warrant of arrest unless Huerta attempted to cross the border into Mexico. Our officials there have been instructed to assist in keeping Huerta under surveillance. The warrant will be held in abeyance ready to serve at any time it is deemed advisable, after consultation with the Department of Justice, to take Huerta into custody for deportation.

I may add that the warrant was not issued until after a conference with Secretary Lansing and Mr. Long, of the State Department, and Mr. Warren, of the Department of Justice.

We have sufficient evidence in the possession of the Department to justify the issuance of the warrant. When arrested he would remain in custody unless or until the Secretary of the Department exercises his discretion to admit him to bail. This authority has never been questioned. Section 20 of the immigration law states "that any alien who shall enter the United States in violation of law, and such as become public charges from causes existing prior to landing, shall, upon the warrant of the Secretary of Labor, be taken into custody and deported to the country whence he came at any time within three years after the date of his entry into the United States. * * * Provided, That pending the final disposal of the case of any alien so taken into custody he may be released under a bond in the penalty of not less than five hundred dollars with security approved by the Secretary of Labor * * * .

Faithfully yours,   W B Wilson

TLS (EBR, RG 130, DNA).

To Charles Richard Crane

My dear Friend: Cornish, N. H., July 3, 1915

Thank you with all my heart for your letter of July second.

I am delighted to know that Mrs. Crane is making such good progress. Please give her my most affectionate regards and congratulations.

Of course, I will try to see Miss Addams, though it is impossible to see her here and I am doubtful when I shall get back to Washington. I shall certainly try to manage the connection.

I am delighted that you are going off for for [sic] the Fourth and that Houston is to have the pleasure of your company. My warmest and most affectionate messages to you both.

Faithfully yours,   Woodrow Wilson

TLS (Letterpress Books, WP, DLC).

To Lillian D. Wald

My dear Miss Wald: Cornish, N. H., July 3, 1915

I understand that Miss Jane Addams is to return tomorrow and it would give me a great deal of pleasure to see her upon her return if I can do so after my return to Washington. I am afraid it is impossible to manage it here with convenience to both of us. Will you not be kind enough to let me know just how long Miss Addam's stay in New York is likely to be?

Cordially and sincerely yours,   Woodrow Wilson

TLS (J. Addams Papers, PSC-P).

From Furnifold McLendel Simmons

My dear Mr. President: New Bern, N. C., July 3rd, 1915.

I am writing you simply to say that I think the feeling against the flagrant violation of our rights upon the high seas by Great Britain is growing very strong and as soon as you should deem the time opportune a vigorous note of assertion and protest would, I think, meet the hearty approval of the people.

Respectfully,   F. M. Simmons

TLS (WP, DLC).

From Samuel Huston Thompson, Jr.

Dear Mr. President: Sunbury, Pa., July 3rd, 1915

As I told you a few weeks ago I have now been on the Chautauqua for ten days. Most of the time I have been up here in this hide bound Republican neighborhood. It would astonish and delight you as it does me to see how the people are following you with the implicit faith of a child towards its father. Their attitude toward you as a personalty is very similiar to their reverence for the memory of Lincoln. It is no longer simply admiration but rather a deep confiding faith. Each day after I have finished speaking these good people who are the very salt of the earth come up to me and with a look in their eyes that would bring a mist over yours, say "God bless the man in the White House. We voted against him or we voted for him but whether we voted for or against we believe in him implicitly." I think every speaker on the Chautauqua mentions your name and every time there is a thunder of applause.

I have yet to find a single individual that wants war and the impression I get is that they will want you to stretch the tether of our national patience till the last thread breaks before we shall go to war.

Though I am only a humble public official still because I come from Washington and belong to the administration, I am supposed to see you frequently and thus the people each day ask me to tell you various messages the import of which I have already described. It is for this reason and also because I know it will cheer and sustain you to know public opinion is with you that I write.

I find the Prohibition idea is growing very rapidly in this exceedingly wet community.

With affectionate admiration I am

Very sincerely yours   Huston Thompson.

ALS (WP, DLC).

To William Bauchop Wilson

My dear Mr. Secretary: Cornish, N. H., July 5, 1915

Thank you sincerely for your letter of July third about the deportation of General Huerta. I feel that his detention, or, at least, the prevention of his entering Mexico, is of the utmost importance and I am sincerely obliged to you for the way in which you have been cooperating with the Department of Justice.

Cordially and sincerely yours,   Woodrow Wilson

TLS (Letterpress Books, WP, DLC).

To Anne Leddell Seward

My dear Miss Seward: Cornish, N. H., July 5, 1915

I am sincerely obliged to you for your letter of July second,[1] which I have read with a great deal of interest, and I shall take the liberty, if I may, of asking the Secretary of State to send someone who is entirely trustworthy but who will attract no attention to Kennebunk Port to see you, so that he may learn fully from you what you think, I believe rightly, we should look into.

May I not say that you seem to me to have performed a public duty in a very considerate and admirable way?

Cordially and sincerely yours,   Woodrow Wilson

TLS (Letterpress Books, WP, DLC).
    [1] The letter is missing in all known collections. However, in it Miss Seward told of meeting a man in Kennebunkport who had told her that he was a secret German agent and had planned the destruction of *Lusitania.* Subsequent

investigation revealed that the man, Commander Franz Rintelen von Kleist, was the head of a German sabotage ring. About this far-flung matter and its impact on the administration and on public opinion when the story was published in the newspapers, see Link, *Struggle for Neutrality*, pp. 561-63, and Reinhard R. Doerries, *Washington-Berlin, 1908/1917* . . . (Düsseldorf, 1975), *passim*. Rintelen told his own story in *The Dark Invader* . . . (London, 1933).

To Robert Lansing

My dear Mr. Secretary   [The White House, c. July 5, 1915]

This puzzles me. Is there any way in which, through your Dept. and the British Embassy, you could have the sender of this identified for me and a clue obtained to his object?

W.W.

I would like your advice how to treat this.

ALI (R. Lansing Coll., NjP).

From Joseph Patrick Tumulty

The White House, July 5, 1915

Following code telegram from United States Attorney Camp[1] at El Paso this afternoon:

"Arrived El Paso Sunday. Huerta and associates still in jail. Can make bond in any reasonable amount. Will probably be released on bond Tuesday. To successfully guard Huerta when released on bond practically impossible. His following in El Paso strong. We can get but little assistance from Police. Believed Huerta can take Juarez without resistance. Huerta ought to be held in detention and removed from border in order to prevent conferences. In my judgment, this can only be done by holding him for deportation or extradition and his removal for safe keeping."

Opinion of Solicitor-General and Secretary of State that if Huerta released on bond Tuesday, on this (his?) second arrest all available present criminal process will have been exhausted. Deportation believed to be unavailable under the statute. Retention for extradition by Governor of Texas possible but if resorted to would probably be regarded by the public as recognition of Villista authorities.   J. P. Tumulty.

T telegram (EBR, RG 130, DNA).
[1] J. L. Camp.

From Robert Lansing

CONFIDENTIAL.

Dear Mr. President: Washington July 5, 1915.

The Mexican situation has been much in my mind and I have been seeking to map out a course of action which will lead to definite results.

The condition precedent to any plan is, of course, that the old aristocratic party must not be recognized in a settlement of the present situation and that the restoration of responsible government must come through the revolutionary element now composed of hostile factions.

The problem is, therefore, the harmonizing of the factions representing the Revolution.

The present activities in this country of the reactionary Mexican element, manifested by the intrigues along the border, have and will have, I believe, a decided influence on the tendency of the revolutionists to unite and will induce them to listen more favorably to a plan of compromise, and this influence will be stronger if the reactionaries obtain a foothold in Mexico. However this influence will be more potent in the North than in the South which is not immediately affected by the reactionary movement. This difficulty is further increased by the character of General Carranza and the present successes of his military forces.

As you know the suggestion has undoubtedly by this time been made to Carranza that he invite the various revolutionary factions to meet in conference, discuss their differences and seek to compose them, each faction in such conference to be represented by only *one* conferee. The idea of the conference is to be consultative and in no sense conventional, thus eliminating any question of majority rule.

If Carranza adopts this suggestion and invites the other factions to confer, an armistice might be proposed during the progress of the conference, for I am convinced that the factions will accept the invitation.

In view, however, of the conditions prevailing in the South and the probable success of the Carranzista arms, together with the stubbornness of Carranza himself, I have little hope that he will adopt the suggestion for a conference or agree to an armistice. I think, therefore, we should plan to act on the supposition that a conference of the revolutionary factions will not take place.

On this supposition I would suggest that the attitude of this Government be embodied in the following propositions:

1. It is manifest that, in view of the personal animosities, jealousies and ambitions of the factional leaders nothing can be accomplished through them to restore peace and stable government.

2. Carranza, Villa, and other factional leaders must retire and not seek dominant leadership.

3. This Government will not recognize as legal any government headed or controlled by any one of these leaders and will exert its moral influence to prevent the establishment of such a government in any part of Mexico.

4. The determination of this Government to eliminate the present factional leaders by withdrawal of moral support should be notified in plain terms to the various factions.

5. An invitation should be issued to the factions by the American Government, agreeing to identical action, to meet in conference through their lesser chiefs for the purpose of organizing a coalition provisional government with the understanding that, provided such government is unquestionably representative of the bulk of the revolutionary element, this Government and the other governments cooperating with it, will recognize it and renew diplomatic relations with Mexico.

6. This Government will aid so far as possible such coalition government by preventing arms and ammunition from reaching parties hostile to it and by employing such other means as it may properly employ to insure the stability and permanency of such government until constitutional government can be restored.

This outline of action I submit with hesitation since there has been no opportunity to discuss the matter with you. It may, however, serve as a basis for discussion.

Faithfully yours,   Robert Lansing

TLS (SDR, RG 59, 812.00/15410½A, DNA).

To Abbott Lawrence Lowell

My dear President Lowell: Cornish, N. H., July 5, 1915

I sincerely appreciate your letter of June thirtieth. Its full recognition of the delicacy of the situation so far as I am concerned was what I would have expected of you and I am warmly obliged to you for letting me see the important resolutions passed by the League to Enforce Peace.

Cordially and sincerely yours,   Woodrow Wilson

TLS (A. L. Lowell Papers, MH-Ar).

From Edward Mandell House, with Enclosure

Manchester,
Dear Governor: Massachusetts. July 5th, 1915.

Before I received your telegram I had decided not to see Iturbide, and after Mrs. Harriman arrived I persuaded her that it would not be a good thing for Iturbide himself or for the Mexican situation in general.

She brought them both down from Washington as far as Beverly, but I am told, they are content with the excuse I gave.

Billy Phillips was here yesterday and we discussed among other things the Mexican situation. He believes, and so does Lansing I hear, that the situation grows more dangerous day by day. He and Lansing suggested that some man acting for the Government, see the heads of the different factions, centered around New York, and keep in touch with what is going on so you might have a more intelligent idea of it. They thought Paul Fuller would fulfil this mission admirably if he would undertake it.

I have asked Lansing here for the next week end and I hope he may be able to come so we may all work together, not only in the Mexican but the South American matter[1] in order that we may take as much of the load from you as possible.

If you will indicate what you want me to do in any of these problems, it will be a great pleasure for me to give them active attention and to report to you as they progress.

I have a letter from Gerard which you may find interesting.

I have been hoping that you and your entire household might find it pleasant to motor from Cornish to Manchester and be with us for a few days. Our house is large enough to care for you all.

Affectionately yours, E. M. House

TLS (WP, DLC).
[1] That is, the proposed Pan-American treaty.

ENCLOSURE

James Watson Gerard to Edward Mandell House

My dear Colonel: Berlin, June 16, 1915.

I have received your letter of June 5th dated from Liverpool.

I think that the firm tone of the President's note will make the Germans climb down. There seems to be a general disposition to be pleased with the note and an expectation that matters can be arranged. The great danger is that the Germans may again get the idea that we do not dare declare war. In such case they will again become difficult to handle.

Von Gwinner[1] said yesterday that if the "Mauretania" sailed it would be treated like the "Lusitania." Zimmermann and von Jagow are both quite pleased with the tone of the note. They both talk now of keeping Belgium, the excuse being that the Belgians hate the Germans so that if Belgium again became independent it would only be an English outpost.

Meyer Gerhard has arrived and has broken into print over the sentiment in America; I am afraid he makes it too peaceful and therefore the Germans will be encouraged to flout America.

I am sorry to report that while authorities here think the idea of freedom of the seas good, they think the idea of freedom of land too vague. They want to know exactly what it means and say the seas should be free because they belong to no one, but land is private property of various nations, and compare the situation to a city street where everyone is interested in keeping the streets free, but would resent a proposal that their houses should also be made common meeting ground if not property.

Unfortunately for Germany and the world, the German armies are winning and this will be considered a complete vindication of the military and caste system and everything which now exists. As Cleveland said, we are confronted by a condition and not a theory. *Germany will never agree directly or indirectly to any freedom of land or disarmament proposal.*

I think everything will work out all right on the Lusitania note and that Bryan will regret leaving and losing part of the credit for a success.

The Emperor will probably see me soon. He has been rabid on the delivery of arms from the U. S. A. question, but like all Germans, when they see we cannot be scared into a change of policy, he is making a nice recovery.

I am glad to see that there is a prospect of Mexico settling. If the President desires I can possibly be of help in getting Lord Cowdrey, Guggenheim and other employers of labor there to take on full crews of laborers, and more, in order to absorb the contending armies, which otherwise would have to continue fighting for a livlihood.

Von Jagow and Zimmermann wish to be remembered to you.

Yours as ever,   James W. Gerard

TCL (WP, DLC).

[1] Arthur von Gwinner, head of the Deutsche Bank, the central bank of Germany.

To Samuel Huston Thompson, Jr.

My dear Thompson: Cornish, N. H., July 6, 1915

It was certainly an act of thoughtful kindness on your part to write me your letter of June third from Sunbury. I thank you for it with all my heart. It has warmed and comforted and encouraged me.

I hope that you are having a fine time lecturing and are enjoying it to the full, though it must be hard work.

Cordially and sincerely yours,   Woodrow Wilson

TLS (S. H. Thompson, Jr., Papers, DLC).

From Robert Lansing

Washington D C July 6 1915

Phillips states Colonel House anxious for me to spend next Saturday and Sunday the tenth and eleventh with him at Manchester. While most anxious to see him do not feel I should leave here unless you return before that time. Kindly advise me.

Robert Lansing

T telegram (WP, DLC).

To Robert Lansing

My dear Mr. Secretary,   [Cornish, N. H.] 7 July, 1915.

I feel, as I have no doubt you also do, that the situation in Mexico grows daily more serious and dangerous. What would you think of designating someone (my choice would be Mr. Paul Fuller, Senior) to keep in touch with the representatives of the several factions so far as they are represented in this country, establish confidential relations with them, if possible, and so be our eyes and ears to watch for an opening for action?

I make this suggestion in the hope that it will commend itself to you.   Faithfully Yours,   W.W.

WWTLI (SDR, RG 59, 812.00/15411½, DNA).

To Edward Mandell House

My dear Friend,   [Cornish, N. H.] 7 July, 1915.

This letter from Gerard is practically a duplicate of one he sent me, enclosure and all.¹ It does not "set us much forreder," does it?

I feel, with Phillips and Lansing, that the Mexican situation grows ominously worse and more threatening day by day, and I have felt, the last few days, as if it were more likely to draw me soon back to Washington than even our correspondence with Germany. I wish most heartily that Lansing could spare you a day but I fear he will feel that he cannot come away until I return.

I like your suggestion about having some man we can trust keep in touch with the factions through their representatives in this country, and I am handing it on to the Secretary of State to-day, in a letter I have just written him

I am well and am profiting immensely by my delightful vacation, the first real one I have had since I went into politics.

Affectionately Yours,   Woodrow Wilson

WWTLS (E. M. House Papers, CtY).
1 This letter is missing.

From Robert Lansing

Washington, D. C., July 7, 1915

In view of usual delay in communicating with Berlin, I considered an immediate answer to Gerard regarding preliminary negotiations should be sent at once. I, therefore, sent the following telegram:

"July 6; 7:00 evening. American Embassy, Berlin. The suggestion contained in your 2543[1] and 2544[2] are receiving attentive consideration. The belief in Germany as reported in your 2544 regarding the resignation of Mr. Bryan is entirely erroneous. Mr. Bryan is not endeavoring to influence public opinion against this Government, and he will support the President. As far as one can judge, the country is almost unanimous in its hearty support of the President. We do not think it advisable at present to enter into negotiations on the subject of the German reply. The position of the United States was fully set forth in its instruction to you of June ninth and we do not feel that the principles upon which this statement stands can be properly the subject of preliminary negotiations. Lansing."

You will perceive that this telegram permits a change of attitude if it seems desirable to you to have Gerard negotiate on the subject. My personal opinion is that Gerard, judging from his previous expressions favoring the German proposals, ought not to be given any latitude in the negotiations if you consider it wise to proceed with them.[3] I am afraid that the principle for which we contend would be sacrificed by him in order to reach a compromise to which Germany would agree. To recede on any of our assertions of principle ought not, in my opinion, to be considered.

If Germany would admit the correctness of the principle asserted by this Government, a negotiation for its application to present conditions might be advisable.   Robert Lansing.

T telegram (WP, DLC).

¹ J. W. Gerard to RL, July 3, 1915, *FR-WWS 1915*, pp. 459-60. Gerard reported the contents of a draft of the German note which assured protection for *American* ships and American lives on neutral vessels, took it for granted that the United States Government would guarantee that American ships with passengers aboard carried no contraband, and suggested increasing the number of neutral ships under the American flag. If this was not possible, the German government was quite ready to discuss the use of belligerent ships "which in such case should be put under the American flag." Speaking personally, Gerard had indicated that the terms did not answer the questions raised by the *Lusitania* case and that he did not for a moment believe that his government would forbid United States ships to carry contraband. He then explained to Lansing some changes that he might be able to bring about if he were given the latitude to negotiate with the Germans.

² J. W. Gerard to RL, July 4, 1915, *FR-WWS 1915*, p. 460, explaining his previous telegram in view of German perceptions of the consequences of Bryan's resignation. Germans universally believed that Bryan would become the leader of a party favorable to Germany and force adoption of an embargo on arms and ammunition and acceptance of unrestricted submarine warfare. Given this belief, Gerard continued, it was necessary that the terms between Germany and the United States be negotiated carefully rather than stated finally. "A mere formal exchange of notes between Germany and our Government," he concluded, "will inevitably lead to a break."

³ Unknown to Lansing and Wilson, Gerard had helped Von Jagow to draft the terms proposed for the German reply. See Link, *Struggle for Neutrality*, pp. 436-37.

To Robert Lansing¹

Windsor, Vermont. July 7, 1915.

Papers received. Am I right in supposing that message from Vienna is merely gratuitous advice from the Austrian Government as to our duty as neutrals?²

In regard to the message from Gerard³ I would suggest if your own judgment coincides that we instruct him to convey unofficially to the Imperial Government our determination not to yield or compromise in any way our rights as neutrals or prestige of our citizens but our hearty willingness to exercise our good offices with regard to effecting any arrangements which will open the sea to common use with as little danger as possible to non-belligerents, keeping these two things entirely distinct, namely, our rights, which we cannot abate, and our services as friends of all parties. We will discuss anything that it is reasonable and practicable to discuss except the curtailment of our clear and established rights.¹   Woodrow Wilson.

T telegram (SDR, RG 59, 763.72/1962½, DNA).

¹ There is a WWsh draft of this telegram in WP, DLC, and a WWT draft in the C. L. Swem Coll., NjP.

² S. Burián von Rajecz to F. C. Penfield, June 29, 1915, *FR-WWS 1915*, pp.

791-93. The Austro-Hungarian Foreign Minister urged the United States to correct the imbalance in its export of arms and ammunition by changing the law to maintain strict parity between both belligerent parties and by forcing the Allies to abandon their illegal blockade.

3 RL to WW, July 7, 1915, T telegram (WP, DLC), transmitting J. W. Gerard to RL, July 5, 1915. In the latest draft of the German note, Gerard wrote, the United States Government would be asked to guarantee that munitions were not carried on ships exempted from visitation, while the German government would promise to let at least one belligerent ship each week pass without attack, if again guarantees could be given that these ships carried no contraband. Gerard asked to be informed about his government's attitude toward the propositions before Germany sent the note, although he doubted that the Germans would make any more concessions. He sought authority to say that, if the note was accepted, it would be on the understanding that Germany would stop its propaganda concerning the export of arms, or at least that it put an end to its anti-American propaganda.

4 This was sent to Gerard in RL to J. W. Gerard, July 8, 1915, T telegram (SDR, RG 59, 763.72/1924, DNA), printed in *FR-WWS 1915*, p. 462.

To Mary Allen Hulbert

Dear Friend,   [Cornish, N. H.] 7 July, 1915.

I am glad the packing and getting ready are done! And how splendidly you have risen to the occasion, as usual, and accepted it with spirit and entire courage. It is like you, and I have no doubt you will be of the greatest possible assistance and inspiration to Allen.

Our thoughts will follow you with the most affectionate interest and solicitude. Please let us know when you get there just how the journey went, how you have fared, and what you have found at the journey's end. This is just a message of the most affectionate good-bye. Los Angeles seems a very long way off, and we shall miss you. But we know that you are doing the right thing and the only thing consistent with your happiness, and so are not unhappy but full of sympathy and hope.

                    Your devoted friend,   Woodrow Wilson

WWTLS (WP, DLC).

From Lindley Miller Garrison

                              Washington D C July 7 1915

Attorney General wants me to furnish quarters at Fort Bliss near El Paso, where Huerta and the deputy marshals may stay until further legal proceedings ensue. Custody is to be that of civil not military authorities. Latter merely furnishing lodging and subsistence. Having no original jurisdiction and not being charged with any initiative in the matter I desire to avoid doing anything which may complicate and confuse the situation or the plans of those managing it, and therefore await your decision as to whether you desire me to act as the Attorney General has requested. Would appreciate immediate reply.

Garrison.

Your telegram received. Request that you act as Attorney General desires.[1]

T telegram (EBR, RG 130, DNA).
[1] Wilson's reply.

From Walter Hines Page

Dear Mr. President: London, July 7, 1915

The King told me to-day after more than a half-hour's talk about the war that in his opinion the Germans would force us in. They will not stop their submarine work nor will they be too careful about their victims. They think they can do the English real harm in this way, and they also hope to stop the shipment of munitions from the United States. He had it from a trustworthy source that when the German Note to our Government was under discussion in Berlin, von Tirpitz even browbeat the Emperor in his earnestness about the submarine warfare—almost threatened the Emperor, in fact, for seeming to differ with him. "I know von Tirpitz and I know the Emperor," said the King, "and this is just what I should expect to happen."

"By coming in," he went on, "you will gain two things—first and less, a financial saving. The war is dislocating your trade and you are losing. You will shorten the war and thus save loss. Second and far more important, you will throw your moral weight against this predatory system of Germany; and the English-speaking world will be drawn together for all time as a controlling force in the world against the recurrence of such an outbreak. Your great influence is needed, for Russia is yet a very backward nation.

"But war is not to be entered into lightly and I admire the President's patience and forbearance. But you will find that the arrogance of the Germans has no limit and they will force you in. If you do come in, I wish it understood how deep my appreciation of your great nation's help will be."

He apologized for not having seen me for several months. "I did not seem to wish to express my real feelings in the delicacy of the situation." And he told me of his several talks with House, which he thoroughly enjoyed. He said much else as we sat by his desk, and he showed a pretty clear notion of the state of feel-

ing in the U. S. and, unlike some Englishmen that I run across,
he has a very high value of the aid the U. S. could bring—a very
high value. He confessed that for the moment the military situation does not look favourable to the Allies; and it was pleasant to
hear his hearty praise of the French.

I suppose half the new Cabinet have spoken to me their hope
that we may "see a way," as one of their phrases is, to come in.
And they all value the moral effect more than the military or
substantial help, high as some of them rate that. They want the
judgment of the U. S. expressed against the Germans. Balfour,
Bonar Law, Lloyd George, Chamberlain, Churchill, Crewe, and
(by an easy inference) Grey have all said this to me, and Carson
too. Carson is the new Attorney-General. Three or four weeks
ago, I met him at dinner where old Princess Henry of Batten-
burg was also a guest. She's the most vigorous and outspoken and
most masculine of King Edward's horde of sisters. Carson was in
a rather gay mood, having no public responsibilities then and he
amused himself by explaining to the Princess and me—as at my
expense—how the war had utterly made an end of the old thing
that we used to call International Law. (This was before the
Lusitania's sinking.) "The Ambassador tries to keep it alive, but,
I tell you, Sir, it's shot to pieces. We'll have to make it all over
again," & so on & so on, in his bantering way. Carson is the brute
of the Ulster rebellion, a great lawyer and a holy terror; and this
was in his playful mood. Well, a week or more ago, after he had
been Attorney-General for a week, I met him again. He took me
off in the corner of the room and said: "I discover that there are
some interesting, friendly differences between our Governments.
I wish to come and see you presently to discuss some of them—
may I?" "Yes, Sir Edward," said I, "come and we'll see if we can
save any shreds of international law—will you?"

"I will!"

He hasn't come. So I am inviting him to dinner.

They're all in a most earnest mood to clean the docket—our
docket with them. I say "all"—I suppose that this includes
Kitchener, out of whom I've never got much; and he knows no
law. But he has lately been expressing himself towards us in quite
a human fashion. Lord Crewe, in charge of the Foreign Office for
a month while Sir Edw. Grey has gone off to rest his eyes, wh.
had failed him, is very friendly and eager. I rehearsed our several
groups of shipping troubles to him the other day and he said:
"I am interested to notice how exactly your statement of them
corresponds to Grey's."

There is one military fact, or plan, that has a bearing on the

British hope that we may come into the war—so, at least, I can't keep from suspecting, altho' no one in authority has ever made an allusion to it in my hearing. Of course the English are doing all they can to get Holland in: I have no doubt of that. Yet I do not know what they are doing. Now Germany has treated Holland much as she has treated us, without (I suspect) being even as polite as she has been to us. Now if we shd. be forced into war, by the same token the English hope that Holland also will come in. If Holland come in, her territory will become a base for a new military move against Germany. Badly as men are needed in France, England now has an army of about a million men in camps on this island—why? And she has been building a great fleet of shallow transports such as she uses in sending troops to France, and shallow big-gun boats—a kind of monitors —what for? The conclusion is irresistible that she is prepared to land this army somewhere—and not in France.

Such an army landed in Holland, with a naval base also in the Zuyder Zee would be the best way to cause the withdrawal of the German army from France back across the Rhine. If we shd. so act as to help Holland to admit such an army, *that* wd. greatly shorten the war.

The psychological state of these people, as I make it out, is not a feeling of hatred—not personal hatred of Germans, but rather an unbounded indignation and undying hatred of the German system and methods. The Bryce report,[1] the use of deadly gases, the killing of English wounded, the Zeppelin raids on unfortified places—these have done their work; and towards the German system, there will be no mercy shown. All the ferocity that the English character has is aroused. If they have their way, the Prussian dynasty and military order will perish.

I haven't felt like breaking in on you during these anxious weeks—especially since House had nothing to do but to tell you everything that he knew and that I knew, too. Peace? God save us, not till France and Germany and Austria become like Servia

[1] *Report of the Committee on Alleged German Outrages Appointed by His Britannic Majesty's Government and Presided Over by the Right Hon. Viscount Bryce* (London, 1915). Appointed in December 1914 to consider evidence about alleged atrocities during the war, Bryce and his committee released their report in May 1915. It listed specific instances of German "outrages" against civilians in Belgium as reported by refugees and examples of breaches of the rules of war in France as recorded by British soldiers. The committee concluded its work with the plea that care be taken after the war that never again could such a military policy as Germany's be pursued. However, it claimed that the killing of noncombatants was deliberate policy in the German army, and the lurid details of the report had the immediate impact of intensifying anti-German feelings in Great Britain and abroad. For the best evaluation of the Bryce Report, see James Morgan Read, *Atrocity Propaganda, 1914-1919* (New Haven, Conn., 1941), especially pp. 201-209.

and Belgium and Poland—lands without men, where women bewail their fate and see their children die of hunger. It will be so bad that it will not be difficult to arrange a plan—a paper-plan at least—to prevent its recurrence. But all these men must first be killed. Perhaps 3,000,000 to 5,000,000 have already been killed outright and perhaps 20,000 [000] are now under arms or are ready to be marched out. When 10,000,000 more are dead—perhaps peace—perhaps not. The men in the trenches were said to want peace till the Germans began to kill the wounded and to use gases. These things bred a new fury.

There will be a vast waste in mid-Europe and the Fiji Islander who comes on a Cook's tour next year or the next will be told by his guide—"That desert was Europe."

Sincerely Yours   Walter H. Page

P.S. Of course the Coalition Government is only one expression of the whole British Empire's renewed resolve. If this fail, there is no alternative. These are the ablest public men in all Britain—of all parties. There's nobody to fall back on: the last good horse is hitched to the waggon.   W.H.P.

ALS (WP, DLC).

From Josephus Daniels

Dear Mr. President: Washington. July 7th, 1915.

I was glad to get your letter and your suggestion about Cary Grayson, who, if he had the place that would please me best, would be Surgeon General of the Navy. In the absence of Dr. Braisted[1] it is not clear what can be done, and I do not like to speak to anybody else. When Braisted returns we will look into the law and do anything that is possible. He will be as anxious to give promotion and recognition to Grayson as we are and will help to find a way or make one.

To-morrow we will take over the Sayville station.[2] Secretary Lansing gave me your letter[3] and this afternoon Capt. Bullard,[4] chief of the radio service, went over to New York. To-morrow he will go to Sayville.

On the Fourth I was at the seashore in North Carolina where my wife and boys have gone for a few weeks. It was a real happiness to find the depths of confidence which the people feel in you. It must be a comfort to you as well as a burden, for when you realize that the people feel you will be able to lead the country into peace with honor that very thought must add to your sense of responsibility and your cry for wisdom.

Everything here is quiet. The weather is delightfully cool. I hope you are getting strength and rest, as well as enjoyment, in your vacation and your freedom to stay out of doors free from observation.

Affectionately your friend,   Josephus Daniels

ALS (WP, DLC).

1 William Clarence Braisted, M.D., surgeon-general and chief of the Bureau of Medicine and Surgery for the U. S. Navy since February 1914.
2 The Sayville radio station, located on Long Island, was owned by the Atlantic Communication Co., which in turn was owned by Germany's two leading electrical companies. At the outbreak of war, the station came under the supervision of the Navy Department, and the operators were required to file all codes and every message with naval censors. Rumors circulated in the late spring of 1915 that messages between the German Admiralty and submarines were being transmitted from the station. When the owners sought a new license for two new powerful transmitting towers, their request was denied on the ground of German ownership, and the navy took over the station. New York Times, July 1 and 8, 1915.
3 It is missing.
4 William Hannum Grubb Bullard.

From Robert Lansing

Washington, D. C., July 8, 1915

The suggestion as to engaging a person to keep in touch with representatives of Mexican factions here seems to me very wise and Mr. Fuller (seems) to be the best fitted. I will, if you desire, ask him to come and see me although I think a communication from you would be more effective in view of the fact that he would be your personal agent in the matter. I assume from your note of the seventh that you had not then received my letter suggesting a course of action in Mexico. I have seen the six diplomats who are communicating with their governments in regard to informal conversations. They all seemed to be personally gratified at the proposed identical action and believed that their governments would readily authorize them to confer.

Robert Lansing.

T telegram (WP, DLC).

To Robert Lansing

My dear Mr. Secretary,   [Cornish, N. H.] 8 July, 1915.

You were right in thinking that I had not received your letter of the fifth, containing your interesting suggestions about Mexico, when I sent you my message of the seventh. I think that in any case, however, Mr. Fuller would serve us admirably in the way I indicated, not only, but also in preparing the way, cautiously and tactfully, for what we intend to do. I would be very much obliged if you would ask him if he can do us this great additional service saying that you do so at my request and advice, as well as on your own judgment.

The suggestions contained in your letter of the fifth furnish an excellent foundation, it seems to me, for planning something definite and final in the Mexican matter, and run very nearly along the lines of my own thought. I would like you to consider the following:

What did Angeles and Bonilla have in mind? I suppose they are still in Washington, or near at hand; and it seems to me that, directly or indirectly, we ought to know everything that is in their mind, especially now that the Huerta cloud has again appeared on the horizon.

Do you know whether Iturbide really represents any-thing substantial? Is it possible that he is in any way in cooperation with the scoundrel, Huerta?

Is there not reason to fear that without the present factional leaders, who seem to represent the strongest that has been thrown to the surface, we would be in a wallow of weaknesses and jealousies down there, unless some man (perhaps Angeles) could be commended by our confidence to the trust of the rest?

Should not the conference proposed in case Carranza does not act (as seems to me certain) be proposed by the A.B.C. group and their associates, and should not they and their associates in some way preside and direct at that conference?

We must be careful not to act in a way which will wound sensibilities. Villa has again and again offered to eliminate himself, and if it should come to our requesting all the present leaders to withdraw in order to effect a satisfactory settlement, these repeated offers should be made the most of and the leaders of the other factions challenged to follow his example. We must play these men as they are.

After the six diplomats we have sounded hear from their governments (assuming, as I think we may, that they will hear favourably) I think their advice will probably be of a good deal of service to us in determining just how to approach the men we shall have to deal with in the way that will be most likely to appeal to them and control them.

I shall be glad to have the benefit of memoranda on all or any of these matters, and thank you sincerely for the thought you are giving this perplexing matter.   Faithfully Yours,   W.W.

WWTLI (SDR, RG 59, 812.00/15412½, DNA).

To Furnifold McLendel Simmons

Private and Confidential.

My dear Senator: Cornish, N. H., July 8, 1915

I have your letter of July third.

I think I feel to the full the force of what you say, but I feel, also, that it would be nothing less than folly to press our neutral claims both against Germany and against Great Britain at one and the same time and so make our situation more nearly impossible.

We are, as a matter of fact constantly in communication with the British Government, pressing upon them our rights and the correction of their wrongs, and I think their position is slowly but steadily altering.

I hope sincerely that you are getting some real rest and refreshment.

Cordially and sincerely yours,   Woodrow Wilson

TLS (Letterpress Books, WP, DLC).

From Robert Lansing

Dear Mr. President: Washington July 8, 1915.

I think that we could dismiss the Austrian statement regarding the sale of arms and ammunition with an acknowledgement, as you suggest in your note of yesterday, but it seems to me that it offers an excellent opportunity to make a full and clear statement of our attitude. While the communication would be addressed to Vienna, we could by making the correspondence public present the matter in a favorable and, I believe, convincing way to the American people.

Home consumption would be the real purpose; and answer to Austria the nominal purpose.

Convinced of the strength of our position and the desirability of placing the case frankly before the people in order to remove the opposition to sales of war materials, which many persons have on moral grounds and not because of pro-German sympathy, it seems to me advisable to prepare an answer to the Austrian communication, which I will submit to you as soon as it is drafted.   Faithfully yours,   Robert Lansing

TLS (WP, DLC).

To Robert Lansing

My dear Mr. Secretary,   [Cornish, N. H.] 9 July, 1915.

I learn to-day from the representative of the Associated Press who accompanied me up here that the German note was deliv-[er]ed to Gerard late last evening.[1] I assume, therefore, that it will be in our hands, and in mine here, by Monday or Tuesday. I shall take a little while to mull over it before returning to Washington to confer with you about it.

May I not suggest that while I am getting my ideas straightened out about it and meditating the necessary reply you will yourself sketch what you think should be said in answer? We can then immediately get our minds together when we meet. Perhaps you would be kind enough to let me have a memorandum of your thought for a reply. You will at once, I take it, see what my own position will necessarily be when you see the note itself.

                              Faithfully Yours,   W.W.

TLS (SDR, RG 59, 763.72/1963½, DNA).
[1] See WW to RL, July 13, 1915, n. 1.

To Joseph Patrick Tumulty

                              Windsor, Vt. July 10, 1915.

Would be obliged to you if you would telegraph me in code if necessary enough to enable me to form my own judgment as to how the note[1] ought to be handled immediately upon its receipt.

                              Woodrow Wilson.

T telegram (WP, DLC).
[1] The newspapers published a summary of the German note on July 10.

From Edward Mandell House

                                          Manchester,
Dear Governor: Massachusetts. July 10th, 1915.

In thinking of your reply to the German Note the following has occurred to me—

The Government of the United States is unwilling to consent to any suggestion looking to the abridgement of the rights of American citizens upon the high seas. If this Government were willing to bargain with the German Government for less than our inalienable rights, then any belligerent nation might transgress the rights of our citizens in other directions and would confidently count upon our trafficking with them for concessions.

This war has already caused incalculable loss to the neutrals of the world, and this Government cannot lend its consent to any abridgement of those rights which civilized nations have conceded for a century or more.

The soul of humanity cries out against the destruction of the lives of innocent non-combatants, it matters not to what country they belong, and the Government of the United States can never consent to become a party to an agreement which sanctions such pitiless warfare.

Since your first note the German Government has not committed any act against either the letter or the spirit of it, and it may be, even though they protest that they are unable to meet your demands, they may continue to observe them.

Affectionately yours,   E. M. House

P.S. In answer to their contention that Great Britain is trying to starve her people, it is well to remember that Germany refused to modify her submarine policy even though Great Britain would agree to permit foodstuffs to enter neutral ports without question.

TLS (WP, DLC).

From Thomas Watt Gregory

Dear Mr. President: Washington July 10/15.

My rather intimate knowledge of Davis & his characteristics furnishes no ground for dissent from any of your conclusions.[1]

He is perhaps the best Solicitor General we have had. The Chief Justice says he combines the best qualities of all his predecessors for twenty years.

While he taught in the law school at Washington & Lee for some time, I think he has made no study of international law & its precedents. If the work appealed to him I hardly think he would mind the smaller salary. From the standpoint of the lawyer his present position is the more desirable of the two.

He would almost certainly be a success & comfort to you as Councilor of the Department of State. I think I could guarantee this, though the work is of a very different character from that he has devoted his life to.

I do think it would be unwise to transfer him. The fall docket in the Supreme Court is unusually heavy & contains some cases of vast importance to the government. Davis has given much time & thought to a number of these, & to lose his services therein would be little short of a calamity. In case you conclude that you need him worse in the State Department I shall of course cheerfully acquiesce in your decision & do the best I can to fill his place.

Hope you are enjoying your vacation.

Faithfully Yours   T. W. Gregory

ALS (WP, DLC).
¹ Wilson's letter, asking Gregory's advice about the appointment of John W. Davis, Solicitor General of the United States, as Counselor of the State Department, is missing.

To Joseph Patrick Tumulty

Windsor, Vermont, July 11, 1915, 9:19 p.m.

According to our telephone conversation shall not expect Secretary of State to come here without previous consultation with me as to the best plan for conference.

Woodrow Wilson.

T telegram (SDR, RG 59, 763.72/1965½, DNA).

To Edward Mandell House

My dear Friend,   [Cornish, N. H.] 12 July, 1915.

Your letters are very welcome and help me always to think my way through the many matters we are facing. I thank you for them with all my heart.

In re. John W. Davis and the Counsellorship of the State Department, I have conferred with Gregory about it, by letter, and have thought it over very carefully myself. I do not think that it would be wise to make the transfer. He would be admirable wherever he might be put, but he is the best Solicitor General of the last twenty years and the docket for the next term of the Supreme Court is crowded with cases of the first moment to the Government which he has studied thoroughly.

Your suggestions for an answer to the German note run very much along the lines of my own thought. I think we might say to them that this Government is not engaged in arrangeing passenger tra[f]fic, but in definding [defending] neutral and human rights!

The relief from the strain at Washington is doing me an immense amount of good. I am really refreshed and renewed. But a few days will necessarily see the end of it now, I fear. I must go down to formulate the reply to Germany.

All join me in warmest regards to all.

Affectionately Yours,   Woodrow Wilson

WWTLS (E. M. House Papers, CtY).

To Thomas Watt Gregory

Cornish, N. H.,

My dear Mr. Attorney General: July 12, 1915

Thank you sincerely for your letter of July tenth. I agree entirely with your conclusions, much as I should like to make the transfer for the sake of strengthening Lansing's hands and giving us the benefit of the admirable counsel we should have.

It was a pleasure to hear from you.

With warmest regards,

Faithfully yours, Woodrow Wilson

TLS (Letterpress Books, WP, DLC).

From Robert Lansing

My dear Mr. President: [Washington] July 12, 1915.

Mr. Tumulty has just sent me your telegram to him of the 11th, 9:19 P.M. I have felt that it was unfortunate that the newspapers gathered the impression that I was to hasten to Cornish to consult with you in regard to the German note. The reporters evidently misunderstood Mr. Tumulty as to the possibility of my visiting you. My own impression has been that it would be unwise, unless it would very materially lengthen your holiday. It would give, I fear, a bad impression to the country as to the situation and, furthermore, in view of our foreign relations, I do not think that it would be well for both of us to be absent from Washington at the same time.

Faithfully yours, Robert Lansing

CCL (SDR, RG 59, 763.72/1965½, DNA).

From Edward Mandell House, with Enclosure

Manchester,

Dear Governor: Massachusetts. July 12th, 1915.

Here is a copy of a letter which comes from Bernstorff this morning.

I have told him that there should be some way out, and if I found he could be of service I would let him know. Do you think there would be any profit in seeing him? Perhaps I might tell him something of the tremendous effort this country would make in the event of war in order to convince the world that we were not as impotent as was thought, and in order to deter any nation in the future from provoking us into hostilities.

Your affectionate,   E. M. House

TLS (WP, DLC).

ENCLOSURE

Count Johann Heinrich von Bernstorff
to Edward Mandell House

My dear Colonel House: Washington, July 10, 15.

If you think there is anything I can do in the present crisis, I should be very much obliged for your advice and help.

I managed to influence our people so far, that our note is extremely friendly and that there is much said in it about the "freedom of the sea." As to the rest we must find some way out.

Yours very sincerely,   J. Bernstorff.

TCL (WP, DLC).

From Warren Worth Bailey

My Dear Mr. President,   Johnstown, Pa., July 12, 1915.

I hope you will pardon this intrusion upon your brief season of rest. It is ventured only because it is felt that, as a representative of the people of this district, the duty rests upon me to convey to you what I believe to be the sentiment which prevails among them touching the situation which has developed in connection with the Lusitania affair.

First of all, permit me to say that, without respect to party, you possess the full confidence of an overwhelming majority of those whom I have the honor to represent. They have faith in your judgment, in your patriotism and in your courage, faith most of all in your moral quality, your strength to do the right, even against a tremendous pressure that would force you to choose a course fraught with gravest possibilities of evil. They implicitly trust in you to disappoint those who would have this country resort to force in the adjustment of a difference which it is confidently believed you can handle with dignity and honor without even a hint of the iron hand.

It has been my privilege to confer with a great many people in my neighborhood and beyond it regarding the pending controversy with the German government. Practically without exception those with whom I have conversed or from whom I have heard express the earnest hope that patience may be exercised and a happy solution found, without abatement of the stand we have taken in the interest of humanity, and yet without the slightest threat of violence. Surely the points of difference which have been brought out are not beyond the range of rational discussion. In all conscience there must be a better way to settle them than the one suggested by those who are urging you to substitute the sword for the pen.

The United States are the light of the world in this hour of darkness. Can we afford to dim the splendor of that light by plunging the country into a situation where its identity would be lost in the murk of this awful conflict involving more than half the world? Can we afford to sacrifice the high estate which peace affords us in order to assert a right which the moral sentiment of mankind must surely recognize and time inevitably vindicate?

It is not overlooked that the metropolitan press is practically a unit in presenting a view contrary to the one I am venturing to offer, but is it certain that the metropolitan press speaks for the country, for the great mass of the American people? I think not. The mass of the people want peace and they have come to love and trust you because they believe you too stand for peace and for the methods of peace rather than for the methods of war. They believe that you have the purpose and the capacity to maintain the national honor without resort to fire and sword; and I feel profoundly that in writing you to urge the exercise of patience and forbearance in a time when these virtues are so much needed and so little in evidence in a war-torn world I am performing a duty the neglect of which would be inexcusable in one who holds a commission from the people as their representative.

Yours sincerely,   Warren Worth Bailey

TLS (WP, DLC).

From Asbury Francis Lever and Others

Sir: Lexington S. C. July 12, 1915.

On last Saturday the following gentlemen met in Columbia South Carolina, viz., Honorable A. F. Lever, Member of Congress, Honorable E. J. Watson,[1] Commissioner of Agriculture for South Carolina and President of the Southern Cotton Congress, Ex-Senator John L. McLaurin,[2] Warehouse Commissioner for South Carolina, Mr. T. B. Stackhouse,[3] Manager of a chain of cotton warehouses, Doctor Wade Stackhouse, President of the South Carolina Cotton Congress, State Senator J. A. Banks[4]–a large cotton grower–Colonel R. M. Cooper,[5] a large and representative cotton grower, Mr. W. B. Sullivan,[6] Publisher of the Columbia Evening Record and Mr. William Banks, Editor of the Columbia Evening Record, for the purpose of counselling as to the best method of meeting the very grave economic situation which is upon the South in the matter of the marketing and financing of her cotton crop. The situation was discussed in all of its details and the opinion was unanimous that the outlook in the South was far more critical and fraught with far more danger than during the season of 1914. It was agreed also that evidence was rapidly coming to light that there is growing among the people– farmers, merchants, bankers and business men, a feeling of unrest and apprehension which might easily develop into a condition of panic. It is felt that the South has never before faced so serious an economic situation and that unless some assurance for the future can be given to the people from those in whom they have confidence, the counsel of wise, conservative leaders will be swept aside by an uncontrollable hysteria such as must develop in men who find themselves facing disaster.

It was thought that a committee of representative and conservative men, not exceeding five from each leading cotton growing State might be of service to you in handling the delicate and critical situation by more fully acquainting you with the facts and yet it was realized that such a committee might embarrass you in working out such plans for relief both in the distribution and financing of the cotton crop as we assume you must have in mind. It is the desire of those who were in the Conference to aid and not to hamper you and only a very full understanding of the tremendous seriousness of the situation of the people of the South induces us to suggest to you the advisability of a personal audience with you. We are of the opinion that out of such a conference strength may be added to your arm and plans evolved which would give assurance against a recurrence of last year's experience.

With assurance of our full confidence in your ability to solve the trying problems which confront the Nation and yet realizing that in a multitude of counsel there is safety, and trusting to hear from you as to the wisdom of this suggestion of conferring with you through a committee and as promptly as may be convenient, for time is pressing,

Very respectfully,   A. F. Lever
E. J. Watson
T. B. Stackhouse[7]

TLS (WP, DLC).
  1 Ebbie Julian Watson.
  2 John Lowndes McLaurin.
  3 Thomas Bascom Stackhouse.
  4 James Arthur Banks.
  5 Robert Muldrow Cooper.
  0 Walter Bernard Sullivan.
  7 A scheduled appointment with Wilson on July 22, 1915, was canceled, and
Lever saw Wilson alone on August 17.

From William Cox Redfield

PERSONAL.

My dear Mr. President: Washington July 12th, 1915.

Pursuant to my statement in a Cabinet meeting some weeks ago, I have caused a careful inquiry to be made into the circumstances surrounding the advertisement of the Cleveland Automatic Machine Company in the "American Machinist" of May 6th, 1915.[1] During the progress of this inquiry, I have received communications concerning it from the British and French Ambassadors, a call from the latter, and there has been a good deal of discussion in the public prints. The inquiry was carried on by the Assistant Solicitor of this Department, Mr. Edward T. Quigley, whose original report and exhibits are herein, together with a copy of the catalogue of the Cleveland Automatic Machine Company, belonging to its president personally and marked with his name, A. L. Garford.[2] The report and the exhibits accompanying same throw full light upon this very surprising matter.

I have not replied personally to the communications that have been addressed to me by the "American Machinist" and the Cleveland Automatic Machine Company, copies of which are herein,[3] because I preferred to wait until the report should have been submitted to you. I have, however, drafted a letter to each concern, copy of which is enclosed.[4] The originals I have signed and left in the care of my confidential clerk to be mailed upon receipt of your approval of them. Should this approval not be sent, nothing will be done.

Permit me to ask whether in your judgment it would be proper for me to show a copy of the report and the exhibits to the English, French and German Ambassadors? The two former have expressed interest in it. Nothing has been heard from the latter, yet the German interest in the advertisement has been more outspoken than any other.

Copy of this letter is given Mr. Sweet,[5] the Acting Secretary in my absence, and he will give the matter care in case you think it wise to have it shown to the Ambassadors named. A copy of this letter is also sent to the Secretary of State, together with a copy of the report and the exhibits.

Yours very truly,   William C. Redfield

TLS (WP, DLC).

1 About this advertisement for a new type of shrapnel shell with lethal poison inside, which caused a furor both in Germany and the United States, see Link, *Struggle for Neutrality*, pp. 353-55. Redfield characterizes it in the passages printed in n. 4 below.

2 They are missing.

3 They are missing.

4 W. C. Redfield to J. P. Brophy, July 12, 1915, CCL (WP, DLC), said in part: "I accept without difficulty also your suggestion that had you realized the normal resentment that this advertisement would cause, you would not have insisted upon it after your attention was called to the fact before it appeared that protest was made against it. It is, I confess, difficult for me to understand how anyone who was not callous in a high degree could have drafted such a statement for publication with a view to selling his own wares, much less how such a one could have insisted upon its publication after he knew that objection was made thereto.

"If, as has been suggested, your thought was to horrify people with the war, no suggestion of such a purpose appears in the advertisement itself. On the contrary, you urge the cruel and agonizing nature of the death caused by certain missiles as an evidence of their effectiveness and suggest this as the basis of a sale for the machines which make those hideous things. At a time when every instinct of patriotism calls for calm and self-restraint, when sobriety of statement is almost a supreme duty, you, as you admit, to gain notice to an advertisement draw a picture of human misery as a means of earning a profit through the sale of machines to produce it."

W. C. Redfield to Hill Publishing Company, July 12, 1915, CCL (WP, DLC), said in part: "Giving due weight to the statements made in your letter, many of which are personally known to me to be correct, it yet seems to me that regardless of your established code, this advertisement was one that should not have been published by you. Whatever truth there may or may not be in the suggestion that statements of the kind are calculated to horrify the public with the war, it is nevertheless true that your columns in this instance were used to promote the sale of a machine whose suggested use in the advertisement named was that of manufacturing shells containing poisonous acids, which shells upon exploding would cause those who were struck by the fragments to die in horrible agony. It cannot be denied that if there were any so cruel as to employ such ammunition, that employment would be promoted by their finding in your columns the apparatus for the manufacture of these horrible missiles. It does not relieve you from responsibility to say that similar or the same statements appear in the press. What others have done is not the measure of what you were called upon to do.

"The time is one of peculiar excitement, with half the world on fire, and we alone of the great nations are outside of the conflict. At such a time, when restraint and calm is the duty of every citizen, your columns are opened to statements calculated to arouse wrath and kindle excitement, as the result has shown."

5 Edwin Forrest Sweet, Assistant Secretary of Commerce.

To Joseph Patrick Tumulty

[[Cornish, N. H., July 13, 1915]]

Please say that from the moment of the arrival of the official text of the German note I have given the matter the closest attention, keeping constantly in touch with the Secretary of State and with every source that would throw light on the situation;

that as soon as the Secretary of State and I have both maturely considered the situation I shall go to Washington to get into personal conference with him and with the Cabinet; and that there will be as prompt an announcement as possible of the purposes of the Government.   [Woodrow Wilson]

Telegram printed in the *New York Times*, July 14, 1915.

To Robert Lansing

My dear Mr. Secretary,   [Cornish, N. H.] 13 July, 1915.

I have of course been giving a great deal of thought to the German note since I received the official text of it.[1] According to my suggestion in my last letter, I am now writing to tell you how the reply lies in my mind in outline.

But, first, certain questions:

Do you think it worth while to take notice of and refute their arguments about the arming of merchantmen destroying the difference between public and private vessels; about this, that, and the other alleged utterance of English ministers or order of the English Government having made their recent course necessary and justifiable; etc., etc., or do you think we had better just speak, and briefly at that, to the merits of the case, in bulk, as they present it, for example as follows:

1. We cannot discuss special arrangements whereby a few vessels may enjoy the rights all are entitled to, nor admit that such arrangements would be in any way adequate to meet the contentions of this Government.

2. We are not merely contending for the rights of Americans to cross the seas as they will without fear of deliberate breaches of international law, but conceive ourselves as speaking for the rights of neutrals everywhere, rights in which the whole world is interested and which every nation must wish to see kept inviolable.

3. These rights the Imperial German Government itself recognizes in theory, professes itself anxious to see safeguarded, and is surely ready to admit as quite as vital to itself, both now and in the years to come, as to any other nation.

4. Violations of neutral rights and of the general obligations of international law by the Government of Great Britain we of course cannot discuss with the German Government; but will discuss with the British Government, so far as they affect the rights of Americans. We will, moreover, as already intimated to the German Government, be glad to be the means of conveying any

00 JULY 13, 1915

suggestions as to modifications of methods of warfare which any one of the belligerants may wish conveyed to the others.

5. We note with interest the fact that in the more recent operations of German submarines it has been feasible to keep within the limits and restrictions of international practice and to act upon the general pri[n]ciples upon which we have insisted. We can see no reason, therefore, why there is not opened a way of immediate agreement between the two governments and of such action as will sufficiently safeguard all legitimate interests and enable the German Admiralty to return to the practice long established and fully recognized in their own instructions already more than once referred to.

I am not selecting words; I am merely trying to outline an argument. What do you think of it?

And what do you think ought to be the concluding terms of demand, that will bring the correspondence to a definite issue? Two things are plain to me, in themselves inconsistent, viz. that our people want this thing handled in a way that will bring about a definite settlement without endless correspondence, and that they will also expect us not to hasten an issue or so conduct the correspondence as to make an unfriendly issue inevitable.

I shall await your own suggestions with the greatest interest. When I have had a chance to see them and reflect upon them, I will confer with you in person, preferably in Washington where we will have all the documents we wish at hand, and all the other persons we might wish to consult with regard to particular phases of this important matter.

With warm regard,

Faithfully Yours,   [Woodrow Wilson][2]

WWTL (WP, DLC).

[1] J. W. Gerard to RL, July 8, 1915 FR-WWS 1915, pp. 463-66. Von Jagow asserted that Germany's submarine warfare was a necessary response to the Allies' intention to interrupt all trade with Germany, whether from neutral nations or not, in violation of the rights of neutrals, and to the British decision to arm merchantmen, obliterating the distinction between them and war vessels. His government could not admit that American citizens could "protect an enemy ship through the mere fact of their presence on board." He promised protection for American vessels and Americans on neutral vessels, but he urged the United States Government to guarantee that the protected ships carried no contraband. To insure adequate passage for Americans traveling to and from Europe, he proposed increasing the number of neutral steamers in service, supplementing them if necessary with four enemy ships transferred to American registration. He concluded:

"The President of the United States has declared his readiness, in a way deserving of thanks, to communicate and suggest proposals to the Government of Great Britain with particular reference to the alteration of maritime war. The Imperial Government will always be glad to make use of the good offices of the President, and hopes that his efforts in the present case, as well as in the direction of the lofty ideal of the freedom of the seas, will lead to an understanding."

[2] There is a WWsh draft of this letter in WP, DLC.

From Edward Mandell House

Dear Governor: Manchester, Mass. July 13th, 1915.

From our Embassy in London I get the following: "This Government offerred various inducements, excepting Constantinople, to Bulgaria to induce her to join with the Allies and has failed. Germany offered her Constantinople and does not ask her to join in for the present. Germany continues her loans. The entire Bulgarian Court which is omnipotent is pro-German. The British Government considers Bulgaria the brick which would knock over all the others in the row if it could be made to fall. Bulgaria will actively join Germany is [if] she be assured Roumania and Greece would not attack her. A million more men from England will be needed in the Dardanelles if Bulgaria cannot be brought in with the Allies."

I was afraid Davis could not be spared from where he is, but the pressure on you in the State Department is so much greater than elsewhere that I would be in favor of weakening any department in order to lighten your burden. You need for Counsellor at this time the best man that the country affords.

I shall try to think of another suggestion unless you already have someone else in mind.

Your affectionate,   E. M. House

TLS (WP, DLC).

A Memorandum by Chandler Parsons Anderson

Washington July 13, 1915.

Memorandum on questions presented by the correspondence between the United States and Germany on the subject of the violation of the American rights by the German submarine methods of warfare.

. . . The position of the German Government, as disclosed by this correspondence, may be briefly summarized as follows:[1]

(1) So far as belligerent enemies are concerned, methods of warfare which otherwise would be illegal are justifiable when carried on as reprisals or in retaliation for illegal actions of the enemy, if such reprisals are necessary in defence of vital interests.

(2) Insofar as these illegal methods of warfare affect neutral interests, no objection can be raised by a neutral government

---

[1] Anderson had just reviewed the German-American exchanges relating to the submarine controversy.

which has submitted to the illegal acts of the enemy in consequence of which these acts of reprisal are adopted.

(3) Neutral vessels not carrying contraband will not intentionally be destroyed, but as they are not always recognizable, it will not always be possible to ensure their safety, and when they enter the war zone they bear their own responsibility for unfortunate accidents. "The German Government on their side expressly decline all responsibility for such accidents and their consequences" (German note of February 16), but where a neutral vessel "through no fault of its own" is attacked by a German submarine "the German Government has expressed its regret at the unfortunate occurrence, and promised indemnity when the facts justified it." (German note of May 28).

(4) Neutral vessels carrying contraband will be sunk after warning, as in the FRYE case, and damages for American losses will be paid when assessed by the German Prize Court.

It appears from the foregoing review of the German position that the issue raised by the United States is solely between the United States and Germany, and rests wholly on questions of law and humanity. In the discussion of this issue Germany has carefully avoided the questions of law and humanity urged by the United States, and has presented a counter issue requiring for its solution action by Great Britain as well as by the United States, and involving questions of diplomacy rather than of law.

The purpose of the German Government in adopting this line of argument remains to be considered.

Germany has presented the issue in a way which suggests as its solution either the abandonment by Great Britain of her interference with neutral trade with Germany, or the abandonment by the American people of their contraband trade with Great Britain. Either one of these solutions would be more advantageous to Germany than the continuance of her submarine warfare against merchant ships, for that has not as yet justified itself from a military point of view, and has threatened her good relations with the United States, but Germany cannot afford to abandon it even if she wants to, unless she can get something in return for so doing. It seems clear that if Germany felt that by continuing her submarine warfare, she could gain more than by being relieved from Great Britain's interference with her neutral trade, she would not have offered to abandon it, as she has already done on several occasions, in exchange for that relief, and she would have sought to justify it as lawful under the principles of international law, instead of by reasons which would disappear if Great Britain abandoned her restraints upon neutral commerce. Germany in effect has admitted that its retaliatory measures would cease to be justifiable the moment they ceased to be retaliatory.

The German Government evidently is proceeding on the assumption that the United States does not want to go to war, and in preference to going to war would either put an embargo on the exportation of war munitions to Germany's enemies, or by the threat of such an embargo or otherwise bring pressure to bear on them to abandon their so-called blockade against Germany. This view is confirmed by Germany's proposal in the last note of a modus operandi which is so obviously impossible for the United States to accept that it is permissible to suspect that Germany did not want the question settled in that way.

From the German point of view this method of settlement would, of course, be preferable to yielding to the demands of the United States, for it would give Germany a free hand in submarine warfare, but it would be far less favorable to Germany than an American embargo on the shipment of war supplies which comes at the head of the list of German preferences followed, as an alternative, by the termination of Great Britain's interference with neutral trade.

It also seems probable that Germany is proceeding on the assumption that Great Britain will not voluntarily agree to an abandonment of the blockade against Germany. Great Britain certainly is not anxious to aid in removing a cause of friction between the United States and Germany which has already proved of great benefit to Great Britain. Compulsion of some kind will be necessary to change Great Britain's attitude, and Germany is counting on bringing pressure to bear either through the United States or through the development of submarine warfare into a menace which cannot be disregarded.

The issue raised by the United States Government interferes with the latter course, so Germany is directing her diplomatic efforts towards putting upon Great Britain the responsibility for the present situation in the expectation that a refusal by Great Britain to voluntarily abandon the restraints on neutral trade which Germany characterizes as illegal, will induce the United States to retaliate in some way upon Great Britain.

The freedom of the seas is the war cry at present, and in Germany's last note the following significant suggestion is found:

The Imperial Government cherishes the definite hope that some way will be found when peace is concluded, or perhaps earlier, to regulate the law of maritime war in a manner guaranteeing the freedom of the seas, and will welcome it with gratitude and satisfaction if it can work hand in hand with the American Government to that end.

The way in which Germany would prefer to have this result brought about is also pointed out in the German correspondence. The note of February 16th dwells at considerable length upon the subject of stopping war munitions trade with Great Britain, or opening up innocent trade with Germany, and sums up the situation as follows:

Germany is to all intents and purposes cut off from oversea supplies with the toleration, tacit or protesting, of the neutrals regardless of whether it is a question of goods which are absolute contraband or only conditional contraband or not contraband at all, following the law generally recognized before the outbreak of the war. On the other hand England with the indulgence of neutral governments is not only being provided with such goods as are not contraband or merely conditional contraband, namely, foodstuffs, raw material, et cetera, although these are treated by England when Germany is in question as absolute contraband, but also with goods which have been regularly and unquestionably acknowledged to be absolute contraband. The German Government believe that they are obliged to point out very particularly and with the greatest emphasis that a trade in arms exists between American manufacturers and Germany's enemies which is estimated at many hundred million marks.

In the same note after stating that the above mentioned trade in contraband, especially, war materials, is carried on in neutral vessels, the following solution is suggested:

In regard to the latter point, the German Government ventures to hope that the American Government upon consideration will see their way clear to a measure of intervention in accordance with the spirit of true neutrality.

The recent protests from Austria-Hungary and Turkey[2] against the sale of war munitions to the Allies which is characterized as unneutral in the existing circumstances, gives added significance to the above suggestion from Germany.

With these considerations in mind the conclusion is inevitable that nothing short of fear of war with the United States will induce Germany to yield to the demands of the United States, so long as there is any chance that through delay and temporizing, the United States may be induced to take sides with Germany against Great Britain on the issues involved.

                                        Chandler P. Anderson

TS MS (WP, DLC).
    2 The Editors have no information about any such protest by the Turkish government.

To Robert Lansing

My dear Mr. Secretary, [Cornish, N. H.] 14 July, 1915.

I fully understood your feeling about this, or thought I did, instinctively, but for once allowed myself to credit what the newspapers contained, under the impression that somehow our currents had got short-circuited.[1] Please never feel that it is necessary to explain. I knew that you would understand my telegram. You evidently have understood it.

Faithfully Yours, W.W.

WWTLI (SDR, RG 59, 763.72/1966½, DNA).
[1] See RL to WW, July 12, 1915.

Two Letters to Edward Mandell House

My dear Friend, [Cornish, N. H.] 14 July, 1915.

Perhaps it might be just as well for you to see Bernstorff, if only to make him fell [feel] not only that some way out *should* be found but that some way out *must* be found and that his Government owe to themselves and to the rest of the world to help to find it.

I think the editor of the Springfield Republican has come as near as any one to pointing out the feasible way of action, or, at least, the necessary and sensible way.[1] Apparently the Germans *are* modifying their methods: they must be made to feel that they must continue in their new way unless they deliberately wish to prove to us that they are unfriendly and wish war.

Thank you for the message from our Embassy in London about Bulgaria. It is painfully interesting.

I think about you a great deal, and I believe *with* you, too. I am now expecting to go down to Washington the first of next week, leaving here on Sunday afternoon next. By that time Lansing and I shall have exchanged notes and will be in good shape for a definitive personsonal [personal] conference and a consultation with the Cabinet.

Affectionately Yours, Woodrow Wilson

WWTLS (E. M. House Papers, CtY).
[1] Wilson referred to "The German Proposals," *Springfield*, Mass., *Republican*, July 11, 1915, commenting on the German note of July 8, 1915. This lengthy editorial said, quite emphatically, that Wilson could not possibly accept the German proposals for the safeguarding of American citizens on the high seas and devoted much space to an analysis of why this was so. However, Wilson's comment in the above letter refers to the latter portion of the editorial which suggested that, while the diplomatic situation was critical, it was not yet hopeless. Present conditions did not seem to require that the President recall Gerard. In all cases except that of the *Lusitania*, substantial satisfaction had been given by the German government. While the two nations remained deadlocked over the *Lusitania* affair, the fact remained that there had been no similar incident in the

two months since the tragedy. This should be the key to American policy for the immediate future: "For what Germany does is more important than what Germany says." There were many possible reasons why the German government might be unwilling to disavow the sinking of the *Lusitania* and publicly promise that there would be no similar atrocities in the future. But the fact that there had been no destruction of a passenger ship running between American and British ports in the two months since the *Lusitania* disaster justified the American government in assuming that Germany had tacitly accepted the soundness of much of the American argument. The United States should strongly reaffirm its determination to maintain the rights of American citizens on the high seas and then await developments. "Yet," the editorial concluded, "the German government should not be left in doubt as to what would follow another massacre of Americans on a small or a large scale; it should know that so sinister an event would be followed by the withdrawal of our ambassador from Berlin."

My dear Friend: Cornish, N. H. July 14, 1915

I know you will read the letter enclosed with interest.[1] I send it to you because it is a sample of, I might almost say, all the letters I am receiving nowadays, and I am receiving them, of course, from many quarters and from many different kinds of persons. It is for that reason that I am sending this to you, in order that you may know the impressions I am getting.

Affectionately yours,   Woodrow Wilson

TLS (WP, DLC).
  [1] W. W. Bailey to WW, July 12, 1915.

To Warren Worth Bailey

My dear Mr. Bailey: Cornish, N. H., July 14, 1915

I thank you sincerely for your letter of July twelfth. There was certainly no need to apologize for sending it or fearing that I would regard it as an intrusion. I have read it with the greatest interest and appreciation, both of its spirit and of its point of view.   Cordially and sincerely yours,   Woodrow Wilson

TLS (W. W. Bailey Papers, NjP).

To Edwin Forrest Sweet

My dear Mr. Sweet: Cornish, N. H., July 14, 1915

I have the letter of the Secretary of Commerce dated July twelfth asking my judgment as to whether he should send a letter, a copy of which he encloses, addressed to the people responsible for inserting an extraordinary and inexcusable advertisement of the Cleveland Automatic Machine Company in the "American Machinist" of May 6, 1915, and he has requested that

I notify you whether I approve of his letter being sent. I do so approve and hope that you will send it.

I am herewith returning the papers which the Secretary was kind enough to submit to me as embodying the results of the inquiry into this matter by Mr. Edward T. Quigley, Assistant Solicitor of the Department.

                    Cordially and sincerely yours,   Woodrow Wilson

TLS (Letterpress Books, WP, DLC).

From Robert Lansing

Personal and Confidential.

My dear Mr. President: Washington July 14, 1915.

I have been making a number of notes on the German reply of the 8th in an endeavor to crystallize my thoughts as to the answer which should be made. I am loath to send you these notes in their present shape as I think that you would find them more useful in a digested form.

The impression which I have gained from careful reading and rereading of the German note is that the thought of "home consumption" entered largely into its composition, while at the same time the German Government failed to appreciate public temper in this country. I think that considerable allowance should be made for the sarcastic tone of certain phrases because written for German readers and to meet the public demand in Germany.

We are to an extent bound to respond to a similar chord in this country. It would be easy to understand American public opinion if the press accurately reflected it. But I am not sure in my own mind that it does. As I read the state of mind of the vast majority of the people it is that they do not want war, that no war spirit exists, but at the same time they want the Government not to recede a step from its position but to compel Germany to submit to our demands. Of course this attitude, if I read it aright, is most difficult to meet. To carry out both ideas is well nigh impossible. Of course I do not feel that public opinion should dictate the Government's action but it is well to consider it.

As to the reply itself I feel that the German note's comments on the action of Great Britain can be dismissed with a statement that they are irrelevant to the subject at issue. That will dispose of nearly half of the note. In the next place I think that we can refuse to discuss a *modus vivendi* for the future until the general principles involved have been considered and the LUSITANIA matter satisfactorily adjusted so far as it is possible. The setting aside of these two subjects in our reply will materially shorten it, and I believe that brevity will impress the German Government with the earnestness of our purpose to insist on our rights (an impression which I have sometimes felt they did not have) and will also cause a feeling in this country that this Government does not intend to prolong the controversy indefinitely. I think in the present state of the discussion a concise and direct statement will be most effective.

As I reached this point your letter to me of the 13th arrived. After reading it I have decided to enclose my undigested notes calling particular attention to Note 13.[1]

I will go over your letter with care and send you any comments which may suggest themselves. I think that you will find on examining the enclosed notes our minds have worked in much the same way.

In order that I may not forward to you at Cornish further memoranda, which might arrive after your departure, can you indicate to me about the time you expect to return here?

I am, my dear Mr. President,

Faithfully yours,   Robert Lansing

TLS (WP, DLC).
¹ He did send them, thirteen in number (WP, DLC). In them, he commented on various sections of the German note of July 8. Lansing's Note 13 dealt with the form and subject matter of a reply to the German communication. The first half of it repeated the argument set forth in the fourth paragraph of the above letter. Lansing's remaining suggestions as to what the next American note should include were all aimed at forcing the German government to respond directly to the issues raised by the *Lusitania* incident, which the German authorities had thus far ignored or obfuscated.

From Joseph Patrick Tumulty

Dear Governor: The White House July 14, 1915.

The enclosed editorial expresses my own feeling so thoroughly with reference to the attitude of England that I send it to you for your information.[1]

When we discussed the proposed English note some weeks ago, I was opposed to sending it but I think it is a matter that we ought now to consider and take action upon without delay.

Cordially and sincerely yours,   J P Tumulty

TLS (WP, DLC).
¹ "The Next Business," Louisville *Courier Journal*, July 12, 1915, suggesting that, now that the diplomatic discussion with Germany over the *Lusitania* seemed about to be concluded, the administration's next move should be to press

Great Britain to end its illegal blockade and recognize American trading rights on the high seas. The editorial asserted that there was growing sentiment in the country for such action.

Robert Lansing to Walter Hines Page

AMEMBASSY LONDON URGENT.

Washington, July 14, 1915.

1848 In order avoid any misunderstanding as to attitude of Government of United States in regard to prize court proceedings in cases involving American interests, inform British Government that in view of differences which are understood to exist between the two Governments as to the principles of law applicable in these cases, the Government of the United States desires to make clear to the British Government that insofar as the interests of American citizens are concerned, it will insist upon their rights under the hitherto established principles and rules of international law governing neutral trade in time of war, without modification or limitation by orders-in-council or other municipal legislation by Great Britain, and it will not recognize the validity of proceedings taken in prize court under restraints imposed by British municipal law in derogation of their rights.

Inform Urion[1] and report any suggestions by him.

Lansing.

T telegram (SDR, RG 59, 763.72112/1343a, DNA).
[1] Alfred Riley Urion of Chicago, long-time general counsel for Armour & Co., at this time attorney for various American meat packing firms in cases before the prize court in London.

From Robert Lansing

Personal and Confidential.

My dear Mr. President: Washington July 15, 1915.

In re your letter of the 13th as to an outline for a reply to the German note may I offer the following comments:

I do not think that it is at all essential to refute the German allegation that the LUSITANIA was to all intents a public ship; at the same time it presents an argument which to the average man appears to have considerable force, and, if it is not met, it may be thought that it could not be answered. There is always danger, I think, in omitting reference to an assertion, since it may be construed into an admission. You will see that my *Note* 6 (July 11th) deals with the question.

Your paragraphs numbered 1, 2 and 3 seem to me to treat the

modus vivendi proposed by Germany in just the right way, and put the subject on the ground of principle, which is a higher ground than the one I suggested and, therefore, a better one.

Paragraph 4, I think, presents the exact way to deal with the charges made against Great Britain. The subject should be stated to be irrelevant to the issue as well as improper for discussion with Germany. The last sentence in the paragraph might possibly obtain greater emphasis by being placed at the end of our answer and show a friendly disposition.

Paragraph 5 might be used in the answer, to emphasize our disappointment that the German Government does not in its note agree to do the very thing it has been doing for the past two months. Possibly this could be used at the beginning in complaining that the rights of Americans are not acknowledged.

I think that you will find that the view of public sentiment contained in the next to the last paragraph in your letter was identical with that expressed in the first part of my letter of yesterday. I am sure the people do not want war with Germany, and I am equally sure that they want the Government to insist firmly on its rights. As you say, the two things are "inconsistent." How they can be brought into harmony is the chief problem.

This brings up the question, which you ask, as to "the concluding terms of demand." Frankly I am not prepared yet to answer that question. I would prefer to wait until the note is drafted in a tentative form and see what demands would be consistent and appropriate. Of course the demands we make will be the most difficult part of the note. Is it possible to be firm and at the same time to compromise?

I think that in formulating the demands the possible consequences must be considered with the greatest care. In case of a flat refusal what will happen? In case of counter proposals what then? Should the demands be so worded as to admit of only "Yes" or "No" as an answer, or should a loophole be given for counter proposals? Can we take a course which will permit further correspondence? These are the questions which are running through my mind and I have not as yet been able to answer them. I wish more time to consider them.

I am now working on a tentative draft, which will put my ideas in a more concrete form than the Notes which I sent you.

Not being sure whether you kept a copy of your letter of the 13th I am returning it to you so that this letter will be intelligible. I have retained a copy.

Faithfully yours,   Robert Lansing

TLS (WP, DLC).

From Edward Mandell House

Manchester, Massachusetts.

Dear Governor: July 15th, 1915.

I am returning Congressman Bailey's letter. He has put the matter strongly and well.

Is it not true, though, that the press of the country generally voices the views of the people better than individuals who write largely for the purpose of influencing your action? I have talked with a great many people and mostly those from a distance and, without exception, they have expressed a wish that a firm answer be sent. When pressed further they have told me that in their opinion the country was willing to accept the consequences.

I shall try and get hold of Bernstorff in a few days.

I have a feeling that Germany will not commit what we would consider an overt act, unless, indeed, such talk as Mr. Bryan is indulging himself in should influence them to do so.

I have a letter from Gerard in which he says:

"I hope the President will not give way to Bryan on this arms export question. If he does, Germany will think it can impose any line of conduct on the United States."

Then again:

"The Chancellor and von Jagow have been in Vienna, probably over the Balkan questions. The situation there hinges on Bulgaria. Germany wants a direct strip of territory for itself or Austria to Constantinople"

And again:

"The enclosed advertisement[1] will bear investigation. It has been reproduced all over Germany to help the hate against us. I am sure it is 'a plant' "

And again:

"Socialists are getting more aggressive in the peace issue."

I notice that Mayre has resigned. That I think is fortunate. I hope you can find a good man, for there is important work to be done in Russia.

It makes me happy when I think of the vacation you are having at Cornish and I hope you will be able to return after a few days in Washington.

John Green, Federal District Attorney for the Southern District of Texas, was with me yesterday. He said that he had yet to find a man in Texas who approved of Mr. Bryan. I have this from many sources and from those that have recently come from what were formerly considered Bryan strongholds.

                              Your affectionate,   E. M. House

TLS (WP, DLC).
  1 In *The American Machinist.*

To Thomas Staples Martin

My dear Senator Martin: Cornish, N. H., July 16, 1915

I am warmly obliged to you for your letter of July fourteenth[1] reminding me of the Negro Exposition at Richmond, which is to close on the twenty-seventh of this month.

The German note has come at just the time it seems likely to detain me in Washington when I had hoped to be in Richmond to attend this exposition.

I shall not entirely give up hope of being able to attend, but at present it looks, I am sorry to say, extremely doubtful.

          Cordially and sincerely yours,   Woodrow Wilson

TLS (Letterpress Books, WP, DLC).
  1 It is missing.

From Robert Lansing, with Enclosure

Dear Mr. President: Washington July 16, 1915.

I enclose herewith a confidential despatch which I have just received from Ambassador Page.

          Faithfully yours,   Robert Lansing

TLS (WP, DLC).

E N C L O S U R E

London, July 15 1915

CONFIDENTIAL. For the President and the Secretary.

Following is in the Secretary's private code.

I interpret thoughtful and responsible opinion here as follows and send it as in the past for your information. Germany reckons on American unpreparedness for war and hopes that pro-German sentiment can prevent munitions from going to the allies, arguing that if pro-German sentiment fail the United States cannot fight and therefore the risk of insulting us is negilgible since as a neutral her enemies obtain help from us through their command of the seas and as an enemy we could do no more harm than we now do.

The feeling seems to be that Germany can never be persuaded to give us a satisfactory answer and that if we do not take effective action of some sort we shall lose the confidence and respect of the allies and in time have to face Germany alone; that if democracy as represented by the United States yield, its standing in the world will be gone for an indefinite time and its advocates weakened in every country.

Men here point out the similarity of Germany's dealing with the United States to her dealing with England, always by evasion, and they point to England's mistake in hoping to avoid war and not equipping an army ten years ago. They say that unless German military power is crushed by the crushing of the professional military party all the world will be terrorized and that we must range out effectively against this menace without delay or suffer ultimately whatever the outcome of the present struggle may be.

I think this opinion is practically universal here among thoughtful men. They are saddened by it but regard it as practically certain that we cannot escape; that the Germans will continue assassination and incendiarism in the United States and will sooner or later destroy more American travelers.

British opinion has great and growing confidence in the President himself but seems to show a doubt about the virility and courage of American public opinion attributing to it a timidity arising from failure to grasp the scope of the issues involved in the struggle and the effect of its outcome on the United States.

American Ambassador   London.

T telegram (WP, DLC).

From Charles William Eliot

Dear Mr. President: Asticou, Maine 16 July, 1915

The irrational and disingenuous Note which you have lately received from Germany seems to afford you a good opportunity, either now or at the next exchange of Notes, of stating to the world the feelings of the American people about the German conduct of war. Those feelings were greatly stirred by the first accounts of the German killing of non-combatants in Belgium, and of the wholesale plundering, with the approval and participation of the German Government, of that quickly conquered country; but in August and September the facts had not been clearly determined, and the responsibility had not been fixed, as it was later, on the German commanders and the Government at Berlin. In consequence, no adequate protest was made by America or by any group of neutral powers; and Germany received no strong impression of the general abhorrence which her proceedings in

Belgium and Northern France excited. You can now make a solemn statement on this subject which Germany will hear, and which will give satisfaction to the many serious people in all parts of the world who thought that a protest should have been made early.

In the Note Germany has just sent to Washington the barbarous performances of the German submarines are justified on the same ground of "military necessity" which to the German mind made inevitable the horrible treatment of Belgium. It says in effect—if the submarine which sunk the "Lusitania" had not fired the torpedo just as it did, it would probably have been sunk itself. Hence, the deed was justifiable. Again it says—the sudden sinking of commercial vessels, containing non-combatants and liable to contain neutrals, is the only effective reply that Germany can make to the blockade maintained by Great Britain; therefore it must go on, whether non-combatants and neutrals are drowned or not. And again, the sinking of fishing vessels, with or without great risk of life for their crews, has become a common German practice in this War, in spite of Germany's subscription to the doctrine that war is to be waged against public forces, and not against private persons or property. There is one indispensable result of this Great War, if civilization is not to be arrested—it must supply a demonstration that international agreements cannot be violated with impunity on the ground of military necessity, no matter how strong the nation which breaks a solemn compact may be.

In replying to this Note, you have an opportunity to state strongly the abhorrence with which America and all neutral countries regard the German mode of carrying on war at sea and on land, and to demand that Germany give solemn and immediate assurances that she will desist from the inhuman methods she is now using in violation of international agreements to which she was a party. To satisfy Germany that she cannot safely maintain her present methods of conducting war may be the shortest way to bring peace; but, at any rate, no satisfactory settlement of this wide-spread conflict can possibly be made which does not include an international agreement that such methods shall never be used again. Germany needs to be told by you that three words—Belgium, Rheims, and Lusitania arouse in all the rest of the civilized world feelings of indignation and resentment which nothing but reformation and reparation by Germany will ever extinguish. It would be a fearful misfortune for the human race, if the outcome of the War should seem to condone the German crimes in Belgium and France and on the seas.

The argument of the German Note concerning our exporting munitions of war is, of course, completely irrelevant. It is incredible that the German Government should not see that arguments against the exportation of munitions of war have nothing whatever to do with the matters treated in the Note to which that Government was replying. For a neutral to sell munitions to either of the combatant alliances or to both is unquestionably legal. Whether such action is right or ethical on the part of the seller depends primarily on the seller's opinion of the rights and wrongs of the conflict. In the present case, the weight of American ethical opinion approves the exclusive sale of munitions to the Entente Powers.

Is it not possible that, if the German Government and ruling class get from you a plain statement of the real feeling of the American people that this War is being waged by the Allies against domination in Europe, or anywhere else in the world, by military force, and in support of eternal principles of public justice and liberty and of universal humanity, it might help them to see that they have the present civilized world against them already, and are sure to have the coming world against them more firmly still? May you not convince them that the sacrifices they have already made and the losses they have already suffered are all in vain, that none of the objects with which they set out on this War can possibly be attained, and that the sooner they turn a new page in the history of Germany, the better it will be for them and for their people? At any rate, you have the opportunity now to make such a statement, and the power to make it; and all the best hopes of humanity will go with you.

I do not imagine that any of these ideas are new to you. I do want to testify that they are entertained by a multitude of thoughtful and responsible Americans, who will rejoice greatly in such action on your part.

I am, with the highest regard,

                                    Very sincerely yours,   [C. W. Eliot]

CCL (C. W. Eliot Papers, MH-Ar).

Robert Lansing to Walter Hines Page

Washington, July 16, 1915.

1860 CONFIDENTIAL. Am informed by British Ambassador that he cabled yesterday to Sir Edward Grey urging the necessity for more considerate and liberal treatment of American trade, particularly cotton, oil and meat products.[1] It is exceedingly important that British Government should understand this necessity, and should realize that this Government considers the general policy of the British Government in seizing American shipments on mere presumption of enemy destination and in restraining American trade with neutral countries is unjustifiable in law. The course pursued by Great Britain has produced wide spread irritation and dissatisfaction through this country, and unless some radical change is made, the situation will become so serious politically that it will be difficult, if not impossible, to find a solution. In view of the increasing gravity of the question, which is reaching a crisis in this country, I would suggest that you communicate unofficially these views to Sir Edward and, if you can do so without offense, intimate to him that the matter be treated as a cabinet question and not left to the decision of subordinates in the governmental departments.   Lansing

T telegram (SDR, RG 59, 763.72112/1354a, DNA).
    ¹ It is paraphrased in Enclosure I with EMH to WW, July 18, 1915. The original is C. A. Spring Rice to E. Grey, July 15, 1915, T telegram (E. Grey Papers, FO 800/85, PRO).

From Edward Mandell House

Manchester, Massachusetts.
Dear Governor: July 17th, 1915.

Hapgood sends me this advance editorial. When he was with me last week I talked to him along these lines. I think he has stated the case as well as it has yet been done.¹

Charles R. Crane and Houston took dinner with us last night. They are all of one mind as to you and the way you are conducting the affairs of the Government during these fateful days.

Jane Addams comes on Monday. Hapgood and Crane thought I should see her. She has accumulated a wonderful lot of misinformation in Europe. She saw von Jagow, Grey and many others and for one reason or another, they were not quite candid with her so she has a totally wrong impression.

It is believed that Germany is willing to make peace now upon the basis of evacuation of Belgium, France and Russian Poland, and this impression gains force by Bernstorff's constant iteration that this is true and his further statement that if England would agree to let foodstuffs enter Germany, they would cease their submarine policy.

These tactics have a tendancy to make people believe that we should treat Germany in the same spirit of compromise as she seems herself to evidence. It also has a tendancy to create the feeling that we are favoring England at the expense of Germany

Sight is lost of the fact that England will be called to an accounting for any infringement of our property rights at sea as soon as Germany has been reckoned with for the more serious offense of killing Americans and other non-combatants.

Sometime I believe you should give out a statement which will clear up these points. If Germany is willing to evacuate Belgium, France and Russian Poland and is willing to give up her submarine warfare if the embargo on foodstuffs is lifted, she should have a chance to say so officially, for immediately she reaches this decision, peace parleys may begin.

Affectionately yours,   E. M. House

P.S. I have just had a telephone from General Wood. It seems that James Garfield is immediately back from Mexico and he has had a conference with both Lansing and Garrison. Wood telephoned at Garrison's suggestion asking me to see him, so I thought I had best do so. He is coming tonight. If anything of value developes I will let you know.

TLS (WP, DLC).
¹ "War and Peace," *Harper's Weekly*, LXI (July 24, 1915), 73. It began with a tribute to Wilson: "A strong man has seldom been more needed. Fortunately we have a strong man." The President was "powerful in thought, principle, and will" but had the calmness of self-possession; the American people recognized this and would support the administration. The editorial then went on to state the magazine's position: "*Harper's Weekly* is not for peace at any price. Far from it. We are for peace as long as that peace can be founded on spiritual strength. We are against peace the minute maintaining it means that the United States would act against her conscience in order to escape her share of the bill." Hapgood had no doubt as to the "desirable outcome" of the war: "The triumph of the organized, calculated force of Germany over the rest of the world's acceptance of the status quo is something we simply cannot contemplate." All of Germany's real or alleged atrocities in the course of the conflict were a consequence of the theorem "that it is right for Germany to do what she deems likely to promote her welfare." The United States simply could not accept this idea without losing moral strength. *Harper's Weekly* supported the declaration of principle set forth by the administration in the first *Lusitania* note. Having made that declaration, the United States could not now recede from it, even if it meant that ultimately she must enter the struggle. "We must give ourselves altogether," the editorial concluded, "to plowing the furrow to the end."

From Nancy Saunders Toy

My dear Mr. President   Seal Harbor, Me. 17 July, 1915

This has been such a Wilson day. May I tell you about it? Encountering Mr. Rhodes on a morning walk, my companion challenged him: "What do *you* think the United States ought to do now?" "I am waiting," he said with his good-humored smile, "to see what the President does, and that will be what I think the U. S. should do." This I promptly repeated when I myself was challenged by the same question a few minutes later on the road —these roads being the real Seal Harbor *salon*. My challenger, a writer on International Law, looked grave. "I am not sure," he said "that this attitude is the helpfulest one to the President. He wants to know what people are thinking and saying, and for that reason Mr. Rhodes would perhaps serve best by not merely 'standing and waiting.' " In a flash, I recalled that I asked you once how you were certain that *vox populi* always reached you, and you answered that the note was not always satisfactorily distinct.

I hear now three notes distinct and clear:—but what am I doing! This is a Wilson, not a war letter. And later there was another Wilson episode. A lawyer from New York, counsel for the du Ponts, declared in the dining-room in a note distinct and clear to all the diners that you would be elected again not by the Democrats, not by the Independents whom you thought so much of, but by a new party—the Wilson Republicans. "We like Wilson, and we don't like Cummins and Borah, and that's the kind of dope they are going to hand out to us the next election."

Your friends have been as much rested by your long automobile rides as you yourself have, as I hope. "I wonder what they talk about, family and guest," I said curiously to Mr. Toy. "Something restful and frivolous, I hope," he answered emphatically, "do you realize that no President was ever confronted by such a situation as is our President now?" *Do* I! Don't we all of us! and isn't the unanimity of confidence shown in press and people something that has never happened before and something (even if it be not lasting, as you hint) that now must cheer and stimulate you? I am reading to Mr. Toy the American Statesmen series —"the series for discrediting Southern statesmen," he calls it. What courage, what confidence, what sturdy determination those old fellows showed! What a splendid adventure it all was! What a splendid adventure it all is now!

God prosper you in it!

Your sincere friend   Nancy Toy

ALS (WP, DLC).

From Edith Bolling Galt

[Cornish, N. H.] Saturday

My precious One: 7 P.M. June [July] 17, 1915

I have just gotten my pen to start this little note when you came down the hall ready for dinner. Oh! my precious Sweetheart how many miles will roll between us when you read this, but no distance can really seperate us.

I cannot let you go without just this little message to take the peace of our good-night talks, and tell you again I love you.

Your visit has been the happiest one for me, and you have forgotten nothing that would add to my comfort or pleasure. Thank you again for all the tender little things that make me feel your love, and for the real confidence and sharing of the big ones that make up your busy life.

Sunday morning

This is a real goodbye, but time or distance need not count, and I am already looking forward to *next Sunday* when you will be coming back! Bless your precious Heart, I love you, and my arms are stretched out to hold and shield you from any hurt or loneliness. And my thoughts will follow you throughout the night and go before to welcome you when you reach the White House

Edith.

ALS (WP, DLC).

From Edward Mandell House, with Enclosures

Manchester, Massachusetts.

Dear Governor: July 18th, 1915.

Here is a curious note from Spring-Rice. He neither addressed, dated nor signed it and it came in a blank envelope. He certainly belongs to the gum shoe brigade.

I hardly know what to do. He has in mind that Sir Edward Grey is trying to meet our wishes, which indeed I know he is, but that he is hampered by Asquith and other members of the Government. I am enclosing two cablegrams for your consideration.

If you think well of them, you might have Mr. Lansing send them from me so the matter may be unofficial. Or if you think best, he could cable Page himself.

I am enclosing you letters recently received from Lord Loreburn and Walter Page which you may care to read at your leisure.

Affectionately yours, E. M. House

TLS (WP, DLC).

ENCLOSURE I

Spring-Rice[1]

July 17th, 1915.

It would be a good thing if Page were to talk matters over with Edward now he has come back to work. I warn him that he must take in hand personally and bring to notice of Premier situation created here if many interests (e.g. cotton, packers and Standard Oil) are all aggrieved and given a basis or excuse for a combination here to press for extra session and prohibition of arms export.

Matter is getting serious and while no doubt there is much to be considered on the other side, yet it is worth paying a certain price in order to obtain certain advantages or avert a certain danger.

A personal and confidential interview to this effect might strengthen Edward's hands in dealing with the other departments who have the matter in hand and may be treating it more from the departmental point of view than that of the general interest of defence taken in the broadest sense.

¹ EMHhw.

E N C L O S U R E   I I

July 18th, 1915.

Spring-Rice suggested my sending you the accompanying despatch so that Sir Edward might use it with the Prime Minister and other members of his Government in an effort to remedy a really serious situation.   Edward House.

July 18th, 1915.

The feeling here regarding the holding up of our cargoes is getting serious and unless something is immediately done there will be a wide spread demand for the calling of Congress in order to retaliate.

This feeling has been repressed largely because of our differences with Germany, but it is doubtful whether it can be much longer restrained. I believe it is important for you to urge this view upon the British Government and endeavor to have them realize how serious the situation is becomming.
                                        Edward House.

T MSS (WP, DLC).

E N C L O S U R E   I I I

Robert Earl Loreburn to Edward Mandell House

My dear Colonel House: London. June 26th, 1915.

You suggested that I might write to you if anything occurred to me that might do any good and though I am not very sure of almost anything I do think that we are on the eve of a movement by outraged human nature to assert itself against what is now going forward on land and sea, and against the incalculable consequences which may ensue.

People are beginning to realize what it all means, the destruction of the rising generation nearly all over Europe and the bedding of their elders with national bankruptcy, for more than one lost mental state, and complete insecurity for property.

It seems almost certain that when di[s]cipline is over, revolution will break out sooner or later in many parts of Europe unless this war comes to an end in time to avert it. And one does not like to think of the problems that will arise, millions more of women without any prospect of home and family life.

It is a defiance of the laws of nature in every sense: slaughter today and anarchy with a break up of family ties to follow. It is this and more also is I think in men's minds here, and from what I am told there is a feeling of this sort in Germany though accompanied by confidence in the issue, as indeed prevails here also.

I have been very seriously thinking whether individuals like myself ought to say these things here. But the feeling always comes to me that there are the powers of good and the powers of evil in Germany and that the latter would immediately fasten upon anything said here in order to strengthen themselves by the thought that England is getting disposed to give way. Nothing could be less true but it would be used in Germany in that way. It is a terrible thought that each nation should feel itself obliged to go on lest any hint of a statement should strengthen the forces that make for prolonging the fight.

Still, somehow or other, I feel that the weaker one must give out. Something must give way, because it is not a machine really but a huge array of human forces artificially drilled to act like a machine. But the fear of leading enemies to think there is a sign of weakness makes any commencement in belligerent countries very difficult and indeed at present impossible.

I cannot help thinking that a neutral source might supply the nucleus round which opinion in Europe could crystalize. The whole horror of the situation is present to all minds in every household here and also I believe—it cannot be otherwise—in every other country where the youth of the house are in deadly peril every hour.

To suggest terms now would probably be premature, though I believe any step, whether it failed or not, would bring the end nearer. But if only a note could be struck in a neutral zone, which could not be misunderstood, bringing home to all, which could penetrate to every corner, the hideous results to the human kind which must stand this war in ever increasing measure the longer it continues,—if that could be done it would gather round it the sympathy of countless millions and furnish a starting point for discussion and cooperation.

It is a truth that the war must end or Western Civilization may be submerged. I feel that this great truth in one of the greatest crisis in the history of mankind ought to be voiced and that no one but a neutral can voice it so as to reach the heart and conscience of the warring nations.

I do not know what you think but I have said my say and am sure you will sympathize even if you do not agree.

It was a great pleasure for me to meet you and I hope we may meet again in happier times.

Yours sincerely,   Loreburn.

E N C L O S U R E   I V

Walter Hines Page to Edward Mandell House

My dear House: London, June 30th, 15.

There's a distinct wave of depression here—perhaps I'd better say a period of set-backs has come. So far as we can find out only the Germans are doing anything in the war on land.

The position in France is essentially the same as it was in November, only the Germans are much more strongly entrenched. Their great plenty of machine guns enables them to use fewer men and to kill more than the Allies. The Russians also lack ammunition and are yielding more and more territory.

The Allies—as you hear now—will do well if they get their little army away from the Dardanelles before the German-Turks eat 'em alive, and no Balkan State comes in to help the Allies. Italy makes progress—slowly, of course, over almost impassable mountains—etc. etc.

Most of this doleful recital I think is true; and I find more and more men here who have lost hope of seeing an end of the war in less than two or three years and more and more who fear that the Germans will never be forced out of Belgium.

And the era of the giant aeroplane seems about to come—a machine that can carry several tons and several men and go great distances—two engines, two propellers and the like. It is'nt at all impossible, I am told, that these machines may be the things that will at last end the war—possibly, but I doubt it. At any rate, it *is* true that a great wave of discouragement is come. They say the factories and the workmen are doing well now—at last; but Lloyd George and his helpers have had to carry on a propaganda that reminds one of Billy Sunday[1] and his friend William J. And now they are carrying on another propaganda—the Prime Minister being chief exhorter—to be thrifty and invest in the Government debt. People are taking the loan, as far as one can make out, quite satisfactorily; and one wonders why a propaganda about it is necessary.

All these events and more seem to prove to my mind the rather dismal failure the Liberal Government made—a failure really to grasp the problem. It was a dead failure. Of course they are waking up now, when they are faced with a certain dread lest many soldiers prefer frankly to die rather than spend another winter in practically the same trenches. You hear rumors, too, of great impending military scandals—God knows whether there be any truth in them or not.

In a word, while no Englishman gives up nor will ever give up —that's all rot—the job he has in hand is not going well. He's got to spit on his hands and buckle up his belt two holes tighter yet.

And I hav'nt seen a man in a month who dares hope for an end of the fight within any time that he can foresee.

I had a talk today with the Russian Ambassador.[2] He wished to know how matters stood between the U. S. and Great Britain. I said to him: "I'll give you a task if you have leisure. Set to and help me hurry up your distinguished Ally in dealing with our shipping troubles." The old man laughed (that seemed a huge joke to him), he threw up his hands and exclaimed—"My God! He is slow about his own business—has always been slow—can't be anything else." After more such banter, the nigger in his woodpile poked his head out: "Is there any danger," he asked, "that munitions may be stopped."

Hoover's been in Belgium a fortnight and he reports privately that Germans and Belgians (many of them at least) seem to feel that Germany will never be driven out. The Belgians who buried their money in the back yard have dug it up and put it back in the bank, the bank goes on all right under German rule.

And the most curious and unexpected thing in the world is happening in Belgium: in a sense the country is getting rich by reason of the war. The people have everything but food; their incomes from investments outside of Belgium are accumulating; they are so shut in that they can't spend any money: their Government (being driven out) can't tax them; the Germans do not levy heavy money indemnities; the outside world is feeding them —has to, or they'd starve—and they've learned to live well on half what they used to eat. Did you ever know such a surprising turn of affairs?

The Germans have been preparing Northern France also for German occupation. No French are left there, of course, except women and children and old men. They must be fed or starved or deported. The Germans put them on trains—a whole village at a time—and ran them to the Swiss frontier. Of course the Swiss pass them on into France. The French have their own and—the Germans will have Northern France without any French population, if this process goes on long enough.

The mere bang, bang, frightful era of the war is passed. The Germans are settling down to permanent business with their great organizing machine. Of course they talk about the freedom of the seas and such mush-mush; of course they'd like to have Paris and rob it of enough money to pay what the war has cost them, and London too. But what they really want for keeps is seacoast—Belgium and as much of the French coast as they can win. That's really what they are gunning for. Of course somehow at some time they mean to get Holland too and Denmark, if they really need it. Then they'd have a very respectable seacoast—the thing that they chiefly lack now.

It seems it was really to find out if England could'nt be made familiar with this thought that the Kaiser invited Lord Haldane to Berlin in 1912. When nothing came of this conference Germany added enormously to her military establishment; but England—did'nt. There you are!

It's hot in London—hotter than I've ever known it. It gets lonelier (more people going away) and sadder—more wounded coming back and more visible sorrow. We seem to be settling down to something that is more or less like Paris—so far less, but it may become more and more like it. And the confident note of an earlier period is accompanied by a dull undertone of much less cheerfulness. The end is—in the lap of the gods.

W. H. Page.

TCL (WP, DLC).

From Edith Bolling Galt

Cornish, New Hampshire Sunday,
My precious Sweetheart: July 18, 1915 10:30 P.M.

There are so many things I want to say first that I can't decide where to begin, but as a preliminary I will ease my heart by saying that which is dearest in all the world, and it is—I love you—love you—love you—and am utterly lonely without you. Just this time last night the "history-readers"[1] got sleepy and dispersed, and you and I were together and I felt your tenderness enfolding me and we knew the world held only each other. Now you seem far away, but in reality I know you are here, and I can still feel the warmth of your dear arms and rest in the protection of your love.

Oh! how hard it was to let you get in the car and drive off alone this afternoon. All the love in me cried out that you needed me—and I wanted to go—to stay with you and say to the world how proud I am that that is my place.

But one look at Mr. Murphy[2] recalled me to my humble self, and I smiled at you through an old wire door (that carried out the idea of my *cage* where I cannot reach you) and tried to look conventional and disinterested. I loved your taking off your hat, and the last look showed me your dear head bared, as though you were on holy ground. And indeed this, *your* home, is, and always will, be *holy ground* to me and I *felt* the thought that prompted your uncovering.

When you had gone Helen and I went out on the porch again and tried to talk. At three your train went by, so we knew you were still waiting at Windsor. Then Gertrude Gordon called me on the phone. I had just talked to her when Frank got back and Helen went to see about her house keeping and I sat in the hammock and *thought*. A tiny little humming bird darted in and out of those same blue flowers that attracted him yesterday when you were in the hammock, and it made me sick to think that these self same flowers and silly little bird were permitted to stay and *you* were *gone*!

Just as this was getting on my nerves Helen came and said let's take a ride. So we went at four thirty through Plainfield and around until we passed the Shipman's[3] about an hour afterward, where we got Altrude,[4] and as Helen wanted to come home, we came right over here and then Altrude and I went down the River Road for a lovely little ride before I took her home. I got back here a little before seven, and Mr. & Mrs. Parish[5] arrived in a few minutes. They are charming people, and I am sure you would like them. We had a lovely little dinner and afterward sat in the morning room and talked. I would not go near the sofa—it was too full of memories—and my right foot behaved so badly that had they not said they must leave at nine thirty, I don't know but what I would have had to call on Mr. Parish for help. The day was saved, however, by their going, and we all soon followed suit by coming upstairs.

I am writing tonight because Jessie and Frank want Helen and me to join them in a picnic tomorrow and they said lets start early. Helen is joining me on the porch tonight so I must stop so as not to keep her up late.

I may add a line in the morning—if I have time. If not p[l]ease Woodrow dearest, remember to take very tender care of your precious self and remember always   I love you,   Edith.

Monday, 9:30

You are just due in Washington, and I am welcoming you home, Sweetheart, before I have to run to join Helen. Don't work too hard and try to take rides. It is raining a little here, but Frank thinks it will stop so we are going.   Always yours   E.

ALS (WP, DLC).
   [1] Cary Grayson, Francis Sayre, Jessie Sayre, and Margaret Wilson were reading aloud Wilson's *A History of the American People.* See Edith Bolling Wilson, *My Memoir* (Indianapolis, 1939), p. 71.
   [2] Joseph E. Murphy, head of the White House detail of the Secret Service.
   [3] The home of Louis Evan Shipman and Ellen McGowan Biddle Shipman in Plainfield, N. H.
   [4] That is, Alice Gertrude Gordon.
   [5] Maxfield Parrish and Lydia Austin Parrish.

To Edward Mandell House

Washington, July 19, 1915.

Confidential message from Page informs us of very serious movement in England to force the Government to make cotton contraband.

You of course realize fatal effect that would have upon opinion here. Probably changing attitude of this country towards the Allies and leading to action by Congress cutting off munitions.

Would it not be well to get your press influence to work in England immediately?   Wilson.[1]

T decode of telegram (E. M. House Papers, CtY), with one correction from the WWsh draft in WP, DLC.
¹ There is also a WWhw coded draft of this telegram in WP, DLC.

From Robert Lansing, with Enclosure

My dear Mr President,   [Washington] p.m. 7/19/15
     This is the corrected draft of reply which you requested.
                         Faithfully yours   Robert Lansing.

ALS (WP, DLC).

E N C L O S U R E

July 16, 1915
Draft of Instruction to Ambassador Gerard.

You are instructed to deliver textually the following note to the Minister of Foreign Affairs:

The note of the Imperial German Government dated July 8, 1915, has received the careful consideration of the Government of the United States which regrets to state that it has found it to be unsatisfactory because of its failure to meet the real differences between the two Governments and to apply to them the principles of law and humanity involved in the present controversy. This Government, by reason of the changed methods of submarine warfare employed by the German naval authorities during the two months preceding the receipt of the note of July 8th, hoped that the Imperial Government was prepared to admit the illegality of the sinking of the LUSITANIA, to make an offer of reparation for the American lives lost, and to give assurances that in the future neutral vessels and neutrals on belligerent merchant vessels would be safeguarded by the exercise of the right of visit and search and by adherence to the other accepted rules of maritime warfare. It was a matter of surprise and disappointment, therefore, to find the note of the Imperial Government silent upon these subjects which constitute, in the views of this Government, the real issue.

The Imperial Government, while it reasserts its desire to conduct its naval operations in accordance with the accepted rules of international law and the principles of humanity, recognizes that the submarine warfare, which it has employed, being retaliatory for asserted illegal practices by Germany's enemies, is contrary to such rules and principles. Illegal and cruel acts, however justifiable they may be against an enemy who has acted in contravention of law, are indefensible when they deprive neutrals of their rights particularly the right of life. If a belligerent cannot retaliate upon an enemy without endangering the lives of neutrals, justice, humanity, and a due regard for the dignity of neutral powers demand that the practice should be discontinued. If persisted in by a belligerent, it would constitute an unpardonable offense against the sovereignty of a neutral nation affected by the practice.

The Government of the United States would be wanting in its earnest desire to preserve the friendly relations which have always existed between the United States and Germany if it failed to make clear to the Imperial Government the fundamental differences between the two Governments which have arisen from the method of submarine warfare practiced by the German navy. It is only by recognizing the fundamental character of these differences and the essential need that they must be removed that this controversy can be brought to an amicable conclusion and mutual goodwill and esteem be preserved.

The Government of the United States believes that the Imperial Government will appreciate the gravity of the situation and will unreservedly accept the principles of right which were violated by the sinking of the LUSITANIA, offer reparation for the wrong done to citizens of the United States, and give assurances that hereafter the lives and rights of neutrals traversing the high seas will not be jeopardized by any retaliatory measure which the Imperial Government may consider itself justified in adopting against its enemies.

Until these subjects have been removed from the field of controversy the Government of the United States cannot consider, much less discuss, any *modus vivendi* such as the one proposed in the note of the Imperial Government, which confers as an act of grace immunity upon particular vessels, to which all are entitled as a matter of right, but in no way satisfies the contentions of this Government or applies those principles which constitute the basis of neutral rights.

While it cannot recede from its determination to maintain the just rights of citizens of the United States on the high seas or permit any power, whatever may be its excuse to violate those rights with impunity, the Government of the United States has noted with satisfaction the intimation of the Imperial Government that it might be possible for the hostile powers through the good offices of the United States to agree to abandon the retaliatory practices which illegally affect neutral rights on the high seas and to return to the settled usage of nations. The Government of the United States gladly seizes this opportunity to assure the Imperial Government of its willingness to be the means of conveying any suggestions as to modification of methods of maritime warfare which any of the belligerent governments may wish conveyed to its adversaries.

The Government of the United States, while thus prepared to act as intermediary in any arrangement which may be sought by any of the parties to the war, feels that candor requires it to state to the Imperial Government that the present issues between the United States and Germany like similar issues between the United States and other belligerents, must be settled independently of any exchanges between the belligerents looking toward the abandonment of lawless methods of warfare and the restoration of the freedom of the seas to neutral commerce which the Imperial Government expressly champions in its note.

The Government of the United States is sure that the Imperial Government will realize that to prolong the discussion of the subjects in dispute between the two governments can serve no good purpose. The issues are plain and require no explanation. The Government of the United States expects, therefore, that the Imperial Government will respond promptly and frankly, and it still earnestly hopes that the answer will be one which will insure to neutrals their full rights on the high seas and cement more strongly the bonds of peace and amity which have for over a century and a quarter united the American and German peoples.

Robert Lansing

TS MS (WP, DLC).

From Robert Lansing, with Enclosure

My dear Mr President,   [Washington] 7/19/15
  This is supplemental to the draft sent to you this afternoon.
Robert Lansing.

ALS (WP, DLC).

E N C L O S U R E

FOR INSERTION

July 19, 1915.
Memorandum

  The general practice of the German naval commanders who have been conducting submarine warfare during the two months suceeding the sinking of the LUSITANIA has demonstrated that the rules of international law governing the detention and visit of merchant vessels on the high seas and the safeguarding of the lives of crews and passengers on vessels subject to capture can be observed by undersea craft without materially reducing the effectiveness of their use.

In view of the manifest possibility of the use of submarines in accordance with the accepted rules of maritime warfare and the assurance of the Imperial Government that it earnestly desires to conform to such rules and to restore to neutral commerce on the high seas that freedom which the observance of international law by belligerent nations confers, the Government of the United States would be wanting in a proper recognition of the honesty of the purpose of the Imperial Government if it doubted that the Imperial Government would in the future apply those principles which have been incorporated in all codes of naval war to safeguard the lives and rights of non-combatants, and give full and frank assurance of its intention to prevent the occurrence of deplorable incidents like the sinking of the LUSITANIA.

Robert Lansing.

TS MS (WP, DLC).

A Draft

Draft of Instructions to Ambassador Gerard, 19 July, 1915.

You are instructed to deliver textually the following note to the Minister of Foreign Affairs:

The note of the Imperial German Government dated the eighth of July, 1915, has received the careful consideration of the Government of the United States and this Government regrets to be obliged to say that it has found it very disappointing, because it fails to meet the real differences between the two Governments and indicates no way in which the accepted principles of law and humanity may be applied in the grave matter in controversy, but proposes, on the contrary, a partial suspension of those principles and arrangements which virtually set them aside.

The Government of the United States notes with satisfaction that the Imperial German Government recognizes without reservation the validity of the principles insisted on in the several communications which this Government has had the honour to address to the Imperial German Government with regard to the establishment of a war zone and the use of submarines against merchantmen on the high seas,—the principle that the high seas are free, that the character and cargo of a merchantman must first be ascertained before she can lawfully be seized or destroyed, and that the lives of non-combatants may in no case be put in jeopardy unless the vessel resists or seeks to escape after being summoned to submit to examination; but it is keenly disappointed to find that the Imperial German Government regards itself as in large degree exempt from the obligation to observe these principles, even where neutral vessels are concerned, by what it believes the policy and practice of Great Britain to be in the present war with regard to neutral commerce.

The Imperial German Government will readily understand that the Government of the United States cannot discuss the policy of Great Britain with regard to neutral trade except with the Government of Great Britain itself and that it must regard the conduct of other belligerant governments as irrelevant to any discussion with the Imperial German Government of what this Government regards as grave and unjustifiable violations of the rights of American citizens by German naval commanders. Illegal and inhuman acts, however justifiable they may be thought to be against an enemy who is believed to have acted in contravention of law and humanity, are manifestly indefensible when they deprive neutrals of their acknowledged rights, particularly when they violate the right to life itself. If a belligerant cannot retaliate against an enemy without injuring the lives of neutrals, as well as their property, humanity itself, as well as justice and a due regard for the dignity of neutral powers, should dictate that the practice be discontinued. If persisted in in such circumstances it would constitute an unpardonable offense against the sovereignty of the neutral nation affected.

Neither can a neutral power be expected in such circumstances to accept the concession of a part of its rights and the suspension of the rest. The Government of the United States, while fully recognizing the friendly spirit in which it is made, cannot accept the suggestion of the Imperial German Government that certain vessels be designated and agreed upon which shall be free of the seas now illegally proscribed. The very agreement would be a curtailment and therefore an abandonment of the principles for which it contends and which in times of calmer counsels every nation would concede as of course.

The events of the past two months have fortunately shown that it is possible and practicable to conduct such submarine operations as have characterized the naval activity of the Imperial German navy within the so-called war zone in entire accord with the accepted practices of regulated naval warfare: that it is possible to make sure of the character of the vessel attacked and to spare the lives of those on board if she must be sunk. The whole world has looked with interest and great satisfaction at the demonstration of that possibility by German naval commanders. It is manifestly possible, therefore, to lift the whole practice of submarine attack above criticism and remove all causes of offense.

The Government of the United States and the Imperial German Government are contending for the same great object, have long stood together in urging the very principles the Government of the United States now so solemnly insists upon. They are both contending for the freedom of the seas. The Government of the United States will continue to contend for that freedom, from whatever quarter violated, without compromise and at any cost. It invites the practical cooperation of the Imperial German Government at this time when cooperation may accomplish most and this great common object be most strikingly and effectively achieved.

The Imperial German Government expresses the hope that this object may be in some measure accomplished even before the present war ends. It can be. The Government of the United States not only feels obliged to insist upon it, wherever violated or ignored, in the protection of its own citizens but is also deeply interested in seeing it made practicable between the belligerants themselves, and holds itself ready at any time to act as the common friend who may be privileged to suggest a way.

In the meantime the very value it sets upon the long and unbroken friendship between the people and Government of the United States and the people and Government of the German nation impel it to press very solemnly upon the Imperial German Government the necessity for a scrupulous observance of neutral rights in this critical matter. Friendship itself prompts it to say to the Imperial German Government that continued acts on the part of the commanders of German naval vessels in contravention of those rights must be regarded by the Government of the United States, when they affect American citizens, as deliberately unfriendly.

WWT MS (SDR, RG 59, 763.72/1940, DNA).

Two Letters from Edward Mandell House

Manchester, Massachusetts.
Dear Governor: July 19th, 1915.

Jane Addams came today and Oswald Vil[l]ard was here last night. Of the two Miss Addams is far more sensible, though neither of them had anything of value to say. I am glad you are to see Miss Addams Wednesday because of her general influence, though I hate to see your time taken up unnecessarily.

James Garfield told me much about Mexico that was interesting and valuable. He said that General Wood, General Scott, Garrison, Lane and he thinks Lansing approve[s] of the plan he has. There is no need to go into it in detail as you perhaps already have it from one of those mentioned.[1]

That matter seems so pressing that I hope you can use some such plan. I have a feeling that as soon as a government is recognized, the people generally will be glad to gravitate to it even though, at the beginning, they do not accept it as the best.

I have made it clear to all those with whom I have talked that if their differences are not composed while you are President, that the first act of a new administration will probably be to intervene and in a way that will overthrow all that for which the Constitutionalists have so long struggled.

Fletcher, our Ambassador to Chili, is returning in a day or two to his post. I believe he is the best man that we could get to help button up the South American matter. Phillips with whom I have talked also agrees that he is.

I have wanted to discuss it with Lansing but have not been able to see him yet. If you think well of pressing this to a conclusion and think well of Fletcher as one of the instruments, will you not have the Department extend his leave for two weeks longer.   Affectionately yours,   E. M. House

[1] Garfield had just returned from northern Mexico, where he had conferred with the leaders of the Villa faction, including General Felipe Angeles. The "plan" that Garfield mentioned was one of several being made by various groups during the summer of 1915. The "plan" provided for the establishment of a new provisional Mexican government representative of all factions, the deposition of Carranza, and American political and financial support for the new Mexican government. James R. Garfield to EMH, Aug. 2 and 11, 1915, and Sept. 10, 1914 [1915], TLS (E. M. House Papers, CtY). For the larger context, see Link, *The Struggle for Neutrality*, pp. 483-90.

Dear Governor:

Manchester, Massachusetts.
July 19th, 1915.

I am cabling Sir Horace Plunkett according to your suggestion and I am impressing upon him the urgency of influencing the British Press in the direction desired.[1]

Do not forget that I can reach Sir Edward Grey direct if at any time you wish me to do so. By direct, I mean literally without any intermediary and in code. I have not done this as yet and do not believe it is desirable to do it unless a real emergency arises.   Affectionately yours,   E. M. House

TLS (WP, DLC).

¹ EMH to H. Plunkett, July 19, 1915, Hw telegram (E. M. House Papers, CtY). Decoded, it reads as follows: "Important British press use influence against action detrimental to cotton. Should Great Britain do this Congress would probably retaliate. The matter is of extreme urgency."

Walter Hines Page to Robert Lansing

London, July 19, 1915.

Confidential. Your 1860, July 16, 5 p m. I have had a long unofficial conversation with Sir Edward Grey in which I fully explained thoroughly the whole political dangers that have arisen and may arise about interference with the cotton trade.

He is having conferences today and tomorrow about cotton and the cabinet will take up the subject on Wednesday. They will probably offer to the cotton interests to buy enough of the new crop to keep the price up to a reasonable figure.

About the more comprehensive subject of the so-called blockade he informed me unofficially that if the British Government permitted unrestricted American trade with European neutral states they had might as well cease to stop anything at all and that they would have to give up all efforts at economic pressure on Germany and indefinitely prolong the war; and he implied that such a course might even put the ultimate issue in doubt.

I suggested that perhaps a clearer understanding might be reached if he would quickly give a frank and full answer to out [our] last general note. He seemed to accept that suggestion and promised to bring the subject before Wednesday's Cabinet.

The seriousness of the situation is appreciated by Sir Edward.

He assured me that no important decisions are left to Departmental officers but are all made by the Cabinet.

American Ambassador, London

T telegram (SDR, RG 59, 763.72112/1355, DNA).

To Edith Bolling Galt

[The White House] Monday,

My precious Darling,   19 July, 1915 9.50 A.M.

I have just this minute come into this empty house,—to find that it is *not* empty, that you *did* run on beforehand to welcome me. I am conscious of the presence of your sweet spirit. I was conscious of it before I left the train, and all night long, after I got into bed and read that sweet, tender note that seemed almost like a touch of your lips in loving pledge. My Darling! I love you more than tongue can tell—and am so unspeakably happy that you love me!

They are clamouring for me, but I must send you this little note to tell you that the journey was made in comfort and safety, that Washington is *not* intolerably hot this morning, that I am perfectly well, and happy in your love as never before, that I am going to *make* business go this week so as to release me at the end of it, and that every hour, every minute of every day and every night my heart is consciously and delightedly full of you. You are all the world to me!   Your own   Woodrow

Dearest love to all

ALS (WP, DLC).

To Melancthon Williams Jacobus

My dear Friend: The White House July 20, 1915

I cannot let your letter of July tenth[1] go by with a mere formal acknowledgment from the office. I must tell you what deep pleasure it gave me. These are indeed days of deep perplexity, but there is no doubt, I suppose, in any wise man's mind on the question as to whether we should maintain our present position with regard to neutral rights or not. The opinion of the country seems to demand two inconsistent things, firmness and the avoidance of war, but I am hoping that perhaps they are not in necessary contradiction and that firmness may bring peace.

Always, with affectionate regard,
                    Faithfully yours,   Woodrow Wilson

TLS (R. S. Baker Coll., DLC).
    [1] It is missing.

To Ellison DuRant Smith

My dear Senator: [The White House] July 20, 1915

I have your letter of July fourteenth[1] and would say in reply that I hope you will never hesitate to write me about anything that you think important, no matter how busy or preoccupied I may be.

And I want to tell you that, though we have said very little about it in public, nothing has been omitted to bring the matters you write about very completely and in their right light to the attention of the Government of Great Britain, and nothing will be omitted that can be done.

Cordially and sincerely yours,   Woodrow Wilson

TLS (Letterpress Books, WP, DLC).
  [1] It is missing.

A Memorandum by Lindley Miller Garrison

Cabinet   July 20, 1915.

All present except Secty Redfield. The Pres. read outlines of proposed note to Germany. Begins by saying that they have recognized the principle for which we contend, but are not living up to it; that their proposition to limit our trade & travel to certain vessels is not entertainable, as we are entitled to whole & not part of rights. That Germany has shown she can identify (synonym for visit & search) & that she should. Her answer unsatisfactory & therefore we will wait & see what she does.

Burleson wanted more in note particularly a threat to refuse to continue to represent her diplomatically if she refused to give assurances disavowal & reparation.

I said I thot Pres note would be taken as abandoning our contention that Germany must adhere to Principle or we couldn't tell where we stood as to past or future.

I read my note (see inclosure)[1]   Long discussion. Pres said it (my note) was dignified & forceful, but he tho't would be taken as continuing the discussion & Am. people dont want discussion continued. He saw Am. people more in a peculiar frame of mind —one that left him in a "cradle" position. They wanted Pres to insist on our rights but to avoid war or any rupture of friendly relations.

I agreed & said that that necessarily limited our proper action. We could not go further than we were supported by pub. op. I tho't therefore best to keep our record absolutely straight by pressing Germany thru to a Yes or No or refusal to answer. We would be no worse off after another note putting question squarely for them unencumbered by a single fact or a discussable suggestion. We could then whatever their conduct govern ourselves accordingly. I said I tho't pub. op. in the country confused on issue.

McAdoo agreed with me that issue should be restated—otherwise agreed with Pres.

Gregory thot Pres right excepting in not referring to Lusitania situation & Pres. agreed to this.

Houston thot Pres. right, but agreed with me that issue should be restated. Lane tho't people were resentful of Germany's attitude, but tho't Pres. note o.k. Wilson agreed with Pres. So did Daniels.

Lansing agreed with Pres. at least Pres said after consultation between self & Lansing mem. he read was result—they agreed.

Pres. said in answer my question that after hearing all of us he would frame note stating Germany recognized prin (I think G[ermany]. didnt & dont in any explicit way)—calling attention to her action & statement about identifying &c &c restate our position, say they haven't lived up to prin & we must await her actions. If another in violation of prin, then we must consider that an intentional unfriendly act.

I didn't agree—still thought & said we should in substance send a note along lines of my draft—(Lansing took my draft).

Lansing said very little. So did Gregory & Daniels & Lane.

Some little talk abt Mex. Pres. hasnt really made up his mind to do anything yet, & nor yet what to do when he does act.

Said as to Eng. we were doing all we could.

I tho't our notes requiring her to live up to our rights should be published. He said it would be like "hedging on a bet" I didnt agree. Think it would have fine effect all round—always have thot so.

Am very interested to see how note to Germany comes out. Pres said no cabinet meeting expected soon He goes to N. H. again Frid. July 23

Hw MS (L. M. Garrison Papers, NjHi).
¹ There is a carbon copy of it, dated July 20, 1915, in the L. M. Garrison Papers, NjHi.

Two Letters to Edith Bolling Galt

[The White House]
My precious Darling,   Tuesday morning, 20 July '15

You should just see this house,—at least the upper storey of it. Downstairs it looks pretty much as it always does,—because visitors look at it all the year around, I suppose; but upstairs! All the hangings are down, everything "stripped to the buff," and all the furniture is in white pajamas. When I arrived there was not a flower in the house,—only empty jars and vases standing about and looking as if they had always been empty and had been left where they were only because no one had thought or cared to put them away. It looked like a house not only vacant but vacated and left unfriended. And yet, as I told you in my note scribbled just after getting here—the very moment I reached the study table—I was not chilled by it all. *You* were not actually here, or everything would have looked and breathed of home, but your thought and love were here to greet me, not to take care of the house, but to comfort and reassure *me* and tell me of happy things which make loneliness impossible except in the stillness and vacant rooms about me. How happy it made me to realize it!

I did not take a long breath until after four o'clock in the afternoon, but went from one piece of business to another without pause. First I cyphered a despatch to House, about a matter I want him to try to help us handle in England (the matter of making cotton contraband which I mentioned to you the other day). Then I spent an hour with Lansing, catching up with many pieces of business, but chiefly discussing, of course, the reply we should make to Germany, our regular correspondent! He had drafted a reply, which was all right as far as it went, but which omitted some of the strong points of our case and stated those it did state too dryly. We agreed, therefore, after I had made clear my own views of how it should be handled, each of us to try our hand at another draft. Then I went to work at the office (12.30) and, with a brief interval for lunch, worked until half past four, clearing up routine matters there. At five the doctor and I took a ride in the landaulette. It had been cooled off enough to sit in, for very soon after lunch a storm came up, a slow, sullen thunder storm with a torrent of rain, and it did not clear until we had been out for half an hour. We had dinner on the terrace, the doctor, Fitz William and I (Tumulty dining out) and after dinner I went at the note to Germany. By half-past ten it was sufficiently in shape to discuss in language and detail with Lansing when I see him this morning at eleven (how I wish I could go over it and discuss it with my sweet partner!) and I was ready to *fall* into bed, as you will readily imagine. But I was not *too* tired. I am *very* well, immensely braced and invigorated by my three weeks with my Darling, and it was only a sort of *satisfied* fatigue after something accomplished. Mac. turned up last night and is lodging with us, and Colonel Brown is expected to-day, so you may think of us as six men condemned to see no one but each other and endure it as best we can! Inasmuch a[s] Tumulty and McAdoo *know* nothing to talk about but business and there is not likely to be silence when we are together, you can easily see how full a week of work your lover is to have. But there seems no reason to doubt (Heaven be praised) that I can get off on Friday at midnight and be with my precious Sweetheart on Saturday at one, for another week of uninterrupted happiness and, that being the case, I don't care what happens to me in the meantime. The weather is quite endurable—and I am a salamander.

I *write* of the occupations of the day, my Darling, but my thought is all the while of you. The first Chapter was full of happiness and sweetness and the wonder and delight of discovery and love, and my sweet One dreaded to see it end; but the second Chapter has been sweeter than the first (don't you think so?), bringing with it every sort of confirmation and fulfilment of the hope and promise of the first. It has filled my heart with a joy unspeakable. I feel myself united to my Love by bonds which nothing can make sweeter or more intimate except *constant* companionship, and I know that she is incomparable and altogether lovely. Ah, my Sweetheart, my precious Sweetheart, you have made me so happy; I love you so deeply and tenderly; I am in every breath of me   Your own   Woodrow

There are a score of things I have not had time to say!

ALS (WP, DLC).

My adorable Sweetheart,
[The White House] Tuesday, 20 July, 1915 5 P.M.

How perfectly and altogether lovely you are! Your letter, written Sunday night, has filled my heart to overflowing: it is so perfect a love letter, and the joy and comfort and strength with which it has blessed me spring from so many sources of loveliness and womanly insight and tenderness, of ineffable charm and *dear*ness, that I do not know which I feel the more keenly, the joy that you love me so or the pain that, loving me so, you cannot come to me and never, never leave my side again! I do indeed *need* you, my precious Darling; you never said a truer thing or had a truer instinct in your life. It was cruelly hard to have to drive away from the house on Sunday and leave you standing there in the doorway as if you were not part of me and I were not leaving my inspiration and real life behind me. I did not lift my hat to my home: I lifted it to *you* and did not cover my head again until the turn of the drive hid you from sight and I was no longer in the presence of the sweet, the incomparable lady without whose presence no place can be my home. You are everything to me. Without you I am maimed and imperfect. For I have learned what you are and my heart is wholly enthraled. You are my ideal companion, the close and delightful *chum of my mind*. You are my perfect *playmate*, with whom everything that is gay and mirthful and imaginative in me is at its best.

You are the sweetest *lover* in the world, full of delicacy and charm and tenderness and all the wonder of intimate self-revelation which only makes you the more lovely the more complete it is. You match and satisfy every part of me, grave or gay, of the mind or of the heart,—the man of letters, the man of affairs, the boy, the poet, the lover. When you are mine for every day I shall be complete and strong and happy indeed. Do you wonder what I am doing in the study at five o'clock in the afternoon, writing to you? I simply *must* write to you every minute I am free to. It is just as instinctive with me, and just as necessary to me, as if you were here in the house and I were free for a little while to go and hold you in my arms and pour out to you everything that was in my mind or heart. We went out to play golf, in Virginia, the Colonel, the doctor, and I, but it rained before we reached the third hole and we were driven home again A hard morning went before—an hour with Lansing and two hours with the Cabinet; and, after lunch, I had to see a Senator and an M.C.[1] to hear plaint and dire prophesy of what the war was doing and was going to do to the cotton interests in the South. It would have been fine if I could have had a couple of hours of golf, to clear the fatigue out of my brain. But a talk with you is infinitely better. That makes me *whole*. I am glad the rain sent me back to you. These sweet intervals when I can give my thoughts altogether to you and pour out my heart to you without restraint or interruption, are, next to your own (wonderful) letters, the means of my salvation when I cannot literally have you, your own sweet self! Lansing and I have virtually agreed upon a note—along substantially the lines you and I talked over—but we did not attempt to put the tentative text of it before the Cabinet to-day. We submitted only an outline of the argument; and the discussion went all ways at once, as usual, Garrison doing, as always, most of the talking. He had brought with him *the complete draft of a note of his own writing*, which he read to us. He seems to feel that he owes us this guidance. He does not expect us to see or think clearly enough to accept what he offers, but he feels bound in conscience to at least afford us the chance to be rightly and intelligently led! Dear fellow! It is hard that we cannot always follow him. On the whole I think most of the men approved of the aswer Lansing and I outlined, I am glad to say, and I hope they will entirely when they read the completed text. We hope to have it complete by to-morrow and to get it off by Thursday or Friday,—Friday at the latest,—and then back to my Darling!

[1] Senator John Hollis Bankhead of Alabama and Representative Samuel Joelah Tribble of Georgia.

What thoughts of you fill and gladden my heart, my Sweet-heart! How deep I have drunk of the sweet fountains of love that are in you—and how pure and wholesome and refreshing they are, how full of life and every sweet perfection! I have seen so many lovely things that make me feel as if I had been in a sanctuary, and yet in a place where there was welcome for everything that was human and natural and unaffected and intimate; and I have learned to love you, my Sweetheart, more and more and more, with each day and hour, with each experience and revelation of your very heart. It seems to me now as if you were indeed a very part of me. Those wonderful mornings when our minds grew to be intimate friends; those conferences in which our affairs and interests seemed to draw together and become merged; those afternoons of mere irresponsible companionship in the simple pleasures of a drive or a game of pool; those never-to-be-forgotten evenings when our hearts were opened to one another without reserve and with the joy of young lovers and when, as you say in this priceless letter that came to me to-day, there was no one else in the world for us,—they have made me feel, not only that you were mine and I was yours as it has seldom been given to two lovers to be united, but also that I had come into a world of joy and intimate happiness wholly created by one lovely, one incomparably lovely, woman to whom my heart must always bow down with a new sense of privilege, a new knowledge of love. My love for you is deeper than all words, my precious One; and I *enjoy* you so! Everything in me enjoys you so,—and misses you so intolerably when you are away from me! Thank God for work! I do not know how I could endure the longing if I were not *obliged* to keep my brains busy all the while. Ah, how I need you! How empty the hours are without you! I can make shift while the working hours last; but when they are over, when there is time and opportunity for a touch of *home*,—when bed-time comes and you are not here to crown the day with your sweet sympathy and tenderness and comprehension of my need, how I get by those crises I do not know—how often, how long I shall be able to get by them I dare not try to think or reckon!

Wed. 21 July, 7.15 A.M.

I was interrupted—and then had to go to dinner with the boys(!), and after dinner had a long conference with the Secretary of the Interior about the Alaska railways, ending with a discussion of life and religion! And then, being desperately sleepy, I went to my room, at nine thirty, elaborately anointed my head with hair tonic, *a la* Mrs. Coon, and went to bed—with your picture on the little stand beside me,—so that, after I had read your dear letter again, it was the last thing my eyes rested on before I put out the light and turned over to go to sleep—with, oh, *such* a longing at my heart, but a sweet longing because I knew that you really and tenderly love me, as only such a woman as you are can, and that some blessed day not far away you would come to me and the longing would be fulfilled. That is what sustains me in the midst of all this terribly responsible work, when the world is gone mad and depends in part on *me* to steady it and bring it back to sanity and peace. I should be in danger of losing my own poise and coolness of judgment if I had not found you and won your precious love. I feel that more and more. You are not only the Darling of my heart but the source of all serenity in me and of the happiness that frees the faculties of a man for action. *I love you with all my heart*!

Your brother Randolph is coming in to take dinner with us tonight. Isn't that fine? I am looking forward with such pleasure to having a chance to really know him;—and perhaps, if the evening is hot, he would like to take a drive with us after dinner. I have not been able to get off any other evening. Grayson had a long talk with Mr. Clapham[2] yesterday which was *most* satisfactory about Rolfe[3] if he will only stay in Panama. It would be folly, and embarrass all his friends besides, for him to come away.

Is my Darling happy? Does she *feel* how her lover's thoughts follow her, and with what infinite tenderness and love? My Darling, my Darling, I am always and altogether

Your own   Woodrow

ALS (WP, DLC).
   [2] Ashton G. Clapham, president of the Commercial National Bank of Washington.
   [3] Rolfe E. Bolling, Edith Galt's eldest brother, at this time manager of branches of the Commercial National Bank of Washington in Balboa and Cristobal, Panama.

From Edith Bolling Galt

Cornish, New Hampshire
My own dearest One: July 20, 1915 9.30 A.M.

Your telegram to Frank[1] yesterday did my heart good for I knew you were safe home.

I followed you all the weary way and do so hope it was cool and comfortable in Washington. Did you come to the sofa at ten minutes to one and rest before lunch? I was in my room by the window in the big chair and tried so hard to find you, but you seemed remote and as though you were thinking of me, but not able to follow out our program.

I am curious to know if this is so, for the wires would work as though there was a bad connection and I could not be sure. Bless your precious heart how I do miss you. And now I am going off before I can get your letter for the rain continued yesterday until so late we had to give up the picnic so we are going today. And the girls want to get back in time for the "Discussion Club" Jessie says she will be ready by eleven so Helen and I are going to walk—starting at ten—and they will pick us up.

I know you will be delighted to know our dear little Helen is quite well again and her old happy self. She and I walked nearly to the Windsor Bridge yesterday afternoon and went to the "Tea Tray" for Tea, and last night Helen was asleep before twelve and did not move until eight thirty this morning.

I think lack of exercise was largly what was the matter, hence we mean to walk every day.

Well the dinner party last night was *very* nice. I was intcrested to meet Mr. Churchill and found him interesting in some respects, but a subtle comparison always comes up in my mind, when I meet men, to a very wonderful person whom I love, and the rest of humanity seems commonplace. This is absolutely true Sweetheart. I have been so interested these past few months trying it, and it has never failed. I kept thinking last night how different the evening would have been had you been here.

Tonight the elder Mr. Parrish[2] comes to dinner, and tomorrow five ladies to lunch. Then, as you remember we go to dinner with Mr. & Mrs. Fitch,[3] and Thursday Miss Parker[4] has asked Helen and me to lunch with her, but if we go for the long walk with Jessie and Frank of course we will not go.

I saw in the papers that you were greeted all along the line by crowds, so I am afraid you had a tiresome trip.

I shall look so eagerly for your dear letter when we come back. Did you know I wrote Dr. Grayson yesterday?

Helen and I went to see Altrude off yesterday, and I had promised him, if I saw her to write and tell him. So I did and it seemed to me what I told him should make him very happy.

Helen is ready, so goodby, Dearest until tomorrow. Take care of my Sweetheart and know that I am always yours,

Edith.

ALS (WP, DLC).
  1 It is missing.
  2 Stephen Parrish.
  3 The Rev. Dr. Albert Parker Fitch and Flora May Draper Fitch.
  4 Marie Parker, proprietress of the Cornish teahouse called "The Tea Tray."

From Robert Lansing

Personal and Confidential.

My dear Mr. President: Washington July 21, 1915.

I have been through the draft of the reply to the German note and enclose a copy with my suggestions. There were two things which I thought ought to be in the reply, namely, reference to the LUSITANIA and a closing paragraph disavowing responsibility on our part for the consequences if Germany should continue her illegal practices. While I think both of these ought to be presented to the German Government, American public opinion will, I am sure, be better satisfied. The last paragraph may seem a little too vigorous, as it undoubtedly contains a veiled (rather thinly veiled) threat, but it is no more than we have already said in other notes. I am confident that it would make a very good impression in this country, and of course we cannot ignore the effect of the reply here, and I do not believe that it would increase German irritation.

The reply has two primary ideas, the illegality of retaliatory acts by a belligerent and the possibility of using submarines in accordance with the rules of maritime war.

You will see that I suggest the transposition of paragraph 6 on page 6 (I have numbered the paragraphs for reference) to page 5 immediately preceding paragraph 4. This, I believe, will give a more logical treatment of the subjects.

Analyzed the subjects are as follows:

Par. 1. Dissatisfaction.
 "   2. Admission of principles.
 "   3. Exemption from principles.
 "   6. Possibility of conformity.
 "   4. The LUSITANIA.
 "   5. Suggested *modus vivendi*.
 "   7. Freedom of the seas.
 "   8. Agreement between belligerents.
 "   9. Observance of neutral rights.
 "   10. Responsibility for consequences of violation.

I have followed my previous practice of putting suggested omissions in brackets and underscoring suggested insertions.

I hope that a final draft may be determined upon today, if possible, for I believe that it should go forward as soon as possible in order to put an end to newspaper speculations which have a tendency to affect public opinion and prevent impartial judgment when the note is actually published.

                    Faithfully yours,   Robert Lansing.

TLS (WP, DLC).

To Robert Lansing, with Enclosure

My dear Mr. Secretary,   The White House. 21 July, 1915.

Thank you for this draft. I have gone over it and am glad to accept practically all of your suggestions.

I have taken the liberty of omitting, however, the last paragraph. It has the tone of an ultimatum, and does not seem to me in fact to add to the meaning of the document as a whole, the manifest meaning of it. I do not think that we need add a *sting*.

I shall be away from the house for a couple of hours, but will get into communication with you so soon as I get back.

Faithfully Yours,   W.W.

WWTLI (SDR, RG 59, 763.72/1940, DNA).

E N C L O S U R E[1]

Draft of Instructions to Ambassador Gerard, 19 July, 1915.

You are instructed to deliver textually the following note to the Minister of Foreign Affairs:

1. The note of the Imperial German Government dated the eighth of July, 1915, has received the careful consideration of the Government of the United States and *it* [this Government] regrets to be obliged to say that it has found it very *unsatisfactory* [disappointing] because it fails to meet the real differences between the two Governments and indicates no way in which the accepted principles of law and humanity may be applied in the grave matter in controversy, but proposes, on the contrary, *arrangements for* a partial suspension of those principles [and arrangements] which virtually set them aside.

2. The Government of the United States ⟨*nevertheless*⟩ notes with satisfaction that the Imperial German Government recognizes without reservation the validity of the principles insisted on in the several communications which this Government has [had the honour to] address*ed* to the Imperial German Government with regard to *its announcement* [the establishment] of a war zone and the use of submarines against merchantmen on the high seas,—the principle that the high seas are free, that

1 The following document is Lansing's revision of Wilson's draft of July 19, which in turn was based upon an undated WWsh draft (WP, DLC). Lansing put excised Wilson text in square brackets and italicized his own substitutions. We have reproduced Lansing's changes following his method. Wilson drew a line through all of Lansing's deletions that he accepted. We have not reproduced these lines.

In addition, Wilson edited Lansing's revised draft. The words that Wilson added are printed in double brackets. Lansing text which Wilson deleted is printed within angle brackets.

the character and cargo of a merchantman must first be ascertained before she can lawfully be seized or destroyed, and that the lives of noncombatants may in no case be put in jeopardy unless the vessel resists or seeks to escape after being summoned to submit to examination; *for a belligerent act of retaliation is* per se *an act beyond the law, and the defense of an act as retaliatory is an admission that it is illegal.*

3. *The Government of the United States is, however,* [but it is] keenly disappointed to find that the Imperial German Government regards itself as in large degree exempt from the obligation to observe these principles, even where neutral vessels are concerned, by what it believes the policy and practice of *the Government of* Great Britain to be in the present war with regard to neutral commerce. The Imperial German Government will readily understand that the Government of the United States cannot discuss the policy of *the Government of* Great Britain with regard to neutral trade except with *that* [the] Government [[itself,]] ⟨[of Great Britain itself]⟩ and that it must regard the conduct of other belligerent governments as irrelevant to any discussion with the Imperial German Government of what this Government regards as grave and unjustifiable violations of the rights of American citizens by German naval commanders. Illegal and inhuman acts, however justifiable they may be thought to be against an enemy who is believed to have acted in contravention of law and humanity, are manifestly indefensible when they deprive neutrals of their acknowledged rights, particularly when they violate the right to life itself. If a belligerent cannot retaliate against an enemy without injuring the lives of neutrals, as well as their property, humanity [itself], as well as justice and a due regard for the dignity of neutral powers, should dictate that the practice be discontinued. If persisted in it would in such circumstances constitute an unpardonable offense against the sovereignty of the neutral nation affected.

[[Insert here attached addition marked "A"]][2]

"A"

[[The Government of the United States is not unmindful of the extraordinary conditions created by this war or of the radical alterations of circumstance and method of attack produced by the use of instrumentalities of naval warfare which the nations of the world cannot have had in view when the existing rules of international law were formulated, and it is ready to make every reasonable allowance for these novel and unexpected aspects of war at sea; but it cannot consent to abate any essential or

[2] WWhw.

fundamental right of its people because of a mere alteration of circumstance. The rights of neutrals in time of war are based upon principle, not upon expediency, and the principles are immutable. It is the duty and obligation of belligerents to find a way to adapt the new circumstances to them.]][3]

See paragraph 6, page 6

4. *In view of the admission of illegality made by the Imperial Government when it pleaded the right of retaliation in defense of its acts, and in view of the manifest possibility of conforming to the established rules of naval warfare, the Government of the United States cannot believe that the Imperial Government will longer refrain from disavowing the wanton act of its naval commander in sinking the* LUSITANIA *or from offering reparation for the American lives lost, so far as reparation can be made for a needless destruction of human life by an illegal act.*

5. ⟨[Neither can a neutral power be expected in such circumstances to accept the concession of a part of its (*manifest*) rights and the suspension of the rest.]⟩ The Government of the United States, while *not indifferent to* [fully recognizing] the friendly spirit in which it is made, cannot accept the suggestion of the Imperial German Government that certain vessels be designated and agreed upon which shall be free *on* [of] the seas now illegally proscribed. The very agreement *would, by implication, subject other vessels to illegal attack and* would be a curtailment and therefore an abandonment of the principles for which *this Government* [it] contends and which in times of calmer counsels every nation would concede as of course.

6. The events of the past two months have *clearly* [fortunately] *indicated* [shown] that it is possible and practicable to conduct such submarine operations as have characterized the naval activity of the Imperial German navy within the so-called war zone in ⟨*general*⟩ [[substantial]] ⟨[entire]⟩ accord with the accepted practices of regulated warfare. ⟨[;that it is possible to make sure of the character of the vessel attacked and to *safeguard* (spare) the lives of those on board if *it is decided to sink her and her cargo.* (she must be sunk.)]⟩ The whole world has looked with interest and *increasing* [great] satisfaction at the demonstration of that possibility by German naval commanders. It is manifestly possible, therefore, to lift the whole practice of submarine attack above *the* criticism *which it has aroused* and remove *the chief* [all] causes of offenses.

Transpose this paragraph so as to follow paragraph 3 on page 5.

7. The Government of the United States and the Imperial Ger-

----

[3] The above paragraph WWT. There is a WWsh draft of this addition in (WP, DLC).

man Government are contending for the same great object, have long stood together in urging the very principles, *upon which* the Government of the United States now so solemnly insists. [upon.] They are both contending for the freedom of the seas. The Government of the United States will continue to contend for that freedom, from whatever quarter violated, without compromise and at any cost. It invites the practical cooperation of the Imperial German Government at this time when cooperation may accomplish most and this great common object be most strikingly and effectively achieved.

8. The Imperial German Government expresses the hope that this object may be in some measure accomplished even before the present war ends. It can be. The Government of the United States not only feels obliged to insist upon it, by *whomsoever* [wherever] violated or ignored, in the protection of its own citizens, but is also deeply interested in seeing it made practicable between the belligerents themselves, and holds itself ready at any time to act as the common friend who may be privileged to ⟨convey the suggestions of either belligerent to its adversary.⟩ [suggest a way.][4]

9. In the meantime the very value, *which this Government* [it] sets upon the long and unbroken friendship between the people and Government of the United States and the people and Government of the German nation impels it to press very solemnly upon the Imperial German Government the necessity for a scrupulous observance of neutral rights in this critical matter. Friendship itself prompts it to say to the Imperial [German] Government that *repetition by* [continued acts on the part of] the commanders of German naval vessels *of acts* in contravention of those rights must be regarded by the Government of the United States, when they affect American citizens, as deliberately unfriendly.[5]

⟨10. *In the event that this situation should unhappily arise the heavy responsibility would rest upon the Imperial Government for the inevitable consequences. The people and Government of the United States are determined to maintain their just rights and will adopt the steps necessary to insure their respect by all nations.*⟩

T MS (SDR, RG 59, 763.72/1940, DNA); page with last paragraph in WP, DLC.
4 Here Wilson is returning to his original wording.
5 The note was sent in this revised form as RL to J. W. Gerard. July 21, 1915, T telegram (SDR, RG 59, 763.72/1940, DNA), printed in *FR-WWS 1915*, pp. 480-82.

ADDENDA

From Walter Hines Page

Dear Mr. President: [London] July 2. 1915

The atmosphere here is now more gloomy than it has before been at any time since the war began. There have been, so far as I can make out, two tragic errors—beginning the attack at the Dardanelles with the fleet instead of surprising the Turks with an army there, and the strange failure to provide enough ammunition of the right kind for the army in France. These caused the downfall of the Government, and each has brought a long train of discouraging consequences to the Allies. The Germans know that the only purpose the war at the Dardanelles will serve will be to keep an Allied army there indefinitely; and this Allied failure prevents any help coming from any of the Balkan States. The lack of proper ammunition in proper quantities prevents the Allied armies in France from trying to drive the Germans back and gives Germany its chance to work its will on Russia. The Dardanelles failure promises to become a sort of permanent discouragement. The manufacture of munitions seems now to be begun aright. But both these failures have had a profoundly discouraging and depressing effect. And certainly they have lengthened the duration of the war.

In a certain direct way, too, they have a bearing on our problems with the British Government. They provoke agitation in favour of many smaller measures which small men imagine may help their cause—*e.g.* there is a renewed and persistent agitation to have cotton declared contraband. What chance this has of success, I cannot say. In fact British action in small and large things as well as the British answer to our Note of long ago about the blockade, seems to wait on the German reply to our Note to Berlin. The British undoubtedly hope that events will help them in their answer.

I have, for instance, just come from Strachey's (the editor of *The Spectator*) who once a week gathers around his tea-table a member or two of the Cabinet, and naval and army and newspaper men whom he trusts. The company talks quite freely under a well-understood arrangement of confidence. There was no effort there to conceal the very depressing situation nor the keen interest felt in Germany's answer to us. This group of men are firmly persuaded that, whatever that answer may be, we shall not be done with serious trouble with the Germans; and they betrayed a good deal of fear of the agitation in the United States in favour of an embargo on munitions—when Congress meets. The Russian Ambassador came to see me yesterday and I discovered that his real errand was to get my judgment on this subject.

Sir Edward Grey has been away for nearly six weeks, because of an ailment of the eyes and he is now, I am glad to say, about to come back again. Lord Crewe has been *locum tenens*—a square, frank, sort of fellow who has words instead of ideas. Routine business has gone on well enough, but matters of larger policy Crewe knows nothing about. The Gov't, as regards us, is 'twixt the devil and the deep sea, the Admiralty being the devil. The real trouble is they can't trust the small neutral States. For these States the Germans, public and private, are too strong and shrewd. Then, again, the British muddle thro' & come even to trust to muddling—to hesitate to cross a stream till they are driven into it.

I've come to have—not less respect exactly—but surely less reverence, and no awe at all, for contemporary British states-manship. It isn't the thing we've read about. I wonder, in fact, if the thing we've read about ever was; and I doubt it. The historians don't give us undressed views. There's no *great* leadership here. Kitchener surely has done an historic thing in raising the new Army. But Jeff. Davis and Lincoln did a parallel thing with far, far less money and a less chance; and not even the military bungling of the Union generals equals the error of the British failure in ammunition. Asquith makes fine speeches. But he doesn't give the sense of leadership. Sir E. Grey has a mastery of his side of the job and he surely has done well. Yet why the Balkan States do not come in but on the contrary give signs of helping the Germans and why Holland isn't won over—occur to one. Lloyd George brings more things to pass than any other man. Yet he's the least heroic figure in the group.

The Prime Minister seems spent. His speeches are admirable. You will not find clearer statements of important facts made by anybody. But there's no passion in them. They seem like a lawyer's speeches, no doubt expressing the convictions of the man. Still you can't quite get away from the feeling that they are merely intellectual uses of obvious material: his words don't burn. In private he merely enunciates an intellectual conclusion or talks to amuse himself. He seems to seek forgetfulness of the stress of things: he plays bridge three hours every night. He runs away every week-end. You never think of him managing the rudder. You know that he is Prime Minister but you never feel it. He has no manner and indifferent manners. He reminds me of a man I once knew who sent his lady flowers every day and a letter every day that he could not call and kept his coach and span at her service—an ardent and ingenious and most attentive wooer. But after he was married he became a commonplace and forgetful husband. When one of his friends reasoned with him, he said: "Yesterday I got to the station just after the train had started. I ran hard to catch it and when I got on I was exhausted. Now would you expect me, having caught the train & got aboard, to be such a fool as to continue to run through the cars, just for the fun of running? I know when the time to rest comes." Mr. Asquith ran hard to reach his present eminence. Apparently he now lets the eminence take care of him. He let his Government fail to grasp the situation. Then he dramatically threw half of them overboard and made the Coalition Government. He must have known his old Cabinet was failing. He *did* know the German readiness and even some of the German plans before the war came. Yet he made no preparations. He knew that every naval authority opposed the Dardanelles-expedition. Yet he let it take place. He was bound to have known (or, if he didn't know, his plight was still worse) the lack of ammunition. Yet he did nothing till the scandal burst. Yet this is the man who has been continuously Prime Minister longer than any other—perhaps that's what's the matter.

I may be wrong, but he is too far spent to be a great negotiator when peace comes near. He seems passed taking a great constructive task. In this judgment I may be wrong. But I can't get away from the feeling that then some heat as well as light will be wanted. Or suppose the war go even worse for a long period— Calais be taken or England (possibly) be invaded, or Holland lost by going over to the enemy, or any other disaster come—some other changes will have to be made in the Government. Of course I can't say that he will go out, but he may.

Yet, of course, all this may be wrong. If the war go on to the Allies' victory without dramatic reverses, he may emerge as England's very great Prime Minister—a great historic figure. Still my guess is against this historic elevation of this man into the select gallery of the Great. He seems to me to be carried on the current, a big chip, but a chip.

I think that Sir Edward Grey will come out of it all as *the* strong man to those who really know the story and to those who think—not as a popular hero, but as the clear-headed, thinking master of British policy. He is too lonely a man for the multitude to know, and he doesn't want to know the multitude but only to serve them. He comes nearer to being the great constructive English statesman that you read of than any other man I know—

silent, strong, simple, linked on to English history and conscious of English greatness. Asquith might have come up in Canada or Australia. Grey could have come only from English soil and English traditions. When he speaks you feel the warmth of burning convictions and you forget to think of his mere manner of speech, which also is exceedingly good. He doesn't have to have manners: he *is* manners and high courtesy and a gentle humour. I have seen on several ceremonial occasions various groups of Knights of the Garter. On all other men the garter seems an affectation: you smile at it. On Edward Grey you admire it—he is chivalry, modesty, courtesy, and the garter fits him. He's the only commoner, by the way, who has it. I've got an interesting measure of him by contrast with Asquith, Haldane, and Crewe, when each of these has had the Foreign Office in charge for brief periods. With these you feel the merely amateur touch: if occasion required, you'd have to watch them. You don't have to watch Grey: he'll be day after tomorrow just where you left him, in any argument or controversy, day before yesterday. He is a philosophical democrat who regrets that society here must be reshapen but who goes at it merely because his conscience will not let him rest—not at all from a love of reforming or of conflict. An old political opponent of his once said to me: "Grey has surprised me. When we were younger I thought he cared chiefly for tennis and fishing, at both which he marvellously excelled. But something has driven him to more serious things." You conceive an affection and high admiration for his personality as for the personality of no other man in public life here.

But—leaving Sir Edward Grey and his peculiar work apart—in this crisis Lloyd George is worth all his associates together. John Sargent and Henry James and I were talking about him the other day. Sargent said that he had never seen him—no other man, I think, in this Kingdom could say that. Old Mr. James smiled and said to me: "If our distinguished friend here had the task of painting Lloyd George, he wd. first rearrange his features." Yet he isn't exactly an ugly man—only an odd-looking one. He's a sort of perpetual motion, but you discover with surprise that he is not only active but that he has thought out his active conduct beforehand. I shd. say that he is the most thoughtful as he is surely the most agile and most thoroughly convinced popular agitator of our time. A year ago he was by far the most hated man in England—among the upper classes. I recall nobody upon whom such vehement abuse was spent. I had been here a year before I met him. He was at no club, no dinner-party, no public dinner that I attended. The House of Have regarded him as a robber, hell-bent on booty, eager to pull down the pillars of the noble structure of things from sheer envy. Yet no man's speeches rang so true to the poor devil who had not been born to grace or fortune. He's as militant a democrat as Jefferson, who, you know, was also a Welshman. If this Kingdom ever becomes a democracy (it has a long way to travel to that goal), Lloyd George will be one of the mightiest forces to bring it about. I'm not sure but England, if she knows what's good for her, could better afford to lose any other man.

He isn't exactly lovely, yet he surely is among the most interesting men living. He has a mind like a cat—nimble and always on its feet—quick as lightning; and his wit and nimbleness have their due relation to a matured philosophy. He is a sort of sword, gleaming all the time and razor-edged. He talked more a few weeks ago at my lunch-table and said more things worth hearing than all the other seven men at the table. He has every mental quality that you admire except repose.

Well, it was George who was on time with his end of the big war-task. He was as ready with plans for the exchequer as Jellicoe was with the fleet;[1] and the plans worked, too. The men that cursed him most loudly voted his budgets and admired his skill and marvellous ingenuity and industry and audacity in making them. When the lack-of-ammunition scandal broke the other week, everybody seemed to say at once: "Set Lloyd George on the job and it'll be done.["] Nobody had any reason to believe that he knew one kind of cartridge from another. He wasn't a soldier, nor a manufacturer, nor provider of any commodity. All that men knew was that he brought things to pass without loss of time. And he became Minister of Munitions. I suspect that the new portfolio was thought of after the man was thought of—was made for him. Parliament had to create the office, but he had the new Department organized and at work before it was created. The very general feeling now is that this is the Department of the Government that is most surely doing its task well.

Hoover, our American dynamo who is feeding the Belgians— the only man, by the way, that I know who makes both the British and the German Government do what he wants—Hoover has a way of knowing what is going on that surprises me. He told me to-day that Lloyd George is worth, for working purposes, every other member of the Cabinet. "They'll have to make him Prime Minister," said Hoover, "before the war ends.["] Hoover, by the way, gave John Bull a recent opportunity to do a characteristic thing. The Government sent for him and askd. if he wd. change his citizenship and become a British subject. He askd. why. They

[1] Admiral Sir John Rushworth Jellicoe, second Sea Lord of the Admiralty when the war broke out.

wanted him to do "a great service" for the Government. He told
them he wd. do any service for them in his power, very loyally
and very gladly. But he added that, apart from a certain sentiment wh. he was sure they wd. understand, he wd. be afraid to
become British. "I shd. soon lose my Yankee energy." He has
heard no more of the "great service." I told him that he had
thrown away a Peerage. His only answer was a disgusted grunt—
"Good God!" From another source I heard something that led
me to think that they wanted him as one of George's chief lieuten-
ants. But he must first be baptised, and Hoover was born in Iowa
and reared in California and he has the brand of Uncle Sam all
over him, inside and out.

John Bull *is* slow, so slow that you can't keep from regarding
him as dense. He isn't degenerate—not by a long shot. He has
character and capacity—enormous stores of both. But he eats too
much beef. He has both his belly and his pocket so well lined that
he is slow to do anything—especially anything new—that disturbs
his comfort. He wrote many books and pamphlets to prove that
the breech-loading gun could never shoot, for 25 years after
everybody else was using only the breech-loading gun. He is now
so sure that a "voluntary" army is vastly superior to a conscript
army that he is using every device, except a law, to force men to
"voluntary." He is surely "set" in his ways. There's never been a
war like this and he persists in preparing for a war of the obsolete
sort—except in the two ways that he has long practiced—in finance
and by his navy. The Germans must first scare the life out of him
before he'll quit writing letters to *The Times* and go get his gun.
He's becoming somewhat alarmed now; and that's a good sign.
But even now he will say nothing. No great convulsion of nations
nor of nature could excite him. He buries his dead without a tear
and pays a fourth of his income to the Government without an
emotion, and he does each in the same heavy way. The universe
couldn't hurry him.

And this slow, phlegmatic habit *is* one form of inefficiency.
It showed itself in the Boer war. It is showing itself in this war.
I can understand why the Germans considered the English effete
and degenerate—they are so slow and so self-satisfied. The Germans won't obliterate him, but I conceive that the Yankees may
some day "run" his business for him. That's where the Germans
missed their chance: they could have (in a sense) have [sic] conquered England in 50 years by peaceful industrial penetration. I
fancy that we may at some time do that very thing. For he is
(in a way) inefficient. His workmen drink and strike and his
employers run to hounds, and the multitude plays cricket. But,

press him hard, and he's an awful fighter. Kipling's Tommy Atkins is true to life

In some way wh. I confess I can't yet clearly foresee, the great gain from the war will come to us—I don't mean merely in trade and finance and such things, but I mean in some sort of world-leadership. Democracy must perish from the earth or it must rule the world and the greatest Democracy must supply the spirit. Everywhere among thoughtful men here, you find the vague rumblings of some such hope or fear.

The great danger that I fear on our side is our long-kept home-keeping public mind, our unconsciousness of foreign things, our fear of foreign relations, our lack of practice in thinking in world-units or in universal terms.

All which is obvious, dull, discourse-like. But there's a little sag here in more immediate things: all the world's waiting to see what Germany will write to the U. S.—a fact wh. throws my obvious discourse into high emphasis. And there's a sag, of course, of high feeling because of the military situation. You hear talk of two, three, even four more years of war; more wounded are seen on the streets; everybody who can go away is leaving London; the murky, second-hand weather is come; there's more real fear of Zeppelin raids on the city; the King doesn't sleep in the Palace, but (I am told) half the time at old Lord Farquahar's,[2] just thro', the wall from me; the Englishman, never a gay creature, is more self-contained than usual. But every man and woman in the Kingdom is this week filling-in a blank form, telling what he or she can do and what he or she is willing to volunteer to do for the country; women punch your tickets at the railway station, deliver your letters, bring your milk and your meat and they've gone to work in ammunition factories. In spite of the present depression nobody becomes permanently discouraged, everybody seems to subscribe to the war-loan and everybody is perfectly willing to die rather than be conquered—*precisely as every German is.*

I try to think out the awful tragedy, turning it round and round again, forever wondering about it in a dazed way, day after day, week after week; and now it looks as if we'd have to live with it a very long time. And the armies in France are in practically the same trenches that their predecessors, whose bones they trample on, occupied last October. The fate of Europe may be fought out right there.   Very heartily yours,   Walter H. Page

ALS (WP, DLC).
[2] Farquhar, Horace Brand, 1st Baron Farquhar.

To John Sharp Williams

Private & Confidential.

My dear Senator: Cornish, N. H., July 8, 1915

Your letter of June twenty-ninth reached me here and you may be sure I have pondered its contents.

I think you are quite right in the whole position you take and I am trying hard to guide myself by the principles both of right and expediency which you so admirably state. I think that such articles as Senator Smith's are calculated to make the situation worse perhaps rather than better.

I hope sincerely that you are getting some real rest and refreshment after the intolerably long pull at Washington.

With warmest regards,
        Cordially and sincerely yours,   Woodrow Wilson

TLS (J. S. Williams Papers, DLC).

INDEX

NOTE ON THE INDEX

THE alphabetically arranged analytical table of contents at the front of the volume eliminates duplication, in both contents and index, of references to certain documents, such as letters. Letters are listed in the contents alphabetically by name, and chronologically within each name by page. The subject matter of all letters is, of course, indexed. The Editorial Notes and Wilson's writings are listed in the contents chronologically by page. In addition, the subject matter of both categories is indexed. The index covers all references to books and articles mentioned in text or notes. Footnotes are indexed. Page references to footnotes which place a comma between the page number and "n" cite both text and footnote, thus: "624,n3." On the other hand, absence of the comma indicates reference to the footnote only, thus: "55n2"—the page number denoting where the footnote appears.

We have ceased the practice of indicating first and fullest identification of persons and subjects in earlier volumes by index references accompanied by asterisks. Volume 13, the cumulative index-contents volume is already in print. Volume 26, which will cover Volumes 14-25, will appear in the near future.

The index supplies the fullest known form of names and, for the Wilson and Axson families, relationships as far down as cousins. Persons referred to by nicknames or shortened forms of names can be identified by reference to entries for these forms of the names.

All entries consisting of page numbers only and which refer to concepts, issues, and opinions (such as democracy, the tariff, the money trust, leadership, and labor problems), are references to Wilson speeches and writings. Page references that follow the symbol Δ in such entries refer to the opinions and comments of others who are identified.

In this index, we have omitted, under WOODROW WILSON, the entries, "Press Conferences," and "Public and Political Addresses and Statements." These are fully listed in the Table of Contents. We will follow this practice in future volumes.

N.B. In the entries for Woodrow Wilson and Edith Bolling Galt, we have not attempted to note their expressions of love for one another. Except for the first letters that they exchanged, all of the letters between Wilson and Mrs. Galt were love letters. The letters are of course indexed for subjects, names, events, and so on.

INDEX

WOODROW WILSON

and *Birth of a Nation* viewing, 86,n1; reaction to sinking of *Lusitania*, 129n1; wishes to stop subscription to *Princeton Alumni Weekly*, 432,-n1; and talk of re-election, 518

APPEARANCE

374

APPOINTMENTS

and Recorder of Deeds in Washington, 71,n1; recommendations for Bryan's successor and appointment of Lansing, 397, 409, 436, 445, 449, 456; Delano suggested for an appointment, 441; House on, 451; recommendations for solicitor-general, 491-92, 492

CABINET

449-51; and *Lusitania* correspondence, 191n1, 295,n3,4, 368, 369, 424-25, 536-37, 540; on Mexican situation, 294-95; and resignation of Bryan, 370,n1, 375-76, 376; Lansing becomes Secretary of State, 397, 409, 436, 445, 449, 456; Crane on Delano for a member of, 441; WW on Garrison, 450-51

FAMILY AND PERSONAL LIFE

memories of his father, 49-50; beginning of relationship with Mrs. Galt, 87, 90; Yesterday, in my deep need and longing, I let myself think of my